LIONEL TRILLING

GARLAND BIBLIOGRAPHIES OF MODERN CRITICS
AND CRITICAL SCHOOLS
(General Editor: William E. Cain)
Vol. 19

GARLAND REFERENCE LIBRARY
OF THE HUMANITIES
Vol. 1303

Garland Bibliographies of Modern Critics and Critical Schools

LIONEL TRILLING
An Annotated Bibliography

Thomas M. Leitch

GARLAND PUBLISHING, INC. • NEW YORK & LONDON
1993

Library of Congress Cataloging-in-Publication Data

Leitch, Thomas M.
Lionel Trilling : an annotated bibliography / by Thomas M. Leitch.
p. cm. — (Garland bibliographies of modern critics and critical schools ; v. 19) (Garland reference library of the humanities ; vol. 1303)
ISBN 0-8240-7128-X (alk. paper)
1. Trilling, Lionel, 1905–1975—Bibliography. I. Title. II. Series. III. Series: Garland reference library of the humanities ; vol. 1303.
Z8885.48.L43 1993
[PS3539.R56]
016.818'5209—dc20 92-23192
CIP

Printed on acid-free, 250-year-life paper
Manufactured in the United States of America

CONTENTS

GENERAL EDITOR'S INTRODUCTION

The Garland Bibliographies of Modern Critics and Critical Schools series is intended to provide bibliographic treatment of major critics and critical schools of the twentieth century. Each volume includes an introduction that surveys the critic's life, career, influence, and achievement, or, in the case of the volumes devoted to a critical school, presents an account of its central figures, origins, relation to other critical movements and trends, and the like.

Each volume is fully annotated and contains listings for both primary and secondary materials. The annotations are meant to be ample and detailed, in order to explain clearly, especially for a reader coming to a critic or critical school for the first time, the point and purpose of a book or essay. In this sense, the bibliographies are also designed to be critical guides. We hope that the volumes will inform and stimulate the reader even as they give basic information about what material exists and where it may be located.

We have tried to include as many of the most important critics and critical schools in this series as possible, but some have been omitted. Some critics and critical schools have already received (or are in the process of receiving) adequate treatment, and we see no need to duplicate the efforts of others.

William E. Cain
Wellesley College

PREFACE

Lionel Trilling was perhaps the last American critic of note to write in the confidence of addressing an audience broader than his fellow critics. Although this bibliography is intended primarily for specialists, I have tried, through comprehensive annotation and illustrative quotation, to make it as accessible as possible to a similarly broad audience. The entries are divided into three parts. The first is a comprehensive bibliography of Trilling's published writing from his poems in the 1924-25 issues of *Morningside*, the Columbia College literary magaizine, to the selections from his journals published by *Partisan Review* in 1987. The second part is a bibliography of books and essays on Trilling in English. I have included only a few responses to Trilling's work published in Germany, France, and Italy, but as his greatest influence by far has been in English-speaking countries, the restriction to materials in English is not as arbitrary as it may seem. The material included in this section ranges from the 1924 college yearbook entry on Trilling and Mark Van Doren's 1927 profile of him as one of six unnamed "Jewish Students I Have Known" to essays and reviews published in 1991. The third part is a bibliography of background material which does not deal centrally with Trilling but influences him, provokes his critical response, comments on him in passing, or seems otherwise useful to an understanding of his work and its influence. This third section, which makes no attempt at comprehensiveness, lists books, essays, reviews, and dissertations published through 1991, and in one case in 1992. In the time it has taken to complete this project, I have twice updated my searches of references to include more recent material, but bibliographies, as Hotspur once remarked, must have a stop, and this one stops around 1990.

This is an annotated bibliography in the strict sense: every entry includes a brief description of the item's contents, based (with two or three exceptions out of a thousand entries) on an examination of the item rather than a reference in some earlier bibliography. These descriptions have of course made the bibliography much longer than it might have been; I can only hope they make it more useful as well. In general the bibliographic information I give--title, date, and so on--comes directly from the item at hand; I note discrepancies between this information and information published in the standard bibliographic references and databases only when these discrepancies seem especially misleading. Whenever I have not been able to give precise information--for example, page references to every reprinting of the widely-reprinted stories "Of This Time, of That Place" and "The Other Margaret"--I have included as much information as possible on the theory that an incomplete reference is more helpful than none. All quotations, unless otherwise indicated, come from the version of each item under discussion--typically its earliest publication.

Within the three general parts, bibliographical listings are organized according to the following categories:

Section A (Books) includes all books and collections of essays published by Trilling during his lifetime and the Uniform Edition of his writings edited by Diana Trilling after his death, including three collections of material not previously reprinted in book form. This section--the only section whose scope is intended to be comprehensive outside English--includes all translations of Trilling's books into foreign languages.

Section B (Prefaces and Books Edited) includes Trilling's Prefaces and Introductions to books he edited or to which he contributed prefatory matter.

Section C (Essays, Stories, Poems, and Review Articles) includes Trilling's early poems and stories, all his essays of whatever length, and his more substantial review essays. Since the line between reviews and review essays is notoriously difficult to ascertain, I have included in this section a large number of review essays, including all Trilling's articles (except for one two-sentence assessment of Philip Rieff's *Freud: The Mind of the Moralist*) for the *Griffin* and the *Mid-Century*.

Section D (Reviews) includes Trilling's book reviews. Review essays, including articles from the *Griffin* and the *Mid-Century*, listed in Section C are cross-indexed here.

Section E (Symposia, Interviews, and Miscellaneous) includes Trilling's published contributions to symposia and professional programs, letters to editors, and a few items (program notes to a recording of

Gounod's *Faust*, an audiotape of a lecture given in 1963) that escaped easy categorization.

Section F (Books, Collections of Essays, Special Issues of Journals) includes books and special issues of journals devoted to Trilling, and the Festschrift (F420) published in his honor. Individual essays in these collections are listed in the following sections.

Section G (Essays and Review Articles) includes essays and review essays focusing on Trilling.

Section H (Reviews of Books by Trilling) includes reviews of books written or edited by Trilling. In an attempt to save time for later researchers, I have listed reviews of such books as *The Partisan Reader* and the first American edition of Orwell's *Homage to Catalonia*, many of which do not mention Trilling's Introductions even in passing, in order to indicate their silence on the subject. When my descriptions of these reviews do not mention Trilling, it can be assumed that the reviews do not mention him either. As in Section D, review essays listed in Section G are cross-indexed here.

Section I (Reviews of Books About Trilling) includes reviews of books entirely or largely about Trilling, including titles from section F, followed by titles from section L.

Section J (Dissertations) includes unpublished dissertations whose primary focus is Trilling.

Section K (Miscellaneous) includes such miscellaneous items as letters responding to Trilling's essays, sidebars to essays on Trilling, and an abridged transcript of Philip French's BBC radio program on Trilling.

Section L (Books) includes books not primarily devoted to Trilling but notable for their influence on Trilling, their brief discussions of him or his ideas, or the information they provide about his literary, cultural, or political background.

Section M (Essays) includes essays analogous to the books listed in Section L.

Section N (Dissertations) includes unpublished dissertations in which Trilling plays a substantial, but not a focal, role.

Section O (Miscellaneous) includes several published letters about Trilling and a misleadingly titled story to which he has only figurative relevance.

The organization of material is chronological according to publication date in Sections A-E, alphabetical according to the author's name in Sections F-G and J-O, and, in Sections H and I, chronological according to the date of the book under review and alphabetically within each chronological section according to the title of the journal, magazine, or newspaper in which the review first appeared.

ACKNOWLEDGMENTS

A trope of acknowledgment pages in academic books is the expression of gratitude toward one's colleagues, who are customarily presented as having no interest higher than devotion to the project in hand. My own experience has suggested that the interest of colleagues is naturally absorbed, except for ritual inquiries at departmental functions and professional conventions, by their own equally valuable work. There does exist, however, a legion who really do display the kind of disinterested fervor ascribed to fellow-scholars: the librarians without whom a project like this one would be unthinkable. I want to extend my heartfelt gratitude here to the librarians who answered my questions, suggested new lines of inquiry, supplied me with material I requested (and occasionally with material I had not thought to request), and prevented me from wandering too far in the wilderness represented by the library of Allentown College of St. Francis de Sales, the Atlanta-Fulton Public Library, the Brooklyn Public Library, the library of the California State University of Pennsylvania, the University of Connecticut Library, Dames & Moore (Atlanta, GA), the Houghton Library at Harvard University, the Indiana University Library, the library of Indiana University of Pennsylvania, the Illinois State Historical Library, the Lafayette College Library, the Lehigh University Library, the Lewis and Clark Library System of Edwardsville, IL, the *Los Angeles Times* Editorial Library, the Mansfield University Library, the University of Miami Library in Coral Gables, the Muhlenberg College Library, the University of North Texas Library, the University of Oregon Library, the College of Physicians of Philadelphia, the Purdue University Library, the library of St. Joseph's College in Philadelphia, the library of the State University of New York at Albany, the library of the State University of New York at Stony Brook, the Swarthmore College Library, the Temple University Library, the University of Utah Library, the Wheaton College Library, and the Wilmington Institute Library. I am especially grateful to Jami Peelle of the Greenslade Special Collections at Kenyon College for responding so promptly and graciously to my urgent appeal; to the staffs of the four libraries where I conducted most of the research for this volume--Butler Library at Columbia University, Morris Library at the University of Delaware, Sterling Library at Yale University, and the Library of Congress--and to Jo McClamroch, Linda Lawrence Stein, Nancy Froysland Hoerl, and the indefatigable ILL staff at Morris Library, without whose repeated assistance my home life during the past three years would have been even more ill-humored and minimal. A welcome grant from the Arts and Science Dean's Office at Delaware saved me further travel expense and enabled me to see something of my children from time to time.

Among my colleagues at Delaware I owe particular thanks to Philip Goldstein for nosing out sources I would otherwise have overlooked and to Thomas Calhoun for help in translation. William Cain, my series editor, responded to niggling questions with encouragement and good humor, and Paula Ladenburg and Phyllis Korper, my editors at Garland, have repaid my delays in the preparation of the manuscript with unfailing patience and support. I have benefited from consulting earlier published bibliographies of Trilling by Marianne Gilbert Barnaby, Jeffrey Cane Robinson, and Edward J. Shoben, Jr. My deepest debt is to Diana Trilling, who allowed me access to her personal bibliographic file on her late husband--material she had been collecting for fifteen years--and offered me the hospitality of her home while I was transcribing material. Without her generous assistance, this bibliography would have been incomparably less useful than I hope it is. It goes without saying, or it should, that neither Ms. Trilling nor anyone else I have mentioned here should be held accountable for my errors of commission or omission. I hope readers discovering such errors will notify me of them in order to facilitate the preparation of a second edition.

BIOGRAPHY

Lionel Mordecai Trilling was born in New York City on 4 July 1905. His father, David Trilling, was a custom tailor who had been dispatched to America from his native town of Bialystok, Poland, after his embarrassing performance during his bar mitzvah dashed his parents' hopes that he was destined for the rabbinate; his London-born mother, Fannie Cohen Trilling, was a voracious and sharp-witted reader whose long-standing wish was that her son take a Ph.D. at Oxford. Trilling grew up in Far Rockaway and the Upper West Side, graduating from DeWitt Clinton High School in 1921 and entering Columbia College at the age of sixteen, and beginning an association with Columbia that would last, with brief intermissions, for the rest of his life. Upon his graduation in 1925 he entered the M.A. program, completing it the following year with a Master's Essay on Theodore Edward Hook. Trilling taught for a year (1926-27) at the University of Wisconsin, then returned to New York to teach for two years at Hunter College, continuing to serve as a part-time instructor in Hunter's night division when he returned to Columbia as an instructor in 1932. In the meantime, the failure of his father's new fur business left Trilling as the sole support of his family, a family which had come to include Diana Rubin, whom he had married in June 1929.

Throughout the 1930's Trilling supplemented his teaching income by reviewing books for a variety of journals and newspapers, most importantly for the *Menorah Journal*, with which he was associated from 1925 through 1931. As a result of his financial responsibilities, his dissertation on Matthew Arnold languished, and in 1936 he was informed by the Columbia English department that his contract would not be renewed. With surprising vigor, Trilling protested his dismissal, and was rewarded in 1939 when the completed dissertation was published and Nicholas Murray Butler, the autocratic president of Columbia, arranged his promotion to assistant professor, noting that Trilling was the first Jew to be promoted within the English department.

Already in 1934 Trilling and his friend Jacques Barzun had begun to teach Columbia's Colloquium on Important Books, an experimental course on the relation between literature and ideas--a relation which remained the focus of most of Trilling's writing as well. At the same time, grown critical of the American Stalinism which had briefly claimed his allegiance, he joined his wife and other disillusioned leftists in signing a letter protesting the Communist Party's attempt to disrupt a Socialist rally at Madison Square Garden in 1934. When *Partisan Review*, which had begun under the aegis of the John Reed Clubs of America, returned to publication in 1937 as an independent journal in 1937, Trilling, now grown strongly anti-Stalinist, joined its staff and became a leading member of the group that would become known as the New York intellectuals.

By the time son James was born in 1948, Trilling, who, practically alone among the New York intellectuals, held a regular academic position, had joined John Crowe Ransom and F. O. Matthiessen in founding the Kenyon School of Letters. Back at Columbia, Trilling decided to give up teaching graduate seminars in American literature and English romanticism, his nominal fields of specialization, and to devote himself instead to undergraduate teaching, especially the teaching of the modernist classics to which he remained highly ambivalent. In the meantime he had been promoted to associate professor (1945) and professor (1948). At the same time, after completing his monograph on E. M. Forster (1943) and his novel *The Middle of the Journey* (1947), he concentrated on the short critical essays collected in *The Liberal Imagination* (1950), *The Opposing Self* (1955), and *A Gathering of Fugitives* (1956).

Trilling's reputation reached a peak during the ten years following the publication of *The Liberal Imagination*. He was elected to the National Institute of Arts and Letters in 1951 and served as a fellow of the American Academy of Arts and Sciences in 1952. In 1955 he became the first layman invited to give the Freud Anniversary Lecture at the annual meeting of the New York Psychoanalytical Society. In 1952, he joined Barzun and W. H. Auden on the editorial board of the Reader's Subscription, a monthly book club, and from 1959 to 1962 assumed the corresponding post at the Mid-Century book club.

With the publication of *Beyond Culture* in 1965, Trilling was appointed George Edward Woodberry Professor of English at Columbia, and he was named one of three University Professors in 1970 on his return from Harvard University, where he spent a year as Charles Eliot Norton lecturer. The resulting lectures were published as the final book Trilling completed, *Sincerity and Authenticity* (1972). Having by now received honorary degrees from Case Western Reserve, Northwestern, Brandeis, Harvard, and Yale, Trilling, in belated response to his mother's dream, was appointed to a visiting lectureship at All Souls College, Oxford, for 1972-73. He was working on a Guggenheim Fellowship when he died on 5 November 1975.

Although several critical books have been written on Trilling, no authorized biography has yet appeared. The best brief accounts of Trilling's life are his own unfinished "Notes for an Autobiographical Lecture," Diana Trilling's essay "Lionel Trilling: A Jew at Columbia" (on Trilling's early years), and the opening chapter of Stephen L. Tanner's *Lionel Trilling*, which can be supplemented by the anecdotes related by such friends and acquaintances as William Barrett, Jacques Barzun, Irving Howe, and William Phillips. The Trilling papers have been sealed in Butler Library at Columbia University until 2005, the hundredth anniversary of Trilling's birth.

Introduction

The difficulty in compiling a bibliography on Lionel Trilling lies not in collecting material by Trilling himself--though he enjoyed an unusually productive career, publishing a prodigious number of essays and reviews that escaped collection in any of his hardcover collections or the ten-volume Uniform Edition of his writings, or indeed listing in previous bibliographies--but rather in knowing where to draw the boundaries in considering commentary on his work. Books and essays whose primary subject is Trilling will of course form the basis of such a bibliographic survey, but what of critical essays that treat him more obliquely or show his influence more generally and diffusely, often without direct acknowledgment? A single 1948 essay, "Manners, Morals, and the Novel," succeeded, as commentators from Ralph Ellison to Russell Reising have pointed out,[1] in making a single paragraph Henry James wrote on Hawthorne central to the rethinking of American fiction, effectively reorienting the study of American literature. R. W. B. Lewis's classic 1955 study *The American Adam*, which never cites Trilling, seems unthinkable in its theorizing of the American literary imagination without this essay; should Lewis's book be included in a bibliography of Trilling? For that matter, what important study of American literature in the generation following Trilling's "Reality in America" escaped its influence? Does justice to what Nicolaus Mills has called "the Trilling thesis"--that "American writers of genius have not turned their minds to society"[2]--require an exhaustive listing of every general pronouncement on American literature and society since Trilling wrote?

Again, consider Trilling's brief periods in the public spotlight as a result first of his birthday speech to Robert Frost in 1959, later of his role in the 1968 demonstrations at Columbia University. Is every document pertaining to the Frost controversy--J. Donald Adams's column in the *New York Times Book Review* rebuking Trilling for calling Frost "a terrifying poet," the barrage of minatory letters that followed, analyses of the controversy in the *Nation* and *Newsweek*, Frost's own comments on the speech[3]--relevant to a bibliography of Trilling? And what of the much more extensive record of Trilling's role in the Tripartite

Commission at Columbia? All but the briefest histories of the Columbia demonstrations report his strenuous attempt as a member of this ad hoc faculty group to mediate between the demands of student protestors and the intransigence of the university administration--an attempt whose failure many observers professed to see mirrored in the political withdrawal and despair of his last works.[4] Should a bibliography of Trilling include every account of the uprising at Columbia?

A more general problem concerns Trilling's status as the exemplary figure among the New York intellectuals--a family of literary, aesthetic, and social critics, poets, and novelists first brought to prominence as contributors to the reborn *Partisan Review* following the collapse of American intellectuals' Stalinist sympathies during the later 1930's who enjoyed their greatest influence as America's pre-eminent group of critics (its only true corps of intellectuals, as Irving Howe has remarked[5]) during the 1950's. The continuing influence of their work, their paradigmatic status as an American intellectual elite, and their legacy to the horde of writers currently at work in New York have all assured the New York intellectuals a lasting place in analyses of American high culture. Should a bibliography of Trilling cite all these analyses, regardless of the prominence they assign Trilling?

My unsurprising answers to these questions will fail to satisfy everyone in some way or other. I have included here not only *The American Adam* but a dozen other volumes on the theory of American literature that mention Trilling only briefly or not at all--and all the studies of American literature I know that debate the Trilling thesis at any length--though I have not included Henry Nash Smith's *Virgin Land*, William Taylor's *Cavalier and Yankee*, or other studies that seem to run parallel to Trilling's theory rather than displaying its influence. The Frost controversy seems to me not only instructive as an example of literary politics but relatively limited in its documentation, and I have included every contemporary comment on the controversy I could find, since together they swell the bibliography by only a page or so. With material on the Columbia demonstrations I have taken very much the opposite tack. Since so many accounts of these events rely on the same sources, I have included only those accounts on which most others draw and those which add some new information, and have made no attempt to provide comprehensive coverage of an event in which Trilling's role was secondary. The New York intellectuals pose a more serious problem, since scholarship on this group has expanded dramatically since 1968 and, fueled by the twin engines of the New York literati and the recent rebirth of interest in cultural studies, shows no signs of abating. With few exceptions, I have included only historical forerunners whose influence Trilling himself acknowledged, essays by contemporaries among the New York circle which mention Trilling or the issues he raises explicitly, and studies of the New York intellectuals which discuss Trilling at some length. Hence my relative neglect, which many readers may find strange, of such figures as Philip Rahv, Harold Rosenberg, and Clement Greenberg, and my focus on the writings of William Phillips, William Barrett, and Irving Howe that deal most directly with Trilling. Though I would welcome a bibliography that dealt comprehensively and even-handedly with the New York intellectuals and their seminal contribution to modern American culture, the present work cannot pretend to fulfill that role.

Nor have I attempted to track down every brief reference to Trilling in the scholarly and general literature of the past sixty-five years; the task would have been herculean and its value dubious. I am comforted in my reservations about this failure by my certainty that computer databases will make such indiscriminate heaps of information available to researchers within a few years. In the meantime, I have attempted a task that will probably take computers a while longer: a broad but selective list of references detailing Lionel Trilling's most enduring contributions to literary and cultural criticism.

It is difficult to indicate the nature of these contributions not only because Trilling's influence has been so broadly diffused but because it seems to lack the ideological or methodological center of the critical movements to which most of Trilling's distinguished contemporaries subscribed: Marxist criticism, New Criticism, existentialist criticism, psychoanalytic criticism, myth criticism, structuralism and post-structuralism. Both by temperament and by design Trilling was a critic without portfolio, profoundly suspicious of the various schools with which commentators sometimes aligned him. During the period of Trilling's greatest influence--roughly the fifteen years following the 1950 publication of *The Liberal Imagination*--when he was widely considered the pre-eminent American critic, it made sense to see him as above the factionalism that had riven American criticism since the 1930's; now, however, his critical distance from these defining factions makes his legacy harder to assess. To join Grant Webster in calling Trilling the Representative Man of the New York intellectuals[6] gives him a place on a map of modern American criticism without indicating the nature or range of his interests, the focus of his critical energies, or the project to which all his major writings were devoted.

Although this project is in truth not easily identified, it is rooted in the texts to which Trilling most often returns--the poetry of Wordsworth and Keats, the novels of Austen and James, the cultural commentary of Rousseau and Arnold, the psychology of Freud--all subsumed within the historical movement of Romanticism. Yet Trilling is himself neither a late-blooming romantic nor a critic of romanticism in the manner of Harold Bloom; nor is he a more avowedly totalizing literary critic like Northrop Frye whose paradigms are drawn from English romanticism. Unlike Frye and Bloom, Trilling is never concerned to valorize the romantic tradition or to define its essential romanticism. If he is not an historian of romanticism, no more is Trilling essentially a reader of its exemplary texts. With the exception of a few striking performances--his essays on the Immortality Ode, on *The Princess Casamassima*, on *Mansfield Park*--he is not primarily an analyst who wishes to establish new readings of disputed texts; even his most brilliant readings are always offered for the sake of some larger generalization about cultural trends or presuppositions.

The tendency has therefore been to label Trilling a cultural critic rather than a purely literary critic. The distinction provides a convenient way to classify Trilling without offering any particular insight into the nature of his interests or shedding any light on the difference between cultural criticism and (presumably) purely literary criticism--a difference Trilling never accepted. For Trilling, writing about literature involved the critic willy-nilly in social, cultural, and ideological issues; he did not emphasize his movement from literary to cultural questions because the possibility of not being implicated from the beginning in cultural questions did not arise.[7] (It is worth pointing out here that Trilling, who generally felt no obligation to define the central abstractions like *self* and *society* so important to his work, returned repeatedly to the vexed question of precisely what the word *culture* means.) Hence Trilling, unlike his friend Jacques Barzun, saw himself not so much an historical analyst of romanticism or a literary analyst of romantic poetry and prose as an inheritor of the romantic tradition struggling to make sense of contemporary manifestations of that tradition--particularly the high modernists--from within its ideology.

The same point has been made more often of Trilling's political commitments: indeed he first made it himself in the preface to *The Liberal Imagination* when he called for a liberal critique of liberalism, defining such a project as quintessentially liberal in its impetus. The apparent contradiction will puzzle only readers who have no idea what liberalism is. Although Trilling never bothers to define the liberal imagination in this preface or elsewhere,[8] its meaning is clear: it refers to the Enlightenment belief in a social order rooted in the irreducible value of individual experience, a value that can be appreciated through the essential similarity of people to each other within a given culture, and perhaps between cultures as well. Liberalism is at heart a belief in social redemption, a humanist belief in human nature, in what used to be called Man. Liberal politicians typically adopt platforms of social meliorism through gradual, rationally directed change within existing institutions; liberal philosophers adopt similarly progressive stances toward given social arrangements in the name of greater happiness; and as for liberal poets and novelists--but it is precisely here that Trilling identifies a problem with contemporary liberalism, since he finds liberal-minded novelists like Dreiser and Sherwood Anderson distressingly atavistic and immature, inadequate in both the content of their ideologies and their uncritical attachment to ideology. Compared to such light-headed liberals, the seminal modernist writers Trilling identifies in "The Function of the Little Magazine"--Proust, Joyce, Lawrence, Eliot, Yeats, Mann, Kafka, Rilke, Gide--comprise a formidably anti-liberal array.[9]

It is not surprising, then, that Trilling enlists the modernists in his critique of liberalism. Commentators who have labeled Trilling a liberal bent on reconciling his politics with his modernist tastes, however, have overlooked Trilling's highly selective fondness for literary modernism. Trilling shows little interest throughout *The Liberal Imagination* in directly confronting either the seminal modernists he identifies or their most distinguished contemporaries--Conrad, Pound, Woolf, or Faulkner--preferring instead to conduct his critique of liberalism through an attack on such dogmatic critics as V. L. Parrington and the defenders of Dreiser and Anderson, an analysis of such pre-modernists or epicentral modernists as James, Twain, and Fitzgerald, and more general allusions to the aesthetics of modernists who are invoked rather than analyzed. Consistently throughout his career, aesthetic modernism seems to interest Trilling more for the issues it raises than for the tastes of his own it gratifies. Trilling is no more a partisan of modernism than of romanticism; as with liberalism, he assumes a position which seems paradoxically both inside and outside the tradition he is analyzing, as if the analysis itself, and the maintenance of his perspective on the cultural frontier, were his pleasure.

This paradox, which is central to each of Trilling's major works and to the unfolding of his career as a whole, is less puzzling than it appears. Trilling's first two books, written after a decade of reviewing novels and critical studies which he regularly criticized for offering politically fashionable sentiments as a substitute for the critical analysis of cultural problems[10], were studies of Matthew Arnold and E. M. Forster, two figures who bore a similarly problematic relation to their aesthetic and political cultures as liberal critics of liberalism. In both cases, Trilling argues that it is precisely the self-critical spirit that warrants the writer's liberalism, and in both cases, he explicitly offers the writer as a corrective to the uncritical uniformity the threat of Nazism may seem to inspire. He represents Arnold as successively turning from poetry to literary and cultural criticism, and finally to religious commentary, in a ceaseless search for certainties he is temperamentally and ideologically too restless to accept; Forster turns his ridicule of liberal bromides into the high, dark comedy of *The Longest Journey* and *Howards End*. It is precisely their ability, not only to carry out a critique of contemporary liberalism from within its beliefs, but to make this critique continuously engaging and amusing, that Trilling most admires and strives to emulate.

In Arnold's case especially, it is clear that Trilling, who described his book as an attempt to produce "a biography of Arnold's mind,"[11] sees his subject as a culture hero, distinguished not by the penetration of his cultural analysis but by the movement of his mind in its critique of literature and society. All of Trilling's major critical work constitutes a valorization of such culture heroes--writers like Arnold, Forster, Fitzgerald, James, Wordsworth, Keats, Austen, Flaubert, Babel, and Hawthorne, fictional characters like Huck Finn and Hyacinth Robinson, Bouvard and Pécuchet and Rameau's Nephew--figures who paradoxically assert themselves most vigorously through their literally self-effacing critique of the enabling conditions of their social, ideological, and intellectual identity.

The period during and just after the Second World War, when the United States emerged from "the good war" confident in the essential rightness of its political power, was an opportune time for Trilling's call to a critique of liberalism through the example of such self-critical culture heroes. The danger that the politics of anti-totalitarianism could spawn their own totalitarianism, so presciently explored by George Orwell in *1984*, made such a critique especially timely, and the completeness of the Allied victory gave American politicians and ideologues a confidence permitting criticisms that might otherwise have been branded disloyal. Contemporary critics who may smile at the use of political terms so colored by careerist paranoia are taking a lamentably short view of history. The rise only a few years after the war of McCarthyism, which had precisely this chilling effect on critiques of American ideology by threatening the critics with the loss of their livelihood, has been widely accepted as fracturing the centrism of the New York intellectuals.

If political forces were instrumental in giving Trilling's critique of liberalism cogency and currency, they were equally important in leading to the eclipse of his influence, an eclipse which cannot simply be ascribed to the temporary depression of any author's valuation in the years immediately following his or her death. F. R. Leavis, reviewing T. S. Eliot's *On Poetry and Poets* in 1958, wondered how a book of criticism could be at once so distinguished and so unimportant;[12] reviewers of *Beyond Culture* and *Sincerity and Authenticity* often adopted the same tone. The decline in Trilling's contemporary reputation is linked most obviously to a precipitous decline in the fortunes of liberalism from the time of McCarthy throughout the period of the Cold War and the war in Vietnam. It is commonplace to note that a decade dominated by Ronald Reagan and his epigones has no place for avatars of "the L word." What is less often observed is that the decline of liberalism has not corresponded to a rise of conservatism, at least as a robust ideology capable of inspiring the allegiance of adherents as intelligent and self-critical as Burke and Coleridge. Contemporary political conservatism continues to take the same form Trilling observed in 1950, expressing itself not "in ideas but only in action or in irritable mental gestures which seek to resemble ideas."[13] Indeed the decline of liberalism has been matched by the decline of conservatism, which, as

Trilling feared was true of postwar liberalism, has become a victim of its own uncritical success. The contemporary critical scene, which offers to editorial writers the edifying spectacle of zealous neoconservatives like Allan Bloom, E. D. Hirsch, Dinesh D'Souza, and William Bennett slugging it out with apocalyptic radicals whose critique of western culture--informed at whatever remove by the decentering projects of Jacques Derrida, Jacques Lacan, and Michel Foucault, presumably aims to debase the western tradition by opening the canon to all comers and reading every work against the grain to suit a tendentious political agenda--perfectly mirrors the contemporary political scene, in which the citizenry expresses its disaffection with public policy not through criticism but through protest votes for anti-establishment figures like Jerry Brown, Pat Buchanan, or H. Ross Perot. In an America in which the center no longer holds--the President builds an electoral consensus not by espousing a centrist ideology but by studiously eschewing all ideological commitments whatever--and ideology in Barthes's sense of unconscious cultural myth has largely taken the place of traditional political thought, Trilling's attempt to awaken liberalism to an awareness of its best possibilities by criticizing it from within must inevitably seem quaint.

The contrast between Trilling's earlier weighty reputation and his recent neglect has been exacerbated by the modishness of postwar literary criticism, which has been notoriously fickle in its intellectual allegiances, and by Trilling's lack of interest, despite the decisive impact of his teaching and writing on a generation of students at Columbia and elsewhere, in founding a school that might advance his critical program. Disinclined to teach graduate students who might spread his gospel, and frankly horrified in his last years by the revolutionary politics his insistence on the political value of literature might have seemed to encourage, Trilling left his posthumous reputation vulnerable to the rivalry of scholars who had cultivated their line of succession more assiduously and the assaults of budding modernists--members of the adversary culture, as he called them--whose skepticism toward the value of liberal culture he had nourished better than he knew. In the wake of the Columbia demonstrations, it became fashionable to concede Trilling a Pisgah view of post-modernism, a prevision of a cultural revolution he could never condone.

What made this view so plausible were Trilling's real contributions to the counterculture whose rise he so deplored. As his contemporaries the American New Critics rose to prominence by setting aside the historicism in which they had been trained for close readings of literary texts, Trilling insisted on the necessary intimacy between literature and "the real world,"[14] keeping alive the faith in historical criticism despite his lack of a pedagogical program comparable in power or authority to that of the New Critics. At the same time, Trilling's dialectical suspicion of ideological orthodoxies presages the rise of deconstructionism, in whose early signs Trilling saw a new orthdoxy from which he could only withhold his allegiance. More specifically, Trilling, as Mark Krupnick and others have agreed, is the largely unacknowledged forerunner of the contemporary cultural criticism that stands in the same relation to literary criticism as Trilling's cultural criticism to the New Criticism of the 1930's and 1940's. Trilling would therefore seem well-equipped to assume not only the role Krupnick has claimed for him--as "the single most important cultural critic of this century among American men of letters"[15]--but the more influential role of a founding father, along with Mikhail Bakhtin and Kenneth Burke, of a modern post-structural criticism mixing ideological critique and cultural studies.

But Trilling could never have accepted such a description of his own activity, and his refusal--over and above his temperamental resistance to nurturing disciples--to subscribe to the anomie of the counterculture, the ideological commitment of the Marxists and Maoists in 1968, and the deconstructive agenda of contemporary cultural criticism all point to the reasons he has not been rehabilitated as a spiritual father of cultural studies. These reasons begin with objections to his unfashionable manner, which deals with intimidating assurance with large abstractions like *society*, *mind*, *will*, *liberalism*, *authenticity*, *self*, and *being*. The objection universally raised to Trilling's oracular use of these terms lies not in their abstractness--for contemporary criticism is notorious for its infatuation with an even more formidable battery of abstractions--but in the imprecision with which he uses them, never defining them exactly and often pressing them into service in contexts whose force is shifting, even contradictory. Reviewers of *The Liberal Imagination* were divided in calling Trilling a liberal, a critic of liberalism, and a critic with a profoundly ambivalent attitude toward liberalism, which he called "not only the dominant but even the sole intellectual tradition" in America only a few pages before urging the necessity of recalling liberalism "to its first essential awareness of variousness and possibility."[16] It has been less widely noted that the title of each of Trilling's subsequent collections of essays, even the minor *A Gathering of Fugitives*, displays a similar contradiction or ambivalence. *The Opposing Self* asks whether the self is something that exists in opposition to society, as one pole of a dialectic, or the product of a dialectic. *Beyond Culture* raises the question explicitly in its preface whether it is possible to go beyond culture in either its narrow, aesthetic sense, or in the broad sense associated with the phrase "cultural conditioning." And *Sincerity and Authenticity* plays endlessly with the tangled implications of its leading terms. Each title dramatizes Trilling's ambivalent attitude toward the concepts he is considering. Is it good--is it even possible--to have a liberal imagination? Should the self define itself in opposition to the larger culture? Given the impossibility of getting beyond culture, what are the likely results of trying? What is gained and lost in the attempt be to be sincere or authentic? Problems arise in each case because instead of attempting to define the terms precisely and then adjudicate, for example, between more and less authentic modes of authenticity, Trilling attempts to study the words and concepts as they have actually been used, recreating all the problematic inconsistencies that underlie the use of them as *idées reçues*. It is precisely these inconsistencies, in fact, that are the subject of so many of his essays, from "Reality in America" to "Authenticity and the Modern Unconscious."

A similar objection is often lodged against Trilling's coercive use of the pronoun *we*, as when he observes in "Mansfield Park" that "the word [duty] grates upon our moral ear."[17] Critics from René Wellek to Marianna Torgovnick have complained that Trilling's *we* is high-handed and inconsistent, conflating the audience of non-specialists he cultivates with a much smaller circle, perhaps the New York intellectuals, whose cultural beliefs are far more tendentious.[18] Despite Trilling's defense of his use of *we* on these terms in the Preface to *Beyond Culture*, the inconsistency is not in the varying groups to which the word refers, but to its equivocal status as empirical stipulation ('I suppose we all assume . . .') and rhetorical exhortation ('If we are prepared to grant this point . . .'). R. P. Blackmur is more illuminating when he points out in his 1950 review of *The Liberal Imagination* that "Mr. Trilling cultivates a mind never entirely his own," a point developed by Elinor Grumet's observation that Trilling's *we* "creates a community-by-incantation which shares and validates the culture as he perceives it."[19] The primary valence of Trilling's *we*, that is, is performative: it is intended to create rather than to describe a community of belief. It is true, of course, that the technique sometimes backfires, as shown by a dialogue in the recent film *Metropolitan*, in which the hero insists that even a fan of Jane Austen's like Lionel Trilling doesn't like *Mansfield Park* because he says that "*nobody* likes Fanny Price." But such misfires are failures of invocation, not imprecise descriptions; Whit Stillman's earnest hero, misconstruing the duplicitous force of Trilling's *we*, has overlooked his intention of championing Austen's novel despite what "we" take to be its flaws.

Trilling's equivocal use of *we* and abstractions like *self* and *culture* have often been linked to his mixture, despite his identification of himself as a liberal critic of liberalism, of liberal and conservative impulses.[20] This argument seems pyrrhic: however deep or sorrowful Trilling's discontent with liberalism becomes, he never espouses a conservative ideology; at most, his increasingly conservative temperament is moved to action by his liberal beliefs. For better or worse, Trilling remains throughout the modulations of his career a liberal critic of liberalism whose fortunes are tied to those of the ideology of liberalism. The fundamental reason for the decline in Trilling's reputation is his refusal to accept the radical, pointedly non-liberal critique of liberalism he seemed from the beginning to be encouraging, and his determination instead to brand that critique as one more imprisoning ideology. There is nothing mysterious about this determination. Trilling's experience of Stalinism in the thirties had left him with a lifelong suspicion of political orthodoxies; his temperament always inclined toward a critique of the dominant ideology, even (or especially) when that ideology itself posed as a critique. Trilling's startling capacity for reinventing himself by putting his earlier beliefs under scrutiny left him impatient with individuals and movements incapable of the same sort of critical self-scrutiny: hence his identification of sixties radicals with thirties Stalinists whose uncritical partisanship he felt he had long outgrown.

Even as Trilling was condemning the dogmatism of would-be radicals, commentators whose own stance was far from radical were criticizing his own dogmatism. William Cain has explained Trilling's declining fortunes by contrasting his attachment to the ideal of a "morally centered self" with the decentered selves stipulated by deconstructionist critiques, and Gregory Jay has predicted that Trilling's lack of a theory of language must prevent his return to favor.[21] Both remarks go to the heart of Trilling's quarrel with contemporary theory. The self dialectically shaped by the constraints of culture and biological imperatives that stubbornly resisted those constraints, a concept Trilling adapted from Freud and brought powerfully to bear on the debate on ideology and literature that raged through the forties, plays a decisive role in all his work, from his dissertation on Arnold to his last unfinished essay on Jane Austen. This shaped self, which makes Keats and Wordsworth so heroic in their ability to engage the world in all its fullness without surrendering to its exigencies, endures in Trilling's late work as the last best hope for the survival of a culture deeply divided against itself and eager at every point to claim institutional power. But it was exactly his attachment to a willfully, heroically shaped self that made Trilling condemn theories which posited the self as a function of cultural imperatives and ultimately decentered it by defining it in terms of its own *différance*.

Conceiving the operations of culture in structural terms on the analogy of language made Trilling even more vulnerable to criticism. From nearly the beginning of his career, he had come under attack for preferring to discuss the ideas of figures like Arnold, Keats, and Wordsworth, shunning the close verbal explications of the New Critics. Although Trilling proved again and again--in his essays on the Immortality Ode, on Graves and Cavafy, on the poems collected in *The Experience of Literature*--that he was an unobtrusively gifted close reader, he never developed a theory of language comparable in power or subtlety to his theory of modern culture and the shaped self. Throughout Trilling's work, language is tacitly regarded as a function of self and culture; post-structuralist theories that consider self and culture as functions of the linguistic codes that enable them by privileging certain differences and repressing others therefore regard this absence as crippling.

The distance between Trilling's cultural criticism and the cultural critique sponsored by post-structuralism is best indicated by setting Trilling alongside Foucault. In many ways the interests of the two men are surprisingly similar. Both are cultural historians who see their own implication in a dominant culture as necessarily equivocal; both, reading cultural norms and imperatives through myriad texts, seek to uncover precisely the imperatives that are not stipulated because they are taken for granted; both see these imperatives as deeply rooted in a quest to seize, consolidate, or justify power, whether personal or institutional; both reject any distinction between the creation or exposition of ideas and their literary use. Foucault's early book *Madness and Civilization* recalls such essays as "The Fate of Pleasure" and "The Two Environments" in the persistence with which it traces the ways political motives determine the operation of apparently disinterested institutions. Here for example is Trilling in "The Two Environments" on the commodification of desire:

> The economy itself is deeply involved with matters of style and with the conditions of the spirit or psyche. Our commodities are not only mere *things* but states of mind: joy, freedom, self-definition, self-esteem. One industry after another is benefited by our ever-growing need to choose a fashion of dress, or décor, or locomotion which will serve to signalize some spiritual or psychic grace. Advertising joins forces with literature in agitating the question of who one is, of what kind of person one should want to be, a choice in which one's possessions and appearance, one's tastes, are as important as one's feelings and behavior.[22]

To the insight that states of mind have become commodities--a commonplace of post-structuralist criticism--Trilling adds a skeptical analogy emphasizing the implication of literature as an agent and an advertisement for this commodification--an analogy so unexpected for a critic of Trilling's humanist temperament that one eminent reviewer of *Beyond Culture* misunderstood him to be praising advertising rather than excoriating literature and had to be corrected in a note to the paperback edition.[23]

For all the boldness of his skepticism about the force of literature in the commodification of desire, however, Trilling never relinquishes his faith in the humanist impulse itself. When he continues here that "the impulse to choose, define, and indicate what kind of person one is can scarcely be thought new, and we shall regard it more charitably if we are aware of how deeply rooted it is in human nature,"[24] the focus on the possibility of moral choice rooted in human nature shows that, however suspicious Trilling may become of literature as an institution, his faith in human nature and in the possibility of self-definition uncorrupted by the will to institutional power continues unabated.

This faith, and the narrower limits within which it operates, is set forth most clearly in the little-known essay "A Portrait of Western Man," which first explores the intimacy between identity as a function of moral choice and identity as a question of style, and in the last and most problematic of Trilling's major essays on Freud, "Freud: Within and Beyond Culture" and "Authenticity and the Modern Unconscious," revised as the final chapter of *Sincerity and Authenticity*. Moved to defend the shaped self against the ever-increasing encroachments and intimations of cultural control, Trilling first proposes a heroic reading of the human organism's biological determinism as "a residue of human quality beyond the reach of cultural control,"[25] but finally, fifteen years later, finds in the irrational and uncompromising internalization of social norms in Freud's superego a harrowing drama of the self against itself as it struggles with colonizing cultural imperatives essential even to its biological identity.

This retreat of the shaped self into a perilously tight corner is the closest Trilling comes to the idea of *différance*, the Derridean notion of identity as a self-dislocation endlessly promising and endlessly deferring a definitive resolution. But Trilling never embraces this state as a condition of existence. Instead, as the plethora of conflictual metaphors in these essays indicate, he celebrates the self's dramatic resistance to the alienation exacted by cultural imperatives in whatever form; it is exactly this fierce resistance that ennobles Freud's fables of identity and makes Freud himself, in Trilling's profoundly un-Foucaultian account, his climactic culture hero, the richest and most heroic example of all. By contrast, Trilling's reference to *Madness and Civilization* in the closing pages of *Sincerity and Authenticity*, far from emphasizing Trilling's sympathy with post-structuralist critiques of the futility of any attempt to define a self outside culture, singles out as "cant" David Cooper's controversial introduction to the English translation of the book, which asserts that in a culture whose dominant institutions are radically dehumanizing, madness is, in Trilling's withering phrase, "health fully realized at last."[26] Though Foucault himself does not subscribe to the "anti-psychiatry" of Cooper and R. D. Laing, neither can he share Trilling's normative attitude toward mental illness or endorse his appeal to experience:

> Who that has spoken, or tried to speak, with a psychotic friend will consent to betray the masked pain of his bewilderment and solitude by making it the paradigm of liberation from the imprisoning falsehoods of an alienated social reality? Who that finds intelligible the sentences which describe madness (to use the word that cant prefers) in terms of transcendence and charisma will fail to penetrate to the great refusal of human connection that they express, the appalling belief that human existence is made authentic by the possession of a power, or the persuasion of its possession, which is not to be qualified or restricted by the co-ordinate existence of any fellow man?[27]

Trilling's critique of culture and its institutions, unlike Foucault's, always operates within and willingly returns to a vantage point within culture, for Trilling, to adopt a remark he makes a few pages earlier about Herbert Marcuse, likes culture; he likes people to have the benefits of culture, cost what it may in alienation. Foucault's archeology of discourse, by contrast, comes to bury culture, in which Foucault is implicated to his cost but with no sense of any corresponding gain.

What Foucault most notoriously comes to bury, of course, is precisely Man, a figure Trilling implicitly takes as the basis of both liberalism and the critique of liberalism, but which Foucault sees as a purely historical function of the modern age's search for an historical subject, a prescriptive function its seekers hope will validate the transcendental categories that in turn enable all knowledge. Instead of analyzing authenticity in historical context, as Trilling does, Foucault defines madness as an historical function; instead of historicizing authors like Austen and James, Foucault historicizes the author-function. In a sense his cultural critique is continuing further along the same path as Trilling's; but this path swiftly brings it back to an annihilating critique of the concepts--culture, mind, self, Man--on whose behalf Trilling first wrote, and outside whose orbit he declined to move.

It would be naive, of course, to describe Foucault, or post-structuralism generally, as simply moving beyond Trilling's blinkered humanism to a more clear-sighted (one is tempted to add "authentic") cultural critique. Critical insight is only purchased, as Paul de Man points out, at the price of some enabling blindness,[28] and if the New Critics were able to valorize the study of literature for literature's sake only by declining to conceptualize literature as such--a blindness which led slowly but inevitably to their displacement at the vanguard--

contemporary cultura; theory may well be enabled by a similar failure to conceptualize culture itself. Even as Foucault painstakingly deconstructs the humanism of Trilling and his contemporaries, Trilling attempts to transcend the post-structuralist critique of cultural studies by putting it in its place as a political aberration, another system designed to enslave its followers and excuse them from the burden of thought. For years Trilling had been conducting an analogous skirmish with political critics like James T. Farrell who excoriated his lack of commitment to change and theorists like Joseph Frank who condemned his dialectical habit of mind as fatalistic, even defeatist, in its quietism.[29] Trilling's response, most pointedly in "The Princess Casamassima" and the climactic scene of *The Middle of the Journey*, was always the same: to argue that seizures of power in the name of a movement toward some political utopia revealed a will to power masking itself in virtue and an ideology whose true goal was the end of ideology, a charmed moment when the need for political and social thought--indeed for thinking of any kind--would wither away. This debate between two dialecticians, a committed believer who dismisses his opponent as passive and a self-critical analyst who attacks his opponent as narcissistically idealistic, allows each to label the other one insufficently dialectical. So too Robert Boyers, in reviewing Krupnick's book on Trilling, can assert that Trilling is more dialectical than Marx.[30]

Despite his many polemical writings on the institutional pretensions of the counterculture, Trilling never engaged the theoretical critique of liberal humanism by the post-structuralists at length. Apart from his furious assault on Cooper's valorization of psychosis and his widely-quoted remark that if he were young again he would fight structuralism, as he had fought Stalinism, as another threat to human freedom,[31] there are only his brief remarks in reply to Robert Scholes's essay "The Illiberal Imagination" in "Art, Will, and Necessity." Trilling's most extended engagement of the issues raised by the contemporary critique of humanism is, surprisingly, in "The Sense of the Past," published fifty years ago in response to widespread wartime breast-beating among Anglo-American intellectuals feeling, as E. M. Forster put it, that "if they had played less and theorized less all this mess would not have come about." After raising several questions designed to "complicate our sense of the past"--problems ranging from "the whole question of causation in culture" to the question of "whether, and in what way, human nature is always the same," both of them still vexing Trilling in his last unfinished essay, "Why We Read Jane Austen"--he turns to the relation of ideas to the historical conditions of their creation and transmission in order to attack the ascription of autonomy to ideas and ideologies (as in Peter Quennell's suggestion that Romanticism was in some way responsible for the Third Reich). Trilling bluntly opposes the belief that ideologies are responsible for historical events with his own belief in the individual will: "Behind every idea that is effective lies the human will and an idea is good or bad, morally speaking, according as the human will that uses it is good or bad." In the same way he attacks the belief in "the tyranny of words": "Words cannot control us unless we wish to be controlled." Present-day intellectuals, "concerned with ideas rather than with thinking," Trilling concludes, blame their troubles on their manipulation by powerful words and ideas in order to avoid taking responsibility for their own bad thinking.[32]

Vesting political power in the individual will rather than in structures of thought like language and ideology naturally sounds unsophisticated to an audience steeped in the belief that the will is everywhere conditioned by precisely these structures and their repressions. But on the subject of the agency of power, its sources and nature, Foucault is no more conclusive. Defining power in several interviews[33] in terms of "relations" rather than "individuals," Foucault declines to identify these relations with social class, ideology, the historical dialectic, or the repressive mechanisms of the state; they are not relations between different individuals, institutions, or modes of discourse. Fallacious as Trilling's claims of power for individual agents may seem, it is not clear that Foucault's analysis is any more satisfying; certainly it has been subject to the same criticisms of political quietism because it apparently fails to open a space for any escape from systematization or any resistance to power.[34]

Trilling's liberal humanist ascription of power to individuals and Foucault's insistence that power always comes from outside both individuals and established institutions impeach each other with such elegant completeness that it is impossible to find a place above or outside both of them from which they can be judged independently of each other; any choice between them is simply a choice, an affirmation of one's beliefs about the nature of power and the possibilities of action. Broadly speaking, Foucault theorizes the operations of power more cogently, but

Trilling's more primitive theory opens a wider space for possible future operations--the kind of space leading cultural theorists are coming to see as more and more necessary to their projects.

An apparent weakness of Trilling's criticism, then--its conceptual incompleteness--is actually one of its greatest strengths. Despite his frequently oracular tone, Trilling never poses as a complete critic with a coherent system that precludes further critique; indeed his principal line of development is projected by his own inveterate habit of self-criticism. Trilling's attack on contemporary intellectuals as more concerned with ideas than thinking reveals by contrast his own insistence on thinking as an uncompleted process, and mind in the modern world best conceived under the aspect of a verb rather than a noun. The question of what Trilling has to offer contemporary criticism, and what he is likely to offer future readers, cannot be answered by citing his own theory--he repeatedly represented himself as having none--or his enduring historical analyses of cultural situations, or his own seminal readings of particular texts, but rather by considering his own position as an avatar of culture. Once again, this is neither to relegate Trilling to a merely historical function as a representative liberal humanist nor to recuperate him on Krupnick's terms as the true progenitor of contemporary cultural studies, but to emphasize the exemplary status of his work and the identity he created for himself. For Trilling's final, and in some ways his greatest, achievement was to turn himself into a culture hero in the line of Arnold, Keats, and Freud.

This is hardly surprising, given the nature of Trilling's attachment to each of his culture heroes and the kindred habit of mind he so valorized in his own work: a critical temper Morris Dickstein has called "lacerating" and Daniel O'Hara "sacrificial," the kind of self-definition that could make Trilling so instantly recognizable in the reply he gave to a critic who complained that he was always taking stands between ideological extremes: "Sometimes between is the only honest place to be."[35] Trilling's liberal critique of liberalism, a project he inherited from Arnold, marks him not only as a latter-day humanist but as an aspiring culture hero who embodies and dramatizes cultural contradictions his discourse cannot resolve. This pose, which Trilling had struck nearly from the beginning of his career--it is already implicit in the *we* of his earliest reviews--becomes increasingly resonant as his critical position turns repeatedly on itself in *The Liberal Imagination*, *The*

Opposing Self, and *Beyond Culture*. Even the ceremonious manner of Trilling's late prose, often taken as equivocation, is more properly read as equivocal, as Trilling attempts to penetrate beneath given concepts of selfhood by using those concepts as analytical tools and historical functions. And Trilling emerges unmistakably as the disintegrated but heroically active modern consciousness from the famous concluding flourish of *Sincerity and Authenticity*, which uses the book's final ironic sentence to set "the falsities of an alienated social reality" with which Trilling has long aligned himself in a kind of heroic resignation with "an upward psychopathic mobility to the point of divinity--each one of us a Christ, but with none of the inconveniences of undertaking to intercede, of being a sacrifice, of reasoning with rabbis, of making sermons, of having disciples, of going to weddings and to funerals, of beginning something and at a certain point remarking that it is finished."[36] The list of responsibilities carefully excludes sacraments, miracles, and resurrection--all activities outside Trilling's sphere--in order to make it clear just who the real modern Christ is.

Such a slyly inflated analogy risks making Trilling's status as culture hero sound all too solemn, a pose which exercised many reviewers of *Beyond Culture* and *Sincerity and Authenticity*. But the slyness is as essential to Trilling's persona as the solemnity. Most of Trilling's commentators have appreciated the wit that bubbles up from such individual performances as his brisk skewering of Otis and Needleman's fatuous *Survey-History of English Literature*[37] or of Karen Horney's vacuously optimistic revision of Freud,[38] his "Valedictory" on the misfit between modern corporate universities and the creative geniuses they profess to lionize or the addendum to the introduction to *Beyond Culture* in which he defends himself for ironies his reviewers have misunderstood, and of course his virtuouso review of the Kinsey Report. But only a few have noticed that all of Trilling's most serious essays, from "Reality in America" to "Mind in the Modern World," are enlivened by an equally playful wit masked by the gravity of the rhetorical occasion. This wit surfaces most frequently in Trilling's fiction--in "Of This Time, of That Place" and "The Other Margaret," and especially in *The Middle of the Journey*, which for this reason alone would deserve a special place among Trilling's works--a place it has rarely been accorded.

Trilling wastes no time in setting a dryly witty tone for his novel. On the first page, Gifford Maxim, arriving with John Laskell by train in Westport, at first gives "not the slightest sign that he had come to his destination," but then leaves with a brief farewell, "the firm, convinced promise of the exile who knows that some day, in some way, he will come to power and then he will not forget the friends who helped him in his adversity" (3).[39] The amusing effect of quiet overinflation depends on Trilling's ability to suggest Maxim's unruffled self-seriousness without definitely attributing the judgment of self-seriousness to Laskell or Maxim himself or indicating whether his readers ought to question or accept this judgment: Laskell, filled with pity for his friend's self-deluding paranoia, is no sooner left by himself than he begins to wonder whether he will be abandoned if the car he is riding in is cut off. This trick of hovering on the edge of characters' judgments while playing them off against each other is not far from the comic technique of *New Yorker* fiction, but Trilling is constantly working to deepen the resonance of these judgments, as in Laskell's observation that "old Mr. Folger was so on the edge of life that he was scarcely a person any longer, yet he was kept a person by his inclusion here, by the little duties he performed such as this one of fetching the eggs" (64)--an unusually apposite remark in a novel about the relation between action and identity--or in the rhythm of the ailing Laskell's thoughts when his no-nonsense nurse Miss Paine is replaced by the "unendurable" Miss Debry:

> Outside of paintings, Laskell had never seen a woman contrived in these proportions. Her skin was superbly white, her hair superbly dark, and she had fishpool eyes. The late light poured in at the window and Miss Debry was willing to stand full in it. It made her very beautiful, very much to be observed. Laskell was glad that it was the late light. Soon after the sun set Miss Debry would be gone, giving place to Miss Paine. He lay there watching her. He hated her. (44-45)

Sometimes Trilling's wit invests commonplace situations and phrases with comically unexpected intimations of metaphorical pretension, as in the adjuration of Laskell's friend Nancy Croom to Laskell as he treads on the edge of her flower bed--"I'll thank you, John, to step out of the cosmos" (73)--or Laskell's unfortunate choice of thirty dollars to given Maxim on the eve of their departure for Connecticut (136). But Trilling seems uncomfortable with such self-consciously playful metaphors, and usually decodes them immediately and awkwardly. He is more consistently successful in playing judgments and voices off against each other in scenes whose economy supplies their wit. When Laskell, drinking in a Crannock bar with Mr. Folger, overhears the loutish Duck Caldwell, prized handyman to Laskell's enlightened friends Arthur and Nancy Croom, telling an off-color story about the Crooms, their noble-savage idealization of Duck is set against his mean-spirited vulgarity. But Trilling complicates this opposition further by noting in gravely oracular terms the reaction of Duck's audience in the bar--"the information about life which they had received was interesting and valuable, but they looked down on the man who had such information to impart"--and adding the remark Mr. Folger characteristically directs to a stag's head over the bar--"There is a kind of man, even his own wife isn't sacred to him"--which both sets an apparently definitive judgment on Duck and portends Laskell's brief affair with Duck's wife Emily, an affair that naturally will complicate his attitude toward Duck still further (101).

The principal beneficiaries of Trilling's use of rhetorical wit to develop and complicate psychological motives are Laskell and Maxim, the cautiously well-meaning liberal and the apostate radical now as fiercely partisan for the Church as he had once been for the Party. Maxim typically argues his opponents down by throwing their own rhetoric in their faces. When Nancy Croom, calling him "Maxim," accuses him of wanting to undo the work of his earlier having drawn them into political activism, Maxim replies, "You are mistaken, Croom," and continues:

> "You are quite mistaken. I didn't draw you in. The dialectic of the situation"--his voice permitted itself a note of intellectual bitterness which swelled as he went on--"mind you, *the dialectic of the situation* detached certain disaffected portions of the middle class from their natural class interests and connections, and attached them to the interests of the oppressed classes." (215-16)

Later, only a few minutes before the catastrophe of Susan Caldwell's death at the bazaar, Maxim, listening to avid, complaisant, right-thinking, left-leaning Rev. Mr. Gurney's remarks about how "religion could be said to be an effort for social justice," responds, "In short, you believe in society and social justice and sociology, but you do not believe in God."

> Mr. Gurney was taken aback. But he recovered himself. He leaned attentively toward Maxim and smiled. "I'm sorry," he said quite urbanely, "I didn't catch the name."
>
> "God," said Maxim with brutal simplicity. (246)

The climactic debate between Maxim and Laskell is similarly shaped by Maxim's ability, in the manner of the Grand Inquisitor, to parody the rhetoric of Laskell's considered liberalism. "Neither beast nor angel!" he sneers at Laskell's rejection of both the Crooms' refusal to blame Duck for Susan's death and Maxim's verdict that Duck, like Maxim himself, is absolutely responsible--and continues, "Like any bourgeois intellectual, you want to make the best of every possible world and every possible view. Anything to avoid a commitment, anything not to have to take a risk" (301). A minute later Maxim will tell Nancy Croom, quoting the line from Blake's *Milton* that had brought Laskell together with Susan and led to her death, "No. John is not above the battle. He will not cease from mental fight"; and he concludes by "gaily" saluting "the supreme act of the humanistic intelligence--it perceives the cogency of the argument and acquiesces in the fact of its own extinction" (302, 305). The point of Maxim's relentless needling is not to allow Laskell a chance to prove his dedication to the "idea in modulation" (302) superior to the zealous dogmatism of Maxim and the Crooms; its point, as Trilling's studiously flat epilogue makes clear, is to fuel the debate without prejudging its conclusion. Trilling's wit not only gives Laskell's opponents their due; it makes their engagement with Laskell, not a particularly interesting character, continuously amusing, even arresting, and in so doing creates the terms under which such engagement can continue. Even Trilling's final scene, which leaves Laskell sitting inconclusively on the train with his heavily symbolic baggage--the empty creel he had first left at the Crooms', then taken on the fishing trip with Duck that led to his encounter with Emily, and the crudely handmade bowl he had bought from Emily at the bazaar--recalls the title *The Middle of the Journey*, which poses the novel as an incompleted action rather than an exposition of liberalism and its discontents.

Trilling's critics, never inclined to take him seriously as a novelist despite his steadfast insistence that he had always thought of himself primarily as a novelist rather than a critic until well into his forties, have condescended to *The Middle of the Journey* as an honorable adjunct to a career in criticism, comparing it unfavorably to its obvious models in James and Forster, recalling its lukewarm reception in America, and pointing to Trilling's failure to publish any more fiction. In all this they are mistaken. Trilling's grave wit in handling ideological motives in the slippery coin of his characters' ideas, if it does not make his novel the equal of *The Bostonians* or *Howards End*, makes it successful in the same ways, as a lively account and example of serious play with large ideas and an invitation to the same kind of critical play. In posing John Laskell as still another culture hero whose ideas must be tested by Trilling's pointed wit, it is the most characteristic of all his books, the one that indicates most clearly what the others are about. If Trilling, like Laskell and all his other heroes, hopes to find his life by losing it in a self-lacerating sacrifice on the altar of liberal culture, his novel dramatizes the ways in which the sacrifice is perfect only to the extent that wit and play make the ordeal fun--and extend the promise of cultural analysis as a form of serious play to readers everywhere.

Critics from Robert Boyers and Mark Krupnick to J. A. Ward have recorded Trilling's attraction to James, especially the James of *The Princess Casamassima*. In particular they have singled out the ways Hyacinth Robinson dramatizes the contradictions among Trilling's ethnic heritage, his early political leftism, his aesthetic modernism, and his frank love of the civilization whose problems so deeply move him.[40] But Trilling's closeness to Hyacinth should not obscure his even closer identification with James the novelist. The opening of Trilling's essay on *The Princess*, in which he recalls James's bitter disappointment at the reception of *The Princess* and *The Bostonians*, surely echoes Trilling's own disappointment at the reception of *The Middle of the Journey*, published the preceding year, as the work Trilling had expected to launch his proper career as a novelist seemed to be received no more favorably than the two great explorations of social ideology on which it had been modeled. Trilling cites James's courage in persisting in his vocation in the face of his reviews even as Trilling is confirming in this very essay another path for himself. Thereafter Trilling recreates himself as an alternative James, a James who became primarily a critic rather than a novelist. His criticism had already taken its cue from James's own voluminous criticism in its unsystematic, anti-dogmatic emphasis on the possibilities of the novel as a means to clarity and freedom. The persistence of a Jamesian sense of play throughout Trilling's work, even in the darkest essays of his final years, may prove to be his most immediate, as it is his most unlikely, legacy to a contemporary critical scene whose horizons have been so dramatically reoriented by a deconstructive sense of play. Trilling is most likely to be remembered historically as the pre-eminent cultural theorist, as the New Critics were the pre-eminent explicators, of high modernism. But James's continuing reputation as a critic who remains indispensible despite his lack of influence on the reigning critical orthodoxies is the surest indication of Trilling's enduring place in the history of criticism.

Notes

[1] Ellison, "Society, Morality, and the Novel," in *The Living Novel: A Symposium*, edited by Granville Hicks (New York: Macmillan, 1957), pp. 83-84; Reising, *The Unusable Past: Theory and the Study of American Literature* (New York: Methuen, 1986), pp. 93-94.

[2] Mills, *American and English Fiction in the Nineteenth Century: An Antigenre Critique and Comparison* (Bloomington: Indiana University Press, 1973), p. 129; see Trilling, "Manners, Morals, and the Novel" (1948), rpt. in *The Liberal Imagination: Essays on Literature and Society* (New York: Viking, 1950), p. 212.

[3] See Adams, "Speaking of Books," *New York Times Book Review*, 12 April 1959, p. 2; Edward Weeks et al., "Letters to the Editor," *New York Times Book Review*, 3 May 1959, p. 24; Anon., "How Terrifying a Poet?," M. L. Rosenthal, "The Robert Frost Controversy," *Nation* 188 (20 June 1959): 559-61; *Newsweek* 54 (27 July 1959): 89; Richard Poirier, "The Art of Poetry II: Robert Frost," *Paris Review*, no. 24 (Summer-Fall 1960): 88-120.

[4] See especially Morris Dickstein, *Gates of Eden: American Culture in the Sixties* (New York: Basic, 1977), pp. 262-66.

[5] See "The New York Intellectuals: A Chronicle and a Critique," *Commentary* 46 (October 1968): 29.

[6] Webster, *The Republic of Letters: A History of Postwar American Literary Opinion* (Baltimore: Johns Hopkins University Press, 1979), p. 252.

[7] *Beyond Culture: Essays on Literature and Learning* (1965: rpt. New York: Viking, 1968), p. 13.

[8] The closest Trilling ever comes to defining the term directly is in his dialectical account of the relation between Romanticism and the Enlightenment. See "A Rejoinder to Mr. Barett," *Partisan Review* 16 (June 1949): 653-58.

[9] See the Introduction to *The Partisan Reader* (1946), rpt. as "The Function of the Little Magazine" in *The Liberal Imagination*, p. 98.

[10] See for example "Another Jewish Problem Novel" (1929), rpt. in *Speaking of Literature and Society*, edited by Diana Trilling (New York: Harcourt Brace Jovanovich, 1980), pp. 16-20.

[11] *Matthew Arnold* (New York: Norton, 1939), p. v.

[12] See "T. S. Eliot as Critic," in *Anna Karenina and Other Essays* (New York: Simon and Schuster, 1967), p. 177.

[13] *The Liberal Imagination*, p. ix.

[14] See Steven Marcus, "Lionel Trilling, 1905-1975" (1976), rpt. in *Art, Politics, and Will: Essays in Honor of Lionel Trilling*, edited by Quentin Anderson, Steven Donadio, and Steven Marcus (New York: Basic, 1977), p. 275.

[15] Krupnick, *Lionel Trilling and the Fate of Cultural Criticism* (Evanston: Northwestern University Press, 1986), p. 13.

[16] *The Liberal Imagination*, pp. ix, xv.

[17] "Mansfield Park" (1954), rpt. in *The Opposing Self* (New York: Viking, 1955), p. 216.

[18] Wellek, "The Literary Criticism of Lionel Trilling" (1979), rpt. as "Lionel Trilling" in *A History of Modern Criticism, 1750-1950* (New Haven: Yale University Press, 1955-92): 6: 142; Torgovnick, "The Politics of the 'We," *South Atlantic Quarterly* 91 (Winter 1992): 50.

[19] Blackmur, "The Politics of Human Power" (1950), rpt. in *The Lion and the Honeycomb: Essays in Solicitude and Critique* (New York: Harcourt, Brace & World, 1955), p. 32; Grumet, "The Apprenticeship of Lionel Trilling," *Prooftexts* 4 (May 1984): 165.

[20] Stephen L. Tanner, for example, argues that Trilling, who "in his literary and cultural views . . . was singularly conservative," has "been identified too exclusively and uncritically with liberalism." See *Lionel Trilling* (Boston: Twayne, 1988), pp. xii, xi.

[21] Cain, "Trilling in Our Time," *Virginia Quarterly Review* 54 (Summer 1978): 569; Jay, review of Krupnick, *Lionel Trilling and the Fate of Cultural Criticism*, *South Atlantic Review* 52 (January 1987): 106.

[22] Trilling, "The Two Environments: Reflections on the Study of English" (1965); rpt. in *Beyond Culture*, p. 224.

[23] See Leon Edel, "Literature and Life Style," *Saturday Review* 48 (8 November 1965): 37-38; and *Beyond Culture*, p. xix.

[24] *Beyond Culture*, pp. 224-25.

[25] "Freud: Within and Beyond Culture" (1955), rpt. in *Beyond Culture*, p. 113.

[26] *Sincerity and Authenticity* (Cambridge: Harvard University Press, 1972), p. 170.

[27] *Sincerity and Authenticity*, p. 171.

[28] Trilling himself borrows from Gregory Bateson the similar idea of the Essential Error which both produces and limits such insight. See "An American Classic" (1960), rpt. in *Speaking of Literature and Society*, p. 379.

[29] See Farrell, "A Comment on Literaure and Morality: A Crucial Question of Our Times," *New International* 12 (May 1946): 141-45, and Frank, "Lionel Trilling and the Conservative Imagination," *Sewanee Review* 64 (Spring 1956): 296-309.

[30] Boyers, "Too Smart to Be Correct," *New York Times Book Review*, 13 April 1986, p. 19.

[31] See Robert Langbaum, "The Importance of *The Liberal Imagination*," *Salmagundi*, no. 41 (Spring 1978), p. 65.

[32] "The Sense of the Past," *Partisan Review* 9 (May-June 1942): 241, 235, 237, 238. The argument is slightly modified in the version reprinted in *The Liberal Imagination*.

[33] See Foucault, *Power/Knowledge: Selected Interviews and Other Writings 1972-1977*, edited by Colin Gordon, translated by Colin Gordon et al. (New York: Pantheon, 1980), pp. 114-15, 122, 198-200.

[34] See for example Fredric Jameson, *The Political Unconscious* (Ithaca: Cornell University Press, 1981), pp. 90-92.

[35] See Dickstein, "The Critics Who Made Us: Lionel Trilling and *The Liberal Imagination*," *Sewanee Review* 94 (Spring 1986): 334; and O'Hara, *Lionel Trilling: The Work of Liberation* (Madison: University of Wisconsin Press, 1988), p. 70. Trilling's remark is quoted in Richard Sennett, "On Lionel Trilling," *New Yorker* 55 (5 November 1979): 209.

[36] *Sincerity and Authenticity*, pp. 171-72.

[37] See "M., W., F. at 10" (1942), rpt. in *Speaking of Literature and Society*, pp. 192-96.

[38] See "The Progressive Psyche" (1942), rpt. in *Speaking of Literature and Society*, pp. 181-85.

[39] Parenthetical references in the following paragraphs are to *The Middle of the Journey* (New York: Scribner's, 1976).

[40] See Boyers, *Lionel Trilling: Negative Capability and the Wisdom of Avoidance* (Columbia: University of Missouri Press, 1977), p. 37; Krupnick, *Lionel Trilling and the Fate of Cultural Criticism*, p. 71; and Ward, "Lionel Trilling and Henry James," *Explorations: The Twentieth Century* (Special Series), 3 (1989): 61-62.

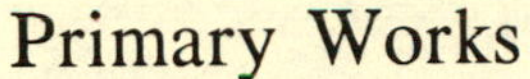

Primary Works

Section A

Books and Collections of Essays

A1. *Matthew Arnold*. New York: Norton, 1939. 4 l., vii-xiv, 15-465 pages.

The Introduction describes the book as "a biography of Arnold's mind" rather than a life based on newly available unpublished material, and an attempt to rescue Arnold from the falsification or "mythopoeia" which reduces Arnold's thought to such catchphrases as "the grand style," "culture," and "sweetness and light." Maintains the unity of Arnold's development from his poetry to his literary, social, and religious criticism, emphasizing "the historical and dialectical nature" of his thought, which often produced contradictions based on Arnold's perceptions of the requirements of different situations, noting that despite Arnold's failures, whose implications Trilling has attempted to draw out, his "eclectic and dialectical method has its vitality exactly because it is the method of history."

Stresses the insouciance and gaiety, especially in reaction against pietism, of Arnold as a young man, in contrast to the elegiac tone characteristic of his poetry, and argues that Arnold's "dandyism" shows the resistance to systems of thought and behavior enabling the "abandonment to melancholy" that produced his best poetry, which indicts the tyranny "of the never-resting intellect over the soul of modern man," alternating between "celebration of the painful glories of man's bondage to the strength of the emotions" and "the abandonment of the romantic temperament" in "the poet's loving, non-personal vision of the world" figured in Arnold's terms as "the general Life." Notes the contradictions implicit in Arnold's attempt to hold both materialistic and Platonic views of nature without reconciling them in his poetry, establishes a basis for Arnold's early ambivalence toward "the general Life" in the social and educational meliorism of his father Thomas Arnold, whose legacy to his son included a vision of a democratic State, a Christianized Roman imperium not antagonistic to individual freedom, and a hatred of Jacobinism, "the demand for 'rights without duties'" of both upper and lower classes.

Contends that the keynote of Arnold's poetry--the attempt to continue the work of the French Revolution by reconciling a romanticized religious faith with Enlightenment rationalism in a synthesis that will overcome the inadequacies of either--persists in his criticism even after his search for peace and health leads him to renounce the melancholy and "desire for romantic violence" at the heart of his poetry. Argues that Arnold's critical judgments are always based on social and political judgments which led him to base a theory of literary style (in *On Translating Homer*) on a theory of morality, to demand "a poetry *adequate* to the time in which it is written," to repudiate the notion of poetic genius independent of its social circumstances, and to describe poetry functionally as a criticism of life: "Criticism is not what poetry *is*; it is what poetry *does*."

Observes that Arnold finds "the modern source of the grand style" in "the *State*," conceived in contradistinction to the State as a force against individual freedom, and roots Arnold's attachment to critical disinterestedness in Hegel's warning that liberty is often used as a mask for private interests. Criticizes the racial theories proposed in Arnold's lectures on Celtic literature as inconsistent in assigning racial characteristics that individual effort may alter; his attempt in *Culture and Anarchy*, "the keystone of his intellectual life," to conceive a State based on social classes without reference to class interests or struggles for power--an attempt which leads Arnold into epistemological problems, as he attempts to base each class's "best self" on an ascertainable reason--Arnold's circular definition of religion as "morality touched by emotion"; Arnold's attack on Protestantism by substituting a psychological and cultural St. Paul for the religious figure of the Church; and Arnold's quest for apodictic knowledge of God despite his dismissal of metaphysical systems in favor of empirical models of knowledge. Notes in each case the development of Arnold's ambivalence in his continued attempt to use poetry, the State, and religion "to supply the lacks of the French Revolution," leading him ultimately to the position that "Christianity *contains* the truth" while declining to affirm that "*Christianity is true*," and the attempt to make poetry fulfill the function of religion by becoming religious, adopting a solemnity precluding comedy.

Uses many footnotes and references to earlier thinkers from Vico to Reynolds and contemporary figures from I. A. Richards to Mussolini to establish parallels between Arnold's historical dilemma--his need to escape entrapment between the competing, inadequate value systems of idealism and materialism by proposing a therapeutic synthesis of ideas neither poetry nor politics could support--and the contemporary situation, in which Arnoldian disinterestedness is once again under attack by ideologues who "believe that thought is inferior to action and opposed to it." Proposes Arnold, whose career was concerned "not so much . . . with combating vile positions as with refining relatively good ones" through a ceaseless criticism of his own ideas, as an exemplary reminder "against the belief that taking sides settles things or requires the suspension of reason."

A1a. British edition of A1. London: G. Allen & Unwin, 1939. 4 l., vii-xiv, 15-465 pages.

A1b. Second edition of A1, including a new Preface. New York: Columbia University Press, 1949. 465 pages.

Expresses relief at Trilling's inability to make changes in A1 despite his desire to do so and his admission that neither the pivotal figure of Clough nor the aesthetics of Arnold's poetry is given enough focus. Emphasizes Arnold's continued relevance now that Soviet Russia has replaced Nazi Germany as a totalitarian threat to the critical intelligence and more insidious and seductive forms of ideological absolutism remain equally dangerous.

A1c. Paperback reprint of A1b. Cleveland: Meridian Books, 1955. 413 pages.

A1d. British edition of A1b. London: Unwin University Books, 1963. xviii, 465 pages.

**** Uniform Edition of A1, including an additional essay, "Matthew Arnold, Poet" (C118). New York: Harcourt Brace Jovanovich, 1977. 12 l., 493 pages. See A11.

**** Paperback reprint of Uniform Edition. New York: Harvest/ Harcourt Brace Jovanovich, 1979. 12 l., 493 pages. See A11.

**** British Uniform Edition. Oxford: Oxford University Press, 1982. 12 l., 493 pages. See A11.

**** Paperback reprint of British Uniform Edition. Oxford: Oxford University Press, 1982. 12 l., 493 pages. See A11.

A2. *E. M. Forster*. New York: New Directions, 1943. 192 pages.

Urges Forster's critical attitude--seriously comic, sympathetically critical, and deeply divided on the question of whether good and evil are opposites or interdependent attributes-- toward liberal pieties as a necessary corrective to a literature undercut by its own limiting political commitments. Describes Forster's culture as "metropolitan" despite his dislike of the city, and defines his central theme as the "undeveloped" heart, "untrained and untutored," as against "the unfeeling or perverted heart." Forster's typical political mode--"an appeal to the Liberal party--to the middle class"--makes it possible for his concern with the private life to venture moral judgments "under the aspect of the nation--or of all the nations," conflating the opposition between public and private spheres. This conflation constitutes Forster's "uniqueness and his intellectual heroism."

Traces three leading themes through Forster's short stories: the nature of death, the inadequacy of modern civilization, and the survival of heroic individuals and moral values. Finds the same themes at the heart of Forster's novels, which excel his stories by virtue of the more complex characters and situations which articulate the themes, the "infinite modulation" of Forster's development, and Forster's discovery of plot, often involving improbable melodrama or coincidence, as a trope superior to the "fantasy and allegory" of the stories. Defends Forster's melodrama in *Where Angels Fear to Tread* against the strictures of realism by arguing that "plot is to the novelist what experiment is to the scientist," a way of "making things act so that we can learn about their nature."

Emphasizes the conflict between illusion and reality, the "confusion of the real with the unreal," in both *The Longest Journey* and *A Room with a View*, contending that in *A Room with a View* the importance of "the physical reality upon which all the other realities rest" aligns the conflict between reality and illusion with a conflict between "crudeness" and "refinement" present in all the novels since *Where Angels Fear to Tread*. Distinguishes between Forster's handling of this conflict and Lawrence's, however, on the basis of Forster's "uncertainty about moral judgment," his saving inability to decide whether humankind is to be divided into sheep and goats or (the position he generally favors) whether good and evil are necessarily mingled in everyone.

Contends that "*Howards End* is undoubtedly Forster's masterpiece" because the problems raised in his earlier work are here treated with "a more mature sense of responsibility"; his heroes and heroines are tested more harshly, their victories more hardly won. The central question posed here--"Who shall inherit England?"--is defined in terms of "a class war" involving competing interests within the middle class, a corresponding "war between men and women," and a series of conflicts between the ideal life and the practical life--contraries whose resolution is enjoined by the novel's enigmatic motto: "Only connect." Finds *A Passage to India* "the most comfortable and the most conventional of Forster's novels," calling it "the least surprising, the least capricious and, indeed, the least personal," and noting that Forster's imaginative intuition of India as seen by a bewildered outsider puts him, for the first time in his novels, to "the test of verisimilitude"--a test he does not entirely pass. Criticizes the novel's story as not "sufficiently worked out in terms of the characters," but confesses bewilderment before the "coda" of the novel, the third part which comments on the plot without advancing it.

Concludes by contrasting Forster's modest criticism with Eliot's more impressive and polemical criticism, remarking that Forster's tendency, against the general tenor of modern criticism, is to accept the universe. Acknowledges that such a tendency not only limits Forster's achievement as a critic, since his acute perceptions are not matched or melded by systematic beliefs, but apparently relegates him to the sidelines in wartime, since he seems to champion disorder and regards all history as "a series of messes." Finds in Forster, however, a miraculous escape from the hegemony of intellectual will and its blind instinct for order, and sees his faith in art as uniquely asserting order and indicating its creators' capacity to achieve a better social order, even though art cannot be produced by a given social order. In a world necessarily galvanized by the will to win a war,

"Forster reminds us of a world where the will is not everything, of a world of true order."

Chapter 7 is reprinted in *Modern British Fiction*, edited by Mark Schorer (Oxford: Oxford University Press, 1961), pp. 195-209.

A2a. *E. M. Forster: A Study*. British edition of A2. London: Hogarth, 1944. 164 pages.

A2b. Second revised edition, with a new Preface. New York: New Directions, 1964. 194 pages.

Notes in the Preface the appearance of several new books by Forster--*Two Cheers for Democracy*, *The Hill of Devi*, and *Marianne Thornton*--and of a great deal of criticism of Forster's novels, but declines to revise A2 substantively in light of this work, or in light of Trilling's own friendship with Forster, except to the extent of expanding the bibliography. Recalls that A2 was written quickly, with "a polemical purpose," in order to enlist Forster's liberal critique of liberalism in assessing an American cultural scene that has now passed, and argues that A2 should stand unrevised as a historical document.

A2c. Paperback reprint of A2b. New York: New Directions, 1964. 194 pages.

A2d. British edition of A2b. London: Hogarth, 1967. 4 l., 164 pages.

**** Uniform edition of A2. New York: Harcourt Brace Jovanovich, 1980. 148 pages. See A11.

**** British Uniform Edition. Oxford: Oxford University Press, 1980. 148 pages. See A11.

A3. *The Middle of the Journey*. New York: Viking, 1947. 310 pages.

A novel of ideas, unobtrusively set in summer 1936, which tells the story of 33-year-old public housing architect John Laskell's convalescence from a near-fatal attack of scarlet fever and a concomitant loss of his sense of himself as his political and emotional assumptions come under attack during a visit to Crannock, Connecticut, where his younger friends Arthur and Nancy Croom have their summer home. The politically progressive Crooms, who are "very much involved in life," have thoughtfully supplied Laskell with trained nurses, oranges, extra pajamas and sheets, and a summer rental--the home of the nearby Folgers, whose daughter Eunice is helping Nancy with her young son Micky during Nancy's second pregnancy. But Laskell, who is recuperating not only from his own near-death but from the death three years before of his unofficial fiancée Elizabeth Fuess, feels disturbingly estranged from them. Arriving at the train station, he is plunged into a nightmarish terror "that he would not escape the state of being unborn" when the Crooms' unreliable handyman Duck Caldwell fails to pick him up. Later he realizes Nancy Croom cannot bring herself to confront his experience of his own illness or of Elizabeth's death--a subject she seems to disapprove of as "politically reactionary," and which she deflects with talk about Duck, whom she takes to incarnate a principle of proletarian life and reality.

A series of flashbacks reveals the story of Laskell's unlikely romance with a rose in a vase near his sickbed--a romance his shrewd night nurse Miss Paine describes as evidence that he does not want to get well--and his involvement with magnetic former Communist Party member Gifford Maxim, who, on leaving the Party, fears he will be assassinated by his former comrades and begs Laskell to help him establish a public existence that will insure him against untimely disappearance by impressing his identity on Miss Paine, asking Laskell to use his influence with wealthy, woolly liberal publisher Kermit Simpson to get Maxim a position on his "Jeffersonian" liberal journal *The New Era*, and traveling to Westport in Laskell's company. Unable to talk to the Crooms about his illness and his fears of death, Laskell withholds the news about their friend Maxim's defection from the Party, partly out of spite, partly because he thinks Maxim's story incomplete without his own. Instead he cultivates a distant friendship with the Folgers, nurtures his dislike of Duck (who repays Nancy's infatuation with him by telling off-color stories about her at a local tavern), and becomes gradually interested in Duck's appealing daughter Susan and his wife Emily, who first appears to him in a tableau suggesting Demeter with Persephone, then is described by the Crooms as silly, affected, and unworthy of Duck, and eventually strikes him as more lively and genuine, for all her harmless pretensions, than her shiftless husband.

A few days after Laskell finally tells the Crooms about Maxim's break with the Party, they receive a copy of *The New Era* containing a long essay by Maxim on a deluxe (and apocryphal) new edition of *Billy Budd*--an analysis written from a severely religious viewpoint. This essay, and the news that Simpson plans to bring Maxim on a visit, precipitates a series of debates between Laskell and the Crooms, later between Maxim and the Crooms, on the nature of individual responsibilites and personal commitments in the light of ideological loyalties; and these debates are the heart of the novel. Nancy, though not a Party member or a fellow-traveler, thinks her leftist sympathies, which have led her secretly to do Maxim a favor both Laskell and her husband had refused him, supersede all other loyalties and preclude any criticism of the Party even in the wake of the Spanish Civil War and the Stalin trials, just as she regards Duck as a free spirit whose peccadilloes are to be ascribed to his social circumstances; in response, Maxim, following Nancy's own line, reduces her arguments and actions to the ideological forces they express. In the meantime, Laskell has cultivated his intimacy with the Caldwells to the point of listening to Susan practice declaiming Blake's Preface to *Jerusalem* for the local Church Bazaar, tendering her advice about the delivery of one line ("I will not cease from mortal fight"), going fishing with Duck and listening to his lucubrations about Eunice Folger ("It was not wickedness. It was emptiness masking itself as mind and desire"), watching Emily and Susan bathe in the river, and later telling Emily about his love affair with death, making love with her, and hearing about Susan's serious heart condition (a secret Emily has kept from Duck and everyone else).

On the morning of the bazaar, Nancy tells Laskell that Julia Walker, the local *grande dame*, has demanded that Eunice leave the Crooms within a few days and go to work for her. At the bazaar, Laskell buys a bowl amateurishly decorated by Emily, then watches in horror as Duck interrupts the children's program by striking Susan because he is ashamed of her performance--she had stumbled on the line Laskell had corrected--and accidentally killing her, and runs after Duck to tell him about Susan's heart; after a brief struggle, Duck is arrested, and Maxim suggests that Laskell had pursued Duck because he felt a guilty implication in Susan's death. After Susan's funeral, whose expenses Laskell shares with Simpson, Emily comes to ask the Crooms if Duck may return to work for them, but Nancy, though she receives her cordially, refuses to let Duck into her house again, leading to a final debate in which Maxim, accusing her of denying the possibility of individual responsibility or forgiveness, announces that his Christian principles assign absolute responsibility but extend the possibility of divine mercy for wrongdoing. When Laskell declines to endorse either position--the absolute freedom from responsibility Nancy's ideological determinism confers, or the absolute responsibility, unconditioned by circumstance, Maxim insists on--the Crooms and Maxim turn on him alike in "the anger of the masked will at the appearance of an idea in modulation"--and although they apologize to him the following morning, he is left to return to New York alone, more isolated from them than ever before but more secure in his own identity.

A3a. British edition of A3. London: Secker & Warburg, 1948. 328 pages.

A3b. *Vid vägens mitt*. Swedish translation of A3. Translated by Vanja Lantz. Stockholm: Wahlström & Widstrand, 1949. 309 pages.

A3c. *Le responsable*. French translation of A3. Translated by Lola Tranec. Paris: Plon, 1951. 328 pages.

A3d. Paperback reprint of A3. Garden City, NY: Doubleday Anchor, 1957. 350 pages.

A3e. *A la mitad del camino*. Spanish translation of A3. Translated by Caridad Marín. Barcelona: Editorial Seix Barral, 1958. 405 pages.

A3f. Paperback reprint of A3a. Harmondsworth: Penguin, 1963. 314 pages.

A3g. *Crisi: romanzo*. Italian translation of A3. Translated by Bruno Lauzi. Milan: Sugar, 1964. 365 pages.

A3h. Paperback reprint of A3. New York: Avon, 1966. 319 pages.

A3i. Another edition, with a new Introduction (C189). London: Secker & Warburg, 1975. xxiii, 310 pages.

A3j. American edition of A3i. New York: Scribner's, 1976. xxiii, 310 pages.

A3k. Paperback reprint of A3j. New York: Avon, 1976.

A3l. New paperback edition of A3f, with a new Introduction. Harmondsworth: Penguin Modern Classics, 1977.

**** Uniform Edition of A3. New York: Harcourt Brace Jovanovich, 1980. xxv, 342 pages. See A11.

**** British Uniform Edition. Oxford: Oxford University Press, 1981. xxv, 342 pages.

A4. *The Liberal Imagination: Essays on Literature and Society.* New York: Viking, 1950. xvi, 303 pages.

Contains the following material:

Preface
Reality in America (C68 and C86)
Sherwood Anderson (C72 and C88)
Freud and Literature (C69)
The Princess Casamassima (B19)
The Function of the Little Magazine (B18)
Huckleberry Finn (B20)
Kipling (D78)
The Immortality Ode (C73)
Art and Neurosis (C80 and D355)
The Sense of the Past (C75)
Tacitus Now (C76)
Manners, Morals, and the Novel (C90)
The Kinsey Report (C91)
F. Scott Fitzgerald (C83 and B17)
Art and Fortune (C92)
The Meaning of a Literary Idea (C95)

Collects a wide range of Trilling's writing from the forties--introductions to reprinted novels, memorial essays, and book reviews, in addition to C73, Trilling's only extended analysis of a single poem--described in the Introduction as unified despite the diversity of their subjects and occasions by "an abiding interest in the ideas of what we loosely call liberalism," which "is not only the dominant but even the sole intellectual tradition" currently flourishing in America. Since contemporary conservative and reactionary political impulses express themselves in actions or gestures rather than ideas, though no less powerful for the poverty of the ideology which masks their programs, and since "it is not conducive to the real strength of liberalism that it should occupy the intellectual field alone," proposes a sympathetic critique of liberal ideas--or more properly of liberal sentiments and the ideas with which they tend to be associated. Takes Peguy's observation that everything begins in sentiment and ends in political action as the basis for the intimate relation between literature and politics, arguing that given the characteristic absorption of the novel since 1800 with politics and the persistent and paradoxical tendency of liberals to deny the full possibilities of emotional life in the name of emotional freedom, the study of literature as "the human activity that takes the fullest and most precise account of variousness, possibility, complexity, and difficulty," can have a therapeutic effect on liberal ideology, helping "to recall liberalism to its first essential imagination of variousness and possibility"--a program pointed and influential enough to make this Trilling's most important book.

Develops this therapeutic function of literature along closely related lines in different essays. Urges in C90 and B19 the need for a more sharply observed analysis of society as a means of questioning commonly shared assumptions about the power of ideology to shape individual behavior, the efficacy of politically correct sentiments, and the political costs and values of the imagination, and commends the moral realism of the great novelists as a uniquely apt diagnostic tool. Argues in C69, C73, and C80 against the belief in a peculiarly poetical mental faculty, maintaining instead the essential continuity between the poetic or artistic imagination and social, political, and moral thought. Notes approvingly in C83 and C92 the ambivalence of novelists like James and Fitzgerald toward the societies they represented, and repeatedly expresses concern over the possible decline of the novel, linking it in C90 and C92 to the blunting of the moral imagination by hegemonic ideologies.

Argues in C75 against the New Critics and for an historical understanding of literature, a sense of the past as past in its importance for the present; but uses numerous figures from the past as exemplars of a prescriptively dialectical stance which opposes uncritical ideological commitment, the besetting sin of contemporary liberals, to the commitment to variety and complexity of the novel as a form, the commitment to an unceasing cultural critique, the commitment to the free operation of mind despite the temptation to rest in political certitudes, and--most widely remarked--the commitment to moral and political ambivalence characteristic of Trilling's heroes of civilization, his avatars of cultural dialectic. Dismisses as heretical the ideological programs of Sherwood Anderson, Theodore Dreiser, and V. L. Parrington--which inhibit the operation of mind by appeals to an immutable set of saving beliefs--and the Kinsey Institute, which takes statistically normal behavior as its own ideological justification. Sets Dreiser against James as counterexamples of the triumph of ideological dogma over complicating circumstance and the resistance to ideology produced by sustained political analysis, aligning James in other essays with his fictional surrogate Hyacinth Robinson and such other ambivalent writers as Tacitus, Wordsworth, Balzac, and Fitzgerald. Notes that such writers are aware of the price of a coercive social order but acknowledge its necessity and recognize the complicity of their own art in its programs, admitting, despite their allegiances, the catastrophic power of anarchy (in Tacitus' case), the necessity of abandoning the childhood illusion of unmediated intimacy between self and world (in Wordsworth's), or the inevitable betrayal of social ideals by the operations of any particular social order (in Balzac's and Fitzgerald's). Offers Freud's tragically ambivalent model of human nature, which sees the mind as essentially poetic in its operations and as inseparable from social determinants and biological compulsions that may lead to its own destruction, as a salutary corrective to ideologies that ultimately deny a full view of social reality in the name of a political program, since it acknowledges more fully than any political ideology the necessary interdependence of culture, mind, and will.

A4a. British edition of A4. London: Secker & Warburg, 1951. xvi, 303 pages.

A4b. Paperback reprint of A4. Garden City: Doubleday Anchor, 1953. xx, 293 pages.

A4c. *Reality in America, and Other Essays* [C69, C90, and C95]. Edited, with Notes, by Saburu Oita. [Kenkyusha Pocket English Series.] Tokyo: Kenkyusha, 1955. 129 pages.

A4d. *La imaginación liberal: essayos sobre la literatura y la sociedad.* Spanish translation of A4. Translated by Enrique Pezzoni. Buenos Aires: Editorial Sudamericana, 1956. 343 pages.

A4e. Japanese translation of A4. Translated by Masaru Otake. Tokyo: Hyoran Sha, n.d. [1958]. 264 pages.

A4f. Korean translation of A4. Translated by Byung-Tak Yang. Seoul: Eul-Yoo, 1960. 437 pages.

A4g. Paperback reprint of A4a. London: Mercury Books, 1961.

A4h. Paperback reprint of A4a. Harmondsworth: Penguin, 1970. 300 pages.

A4i. Another edition, with a new Foreword. New York: Scribner's, 1976. xvi, 303 pages.

The Foreword ascribes the impact of A4 not to the originality of its insights but to its "polemical purpose" in attacking Stalinism, which "was coming to dominate the old ethos of liberal enlightenment," as a rejection of politics and will in the name of a revolution and "an imposed monolithic government" which promised to "end the exertions of our individual wills."

**** Uniform Edition of A3. New York: Harcourt Brace Jovanovich, 1979. 91., 284 pages. See A11.

**** British Uniform Edition. Oxford: Oxford University Press, 1981. 284 pages. See A11.

A5. *The Opposing Self: Nine Essays in Criticism.* New York: Viking, 1955. xv, 232 pages.

Contains the following material:

Preface
The Poet as Hero: Keats in His Letters (B22)
Little Dorrit (B111)
Anna Karenina (B23)
William Dean Howells and the Roots of Modern Taste (C98)
The Bostonians (B25)
Wordsworth and the Rabbis (C96)
George Orwell and the Politics of Truth (C100)
Flaubert's Last Testament (C112)
Mansfield Park (C116)
(Author's Note)

The book's title and Preface define the unity of the collection in terms of its absorption with the self in the literature of the past 150 years, a period during which the self has defined itself in opposition to the assumptions of the dominant culture through a critique of the mechanisms whereby culture shapes the self. Adverts in the Preface and throughout to Hegel's distinction between "character" and "personality," and the importance he assigns to "quality" in establishing not only the ethical status of particular actions but also the nature or being of moral agents. Argues in the Preface that this conception of the self as constituted by "the manner and style of the moral action" prefigures "a new idea in the world": "the modern imagination of autonomy and delight, of surprise and elevation, of selves conceived in opposition to the general culture," noting that such an opposition is necessary to the culture as well as the self.

Reintroduces a series of themes presented earlier in A2 and A4: the inescapable dialectic between self (now the specifically modern self) and social culture; the skeptical critique of ideological orthodoxy, here figured as the prison in which society encourages its members to immure themselves; the focus on such exemplary heroes of dialectical selfhood as Keats, Flaubert, and James. Departs in important ways, however, from the terms and methods of A4. Develops the argument against the constraints of social orthodoxy not in terms of the ideological critique of A4 but in psychological, often religious terms (especially in C96, C111, and C112). Following the impulse seen earlier in B19 (and perhaps traceable to the number of these essays first conceived as introductions to reprinted classics), seeks autobiographical roots for dialectical conflicts not only in the obvious cases of B22 and C112, but also in B25, C111, and C116.

Explores in almost all the essays the more general paradox of a self defined in opposition to a culture which aims to shape the self. As if anticipating the question of which self is more genuine, the self shaped by cultural norms or the self arising in opposition to culture, proposes an exfoliation of selves defined each by an appropriate will. Distinguishes in C111, for example, between the "social will" which internalizes cultural imperatives and the "individual human will" which Arthur Clennam feels he has lost; between Clennam's "ethical will," which remains healthy, and his "personal will," which has atrophied; and between the "personal will" defining itself in opposition to society (and represented by such self-tormented characters as Miss Wade and Tattycoram) and the negation or transcendence of that will in the figure of Little Dorrit, "the Paraclete in female form." Returns in C116 to a distinction between the strenuous anxieties and self-dramatizations required to maintain a modernist conception of selfhood defined by a Hegelian notion of personality, which requires a dialectical opposition to cultural sanctions, and "the bliss of being able to remain unconscious of the demands of personality" by relying on the principled sanctions marking "the path to the wholeness of the self which is peace." Commends Keats for his ability to maintain the dialectic between self and world, evil and transcendence, and, more surprisingly, Wordsworth and Howells for their rejection of the modern heresy of a completely transcendent self unconditioned by, and wholly in opposition to, social circumstance, contrasting the "apocalyptic" temper of the modernist imagination to a persistent strain showing "the will seeking its own negation--or, rather, seeking its own affirmation by its rejection of the aims which the world sets before it and by turning its energies upon itself in self-realization." Identifies Wordsworth's "sentiment of Being" as an exemplary figure for the "quietism" he shares with the Judaic tradition, a quietism offered as a useful corrective to the alienating dislocations of the modern self.

A5a. British edition of A5. London: Secker & Warburg, 1955. xvi, 232 pages.

A5b. *O eu romântico*. Portuguese translation of A5. Translated by Maria Beatriz Nizza da Silva. Rio de Janiero: Lidador, 1955. 221 pages.

A5c. *Imágines del yo romántico: nueve ensayos de critica literaria*. Spanish translation of A5. Translated by E. L. Revol. Buenos Aires: SUR, 1956. 202 pages.

A5d. Paperback reprint of A5. New York: Viking Compass, 1959. xv, 232 pages.

A5e. *El yo antagónico: nueve ensayos criticos*. Spanish translation of A5. Translated by Alicia Bleiberg. Madrid: Taurus, 1974. 226 pages.

**** Uniform edition of A5. New York: Harcourt Brace Jovanovich, 1978. 256 pages. See A11.

**** Paperback reprint of Uniform Edition. New York: Harvest/ Harcourt Brace Jovanovich, 1979. 204 pages. See A11.

**** British Uniform Edition. Oxford: Oxford University Press, 1980. 256 pages. See A11.

**** Paperback reprint of British Uniform Edition. Oxford: Oxford University Press, 1982. 204 pages. See A11.

A6. *Freud and the Crisis of Our Culture*. Boston: Beacon, 1955. 59 pages.

Observing that "no other profession has had so long or so intimate a connection with psychoanalysis as the profession of literature," traces four leading connections between psychoanalysis and literature. (1) Defines literature's "dedicat[ion] to the conception of the self" as "an achievement . . . in advance of what society, or the general culture, can conceive" parallel to Freud's systematization of the "willing suspension of disbelief in the selfhood of someone else." (2) Notes the connection between Freud's theory of the death instinct and the link tragic poets have forged between the pleasure principle and the reality principle: "Literature has always recorded an impulse of the self to find affirmation even in its own instinction. . . . The assertion of the death instinct is the effort of finely tempered minds to affirm the self in an ultimate confrontation with reality." (3) Argues along similar lines that literature and Freudian psychoanalysis both oppose love to power yet conceive "love as a principle of order for the self" and as "a civic and civilizing power" nurturing the self, for example, through a love of fame or creative activity. (4) Defines literature, like psychoanalysis, as "subversive" in its insistence on "the high authority of the self in its quarrel with society and its culture," emphasizing Freud's ambivalence toward modern culture conceived "as a new sort of selfhood bestowed upon the whole of society," and discussing at length the relation between honorific and adversive attitudes toward the formative power of culture in Freud's thought and "his sense of himself as a biological fact" as offering welcome resistance to the seductive nightmare of comprehensive cultural conditioning: "Somewhere . . . there is a hard, irreducible, stubborn core of . . . biological *reason*, that culture cannot reach and that reserves the right . . . to judge the culture and resist and revise it." Notes that although the Freudian superego is conceived as "the surrogate of . . . the culture," it envisions "a sanction beyond the culture," a conviction of selfhood that is the most important feature it shares with literature.

Revised and reprinted as "Freud: Within and Beyond Culture" in A8.

A6a. British edition of A6. London: Mark Paterson, 1955. 59 pages.

A7. *A Gathering of Fugitives*. Boston: Beacon, 1956. 6 l., 167 pages.

Contains the following material:

(Acknowledgments)
(Preface) (C125)
The Great-Aunt of Mr. Forster (C124)
In Defense of Zola (C109)
A Ramble on Graves (C120)
The Morality of Inertia (C123)
The Dickens of Our Day (C105)
Edmund Wilson: A Backward Glance (C104)
Freud's Last Book (C93)
The Situation of the American Intellectual at the Present Time (C107)
A Novel in Passing (D362)
Two Notes on David Riesman (C101 and C114)

Dr. Leavis and the Moral Tradition (D361)
Profession: Man of the World (C121)
Adams at Ease (C103)
The Novel Alive or Dead (C119)
Criticism and Aesthetics (C115)
On Not Talking (C129)
"That Smile of Parmenides Made Me Think" (C127)

The Preface acknowledges that, unlike Trilling's other collections of essays, A7 has no principle of unity, being mostly a miscellany of pieces from the *Griffin*, the monthly publication of the Reader's Subscription--whose board of editors consisted of Trilling, Jacques Barzun, and W. H. Auden--and notes that these essays, and the others (C93, C123, C129, D361, and D362) Trilling chose to complement them, are written less formally and "more personally, even autobiographically," than most of Trilling's work. Makes an exception to this rule of informality for C107, chosen for reprinting because it has frequently come under attack and been quoted out of context. C107, the most extended and ambitious essay collected here, marks an important transitional stage, in its injunction to intellectuals to survey critically the particulars of American social culture instead of retreating into a fashionable alienation, between Trilling's critique of liberal culture in A4 and his critique of the adversary culture in A8, but, as the self-effacing tone of the Preface implies, this injunction is not echoed or developed systematically in the other essays.

A7a. British edition of A7. London: Secker & Warburg, 1957. 6 l., 167 pages.

**** Uniform Edition of A7. New York: Harcourt Brace Jovanovich, 1978. 6 l., 179 pages. See A11.

**** British Uniform Edition. Oxford: Oxford University Press, 1980. 6 l., 179 pages.

A8. *Beyond Culture: Essays on Literature and Learning*. New York: Viking, 1965. xviii, 235 pages.

Contains the following material:

Preface
On the Teaching of Modern Literature (C159)
Emma and the Legend of Jane Austen (C131)
The Fate of Pleasure (C175)
Freud: Within and Beyond Culture (A6)
Isaac Babel (C122)
The Leavis-Snow Controversy (C170)
Hawthorne in Our Time (C177)
The Two Environments: Reflections on the Study of English (C179)
Bibliographical Note

The Preface begins by noting that critics have often complained about Trilling's indiscriminate or tendentious use of "we" and defends this use by nominating the New York intellectuals as a group whose authority and influence make it representative of a larger culture and proceeding to a more general discussion of the two meanings of culture, one pertaining to the arts and allied intellectual activities (as in "high culture" or "popular culture"), the other concerning "a people's technology, its manners, and customs, its religious beliefs and organization, its systems of valuation, whether expressed or implicit." Notes that the pun in the book's title, like the ambiguous titles of A4 and A5, expresses ambivalence toward its subject: though it is clearly impossible to escape the determining forces of culture in its broader sense, people commonly believe that it is possible to do so, especially through the agency of culture in the narrower sense. Observes that the adversarial stance of "art and thought" to the larger culture has been complicated in recent years by intellectual culture's own investment, through its increasing size, importance, and institutionalization, as a class whose ideology has developed an ambiguously compromised relation to its central ideal of autonomy. Takes exception to Lawrence's dictum that the world can pigeonhole new ideas but not new experiences, arguing that the world pigeonholes new experiences by organizing them through cultural institutions like art museums and universities into ideas and ideologies with all the potentially tyrannical force of the culture whose hegemony they purport to challenge or escape.

Maintains the Preface's ambivalent attitude toward culture in both senses--in part prescriptive, seeking a perspective beyond culture from which to judge cultural forces and escape their ultimate determination, in part descriptive, observing the failure of aesthetic and intellectual culture to reach just such a perspective despite its claims--throughout the book, most notably in A6, C159, C175, and C179. Advances a prescriptive viewpoint most directly in A6 in commending Freud's biological theory of some "human quality beyond the reach of cultural control," providing an explicit basis for the Wordsworthian "sentiment of Being" first discussed in C96. Qualifies any belief in a biological theory of selfhood even in this essay, however, by expressing reservations about the clinical evidence for this theory and describing the "intense conviction of the existence of the self apart from culture" as the "noblest and most generous achievement" of culture itself.

Continues throughout the remaining essays the critique, developed earlier in A4 and A5, of cultural hegemony in all its forms by skeptically scrutinizing the claims of contemporary aesthetic culture to maintain a truly adversarial, anti-cultural stance. Notes in C177 that Hawthorne is unsatisfying to modern readers because his ironies, ambiguities, and lacunae suggest "the limitations of art" by refusing to establish the mediating function of art between self and world, but concludes only that this refusal is somehow liberating, suggesting that no such mediation is finally possible. Rejects in C175 the adversarial claims of "modern spirituality, with its devaluation of the principle of pleasure," as offering a merely "negative transcendence" that is just as deeply implicated in consumer values as the aesthetic culture of luxury and delight it opposes, but does not offer a superior, unacculturated alternative. Analyzes in C159 and C179 the ways in which the university, the humanities, and the study of literature provide themselves with the supporting accoutrements of culture in their attacks on culture, but does not indicate a program for liberation from the blandishments of this adversary culture beyond the exercise of critical intelligence. Stresses, in repeated acknowledgments in the Preface and elsewhere, that even "the rational intellect," which anatomizes the operations of cultural forces with the "informing purpose of standing beyond any culture" in an expression of its own autonomy, cannot avoid being shaped by the cultural forces on which it presumes to pass judgment, confirming that Trilling's program is a continuing critique of cultural hegemony, not an inversion of contemporary aesthetic culture's faith in its own adversarial stance through a recommendation of quietistic assent or acquiescence to the pieties of the dominant culture. The emphasis throughout is not on Trilling's prescription for reaching a standpoint outside culture but on exposing the pretenses of the adversary culture's claim to have done so.

A8a. British edition of A8. London: Secker & Warburg, 1966. xvii, 235 pages.

A8b. Paperback reprint of A8a. Harmondsworth: Penguin, 1967. 202 pages.

A8c. Paperback reprint of A8. Viking Compass, 1968. xx, 235 pages.

An addendum to the Preface (pages xviii-xx, reprinted as "On Irony: An Addendum" in A15) notes that several reviews [H757, H777, and H780] have taken seriously Trilling's ironic approval of the growing intimacy between universities and the arts, his linking of advertising to literature, and his description of the study of modern literature as a fad, and disavows the positions the reviewers have imputed to him.

A8d. *Más allá de la cultura, y otros ensayos*. Spanish translation of A8. Translated by Carlos Ribalta. Barcelona: Editorial Lumen, 1969. 323 pages.

Contains seven essays from A8 (omitting C177) and three essays from A4.

**** Uniform Edition of A8. New York: Harcourt Brace Jovanovich, 1978. 256 pages. See A11.

**** Paperback reprint of Uniform Edition. New York: Harvest/ Harcourt Brace Jovanovich, 1979. 204 pages. See A11.

**** British Uniform Edition. Oxford: Oxford University Press, 1980. 256 pages. See A11.

A8e. *Al di là della cultura*. Italian translation of A8. Translated by Guido Fink. Firenze: La Nuova Italia Editrice, 1980. 197 pages.

**** Paperback reprint of British Uniform Edition. Oxford: Oxford University Press, 1982. 204 pages. See A11.

A9. *Sincerity and Authenticity*. Cambridge: Harvard University Press, 1972. 6 l., 188 pages.

A revised version of the Charles Eliot Norton Lectures Trilling gave at Harvard in 1969-70 which together trace the vicissitudes of the ideal of sincerity--"a congruence between avowal and actual feeling"--and the related ideal of authenticity since the sixteenth century, when social urbanization and opportunities for social mobility, including the self-dissembling of villains, parvenus, and Tartuffian hypocrites, first made attestations of sincerity seem necessary and possible. Sets forth an intricate and digressive argument, organized around a series of sympathetically dialectical figures--Diderot, Rousseau, Austen, Marx, Wilde, Nietzsche, Conrad, Freud--about the superseding of sincerity by authenticity as an index of contemporary hostility to social imperatives.

After asking in the opening chapter what is the self to which sincerity calls one to be true, links the rise of sincerity and "plain speaking" to the growing awareness through the seventeenth century of society as such, the increased importance of autobiography and privacy, and the development of the concept of individuality. Considers Diderot's dialogue *Rameau's Nephew* in the second chapter as dramatizing the "systematic separation of the individual from his actual self" through a dramatic confrontation between *Moi*, "the honest soul" who espouses the virtue of sincerity as an endorsement of the social order to which it provides honest entry, and *Lui*, "the disintegrated consciousness" who condemns the social order as alienating, and mere straightforwardness in social self-presentation as insincere. Analyzes the ways in which Hegel's *Phenomenology of the Spirit* upsets Diderot's dialectical balance between *Moi* and *Lui* by exalting the "baseness" of the disintegrated consciousness over the "noble self," whose loyalty to existing social norms is retrograde, an obstacle to the evolution of consciousness toward pure Spirit in culture (a unified field of "depreciatory judgment," in contrast to a society unified by its "external power"). Notes Werther's transformation from nobility to Hegelian baseness and the simultaneous attack on the noble ethos of sincerity by the rise of "plebeian democracy," which rejects "the old visionary norm" or "material and social establishment."

Examines in the following two chapters Rousseau's legacy as a champion of both sincerity (in the *Confessions*) and authenticity (in his political writings). Emphasizes the "English sincerity" (communication without deception, as against the more stringent "French sincerity," which requires one to confront and confess one's worst failings) at the heart of Rousseau's political thought, which condemns literature and the arts as dangerous because they imperil the self in encouraging an influx of other, enlarging and obscuring, selves, reducing its "actuality and autonomy." Glosses Rousseau's exception of novels from his condemnation of literature by examining the survival of a noble, archaic "sentiment of being" in Austen, whose pedagogic solicitude in *Mansfield Park* for her readers' well-being categorically echoes Rousseau's hostility to the theater. Argues more generally that the novel, the Hebrew bible, the practical ego of the Renaissance, and the epiphanies of Wordsworth and Joyce all oppose the ideal of heroism, proposing instead a Rousseauesque sentiment of being, a self-identity independent of social definition, which prefigures the modern preoccupation with authenticity. Sees this preoccupation as increasingly dominant through the nineteenth century, for example in the autonomy of the work of art, in the social autonomy of the artist, and in the aspiration to autonomy through confrontation with an artwork like *La nausée*, which "instructs us in our authenticity and adjures us to overcome it" by extirpating "the sentiment of individual being [which] depends upon other people" through social norms. Notes the ways this attitude creates a new class of "culture-Philistines" by making the sentiment of being depend on aesthetic norms as fully determined by other people as the social norms they condemn.

Dramatizes in the final two chapters the triumph of aesthetic modernism as valorizing Nietzsche's "base" or "authentic" Dionysiac principle over the "noble" or socially sincere Apollonian principle. Contends that just as Hegel misread Diderot in siding with *Lui* against *Moi*, Nietzsche's readers have ignored the dialectic he establishes between Apollo and Dionysus--echoed by Conrad's dialectic between the noble Marlow and the base Kurtz--and expressed an increasingly uncritical preference for the latter. Attributes the rise of Freudian psychoanalysis to the perception that Freud was concerned with the hidden, Dionysiac side of human desire, and its fall from favor to the revelation that

Freud was allied with Apollonian conservators of the noble self and its society. Examines the growing perception that society itself, then culture (conceived successively as an infernal machine and a seduction to atavistic organicism), finally storytelling, history, literary culture, the family, and the past, all come under suspicion as trammels to "the authentic unconscious" posited by critics of Freud like Sartre and revisionary Freudians like Marcuse. Reviews Freud's tragic model of the self as riven by biological conflicts between a rational, conscious ego and an equally irrational, unconscious id and superego--conflicts neither attributable to society nor amenable to social meliorism--and concludes by defending this model against recent proclamations by David Cooper and R. D. Laing that since society is "the destroyer of the very humanity it pretended to foster," the only true authenticity is to be found in psychosis or schizophrenia as critical responses to deforming social pressures, warning that such a theory takes no account of the devastating isolation of actual schizophrenics and psychotics, treating them instead as beneficiaries of "an upward psychopathic mobility to the point of divinity, each one of us a Christ--but with none of the inconveniences of undertaking to intercede, of being a sacrifice, of reasoning with rabbis, of making sermons, of having disciples, of going to weddings and funerals, of beginning something and at a certain point remarking that it is finished."

A9a. Paperback reprint of A9. Cambridge: Harvard University Press, 1972. 6 l., 188 pages.

A9b. British edition of A9. Oxford: Oxford University Press, 1972. x, 188 pages.

A9c. Paperback reprint of A9b. Oxford: Oxford University Press, 1974. 188 pages.

A9d. *Das Ende der Aufrichtigkeit.* German translation of A9. Translated by Henning Ritter. Vienna: Carl Hanser, 1980. 163 pages.

**** Uniform Edition of A9. New York: Harcourt Brace Jovanovich, 1980. 192 pages. See A11.

A10. *Mind in the Modern World: The 1972 Thomas Jefferson Lecture in the Humanities.* New York: Viking, 1973. 41 pages. See C185.

A11. *The Uniform Edition of the Works of Lionel Trilling.* New York: Harcourt Brace Jovanovich, 1977-80; Oxford: Oxford University Press, 1980-82.

Reprints all books previously written by Trilling, adding two new volumes (A12 and A14) collecting essays and stories not previously published in book form and another volume (A13) reprinting essays previously published in B40.

Includes the following volumes, in the order of their American publication:

Beyond Culture (HBJ, 1978 [paper, 1979]; Oxford, 1980 [paper, 1982])
The Opposing Self (HBJ, 1978 [paper, 1979]; Oxford, 1980 [paper, 1982])
Matthew Arnold (HBJ, 1978 [paper, 1979]; Oxford, 1982 [paper, 1982])
A Gathering of Fugitives (HBJ, 1978; Oxford, 1980)
The Liberal Imagination (HBJ, 1979; Oxford, 1981)
Of This Time, of That Place, and Other Stories (HBJ, 1979 [paper, 1980]; Oxford, 1981 [paper, 1982])
Prefaces to The Experience of Literature (HBJ, 1979 [paper, 1981]; Oxford, 1981 [paper, 1982])
The Last Decade (HBJ, 1979 [paper, 1981]; Oxford, 1981 [paper, 1982])
The Middle of the Journey (HBJ, 1980; Oxford, 1981)
Sincerity and Authenticity (HBJ, 1980; omitted from British

edition)
E. M. Forster (HBJ, 1980; Oxford, 1980)
Speaking of Literature and Society (HBJ, 1980; Oxford, 1982)

A12. *Of This Time, of That Place and Other Stories*, selected by Diana Trilling. New York: Harcourt Brace Jovanovich, 1979. 116 pages.

Contains the following material:

Impediments (C53)
The Other Margaret (C84)
Notes on a Departure (C58)
The Lesson and the Secret (C85)
Of This Time, of That Place (C77)

Omits two stories (C54 and C56) originally published, like C53 and C58, in the *Menorah Journal*. The stories selected focus on the problem of maintaining individual identity--figured in terms of ethnic heritage (C53 and C58), aesthetic sensibility (C85), and moral responsibility (C77 and C84) in a world whose pressures toward compromise and social assimilation are intense, leading variously to attempted escape (C53 and C58), deadlock (C85), or a heightened awareness of the necessary costs of compromise (C77 and C84).

A12a. Paperback reprint of A12. New York: Harvest/Harcourt Brace Jovanovich, 1980. 116 pages.

A12b. British edition of A12. Oxford: Oxford University Press, 1981. 116 pages.

A12c. Paperback reprint of A12b. Oxford: Oxford University Press, 1982. 116 pages.

A13. *Prefaces to* The Experience of Literature. New York: Harcourt Brace Jovanovich, 1979. xvi, 302 pages.

Reprints all fifty-two of Trilling's brief commentaries from *The Experience of Literature* [B40], together with Trilling's 1967 introduction and a brief Foreword by William Jovanovich.

Includes commentaries on the following works:

1. Drama

Sophocles, *Oedipus Rex*
William Shakespeare, *The Tragedy of King Lear*
Henrik Ibsen, *The Wild Duck*
Anton Chekhov, *The Three Sisters*
George Bernard Shaw, *The Doctor's Dilemma*
Luigi Pirandello, *Six Characters in Search of an Author: A Comedy in the Making*
William Butler Yeats, *Purgatory*
Bertolt Brecht, *Galileo*

2. Fiction

Nathaniel Hawthorne, "My Kinsman, Major Molineux"
Herman Melville, "Bartleby the Scrivener: A Story of Wall Street"
Fëdor Dostoevski, "The Grand Inquisitor"
Leo Tolstoi, "The Death of Ivan Ilych"
William Somerset Maugham, "The Treasure"
Guy de Maupassant, "Duchoux"
Anton Chekhov, "Enemies"
Henry James, "The Pupil"
Joseph Conrad, "The Secret Sharer"
James Joyce, "The Dead"
Franz Kafka, "The Hunter Gracchus"
D. H. Lawrence, "Tickets, Please"
E. M. Forster, "The Road from Colonus"
Thomas Mann, "Disorder and Early Sorrow"

Isaac Babel, "Di Grasso: A Tale of Odessa"
Isak Dinesen, "The Sailor-Boy's Tale"
Ernest Hemingway, "Hills Like White Elephants"
William Faulkner, "Barn Burning"
John O'Hara, "Summer's Day"
Lionel Trilling, "Of This Time, of That Place"
Albert Camus, "The Guest"
Bernard Malamud, "The Magic Barrel"

3. Poetry

Anonymous, "Edward"
Sir Thomas Wyatt, "They Flee from Me"
John Donne, "A Valediction: Forbidding Mourning"
John Milton, "Lycidas"
Andrew Marvell, "To His Coy Mistress"
Alexander Pope, "An Essay on Man: Epistle I"
William Blake, "Tyger! Tyger!"
William Wordsworth, "Resolution and Independence"
Samuel Taylor Coleridge, "Kubla Khan or A Vision in a Dream: A Fragment"
George Gordon, Lord Byron, "*Don Juan*: An Episode from Canto II"
Percy Bysshe Shelley, "Ode to the West Wind"
John Keats, "Ode to a Nightingale"
Matthew Arnold, "Dover Beach"
Walt Whitman, "Out of the Cradle Endlessly Rocking"
Gerard Manley Hopkins, "The Leaden Echo and the Golden Echo"
Emily Dickinson, "'Go Tell It'--What a Message--"
William Butler Yeats, "Sailing to Byzantium"
Thomas Stearns Eliot, *The Waste Land*
Robert Frost, "Neither Out Far Nor In Deep"
e. e. cummings, "my father moved through dooms of love"
W. H. Auden, "In Memory of Sigmund Freud (d. 1939)"
Robert Lowell, "For the Union Dead"

A13a. Paperback edition of A13. New York: Harcourt Brace Jovanovich, 1981. xvi, 302 pages.

A13b. British edition of A13. Oxford: Oxford University Press, 1981. xvi, 302 pages.

A13c. Paperback edition of A13b. Oxford: Oxford University Press, 1981. xvi, 302 pages.

A14. *The Last Decade: Essays and Reviews, 1965-75*. Edited by Diana Trilling. New York: Harcourt Brace Jovanovich, 1979. 4 l., 241 pages.

Contains the following material, arranged in order of composition:

[Editor's Note]
A Novel of the Thirties (C180)
James Joyce in His Letters (C181)
What Is Criticism? (B41)
Mind in the Modern World (C185)
Art, Will, and Necessity (C193)
Aggression and Utopia (C186)
The Uncertain Future of the Humanistic Educational Ideal (C189)
The Freud/Jung Letters (C188)
Whittaker Chambers' Journey (C190)
Why We Read Jane Austen (C191)
Appendix: Some Notes for an Autobiographical Lecture (C194)

Collects the most important writing, apart from A9, from the last ten years of Trilling's life. The essays included are marked by two consistent preoccupations during this period. In three separate essays (C185, C186, and C193) Trilling cites William Morris's *News from Nowhere* as an attack on the socially threatening power of the personal will, which Trilling wishes to defend in all its aggressiveness and potential disruptiveness. C185 and C186 similarly defend "mind" (a term which displaces "imagination" in Trilling's late work) against anti-intellectualism, and C193 and C189 defend artistic and educational ideals of humanism against recent attacks made in the name of social or aesthetic egalitarianism. A second tendency is to replace the autobiographical surrogates of such earlier essays as A1, A2, A6, B17, and B19 with figures to whom Trilling feels less clearly sympathetic (Joyce and Chambers) and to indulge the autobiographical impulse more directly in retrospection in C180, C190, and C193. In C191, the latest essay included here, Trilling proposes a new dialectic between life (a term whose associations in the other essays include character, individuality, will, struggle, and humanism) and art, identified here explicitly with the wish for the fixity of death. This dialectic--the shaped self urged throughout the essays in A5 now appears as the product of a death-wish in both C181 and C191--is the most radical development of the series of dialectics Trilling had earlier proposed between integrity and political commitment, self and culture, the adversary impulse and the seductions of institutional power. As in A9, the self can no longer seek refuge in an escape from culture, for the greatest threat to its existence is its own constitutive impetus toward definition. The pessimism following from this formulation colors all Trilling's last essays except for B41.

A14a. Paperback reprint of A14. New York: Harvest/Harcourt Brace Jovanovich, 1981. 4 l., 241 pages.

A14b. British edition of A14. Oxford: Oxford University Press, 1981. 4 l., 241 pages.

A14c. Paperback reprint of A14b. Oxford: Oxford University Press, 1982. 4 l., 241 pages.

A15. *Speaking of Literature and Society.* Edited by Diana Trilling. New York: Harcourt Brace Jovanovich, 1980. 8 l., 429 pages.

Contains the following material, arranged in order of composition:

Editor's Foreword
(Editorial Note)
The Poems of Emily Brontë (C46)
A Study of Terror-Romanticism (D198)
Cities of the Plain (D202)
Another Jewish Problem Novel (D234)
Flawed Instruments (D244)
The Promise of Realism (D248)
The Social Emotions (D250)
D. H. Lawrence: A Neglected Aspect (C60)
The Problem of the American Artist (D253)
The Changing Myth of the Jew (C192)
Carlyle (D261)
The Coleridge Letters (D282)
The Autonomy of the Literary Work (D283)
Politics and the Liberal (D285)
Willa Cather (C65)
Marxism in Limbo (D304)
The America of John Dos Passos (C66)
Evangelical Criticism (D305)
The Situation in American Writing: Seven Questions (E380)
Hemingway and His Critics (C67)
The Victorians and Democracy (D312)
The Unhappy Story of Sinclair Lewis (D311)
Literature and Power (C70)
T. S. Eliot's Politics (C71)
An American in Spain (D313)
The Wordsworths (D327)
The Progressive Psyche (D328)
Artists and the "Societal Function" (D330)
M., W., F. at 10 (D331)

Under Forty (E384)
The Head and Heart of Henry James (D341)
Sermon on a Text from Whitman (C81)
The Problem of Influence (D348)
Making Men More Human (D349)
Neurosis and the Health of the Artist (D355)
Treason in the Modern World (C89)
Family Album (D357)
The State of Our Culture: Expostulation and Reply (E388)
Orwell on the Future (D359)
Fitzgerald Plain (D363)
An American View of English Literature (C99)
The Formative Years (D368)
The Years of Maturity (D371)
Social Actualities (B31)
The Person of the Artist (D132)
Last Years of a Titan (D373)
Communism and Intellectual Freedom (C136)
Proust as Critic and the Critic as Novelist (C137)
The Last Lover (C138)
Reflections on a Lost Cause: English Literature and American Education (C135)
Paradise Reached For (C145)
The Assassination of Leon Trotsky (C148)
An American Classic (C154)
Yeats as Critic (C163)
A Comedy of Evil (C166)
Literary Pathology (E419)
A Valedictory (C178)
On Irony: An Addendum (A8a)
Appendix: Lionel Trilling: A Jew at Columbia, by Diana Trilling (G540)

A miscellany of book reviews and other essays written between 1924 and 1968 and not previously published in any of Trilling's books.

The Editor's Foreword notes the discrepancy between the small number of Trilling's essays that remained unpublished and the large quantity of his published work--essays, reviews, speeches, and contributions to symposia--that remained uncollected in his lifetime. The editor recalls that Trilling was often handicapped in his writing by a "serious difficulty in putting words on paper," and that "his dedication to reading was the nearest thing to an absolute in his character"; remarks her inability to fulfill any of her original goals in selecting material for this volume (to trace Trilling's evolution and the development of the literary culture he observed, to inform younger readers and remind older ones about "the Stalinization of the American intellectual classes"); and expresses the hope that despite its necessarily miscellaneous character, the collection "*is* more than it *tells* us of social and cultural history."

A15a. British edition of A15. Oxford: Oxford University Press, 1982. 8 l., 429 pages.

Section B

Prefaces and Books Edited

B16. O'Neill, Eugene. *The Emperor Jones, Anna Christie, The Hairy Ape*. Introduction (pp. vii-xix) by Lionel Trilling. New York: Modern Library, 1937. xx, 260 pages.

Suggests that the stylistic innovations which brought O'Neill to prominence are a function of his "profound if groping philosophical intention": the "metaphysical" misery of his principals confronted by a vast, hostile universe. Indicates the extent of O'Neill's assault on positivism and rational intellect before the inescapable threat of death. Notes the political dangers of this assault--"unreasoning chauvinism" and "fascism"--and emphasizes the ways in which O'Neill's position may be turned to a critique more sympathetic to "the very positivistic philosophies he rejects."

B17. Fitzgerald, F. Scott. *The Great Gatsby*. Introduction (pp. vii-xiv) by Lionel Trilling. New York: New Directions, 1945.

Ascribes Fitzgerald's enduring appeal to his personal qualities of honesty and "preoccupation with virtue," observing that his powers are fully realized only in *The Great Gatsby*, which is memorable for the symbolic economy which presents Gatsby as an allegorical figure for the American dream, its dramatic foreshortening, its ideographic evocations of character and landscape, and "the courage with which it grasps a moment of history as a great moral fact." Identifies Fitzgerald's voice, which modifies "a true firmness of moral judgment" by lightness and tenderness, as "the normal or ideal voice of the novelist."

Some material from the Introduction is reprinted in "F. Scott Fitzgerald" in A4, and in *F. Scott Fitzgerald: The Man and His Work*, edited by Alfred Kazin (Cleveland: Meridian, 1951), pp. 194-204; *The Great Gatsby: A Study*, edited by Frederick J. Hoffman (New York: Scribner's, 1962), pp. 232-43; and *Fitzgerald: An Anthology of Critical Essays*, edited by Arthur Mizener (Englewood Cliffs: Prentice-Hall, 1963), pp. 11-19.

B18. Phillips, William, and Rahv, Philip, editors. *The Partisan Reader: Ten Years of Partisan Review, 1934-1944: An Anthology.* Introduction (pp. ix-xvi) by Lionel Trilling. New York: Dial, 1946.

Notes with alarm "the great gulf between our educated class and the best of our literature" that has opened since the nineteenth century in America and praises journals of limited circulation for their attempt to bridge this gap. Singles out *Partisan Review* for its attempt, through its special emphasis on political ideas, to forge a link between "our liberal educated class" and the modern literary imagination, whose avatars--Proust, Joyce, Lawrence, Yeats, Eliot, Mann, Rilke, Gide--are generally inimical to the liberal ideas pietistically espoused in the official liberal literature currently dominant. Traces the vitality of *Partisan Review* to its critique of the American Communist Party, with which it had initially been closely linked, observing that even though its focus is now less overtly political, its orientation remains political in its definition of politics as including "every human activity and every subtlety of every human activity," and adds that "unless we insist that politics is imagination and mind, we will learn that imagination and mind are politics, and of a kind that we will not like." Concludes by indicating the ways in which Homer, Chaucer,

Shakespeare, Milton, the Romantics, Dostoevski, and Whitman are coterie writers whose tradition of broad cultural engagement for an initially small audience the little magazines continue.

The Introduction is reprinted as "The Function of the Little Magazine" in A4.

B19. James, Henry. *The Princess Casamassima*. Introduction (pp. v-xlviii) by Lionel Trilling. 2 volumes, xlviii, 321 + 382 pages. New York: Macmillan, 1948.

Expresses surprise that *The Bostonians* and *The Princess Casamassima*, of all James's novels "the most likely to make an immediate appeal to the reader of today" for their straightforwardness of style and motive and the fullness and directness of their representation of society, should have been so savagely attacked on their first publication, and, after establishing the fairy-tale roots of James's story (and those of such other Young Men from the Provinces as Pip, Julien Sorel, and Jay Gatsby) in folktales about the woodcutter's youngest son, defends *The Princess* as "a brilliantly precise representation of social actuality" by drawing extended parallels between James's shadowy revolutionaries and anarchist conspiracies of the 1880's. Contends that Hyacinth Robinson's double loyalty to art and moral action, culture and anarchy, can be traced to "the author's fantasy about himself," which pits him against his brother William and his sister Alice (here recast as Paul Muniment and the Princess), whose denigration of European culture overvalued their own presumed awareness of political reality and overlooked their own implication in the "coercive power" of a civilization willing to sacrifice "the ideal of adventurous experience" that makes art and freedom possible. Sees Hyacinth as comprehending a wider view of political actuality than the anarchists who commission him and such dilettantes in politics as Paul and the Princess, since the "revolutionary passion" associated with his mother is complemented by a "passion for life at its richest and noblest" inherited from his father, and the two together make him "a hero of civilization" who "dares to do more than civilization does: embodying two ideals at once, he takes upon himself, in full consciousness, the guilt of each. . . . By his death he instructs us in the nature of civilized life and by his consciousness he transcends it." Describes the "moral realism" informing James's portraits of Rosy Muniment, her brother, and the Princess--"the very embodiment of the moral will which masks itself in virtue . . . and longs for an absolute humanity," defined by "its false seriousness--the political awareness that is not aware, the social consciousness which hates full consciousness"--and concludes that James's critique of the masked will stems from "the imagination of love" that grasps the "pride and beauty" of its subjects together with "their ambiguity and error."

The Introduction is revised and reprinted as "The Princess Casamassima" in *Horizon* 17 (April 1948): 267-95; in A4; and in *Henry James's Major Novels: Essays in Criticism*, edited by Lyall H. Powers (East Lansing: Michigan State University Press, 1973), pp. 103-32.

B20. Twain, Mark. *The Adventures of Huckleberry Finn*. Introduction (pp. v-xviii) by Lionel Trilling. xxiv, 293 pages. New York: Rinehart, 1948.

Defines the greatness of Twain's masterpiece as "its power of telling the truth" not only about a boy's perspective on the world of adults and adult affairs, compromises, and conspiracies, but also about the conflict between the primeval river-god, which "appears to embody a great moral idea" of affection and social activity--and which is associated here with nostalgia and the sense of reality--and "the money-god" arisen from the concentration of capital in cities and businesses and the fascination with machines in the Gilded Age--identified here as "the father of ultimate illusion and lies." Describes the concluding section of the novel, despite its inevitable falling off from the journey down the river, as having "a certain formal aptness" in rescuing Huck from the role of hero and allowing him to escape civilization once more, and praises Twain's style, despite its reliance on dialect, as marked by "the strictest literary sensibility," moving with "the greatest simplicity, directness, lucidity, and grace," so as to strike readers with the unmediated force of truth.

The introduction is revised and reprinted as "Huckleberry Finn" in A4; in *Readings for Thought and Expression*, compiled by Stewart S. Morgan, John Q. Hays, and Fred E. Ekfelt (New York: Macmillan, 1955), pp. 409-18; in *American Critical Essays (20th Century)*, edited by Harold Lowther Beaver (London: Oxford University Press, 1959), pp. 233-48; and in *The Open Form*, edited by Alfred Kazin (New York: Harcourt, Brace & World, 1965), pp. 123-34.

B20a. Paperback reprint of B4. New York: Holt, Rinehart & Winston, 1948. xxiv, 293 pages.

B21. Arnold, Matthew. *The Portable Matthew Arnold*. Edited and with an introduction (pp. 1-30) by Lionel Trilling. New York: Viking, 1949. 659 pages.

Notes Arnold's continuing influence despite his small and uneven canon of poetry, the lack of appeal of his religious writing, and the generally occasional forms of his literary and social criticism, and ascribes this influence not to his talents or personality but to his transmission and critique of liberalism, a liberalism rendered poignant by Arnold's double sense of isolation through social fragmentation and scientific discoveries proclaiming "a universe in which man is a stranger." Observes that although Arnold's humanism took as its audience and exemplary subject the rising middle class, the middle class has always been resistant to humanistic ideals, tending recently toward cultural anarchism instead. Summarizes the particulars of Arnold's life, remarking the popular press's suspicion of his poetry's "cultural subversiveness" and Arnold's status as one of the first modern writers who attempted to make a living by means other than writing. Emphasizes the practical, social matrix of Arnold's literary essays, concluding that "for him criticism had to do with the quality of life however manifested. This is the mark of the great critic." Regrets the omission from B21 of Arnold's religious writings, though distinguishing Arnold's "natural piety" from religious belief and criticizing Arnold for attempting through his religious work to "advance the cause of social peace and order" on the grounds that he is applying social standards to metaphysics, ruling that although "the ultimate nature of the universe does not yield to the criteria of reasonableness," these criteria are entirely apt to the social problems with which Arnold was centrally concerned.

B21a. Paperback reprint of B21. New York: Viking, 1956. 659 pages.

B21b. *The Essential Matthew Arnold*. British paperback edition of B21. London: Chatto and Windus, 1969. ix, 659 pages.

B22. Keats, John. *The Selected Letters of John Keats*. Edited and with an introduction (pp. 3-41) by Lionel Trilling. New York: Farrar, Straus and Young, 1951. 282 pages.

Ascribes the unique importance of Keats's letters to his "conscious desire to live life in the heroic mode," his certainty that "to be, or to become, a man was an adventurous problem." Uses Keats's geniality, the easy manners and the joy in his own powers and sensuous appetites observed by Shaw, to dispute Edmund Wilson's contention that "the poet derives his power from some mutilation he has suffered," arguing that Keats's capacity for pleasure implies his capacity for the "apprehension of tragic reality" through a conflict between youthful appetites and preoccupations and the wisdom of maturity. Observes that although "Keats did institute some kind of antagonism between the idea of luxury and the idea of energetic morality," this "conflict is never to the death, is never cruel," because "he seems never to have wished to injure or destroy any part of himself." Aligns this conflict with a "dialectic . . . between passivity and activity" and an "opposition between thought and sensation," defending Keats against charges of anti-intellectualism by pointing out that his conception of mind is not hostile to the emotions: instead, "mind came into being when the sensations and emotions were checked by external resistance or by conflict with each other, when . . . the pleasure principle is confronted by the reality principle." Contends that Keats's notion of Negative Capability, which may seem an invitation to indecision or quietism--for "making up one's mind is not only the end of intellection but one of the means of intellection"--is in fact a sign of positive intellectual power depending on a confidence in one's personal identity that does not depend on settled opinions, concluding that Negative Capability is at the heart of Keats's attempt to comprehend the problem of evil, reconciling "the sense of personal identity and the certainty of pain and extinction." Traces the doctrinal implications of Negative Capability for what Keats calls "soul-making," noting that Keats's doctrine is unlikely to compel belief any longer because "we have lost the *mystique* of the self" that endows it with the power and importance Keats assumes. Grants that historical events have made Keats's faith in the power of the self impossible, and pronounces Keats "the last image of health at the very moment when the sickness of Europe began to be apparent."

The Introduction is revised and reprinted as "The Poet as Hero: Keats in His Letters" in *Cornhill* 165 (Autumn 1951): 281-302, and in A4.

B22a. Another edition. 344 pages. Garden City: Doubleday, 1956.

B23. Tolstoi, Lev Nikolayevitch. *Anna Karenina*. Two volumes. Translated by Constance Garnett. Text edited and revised by Gustavus Spett. Translation revised by Bernard Guilbert

Guerney. Introduction (pp. v-xii) by Lionel Trilling. Printed for the Limited Editions Club. Cambridge: Cambridge University Press, 1951. xiv, 935 pages.

Concedes that "criticism . . . must lay down its arms before this novel," since the power of Tolstoi's moral vision is to present an image of normal life equalled in the assent it compels only by the earlier conflation of Nature and Homer. Points out that Tolstoi's supposed objectivity of presentation is actually "the most lavish and prodigal subjectivity possible," for it is everywhere informed by the author's love for his characters and their world. Acknowledges that Tolstoi may seem less relevant than Dostoevsky to modern readers because his lack of James's "imagination of disaster" may make his reality actually "an idyl of reality," but argues that Tolstoi's compelling sense of normality stems from his unique awareness of the ways "the spirit of man is always at the mercy of the actual and trivial," concluding that "to comprehend unconditioned spirit is not so very hard, but there is no knowledge rarer than the understanding of spirit as it exists in the inescapable conditions which the actual and the trivial make for it."

The Introduction is revised and reprinted as "Anna Karenina" in A5.

B23a. Another edition. New York: Heritage Club, n.d. xiv, 935 pages.

B24. Orwell, George. *Homage to Catalonia.* New York: Harcourt, Brace, 1952. Introduction (pp. v-xxiii) by Lionel Trilling. xxiv, 232 pages.

For Introduction, see C100.

B24a. Paperback reprint of B24. New York: Harcourt, Brace, 1952. xxiv, 232 pages.

B25. James, Henry. *The Bostonians*. Introduction (pp. vii-xv) by Lionel Trilling. The Chiltern Library. London: John Lehmann, 1953.

Emphasizes the Americanness of James's novel, its close observation of specific locations and social manners and relations, contending that, like its companion novel, *The Princess Casamassima*, it presents an explicitly social and political version of James's characteristic dialectic between "radical" and "conservative" principles, typically aligned in his work with America and Europe, that may be called "energy and inertia; or spirit and matter; or spirit and letter; or force and form; or creation and possession; or Libido and Thanatos." Notes that James, who typically uses psychological conflicts to focus large-scale cultural conflicts, here uses the feminist reform movement to examine "the bitter total war of the sexes" explored by Strindberg and Lawrence, and linked here by Basil Ransom's background to the Civil War, as "the fear of the loss of manhood" is linked to Ransom's "distrust of theory" and "tragic awareness of the intractability of the human circumstance." Suggests that this conflict was awakened in James by the deaths of his parents--first his mother, representing to him "the strength of conservation, the unseen, unregarded, seemingly unexerted force that holds things to their center"; then his father, who "had had the masculine power," in James's words, "'to know and yet not to fear reality'"--producing "a story of the parental house divided against itself . . . of the sacred mothers refusing their commission and the sacred fathers endangered."

The Introduction is revised and reprinted as "The Bostonians" in *Henry James's Major Novels: Essays in Criticism*, edited by Lyall H. Powers (East Lansing: Michigan State University Press, 1973), pp. 89-99, and in A5.

B26. Dickens, Charles. *Little Dorrit*. Introduction (pp. v-xvi) by Lionel Trilling. New Oxford Illustrated Dickens. London: Oxford University Press, 1953. xxvi, 826 pages.

For Introduction, see C111.

B27. *Perspectives USA*, no. 2 (Winter 1953). Lionel Trilling, Supervising Editor. 190 pages.

The contents of this issue include the following:

Lionel Trilling, "Editor's Commentary" (E396)
Mary McCarthy, "America the Beautiful"
Theodore Spencer, "Technique as Joy"
e. e. cummings, "Thirteen Poems"
Jacques Barzun, "Some Principles of Musical Biography"
Randall Jarrell, "Some Lines from Whitman"
Robert Goldwater, "Arthur Dove" (illustrated with reproductions of Dove's paintings)
Richard Gibson and James Baldwin, "Two Protests Against Protest"
Saul Bellow, "The Einhorns"
Robert Warshow, "The Movie Camera and the American"
Philip Rahv, "Notes on the Decline of Naturalism"
F. W. Dupee, "Thomas Mann's *The Holy Sinner* and Henry Hatfield's *Thomas Mann*"
William Barrett, "John W. Aldridge's *After the Lost Generation*"
Richard Chase, "Recent Books on Melville"
A Selective Listing of Recent Books
Notes on the Contributors
Photographs of the Contributors
Acknowledgments

B28. Flaubert, Gustave. *Bouvard and Pécuchet*. Translated by T. W. Earp and G. W. Stonier. Introduction (pp. v-xxxvii) by Lionel Trilling. Norfolk, CT: New Directions, 1953. xxxviii, 348 pages.

For Introduction, see C112.

B29. Babel, Isaac. *The Collected Stories of Isaac Babel.* Translated and edited by Walter Morison. Introduction (pp. 9-37) by Lionel Trilling. New York: Criterion, 1955. 381 pages.

For Introduction, see C122.

B29a. British edition of B29. London: Methuen, 1957. 381 pages.

B29b. Paperback reprint of B29a. Harmondsworth: Penguin, 1961. 332 pages.

B29c. Paperback reprint of B29. Cleveland: Meridian/World, 1970.

B30. Stock, Irvin. *William Hale White (Mark Rutherford): A Critical Study.* Foreword (pp. v-x) by Lionel Trilling. New York: Columbia University Press, 1956. xii, 268 pages.

Dissents from the prevailing estimate of Hale White's works as valuable "rather as documents in the history of certain phases of Victorian thought than as works of imaginative literature," adducing the contrary tendency "to search out what life there may be in the works of the past and to cherish it." Characterizes Hale White as a transitional figure between the Victorian and modern periods, cites his affinities with Shaw, Lawrence, Forster, and Gide in their shared fascination with salvation, and observes the recent loss of "the sense of personal fate, and of the possibility of personal salvation, which animated the great literature of a quarter of a century ago."

B31. O'Hara, John. *The Selected Stories of John O'Hara.* Edited with an Introduction (pp. vii-xiii) by Lionel Trilling. New York: Modern Library, 1956. xiv, 303 pages.

Praises O'Hara's work as "preeminent for its social verisimilitude" and "brilliant awareness of the differences within the national sameness." Notes the importance of social details and distinctions in Kipling, Hemingway, Flaubert, *Huckleberry Finn*, and *Moby Dick* despite "the tendency of our critical theory to belittle it" and to dismiss O'Hara as excessively concerned with it. Argues that although O'Hara's concern with social detail is sometimes excessive, as in *A Rage to Live*, it is never gratuitous, for "his characteristic way of representing the elemental is through its modification by social circumstance." Describes O'Hara's attitude toward the absurdities of social distinctions as compounded of love and fear, and compares him to Kafka in his "imagination of society as some strange sentient organism which acts by laws of its own being which are not to be understood."

The Introduction is reprinted as "Social Actualities" in A15, and excerpted in *John O'Hara Journal* 3 (1980): 168.

B32. Bellow, Saul. *The Adventures of Augie March*. Introduction (pp. vii-xiii) by Lionel Trilling. New York: Modern Library, 1956. xiv, 536 pages.

For Introduction, see C110.

B33. Austen, Jane. *Emma*. Introduction (pp. x-xxiv) by Lionel Trilling. Boston: Houghton Mifflin, 1957. xxvi, 381 pages.

For Introduction, see C131.

B33a. Paperback reprint of B33. Boston: Houghton Mifflin, 1957. xxvi, 381 pages.

B34. Mayewski, Pawel, editor. *The Broken Mirror: A Collection of Writings from Contemporary Poland*. Introduction (pp. 1-10) by Lionel Trilling. New York: Random House, 1958. 209 pages.

For Introduction, see C136.

B35. Jones, Ernest. *The Life and Work of Sigmund Freud*, edited and abridged by Lionel Trilling and Steven Marcus, with an introduction (pp. vii-xviii) by Lionel Trilling. New York: Basic, 1961. xxvi, 541 pages.

The Introduction disputes Freud's claim that his importance lay only in his work, not in his personal life, citing the curiosity Freud's prodigiously influential work arouses about his life, the light his biography throws on the historical understanding of psychoanalysis, and the legendary quality of Freud's life in its "style and form," the old-fashioned accord Freud achieved between his life and his work. Remarks the "archaic quality" of Freud's youthful determination to be first a hero, later a genius, but stresses his relatively late professional development and his frustrated sense of the limitations of his intelligence. Notes Jones's aptness as Freud's authorized biographer, recalls the circumstances of the filming of E403, and gives a rationale for the abridgement: many exhaustive technical, documentary, and summary sections have been cut, as well as letters printed in appendices to the original edition; more arguable cuts have relieved Jones of his burdens as an archivist in order to let him function more effectively as a biographer; and a few new transitional passages necessitated by omissions have been written "in what we hope is the spirit of Dr. Jones's own prose."

B35a. British edition of B35. London: Hogarth, 1961. xxvi, 541 pages.

B35b. Paperback reprint of B35. Garden City: Doubleday Anchor, 1963. xxiv, 532 pages.

B35c. Paperback reprint of B35a. Harmondsworth: Penguin, 1964.

B36. Warshow, Robert. *The Immediate Experience: Movies, Comics, Theatre and Other Aspects of Popular Culture.* Introduction (pp. 11-22) by Lionel Trilling. Garden City, NY: Doubleday, 1962. 282 pages.

For Introduction, see C164.

B36a. Paperback reprint of B36. Garden City: Doubleday Anchor, 1964. xxviii, 212 pages.

B36b. Another paperback reprint. New York: Atheneum, 1970. 282 pages.

B37. Anderson, Quentin, and Joseph A. Mazzeo, editors. *The Proper Study: Essays on Western Classics.* Preface (pp. v-x) by Lionel Trilling. New York: St. Martin's, 1962. xiv, 606 pages.

Recalls how the original rationale for Columbia's Humanities course discouraged students from consulting secondary sources, and explains that the present anthology of critical essays is intended to remind students of the "*otherness*" of past cultures--although it is true that "human nature is always the same," it is equally true that "human nature changes, sometimes radically, with each historical epoch"--and to foster more active engagement with "the community of mind" comprised by earlier responses to the works under study.

B38. Slesinger, Tess. *The Unpossessed.* Afterword (pp. 311-33) by Lionel Trilling. New York: Avon, 1966. 333 pages.

For Afterword, see C180.

B39. Follett, Wilson. *Modern American Usage.* Edited and completed by Jacques Barzun, in collaboration with Carlos Baker, Frederick W. Dupee, Dudley Fitts, James B. Hart,

Phyllis McGinley, and Lionel Trilling. New York: Hill & Wang, 1966. xi, 436 pages.

An unsigned preface announces that after Follett's death in 1963, Barzun agreed to complete the encyclopedic reference on American English grammar and stylistics that had long engaged his friend, with the stipulation that "he would be aided by a small group of writers and teachers of English," each of whom gave the book "the benefit of his literary skill and educated judgment."

B40. *The Experience of Literature: A Reader with Commentaries.* Garden City: Doubleday, 1967. xxiv, 1320 pages.

An introductory anthology of literature unusual for its size--it includes 8 plays, 22 stories, and 281 English and American poems from "Edward" to Allen Ginsberg--and its extensive commentaries on 52 of the individual selections, sometimes providing historical or biographical background but more often taking the form of detailed interpretations. The brief Introduction (pp. ix-xi) defends the teaching of literature even though its experience is "a species-characteristic trait of mankind," explaining that the purpose of the commentaries is to foster the passage from instinctual pleasure to conscious response and public discussion by "mak[ing] it more likely that the act of reading will be an experience." The most widely discussed of the individual commentaries is Trilling's discussion of C77, which identifies Tertan and Blackburn with two of Trilling's students at Columbia--critics have generally proceeded to identify Tertan with Ginsberg--describes the plot of the story as arising from their juxtaposition, insists on Tertan's literal madness despite his "passionate devotion to the intellectual life," and defines the story's power as "its ability to generate resistance to the certitude that Tertan is deranged."

The Commentary on "The Secret Sharer" in reprinted in *Media for Our Time*, edited by Dennis De Nitto (New York:

Holt, Rinehart and Winston, 1971), pp. 90-93. All 52 commentaries are reprinted in full in A13.

B40a. Textbook edition of B40. New York: Holt, Rinehart and Winston, 1967. 1320 pages.

B40b. Briefer version of B40. New York: Holt, Rinehart and Winston, 1969. xx, 663 pages.

An appendix to the introduction (p. xi) notes that the abridgment is by Charles Kaplan, who also prepared a separate Teacher's Guide. The briefer version includes 3 plays, 11 stories, and 182 poems, as well as 15 of Trilling's original commentaries.

B40d. Paperback edition of B40. Three volumes (Drama, Fiction, Poetry). Holt, Rinehart and Winston, 1969.

B41. *Literary Criticism: An Introductory Reader*. Edited and with a Preface, "On the Place of Criticism in Literary Education" (pp. v-xii), and an Introduction, "What Is Criticism?" (pp. 1-28) by Lionel Trilling. New York: Holt, Rinehart and Winston, 1970. xiv, 629 pages.

The Preface roots the introductory purpose of B21 in the antagonism between scholars and critics which provoked John Crowe Ransom's founding of the School of Letters at Kenyon College as a forum for the latter, and the resolution of this antagonism by the phenomenal rise of criticism, observing that although the New Criticism Ransom championed has been unfashionable since "the mid-Fifties," literary criticism has come to occupy an ever larger place in scholarly discourse and ought perhaps to be introduced to beginning as well as advanced students. Accounts for the omission of Horace, Sidney, Pope, and Shelley as unlikely to appeal to beginning students, and such modern critics as Ransom, Blackmur, Burke, and Empson as too difficult for them.

The Introduction stresses the primacy of comparative judgment as the end of criticism, ascribing the shifting tendencies of critical theory--which are described at length in terms borrowed from the opening chapter of M. H. Abrams's *The Mirror and the Lamp*--to the changing criteria which have controlled judgment. Points out that although judgment is the salient motive of criticism, criticism begins before judgment of a given work in questions of definition and procedure and continues beyond judgment in "celebration" or "love" or analysis of historical novelty or formal coherence or thematic interpretation. Remarking that criticism, like science, is concerned with "questions of causation," argues against the New Critical attack on the "conditioned" nature of literature by emphasizing several contexts which influence the shaping of a work: the culture by and for which it is produced (and for which "the work of art is a commodity"), the circumstances of its author's career, and the psychoanalytic matrix of its inception. Notes however that psychoanalysis, although it can help to explain an author's preoccupations, cannot account for either poetic talent or personal style, and warns that most Marxist criticism, despite the promise of its cultural analysis, has tended to reduce literature to a "demonstration of how the social turpitude manifests itself in the corruption of the artistic consciousness." Concludes by insisting on the continuity and amity, rather than the rivalry, between criticism and literature.

The Introduction is reprinted in A14.

B42. *The Oxford Anthology of English Literature: Romantic Poetry and Prose*. Edited by Harold Bloom and Lionel Trilling. New York and London: Oxford University Press, 1973. 813 pages.

Volume 4 of the six-volume Oxford Anthology. The commentaries to all the prose selections are by Trilling.

B42a. Paperback reprint of B42. New York and London: Oxford University Press, 1973. 813 pages.

B43. *The Oxford Anthology of English Literature: Victorian Prose and Poetry.* Edited by Lionel Trilling and Harold Bloom. New York and London: Oxford University Press, 1973. 750 pages.

Volume 5 of the six-volume Oxford Anthology. The commentaries to all the prose selections are by Trilling.

B43a. Paperback reprint of B43. New York and London: Oxford University Press, 1973. 750 pages.

B44. Weiner, Dora B., and William R. Keylor, editors. *From Parnassus: Essays in Honor of Jacques Barzun.* Prefaced by "A Personal Memoir" (pp. xv-xxii) by Lionel Trilling. New York: Harper and Row, 1976.

An unfinished memoir of Jacques Barzun, emphasizing the ways Trilling's friendship with him was deepened by their shared teaching of the Colloquium on Important Books at Columbia. Suggests that Barzun, whose mind had been shaped earlier than Trilling's, had a greater impact on Trilling than Trilling had on him. Contrasts Trilling's withdrawal from undergraduate activities with Barzun's wide range of interests and competences, and speaks at length of his early decisive influence by prewar French culture, ascribing his distaste for modern art to his revulsion from the "nihilistic disgust" with life modernists affected in reaction to the war's suppression of modernism's original "regenerative creativity." Describes the Colloquium as opposed to this nihilistic impulse of modernism through its commitment to "the heroic principle," its emphasis on "achievement against odds." The memoir breaks off just as Trilling is returning to Barzun's conduct of the Colloquium.

Section C

Essays, Stories, Poems, and Review Articles

C45. "Old Legend; New Style." *Morningside* 13 (November 1924): 11.

A sonnet retelling the story of a bored Pandora and her teasing box.

Reprinted in *Morningside* 13 (April 1925): 129.

C46. "Resuscitations: I. The Poems of Emily Brontë." *Morningside* 13 (November 1924): 23-26.

Compares Brontë's poetry to that of Milton, Shakespeare, Pope, and Byron, as well as that of Thomson, Campbell, Southey, and "the poorer Wordsworth," and characterizes her achievement as her ability to break through "a tough crust of triteness and . . . an idiom of poetic imagery worn to almost meaningless abstraction." Concludes that "her art at its best is of great accuracy and precision; at its worst, it is never insipid, only unhappily and dully presented."

Reprinted as "The Poems of Emily Brontë" in A15.

C47. "A Sentimental Poet to His Wife/When Both Have Reached the Age of Thirty-Six." *Morningside* 13 (December 1924): 55.

A poem contrasting the poet's infatuation with overblown literary images of romance and the "sullen legs" and "ratty eyes" of his wife.

Reprinted in *Morningside* 13 (April 1925): 128.

C48. "Resuscitations: III. Augustine Joseph Hickey Duganne." *Morningside* 13, n.d. (ca. February 1925): 77-82.

Satirically reviews the career of the prolific, forgotten "Crichton of America," a leader of the Know-Nothing Party whose works included "history, philosophy, drama, aesthetics, economics, politics, religion," and dime novels. Lampoons *Injuresoul*, Duganne's 1884 rear-guard attack on Robert Ingersoll, which derided not only Darwin's theory of evolution but scientific theories of "the circulation of the blood, of planetary movement, of Newton's law of gravitation, of potential energy, of all chemical and physical evidence."

C49. "Pathetic Fallacy." *Morningside* 13 (April 1925): 128-29.

A poem recounting how a man universally shunned by women seeks peace in the grave but is rejected as well by Mother Earth in the form of a shelf of bedrock.

C50. "Junior to Senior." *Morningside* 13 (April 1925): 130-31.

A poem explaining the young speaker's love and hate toward his mentor by recalling how the elder's revelation of his "undone promise" had chastened the speaker's arrogant assessment of his unique powers of insight into "the guest-book" of his "poor fellow-travellers," kindling first his hatred and then "the gratitude for my fine hate."

C51. "Trout." *Morningside* 13 (April 1925): 131.

A paean to "a graceful, wise, majestical and blind old trout" kept in a well to keep it clear of insects.

C52. "Letter to a Friend in a Provincial University." *Morningside* 13 (May 1925): 144-50.

A burlesque of intellectual life at Columbia, satirizing naively enthusiastic students, hard-bitten philosophers, impressionable *Spectator* reporters, dulcet-toned poets who find poetry in every activity, "disillusioned" and vulgarly opinionated enemies of aestheticism, and uninspired scholars. Concludes that despite the presence of some talented writers and a few thinkers, "I am being unwarrantably weighed down and oppressed by . . . Columbia's intellectual life."

C53. "Impediments." *Menorah Journal* 11 (June 1925): 286-90.

Dramatizes the relationship between two college students, the anonymous narrator and the "scrubby little Jew" Hettner, focusing on Hettner's confrontation of the narrator late one night as he has been writing a "painlessly achieved" paper on Browning. Hettner, better read than the narrator, more serious and humble, clearly wants "to tell me things about his soul," but the narrator keeps him at a distance, "defend[ing] my citadel" with determined small talk because "I do not want to know about people's souls. . . . I was particularly reluctant to see this man's insides; they would be, probably, too much like mine." The combination of defensive flippancy and gin eventually exhausts Hettner, but as he leaves, he tells the narrator simply, "What a miserable dog you are."

Reprinted in A12.

C54. "Chapter for a Fashionable Jewish Novel." *Menorah Journal* 12 (June 1926): 275-82.

Describes a moribund Sunday evening on which the nameless hero visits his friend Julia for cocktails and dinner. The party also includes Julia's teenaged sister Janet and Julia's friends Arthur and Paula. A conversation about the columnist Milt Gross's description of "a certain large class of Jews"--who are "not the sort of Jews you might know, nor are they ghetto Jews. . . . The men belong to lodges and the youths to fraternities that they themselves found"--reveals the source of the narrator's anomie: he is stranded between the ghetto culture he has repudiated and an aspiringly secular culture he finds depressingly impoverished, so that in bringing up Gross's column to his worldly Jewish friends, he feels "not like a prophet come howling from the wilderness to warn a people defiling holiness, but like a satyr leaped into a respectable home . . . disgusting the inhabitants by the abandon and licentiousness of his Semitic existence. He smirked at himself: patriot by perversity." The story ends by setting an image of men drilling a construction pit, "making the drills sing a mad song," against the forlorn figure of a young Jewish woman trapped for life in her family's stationery store.

C55. "A Friend of Byron." *Menorah Journal* 12 (August 1926): 371-83.

Surveys, in the facetious style of C48--a style Trilling was never to use again in his published writing--the life and work of Isaac Nathan (1791?-1864), the composer and music critic who set Byron's *Hebrew Melodies* to music and published *Fugitive Pieces and Reminiscences of Lord Byron*. Expressing contempt for Nathan's "meretricious" music and his "lyrically banal" commentary on it, describes Nathan's career as a betrayal of both the Jewish liturgical tradition and the tradition of British secular culture on which it was doubly parasitic, and concludes that Nathan is "not quite a tradesman, not quite a gentleman, nor yet quite an artist."

C56. "Funeral at the Club, with Lunch." *Menorah Journal* 13 (August 1927): 380-90.

Dramatizes the isolation of a Jewish college instructor come from "the metropolis" to a "provincial" university who realizes, lunching at the faculty club just before the funeral of Professor Fitch, that he is afraid his colleagues will close ranks against him in their collective mourning--that he has remained "an outlander" because of his religion. Torn between the sense of freedom that comes from acknowledging his isolation as a Jew and the fear that "he was foully seeking martrydom," he feels unable either to make a formal religious profession toward his colleagues ("We are all alike, and thou art better than I") or an attestation of intellectual achievement ("Thou fool"), but, realizing that none of his colleagues has ever truly liked Fitch or objected to himself, rejects them on that account, achieving a new distance that "said for him 'Thou fool.' The new distance allowed him to say the other yet kept him uncaught." Deciding not to attend the funeral, he leaves the club with the sense of setting out on a journey.

C57. "A Light to the Nations." *Menorah Journal* 16 (April 1928): 402-8.

Amusingly recounts Trilling's unlikely success with two students at "a Western university [the University of Wisconsin]." One of them, Anita Barberino, miserable because of her family's strict allegiance to the ways of Little Italy, does not respond to the narrator's appeals to her national or cultural pride, but becomes "gayer and freer," and capable of writing "hard and real" stories about Italian-Americans, at the news that the narrator, "this young man, so nice and so intelligent, who was a member of a faculty and lived in a forbidding club with other members of a faculty," is Jewish. When she imparts this revelation to her friend Miss Stopford, who had confided her anti-Semitism to the narrator in an earlier conference, Miss Stopford, whether in atonement or embarrassment or revenge, improves dramatically as a writer. Trilling lets his friend Judson, whose Oxford training had failed with Miss Stopford, think him "a tower of pedagogy."

C58. "Notes on a Departure." *Menorah Journal* 16 (May 1929): 421-34.

A story dramatizing a Jewish teacher's departure from his college through his farewell to his undergraduate student McAllister, whose broken, unmendable rib near his heart makes McAllister "older than he," and his brief, archly formal conversation with Enid, whose perfect beauty he has sought to possess without wanting to become aware of her humanity. Acknowledging that his identity as a Jew has given him a freedom from unwelcome intimacy from the town and is now preventing him from remaining in a place which "would have given him a very sweet and gracious contentment," he realizes that this identity, envisioned as a comic familiar, has died in the act of insuring his freedom, isolation, and departure, and feels "complete not as a story is complete that a writer sends to the printer, but as the idea for that story becomes complete in the mind of the writer over many months," freed for action and self-creation in what he recognizes is "the best moment of his life."

Reprinted in A12.

C59. "Tragedy and Three Novels." [Review of Ernest Hemingway, *A Farewell to Arms* (New York: Scribner's, 1929); Edward Dahlberg, *Bottom Dogs*, with an Introduction by D. H. Lawrence (New York: Simon & Schuster, 1930); and William Faulkner, *The Sound and the Fury* (New York: Jonathan Cape and Harrison Smith, 1929).] *Symposium* 1 (January 1930): 106-14.

Ascribes the modern inability to feel terror to a pessimism that "finds life bad and death good," affirming human values but making tragedy more remote. Praises Hemingway as "our most skilful writer of tragedy" because of his "willingness to use terror and his development of new terms for it." Contrasts Dahlberg's "balance of pity and terror" with Dreiser's unmitigated plea for pity in *An American Tragedy*. Finds Faulkner's tragedy of "a bred-out provincial family" too "bent by the weight of technique" to evoke "anything save special and very cramped response," and wonders whether the modernist techniques of Joyce and his followers can express tragedy as well as "the older convention."

C60. "D. H. Lawrence: A Neglected Aspect." *Symposium* 1 (July 1930): 361-70.

Identifies Lawrence as pre-eminently "a poet of rebellious social theory" who traces the atrophy of "the 'dark' forces, self-assertion, masterfulness, pride, and joy" to "democracy and capitalistic industrialism," which foster the virtues of "idealism, benevolence, dutiful submission" at the cost of defeating the "dark" virtues and turning love into a "spiritual bullying." Points out that Lawrence, although proletarian in his own background, addresses himself didactically to "the sensitive middle class" and "those who are close to the rulers of the world." Argues that Lawrence never sees sex as "the ultimate activity of man," but sets it in a dialectic with "purposive" activity.

Reprinted in A15.

C61. "Is Literature Possible?" *Nation* 131 (15 October 1930): 405-6.

Discusses the Spenglerian claims that the "tyranny of the machine over life" makes modern American art impossible, and argues that artists, however mediocre, flourish in America and that the "repulsiveness" of American culture provides a subject as rich as that of modern European writers like Lawrence and Joyce. Chastises artists and critics who, like modern criminologists, shift the blame for the failure of modern art from the artist to the environment, defines the modern critic's role as fostering the artist's "old function of seer and teacher," and concludes that the most promising American art will be the most acutely subversive, like the fiction of Dos Passos and Dahlberg.

C62. [With Milton Rugoff] "Columbia '25--Columbia '33." *Modern Youth* 1 (May-June 1933): 7-11, 44.

Contrasts the college generation of 1921-25 with that of Rugoff, a Columbia graduate of 1933, by distinguishing it from both the Lost Generation of a few years earlier and Rugoff's Depression-era generation, "realistic, practical and even a little grim." Agrees with Mark Van Doren that students during this period were "serene" in their freedom from superstition about religion and social nostrums and armed against social vulgarity and stupidity with irony and a conviction that "reality was a literary quality--a quality especially associated with Dostoevsky, Lawrence, Proust, and Gide.

C63. "Boar's Head." *Columbia Review* 16 (May 1935): 6-8.

Commemorates the influence of George Edward Woodberry and Randolph Bourne on Columbia's poetry society. Maintains that although only Louis Zukofsky has emerged from Boar's Head to fulfill his vocation as a poet, the society's value lies in the promulgation of "artistic creation" as "a general and normal activity." Suggests that "the best poets of our day are speaking more relevantly to the best minds in the college than were equally eminent poets of twenty or even ten years ago."

C64. "Eugene O'Neill." *New Republic* 88 (23 September 1936): 176-79.

Traces O'Neill's philosophical development, his attempts to solve the problems of life, from his early attacks on middle-class complacency (leading eventually to his enshrinement as "a physician of souls" by the class he criticized, which "wanted certain of its taboos broken") to his affirmation, in the face of individual defeat, of the goodness of life through religious faith: "O'Neill feels that life is empty--having emptied it--and can fill it only by faith in a loving God." Notes that the unflinchingly metaphysical cast of O'Neill's theater, which isolates his characters from any social context--"they act their crimes on the stage of the infinite"--eventually leads, in *Days Without End*, to the banishing of life "by the vision of the Life Eternal," which approves "all the warping, bullying idealism that O'Neill had once attacked." Concludes that "O'Neill has crept into the dark womb of Mother Church and pulled the universe in with him."

Reprinted in *After the Genteel Tradition: American Writers Since 1910*, edited by Malcolm Cowley (New York: Norton, 1937), pp. 127-40; and in *O'Neill and His Plays*, edited by Oscar Cargill, N. B. Fagin, and W. J. Fisher (New York: New York University Press, 1961), pp. 292-300.

C65. "Willa Cather." *New Republic* 90 (10 February 1937): 10-13.

Contends that Cather's determination to rid the novel of its "furniture" of social facts has sent her, like many other noted novelists, "down to defeat before the actualities of American life." Defines Cather's work as "an attempt to accommodate and assimilate her perception of the pioneer's failure" which impels her "toward the spiritual East . . . toward authority and permanence, toward Rome itself." Suggests that Cather's perception of the inadequacies of the pioneer ideal leads her to "the new frontier" of "the mind," although the "striving after new worlds which cannot be gratified seems to spread a poison through the American soul, making it thin and unsubstantial, unable to find peace and solidity." Hence "the 'spirituality' of Miss Cather's latest books consists chiefly of an irritated exclusion of those elements of modern life with which she will not cope" and a glorification of domestic gentility and domesticity: "Life without its furniture is strangely bare."

Reprinted in *After the Genteel Tradition: American Writers Since 1910*, edited by Malcolm Cowley (New York:

Norton, 1937), pp. 52-63; in *Willa Cather and Her Critics*, edited by J. M. Schroeter (Ithaca: Cornell University Press, 1967), pp. 148-55; in *Literature and Liberalism: An Anthology of Sixty Years of The New Republic*, edited by Edward Zwick (Washington: New Republic, 1976); and in A15.

C66. "The America of John Dos Passos." [Review of John Dos Passos, *U.S.A.* (New York: Harcourt, Brace, 1937).] *Partisan Review* 4 (April 1938): 26-32.

Locates *U.S.A.* within "the cultural tradition of the intellectual Left," but notes that it modifies that tradition in three important ways: emphasizing individual over collective experience; neglecting the class struggle or class in the political sense; and denying the ultimate triumph of goodness or progressivism. Distinguishes between the consequent despair of the trilogy and the response it is intended to evoke in its readers. Observes that Dos Passos is less interested in political struggles between classes than in moral indecision within characters divided by their conflicting loyalties and uncertain sense of themselves, and characterizes the attempt to resolve moral dilemmas by an appeal to alternative notions of personal identity as a peculiarly modern approach to morality. Concludes that Dos Passos's essentially romantic notion of morality, which condemns safe choices as marking a "loss of human quality" and refuses to sanctify commitment to a particular party as a moral panacea, has alienated even his most acute critics (Malcolm Cowley and T. K. Whipple) on the left.

Reprinted in *Dos Passos: A Collection of Critical Essays*, edited by Andrew Hook (Englewood Cliffs, NJ: Prentice-Hall, 1974), pp. 93-100, and in A15.

C67. "Hemingway and His Critics." [Review of Ernest Hemingway, *The Fifth Column and the First Forty-Nine Stories* (New York: Scribner's, 1938).] *Partisan Review* 6 (Winter 1939): 52-60.

Distinguishes Hemingway the artist, conscious yet disinterested, who has written his short stories, from Hemingway the man, self-conscious, naive, and fumbling, who is responsible for *The Fifth Column*. Argues that Hemingway's critics have been largely responsible for the eclipse of the artist, who attempted to describe a complex and threatening world, through their demands that he prescribe a course of action for dealing with that world and their inclination to see his heroes as role-models for his audience. Argues that Hemingway's work is weakened by the interjection of the "fine feelings" whose absence progressive critics had deplored in his stories, since despite most readers' Platonic desire to have "our attitudes formulated by the tribal bard," literature is ill-equipped to assume the "messianic responsibility" of solving social and political problems that afflict writers as well as their audiences.

Reprinted in *Hemingway and His Critics: An International Anthology*, edited by Carlos Baker (New York: Hill and Wang, 1961), pp. 61-70.

C68. "Parrington, Mr. Smith, and Reality." [Review of V. L. Parrington, *Main Currents in American Thought* (New York: Harcourt, Brace, 1939), and Bernard Smith, *Forces in American Criticism* (New York: Harcourt, Brace, 1939).] *Partisan Review* 7 (January-February 1940): 24-40.

Notes that Parrington has "broadened the conception of letters" to include political and theological works and judged according to a single "standard of historical relevance," simplifying complexity and overlooking the importance of personal style, and preferring a model of literary creation that prescribed a close imitation of reality: "Fig. 1, Reality; Fig. 2, the Artist; Fig. 1a, the Work of Art." Argues that Parrington limits the reasons for "turning away from reality" to a generous but ambivalent romanticism (Emerson) or a psychological aberration (Hawthorne, Poe, Henry James) and that the severely materialistic portrait of American culture that emerges from such an analysis is politically as well as aesthetically suspect. Dismisses Smith's conception of scientific method as discredited by its positivism and refusal to deal with any "nonsense about 'mind,'" discusses the ways criticism can and cannot be modeled on scientific empiricism, and concludes that Smith's simplistic confidence about reality and his own disinterested powers of observation and analysis "carries his materialism to the point of Platonism, rejecting the partial, rejecting 'mere opinion,' demanding the One, the True and the Good."

Reprinted as Part I of "Reality in America" in A4, and in that form in *The Achievement of American Criticism*, edited by Clarence Arthur Brown (New York: Ronald, 1954), pp. 665-77, and in *Literary Opinion in America*, edited by Morton Dauwen Zabel (New York: Harper, 1951), pp. 404-16.

C69. "The Legacy of Sigmund Freud: An Appraisal." *Kenyon Review* 2 (Spring 1940): 135-85. [Trilling's contribution, "Part 2. Literary and Aesthetic," pp. 152-73. "Part 1. Therapeutic," is by Alexander Reid Martin; "Part 3. Philosophical," is by Eliseo Vivas.]

Calls Freudian psychology "the only systematic account of human nature" comparable to "the chaotic accumulation of insights which literature has made over the centuries." Traces the literary roots of Freudian theory to Diderot, Rousseau, and the Romantic poets, who created "a literature passionately devoted to . . . knowledge of the self," and notes his influence on Kafka, Mann, and Joyce. Insists against Mann that Freud's romanticism is complemented by a militant rationalism which holds "rather naively . . . to a correspondence-theory of knowledge" that vitiates his writings specifically devoted to art. Analyzes the "contempt" for art as a "narcotic" required by Freud's positivism as a result of Freud's two contradictory notions of mind--as capable of shaping a malleable external reality, and as required to deal with "a reality quite fixed and static"--generated in turn by "Freud's belief that the biological impulses are constants and that they are in a sense finally determining," and argues instead that "the poet is in command of his illusion, while it is exactly the mark of the neurotic that he is possessed by his illusion." Criticizes Ernest Jones's Freudian reading of *Hamlet* as presumptive in its claim that "the Oedipus motive is *the* meaning of *Hamlet*" and weakened by the incomplete nature of psychoanalytic accounts of meaning, which limit meaning to the author's intention rather than considering the work's effect as well and too easily assume access to the author's unconscious motives: "*Hamlet* is not merely the product of Shakespeare's thought, it is the very instrument of his thought." Praises Freudian psychology, however, as making "poetry indigenous to the very constitution of the mind," which is "exactly a poetry-making organ," and emphasizes the power of Freud's theories of repetition compulsion (which accounts for the "mithridate" or homeopathic function of tragedy and comedy) and of the death instinct in accounting for the power and complexity of literature too often denied by latter-day Freudians, concluding that the development of these two theories places Freud "clearly in the line of the classic tragic realism."

Revised and reprinted as "Freud and Literature" in *Horizon* 16 (September 1947): 182-200; in *Criticism: The Foundations of Modern Literary Judgment*, edited by Mark Schorer, Josephine Miller, and Gordon McKenzie (New York: Harcourt, Brace, 1948), pp. 172-82; in A4; in *Literary Opinion in America*, edited by Morton Dauwen Zabel (New York: Harper, 1951), pp. 677-92; in *Psychoanalysis and Literature*, edited by H. M. Ruitenbeck (New York: Dutton, 1964), pp. 251-71; in *Critical Theory Since Plato*, edited by Hazard Adams (New York: Harcourt Brace Jovanovich, 1971), pp. 949-58; and in *20th Century Literary Criticism: A Reader*, edited by David Lodge (London: Longman, 1972), pp. 276-90.

C70. "Literature and Power." *Kenyon Review* 2 (Autumn 1940): 433-42.

Examines the dilemma of professors of English whose function seems marginal, and their claim, prevalent ever since the institutionalizing of English studies under Arnold, that literature is "not merely a symptom of civilization but actually a civilizing agent," the repository of the ethical values once associated with religion--a belief which led to the current myth that "the essence of literature is . . . power, moral, political or scientific, and that [professors are] moralists, politicians and scientists." Observes that this myth has lately been supplemented by two other attitudes toward literature, which see in it raw material for scientific or historical investigation. Notes the dangerous modern tendency to separate the "contemplative experience" offered by literature from its status as "purposive activity," and warns of the future "development of two kinds of literature--a literature of duty and a literature of pleasure"--which will threaten both the experience literary art offers "of nearly unconditioned living" and "the awareness of the qualities of things," whether these qualities are artistic, moral, or political.

Reprinted in A13, and in *Kenyon Review*, new series 11 (Winter 1989): 119-25.

C71. "'Elements That Are Wanted.'" [Review of T. S. Eliot, *The Idea of a Christian Society* (New York: Harcourt, Brace, 1939).] *Partisan Review* 7 (September-October 1940): 367-79.

Contends that for all Eliot's hostility to romanticism, his politics and religion are essentially romantic and anti-materialistic. Describes the past century as dominated by the inconclusive struggle between materialism and romanticism, to which Eliot's "book is the tragic coda" because, despite its flaws and limitations--its blindness to the failure of earlier Christian societies and to the critique of

Christianity which has arisen within such societies, its "cold ignorance of what people are really like," its confusion of morality with snobbery, conformity, or Puritanism, its inadequate account of "the relation of social forms to power and of power to wealth"--it establishes moral perfection as an absolute goal rather than a political instrumentality. Discusses the decline of ideals of personal morality from Montaigne, Rousseau, and Diderot through Marx and Lenin, noting Wordsworth's anti-revolutionary "affirmation that every man was an end" in the face of the paradoxical use of "the *ultimate man*" as an ideal to diminish the "free will and individual value" of each existing person, especially in contemporary Marxism, and concludes that "a rational and naturalistic philosophy" needs to incorporate both materialistic and supernatural elements.

Reprinted as "T. S. Eliot's Politics" in A15.

C72. "Sherwood Anderson." *Kenyon Review* 3 (Summer 1941): 293-302.

Criticizes Anderson's enduringly adolescent sensibility, whose character is fixed beyond the hope of development by the importance he ascribes to the conflict between sincerity and commercialism or gentility: "He had dared too much for art and therefore expected too much from his mere daring." Compares Anderson to one of the grotesques in the Introduction to *Winesburg, Ohio*, who has been distorted by his uncritical affirmation of "love, passion and freedom," which "make the world unbearably abstract," depriving Anderson's work of sensory richness or solidity of social specification and forcing him to use "the language of the very greatest and most strenuous religious experience" for "the salvation of a small legitimate existence." Concludes that the disparity between the grandiose general terms in which Anderson speaks of salvation and the modest particulars of love and freedom he describes--"a farm, neighbors and a small daily work to do"--reflects the reality of the cultural situation he describes and the difficulty of achieving the small legitimate existence so necessary to most people.

Reprinted with additional material from C88 in A4; in *Critiques and Essays in Modern Fiction, 1920-1951*, edited by John W. Aldridge (New York: Ronald, 1952), pp. 319-27; in *The Achievement of Sherwood Anderson*, edited by R. L. White (Chapel Hill: University of North Carolina Press, 1966), pp. 212-21; and in *Sherwood Anderson: A Collection of Critical Essays*, edited by Walter B. Rideout (Englewood Cliffs: Prentice-Hall, 1974), pp. 130-38.

C73. "Wordsworth's Ode: 'Intimations of Immortality.'" *English Institute Annual* 3 (New York: Columbia University Press, 1942): 1-28.

Dismisses the theory that the Immortality Ode is an elegy to Wordsworth's failing poetic powers on the grounds that the poem neither cites the specific failure of those powers as a danger that besets the poet nor identifies the composition of poetry with any particular mental faculty. Arguing instead that the poem is "about growing. . . . It is concerned with ways of seeing and then with ways of knowing," discusses the poem's movement from posing a question ("Whither is fled the visionary gleam?") about the passing of the "oceanic" sensation of "the perfect union of the self and the universe"--as opposed to Coleridge's lament in the Dejection Ode for the loss of his poetic gifts--to giving two contradictory answers representing "the resistance to and the acceptance of growth." Notes that since "Wordsworth is speaking of a period common to the development of everyone," his final ambivalence constitutes an exemplary "double vision" of "man both in his ideal nature and in his earthly activity."

Revised and reprinted as "The Immortality Ode" in A4; in B37, pp. 483-502; and in *Discussions of William Wordsworth*, edited by Jack Davis (Boston: Heath, 1964), pp. 142-59.

C74. "E. M. Forster." *Kenyon Review* 4 (Spring 1942): 160-73.

Calls "Forster's bright, modest, stubborn mind . . . particularly useful as we face the trials of war," even though he has generally been undervalued because of his comic seriousness and his playful manner, which makes him "sometimes irritating in his refusal to be great." Notes Forster's affinities with the self-conscious use of comic conventions of narration in Fielding and with the presentation of good and evil as inextricably linked in Dickens, Hawthorne, James, Meredith, and *The Winter's Tale*, since his plots are characterized by moral duality, clearcut choices between good and evil, while his ironic manner bespeaks reconciliation. Characterizes Forster as a liberal constantly at war with the certitudes of the liberal imagination, contrasting him with Lawrence, whose social critique gains "coercive power" at the cost of "intellectual power," and with Anderson, whose development is arrested by his failure to see as his true community "the members of the European tradition of thought," and who, "for all his great explicit impulse toward actuality," lacks Forster's detailed knowledge and ultimate acceptance of people and their world as they are: "The way of human action does not, of course, satisfy him, but he does not believe there are any new virtues to be discovered." Concludes that Forster's ideological skepticism makes him "one of the thinking people who were never led by thought to suppose they could be more than human and who, in bad times, will not become less."

Revised and reprinted as Chapter 1 of A2, and in *Forster: A Collection of Critical Essays*, edited by Malcolm Bradbury (Englewood Cliffs: Prentice-Hall, 1966), pp. 71-80.

C75. "The Sense of the Past." *Partisan Review* 9 (May-June 1942): 229-41.

Seeks to define more precisely, in response to recent debates about the relation between history and criticism in literary study, the sense of the past that informs all discussions of literature. Defines literature as historical on three counts: because of its concern to record important events, its awareness of its own past, and its historicity, its pastness, as it affects the responses of present-day readers. Argues that even if interpretation and evaluation should perhaps be free of the awareness of historicity, they cannot be separated from it: "Without the sense of the past we might be more certain, less weighed down and pessimistic. But we might also be less generous and complete." Since "it is only if we are aware of the reality of the past as past that we can feel it as alive and present," recommends sharpening and complicating the sense of the past by considering more critically the ways in which human nature changes over time, the assumed (rather than the expressed) ideas of an age, the ways literature develops ideas rather than simply borrowing or using them, the role poets play in shaping the environment that in turn affects them, the puzzling and pervasive nature of influence and of causality in culture generally, and the relation between abstract ideas and the conditions of their development and transmission. Concludes that neither words nor ideas can take responsibility for historical events away from the people who give them their assent, since "behind every idea that is effective lies the human will," so that ideas never "exist apart from the thinker and the situation," and warns that ascribing historical effects to ideas apart from their proponents and espousers, a habit made fashionable by the coming of war, is "obscurantist and demagogic."

Revised and reprinted in A4; in *Essays in Modern Literary Criticism*, edited by Ray B. West, Jr. (New York: Rinehart, 1952), pp. 290-301; and in *Influx: Essays on Literary Influence*, edited by Ronald Primeau (New York: Kennikat, 1977), pp. 22-33.

C76. "Tacitus Now." [Review of *The Complete Works of Tacitus*, translated by Alfred John Church and William Jackson Brodribb; edited, with an Introduction, by Moses Hadas (New York: Modern Library, 1942).] *Nation* 155 (22 August 1942): 153-54.

Observes that although Tacitus has never been important to American readers, "our political education of the past decades" has brought the European experience and its historians closer to Americans. Calls Tacitus "one of the few great writers who are utterly without hope," and defines the power of his analysis as psychological rather than political, linking him to Flaubert. Notes that more recent historians have characterized the period which seems so turbulent in the *Histories* and the *Annals* as largely peaceful and concludes that Tacitus lacks "'the long view' of history," adding that "to minds of a certain sensitivity 'the long view' is the falsest historical view of all, and indeed on the length of perspective is intended precisely to overcome sensitivity." Argues instead that the relevance of Tacitus to the present lies precisely in his passionate energy, "his power of mind and his stubborn love of virtue maintained in desperate circumstances."

Revised and reprinted in A4.

C77. "Of This Time, of That Place." *Partisan Review* 10 (January-February 1943): 72-81, 84-105.

Dramatizes the relationship between Dr. Joseph Howe, an instructor in English at fictional Dwight College, and his brilliant but incoherent freshman Ferdinand Tertan, who reveres Howe as a poet despite the dismissal of his work as socially irresponsible in a recent issue of an influential journal and comes to love him as a mentor despite Howe's growing perception of Tertan as mad. Sets Tertan's socially threatening madness against the socially acceptable madness of Dwight senior Theodore Blackburn, whose pretension to literary study as part of his cultural baggage does not conceal his complete lack of interest in or sensitivity to literature. Shows the deeply divided responses both students evoke in their teacher, who shares his uneasiness about Tertan with the Dean despite his conviction that "he must not surrender the question" of Tertan's identity to an institutional authority determined to resolve it once and for all, and who finally gives Blackburn a passing grade in his course in the Romantic poets despite his certainty that Blackburn knows nothing of the material and his revulsion from Blackburn's attempts to blackmail him into a passing grade by revealing his sponsorship of the unstable Tertan for a college literary society. Shows Howe in the final scene preparing for the commencement procession, knowing that, partly because of his complicity in both cases, Tertan will be institutionalized on completion of the term, while Blackburn is warmly congratulated by the Dean for being the first member of his class to have secured a job.

Reprinted in *The Three Readers: An Omnibus of Novels, Stories, Essays & Poems Selected with Comments by the Editorial Committee of the Readers Club*, edited by Clifton Fadiman, Sinclair Lewis, and Carl Van Doren (New York: Readers Club, 1943), pp. 82-115; in *The Best American Short Stories 1944*, edited by Martha Foley (Boston: Houghton Mifflin, 1944), pp. 385-422; translated into French by G.-M. Tracy in *La revue de Paris* 53 (December 1946): 80-107; in *The Penguin New Writing*, edited by John Lehmann (Harmondsworth: Penguin, 1948); in *Reading Modern Short Stories*, edited by Jarvis A. Thurston (Chicago: Scott, Foresman, 1955), pp. 451-85; in *Pleasures of New Writing: An Anthology of Poems, Stories and Other Prose Pieces from the Pages of New Writing*, edited by John Lehmann (London: John Lehmann, 1951); in *Modern Short Stories*, edited by Marvin Felheim, Franklin B. Newman, and William R. Steinhoff (New York: Oxford University Press, 1951), pp. 126-62; translated into Polish by Juliusz Mieroszewski in *Kultura* 69 (July-August 1953): 103-42; in *More Stories in the Modern Manner from Partisan Review* (New York: Avon, 1954), pp. 196-234; in *Short Story*

Study: A Critical Anthology, compiled by Albert J. Smith and W. H. Mason (London: Edward Arnold, 1961); in *Best Short Stories of the Modern Age*, edited by Douglas Angus (New York: Fawcett, 1962); in *Stories of Modern America*, edited by Herbert Gold and David L. Stevenson (New York: St. Martin's, 1961), pp. 59-94; in B2; *Anthology: An Introduction to Literature*, edited by Lynn Altenbernd (New York: Macmillan, 1977); in *Composition and Literary Form: An Anthology*, edited by Nicholas A. Salerno and Nancy J. Hawkey (Cambridge, MA: Winthrop, 1978), pp. 260-89; 103-42; in extract in Arthur Finley Scott, *English Composition, Book III* (Cambridge: Cambridge University Press, 1953); and in A12.

C78. "Mr. Eliot's Kipling." [Review of *A Choice of Kipling's Verse*, made and with an essay by T. S. Eliot (New York: Scribner's, 1943).] *Nation* 157 (16 October 1943): 436-42.

Discusses reading Kipling as a crucial childhood experience and reacting against him as the "first literary-political decision" of many "liberals of a certain age." Cites Kipling's fascination with "being 'in' on literature" and mastering a craft or mystery as an introduction to "the cult of art." Traces liberal disenchantment with Kipling to Shaw and Wells, and calls Eliot's introduction an essay on politics rather than literature, since his defense of Kipling as a Tory is weakened by considering other Tories--Johnson, Burke, Scott--whose generosity of mind and temperament Kipling lacks. Observes that Kipling's low opinion of liberal intellectuals provoked the liberal audience into "hating everything that Kipling loved," undermining "the national virtues" of physical courage, civic responsibility, and judgment in governance both by his own pettiness, narrow-mindedness, and anti-intellectualism, and by encouraging his disparagers to react against his principles, so that Kipling ends by "making impossible the virtues he prized." Concludes by comparing Eliot to Kipling in his dependence on public performance, his pose as politically beleaguered and elitist, and his usefulness--now found to be waning--in challenging the liberal sensibility.

Revised and reprinted in A4; in *Kipling's Mind and Art*, edited by Andrew Rutherford (London: Oliver & Boyd, 1964), pp. 85-94; and in *British Victorian Literature: Recent Revaluations*, edited by Shiv K. Kumar (New York: New York University Press, 1969), pp. 145-54.

C79. "The Mind of Youth." *Harper's Bazaar* 78 (July 1944), pp. 30, 80, 84.

Deplores the ignorance and intellectual immaturity of students whose preparation for college has been undermined by the belief that "we do not want to teach subjects, we want to teach students." Argues that such an anti-authoritarian emphasis respects neither "the person the student will be" nor the student's mind, which is dissolved into a set of social attitudes.

C80. "A Note on Art and Neurosis." *Partisan Review* 12 (Winter 1945): 41-48.

Responds to M1054 by disputing the argument made popular by L981 that artistic power is rooted in disabling neurosis. Points out that the myth of the neurotically withdrawn artist is of recent origin, having no currency in the Renaissance or the eighteenth century, and that the myth serves the interests of both aspiring artist-prophets and the philistine who "wants to listen at the same time that he wants to shut his ears." Objects that although "it is the writer's job to exhibit his unconscious," psychoanalysis assumes unconscious motives for all activity, so that observers who impute artistic ability to neurotic causes should "be willing to relate all intellectual achievement to neurosis"; and that neurotic theories of artistic inspiration cannot account for the power with which artists shape and express their fantasies, suggesting instead that the most healthy part of any artist is whatever "gives him the power to conceive, to plan, to work, and to bring his work to completion." Concludes that the story of Philoctetes is not "an explanatory myth" of the sources of artistic power but rather "a moral myth" warning that "weakness does not preclude strength nor strength weakness."

Incorporated into "Art and Neurosis" in A4, and reprinted in that form in *American Literary Criticism, 1900-1950*, edited by Charles I. Glicksberg (New York: Hendricks House, 1952), pp. 550-66; in *The Study of Literature: A Handbook of Critical Essays and Terms*, edited by Sylvan Barnet, Morton Berman, and William Burto (Boston: Little, Brown, 1960), pp. 214-33; and in *Critical Theory Since Plato*, edited by Hazard Adams (New York: Harcourt Brace Jovanovich, 1971), pp. 959-67.

C81. Sermon on a Text from Whitman." [Review of *Walt Whitman, Poet of American Democracy*, selected and edited by Samuel Sillen (New York: International Publishers, 1944).] *Nation* 160 (24 February 1945): 215-20.

Notes the ways *Democratic Vistas* makes the future of democracy depend on literature: literature is to provide not only what Whitman calls "an American stock personality" but "the intermediary between the necessary authority of government and the ideal condition of human freedom." Argues that the dialectical conflict between authority and "personalism," or individual identity, is at the heart of *Democratic Vistas.* Criticizes Sillen's partisan, proto-Russian view of Whitman as oversimplified and anti-political in its distrust of individual identity (as opposed to individual value or ideals), points out that Whitman is potentially valuable to victims of the war, who, "where they have not lost their lives, have lost their sense of personal identity to an extent painful beyond imagination," and accounts for the appeal of the tradition it represents by asserting that "all of us, latently and unconsciously, fear in ourselves the sense of identity, and wish to lose it." Finds Whitman's legitimate heirs in Marianne Moore, e. e. cummings, and other poets who seek "to shock us out of the way of seeing forced upon us by the political past and the institutional present," and his "negation" in Sillen's volume.

Reprinted in A15.

C82. "Teacher vs. Scholar," *Bulletin of the Association for General and Liberal Education* 1 (June 1945): 23-25.

Resolves the dispute between the primacy of teaching and scholarship by attacking the belief that "the student is more important than anything he may learn," contending instead that "it is only if you put the subject first that the student comes anywhere at all." Condemns "seductive teaching" apart from the authority conferred on teachers by their mastery of their subjects, and insists that "it is the nature of true scholarship to be interesting and instructive."

C83. "F. Scott Fitzgerald." [Review of F. Scott Fitzgerald, *The Crack-Up*, edited by Edmund Wilson (New York: J. Laughlin, 1945).] *Nation* 161 (25 August 1945): 182-84.

Identifies "the root of Fitzgerald's heroism," his awareness of the exemplary tragedy of his ill-husbanded talent, in "his power of love"--his admiration of the good, his consequent sense of moral responsibility, his fascination with an aristocracy of personal distinction or, more critically, of material wealth and social privilege. Compares Fitzgerald to Yeats for his continued nourishing of his youthful vanities, Goethe for his early success and consciousness of his role as spokesman of a rising generation, and Milton's Samson for his nobility in self-destruction, and defends the comparisons by invoking Fitzgerald's own estimation of his strengths and weaknesses and concluding that his lack of prudence is generous, even heroic.

Reprinted with additional material from B17 as "F. Scott Fitzgerald" in A4; in *F. Scott Fitzgerald: The Man and His Work*, edited by Alfred Kazin (Cleveland: Meridian, 1951), pp. 195-204; and in *Fitzgerald: An Anthology of Critical Essays*, edited by Arthur Mizener (Englewood Cliffs, NJ: Prentice-Hall, 1963), pp. 11-19; and excerpted in *The Great Gatsby: A Study*, edited by Frederick J. Hoffman (New York: Scribner's, 1962), pp. 232-43.

C84. "The Other Margaret." *Partisan Review* 12 (Fall 1945): 481-501.

Presents the story of fortyish Stephen Elwin, who, stopping on the way from his job as a publisher of scientific books to pick up a framed reproduction of "one of Rouault's kings," and witnessing a bus conductor's humiliation of a little boy asking the fare, returns home to his wife Lucy and their 13-year-old daughter Margaret, who is just beginning to grow up. Develops two disagreements between Margaret and Lucy--first about the likelihood that another bus conductor was ridiculing a passenger by pretending she was Jewish, then about whether the Elwins' black maid, "the other Margaret," is, unlike their former black maid, "a thoroughly disagreeable person." Both times Margaret argues that members of underpaid and socially oppressed classes are not responsible for their actions, and both times a quarrel is averted by a diversion, first by a family joke, then by Lucy's discovery of a green-glazed clay lamb Margaret has made for her birthday a week hence. Elwin's frustrated reflections on his inability to explain to Margaret "the nature of the double truth"--that "society is responsible" for the condition of individuals, but that individuals are responsible for their own behavior as well--are interrupted by the maid's announcement that she is quitting her job. Elwin senses that his daughter identifies with Margaret's expulsion, but a moment later she turns against the maid on seeing her deliberately smash the lamb, and neither her parents' protestations ("It was an accident," "It just happened") nor Elwin's sense of the Rouault king's "old, fine, tragic power," now grown irrelevant, can prevent her from mourning her own loss of innocence in seeing "with her own eyes . . . the actual possibility of what she herself might do, the insupportable fact of her own moral life."

Reprinted in *The Best American Short Stories 1946*, edited by Martha Foley (Boston: Houghton Mifflin, 1946), pp. 464-96; in *The Art of Modern Fiction*, edited by Ray B. West, Jr., and R. W. Stallman (New York: Rinehart, 1949), pp. 374-92; in *Life and Letters and the London Mercury*, vol. 63, no. 147 (November 1949), edited by R. Herring; in *The New Partisan Reader, 1945-1953*, edited by William Phillips and Philip Rahv (New York: Harcourt, Brace, 1953), pp. 10-30; in *Stories in the Modern Manner from the Partisan Review* (New York: Avon, 1953), pp. 101-27; in *Stories British and American*, edited by Jack Barry and W. Richard Poirier (Boston: Houghton Mifflin, 1953); in *Contrasts: Idea and Technique*, edited by Robert E. Knoll (New York: Harcourt, Brace, 1955), pp. 501-20; and in A12.

C85. "The Lesson and the Secret." *Harper's Bazaar* 79 (March 1945): 90, 136-52.

Recounts a meeting of a creative writing course whose instructor, Vincent Hammell, meets a challenge by his class of wealthy older women to teach them the secret of writing stories they can sell to magazines by reading them a story about two American girls visiting an Austrian priest who, while he is called away, step into his bathtub filled with newly pressed wine, hasten to clean themselves, and then sit decorously while he serves them the wine. Initially fearful that he has chosen an inappropriate story for his class, Hammell observes that the story has awakened a response in all of them by celebrating "their youth, their beauty, their femininity. . . . It was thus that the women of Thrace must have sat around Orpheus before they had had occasion to be enraged with him." The students' attempts to account for the story's power over them, however, assume hopelessly conventional terms. One of the more refractory students, praising the story "in the only language she knew" as neither "highbrow *or* commercial," asks Hammell, "Does this writer sell well?" to produce a final expectant tableau.

Reprinted in *Horizon* 20 (August 1949): 111-22; in *The Writer's Book. Presented by the Authors Guild*, edited by Helen R. Hull (New York: Harper, 1950), pp. 181-93; and in A12.

C86. "Dreiser and the Liberal Mind." [Review of Theodore Dreiser, *The Bulwark* (Garden City: Doubleday, 1946).] *Nation* 162 (20 April 1946): 466, 469-70, 472.

Sets Dreiser against Henry James--a juxtaposition that evokes "the dark and bloody crossroads where culture and politics meet." Wonders why, if, as Robert Gorham Davis argues, "it is a little too late" for James's moral perceptiveness to be of practical value, it is not also a little too late for Dreiser's "self-pity" and "honest stupidity," and traces the contrasting evaluation of the two writers to the American suspicion of mind, which imposes on James the responsibility for resolving the moral problems he discerns while sentimentalizing Dreiser as a "peasant," praising his awkward, often bookish style as a direct representation of reality, and protectively describing his ideas ("religion is nonsense, 'religionists' are fakes, tradition is a fraud . . .") as immaterial. Condemns the progressive critics who accepted Dreiser by first establishing "the ultimate social responsibility of the writer" and then arguing that "he is not really responsible for anything, even his ideas."

Revised and reprinted as Part II of "Reality in America" in A4, and in that form in *The Achievement of American Criticism*, edited by Clarence Arthur Brown (New York: Ronald, 1954), pp. 665-77, and in *Literary Opinion in America*, edited by Morton Dauwen Zabel (New York: Harper, 1951), pp. 404-16; and in its original form in *Dreiser: A Collection of Critical Essays*, edited by John Lydenberg (Englewood Cliffs: Prentice-Hall, 1971), pp. 87-95.

C87. "The Life of the Novel." [Review of Eleanor Clark, *The Bitter Box* (Garden City: Doubleday, 1946).] *Kenyon Review* 8 (Autumn 1946): 658-67.

Ascribes the contemporary decay of the novel to the lapse in the general interest in morals and manners, as indicated by the pointed lack of interest recent fiction has taken in the Communist Party "except as a figment." Commends Clark's novel for dealing directly with the culture of American Communism as "a field of freedom in which, as in all human experience, cordial and corrosive are found together." Traces the shortcomings of the novel's reliance on the paraphernalia of anxiety" which becomes "touched with academicism," and notes that although modern fantasists define their approach as a reaction against naturalism, their fantasy is itself rooted in social reality. Points to Clark's laughter as liberating her novel from its anxiety, joining Henry James's tales of writers and artists in rejecting mere representation in order to "put fantasy to work projecting a potentiality of states of being."

C88. "The World of Sherwood Anderson." [Review of *The Sherwood Anderson Reader*, edited by Paul Rosenfeld (Boston: Houghton Mifflin, 1947).] *New York Times Book Review*, 9 November 1947, pp. 1, 67-69.

Notes Anderson's appeal to audiences who first read him in their own adolescence or "the adolescence of contemporary American literature." Places Anderson in the context of such other writers as Blake, Thoreau, Whitman, and Lawrence, who "maintain a standing quarrel with society and have a perpetual bone to pick with the rational intellect," but judges his achievement in retrospect as undermined by his contempt for mind and energy, his commitment to an ideal "which is less alive than our daily actuality," his tendency to abstract the objects of his greatest affection, and his falsely theatrical adoption of a "credo of defenselessness" which valorized his lack of historical and cultural knowledge.

Some material is reprinted in "Sherwood Anderson" in A4 and reprinted in that form in *Critiques and Essays in Modern Fiction, 1920-1951*, edited by John W. Aldridge (New York: Ronald, 1952), pp. 319-27; in *The Achievement of Sherwood Anderson*, edited by R. L. White (Chapel Hill: University of North Carolina Press, 1966), pp. 212-21; and in *Sherwood Anderson: A Collection of Critical Essays*, edited by Walter B. Rideout (Englewood Cliffs: Prentice-Hall, 1974), pp. 130-38.

C89. "Treason in the Modern World." [Review of Rebecca West, *The Meaning of Treason* (New York: Viking, 1947).] *Nation* 166 (10 January 1948): 46-48.

Praises the seriousness with which West offers "the national idea" as a motive equal in its power to the economic motives subscribed by "the old basic liberal belief" and her skepticism of progressivism as blind to "the deep instinctual roots of man," but criticizes her "incantatory glorification" of nationalistic motives and her analysis of World War II traitors as psychologically deviant as obscuring an emerging rift between nation and ideology. Reviews the three types of traitors West describes--"children," mental aberrants, and "revolutionaries"--as representative instances of "the struggle between nationality and ideology."

Reprinted in A15.

C90. "Manners, Morals, and the Novel." *Kenyon Review* 10 (Winter 1948): 11-27.

Defining "manners" as "a culture's hum and buzz of implication," and the central problem of the novel as a literary mode as "the old opposition between reality and appearance," argues that "the novel . . . is a perpetual quest for reality, the field of its research being always the social world, the material of its analysis being always manners as the indication of the direction of man's soul." Observes that "the novel as I have described it has never really established itself in America," first because of the thinness of American society remarked by Cooper and James, more recently because "Americans have a kind of resistance to looking closely at society"--not because they have no interest in society, but because they conceive of society in terms of a bedrock "reality" that can be described only in the most abstract terms, so that "in proportion as we have committed ourselves to our particular idea of reality we have lost our interest in manners. . . . The reality we admire tells us that the observation of manners is trivial and even malicious, that there are things much more important for the novel to consider." Describes novelists like Steinbeck, who define society in abstract terms rather than in James's and Forster's terms of particular differences in manners, as illustrating a broadening of social feeling at the expense of the power of love. Warns that the neglect of the "moral realism" whose most effective agent for over two hundred years has been the novel allows "the moral passions," warranted by self-righteousness against their possible shortcomings, to become "even more wilful and imperious and impatient than the self-seeking passions," and links the decline of the novel to the waning of moral freedom.

Reprinted in *Forms of Modern Fiction: Essays Collected in Honor of Joseph Warren Beach*, edited by William Van O'Connor (Minneapolis: University of Minnesota Press, 1948); in A4; in *Readings for Liberal Education*, edited by Louis Glenn Locke, William Merriam Gibson, and George Warren Arms, revised edition (New York: Rinehart, 1952); and in *Essentials of the Theory of Fiction*, edited by Michael J. Hoffman and Patrick D. Murphy (Durham: Duke University Press, 1988), pp. 115-30.

C91. "Sex and Science: The Kinsey Report." [Review of Alfred C. Kinsey, Wardell B. Pomeroy, and Clyde E. Martin, *Sexual Behavior in the Human Male* (Philadelphia: Saunders, 1948).] *Partisan Review* 15 (April 1948): 460-76.

Describes the Kinsey Report as significant as both a therapy in its likely permissive effects, and a symptom of the isolation that requires "the community of sexuality . . . to be established in explicit quantitative terms." Notes that the Report contravenes its claims to moral disinterestedness in its definition of sexuality as a measurable physiological experience and its corresponding neglect of psychological factors, in its appeals to animal behavior as a norm and its distrust of the peculiarly human features of human sexuality, and in its elision of "the Natural" to "the Normal" through its simplication of male sexuality by a model of the physical release of sexual tension, so that although, for example, "the Report is partisan to sex, it wants people to have a good sexuality," still "by good it means nothing else but frequent." Notes, in unusually caustic terms, the link between the "generosity of mind" behind the Report's "impulse toward acceptance and liberation" and its "almost willed intellectual weakness" about intellectual distinctions that may turn out to have social consequences: "Somehow the democratic virtues are inclined, in the intellectual life, to lead from the large acceptance of the facts of society to the belief that any use of these facts which perceives values and demonstrates consequences is dangerous." Hence the Report, in its emphasis on the factuality and quantitative authority of its data, succeeds in "removing the human subject from its human implications" and "preventing the consideration of the consequences" of sexuality, making present-day social behavior its own norm.

Revised and reprinted as "The Kinsey Report" in A4, and in *Perspectives USA*, Pilot Issue (January 1952): 193-206.

C92. "Art and Fortune." *Partisan Review* 15 (December 1948): 1271-92.

Extends the argument of C90 by investigating the widely-proclaimed death of the novel and examining the conditions under which it might continue to flourish. Examines three explanations for the death of the novel, and concludes that the novel has not simply exhausted its material, but that that material itself--the focal questions of class, money, manners, and ideas--has grown less compelling, and that the novel's repeatable (because largely ineffectual) revelation of the reality of human depravity has been superseded by the revelation of actual Nazi atrocities and dulled by the modern novel's lack of interest in "human life as an aesthetic object." Notes that the death of the novel coincides with the decline of the social will through its own single-minded excess, and defines "the great work of our time" as "the restoration and reconstitution of the will." Argues that the romantic impetus of the novel, its fascination with "the world of unfolding possibility," is the source of its power for social renewal--a power denied "the authorless novel" of Sartre, the "consciously literary" fantasy of Djuna Barnes, and the formal experiments of post-Joyceans. Predicts that "the novel of the next decades will deal in a very explicit way with ideas," not only as they are incarnated in character and dramatic action, but directly--for example, by substituting "the organization of society into ideological groups" for class conflicts as its primary subject. Contends that acknowledging the interdependence of Art and Fortune--form and free invention, programmatic content and gratuitous development--can help free the novel from the demand that it surrender its enabling ambivalence and playfulness in order to save the world, "establishing the state of the soul in which the novel becomes possible."

Revised and reprinted in A4, and in *Critiques and Essays in Modern Fiction*, edited by John W. Aldridge (New York: Ronald, 1952), pp. 526-43.

C93. "Sigmund Freud: His Final Credo." [Review of Sigmund Freud, *An Outline of Psychoanalysis*, translated by James Strachey (New York: Norton, 1949).] *New York Times Book Review*, 27 February 1949, pp. 1, 17.

Calls Freud "pre-eminent among the modern theorists of the mind" for his unique sensitivity in representing "the stress and pain of the soul," especially in his conception of the tragic relation between free will and necessity. Commends Freud's "drive to reality" even when it "yields unacceptable results," as in his widely-debated theory of the death-instinct, here made coequal with the libido: "Even if we should be led to reject the theory, we still cannot miss its grandeur, its ultimate tragic courage in acquiescence to fate."

Revised and reprinted as "Freud's Last Book" in A7.

C94. "Humanism and the Middle Class." *Nation* 168 (7 May 1949): 528-30.

Ascribes the continuing power and relevance of Matthew Arnold to his attempt to transmit humanistic ideals to the middle class. Uncovers a fundamental contradiction in humanism--its insistence that justice be absolute, and its conception of society as "pragmatic and even anomalous"--which underlies its tendentious belief that "society can change itself gradually by taking thought and revising sensibility." Traces the modern bourgeoisie's remoteness from Arnold's humanistic ideals to its growing anarchism, which, instead of a humanist critique, "takes the more diffused form of disgust with the very idea of society" on every level of taste, from the refined disgust of Baudelaire, Rimbaud, Kafka, and Céline to the violence of popular and commercial art. Notes that although the revolt against the humanist ideals of "sweetness and light" generally takes Arnold as its target, Arnold borrowed this phrase from Swift, whose uncompromising revulsion and disgust were based precisely on "the refusal of men to live by the virtues of humanism," whereas "the extremity of our own situation has led us to love extremity in ourselves."

Incorporated into the Introduction to B5.

**** "A Rejoinder to Mr. Barrett." *Partisan Review* 16 (June 1949): 653-58. See E390.

C95. "Contemporary American Literature and Its Relation to Ideas." *American Quarterly* 1 (Fall 1949): 195-208.

Responds to an invitation to discuss "the debt of four American writers [O'Neill, Faulkner, Dos Passos, and Wolfe] to Freud and Spengler" with a much more general discussion of "the proper relation" between literature and ideas. Begins by observing that literature is always implicated with ideas because it deals with "man in society," either implicitly or explicitly dramatizing competing ideas; that combining any two emotions produces an idea; and that the dialectical, purposive form of a literary work is itself an idea. Glosses Eliot's remark that Henry James had a mind so fine that no idea could violate it by suggesting that Eliot's fear is not of ideas or thought as such but of "so intellectualizing life that it loses all spontaneity and actuality." Notes the tendency in modern culture for ideas to "deteriorate into ideology," but defends the values of concreteness and cogency that conscious, systematic thought can impart to a literary work. Argues that contemporary European literature is essentially "active" in its resistance to comprehension and typology, drawing much of its emotional power from the "primitive" roots of its intellectual power, whereas contemporary American literature is "passive," the subject rather than the object of study, largely because of its "intellectual thinness." Ascribes the power of Faulkner and Hemingway, exceptional among recent American prose writers, to the "piety" which roots them in inherited beliefs and value systems they subject to scutiny, but finds in both of them "a deficiency of conscious mind." Concludes by noting that the most compelling modern European writing is "indifferent to or even hostile to the liberal democratic tradition," and by asking "why it is that these particular ideas have not infused themselves with force and cogency the literature that uses them."

Revised and reprinted as "The Meaning of a Literary Idea" in A4; in *The American Writer and the European Tradition*, edited by Margaret Denny and William H. Gilman (Minneapolis: University of Minnesota Press, 1950), pp. 132-53; and in *The Critical Tradition: Classic Texts and Contemporary Trends*, edited by David H. Richter (New York: St. Martin's, 1989), pp. 520-30.

C96. "Wordsworth and the Iron Time." *Kenyon Review* 12 (Summer 1950): 477-97.

Suggests first that Wordworth's popularity has faded because of his Christian characteristics; then, after reviewing the case to be made against Wordsworth as a Christian poet, that "the quality in Wordsworth that now makes him unacceptable is a Judaic quality." Examines in detail analogies between Wordsworth and the rabbis who wrote *Pirke Aboth*: their Law, like Wordsworth's Nature, conceals a divine presence which cannot be apprehended directly; Hillel's famous questions--"If I am not for myself, who, then, is for me? And if I am for myself, what then am I?"--express Wordsworth's sense of "the interplay between individualism and the sense of community; both display "a certain insouciant acquiescence in the anomalies of the moral order of the universe," leading in each case to a neglect of the problems of a moral struggle with evil and the need for personal courage and the commendation of a "quietism, which is not in the least a negation of life, but, on the contrary, an affirmation of life so complete that it needed no saying." Notes the remoteness of this "sentiment of Being" from a culture increasingly "committed to an idea of consciousness and activity, of motion and force," concluding that although modern culture shares Wordsworth's "preoccupation with being," still "his conception of being seems different from ours." Contrasts Wordsworth's *Gemüt*, in which "the soul's energy is directed to the delight of the soul in itself," with the modern fascination with the active struggle against "the dull not-being of [normal] life" and "the intense not-being of death," and the consequent inability to "imagine being--we do not imagine that it can be a joy," noting that "every tragic literature owes its power to the high esteem in which it holds the common routine, and the sentiment of being which arises from it, the elemental *given* of biology," and citing modern instances--Leopold Bloom, Jennie Gerhardt, Hemingway's waiters, Faulkner's enduring black people--of "the will seeking its own negation--or, rather, seeking its own affirmation by its rejection of the aims which the world sets before it and turning its energies upon itself in self-realization"--which valorize Wordsworth's sentiment of being.

Revised and reprinted in *Wordsworth: Centenary Studies Presented at Cornell and Princeton Universities*, edited by Gilbert T. Dunklin (Princeton: Princeton University Press, 1951), pp. 131-52; in *The Kenyon Critics*, edited by John Crowe Ransom (Cleveland: World, 1951), pp. 233-51; and in *Wordsworth: A Collection of Critical Essays*, edited by M. H. Abrams (Englewood Cliffs: Prentice-Hall, 1972), pp. 45-66; as "Wordsworth and the Rabbis: The Affinity Between His 'Nature' and Their 'Law,'" in *Commentary* 19 (February 1955): 108-19; and as "Wordsworth and the Rabbis" in A5.

C97. "An American View of Two Literatures." *Books: Journal of the National Book League*, no. 263 (August 1951), pp. 178-81.

Briefly sets American writers' diffidence toward social reality--which leads them either to turn from social subjects or treat society as an abstraction or "a problem to be solved"--against British writers' appreciative sense of "the mystery of social life."

Incorporated into C31a.

C98. "William Dean Howells and the Roots of Modern Taste." *Partisan Review* 18 (September-October 1951): 516-36.

Considers a Howells revival unlikely despite his historical importance, and his friendship with the newly revived James and Twain, because his brand of realism, with its attachments to "the common, the immediate, the familiar, and the vulgar," its emphasis on "the family life of the middle class," and its "love . . . of the social idea," is antithetical to modern taste, which places a premium on "the rare and strange" in revolt from any "particular society of the present." Sees the lack of interest in the family characteristic of modern fiction as "but one aspect of our attitude toward the idea of *the conditioned*," the modern "demand for life as pure spirit" untrammeled by social circumstances. Suggests that readers' acceptance of the Bundren family in *As I Lay Dying* indicates a paradoxical "intimation of liberty--when conditions become extreme enough there is sometimes a sense of deep relief, . . . as if spirit were freed when the confining comforts and the oppressive assurances of civil life are destroyed." Warns that the impulse to take all fictional experience as figuratively meaningful tends to make it "merely typical, formal, and *representative*," denying the actuality of material conditions: "Our metaphysical habits lead us to feel the deficiency of what we call literal reality and to prefer what we call essential reality," and to consider the mind's formative faculty more characteristic than its faculty of observation, leading to the "sterility" typical of abstract painting which utterly rejects representing the "resisting object." Sets Howells's indifference to evil against the modern fascination with the glamor of evil as a dramatic subject, citing Richard Chase and Hannah Arendt on the temptation to yield to hyperaesthesia and disintegration as experiences. Praises the dialectical balance of the sense of evil with the sense of self in Shakespeare and Keats, asking "whether our quick antagonism to [Howells's] mild recognition of pleasure does not imply an impatience with the self," an eagerness to surrender to the "historical necessity" of "the godhead of disintegration."

Reprinted as "The Roots of Modern Taste and William Dean Howells" in *Adelphi* 28 (First Quarter, 1952): 499-516, and under its original title in A5; and translated into German by Marlene Lohner in *Der amerikanische Roman in 19. and 20. Jahrhundert*, edited by Edgar Lohner (Berlin: Schmidt, 1974), pp. 106-25.

C99. "Dreiser, Anderson, Lewis, and the Riddle of Society." *Reporter* 6 (13 November 1951): 37-40.

Focuses on American literature's distinctive "tendency to transcend or circumvent the social fact and to concentrate upon the individual in relation to himself, to God, or to the cosmos," as against English literature's "tendency to take society for granted and then go on to demonstrate its burdensome but interesting and valuable complexity." Comparing *Kim* and *Huckleberry Finn*, notes that "the English book says that initiation into society is possible, fascinating, and desirable, while . . . the American book says that virtue lies in alienation from society." Charges that most academic historians of American literature (V. L. Parrington, "an honest man," is excepted) have not acknowledged its "pervasive asociality," so clear to D. H. Lawrence. Reviewing *World So Wide*, Sinclair Lewis's last novel, and critical studies of Theodore Dreiser (by F. O. Matthiessen) and Sherwood Anderson (by Irving Howe), contends that although American literature since the 1920's has taken a greater interest in social circumstance, it continues to treat society as "a grim problem to be solved, the solution being the individual's escape from or triumph over the social conditions" in the absence of any development of "personality."

Reprinted as "An American View of English Literature" in A15.

C100. "George Orwell and the Politics of Truth." *Commentary* 13 (March 1952): 218-27.

Remarks the widespread resistance, especially among intellectuals, to admitting connections between the power of ideas and ideals and "the old, unabashed, cynical power of force," and considers the ways in which Orwell is a figure--emphatically not a genius, but an intelligent, virtuous man, free of self-delusion and cant, with whom readers can more readily identify--whose testimony is a scandal to such political irresponsibility. Notes Orwell's similarities to Cobbett and Hazlitt for his affirmation of middle-class virtues and his respect for the truth against partisan claims, summarizing his "criticism of the liberal intelligentsia" as the exposure of their "tendency to abstractness and absoluteness," their refusal "to connect idea with fact, especially personal fact," or "to understand the conditioned nature of life," observing that Orwell "came to respect the old bourgeois virtues because they were stupid--that is, because they resisted the power of abstract ideas" which, held too uncritically, could blind their adherents to the truth of the Communists' treachery during the Spanish Civil War, here recounted by Orwell.

Revised and reprinted as the Introduction to B8, and in A5.

C101. "A Change of Direction." [Review of David Riesman, *The Lonely Crowd* (New Haven: Yale University Press, 1950).] *Griffin* 1 (March 1952): 1-5.

Calling *The Lonely Crowd* "one of the most important books about America to have been published in recent times," defends it as "a work of literature" comparable to the work of Hume, Gibbon, and Tocqueville. Argues that sociology has taken over literature's traditional function of investigating morals and manners because novels since *Babbitt* have taken so little interest in this function. Summarizes Riesman's analysis of the twentieth-century rise of the other-directed personality that craves social validation as "the hard, resistant materiality of the world" no longer "validated the hard, strenuous will of inner-directed people," agreeing that "inner-direction . . . must seem the more fully human" of the two.

Revised and reprinted as Part I of "Two Notes on David Riesman" in A7.

C102. "Fiction and History." [Review of Geoffrey Blunden, *The Time of the Assassins* (Philadelphia: Lippincott, 1952).] *Griffin* 1 (June 1952): 1-4.

Compares Blunden's novel about the German occupation of the Ukraine to the histories of Tacitus and Josephus because of its "historical imagination," which maintains the power of the mind in the face of the disintegration of society. Contrasts Blunden's insensate party hacks with Malraux's intellectual Communists, observing that "almost three decades have passed" since anyone has been able to enter into an active, critical relation with Communism.

C103. "Adams at Ease." [Review of *The Selected Letters of Henry Adams*, edited by Newton Arvin (New York: Farrar, Straus and Young, 1951); and Henry Adams, *Democracy* (rpt. New York: Farrar, Straus and Young, 1952).] *Griffin* 1 (August 1952): 1-6.

Finds Adams's model of "American loneliness and isolation" compelling despite his snobbishness and errors in his theories of history and society and recommends balancing admiration and suspicion for him in "strict ambivalence." Observes that Adams's letters provide a more accurate account of his mental development than his *Education*, showing his pessimism tempered by an abiding faith in democracy, despite his novel's "satiric rejection of the actualities of American government in 1879." Concludes, however, that *Democracy* answers its leading question ("The nature of American life being what it is, is it possible for a person of moral sensibility to participate in it?") in the negative--an answer that "in some important part" is still valid.

Revised and reprinted in A7.

C104. "The Early Edmund Wilson." [Review of Edmund Wilson, *The Shores of Light: A Literary Chronicle of the Twenties and Thirties* (New York: Farrar, Straus and Young, 1952).] *Griffin* 1 (September 1952): 1-5.

Acknowledges Trilling's indebtedness to Wilson as literary editor of the *New Republic* and describes him as an exemplary man of letters, noting with dismay the present disenchantment with the ideal of the literary life--marked, for example, by the passing of the assumption, current under Wilson's editorship, that politics and literature are intimately connected. Finds the only flaw in Wilson's voracious and catholic appetite for literature in general his lack of passionate enthusiasm for particular works or writers.

Revised and reprinted as "Edmund Wilson: A Backward Glance" in A7.

C105. "The Measure of Dickens." [Review of Edgar Johnson, *Charles Dickens: His Tragedy and Triumph*, two volumes (New York: Simon and Schuster, 1952).] *Griffin* 2 (January 1953): 1-7.

Ranks Dickens with Austen as "one of the two greatest novelists of England" but emphasizes the energy and commitment he accorded such other activities as writing letters, directing charities, organizing amateur theatricals, and editing several magazines: "It is also true that he wrote novels." Expresses admiration for the copiousness of Johnson's criticism and scholarship, concluding that "no single book . . . tells us so much as Mr. Johnson's about the nature of Victorian life."

Revised and reprinted as "The Dickens of Our Day" in A7.

C106. "The Personal Figure of Henry James." [Review of Leon Edel: *Henry James: The Untried Years* (Philadelphia: Lippincott, 1953] *Griffin* 2 (April 1953): 1-4.

Notes the "benign fatigue" which has followed the posthumous revival of James as an artist and "culture-hero," contrasting Edel's intimate treatment of James. Criticizes the lack of "intellectual intensity" in Edel's presentation of James's life as constituting "an impassioned idea."

C107. "The Situation of the American Intellectual at the Present Time." *Perspectives USA*, no. 3 (Spring 1953), pp. 24-42.

Reprints and expands E394, pointing out in a prefatory note that the editors' questions defined culture institutionally, but that a renewed, albeit critical, attachment to the "more intangible aspect[s] of 'culture'" underlies the responses of most of the participants. Cites the Stevenson candidacy and the higher prestige of college teaching as examples of the increased social and political power of intellectuals, but warns of the dangers of the resulting "impurity" of universities and of literary intellectuals' continuing tendency to conceive society in terms of unhelpful abstractions. Applauds the declining influence of European culture as freeing American intellectuals from abstract, Marxist, and anti-intellectual notions of culture. Recommends a closer study of such practical questions as the formation of American educational policy and current developments in post-Freudian psychology, charging that revisionary Freudians, in their emphasis on social meliorism, have failed to come to terms with Freud's biological theory of personality formation, and linking a more particular awareness of social policy to the American nonconformist tradition.

Revised and reprinted in A7.

C108. "A Portrait of Western Man." *Listener* 49 (11 June 1953): 969-71, 974.

Traces the rise and development of Dewey's idea that moral choices depend on "the question of what we want to be" as the basis for the modern idea of personality. Considers the dialectic between spirit and matter in Hegel, the "drama of spirit at war with itself" in *Sense and Sensibility* and *Mansfield Park*--a drama which places Austen, in her concern with sincerity and vulgarity, at the beginning of the modern period--and Dickens's attack on the gentlemanly ideal in *Little Dorrit*, before identifying "the spirit of Blandois," of self-pity as a destructive principle, as a keynote of modern politics and literature. Hails Lawrence as a modernist who, despite his hostility toward established society, resisted the contrary expression of personality "in the demand for *being*, which is most simply conceived as status," seeing consciousness as "death as any of its excesses or deficiencies" but "a thing of ultimate grace" in "its glorious mean, in the real truth of its nature." A little-known essay, never reprinted, which not only contains the gist of C111 and C116 and comprises an early, and considerably more optimistic, sketch for A9, but sets forth a conspectus of the leading ideas about literature Trilling would develop over the next twenty years.

C109. "Zola's Quality." [Review of Angus Wilson, *Emile Zola: An Introductory Study of His Novels* (New York: Morrow, 1952); and Emile Zola, *Restless House*, translated by Percy Pinkerton and introduced by Angus Wilson (New York: Farrar, Straus & Young, 1953).] *Griffin* 2 (August 1953): 4-11.

Doubts that Zola's reputation can be restored by merely rescuing him from his disciples--including Arnold Bennett, Frank Norris, and Theodore Dreiser--and "his formulated theory," agreeing with Wilson that Zola's work needs fundamental reassessment: he is not a literalist but a blackly comic fantasist like Breughel, Bosch, Baudelaire, and Joyce, and his work is to be judged on the basis of the energy, not the accuracy, of its indictment of the bourgeoisie.

Concludes that a Zola revival is unlikely because, unlike Stendhal, Flaubert, Yeats, Eliot, Kafka, and other modern writers, he created no personal legend: his work must succeed on its own merits, not through the public personality of its author.

Revised and reprinted as "In Defense of Zola" in A7.

C110. "A Triumph of the Comic View." [Review of Saul Bellow, *The Adventures of Augie March* (New York: Viking, 1953).] *Griffin* 2 (September 1953): 4-10.

Ascribes "the peculiarly radiant quality" of Bellow's novel to his "conscious commitment . . . to the comic tradition" long in revolt against the dominant heroic tradition, though lately in retreat before social progressivism. Places Bellow in "the tradition of American personalism," setting him against "proletarian" writers in his acceptance of his lower-class characters on their own terms and his conviction that functional categories ("a social class, a profession, a theory, or a principle") deny the individual identity and life. Admires Bellow's achievement but dissents from his point of view, averring that "without function it is very difficult to be a person and have a fate."

Revised and reprinted as the Introduction to B32.

C111. "*Little Dorrit*." *Kenyon Review* 15 (Autumn 1953): 577-90.

Urges the particularly modern relevance of *Little Dorrit* among Dickens's late novels as the one most especially concerned with society and most dominated by a peculiarly abstract moral idea stemming from the observed equation of society with prison. Observes how Dickens's portrait of the alienating and imprisoning social will, which constrains the personal will of individuals by internalizing social imperatives, forms a parodic version of individual neurosis, as the mind, "at once the criminal, the victim, the police, the judge, and the executioner," becomes "the matrix of society." Analyzes the implication of characters as diverse as Mrs. Clennam, Mr. Meagles, Blandois, and Miss Wade in Dickens's critique of the imprisoning social will, linking the announced failure of Arthur Clennam's will to Dickens's crucial inability, revealed by his failure to respond to the returning Maria Beadnell, to sustain the dreams and vanities of his own youth, and his consequent "wish to negate the will in death." Emphasizes the religious nature of Dickens's resolution of this crisis of the will in such mildly self-denying figures as Daniel Doyce and Little Dorrit, who represent not only "the negation of the social will" but also "the transcending of the personal will, . . . the search for the Will in which shall be our peace."

Revised and reprinted as the Introduction to B26; in A5; and in *Dickens: A Collection of Critical Essays*, edited by Martin Price (Englewood Cliffs, NJ: Prentice-Hall, 1967), pp. 147-57.

C112. "Flaubert's Last Testament." *Partisan Review* 20 (November-December 1953): 605-30.

Places Flaubert's last novel in the context of his other critiques of ideology in modern life, observing that "books themselves are virtually the *dramatis personae*" instrumental in dramatizing the heroes' naive belief that "the world yields to mind." Notes the novel's continuities with *Don Quixote*, *Tristram Shandy*, Book 3 of *Gulliver's Travels*, *The Bourgeois Gentleman*, and *Gargantua and Pantagruel*, whose faith in encyclopedic knowledge it inverts. Maintains that it fails as a satire of its heroes because their friendship makes them too lovable for contempt; they are ridiculous not because of their impossible quest to master all knowledge but because they are essentially comic in themselves. Nor is the novel "a fierce indictment of the bourgeois democracy"; its satire is rather leveled against culture itself. Traces this rejection of culture, which renders Flaubert's bourgeois heroes "a *reductio ad absurdum* of our lives in culture," to Flaubert's self-sacrificing attachment to his niece Caroline, emphasizing the combination of genuine religious feeling and satire of the cultural manifestations of particular religious beliefs in *Bouvard and Pécuchet* and its pendant, the *Three Tales*, concluding that Flaubert's heroes in their final role as copyists of information they no longer believe in, "stripped of every idea . . . beyond what is necessary to keep men alive and still human, are, in their own mild negation of self, intended by Flaubert to be among the company of his saints."

Excerpted as "Flaubert's Encyclopedia," *Griffin* 3 (January 1954): 5-23; and revised and reprinted as the introduction to B28, and in A5.

C113. "The Van Amringe and Keppel Eras." Chapter 1 of *A History of Columbia College at Morningside*. Edited by Dwight C. Miner. New York: Columbia University Press, 1954. Pp. 14-47.

Traces the emergence of Columbia College as a distinct entity with its own cohesive rationale to the Deanship of John Howard Van Amringe (1894-1910), whose conception of the College as "making men" through a specifically undergraduate course of study is set against Professor John Burgess's conception of the college as a gymnasium designed to train specialists, on the model of European universities. Notes that Columbia College, which was called the School of Arts until 1896, was not central to its university in the same ways as the colleges of Harvard, Yale, and Princeton, and recounts Van Amringe's struggles to strengthen the College's identity by campaigning against plans to abolish the College, apportioning its functions between high schools and graduate schools, and resisting attempts to shorten the time pre-professional students spent in the college. Describes the ways in which the abolition of the Latin entrance requirement under the Deanship of Van Amringe's successor Frederick P. Keppel (1910-17) fundamentally changed the nature of the undergraduate population, opening the College to graduates of public high schools and eliminating much of its social elitism. Reports Van

Amringe's disparagement of large lecture courses, which confirmed the College's dedication, despite rising enrollments, to small discussion groups, and recounts the inauguration of Professor John Erskine's general education curriculum, based on a survey of great books from the European tradition, with the establishment of the General Honors and Contemporary Civilization courses under Dean Herbert E. Hawkes in 1919.

C114. "American Portrait." [Review of David Riesman, *Individualism Reconsidered, and Other Essays* (Glencoe, IL: Free Press, 1954).] *Griffin* 3 (May 1954): 4-12.

Notes the superiority of Riesman's sociological essays to any recent American novel in conveying a "sense of the actuality of our society." Applauds his status as an intellectual who can "bring us the news of ideas," his "pragmatic acceptance of society" rooted in a hard-won ambivalence toward American society in the face of widespread social withdrawal, and his unfashionable assumption that "the principle of individualism is morally prepotent."

Revised and reprinted as Part II of "Two Notes on David Riesman" in A7.

C115. "Art and the Philosopher." [Review of Louis Arnaud Reid, *A Study in Aesthetics* (1931; reprinted New York: Reader's Subscription, 1954).] *Griffin* 3 (August 1954): 5-13.

Regrets the displacement of aesthetics, "the theory of the Beautiful," by criticism, the analysis of the "interest" of individual works, as beauty has fallen into disrepute and literary criticism, with its emphasis on questions of value and "immediate practicality," has become the exemplary critical mode. Recommends "the quickening and liberating influence of aesthetic theory" on the individual response to art.

Revised and reprinted as "Criticism and Aesthetics" in A7.

C116. "Mansfield Park." *Partisan Review* 21 (September-October 1954): 492-511.

Notes the ways in which Austen's characteristic irony--her recognition that human spirit is only meaningful in its conditioning by circumstance--is apparently absent from *Mansfield Park*, whose greatness is "commensurate with its power to offend." Acknowledges that Fanny Price is not easy to like and that the Crawfords (especially Mary, who "cultivates the *style* of sensitivity, virtue, and intelligence") are seductively ingratiating, but defends Austen's conservative morality in its devotion to duty and a "hygiene of the self"--a notion long made unfashionable by the belief that "right action is typically to be performed without any pain to the self." Discusses the novel's suspicion of role-playing as injurious to personal integrity. Contrasts *Pride and Prejudice*, whose ironic comedy "permits us to conceive of morality as style," with *Mansfield Park*, whose "more profound" irony is "directed against irony itself." Speculates that the novel "points to a crisis in the author's spiritual life" and that Lady Bertram may be a parodistic self-portrait of her wish "to withdraw from the exigent energies of her actual self." Claims more generally that "it was Jane Austen who first represented the specifically modern personality and the culture in which it had its being," calling her "the first to be aware of the Terror that rules our moral situation," the need to demonstrate moral purity not only in individual actions but in a personal style of acting that constitutes "the quality of the agent," noting that the strain of the consequent anxiety, "the exhausting effort which the concept of personality requires us to make," leads to "the *disgust* which is endemic to our culture"--and, incidentally, to Austen's imagining in *Mansfield Park* "the self safe from the Terror of secularized spirituality," shaped by the sanctions of principle rather than those of culture or personality.

Reprinted as "Jane Austen and *Mansfield Park*" in *The Pelican Guide to English Literature, Volume 5: From Blake to Byron*, edited by Boris Ford, revised and expanded edition (Harmondsworth: Penguin, 1982), pp. 154-71, and under its original title in A5, and in *Jane Austen: A Collection of Critical Essays*, edited by Ian Watt (Englewood Cliffs: Prentice-Hall, 1963), pp. 124-40.

C117. "Measuring Mill." [Review of Michael St. John Packe, *The Life of John Stuart Mill* (New York: Macmillan, 1954).] *Griffin* 3 (December 1954): 4-11.

Notes the continuing resistance to the appreciation of the Victorians despite the examples of Koestler, Orwell, and Churchill--a resistance that extends even to the often unnecessarily apologetic or ironic tone of Packe's "definitive" biography. Links Mill's "charm" to the appeal of Orwell's matter-of-fact honesty, and reviews briefly Mill's "disturbing," though undeniable, intellectual debt to Harriet Taylor, which "was made possible by his submission to her."

C118. "Matthew Arnold, Poet." *Major British Writers*. Edited by G. B. Harrison. 2 volumes. New York: Harcourt, Brace and World, 1954. 2: 419-32.

Recapitulates the major themes and moments of A1, giving surprisingly scant attention to any particular poems. Describes Arnold as having a better understanding of systematic social relationships than any other Victorian writer. Briefly summarizes Arnold's background and the events of his life, sketching the figure of Clough more fully, and emphasizing Arnold's attraction toward ideals of energy, gaiety, and sexual freedom--ideals whose passing his poems lament, often using sexual or romantic frustration as a figure for alienation from an increasingly mechanistic social order. Links the elegiac tone of Arnold's poetry to his literary criticism, which is concerned not only with poems themselves but with their effects on readers and ultimately on society, and his cultural and religious writing, stressing throughout the unity of Arnold's thought.

Slightly abridged and reprinted in A1b.

C119. "The Novel Alive or Dead." [Review of C. P. Snow, *The New Men* (New York: Scribner's, 1955).] *Griffin* 4 (February 1955): 4-13.

Notes that Snow's "plain and modest" novels seem to have been written expressly in order to prove that the novel is not dead, and proceeds to imagine a fanciful series of events--an argument, a wager, a mental stocktaking--that launched the physicist on his career as novelist with few resources except "a sense of social fact," "a sense of the present in relation to a sense of the past," and a strong interest in matters and relations beneath the notice of most novelists since Trollope. Singles out Snow's "tendency to forgiveness," as against the American inclination to lay blame, as "a condition of the reality of his characters."

Revised and reprinted in A7, and excerpted in *The Theory of Criticism from Plato to the Present*, edited by Raman Selden (London: Longman, 1988), pp. 517-18.

C120. "A Ramble on Graves." [Review of Robert Graves, *Collected Poems* (Garden City: Doubleday, 1955).] *Griffin* 4 (June 1955): 4-12.

Contends that Graves, whose novels and autobiography had made him "a first-rate secondary figure," now claims attention as "a poet of the first rank." Notes that Graves's voice--graceful, elegant, colloquial, ironic--carries the authority of experience, and compares "his feeling for the genius of English" to that of Landor, Skelton, and Hardy, remarking especially his affinity for nature and the commonplace, and concluding the essay--Trilling's most extended stylistic discussion of any poet--by comparing him to Lawrence, cummings, and Horace, placing him "in the tradition of the men who, by the terms upon which they accept their ordinary humanity, make it extraordinary."

Revised and reprinted in A7.

C121. "Profession: Man of the Wor[l]d." [Review of James Pope-Hennessy, *Monckton Milnes: Volume 1: The Years of Promise, 1809-1851* (New York: Farrar, Straus & Cudahy, 1955).] *Griffin* 4 (September 1955): 4-11.

Traces his contemporaries' condescension toward Mockton Milnes and later writers' dismissal of him to his unlikely combination of goodness and worldliness. Defines Milnes's insatiable interest in social life as a fascination with "power . . . either intellectual or political." Contrasts Milnes's ineptness as a politician with his understanding of politics, and his acquiescence in remaining second-rate despite his high intelligence, and considers him in his official life a "forerunner of the modern Foundation," with the addition of the un-Foundationlike qualities of "courage, intelligence, and sincerity."

Revised and reprinted as "Profession: Man of the World" in A7.

C122. "Isaac Babel: 'Torn Between Violence and Peace': The Intellectual and the Revolution." *Commentary* 19 (June 1955): 550-61.

Emphasizes the ability of Babel's stories to disturb individuals and threaten "the impassivity of the state" by their "intensity, irony, and ambiguousness," which "constitute a *secret*." Ascribes Babel's ambivalence to his attraction both to "the way of violence" as a test or initiation represented in his work by the murderous Cossacks and "rooted in the memory of boyhood," and "the way of peace," associated with his status as a Jewish intellectual. Explains Babel's preoccupation with violence as a fascination with the Lawrentian ideals of passion and grace and a way of his testing his potency for action--"not whether he can endure being killed but whether he can endure killing." Noting that "violence is . . . the negation of the intellectual's characteristic enterprise of rationality," urges the violence of the attempt to grasp reality or embody it in an aesthetic epiphany, describing Babel's admiration of the reality represented by the Cossacks' violence as "a criticism of his own ethos not merely as an intellectual but as a Jew," concluding by linking the dialectic in Babel's stories between violence and spirituality to the influences of his father and mother.

Excerpted as "Product of the Revolution?" *Griffin* 4 (July 1955): 5-11; and revised and reprinted as the Introduction to B29, and as "Isaac Babel" in A5.

C123. "The Morality of Inertia." *Great Moral Dilemmas in Literature, Past and Present.* Edited by R. M. MacIver. New York: Harper, 1956. Pp. 37-46.

Notes the factitious cruelty of Edith Wharton's *Ethan Frome*, whose characters suffer "at the behest of their author" without the justification of a serious moral intention (practical recommendations, a search for the true causes of actions, a challenge to the audience's fortitude of piety). Finds the value of the novel in its inadvertent premise that "moral inertia, the *not* making of moral decisions, constitutes a large part of the moral life of humanity." Contrasts Wharton's "morality of habit and biology" to the saintly dullness often found in the characters of Flaubert, Balzac, Dickens, and Dostoevsky, contending that Aristotle's myth of rational choice as the basis of moral action plays little part in the lives of most people, who "live in the moral universe of the Book of Job."

Reprinted in *London Magazine* 2 (November 1955): 69-76, and in A7.

C124. "Mr. Forster's Aunt Marianne." [Review of E. M. Forster, *Marianne Thornton: A Domestic Biography, 1797-1887*

(New York: Harcourt, Brace, 1956).] *Griffin* 5 (Summer 1956): 4-12.

Takes Marianne Thornton, whose legacy to her nephew made it possible for him to pursue a career as a writer, as an avatar of "a massive cultural tradition" transmitted in England through families and family life, fostering a "hereditary talent which takes pleasure in exercising itself and is encouraged and given the opportunity to do so" by the social institutions of family, class, and an Evangelical sense of duty.

Revised and reprinted as "The Great-Aunt of Mr. Forster" in A7.

C125. "Preface to *A Gathering of Fugitives*." *Griffin* 5 (September 1956): 12-13.

Acknowledges that, unlike Trilling's other collections of essays, A7 has no principle of unity, being mostly a miscellany of pieces from the *Griffin*, the monthly publication of the Reader's Subscription--whose board of editors consisted of Trilling, Jacques Barzun, and W. H. Auden--and notes that these essays, and the others (C93, C123, C130, D361, and D362) Trilling chose to complement them, are written less formally and "more personally, even autobiographically." than most of his work. Makes an exception to this rule of informality for C107, chosen for reprinting because it has frequently come under attack and been quoted out of context (see for example L957).

Revised and reprinted in A7.

C126. "The Farmer and the Cowboy Make Friends." [Review of Douglas Bush, *English Literature in the Earlier Seventeenth Century* (Cambridge: Cambridge University Press, 1952).] *Griffin* 5 (Fall 1956): 4-12.

Reviews the controversy between historians and New Critics about the proper focus of literary study, quoting C75 in defense of the necessity of historical awareness, advising compromise between the two viewpoints--criticism must inevitably take account of history, but the point of literary history is ultimately critical--and commending Bush's notable success in reconciling the demands of "scholarship and criticism."

C127. "'That Smile of Parmenides Made Me Think.'" [Review of George Santayana, *Letters*, edited with an introduction and commentary by Daniel Cory (New York: Scribner's, 1955).] *Griffin* 5 (February 1956): 4-16.

Acknowledges that Santayana, not a likeable man, is especially easy for Americans to dislike because of his condemnation of America. Attributes Trilling's own inability as an undergraduate to comprehend Irwin Edman's sympathetic exposition of Santayana's philosophy to his prejudice against his detachment, which the youthful Trilling identified with Pater's aestheticism. Contrasts American materialism, which sees the material world as "the natural field of the spirit," with Santayana's more severe European materialism, which, distinguishing between moral goodness and mere sweetness of disposition, sees the world as "resistant to spirit" and so paradoxically requires "its negation in an intense respect for the life of spirit."

Revised and reprinted in A7, and, as "The Smile of Parmenides: George Santayana in His Letters," in *Encounter* 7 (December 1956): 30-38, and in *Encounter: An Anthology from the First Ten Years of Encounter Magazine, 1953-1963*, edited by Stephen Spender, Irving Kristol, and Melvin J. Lasky (New York: Basic, 1963), pp. 350-61.

C128. "Mr. Colum's Greeks." *Griffin* 5 (Christmas 1956): 4-15.

Discusses the rewards and problems of reading "real books" aloud to young children: "A real book has the power of stirring the emotions, and suppose you stir them in the wrong way?" Emphasizes the appeal of *The Jungle Books* and *Treasure Island* to the sense of curiosity and fantasy progressive education tends to suppress, and defends the reading of Greek mythology before explorations in the folk literatures of India, China, and Babylonia. Warns against the "archness and facetiousness" of Hawthorne's *Wonder-Book* and *Tanglewood Tales* (which, unlike the best 19th-century children's books, are addressed to girls), commending instead Padraic Colum's "vigorous and straightforward" adaptations in *The Golden Fleece and the Heroes Who Lived Before Achilles* and *The Adventures of Odysseus and the Tale of Troy.*

Revised and reprinted as "Rearing and Reading," *Vogue* 131 (May 1958): 150-51, 196, 198-99.

C129. "On Not Talking." *Proceedings of the American Academy of Arts and Letters and the National Institute of Arts and Letters*, Second Series, no. 6 (New York: American Academy of Arts and Letters, 1956), pp. 49-60.

Discusses one symptom of the alienation of American artists and intellectuals--their "habit of not talking to each other"--as marking an eclipse of the artist's "love of the idea of community," associated here with the catholic interests and connections of Delacroix, by the image of the artist as withdrawn from the community. Considers the premise that writers, painters, and composers have grown too specialized and too short of time to comment intelligently on each others' work, but suggests instead that the "manners" of modern culture (a word now traced to Tocqueville) which proscribe blunt disagreements among intellectuals indicate "a lack of innocence and ready human respect, a fear of being wrong, an aspiration to *expertise.*"

Revised and reprinted in A7.

C130. "Old Calabria." [Review of Norman Douglas, *A Selection from His Works*, with an introduction by D. M. Low (London: Chatto & Windus/Secker & Warburg, 1955), and *Old Calabria*, 4th edition, edited by John Davenport

(London: Secker & Warburg, 1955).] *Griffin* 6 (February 1957): 4-10.

Observes that despite the fashionable popularity of *South Wind* in the 1920's, "fiction was not Douglas's *forte*," and describes his strength as "that of the English familiar essayists," especially Hazlitt, with "a touch of Arabian Doughty, and a considerable infusion of Pliny." Praises Douglas's responsiveness to "the present life of the country" in all its poverty, inequity, and official chicanery.

C131. "Emma." *Encounter* 8 (June 1957): 49-59.

Distinguishes between Austen as an author and as a mythic figure defined by the range of responses to her work, noting that the attempt to complicate that myth in C116 met with great resistance. Notes that Emma's charm is a function of her self-love, which leads her also to a peculiarly un-English snobbery, and contends that in her unusually discriminating and attractive self-love and the "poet's demand" that underlies her errors of judgment and action, she represents "the relation . . . between our ideal self and our ordinary fallible self." Analyzes the novel as a combination of pastoral idyll, represented by such village types as Mr. Woodhouse and Miss Bates, and comedy, represented by Emma's critical attitude toward the other characters and their world. Aligning the idyll with the utopian dream of an unconditioned world and comedy with the acceptance of social actuality and "the modern self," concludes by describing the novel as a debate between these worlds and their values, its arena the "battlefield" of Austen's mind, which was capable of encompassing such a debate because "she could imagine the possibility of victory--she did not shrink from the idea of victory--and because she could represent harmony and peace."

Revised and reprinted as the Introduction to B33, and as "Emma and the Legend of Jane Austen" in A8.

C132. "Impersonal/Personal." [Review of *Letters of James Joyce*, edited by Stuart Gilbert (New York: Viking, 1957).] *Griffin* 6 (June 1957): 4-13.

Defines Joyce's artistic impersonality as a personal attribute he cultivated, and asserts that his letters provide more connections between Joyce the man and the artist than Herbert Gorman's biography. Observes that after "the Siegfried call" of Joyce's youthful letter to Ibsen, his letters focus on the "dirty details" and "mean chores" of writing--"Joyce . . . thought of his genius not only as a sacred spiritual trust but as a property, as an investment that had to be made to pay"--until he sounds a note of "ruefulness and self-doubt" in a 1921 letter, after which the letters become more relaxed: "There is no difficulty at all in connecting the person with the artist of *Finnegans Wake*." Cites Joyce's concern for his family and his "monumental" propriety as qualities manifest in *Ulysses*, "one of the most delightful and charming books of the age."

Reprinted as "The Person of the Artist," in *Encounter* 9 (August 1957): 73-79, and in A15.

C133. "The Nude Renewed." [Review of Kenneth Clark, *The Nude: A Study in Ideal Form* (New York: Pantheon, 1956.] *Griffin* 6 (July 1957): 4-12.

Hails Clark's celebration of the nude, "that genre of traditional art which is most extravagantly 'human,'" as a welcome response to the anti-humanistic tendencies of the modern visual arts identified by Ortega y Gasset, remarking Clark's insistence on the erotic feelings aroused by the nude, his continuity in this respect with Blake (against Ortega's characterization of modern art as scornfully discontinuous with its predecessors), and his tonic departure in tone and emphasis from the round of conferences plaintively demanding "that mankind affirm the Western tradition" without cognizance of the radical and equivocal powers of representational art.

Reprinted as "The Nude Renewed: Sex, Style, and Geometry" in *Encounter* 9 (October 1957): 31-34.

C134. "The Story and the Novel." [Review of Isak Dinesen, *Last Tales* (New York: Random House, 1957), and James Agee, *A Death in the Family* (New York: McDowell, Obolensky, 1957).] *Griffin* 7 (January 1958): 4-12.

Notes the many contrasts between Dinesen's work and Agee's, emphasizing especially the difference between the "divine art" of the story or tale, which clarifies and abstracts its people to heroic status, and the anti-heroic premise of the novel, which exists for the sake of the complex characters it observes and develops in such detail. Observes however that Agee's rare fascination and sympathy with goodness fosters a "negation of ambivalence" which gives his novel the same "legendary quality" as Dinesen's tales.

C135. "English Literature and American Education." *Sewanee Review* 66 (Summer 1958): 364-81.

Notes the decline of the study of English literature in American universities despite the generally increased responsiveness to literary study, ascribing this decline to the political decline of England, whose image in America "is not powerful enough to support a lively imagination of the historical periods that to us were so vivid"; to the rise in programs in American studies emphasizing the distinctive qualities of American literature; to courses in world literature modeled on Humanities A at Columbia; to "a global view of culture" calling into question the centrality of "the Judaic-Hellenic-Christian tradition"; and to the engaging and demanding study of modern literature as a competitor to literary history. Deplores the fading American awareness of England as "*the other culture*," an ideal discussed in A6, contending that neither Humanities nor World Literature courses can provide this knowledge, since Humanities necessarily "deals chiefly with ideas" and World Literature, by affirming the equal value of all cultures, denies "the actuality . . . the force and value" of any single culture. Nor can "the systematic study of American literature" supply detailed information about another culture, for "American literature is not sufficiently extensive in its history" to provide diverse examples of the interrelations between language, ideas, and historical reality.

Revised and reprinted as "Reflections on a Lost Cause: English Literature and American Education," *Encounter* 11 (September 1958): 3-12, and in A15.

C136. Introduction to *The Broken Mirror*." *New Leader* 41 (7-14 July 1958): 30-33.

Notes that the seven Polish writers whose essays are collected in *The Broken Mirror* all fulfill "the ideal conception of the intellectual: they assert an intense critical preoccupation with the relationship that should properly exist between society and the intellect," defining this relationship in terms of intellectual freedom. Argues that, although its appeal to the idea of history often makes it attractive to members of an established society, the primary appeal of Communism is to citizens of disadvantaged countries who associate democracy with a capitalism they reject or find impossible to achieve. Describes Polish intellectuals' revolt against the "moral corruption" of their allegiance to the party, marks the distinctions between Russian and Polish Communism that have allowed Polish intellectuals a greater freedom of expression, and credits the Polish party itself for asserting an independence from Russia that fostered in turn a greater independence among its members. Expresses the hope that the Polish party may be or become more "responsive to the actual wishes of the Polish people," but doubts that the Russian party, under the agenda of world conquest, will become more democratic as well.

Revised and reprinted as the Introduction to B34, and as "Communism and Intellectual Freedom" in A15.

C137. "Proust as Critic and the Critic as Novelist." [Review of *Contre Sainte-Beuve* in *Proust on Art and Literature*, translated by Sylvia Townsend Warner (New York: Meridian/World, 1958).] *Griffin* 7 (July 1958): 4-13.

Notes the novelistic form of *Contre Sainte-Beuve* and its close affinities with *Remembrance of Things Past*. Reviews Proust's attack on Sainte-Beuve's assumption that the sense of an author's work could be derived from a study of his or her personal life, commenting that although literary scholarship has become more aware of the pitfalls of biographical criticism Proust adumbrates, psychoanalysis has not: "It is wholly at a loss" to establish the connection "between personality and creative power" because "it virtually never addresses itself to questions of language, of style, of dramatic form."

Reprinted in A15.

C138. "The Last Lover: Vladimir Nabokov's *Lolita*." [Review of Vladimir Nabokov, *Lolita* (New York: Putnam, 1955).] *Griffin* 7 (August 1958): 4-21.

Calls *Lolita* "a shocking book" not because it is pornographic (asserting in a long and unusually candid excursis that "the arousing of thoughts of lust" is a legitimate function of literature) but because Humbert Humbert's "love-affair with America" in the person of Dolores Haze violates "one of the few prohibitions which still seem to us to be confirmed by nature itself." Contends that Nabokov's wish to write about the "passion-love" described in eclipse by Denis de Rougement requires a scandalous union that excludes the possibility of marriage: "A man in the grip of an obsessional lust and a girl of twelve make the ideal couple for a story about love written in our time." Observes that, "although it strikes all the most approved modern postures and attitudes," *Lolita* is archaic in its erotic imagery and reactionary in its mocking of "all forms of progressive rationalism not only because they are stupid in themselves but because they have brought the madness of love to an end." Wonders if Humbert is intended as a tragic hero rather than the anti-hero he makes himself out to be.

Revised and reprinted in *Encounter* 11 (October 1958): 9-19, and as "The Last Lover" in A15.

C139. "Mind and Market in Academic Life, Parts 1 and 2." [Review of Paul Lazarsfeld and Wagner Thielens, Jr., *The Academic Mind* (Glencoe, IL: Free Press, 1958), and Theodore Caplow and Reece McGee, *The Academic Marketplace* (New York: Basic, 1958).] *Griffin* 7 (December 1958): 4-17.

Points out that although Americans may perceive universities and university professors as increasingly important in the national life, "no professor believes this": academics see themselves as marginal, stigmatized, and "therefore . . . morally justified." Takes issue in Part 1 with Seymour Lipset's argument that the prestige of American academics has remained constant since the twenties, claiming that its prestige has increased despite the ways, documented by Lazarsfeld and Thielens, McCarthyism "crushed" its spirit. Attacks liberal "anti-anti-communists" who defended Communism because they accepted the implosion of Communism and liberalism, noting that Lazarsfeld and Thielens's extensive survey of academics in the social sciences documents their sense of fear and depression rather than any specific cause for those feelings. Deplores the "patterns of caution"--ignoring Soviet Russia, offering carefully "balanced" perspectives on economic matters, ascribing their views to other sources--followed by many professors fearful of being labeled Communists, concluding that professors were peculiarly vulnerable to political pressure because of "the insufficiency of professional pride, the lack of a felt connection with an intellectual tradition, the failure to imagine a special relation to mind." Considers in Part 2 Caplow and McGee's study of "academic life in its normal course," focusing on the way a university fills a vacant academic position. Observes that although it does not deal directly with the question Jacques Barzun raises in his Introduction--"Why has the American college and university so little connection with Intellect?"--its analysis of reputation rather than achievement as the paramount consideration in hiring decisions suggests that the question should be, "Why has the American college and university so little connection with Intellect and so much connection with Prestige?"

Revised and reprinted in *New Leader* 42 (9 February 1959): 19-23, and 42 (16 February 1959): 20-21.

C140. "A Speech on Robert Frost: A Cultural Episode." *Partisan Review* 26 (Summer 1959): 445-52.

Describes the speech at Frost's 85th birthday party which aroused J. Donald Adams (G431) and numerous correspondents (K891) to attack Trilling as ignorant of the American experience dramatized by Frost with a brief introduction which summarizes the tone of the responses and quotes from them briefly, expressing particular distress over the letter by Emery Neff, Trilling's dissertation director at Columbia. Reprints the speech, which playfully describes Frost as a mythic figure, "a tutelary genius of the nation and . . . a justification of our national soul," accounts for Trilling's long resistance to Frost by contrasting urban and rural sensibilities, and distinguishes "my Frost" from "the Frost who reassures us by his affirmation of old virtues, simplicities, pieties, and ways of feeling," asserting that his characteristically American concern with what D. H. Lawrence calls "a disintegration and a sloughing off of the old consciousness" makes him instead "a terrifying poet," or "if it makes things any easier, a tragic poet" in the line of Sophocles, whose national audience "loved him chiefly because he made plain to them the terrible things of human life."

Reprinted in *Robert Frost: A Collection of Critical Essays*, edited by James M. Cox (Englewood Cliffs, NJ: Prentice-Hall, 1962), pp. 151-58.

C141. "The Lost Glory." [Review of John Osborne, *Three Plays* (New York: Mid-Century Book Society, 1959).] *Mid-Century*, no. 1 (July 1959), pp. 3-7.

Contrasts Osborne's "confrontation of failure, defeat, and despair" in the lower classes with Lawrence's belief in salvation through identification with "an ideal and legendary aristocracy," and concludes that "Jimmy Porter's subversive alienation from English life [is] his response to the loss of an old glory, an old power, even an old internal struggle" that invigorated Lawrence. Compares the "curious moral energy" of Osborne's dramatization of despair to that of Chekhov.

C142. "The Rational Enchantress." [Review of Geoffrey Scott, *The Portrait of Zélide*, new edition (New York: Scribner's, 1959).] *Mid-Century*, no. 1 (July 1959), pp. 21-23.

Pronounces the *Portrait* (1925), the story of an intelligent, independent woman's intermittently successful quest for a fulfilling relationship with a man whose accomplishments equalled her own--the candidates included the Marquis de Bellegarde, James Boswell, and Benjamin Constant--the "one masterpiece" of Strachey's genre of "compact, carefully planned, elegantly executed biography."

C143. "'An Investigation of Modern Love.'" [Review of Lawrence Durrell, *Justine* (New York: Dutton, 1957), and *Balthazar* (New York: Dutton, 1958).] *Mid-Century*, no. 2 (August 1959), pp. 4-10.

Notes the dependence of the novel's formal structure and aesthetic appeal on its role as "a *naturalizing* agent" for new perceptions and experiences, and calls Durrell "the first contemporary novelist in a long time to lead me to believe that he is telling me something new." Contrasting Durrell's self-proclaimed "investigation of modern love" with "those therapeutic alliances" of other modern lovers, observes that like Proust's lovers, Durrell's strongly resemble the figures of neoclassic French drama. Suggests that Durrell's multiple perspectives do not so much contrast opposing points of view as emphasize the difficulty of ascertaining the truth of human relations.

Reprinted with C150 in *The World of Lawrence Durrell*, edited by Harry T. Moore (Carbondale: Southern Illinois University Press, 1962), pp. 49-65.

C144. "All Aboard the Seesaw." [Review of William Gibson, *The Seesaw Log* (New York: Knopf, 1959).] *Mid-Century*, no. 3 (September 1959), pp. 3-12.

Confesses Trilling's own repulsion from the mystique of the theater, the histrionic personality, habitual theatergoers, and especially "serious plays of contemporary life." Contrasts the privacy of novel-writing and the solicitous criticism of novels-in-progress with the public and peremptorily financial interest of producers, directors, and actors in the development of dramatic texts. Remarks that Gibson's principal problem in successive revisions of his play *Two for the Seesaw* was to make his hero as compelling as his heroine, suggests that "the modern female style is much more emphatic than the male style," and contrasts Gibson's Jerry Ryan with John Osborne's Jimmy Porter, who is "real and morally significant" to "the degree that he seems to negate principle and 'superego.'"

Reprinted in *Tulane Drama Review* 4 (May 1960): 16-22.

C145. "Paradise Reached For." [Review of Norman O. Brown, *Life Against Death: The Psychoanalytical Meaning of History* (Middletown, CT: Wesleyan University Press, 1959).] *Mid-Century*, no. 5 (Fall 1959), pp. 16-21.

Links Brown's book, which "gives the best interpretation of Freud that I know," with Marcuse's *Eros and Civilization* as using Freudian analyses to "controvert Freud's pessimistic view of the possibility of human happiness." Traces Brown's analysis of modern culture's "revolt against itself" to Nietzsche, Conrad, and Gide, emphasizing the therapeutic originality of Brown's cultural pathology, which prescribes an acceptance of death in order to avoid the strengthening and perversion of the death-instinct. Commends the usefulness of Brown's Utopian perspective even to "my thoroughly anti-Utopian mind," and expresses the hope of treating his book at greater length elsewhere.

Reprinted in A15.

C146. "Practical Cats More Practical Than Ever Before." [Review of T. S. Eliot's recorded reading of *Old Possum's Book of Practical Cats* (New York: Spoken Arts, 1959).] *Mid-Century*, no. 6 (November 1959), pp. 11-13.

Recalls Trilling's experiences reading Eliot's book aloud to his young son, and whimsically compares Eliot's "bold dramatic manner" of performance to Trilling's "hammish richness of utterance."

C147. "Angels and Ministers of Grace." [Review of *The Henry Miller Reader*, edited by Lawrence Durrell (New York: New Directions, 1959).] *Mid-Century*, no. 7 (December 1959), pp. 3-9.

Calls Miller "pre-eminent" among American modernists marked by their "ultimate condemnation of our civilization." Describes him as a visionary and a writer, "but not an artist," and therefore a difficult subject for literary criticism. Agrees that Miller is "on the side of the angels," but sets Miller's "angels," who "have no superego," against the "swift, imperious, and very neat" angels of Lawrence, placing their "Nirvanic abstractness" in the American transcendentalist tradition.

Reprinted in part in *Mid-Century*, no. 31 (October 1961), pp. 11-12.

C148. "The Mind of an Assassin." [Review of Isaac Don Levine, *The Mind of an Assassin* (New York: Farrar, Straus & Cudahy, 1959).] *Mid-Century*, no. 8 (January 1960), pp. 11-17.

Maintains that Ramón Mercader, Trotsky's assassin, is interesting as "a human fact" precisely because of his "lack of interest as a person." Reviews Mercader's background and the circumstances of the assassination, imputing to Trotsky "the pride of the intellectual" for his insistence on the autonomy of literature and his willingness to debate means and ends with John Dewey. Calls Levin's book useful mainly for its portrait of Soviet ruthlessness in its human particularities.

Reprinted as "The Assassination of Leon Trotsky" in A15.

C149. "Love and Death in the American Novel." [Review of Leslie A. Fiedler, *Love and Death in the American Novel* (New York: Criterion, 1960).] *Mid-Century*, no. 10 (March 1960), pp. 4-14.

Hails Fiedler's "insolence" as a welcome corrective to the "conventional and boring" studies of American literature invited by the general mediocrity of American writers apart from a small group but stifled by the recent emergence of studies of American culture. Agrees with the decisive importance Fiedler assigns American writers' "negative and secret" treatment of sexuality, as against European writers' constant linking of sexuality and politics. Distinguishes Norman O. Brown's radical attack on genital sexuality from Fielder's "conservative" endorsement of a culture based on adult heterosexuality.

C150. "Lawrence Durrell's *Alexandria Quartet*." [Review of Lawrence Durrell, *Mountolive* (New York: Dutton: 1959), and *Clea* (New York: Dutton, 1960).] *Mid-Century*, no. 11 (April 1960), pp. 4-12.

Notes with some dismay Durrell's inversion of the novel's "preoccupation with the will" as "a peculiarly European faculty" which is here deprived of its potency and moral weight by the recalcitrance of "ancient" (though modern) Alexandria, the amoral claims of love and art, and a narrative manner which largely dispenses with "the rhetoric of the will" in its freedom from moralizing.

Reprinted with C143 in *The World of Lawrence Durrell*, edited by Harry T. Moore (Carbondale: Southern Illinois University Press, 1962), pp. 49-65.

C151. "Fifty Years of *The Wind in the Willows*." [Review of Kenneth Grahame, *The Wind in the Willows* (New York: Scribner's, 1960).] *Mid-Century*, no. 13 (June 1960), pp. 19-22.

Defines the sacred books of childhood--a group which for Trilling includes *The Jungle Books* and the opening chapters of *David Copperfield* and *Treasure Island*--as those presenting "fear and sadness in an ambience that prevents them from being terror and grief" and so encourages children to think of themselves as people "with emotions and a fate." Regrets that such books have not been written for fifty years because contemporary writers choose as their subjects "troubled children" pitted against "nasty Society," and "a culture that cherishes *The Catcher in the Rye* can't understand and doesn't deserve Mowgli or David or Jim Hawkins, or even Peter Rabbit."

C152. "The Inimitable as an Immortal." [Review of *The Selected Letters of Charles Dickens*, edited by F. W. Dupee (New York: Farrar, Straus & Cudahy, 1960).] *Mid-Century*, no. 14 (July 1960), pp. 9-14.

Compares Dickens to a god supremely confident in and gratified by his "supernal powers," grouping him with Austen and Lawrence as the "great geniuses of the English novel" and ascribing his prodigious powers of action, organization, and leadership to his freedom from conscious guilt, suggesting that despite his neuroses, Dickens had "the great gift of keeping his unconscious life unconscious; it made its way into his fantasy but not into his sense of himself."

C153. "The Poem Itself." [Review of *The Poem Itself: 45 Modern Poets in a New Presentation*, edited by Stanley Burnshaw (New York: Holt, Rinehart & Winston, 1960).] *Mid-Century*, no. 15 (August 1960), pp. 10-14.

Sets the poetic translations collected in Burnshaw's anthology, each a "reading" of the given poem whose "end and glory [is] the reader's forgetting that there ever was an original," against literal translations whose role is "frankly ancillary" to the original text. Identifies Trilling as "one of those shy dullards in my relation to languages" who is especially grateful for the active engagement Burnshaw's translations stimulate.

C154. "An American Classic." [Review of James Agee and Walker Evans, *Let Us Now Praise Famous Men*, revised edition (Boston: Houghton Mifflin, 1960).] *Mid-Century*, no. 16 (September 1960), pp. 3-10.

Reprints D321 with a brief prologue and an epilogue which ascribes Agee's "failure" to believe his subjects anything but good to his enabling ability "to affirm, if not actually to believe, that the human soul could exist in a state of radical innocence" and hopes the "terrible actuality" of the book will not by undermined by its acceptance as "art."

Reprinted in A15.

C155. "The Word as Heard." [Review of T. S. Eliot, *Four Quartets*, sound recording read by Robert Speaight (New York: Spoken Arts, 1960).] *Mid-Century*, no. 17 (Fall 1960), pp. 17-22.

Acknowledges Trilling's "resistance to poetry as an oral-aural art" promoted by the "growing hostility to print" that leads to a search for "an audio-visual aid" such as "an actual writer." Praises Speaight's ability to make the poems more immediately accessible and to modulate the leading tones of the *Quartets*--"apparently affectless precision of statement" and "controlled but intense despair and bitterness."

C156. "Masterpieces of Greek Art." [Review of Raymond V. Schoder, *Masterpieces of Greek Art* (Greenwich, CT: New York Graphic Society, 1960).] *Mid-Century*, no. 18 (October 1960), pp. 4-10.

Notes that it is no longer true, as Shelley claimed, that "*we are all Greeks*" who accept the standards of Greek plastic art as setting a universal standard of perfection, and concludes that "the dispensation that destroyed the tyranny of Greece makes it possible for us to accept the Greeks" among other national styles of art for the power of their assertion of an Apollonian triumph over Dionysiac irrationality.

C157. "Bergman Unseen." [Review of Ingmar Bergman, *Four Screenplays*, translated by Lars Malmstrom and David Kushner (New York: Simon and Schuster, 1960).] *Mid-Century*, no. 20 (December 1960), pp. 2-10.

Confesses Trilling's ignorance of contemporary cinema after the infatuation of his adolescence and early adulthood. Points out that Bergman's account of his avowedly "non-literary" methods of composition have much in common with modern accounts of creation in many arts, including literature, adding that cinema typically depends on narrative structures and on "the criterion of 'truth'" that gives photography a peculiar, and often abused, power. Agrees with Bergman in "connect[ing] his artistic powers with his religious upbringing," which gave him the "sense of immanent or present crisis in human lives."

C158. "Three Memoranda on the New Arden Shakespeare." *Mid-Century*, no. 21 (January 1961), pp. 3-11. [Trilling's contribution, pp. 8-11. The other contributors are W. H. Auden and Jacques Barzun.]

Observes that since everyone is expected to have read Shakespeare long since, the actual reading of the plays, as opposed to seeing them in performance, is a private experience not easily discussed. Concludes that "because no one may in decency report the act of reading Shakespeare, no one is likely to commit the act for reasons of pride and prestige--one reads Shakespeare for personal and private reasons or not at all."

C159. "On the Modern Element in Modern Literature." *Partisan Review* 28 (January-February 1961): 9-35.

Recounts Trilling's experiences of the problems involved in teaching a course in modern literature to students avid but superficial in their grasp of new ideas and indifferent to knowledge which has no "practical relevance to modernity." Sets the "power and magnificence" of modern literature and the difficulty that makes it a logical subject of study against its "shockingly personal" themes and stances and the intense concern with spirituality that make it difficult to teach. Notes that teaching modern classics makes them less immediate and threatening and domesticates their terrors. Cites New Critical modes of close analysis as a salutary corrective to his own pragmatic view of literature, but recalls that "since my own interests lead me to see literary situations as cultural situations, and cultural situations as great elaborate fights about moral issues, and moral issues as having something to do with gratuitously chosen images of personal being, and images of personal being as having something to do with literary style, I felt free to begin with what for me was a first concern, the animus of the author, the objects of his will, the things he wants or wants to have happen." Discusses the books he chose as a "background" to modern literature (*The Golden Bough*, *The Birth of Tragedy*, *Heart of Darkness*, *Death in Venice*, *The Genealogy of Morals*, *Civilization and Its Discontents*, *Rameau's Nephew*, *Notes from Underground*, *The Death of Ivan Ilytch*, and two plays by Pirandello) and observes mordantly that none of them succeeded in disturbing most of his students, or in making them realize the force of the desire they expressed to achieve "not merely freedom from the middle class but freedom from society itself"--noting the contradictions involved in enshrining such an anti-institutional literature in academic institutions.

Revised and reprinted in *The Partisan Review Anthology*, edited by William Phillips and Philip Rahv (New York: Holt, Rinehart and Winston, 1962), pp. 263-79; in *The Idea of the Modern in Literature and the Arts*, edited by Irving Howe (New York: Horizon, 1968), pp. 59-82; and as "On the Teaching of Modern Literature" in A8, and in *Issues in Contemporary Literary Criticism*, edited by Gregory T. Polletta (Boston: Little, Brown, 1973), pp. 539-56.

C160. "Looking at Pictures." [Review of Sir Kenneth Clark, *Looking at Pictures* (New York: Holt, Rinehart & Winston, 1960).] *Mid-Century*, no. 23 (March 1961), pp. 2-7.

Suggests that an educated class in England, unlike America, can still maintain an interest in the arts "innocent" in its appetite for pleasure rather than prestige. Remarks that despite their air of cozy intimacy, English journals are "humane" in "propos[ing] . . . the idea of the democracy of intellect" opposed in America by the ideal of the isolated artist. Cites Clark's emphasis on the role "subordinate interests properly play in the aesthetic activity" as a refutation of the view that "information about a work of art is not only irrelevant to the aesthetic experience but destructive of it."

C161. "Curtains." [Review of Kenneth Tynan, *Curtains: Selections from the Drama Criticism and Related Writings* (New York: Atheneum, 1961).] *Mid-Century*, no. 24 (April 1961), pp. 2-9.

Contends that Trilling does not hate the theater but loves it "*really*, which is to say unconsciously, deep down, angrily, bitterly." Describes contemporary theater as intellectually naive and inferior to opera in its "truth of passion." Praises Tynan's "middlebrow" reviews for the "old-fashioned" force of their prose and their civilizing good nature, but finds their social radicalism undeveloped and uncritical. Humorously suggests that Tynan thought of David Susskind's television interview with the *Mid-Century* editors (see L977) as "a problem drama, when actually it was a wild, grim comedy."

C162. "A Poet Newly Given." [Review of *The Complete Poems of Cavafy*, translated by Rae Dalven (New York: Harcourt, Brace & World, 1961).] *Mid-Century*, no. 25 (May 1961), pp. 3-12.

Recalls Trilling's discovery of Cavafy in 1943 through Forster's essay on him, which quotes several poems that made Trilling believe briefly that he too could write poetry (though "I never did make the attempt"). Emphasizes the influence of Cavafy's homosexuality on his poems, linking his "certitude of the law of his own being" to his citizenship in "many different Greeces" comprising both less and more than a national culture, and agrees with Cavafy's estimate of himself as "a poet-historian."

C163. "Yeats as Critic." [Review of William Butler Yeats, *Essays and Introductions* (New York: Macmillan, 1961).] *Mid-Century*, no. 28 (Summer 1961), pp. 3-8.

Distinguishes Yeats's criticism from Eliot's by emphasizing its more personal, occasional quality and its author's resistance to adopting the role of critic. Ascribes this resistance to Yeats's "unremitting and troubled and bitter awareness of his culture," which links him to Arnold as well as Eliot and Joyce: "Yeats from the first spoke out *in propria persona* to denounce Philistine culture, first the British variety, then the Irish." Describes Yeats's essays as "propaganda . . . for a mode of poetry, for a kind of personality, for a way of life."

Reprinted in A15.

C164. "The Mind of Robert Warshow." *Commentary* 31 (June 1961): 501-6.

Defines Warshow's personal style in terms of an "avowed *plainness*" which insists on actuality. Ascribes his own earlier quarrels with Warshow to a generational conflict exacerbated by Trilling's refusal to serve on the advisory board of *Commentary*--a refusal which led to the cooling of Trilling's relations with Elliot Cohen, founding editor of the journal, and his sharper disputes with managing editor Clement Greenberg and the younger members of Cohen's staff--and Warshow's negative review of A3 (see G544). Observes that their friendship grew despite these strains because of their common concern for the pragmatics of child-rearing--they both rejected "progressive" dogmas as marked by "animosity to parents" and "malice toward children"--a concern which illustrated Warshow's "continuing connection with his own boyhood." Links this connection to Warshow's fascination with Hollywood movies, which he studied analytically without surrendering his boyhood involvement with them. Identifies the imperative in Warshow's criticism as "never to separate himself from the matter in hand," noting that Warshow's characteristic "self-implication" accounts for the plainness, the absence of histrionic effect, the intellectual honesty, of his voice, and concludes by comparing him in this regard to Hazlitt and Orwell.

Revised and reprinted as the Introduction to B36.

C165. "Beautiful and Blest." [Review of *Great English Short Novels*, edited by Cyril Connolly (New York: Dial, 1953); *Great French Short Novels*, edited by Frederick W. Dupee (New York: Dial, 1952); and *Great Russian Short Novels*, edited by Philip Rahv (New York: Dial, 1951).] *Mid-Century*, no. 30 (September 1961), pp. 3-9.

Sets the short novel's development of a single idea against the short story's ironic "indifference to development" and the novel's "creation of a world" which generally conceals its informing idea. Complains that despite the attractions of the form, modern short novels are rare because they are not taken seriously by publishers, reviewers, or most readers.

C166. "A Comedy of Evil." [Review of *The Short Novels of Dostoevsky*, with an Introduction by Thomas Mann (New York: Dial, 1945).] *Mid-Century*, no. 32 (November 1961), pp. 7-11.

Asks why such enormous crowds mourned Dostoevsky's death, and finds the answer not in his personal conduct or in the compassion often claimed for his work but in his "pitiless confrontation of his own moral repulsiveness," which "made the spiritual life . . . an adventure" and a liberating experience to the audience who could recognize themselves in Stavrogin and the Underground Man. Concludes by remarking the predominance of corrosive comedy over tragedy in Dostoevsky's short novels.

Reprinted in A15.

C167. "Rimbaudelaire." [Review of Enid Starkie, *Arthur Rimbaud*, third edition (Norfolk, CT: New Directions, 1961), and *Baudelaire* (New York: New Directions, 1958).] *Mid-Century*, no. 34 (December 1961), pp. 3-10.

Identifies modern spirituality with violence and "the insistence upon the sordid or the disgusting or the obscene" as an affront to the "specious good" of bourgeois habits. Sets Baudelaire's "essential accord with civilization and tradition" against both his "heterodox and shocking" manner of expression and Rimbaud's more radical "achievement of the divine unconnectedness," which embodies "the charismatic effect of those who do harm without feeling guilt."

C168. "No Mean City." [Review of Jane Jacobs, *The Death and Life of Great American Cities* (New York: Random House, 1961).] *Mid-Century*, no. 37 (March 1962), pp. 14-19.

Agrees with Jacobs' attack on the assumption, sanctified not by logic or practicality but by a "moralizing aura," that large cities are "inimical to the good life." Observes that Trilling's own street, Claremont Avenue, is both safer and more interesting than such dedicated public spaces as Riverside Park and Morningside Park, and approves the criteria of "complexity and variety and denseness and strangeness and activity" Jacobs recommends for city planning.

C169. "'What a Piece of Work Is Man.'" [Review of Claude Lévi-Strauss, *A World on the Wane*, translated by John Russell (New York: Criterion, 1961).] *Mid-Century*, no. 38 (April 1962), pp. 5-12.

Notes the gravity of Levi-Strauss's analysis of the cultural decline in the power and complexity of native Brazilian cultures, emphasizing his kinship to Montaigne, Rousseau, and Montesquieu, and his similar turn from "wonder" at the range of human behavior in different societies to a view of "ourselves as others might see us."

C170. "Science, Literature and Culture: A Comment on the Leavis-Snow Controversy." *Commentary* 33 (June 1962): 461-77.

Refers the dispute between C. P. Snow's *The Two Cultures* and F. R. Leavis's "The Signficance of C. P. Snow" concerning the respective claims of science and literature as foundations of culture to the similar debate eighty years earlier between Arnold and T. H. Huxley. Agrees with Leavis that nineteenth-century writers were far more active as social critics than Snow recognizes, citing Orwell's political commitment as refuting Snow's claim that *1984* expresses "the strongest possible wish that the future shall not exist." Reaffirms Arnold's conception of literature as a criticism of life "on behalf of the illumination and refinement of that Reason by which man might shape the conditions of his own existence." Contends that Snow claims for scientists "the right to go their way *with no questions asked*," and that his utopian vision of Soviet and Western scientists building a better future together denies the reality of politics. Charges that the carping, *ad hominem* nature of Leavis's attack on Snow prevents him from responding to the seriousness of his argument. Suggests that the "passionate hostility to society" characteristic of contemporary literature may represent a self-criticism of society rather than a rejection of society. Noting Snow's and Leavis's similarly middle-class backgrounds, hostility to modernism, and sensitivity to questions of social class, concludes that both men, in their interest "in shaking the old certainties of class, in contriving new social groups on the basis of taste," assume too great a power for "the idea of *culture* as a category of thought," giving up the disinterestedness of Faraday's determination not to align himself with a particular class or culture.

Revised and reprinted as "The Leavis-Snow Controversy" in A8, and in *The Commentary Reader: Two Decades of*

Articles and Stories, edited by Norman Podhoretz (New York: Atheneum, 1966), pp. 467-88; and excerpted in *The Theory of Criticism from Plato to the Present*, edited by Raman Selden (London: Longman, 1988), pp. 516-17.

For replies by Leavis and Snow appended to reprints of their original statements, see L951 and L975.

C171. "Commitment to the Modern: The Problem of Perspective in Literature." *Harvard Alumni Bulletin* 64 (7 July 1962): 739-42.

Applauds the "direct relation between the intellectual force and prestige of any particular college and the degree of its responsiveness to modern life," contrasting this commitment with Henry Adams's sense of Harvard's indifference to the modern world during his undergraduate career there, but warns that the spiritual subversiveness of modern literature, the doubt it casts on social values and the idea of society itself, often arouses a hostility to disinterested perception and intellect that deprives students of the intellectual categories they need to analyze it, so that "students are not mastering subjects, they are experiencing them." Prescribes the "countervailing force" of a mind that acknowledges that "the world is intractable as well as malleable" as a way of complicating the "radical subjectivity" fostered by modern literature, protecting it from corruption "by mere bland tolerance, or by a Philistine delight in its intent of outrageousness."

Revised and reprinted in *Harvard Today*, Autumn 1962, pp. 27-31, and *Teachers College Record* 64 (February 1963): 404-8.

C172. "The Wheel." [Review of Christopher Isherwood, *Down There on a Visit* (New York: Simon & Schuster, 1962); and Iris Murdoch, *An Unofficial Rose* (New York: Viking, 1962).] *Mid-Century*, no. 41 (July 1962), pp. 5-10.

Notes the reaction against the Jamesian ideal of The Novel as an impersonal, highly wrought mode of art. Suggests that Isherwood, whose "novel-as-memoir or memoir-as-novel" displays a familiar novelistic ambivalence toward self-love, adopts his first-person point of view in order to display himself "with all his stains of fallible humanity" instead of dissimulating his presence behind an elaborately contrived fictional viewpoint, and that Murdoch "follows all the rules for the Novel-as-work-of-Art" for the untraditional purpose of showing that "moral success is not possible."

C173. "James Baldwin." [Review of James Baldwin, *Another Country* (New York: Dial, 1962).] *Mid-Century*, no. 44 (September 1962), pp. 5-11.

Argues that despite the uncomfortable pressures of Baldwin's status as "the only American Negro with a considerable body of respected work to his credit," his re-emergence as spokesperson for his ethnic group has strengthened him as a novelist, because his "angry awareness of the Negro situation" has led him to affirm "the primacy of the will" in his characters' struggles with the "white society" which corrupts or destroys them.

C174. "Lord of the Flies." [Review of William Golding, *Lord of the Flies*, new edition (New York: Coward-McCann, 1962).] *Mid-Century*, no. 45 (October 1962), pp. 10-12.

Contrasts Golding's "affirmation of . . . Original Sin" with Salinger's assurance in *The Catcher in the Rye* that "*no blame attaches*" to "any Nice Individual" but only "to parents, to teachers, to institutions, to The Culture, to Society." Concludes that "the enthusiasm for Mr. Golding's novel . . . amounts to something like a mutation in culture."

**** "Literary Pathology." [Response to M1035. First published in A15.] See E419.

C175. "The Fate of Pleasure: Wordsworth to Dostoevsky." *Partisan Review* 30 (Summer 1963): 167-91.

Analyzes the evolution of pleasure as an aesthetic and moral ideal from Wordsworth's substitution of pleasure for God as the "grand elementary principle" by which people are animated and moved through Keats's ambivalence toward pleasure as both consuming and "self-negating" to the antagonism toward pleasure in *Notes from Underground* and modernist aesthetics. Links the Romantic fascination with sensual pleasure to the growing European preoccupation with luxury as a mediated expression of economic power, noting the widening gap in modern culture between a political morality based on self-affirmation, affluence, and pleasure, and an artistic morality that opposes these ideals as expressions of "the *conditioned* nature of man." Proposes Dostoevski rather than Nietzsche as defining "the characteristically modern conception of the spiritual life," arguing that unlike Nietzsche, he criticizes both Christianity and modern humanism as enshrining principles of pleasure he rejects. Contends that modern spirituality, which denigrates pleasure in the name of "negative transcendence," is a "competition for spiritual status" based on the claim of "more life"--a claim which has now passed from a mode of experience for the minority represented by the Underground Man to an ideal, even an ideology, for a growing class, united by their hostility toward middle-class values, whose "accredited subversiveness" licenses an uncritically adversary stance Trilling contrasts with the "awesome paradoxes" Freud considers in *Beyond the Pleasure Principle*.

Reprinted in *Romanticism Reconsidered*, edited by Northrop Frye (New York: Columbia University Press, 1963), pp. 73-106; in *Literary Views: Critical and Historical Essays*, edited by Carroll Camden (Chicago: University of Chicago Press for William Marsh Rice University, 1964), pp. 93-114; and revised and reprinted as "The Fate of Pleasure" in A8; in *Perspectives in Literary Criticism: A Collection of Recent Essays by American, English, and*

European Literary Critics, edited by Sheldon Norman Grebstein (New York: Harper, 1968), pp. 171-87; and in *Literary Criticism: Idea and Act*, edited by W. K. Wimsatt (Berkeley: University of California Press, 1974), pp. 189-211.

C176. "The Scholar's Caution and the Scholar's Courage." *The Cornell Library Conference: Papers Read at the Dedication of the Central Libraries, 1962* (Ithaca: Cornell University Library, 1964), pp. 51-65.

Contrasts the intellectual ferment of undergraduate education with the moribundity of graduate study, however widely respected, and ascribes this difference in large part to the difficulty in students' grasping the "public character" of graduate study when it is so seldom discussed and so vaguely conceived. Arguing that "it is only when criticism exists in conjunction with history that it maintains its force" and agreeing with Nietzsche that "scholarship serves life in the degree that its conception of History is right-minded," recommends that graduate study in literature be recalled to its public character by re-dedication to the study of history as an organizing principle and a goad toward the more active understanding of the present.

C177. "Afterword: Our Hawthorne." *Hawthorne Centenary Essays*, edited by Roy Harvey Pearce (Columbus: Ohio State University Press, 1964), pp. 429-58.

Contrasts Henry James's estimate of Hawthorne as serene and playful in his handling of Puritanism with the modern view of Hawthorne as darkly ambiguous as a symptom of contemporary criticism's contribution to the "respect revolution" which has come to challenge "democratic-capitalist" pieties. Notes the paradox of a criticism emphasizing the creator's private life even as it makes that life increasingly public, relegating literary works like Hawthorne's to "the purview of one or another of the public agencies [such as literary criticism] we have set up for the service of the inner life" and losing the charm to which James responded. Defining this charm in reference to James's injunction to "'have your life,'" his "certitude that the world is *there*," and his assent to the moral sanctions which govern the search for pleasure, sets James's Hawthorne against "our Hawthorne," the skeptical ironist licensed by modernist readings of Kafka. Urges that despite Hawthorne's similarities to Kafka, he differs in the intransigence of his physical world and his appeals to conscience as a spiritual standard, and suggests that Hawthorne, unlike Kafka, focuses on the interpenetration of the literal and the spiritually transcendent. Concludes that to the degree Hawthorne grants his principals spiritual autonomy, he can be made to appeal to the modern imagination, but argues that autonomy in Hawthorne is always conditioned by a worldly awareness that makes him antipathetically playful and resistant to any "tyrant-dream" that might satisfy a modern audience: "It is questions which Hawthorne leaves us with."

Revised and reprinted as "Hawthorne in Our Time" in A8.

C178. "A Valedictory." *Tri-Quarterly*, no. 1 (Fall 1964), pp. 26-31.

Remarks that the conventional structure for a valedictory speech--the opposition between the sheltered, idealistic environment of the university and the indifferent world the graduates are to enter--has been outmoded by the eagerness with which "so much of the world is trying to crowd itself into the university." Ridicules Clark Kerr's proposal that universities make a new attempt "to accommodate pure creative effort" by indicating the problems the private lives or dispositions of Joyce, Gide, Sartre, Yeats, and others would pose to universities seeking to install them at the center of "the knowledge industry."

Revised and reprinted in *Encounter* 24 (March 1965): 57-61; in *The Harbrace College Reader*, 4th edition, edited by Mark Schorer, Philip Durham, and Everett L. Jones (New York: Harcourt Brace Jovanovich, 1972), pp. 241-48; and in A15.

C179. "The Two Environments: Reflections on the Study of English." *Encounter* 25 (July 1965): 3-13.

Traces the early development of university departments of English as mainstays of liberal education from their establishment in opposition to the study of classical languages to philological principles of scholarship and finally to the humanistic study of literature under the auspices of New Criticism. Identifies the motives for the present-day study of literature, especially of modern literature, as less concerned with the search for ethical principles animating nineteenth-century partisans of literary study than with the desire for "control of the sources of life" as expressed by culture as a "style of life" fostered by a particular society which manufactures and packages such commodities as "joy, freedom, self-definition, self-esteem." Contends that unlike liberal education a hundred years ago, whose purpose was a reasoned critique of the pieties of the prevaling culture, modern universities offer students a choice of two cultures: a Philistine middle-class culture and an equally institutionalized (albeit less powerful) "party of opposition," an adversary culture dedicated to "the imagination of fullness, freedom, and potency of life," and the concomitant concern with "moralized taste" and mastery of the styles appropriate to the control of the sources of life. Indicts modern criticism as timid in limiting itself to verbal analysis, which fosters "an intelligent passivity before the beneficent aggression of literature." Citing the ways in which Saul Bellow's recent withering attack on the pietistic alienation of modern fiction has already passed into the reassuring "realm of gossip" instead of being seriously addressed, asks if the original mission of education in modern literature--its encouragement to students to detach themselves from "the idols of the Marketplace, the Tribe, the Theatre, and even of the Cave"--has now been inverted by the success of literary studies in establishing its own idols.

Revised and reprinted in A8.

C180. "Young in the Thirties." *Commentary* 41 (May 1966): 43-51.

Responding to Murray Kempton's citation of Slesinger's *The Unpossessed* in L945, notes that the novel has greater value than its historical testimony concerning American intellectuals in the thirties, "the indispensable decade" which "created the American intellectual class as we now know it in its great size and influence." Compares Slesinger to Mary McCarthy, though remarking that "her animus" against the targets of her satire "was checked by compunction" and continuing affection. Briefly recounts the tensions between Henry Hurwitz and Elliot Cohen that determined the shifting nature of the *Menorah Journal* during the thirties, defining the common ground of its contributors as the search for an authentic Jewishness, and cites Trilling's own appointment as an instructor at Columbia as "pretty openly . . . an experiment." Describes *The Unpossessed* as the first novel to deal with thirties radicalism in its typical contradictions--"the discrepancy, eventually the antagonism, between life and the desire to make life as good as it might be," and between the liberating doctrine of its politics and the rigidly conformist conduct of those politics--treated by Slesinger in social or moral rather than political terms. Praises Slesinger's ability, despite her dedication to the terms of radicalism, to criticize the "spiritual intellect" of radicalism itself.

Revised and reprinted as the Afterword to B38, and as "A Novel of the Thirties" in A14.

C181. "James Joyce in His Letters." [Review of *Letters of James Joyce*, volumes 2 and 3, edited by Richard Ellmann (New

York: Viking, 1968).] *Commentary* 45 (February 1968): 53-64.

Explores Joyce's contradictory fascination with "nullity," combining "the impulse to resist nullity" with "the impulse to make nullity prevail." Links Joyce's success in "kill[ing] the nineteenth century" to his attack on ideals of worldly or spiritual success, excepting only the artistic will embodied in Stephen Dedalus. Noting Joyce's increasing detachment from the world during his long exile, traces Joyce's development from the "early egotism of the world" revealed in his letter to the aging Ibsen to his "later egotism of nullity" marked by "the sensitivity of his class feelings" in his quarrel with Gogarty, the erotic "rapture" of his relationship with Nora, and the obscenity and self-degradation of his letters to her. Describes this development as an attempt "to move through the fullest realization of the human, the all-too-human, to that which transcends and denies the human," commending Joyce for heroically discovering the vanity and futility of human life rather than taking it for granted, as succeeding generations have done.

Reprinted in Joyce: A Collection of Critical Essays, edited by William M. Chace (Englewood Cliffs, NJ: Prentice-Hall, 1974), pp. 142-65, and in A14.

C182. "A Recollection of Raymond Weaver." *University on the Heights: A Collection of Essays About Life at Columbia by Prominent Columbia Alumni*, edited by Wesley First (Garden City: Doubleday, 1969), pp. 5-13.

Describes the scholar who led the Melville revival in 1921 as "sacramental" in his dandyism, self-discipline, and "piety toward life." Recalls Weaver's early hostility to Trilling as an intellectual whose passions were diluted by skepticism and irony and his unexpected respect for the anger which led Trilling to protest his dismissal from Columbia and finish his dissertation "in a maniacal burst of energy."

C183. "William Wordsworth." *Atlantic Brief Lives*, edited by Louis Kronenberger (Boston: Atlantic Monthly Press/Little, Brown, 1971), pp. 882-84.

Acknowledges that despite his consensual reputation, Wordsworth is often disliked because his later work is inferior and antipathetic in its didactic intent and because he is not as personally endearing as the younger romantics. Links the "*caritas* of unique strength and tenderness" arising from Wordsworth's stern personality to his "preoccupation with the concept, and even more with the sensation, of *being*" in himself and others.

C184. "Authenticity and the Modern Unconscious." *Commentary* 52 (September 1971): 39-50.

Argues that modern culture is obsessed with "authenticity as a quality of the personal life and as a criterion for art," citing in evidence contemporary distrust of storytelling, narrative history, and the narrative past as inauthentic before discussing at length the suspicion accorded the therapeutic narratives of Freudian psychoanalysis. Dismisses Sartre's critique of Freud's distinction between ego and id, which charges that Freud's model inauthentically depersonalizes the id in order to identify the self with the ego, as outmoded by Freud's theory of the "gratuitous harshness" of the super-ego, whose accusations of guilt against the ego are described in *Civilization and Its Discontents* as "anything but rational." Concludes that Freud roots authenticity not in the ego or super-ego but in "the essential immitigability of the human condition as determined by the nature of mind"--a tragic mental dialectic that filled the space left by what Nietzsche called the death of God and the resulting "weightlessness" of experience. Deplores recent psychiatrists' attacks on Freud's tragic stoicism, charging that Marcuse's revulsion from the permissive social culture he prescribes in *Eros and Civilization* stems from "preference for the personality-type shaped by a relatively repressive society. . . . He *likes* people to have character, cost what it might in frustration," and excoriating the belief shared by Norman O. Brown, David Cooper, and R. D. Laing that extreme social repressions make madness the only possible mode of personal authenticity. Ends by pointing out that the kinds of identity these writers describe as authentic--Cooper's "I am (or you are) Christ"--free the subject's identity from the responsibilities of action and and the analyst's assent from "actual credence."

Revised and reprinted as Chapter 6 of A9.

C185. "Mind in the Modern World." *TLS*, 17 November 1972, pp. 1381-85.

Contrasts H. G. Wells's 1946 *Mind at the End of Its Tether* with Jefferson's faith in the essential health, unity, and social utility of mind in order to dramatize the modern loss of faith in the powers of mind, noting the present fragmentation and mutual ignorance and distrust of different academic disciplines and citing Louis Kampf's 1971 Presidential Address to the Modern Language Association as indicating the current contempt for literature and criticism by their own practitioners. Discusses Morris's *News from Nowhere* as a precursor of the modern resentment toward mental powers as dangerously aggressive, authoritarian, and socially inequitable, finding its echo in contemporary resentment to the power and social mobility conferred by university study. Acknowledges inequalities of opportunity in modern universities, but sees the universities' uncritical acceptance of affirmative action programs as a quietistic rejection of the powers of mind. Defends Arnoldian ideals of mental objectivity--"the effort 'to see the object in itself as it really is'"--against recent attacks on objectivity as scientistic and dehumanizing, suggesting that a "contemporary ideology of irrationalism" has grown out of impatience with the impossibility of achieving complete objectivity and the compromises necessarily implicit in all rational perception and action. Concludes that "the *mystique* of mind" displayed in the sudden entrance of the aristocracy into universities during the English Renaissance and now apparently in eclipse remains discernible both in the modern tendency to judge societies and nations in terms drawn from "the right conduct of mind" and in the mind's awareness of its own vicissitudes, and urges a renewal of the mind's grasp of freedom, power, and delight in itself.

Revised and reprinted as A10, and in A14.

C186. "Aggression and Utopia: A Note on William Morris's *News from Nowhere*." *Psychoanalytic Quarterly* 42 (April 1973): 214-25.

Contends that Morris's vision of a utopian world based on "a life in which aggression plays no part" is disturbing because it denies social and artistic goals "beyond pleasure" and the importance of past and future in forming "the imaginative will of genius in aggressive adversary relation to the world as it is." Asserts that these aggressive energies are for better or worse the foundation of humanistic ideals of transcendence, including "immortality," "glory," and "dignity." Links Morris's utopian vision to the unlikely latter-day utopian B. F. Skinner, and especially to Skinner's attack on humanistic ideals and aggressions in *Beyond Freedom and Dignity*, suggesting that such efforts to overcome or banish aggression merely lead to its return in new and covert forms.

Reprinted in A14.

C187. "General Education and the American Preparatory System." [Columbia University] *Seminar Reports* 1 (7 December 1973): 1-3.

Reviews the history of the debate over the value of liberal or general education as the specific mission of Columbia College, noting that the continuing, often intense debate on the subject has never taken account of the potentially crucial role of secondary education in general education. Concludes that the "radically accelerated . . . process of social and cultural maturation" characteristic of contemporary American adolescents gives them an intellectual potential that makes it highly appropriate to link secondary education much more closely with the liberal education traditionally assumed to be the exclusive purview of undergraduate colleges.

For replies, see M1033, M1055, and M1056.

C188. "The Freud/Jung Letters." [Review of *The Freud/Jung Letters: The Correspondence Between Sigmund Freud and C. G. Jung*, edited by William McGuire, translated by Ralph Manheim and R. F. C. Hull (Princeton: Princeton University Press, 1974).] *New York Times Book Review*, 21 April 1974, pp. 1, 32-35.

Reviews the deterioration of the friendship between Freud and his most distinguished disciple as chronicled in their letters from 1906 through 1913, noting Freud's consistently paternal attempts to insure Jung's personal and professional loyalty despite the urging of Jung's wife Emma "to give up his paternal relation to her husband," and Jung's success through a quarrel over Freud's fainting spells in "transform[ing] the judging father into the condemned brother"--a revolt Trilling calls "an elaborate act of intellectual supererogation" for both his cultural concepts and his clinical theory.

Reprinted in A14.

C189. "The Uncertain Future of the Humanistic Educational Ideal." *American Scholar* 44 (Winter 1974-75): 52-67.

Predicts that society will become increasingly alienated from a humanistic educational ideal which seemed until recently firmly entrenched. Traces the vicissitudes of this ideal at Columbia from Frederick Barnard's and Nicholas Murray Butler's proposals to abolish its liberal arts college to the rise of John Erskine's General Honors curriculum, organized around the Great Books, to the recent indifference greeting L902. Sets modern culture's unceasing emphasis on self-affirmation and self-actualization against the humanistic ideal of shaping the self through ordeal and effort, noting that many people barred from higher education want it not as an opportunity for achievement but as a means to upward mobility based on accredation irrespective of achievement, and charging that Archibald Cox's high estimate of modern students has "celebrated as knowledge and intelligence what is actually a congeries of 'advanced' public attitudes." Laments the passing of the desire to shape a self by closing out options to alternative selves, and observes that a humanistic educational ideal that espouses such a strenuously shaped self as a model will be found increasingly retrograde.

Reprinted in A14.

C190. "Whittaker Chambers' Journey." *Times Saturday Review* [London], 5 April 1975, pp. 5, 9.

Acknowledges that Gifford Maxim in A3 was based on Trilling's old college acquaintance Whittaker Chambers, not yet widely-known as the accuser of Alger Hiss of Communist connections, but denies that the Crooms are based on Hiss and his wife, whom Trilling never knew. Recalls that although Chambers was not a friend of his, Trilling refused to testify about him to the HUAC, describing him as "a man of honor." Recounts how A3 was originally conceived without Maxim as a *nouvelle* about "the way death is conceived by the enlightened consciousness of the modern age," but that once Trilling thought of including a figure based on Chambers, "whose commitment to radical politics was meant to be definitive of his whole moral being" and whose passion and terror could thus represent "the principle of reality," the *nouvelle* grew in length and resonance, for Maxim's challenge to the Crooms' shallow Stalinism revealed "the clandestine negation of the political life which Stalinist Communism had fostered among the intellectuals of the West" as "one aspect of an ever more imperious and bitter refusal to consent to the conditioned nature of human existence." Notes that although he conceived Maxim as a "sad comedian," the Hiss affair made it impossible to think of Chambers comically, and defends Chambers's integrity despite his fondness for portentous nonsense and his links to Richard Nixon, whose recent disgrace should not impugn Chambers's "magnanimous intention."

Enlarged and reprinted as "Whittaker Chambers and *The Middle of the Journey*," *New York Review of Books* 22 (17 April 1975): 18-24; as the Introduction to A3i; and as "Whittaker Chambers' Journey" in A14.

C191. "Why We Read Jane Austen." *TLS*, 5 March 1976, pp. 250-52.

Explores the reasons for the renewed appeal of Austen's novels, recalling that even though Trilling and his students approached them in the "traditional humanistic" belief that the culture they presented was continuous with theirs, they also saw its culture as an attractive alternative to their own in its rural landscapes and values, its assumptions about social aristocracy, and its lack of interest in "achievement" as a means of "personal definition," rendering life a matter of "being" rather than "doing." Considers a similarly paradoxical hermeneutic circle in M1007, which identifies modes of personal and social identity remote from Geertz and his Eurocentric audiences in their negation of the personal will yet readily comprehensible because of their affinities with the tragic ideal of a life transmuted by destiny into a work of art that may be grasped as an intelligible whole. Proposes that the humanistic ambivalence toward the quietism of art as an ideal image of human life represented by Keats's Grecian Urn is dialectical, but breaks off before developing this point or returning to Austen.

Reprinted in A14.

C192. "The Changing Myth of the Jew." *Commentary* 66 (August 1978): 24-34. [Originally written in 1929 and accepted for publication in *Menorah Journal* in 1931, but not previously published.]

Disputing the assumption that earlier writers' attempts to treat Jewish characters realistically were blunted by their ignorance and hatred, argues that "the Jew in fiction was always an abstraction, a symbol, a racial stereotype" intended to serve the emotional, political, and economic interests of Gentile writers and their audiences. Traces the development of myths of the Jew in English literature from the "active anti-Christ" in "The Prioresse's Tale" to the economically based Machiavels of *The Jew of Malta* and *The Merchant of Venice* and to the increasingly equivocal Wandering Jew of English gothic and romantic novels (whose "punishment is so dreadful that he becomes by means of it a virtuous person"), the comic parvenus and dupes of Sheridan and Cumberland, and finally to the impossibly virtuous "counter-myths" of Riah, Coningsby, and Daniel Deronda. Concludes that it is impossible to consider contemporary Jewish fiction critically without considering the ways in which it is implicated in these earlier myths.

Reprinted in A15.

C193. "Art, Will, and Necessity." [Given as a lecture at Cambridge University, 1973; revised and first published in A14.]

Analyzes the attack on the individual will in creating art lamented by Harold Rosenberg in *The De-Definition of Art* and urged by Robert Scholes in G530. Ascribes Rosenberg's revulsion from the culture of contemporary American visual art with that culture's resounding and gratuitous rejection of "'the heroic concept of masterpieces'" as "an exercise of the creative will," contending that the schools of art he discusses, from pop art to conceptual, non-visual art and "happenings," join in "deny[ing] the will as we traditionally know it" by impugning the validity of "the traditional aesthetic experience" in favor of "a concept of art as simultaneously a total environment and a total participation." Links this attack on the will expressed in traditional art and earlier avant-gardes to Scholes's call for a structuralist devaluation of the individual will (of fictional characters, their creators, their readers) and its concomitants--"individual *quirkiness*" and "momentous" personal experiences that affirmed individual uniqueness--in favor of a transcendently syncretistic perspective Trilling compares to "the program of Stalinist liberalism." Noting the determined narcissism of the artists Rosenberg considers, concludes that the attack on "*will-power*" is actually a regressive call to "the will of the undeveloped ego, unresponsive to necessity."

C194. "Appendix: Some Notes for an Autobiographical Lecture." [Notes for a lecture in a 1971 Purdue University series in which contemporary literary theorists discussed their own work; first published in A14.]

A memoir, consisting of twelve brief paragraphs and a series of jottings, which begins by expressing Trilling's continuing surprise at being labeled a critic, given his desire to become a novelist, his derivation of ideas mainly from novels rather than poetry, criticism, or philosophy, and his "*anti-literary*" preoccupation with moral rather than formal or aesthetic questions in those novels. Describes the renewed emphasis throughout the 1920's on "the QUALITY OF LIFE" together with "questions of social justice." Discusses John Erskine's introduction of the General Honors course, its implications at Columbia--"the great word in the College was INTELLIGENCE," offering an escape from students' middle-class backgrounds through encounters with great ideas and models of thought, feeling, and imagination--and elsewhere the General Education movement took root, and considering its present eclipse. Recalls modernist writers' sense of crisis in confrontating a hostile culture which seemed to require the kind of "unmasking" practiced by Marx and Freud. Explains the motive behind A1 as the wish "to discover and explain in historical-cultural terms why [Arnold] was so sad." Recalls the growing saturation of "every aspect of existence" in the later 1930's and 1940's with "ideas, or the simulacra of ideas," and recounts Trilling's impulse to unmask apparently political positions that "actually expressed a desire to transcend the political condition" or a "desire to exercise power." Remarks in closing that "power blinds us to the object: to the work of art, to the complexity. . . ."

C195. "From the Notebooks of Lionel Trilling." Edited by Christopher Zinn. *Partisan Review* 51/52 (Fall 1984/Winter 1985): 496-515, and 54 (Winter 1987): 7-17.

Reprints excerpts from Trilling's notebooks--not a diary, but comments on books, people, and important events, and suggestions for his own fiction--from 1927 through 1975. The first series (1927-1951) includes Trilling's early injunctions to "become a friend to yourself" and to withhold fairy tales and most novels from any son he might educate and his observation that "being a Jew is like walking in the wind or swimming: you are touched at all points and conscious everywhere" before focusing on his successful attempt in 1936 to persuade the Columbia English department to reconsider his termination. Later entries record Trilling's recollection of himself as "enormously mature" from an early age and of his mother having reserved "something, not life, better than life . . . for me"; his conviction that novels may legitimately dwell on the upper classes because "money & snobbery" are the basis of the novel, and that the middle class is shaped "not by its financial situation but by its relation to government"; his confession in 1944 that "the Victorians have lost all charm for me"; his hunger for the praise of such valued contemporaries as Mark Schorer and Leslie Fiedler and his depressed indifference to praise from others; and his sense of liberation on deciding to give up graduate teaching and courses in American literature.

The second series (1952-75) refers briefly (in 1953) to Trilling's plan to write more novels; recalls the diffidence the staff at Viking had expressed in accepting A3 for publication and their surprise that it found a British publisher; expresses Trilling's grief at the death of Hemingway and the "shame and regret for what I have not done" exposed by Sartre's *Les mots*; identifies "the politicization of desire" as "the great fact of modern life"; recalls Trilling's early dismissive review (written for *New Freeman*, but left unpublished by the journal's collapse) of *Civilization and Its Discontents*; and attributes Trilling's "incoherent and pointless" attack on a 1969 proposal to give voting privileges to "all teaching personnel of the college" to his "not being in control of my mind," evidence of "the approach of old age."

Taken as a group, the excerpts present Trilling as chronically insecure about his status as a critic, painfully aware of his ignorance of foreign languages and scholarly materials, yet simultaneously confident of his superiority to critics whose credentials apparently outshine his own.

Section D

Reviews

D196. "What Price Jewry?" [Review of Hugo Bertauer, *The City Without Jews*, translated by Salomea Neumark Brainin (New York: Bloch, 1926).] *Menorah Journal* 13 (April 1927): 218-19.

Criticizes the publication of Bertauer's pro-Semitic pamphlet in the form of a novel about the baneful effects of banishing all Jews from Vienna and notes its unintended anti-Semitism in the portrait of Jews as "civilized, creative, free, colorful"--a dangerous description in an American culture "where it is considered best that color be whitewashed, civilization taught quaint new purposes, and freedom and creation shown their limits."

D197. "Competent, But--" [Review of Lester Cohen, *The Great Bear* (New York: Boni and Liveright, 1927).] *Menorah Journal* 13 (November 1927): 522-23.

Compares Cohen's family saga unfavorably to similar novels by Mann, Bennett, Galsworthy, and others, observing that although he has "attacked a commendably ambitious and deplorably unnecessary task with honest energy," Cohen's lack of insight and originality fail to make the saga form vital. Notes that competence in fiction creates a trap for critics who cannot account for a competent novel's failure without dealing in "imponderables" like "'tone,' 'spirit,' 'truth.'"

D198. "A Study of Terror-Romanticism." [Review of Eino Railo, *The Haunted Castle: A Study of the Elements of English Romanticism* (New York: Dutton, 1927).] *New York Evening Post*, 10 December 1927, section 3, p. 16.

Suggests that Railo's subtitle indicates his wish to use the "pathologically exaggerated" qualities of English Gothic as a figure for the "more normal manifestations" of romanticism generally. Calls romanticism "a return to the more characteristic accent and tone of English literature" rather than a new development, save only in Gothic writers' concentration on terrifying their readers, and criticizes Railo for focusing on the sources of the motifs of romanticism rather than "the intellectual and emotional climate that fostered it."

Reprinted in A15.

D199. "Modish Makeup on One More Novel of Marriage." [Review of Mathilde Eiker, *Over the Boat-Side* (Garden City: Doubleday, Page, 1927).] *New York Evening Post*, 17 December 1927, section 3, p. 10.

Finds beneath Eiker's "gracefully hard-boiled" veneer, which suggests "the luncheon conversation of clever and cultured alumnae who have been somewhat successful in the advertising business," the outworn elements of "the female literature of marriage," and suggests that refurbishing the genre so pertly is "a little like rouging a corpse."

D200. "Three More Interesting Tales of de Gobineau's." [Review of Comte de Gobineau, *The Crimson Handkerchief and Other Stories*, translated by Henry Longan Stuart (New York: Harper, 1927).] *New York Evening Post*, 7 January 1928, section 3, p. 13.

Emphasizes Gobineau's constant concern with "people who act vigorously for the realization of an ideal," commending especially "A Daughter of Priam," his story of a modern man's retreat into the distant past with a woman of Naxos, but denies Gobineau Stendhal's intensity and passion.

D201. "Of Sophistication." [Review of Ludwig Lewisohn, *Roman Summer* (New York: Harper, 1927).] *Menorah Journal* 14 (January 1928): 106-9.

Warns that the most characteristic recent American fiction, like *An American Tragedy* and Lewisohn's novel, is unsophisticated in lacking "that state of mind which prevents a mature man from explaining things every intelligent person should know," and its consequent fascination with adolescent or preadolescent disillusionment, and calls for "a new attitude" transcending knowledge of elemental social facts by using them, synthesizing them, and giving them a meaning.

D202. "Vulgarity Ascendant, Jealousy's Thrall, M. de Charlus's Anomaly Occupy Proust in This Section." [Review of Marcel Proust, *Cities of the Plain*, translated by C. K. Scott Moncrieff (New York: A. and C. Boni, 1927).] *New York Evening Post*, 21 January 1928, section 3, p. 14.

Notes the direct, gossipy appeal of Proust's characters and incidents, which makes his novel approximate a memoir. Emphasizes the basis of Proust's melancholy in his minatory attitude toward homosexuality--a surprising exception to his general "ethical indifference"--and the arrival of his narrator at maturity. Ascribes Proust's focus on "technical" rather than moral heroism to the strength of society, which makes Proust's heroes "fight against society itself."

Reprinted as "Cities of the Plain" in A15.

D203. "Our Colonial Forefathers." [Review of Hannah R. London, *Portraits of Jews by Gilbert Stuart and Other Early American Artists*, with an Appreciation by Dr. A. S. W. Rosenbach and an Introduction by Lawrence Park (New

York: Rudge, 1927).] *Menorah Journal* 14 (February 1928): 217-20.

Praises the thoroughness and usefulness of London's research, but remarks that her commentaries tend to rely on the abstraction of "the Absolute Jew." Points out that the omission of any information about Gentiles and any Gentile perspectives on the artistocratic subjects of the illustrated paintings have allowed the subjects to achieve "what all Jews (and all people) seek to achieve, and the thing that has departed is the Jewishness of each."

D204. "Dear Old Tom, an Artist." [Review of Roger Burlingame, *High Thursday* (New York: Scribner's, 1928).] *New York Evening Post*, 4 February 1928, section 3, p. 13.

Deplores the revival of "the very type of what the sofa-reader supposes the artist to be" in Burlingame's sentimental portrait of an untutored genius.

D205. "Brilliancy--Or a Barbarian?" [Review of Philip Guedalla, *Conquistador* (New York: Harper, 1928).] *New York Evening Post*, 18 February 1928, section 3, p. 10.

Compares Guedalla's arch dismissal of America in his travel memoirs to Twain's philistine resistance to European culture, concluding that Americans have themselves anticipated his criticisms while avoiding the manner of "a sophomore's letters home."

D206. "Buy My English Whimsies." [Review of Sandys Wason, *Palafox* (London: Cope & Fenwick, 1927).] *New York Evening Post*, 18 February 1928, section 3, p. 10.

Dismisses the novel's arch-English absurdities as "chiefly silly and almost always dull" despite the promise of its chief invention: "a machine that allows the holder to read thoughts."

D207. "Smoking Browning's Traits Out of His Parleyings." [Review of William Clyde DeVane, Jr., *Browning's Parleyings: An Autobiography of a Mind* (New Haven: Yale University Press, 1927).] *New York Evening Post*, 17 March 1928, section 3, p. 12.

Welcomes DeVane's doctoral thesis, which sets Browning's "proud, arrogant and self-deceiving" self-portrait in his *Parleyings* alongside the events of his life, leaving readers to draw their own conclusions about the poet, as heralding a movement away from the current tendency of biographers to freeze their subjects in a "finality of generalization."

D208. "Clinch Calkins's Religious Lyrics: An Appreciation." [Review of Clinch Calkins, *Poems* (New York: Knopf, 1928).] *New York Evening Post*, 24 March 1928, section 3, p. 12.

Observes that religious poems, which cannot be judged by the standards of truth, value, or accuracy, are either "wholly successful or wholly nonsensical," and commends Calkins's directness in choosing and dramatizing unfashionably religious material.

D209. "A Perfectly Nice Girl." [Review of V. Sackville-West, *Aphra Behn: The Incomparable Astraea* (New York: Viking, 1928).] *New York Evening Post*, 14 April 1928, section 3, p. 14.

Regrets that Sackville-West's whitewashing apologetic has "destroyed the Aphra Behn legend," and wonders facetiously "where Modern Thought is going to stop in its cynical unbelief" in all ideals, even that of bawdiness.

D210. "Four Volumes of 'Saki's' Stories, Neat and Witty." [Review of H. H. Munro, *The Works of "Saki": I. The Chronicles of Clovis; II. The Unbearable Bassington; III.*

The Toys of Peace; IV. Beasts and Super-Beasts (New York: Viking, 1928).] *New York Evening Post*, 5 May 1928, section 3, p. 8.

Ascribes Saki's "grimness" to his exact and limited grasp of neat and illuminating juxtapositions, especially in his comic stories. Compares *The Unbearable Bassington* to Wharton's "slower and fuller and yet less successful" *House of Mirth*, and suggests that only the "solemn savagery of Balzac" might have made the hero's struggle with poverty tragic.

D211. "Early and Recent Stories by Thomas Mann." [Review of Thomas Mann, *Children and Fools* (New York: Knopf, 1928).] *New York Evening Post*, 19 May 1928, section 3, p. 8.

Notes Mann's uncommon sureness in handling "emotional values" even in his earliest stories, singling out the unusual "tenderness" of the recent "Disorder and Early Sorrow" for special praise.

D212. "Common Sense on Hardy." [Review of Samuel C. Chew, *Thomas Hardy, Poet and Novelist* (New York: Knopf, 1928).] *New York Evening Post*, 26 May 1928, section 3, p. 8.

Affirms the modest achievement of Chew's exposition of Hardy's ideas, congratulating him for not rephrasing Hardy's own explicit revelations about himself. Contends that only two more books on Hardy--a full-scale biography and "a hard, critical, philosophical and social attack"--are likely to be useful.

D213. "Mr. Untermeyer As Poet." [Review of Louis Untermeyer, *Burning Bush* (New York: Harcourt, Brace, 1928).] *Menorah Journal* 14 (June 1928): 604-8.

Dismisses Untermeyer's claims as either an American or a Jewish poet on the grounds of his pretentiousness, his "unimportant conclusions about foregone matter," his straining after verbal effects, his inability to observe closely, and his lack of faith in the reality of the objects and experiences he describes, a lack of faith that leads him to importing meaning to objects instead of discovering it within them.

D214. "Whether to Laugh." [Review of David Pinski, *Arnold Levenberg, Man of Peace*, translated by Isaac Goldberg (New York: Simon and Schuster, 1928).] *Menorah Journal* 15 (September 1928): 290-92.

Ridicules, largely through extended plot summary, the "feebleness" and "puerility" of Pinski's war novel and "the author's ignorance of the simplest social and emotional habits."

D215. "Thackeray as a Commonplace Clubman With a Talent, Whom One More Biographer Dandles." [Review of Lewis Melville, *Thackeray* (Garden City: Doubleday, Doran, 1928).] *New York Evening Post*, 1 September 1928, section 3, p. 5.

Criticizes the attempts of Melville and other biographers to make the character and personal life of Thackeray more interesting than they actually were, suggesting that they focus instead on the surprising "superimposition of ability upon a London clubman" that makes his books so much more interesting than he is.

D216. "Wyndham Lewis, in a Prodigious Novel, Carries His War on Time-Mindedness Into the Next World." [Review of Wyndham Lewis, *The Childermass, Section I* (New York: Covici, Friede, 1928).] *New York Evening Post*, 22 September 1928, section 3, p. 4.

Describes the novel as a fictional adjunct to Lewis's attack on "the modern preposession with time, flux, and relativity" in *Time and Western Man*. Summarizes the eschatological plot at length, predicting that Lewis's vitriolic anger will restrict his influence, rendering him a faddish "symptom of modern malaise."

D217. "Short Stories by Glenway Wescott." [Review of Glenway Wescott, *Good-bye, Wisconsin* (New York: Harper, 1928).] *New York Evening Post*, 29 September 1928, section 3, p. 9.

Observes the domination of Wescott's vast, mild, neutral midwestern landscape over his human figures, contrasting his refusal to encourage identifications with his principals with Sherwood Anderson's dependence on such identifications. Considers the volume a modest success, but hopes that Wescott will outgrow his graceful minimalism.

D218. "A Gobineau Novel of Rare Vintage." [Review of Count Arthur de Gobineau, *Pleîads* (New York: Knopf, 1928).] *New York Evening Post*, 27 October 1928, section 3, p. 9.

Contrasts Gobineau's prescient maturity and prudence in dealing with "modern confusion" sixty years earlier with Wyndham Lewis's current rage over similar problems. Endorses Gobineau's modernist ideal of lonely self-cultivation, contrasting his stoicism in making this recommendation with Arnold's and Nietzsche's sentimentality and self-pity.

D219. "Burning Doorbells." [Review of Paul Rosenfeld, *The Boy in the Sun* (New York: Macaulay, 1928).] *Menorah Journal* 15 (November 1928): 483-86.

Notes the increasingly formulaic nature of the *Bildungsroman* since *Wilhelm Meister* and its adoption by modern writers retreating from adult realities: "The novel of adolescence affords the luxury of the whimper." Criticizes Rosenfeld's reliance on musical devices and his extravagant language (e.g., "shortly the doorbell burned"), and concludes that "Rosenfeld, while always writing authoritatively, sometimes beautifully, does not consider English a sufficient language for him." Defends this stricture, although it seems to be "denying the process of poetry," with the argument that "to say a simple thing by a precious and fantastic use of words probably indicates the unclear perception of even a simple thing."

D220. "Mrs. Peterkin Tells Story of Scarlet Sister." [Review of Julia Peterkin, *Scarlet Sister Mary* (Indianapolis: Bobbs-Merrill, 1928).] *New York Evening Post*, 3 November 1928, section 3, p. 8.

Ascribes the "crisp, limited beauty" of Peterkin's novel less to its story or its rather abstract principals than to the "engaging directness" with which it treats its African-American characters and their community, foregoing condescension, exoticism, or "hysterical resentment of injustice."

D221. "Virginia Woolf's Propaganda for Grace and Wit." [Review of Virginia Woolf, *Orlando* (New York: Harcourt, Brace, 1928).] *New York Evening Post*, 10 November 1928, section 3, p. 8.

Suggests that Woolf's "*jeu d'esprit*," like all such singular works, disarms analytical criticism. Wonders whether the book is intended "as the spiritual autobiography, abstracted and formalized, of all talented women," or whether, as "the story not of Orlando but of his poem," it is "an allegory of the artist and his necessary bisexuality." Concludes that Woolf is writing "propaganda for a point of view and for a way of feeling."

D222. "Neo-Irreverent Style Pervades Life of Arnold." [Review of Hugh Kingsmill, *Matthew Arnold* (New York: Dial, 1928).] *New York Evening Post*, 10 November 1928, section 3, p. 10.

Describes Kingsmill's breezy tone as a reaction against recent attempts to temper the irreverence of earlier Victorian studies, severely criticizes his determination to reconstruct a historical Marguerite entirely from evidence in Arnold's poems, and calls his criticism of Arnold's ideas "personal and gossipy."

D223. "Five Significant Works on Problems of Aesthetics." [Review of five volumes in the series *An Outline of Aesthetics*, edited with introductory notes by Philip N. Youtz (New York: Norton, 1928): Irwin Edman, *The World, The Arts, and the Artist*; Henry Wells, *The Judgment of Literature*; M. Cecil Allen, *The Mirror of the Passing World*; Henry Ladd, *With Eyes of the Past*; and Thomas Munro, *Scientific Method in Aesthetics*.] *New York Evening Post*, 24 November 1928, section 3, p. 8.

Emphasizes the miscellaneous and eclectic nature of the volumes in the series, observing that neither a common method or approach nor Youtz's general introductions make them coherent with each other. Takes particular exception to Wells's dictum that modesty and silence are the cardinal virtues of the critic, calling it sentimental and ultimately paralyzing. Expresses polite skepticism toward Munro's attempt to put aesthetics on a scientific basis.

D224. "Amiel Reappears Sadly." [Review of Henri Frédéric Amiel, *Amiel's Journal*, translated by Mrs. Humphry Ward (New York: Brentano's, 1928).] *New York Evening Post*, 15 December 1928, section 3, p. 8.

Describes the reprinting of Mrs. Ward's translation, based on Mlle. Mercier's moralistic selection from the journals, as a wasteful anachronism superseded in 1923 by Bouvier's fuller selection, which gave a fresher, more comprehensive picture of the author.

D225. "The Lyric Genius of 17th Century." [Review of Norman Ault, *Seventeenth-Century Lyrics* (New York: Longmans, Green, 1928); and A. C. Judson, *Seventeenth-Century Lyrics* (Chicago: University of Chicago Press, 1927).] *New York Evening Post*, 15 December 1928, section 3, p. 10.

Praises Judson's selection as a college textbook though quarreling with its inclusion of five times as many poems by Herrick as by Donne. Noting the frequent appearance of striking lines in otherwise mediocre poems of the period, commends Ault for reprinting so many such poems drawn from such a wide variety of sources.

D226. "Heroic and Respectable Both, This Man Dickens." [Review of John Forster, *The Life of Charles Dickens*, edited and annotated with an introduction by J. W. T. Ley (Garden City: Doubleday, Doran, 1928); Ralph Straus, *Charles Dickens: A Biography from New Sources* (New York: Cosmopolitan, 1928); and Myron Brightfield, *Theodore Hook* (Cambridge: Harvard University Press, 1928).] *New York Evening Post*, 22 December 1928, section 3, p. 8.

Emphasizes the contradiction of Dickens's respectability, celebrated in Forster's biography, and his heroism, which appeals more to modern biographers. Remarks approvingly that recent criticism of Dickens has "smothered the social philosopher and the dictator of absurd morals and humid emotionalities and have set up the unmoral Rabelaisian lover of life and gusto." Notes the roots of Dickens's early farcical portraiture in the figures of his contemporary Hook.

D227. "Obsession." [Review of L. Steni, *Prelude to a Rope for Myer* (New York: Dial, 1928).] *Menorah Journal* 16 (January 1929): 84-85.

Observes that Steni's novel about a young man's obsessive and fatal romance, despite its length, has rather "a lyric singleness of mood and a linear direction proper to a good short story." Despite criticisms of the novel's "theoretical and clinical tone," commends Steni's associative, Proustian method of description, contrasting it to the synaesthesia and hyperbole of Untermeyer and Rosenfeld (see D213 and D219).

D228. "Beddoes' Genius Never Matured." [Review of Royall H. Snow, *Thomas Lovell Beddoes, Eccentric and Poet* (New York: Covici, Friede, 1928).] *New York Evening Post*, 5 January 1929, section 3, p. 8.

Notes the deeply conflicting influences on Beddoes--his eccentic scientist father and his friend Coleridge, the rational optimist Richard Lovell Edgeworth, Charles Maturin's Gothic tales--and ascribes his deepening pessimism and suicide to "his temperament and training" as well as his medieval and philosophical studies and his unsuccessful political career. Calls Beddoes even more poignant a symbol than Keats and Shelley "of the first contacts of the purely poetic soul with modernity."

D229. Spinoza's Lure for Moderns Explained in McKeon's Study." [Review of Richard McKeon, *The Philosophy of Spinoza* (New York: Longmans, Green, 1928).] *New York Evening Post*, 9 February 1929, section 3, p. 9.

Identifies Spinoza's attraction to modern thinkers as his courage in proclaiming "an ultimate absolute" beyond the quotidian pragmatism of contemporary philosophy, and describes his absolute of faith beyond wisdom as demanding an "intellect terribly at battle" with its own comfort.

D230. "Richardson is a Dull Man." [Review of Brian W. Downs, *Samuel Richardson* (New York: Dutton, 1928).] *New York Evening Post*, 16 February 1929, section 3, p. 11.

Calls Richardson a great novelist despite his personal dullness and his pietistic "debauchery of the mind of Europe" because of his "faculty of picturing the soul in flight" and his insight into the divided mind--a "Dostoevskian" insight not further developed for a hundred fifty years after him.

D231. "Robert Browning Seen as Uxorious Husband." [Review of David Loth, *The Brownings: A Victorian Idyll* (New York: Brentano's, 1929).] *New York Evening Post*, 23 February 1929, section 3, p. 11.

Deplores Loth's exclusive emphasis on the "externalities" of Browning's life as a concesssion to a defective popular taste, and criticizes him for ignoring Browning's poetry in his portrait of the author as merely "a playboy of respectability."

D232. "Robinson's 'Buck Fever' Has Masefieldian Bravado." [Review of Henry Morton Robinson, *Buck Fever* (New York: Duffield, 1929).] *New York Evening Post*, 2 March 1929, section 3, p. 11.

Disapprovingly recalls Robinson's earlier attempt in *Children of Morningside* "to sentimentalize one of the most admirably unsentimental schools in the world," and notes that his sentimentality undermines the stories and, even more fatally, the poems in this volume--"when Mr. Robinson writes about Beauty he seems to be turning out very attractive advertising copy for the commodity"--except when he deals with "the visual and the objective."

D233. "Stendhal Built Monument to a Bored Maiden." [Review of Stendhal, *Lamiel*, translated with a Preface by Jacques Le Clerq (New York: Brentano's, 1929).] *New York Evening Post*, 16 March 1929, section 3, p. 10.

Defends Stendhal's extravagance in dramatizing the career of his bored heroine, which makes his supporting figures callous and stupid in order to justify the "flame, death and desperation" of his stories, as the only alternative to explaining boredom by means of boredom.

D234. "Another Jewish Problem Novel." [Review of Milton Waldman, *The Disinherited* (New York: Longmans, Green, 1929).] *Menorah Journal* 16 (April 1929): 376-79.

Discusses the leading motif of novels of Jewish spirituality--"that the hero *comes* to Judaism"--as parallel to the romantic theme of the scullion whose birthmark reveals him as a prince, and argues that "though a Jew's coming to Judaism is perhaps just as dramatic as a mystical Christian conversion, it is certainly an experience more related to normal life" which therefore calls for more circumstantial and less hagiographic treatment. Calls for a novel in which "the Jewish problem is included in a rich sweep of life . . . to which the problem of Jewishness adds further import and moment."

Reprinted in A15.

D235. "Stendhal Made Valiant War on Vulgar Boredom." [Review of Paul Hazard, *Stendhal*, translated by Eleanor Hard (New York: Coward, McCann, 1929).] *New York Evening Post*, 20 April 1929, section 3, p. 11.

Describes Stendhal as a progenitor of modernism in his determined opposition to vulgarity--"the functioning of the individual as though he embodied all the characteristics of the mob"--through the identification of life with youth and love. Suggests that the spiritual impotence of Stendhal's heroes required "the arousing lash of violent deed" in the absence of the maturity and insight that would fortify them against vulgarity.

D236. All the Critics Find Swinburne Confusing Poet." Review of Samuel C. Chew, *Swinburne* (Boston: Little, Brown, 1929).] *New York Evening Post*, 18 May 1929, section 3, p. 8.

Ascribes commentators' widespread difficulty in dealing with Swinburne to the deficiency of his life in incident and the resulting insularity of his poetic process, which depends to an unusual extent on the verse of earlier poets as Swinburne's chosen "common speech."

D237. "A Tough Hero Is a Little Soft." [Review of Joseph Auslander, *Hell in Harness* (Garden City: Doubleday, Doran, 1929).] *New York Evening Post*, 21 September 1929, section 3, p. 7.

Criticizes Auslander's presentation of his lower-class hero as maudlin and sentimentalized, lacking the objectivity that prevents Hemingway's heroes from sharing his status as a "low-life Sidney Carton."

D238. "Despair Apotheosized." [Review of Gertrude Diamant, *Labyrinth* (New York: Coward-McCann, 1929).] *Menorah Journal* 17 (October 1929): 91-94.

Traces the identification of despair as a keynote of the nineteenth and twentieth centuries to "the creation of the crowd" which in turn created "the individual as he stood in contradistinction to, in fear of, in defense against the crowd." Notes the return of despair as "the dominating matter" in Joyce and Eliot, but criticizes the evocation of despair in Diamant's novel as enthusiastic, admiring, and self-justifying, contrasting it with the work of the Victorians, who "had muscles and the willingness to live."

D239. "A Too Simple Simplicity." [Review of Robert Nathan, *There Is Another Heaven* (Indianapolis: Bobbs-Merrill, 1929).] *Menorah Journal* 17 (December 1929): 292-94.

Finds Nathan bereft of most of those qualities--"sophistication, wit, 'spiritual dexterity,'" and expressive silence--popularly imputed to him; although he has "'spiritual refinement'--a reverence for life and its beauty, an ardor for gentleness, passion and love," he writes "in terms so simple, even so banal, that one turns away from them in impatience," relegating his fiction to "a charity box for the education of the simpler folk of the community--bishops, for example, or clubwomen to learn from it, and liberal editors to admire it."

**** "Tragedy and Three Novels." [Review of Ernest Hemingway, *A Farewell to Arms* (New York: Scribner's, 1929); Edward Dahlberg, *Bottom Dogs*, with an introduction by D. H. Lawrence (New York: Simon & Schuster, 1930); and William Faulkner, *The Sound and the Fury* (New York: Jonathan Cape and Harrison Smith, 1929). *Symposium* 1 (January 1930): 106-14. See C59.

D240. "The Necessary Morals of Art." [Review of Jean-Richard Bloch, --- *and Co.*, translated by C. K. Scott-Moncrieff (New York: Simon and Schuster, 1929).] *Menorah Journal* 18 (February 1930): 182-86.

Judges contemporary American fiction as wanting in the morality characteristic of Mann, Lawrence, and lesser writers like Bloch--"the admission that life is immediate to man . . . and that it merits and commands his best thought" rather than being reduced to a series of local problems. Contends that "no one writing novels of Jews in America has been even able to see them clearly" because American authors persist in isolating national, economic, and spiritual determinants instead of analyzing their interrelations.

D241. "Stendhal Strove for Technique of Egoistic Life." [Review of Rudolf Kayser, *Stendhal or the Life of an Egoist* (New York: Henry Holt, 1930).] *New York Evening Post*, 1 March 1930, section 3, p. 6.

Commends Kayser's "noble and important" portrait of Stendhal, vivid and compelling despite the limits of his genre of novelized biography, but notes with regret the absence of "the old apparatus" of biographical scholarship that "would have added weight and reality" to the figure.

D242. "Publisher's Classic." [Review of Manuel Komroff, *Coronet*, two volumes (New York: Coward McCann, 1929).] *Menorah Journal* 18 (March 1930): 282-85.

Condemns the overscaling of Komroff's ambitious novel, which bloats and falsifies his own intentions, and the American obsession with "size and pretension," which requires big ideas "to fill the head," since "one big idea does the work quicker than a lot of little ideas." Suggests that Americans define literature as "fiction with a big idea."

D243. "Kallen Views Aesthetics as a Pragmatist." [Review of Horace M. Kallen, *Indecency and the Seven Arts, and Other Adventures of a Pragmatist in Aesthetics* (New York: Liveright, 1930).] *New York Evening Post*, 19 April 1930, section 3, p. 10.

Praises Kallen's attempts at pragmatic "detachment from the combative ruck of artistic sects and from the fruitless convolution of aesthetic dogma," but finds his work, except for a concluding essay on tragedy, undermined by a commonplace intelligence and an "inflated, garrulous and unsuccessfully jocular" style which would benefit from Kallen's closer attention to his own strictures in "Style and Meaning."

D244. "Flawed Instruments." [Review of Ludwig Lewisohn, *Adam: A Dramatic History in a Prologue, Seven Scenes, and an Epilogue* (New York: Harper, 1929), and *Stephen Escott* (New York: Harper, 1930).] *Menorah Journal* 18 (April 1930): 380-84.

Defines "the real objection to the use of art for specific moral teaching" as the fact that "the art is likely to falsify the morality," and notes that in Lewisohn's moralistic fiction, "his insufficiencies as a novelist are constantly invalidating his strength as a moralist," since "Mr. Lewisohn's preaching, based on truth though it be, is washed out and made dim by a work that deals not only with truth but with people."

Reprinted in A15.

D245. "Mr. Lewisohn Reiterates." [Review of Ludwig Lewisohn, *Adam: A Dramatic History in a Prologue, Seven Scenes, and an Epilogue* (New York: Harper, 1929).] *New Republic* 62 (9 April 1930): 226.

Observes that although Lewisohn's characteristic theme--"it is impossible for a Jew to function as a man in modern society unless he affirms his Jewishness"--has "deep truth and importance," Lewisohn is content to reiterate this idea without giving it "significant positive development."

D246. "An Old Dirge Newly Sung." [Review of D. H. Lawrence, *Pansies* (New York: Knopf, 1929).] *New Freeman* 1 (17 May 1930): 234-35.

Acknowledges that Lawrence's poetry lacks the "force and finality" of his prose but defends his last volume of poems, however frequently "flat and downright," as "a fascinating book, as a record of a strange and great soul" whose keynote throughout is too "wearied by disgust" for a conventionally elegiac tone: "People are fraudulent and without dignity; empty of passion and full of hunger. They have no touch with the world and no peace. Individuality has died; gaiety has died; joy has died."

D247. "Wycherley." [Review of Willard Connely, *Brawny Wycherley* (New York: Scribner's, 1930).] *New Republic* 63 (28 May 1930): 52.

Commends Connely's study as "admirably in the older fashion" of eschewing the kind of psychological conjecture that unwisely attempts to pierce its subject's reserve.

D248. "The Promise of Realism." [Review of Edward Dahlberg, *Bottom Dogs*, with an Introduction by D. H. Lawrence (New York: Simon and Schuster, 1930); Nathan Asch, *Pay Day* (New York: Brewer and Warren, 1930); and Meyer Levin, *Frankie and Johnnie* (New York: John Day, 1930).] *Menorah Journal* 18 (May 1930): 480-84.

Analyzes the reasons that contemporary American fiction has assumed a dominantly realistic mode. Distinguishes between Levin's "sentimental" realism, which assumes, with Anderson and Dreiser, that "there was something divine about America" even if it destroyed its people, and the newer, more radical mode of Dahlberg and Asch, which contends that "the only way to be close to America is to hate it; it is the only way to love America. . . . For at the bottom of America there is insanity." Argues that although Dahlberg's and Asch's novels have been dismissed as "sociological studies," virtually everyone in their audience is, like their heroes, "in an asympathy of disgust and hate with his fellows." Concludes that "America must . . . be committed to realism for a long time yet," and predicts that the next great American novelist "will not abandon realism. He will be above the tendency, but he will be rooted deep in it."

Reprinted in A15.

D249. "A Transcendental Prude." [Review of Henri Frédéric Amiel, *Philine: From the Unpublished Journals*, translated by Van Wyck Brooks, with an Introduction by Edmond Jaloux (Boston: Houghton Mifflin, 1930).] *Nation* 130 (11 June 1930): 682-84.

Describes Amiel as "the very symbol of the sick will" analyzed or dramatized by Stendhal, Arnold, Turgenev, de

Vigny, Eliot, and Hemingway--a malady "called, variously, spleen and Weltschmerz; Wertherism, Faustism, Hamletism," the emotionally intuitive sense that "between the soul of man and the uses of this world there is a necessary and rigid divorce." Sees in the prudish Amiel's atypical sexual fascination with an importunate woman, documented in these journals, "not a new Amiel . . . but merely an Amiel whose sick will is turned from the cosmic and eternal to the mundane and diurnal."

D250. "The Social Emotions." [Review of A. Fadayev, *The Nineteen* (New York: International Publishers, 1929).] *New Freeman* 1 (16 July 1930): 429.

Praises Fadayev's novel of revolutionary Russia for "rehabilitating social love and loyalty," remarking that "one almost distrusts" the purity and virtue of his characters, contrasted with Babel's figures in *Red Cavalry* and "the American masses." Notes that in Fadayev's novel, the ideals of communism release the heroes' individuality instead of dehumanizing or "standardizing" them.

Reprinted in A15.

D251. "Fighting It Over." [Review of Private No. 19022, *Her Privates We* (New York: Putnam's, 1930); Charles Yale Harrison, *Generals Die in Bed* (New York: Morrow, 1930); Ex-Private X, *War Is War* (New York: Dutton, 1930); Richard Blaker, *Medal Without Bar* (New York: Doubleday, Doran, 1930); and C. R. Benstead, *Retreat* (New York: Century, 1930).] *New Republic* 63 (23 July 1930): 296.

Asserts that "the novel is the only medium through which the truth about war can be told," since films compromise unpleasant truths in order to satisfy public taste, and dramatic treatments "implicitly glorify war" by steeping it in "the tragic glamor." Observes that although most war novels are "negligible, even detestable," the novel has the advantages of an unlimited canvas and direct access to its characters' minds.

D252. "Genuine Writing." [Review of Charles Reznikoff, *By the Waters of Manhattan* (New York: Charles Boni/Paper Books).] *Menorah Journal* 19 (October 1930): 88-92.

Salutes Reznikoff's novel as "the first story of the Jewish immigrant that is not false," arguing that it escapes the convention of recent American fiction that "good prose" is limited to fantastic or romantic subjects, as in Cabell, Wilder, and Nathan, whereas "anything that touches on the natural bases of life [as in Lewis, Dreiser, or Sinclair] must be written of in crude ('stark') or melodramatic prose." Commends Reznikoff's avoidance of a conventionally "dramatic" style which sentimentalizes pain and deprivation by making them seem "glamorous and even good."

D253. [Review of Matthew Josephson, *Portrait of the Artist as American* (New York: Harcourt, Brace, 1930).] *Symposium* 1 (October 1930): 558-61.

Disputes Josephson's contention that "ruthless mechanical enterprise," intensifying the "ruthless personal enterprise" of the Gilded Age, has created an "unfeeling order" blighting contemporary American art, ruling that literature "is not an aspect of life, but an instrument of life" dedicated to "discovering and judging values," good or bad. Suggests that modern European novels, discovering "a harmony of discord" with society, have become more "philosophical," and that the American novel falls short of their standard not because its milieu is hostile to art but because "it resists its milieu much too successfully--resists it by evading it or looking at it with a careful half-an-eye."

Reprinted as "The Problem of the American Artist" in A15.

D254. "The Latest Matriarch." [Review of G. B. Stern, *Mosaic* (New York: Knopf, 1930).] *Menorah Journal* 19 (November-December 1930): 206-8.

Acknowledges "the charm and worth of the bright, unhaunted mind" another critic attributes to Stern but doubts that "our age can produce or accommodate" such a mind: "When once 'real life' is evoked as an aid to illusion, then the unhaunted mind becomes inadequate, even insulting." Criticizes the trilogy concluded by *Mosaic* as reducing a broad span of experience "to the terms of Viennese operetta." Traces Stern's reductiveness to the prevailing assumption that "there must be a distinct feminine manner in literature," arguing that "Fielding, the most manly of the English novelists, never makes a male assertion as a writer," and that Austen, Eliot, Charlotte and Emily Brontë "were all content to practice writing free of the accidents of sex."

D255. "Lawrence's Last 'Novel.'" [Review of D. H. Lawrence, *The Virgin and the Gypsy* (New York: Knopf, 1930).] *Nation* 131 (24 December 1930): 710-11.

Observes that Lawrence's later work shows an increasing tendency away from "Meredithian" lambency and toward simplicity; criticizes the near-parodistic spareness with which Lawrence presents still another sexual awakening of a woman by a "darker" man; and notes in mitigation that the novel is very short, unrevised by its author, and perhaps incomplete even in its story, which bears marks of inconclusiveness.

D256. "Art and Justice." [Review of Lion Feuchtwanger, *Success*, translated by Willa and Edwin Muir (New York: Viking, 1930).] *Menorah Journal* 19 (June 1931): 470-72.

Notes that novels about legal injustice as a barometer of "modern society and the modern state" are now fashionable in Germany, and that authors like Feuchtwanger espouse "propaganda in the cause of political decency" as one of their primary functions. Argues that the contrary attitude--"that literature is a solace, an escape, a high amusement, et cetera"--has made contemporary literature "widely scorned" and "ineffectual," and that, in the face of widespread aesthetic and political hostility toward socially signficant art, every writer has a responsibility "to use the language of the market-place and scrabble there like any realtor for his right to exist."

D257. "Modern Palestine in Fiction." [Review of Meyer Levin, *Yehuda* (New York: Jonathan Cape and Harrison Smith, 1931).] *Nation* 132 (24 June 1931): 684.

Notes that despite the title stressing its violinist hero's individual dilemma, Levin's novel is really about the Palestinian commune in which he lives and works. Argues that only Russia and Palestine are based on political ideologies which emphasize "the conception of society and the individual in vital relationship to each other," allowing their writers to deal with "the social emotions"--glory, loyalty, political honor--which are especially moribund in modern America, and renewing the importance of private emotions whose value derives from the group.

D258. "Mr. Faulkner's World." [Review of William Faulkner, *These Thirteen* (New York: Jonathan Cape and Harrison Smith, 1931).] *Nation* 133 (4 December 1931): 491-92.

Contends that the implications of Faulkner's work are frequently minor not because it depends on an esoteric and self-enclosed world but because its social ideology of self-isolated aristocracy precludes contact with the larger world of common experience. Concludes that Faulkner's strongest work--*The Sound and the Fury*, *As I Lay Dying*, "Dry September," and "Victory"--breaks away from this ideology by exploring the symbols of physical experience.

D259. "Two Novelized Biographies." [Review of Ernst Penzoldt, *The Marvelous Boy*, translated by John J. Trounstine and Eleanor Woolf (New York: Harcourt, Brace, 1931); and George O'Neil, *Special Hunger: The Tragedy of Keats* (New York: Liveright, 1931).] *Nation* 134 (6 January 1932): 24.

Excoriates the "complacent mediocrity" of the novelized biography, "now as established an industry as detective fiction," as represented by Penzoldt's extravagant embroidering of Chatterton's life and O'Neil's dully servile account of Keats.

D260. "Sainte-Beuve." [Review of William Frederick Giese, *Sainte-Beuve: A Literary Portrait* (Madison: University of Wisconsin Studies, 1931).] *Nation* 134 (20 April 1932): 471-72.

Argues that Sainte-Beuve, despite his taste and penetration, has lost his influence because of his "anarchistic" resistance to systematic thought--"he thought brilliantly but in no direction"--and ascribes Arnold's continuing influence to his ability to turn his point of view into a system brought to bear on politics and religion as well as literature. Notes the advantages of such a system, however wrongheaded, for Eliot and contemporary Marxist critics.

D261. "Carlyle." [Review of Emery Neff, *Carlyle* (New York: Norton, 1932).] *Modern Quarterly* 6 (Summer 1932): 109-11.

Notes the contemporary relevance of Carlyle's anomalous position as a bourgeois intellectual in a proletarian movement and his "metamorphosis from radical to capitalist apologist," which Trilling attributes to "a preoccupation with religious values which kept Carlyle from looking realistically at events." Discusses Carlyle's transcendentalism as a bridge between his political radicalism, which it originally nourished, and "the firm old ground of Calvinism," whose virtues become under the pressure of imperialism "the capitalistic virtues."

Reprinted in A15.

D262. "Intellect or Religion?" [Review of Emile and Georges Romieu, *The Life of George Eliot*, translated by Brian W. Downs (New York: Dutton, 1932).] *New Republic* 72 (14 September 1932): 131-32.

Observes that Eliot's reputation remains low despite the fact that the argument advanced against her work--that "art must be aristocratically non-moral"--has itself been largely rejected, and concludes that Eliot's failure stems not from her theory of art but from her "provincial evangelism," which prevented her "from *seeing* people and things" except in relation to an enervating moralism.

D263. "The British Sixties." [Review of *The Eighteen-Sixties: Essays by Fellows of the Royal Society of Literature*, edited by John Drinkwater (New York: Macmillan, 1932).] *Nation* 135 (28 September 1932): 288.

Suggests that although erasing the sharp distinction maintained in America between "creative writer, critic, and scholar" is in theory desirable, the determination here to practice "polite letters" substitutes "easy camaraderie" with literary subjects for critical intelligence.

D264. "The Dispossessed." [Review of Heinz Liepmann, *Peace Broke Out*, translated by Emile Burns (New York: Harrison Smith, 1932), and Karl Aloys Schenzinger, *Fired*, translated by S. Guy Endore (New York: Century, 1932).] *New Republic* 72 (19 October 1932): 267-68.

Ascribes the failure of these two proletarian novels to their "refusal to discover the cause of their cataclysm" in political terms, and concludes that explicitly political doctrine may be aesthetically necessary to fiction, because "the spectacle of mass suffering set down without doctrine of cause or cure, degenerates into hysteria or stupidity."

D265. "Treachery--and Destiny." [Review of Lion Feuchtwanger, *Josephus*, translated by Willa and Edwin Muir (New York: Viking, 1932).] *Nation* 135 (7 December 1932): 570-71.

Characterizes Feuchtwanger's talent for representing "political emotions" as especially suiting him to the historical novel, and praises his fictionalized account of the Jewish historian, whose determinants, though developed in largely psychological terms, were historical rather than psychological.

D266. "Faculty Critic Maintains 'Review' Is Greatly Changed in Viewpoint." [Review of *Columbia Review*, November 1932.] *Columbia Spectator*, 9 December 1932, p. 4.

Compares the current issue of the *Columbia Review* to the 1924-25 issues of *Morningside*, concluding that the writing, though inferior, marks a telling change away from the futile attempt to use "the critical attitude" to expose stupidity, vulgarity, and Babbitry to the further-reaching attempt to grasp and change the "misery and hardship" pervading American society.

D267. "Swinburne and the Moderns." [Review of Georges Lafourcade, *Swinburne: A Literary Biography* (New York: Morrow, 1932).] *Nation* 135 (14 December 1932): 594.

Accepts as inevitable Lafourcade's revisionary portrait of "a less elfin and more weighty" Swinburne, but dismisses his reassessment of the poet as an important modern precursor of Gide, Proust, Lawrence, Joyce, and Huxley because of his recognition of "the cruel and perverse aspects of love," which appear only in minor or unrepresentative works whose grasp of evil is psychologically naive.

D268. [Unsigned review of E. F. Benson, *As We Are* (New York: Longmans, Green, 1932).] *Nation* 135 (14 December 1932): 596-97.

Remarks that Benson's "'parable' of the Buryan family . . . falls between the stools of generalization and concreteness" that would allow him to show the change in the English aristocracy since 1900: "It is not quite social history and not quite a novel."

D269. [Unsigned review of J. W. and Anne Tibble, *John Clare: A Life* (New York: Oxford University Press, 1932).] *New Republic* 73, (11 January 1933): 251.

Notes that despite the brevity of Clare's vogue, "he was a lyric poet of real genius and his life . . . is one of the saddest in the history of English literature."

D270. "Zweig's Tetralogy." [Review of Arnold Zweig, *Young Woman of 1914*, translated by Eric Sutton (New York: Viking, 1932).] *Nation* 136 (18 January 1933): 70-71.

Expresses disappointment that the latest installment of Zweig's war tetralogy falls so far in weight of conception below *The Case of Sergeant Grischa*, which is distinguished by "his strong intelligence playing over the confused aspects of a great theme, the problem of human justice."

D271. "Victorians and 'Moderns.'" [Review of *The Great Victorians: Forty Essays*, edited by H. J. Massingham and Hugh Massingham (Garden City: Doubleday, Doran, 1932).] *Nation* 136 (25 January 1933): 98.

Rejects the editors' claim that their volume shows one generation summing up another with the judgment that their contributors--Hugh Walpole, St. John Ervine, and Edmund Blunden among them--are the spiritual contemporaries, not the successors, of the Victorians, and that, for example, when Blunden discusses Arnold "from a poetic vacuum, and all of Arnold's political, religious, and even critical thought fades away, he is being considerably less modern than Arnold himself."

D272. "The Youth of Arnold." [Review of *The Letters of Matthew Arnold to Arthur Hugh Clough*, edited by Howard Foster Lowry (New York: Oxford University Press, 1932).] *Nation* 136 (22 February 1933): 211.

Describes the principal interest of Arnold's letters to Clough as "the personal changes in a man as he struggled to establish himself spiritually in the modern world" by changing from a dandyish, high-spirited undergraduate to a "centric" figure purged not only of intellectual idiosyncrasies but of "personality in our modern sense of the word as well"--an "abrogation" traced in his estrangement from Clough, "the symbol of Arnold's youth."

D273. [Unsigned review of *The Letters of Matthew Arnold to Arthur Hugh Clough*, edited by Howard Foster Lowry (New York: Oxford University Press, 1932).] *New Republic* 74, (15 March 1933): 139.

Briefly notes that the letters mark "the passage of Arnold from melancholy but ebullient youth to serene but weary maturity," recording "Arnold's obsessive fear of passing youth" and his counsels of serenity.

D274. "Why We Laugh." [Review of A. M. Ludovici, *The Secret of Laughter* (New York: Viking, 1932).] *Nation* 136 (15 March 1933): 293-94.

Contrasts Ludovici's comprehensive discussion of laughter as the expression of an actual or defensively desired "superior adaptation" based on Hobbes's notion of "sudden glory," with discussions limited to "explicitly 'funny' situations. Criticizes the link between laughter and animal snarling as oversimplified, but agrees in Ludovici's estimate of laughter as assuming "unprecedently exaggerated" importance in modern life as "the anodyne for a confused civilization (or class?) and a force for inaction or reaction."

D275. "A Clue to Hitlerism." [Unsigned review of Hans Fallada, *Little Man, What Now?*, translated by Eric Sutton (New York: Simon and Schuster, 1933); Lion Feuchtwanger, *Success*, translated by Willa and Edwin Muir (New York: Viking, 1930); Hans Liepmann, *Peace Broke Out*, translated by Emile Burns (New York: Harrison Smith, 1932); Josef Maria Frank, *Fever Heat: A Drama of Divided Germany*, translated by F. H. Lyon (London: Macmillan, 1932); Leonhard Frank, *The Singers* (New York: Henry Holt, 1933); Hans Marchwitza, *Storm over the Ruhr* (New York: International Publishers, 1932); Klaus Neukrantz, *Barricades in Berlin* (New York: International Publishers, 1932); Karl Aloys Schenzinger, *Fired*, translated by S. Guy Endore (New York: Century, 1932); and Hanns Heinz Ewers, *Riders of the Night*, translated by George Halasz (New York: John Day, 1932).] *New Republic* 74 (10 May 1933): 352-53.

Observes that recent events in Germany have made every current German novel, "in effect and often in intent, . . . a political work." Examines the preoccupation with the defeat of the German liberal center in Fallada, Feuchtwanger, Liepmann, Frank, and Frank, the "lack of dialectical insight" in Communist novels by Marchwitza and Neukrantz, and the "psychotic" triumph of the "knightly" forces of Nazism in the face of Communist attempts at rational persuasion in Schenzinger and Ewers.

D276. "Charlotte's Dream Empire." [Review of Charlotte Brontë, *Legends of Angria*, compiled by Fannie E. Ratchford, with the collaboration of William Clyde DeVane (New Haven: Yale University Press, 1933).] *Nation* 136 (31 May 1933): 619.

Recounts the circumstances under which the Brontës first invented the kingdom of Angria, whose legends are valuable because "from them springs half the greatness of Charlotte Brontë's mature work," in which their "complex and wild passions" are tempered by a "worldly realism" that appears in the latest of them.

D277. [Review of Walter Wilson, *Forced Labor in the United States* (New York: International Publishers, 1933).] *Modern Monthly* 7 (June 1933): 314-15.

Argues that capitalist definitions of "forced labor" are inadequate because they exclude the exploitations of capitalism itself. Notes that even under a capitalist definition, forced labor is deplorably pervasive in American prisons and in the sharecropping system. Finds Wilson's chapter contrasting the "smiling peasant face" of Russian labor insufficently "intimate and analytical."

D278. [Unsigned review of *Selected Poems of George Edward Woodberry* (Boston: Houghton Mifflin, 1933), and *Selected Letters of George Edward Woodberry*, edited by Walter De La Mare (Boston: Houghton Mifflin, 1933).] *Nation* 137 (5 July 1933): 25.

Calls Woodberry, despite his narrow influence, "brave" and "almost saintly" in his "elegiac," defeated response to "the new America."

D279. "Ruskin: A Career of Error." [Review of R. H. Wilenski, *John Ruskin: An Introduction to Further Study of His Life and Work* (New York: Stokes, 1933).] *Nation* 137 (25 October 1933): 488-89.

Agrees with Wilenski that Ruskin's work on every subject combines "liberating insight" with "insular prejudice," but argues that Ruskin's psychopathology probably produced as many insights as fallacies, and that his neurotic conflicts "not only made Ruskin mentally ill but also determined the content of his mind." Finds Ruskin's most enduring value not in individual insights Wilenski ascribes to the "true Ruskin," but in his success in placing "the whole of human activity in a great organic synthesis: art, science, religion, morality become in that synthesis integrally related to one another within the integrating social order."

D280. "Kultur in Eclipse?" [Review of Anonymous, *Germany--Twilight or New Dawn?* (New York: Whittlesey House, 1933).] *Brooklyn Eagle Sunday Review*, 19 November 1933, p. 17.

Dismisses the author's claim to objectivity in his naive and superficial "exculpation of some of the worst aspects of the Nazi philsophy" and such political manifestations as militarism, book-burning, imperialism against Austria, and persecution of the Jews.

D281. "A German and a Jew." [Review of Jacob Wasserman, *My Life as German and Jew*, translated by Salomea Neumark Brainin (New York: Coward-McCann, 1933).] *Brooklyn Eagle Sunday Review*, 26 November 1933, p. 19.

Condemns as inadequate to modern anti-Semitism Lewisohn's counsel of a return to Judaism's medieval heritage and Wasserman's equally mystical and atavistic attempt "to express the German soul" through his writing, which ignores the social and economic causes of anti-Semitism and the need for political opposition.

D282. "The Coleridge Letters." [Review of *Unpublished Letters of Samuel Taylor Coleridge*, edited by Earl Leslie Griggs (New Haven: Yale University Press, 1932).] *Nation* 137 (27 December 1933): 738-39.

Notes the links between Coleridge's "idealistic, absolutistic, and anti-materialistic philosophy" and modern fascism and ascribes his "religious [and social] authoritarianism" to "his neurotic inability to order his own life" in accord with his dual loyalty to poetry and philosophy: "It is as though Coleridge were declaring that the modern world needed . . . a setting in order before poetry could flourish" and accepting the eclipse of his poetic talent in the service of such an order.

Reprinted in A15.

D283. [Review of Martin Schütze, *Academic Illusions* (Chicago: University of Chicago Press, 1933).] *Modern Monthly* 7 (January 1934): 758-60.

Agrees with Schütze and I. A. Richards that literary study is impoverished when it is restricted to historical background and philosophical generalities, but points out that "although literature does not *discover* concepts or truths, it may *use* them," since concepts operate within individual personalities, facts of the writer's environment, and ethical decisions: "The person establishes his kind or quality by choosing among concepts." Praises Mann's insight in *Buddenbrooks* that "'total personality' responds within the iron limits of laws and necessities" which can be formulated, though not in absolute or a priori terms.

Reprinted as "The Autonomy of the Literary Work" in A15.

D284. "The Comic Genius of Dickens." [Review of Stephen Leacock, *Charles Dickens: His Life and Work* (Garden City: Doubleday, Doran, 1934).] *Nation* 138 (7 February 1934): 161.

Defines Dickens's essential genius as comic, especially in his ability to endow fictional grotesques with a "mythical" reality rather than creating mere ideological caricatures (as in *Hard Times*). Suggests that modern revolutionary novelists, evidently feeling "a necessary antagonism between ideas about people and the personality of people" and therefore impatient with "character drawing," would do well to borrow Dickens's force by imitating his creation of "real people and not mere social units and types."

D285. "Politics and the Liberal." [Review of E. M. Forster, *Goldsworthy Lowes Dickinson* (New York: Harcourt, Brace, 1934).] *Nation* 139 (4 July 1934): 24-25.

Defends Dickinson as an apt subject for biography because he is "representative of a temper of the human mind and the impasse which that temper has reached." Observes that Dickinson's avowed desire "to raise the [political] mind above the fighting attitude" depended on "the divorce it made between 'ideals' and 'passion and interests" and argues that "since no such divorce exists in politics," the effect of Dickinson's "liberal-humanitarian" attitude was "not to give the minds of this generation a higher function but to betray these minds into becoming the tools of the interests they truly hated."

Reprinted in A15.

D286. "Why Feuchtwanger Is Not First-Rate." [Review of Lion Feuchtwanger, *The Oppermanns* (New York: Viking, 1934).] *American Mercury* 34 (August 1934): 506-8.

Finds Feuchtwanger's novels inadequate in their grasp of history and "the social structure," a requirement forced on fiction by the press of postwar politics. Ascribes their "failure of historical logic" to Feuchtwanger's determined implication that the "liberal, educational intellect" will ultimately defeat the political threats he so accurately diagnoses as destroying his principals.

D287. "Gamaliel Bradford." [Review of *The Letters of Gamaliel Bradford, 1918 to 1931*, edited by Van Wyck Brooks

(Boston: Houghton Mifflin, 1934).] *Nation* 140 (2 January 1935): 24.

Characterizes Bradford's biographical essays as "sound journeyman work" limited in penetration by his sense of himself as "between two cultures" and the remoteness from contemporary America enforced by his invalidism, which led him to an uncritical enthusiasm for "the New America."

D288. "A Good Revolutionary Novel." [Review of Ignazio Silone, *Fontamara*, translated by Michael Wharf (New York: Harrison Smith and Robert Haas, 1934).] *American Mercury* 34 (February 1935): 250-52.

Suggests that Silone's emphasis on the revolutionary question "What must we do?" makes his novel more interesting as anthropology than as literature, and commends its insistence that "the revolutionary act grows out of the people and their suffering" rather than being imposed by an ideology or a political party.

D289. "Trilling Says Authors Show Talent in Review's New Writers' Number." [Review of *Columbia Review*, March 1935.] *Columbia Spectator*, 20 March 1935, pp. 1, 2.

Notes the freedom of the contributions to the current *Columbia Review* from the supposedly tyrannical "pressure of desperate world forces," and suggests that although "these men are interested in themselves and are not interested in society," their "canvassing of their own confusion . . . is an inventory of the instruments available to them" for dealing with social reality.

D290. "History of Heroism." [Review of William J. Calvert, *Byron: Romantic Paradox* (Chapel Hill: University of North Carolina Press, 1935).] *Nation* 141 (10 July 1935): 52-53.

Agrees with Calvert in locating the crux of Byron's heroic self-conflict in his defense of Pope's neo-classicism as the expression of common sense, an ideal presumably to be reached "by a curtailment and subordination of the mere individual's observation and feeling" which Byron felt as "the heavy burden of self." The conflict between heroic individualism and social integration enacted by his solitary heroes "has reference not to the personal will but to the social will in its European corruption."

D291. "Studs Lonigan's World." [Review of James T. Farrell, *Guillotine Party* (New York: Vanguard, 1935).] *Nation* 141 (23 October 1935): 484-85.

Finds Farrell's writing, despite its "importance," "inadequate" in Arnold's sense, since it neither conveys a sense of the principle underlying the chaos of life (as *Ulysses* does) nor presents characters whose free and ethical actions "affirm the qualities essential to decent human life" (as *Man's Fate* does); his social milieu is too simple, and his characters are conceived in terms of a society that "has robbed them of principles and free will."

D292. "Mr. O'Hara's Talent." [Review of John O'Hara, *Butterfield 8* (New York: Harcourt, Brace, 1935).] *Nation* 141 (6 November 1935): 545.

Notes the discrepancy between O'Hara's powers of social observation, both in its selection of social distinctions and its implications about the social determinants of those distinctions, and his refusal to think, which gives *Butterfield 8* "a burden of social thought about equivalent to that borne by Walter Winchell's column." Concludes that "a writer who sees as much as Mr. O'Hara sees must see more or mean nothing."

D293. "The Ambiguity of Feuchtwanger." [Review of Lion Feuchtwanger, *The Jew of Rome*, translated by Willa and

Edwin Muir (New York: Viking, 1936).] *Nation* 142 (8 January 1936): 52-53.

Praises Feuchtwanger's consistent grasp of the theme of social justice, exhibited again in this sequel to *Josephus* (see D265) but regrets the absence of "the apocalyptic vision of the great novelist." Cites the divided loyalties of Josephus to a Roman vision of a future world of justice and a Jewish "core of aspiration for a world order transcending nationalism," and suggests that the ambiguous gesture with which his hero resolves this division indicates Feuchtwanger's inability to commit himself to either a revolutionary or a tragic answer to the question of a just world order.

D294. "Trilling Notes 'Pleasant' Change in Reviewing Current Jester." [Review of *Columbia Jester*, January 1936.] *Columbia Spectator*, 13 January 1936, p. 2.

Recalls Trilling's long-standing belief that "the undergraduate of letters was on firmer ground as journalist, poet, fiction writer, than as humorist," but acknowledges that Columbia's humor magazine has developed "a strong relationship with the more serious intellectual life of the campus." Praises "the skill of Tom Merton's use of prose, which is far superior to his idea in 'The Chaste.'"

D295. "Nazi Novels." [Review of Hans Fallada, *Once We Had A Child*, translated by Eric Sutton (New York: Simon and Schuster, 1936); Max René Hesse, *Doctor Morath*, translated by Ernest Crankshaw (Boston: Houghton Mifflin, 1936); and Ernst Wiechert, *The Baroness*, translated by Phyllis and Trevor Blewitt (New York: Norton, 1936).] *New Republic* 86 (15 April 1936): 285.

Describes all three novels as devoid of literary interest but compelling "flotsam from a wrecked culture." Deplores Fallada's turn from his earlier lukewarm liberalism; Hesse's "objectivity" in erasing moral gradations--"The reader feels that he has experienced a complex adventure while drugged"--and Wiechert's best-selling, "'delicate' dream of piety, romanticized feudalism and irrationalism."

D296. "Prologue to 'Sergeant Grischa.'" [Review of Arnold Zweig, *Education Before Verdun*, translated by Eric Sutton (New York: Viking, 1936).] *Nation* 142 (13 May 1936): 617.

Criticizes this sequel to *Young Woman of 1914* (see D270) and prologue to *The Case of Sergeant Grischa* as "indecisive and confused" despite the promising central irony of its situation: Werner Bertin's invocation of the principles of abstract justice in defending the name of a young sergeant who accused his fellow-officers of depriving their men of the best rations, as against the call for personal justice by the sergeant's brother and the requirements of wartime. Concludes that Zweig's indictment of moral corruption is blunted by the hazy presentation of its spokespersons.

D297. "Motor and Metaphor." [Review of George Weller, *Clutch and Differential* (New York: Random House, 1936).] *Nation* 143 (14 November 1936): 583.

Describes the complex uses Weller's novelistic collage makes of the analogies between people and automobiles and concludes disapprovingly that, unlike Joyce and Dos Passos, who also make extensive use of symbolic patterns, Weller "relies on pattern to the total exclusion of continuing narrative."

D298. "A Critical Bookman." [Review of Van Wyck Brooks, *The Flowering of New England* (New York: Dutton, 1936).] *New York Teacher* 1 (December 1936): 25.

After calling Brooks's study "a masterpiece," criticizes its "occasionally dithyrambic style and impressionistic manner," its neglect of social, political, and economic problems, and his recreation despite his own intentions of New England as an idyllic cultural myth rather than a historical actuality.

D299. "Realism and the Old Order." [Review of I. J. Singer, *The Brothers Ashkenazi*, translated by Maurice Samuel (New York: Knopf, 1936).] *Jewish Frontier* 4 (January 1937): 21-22.

Observes that Singer is more successful as historian than novelist because he is less interested in his characters than in the historical events that animate them. Praises Singer's refusal to idealize ghetto life or to offer "any solution of the present in terms of the past"--a refusal "that has the laudable power to make some Jews unhappy about their favorite schemes of Jewish salvation."

D300. "An XVIII Century Proust." [Review of James Boswell, *Journal of a Tour to the Hebrides*, edited by Frederick A. Pottle and Charles H. Bennett (New York: Viking, 1936).] *New York Teacher* 1 (March 1937): 23.

Records Trilling's "capitulation to Boswell" as a descendant of Rousseau, James, and Proust, and a "cousin" of Leopold Bloom, and his continued resistance to Johnson as "in many ways a fraud" who "nevertheless had the qualities of a tragic myth." Notes that Johnson's and Boswell's tour of "the last home of real feudalism" leads them to "raise . . . all the questions of society and government," though no modern reader is likely to agree with any of their conclusions.

D301. "Off and On the Record." [Review of B. H. Haggin, *A Book of the Symphony* (New York: Oxford University Press, 1937).] *New Republic* 91 (13 May 1937): 27.

Reports that Trilling, who enjoys music but cannot read scores, has benefited from the mechanical device Haggin supplies with his book to coordinate his discussions with musical examples from a phonograph record, and approves Haggin's concentration on the "architectonics" of music to the exclusion of interpretations inclining toward "literature": "No Fate knocks on the door" in his analyses.

D302. "Earlier Work." [Review of Heinz Liepmann, *Nights of an Old Child,* translated by A. Lynton Hudson (Philadelphia: Lippincott, 1937).] *New Republic* 91 (9 June 1937): 137.

Calls this autobiographical memoir "even less perceptive" than *Peace Broke Out* (see D274), which it precedes: "This story of a childhood and youth made old by war, famine and chaos is so limited by self-pity that it is ineffective as anything but a private document."

D303. "Marxism in Limbo." [Review of Robert Briffault, *Europa in Limbo* (New York: Scribner's, 1937).] *Partisan Review* 4 (December 1937): 70-72.

Dismisses the supposed intelligence of Briffault's novel as "authoritarian nihilism" and his anger as "spleen," observing that his work has been highly praised despite its shortcomings because it is politically correct. Maintains that Briffault reduces "the motives of the Revolution and the chaos in Europe" to a question of sexual mores. Recommends instead of Briffault's undifferentiated hatred of "the human spirit and its whole career" a more "difficult and complex" attitude toward cultural problems.

Reprinted in A15.

**** "The America of John Dos Passos." [Review of John Dos Passos, *U.S.A.* (New York: Modern Library, 1937).] *Partisan Review* 4 (April 1938): 26-32. See C66.

D304. "Evangelical Criticism." [Review of H. V. Routh, *Towards the Twentieth Century* (New York: Macmillan, 1937).] *New Republic* 95 (20 June 1938): 314-15.

Regrets that Routh's prescriptive attitude toward literature--it must "provide the synthesis of intellect and emotion, of truth and desire, which man needs for happiness"--blinds him, like Arnold, to the variety of functions literature may serve; the stringency of his requirements explains why the Victorians never "solved the human dilemma and left a recipe for wholeness."

Reprinted in A15.

D305. "Allen Tate as Novelist." [Review of Allen Tate, *The Fathers* (New York: Putnam's, 1938).] *Partisan Review* 6 (Fall 1938): 111-13.

Defends Tate's novel about the South, in which "the wild abnormalities of the Greek dramatic fables [are] set within the limitations of strictest form," against attacks that it is distinguished but unsuccessful by observing that the point of the novel is "in the intended paradox of form and content." Judges Tate's world as perishing from "a codification so thorough that consciousness no longer need function. The old South destroys itself in this novel from lack of mind." Observes that, in view of Tate's disenchantment with Southern literature, politics, and religion, the value he ascribes to the Southern tradition is evidently purely stylistic, and commends Tate's novel, despite its "factitiousness," as a model for other writers wishing to establish a stylistic counterweight to "the brutality of the 'abyss'" they are confronting.

For a response by Tate, see K890.

D306. "'The Primal Curse.'" [Review of Rose Macaulay, *The Writings of E. M. Forster* (New York: Harcourt, Brace, 1938).] *New Republic* 96 (5 October 1938): 247.

Describes Forster's work as a reversal of the "hard-boiled" paradox: it "looks soft but inside is hard as nails." Maintains that Macaulay's book "bring[s] out Forster's apparent softness while it obscures his toughness." Suggests that Forster's "refus[al] to simplify the moral life" through moral absolutism makes him potentially a more attractive exemplar of liberal humanism than Thomas Mann, whose ascendancy, though a necessary corrective to political radicals' "negation of the humanistic virtues," is politically "saddening" because it marks "the retreat to the uncritical acceptance of the old slogans of liberal democracy."

**** "Hemingway and His Critics." [Review of Ernest Hemingway, *The Fifth Column and the First Forty-Nine Stories* (New York: Scribner's, 1938).] *Partisan Review* 6 (Winter 1939): 52-60. See C67.

D307. "Feminine Without the Charm." [Review of Dorothy Richardson, *Pilgrimage* (New York: Knopf, 1938).] *Kenyon Review* 1 (Summer 1939): 345-48.

Criticizes *Pilgrimage* as charmless and sterile despite its similarities to the work of James, Joyce, and Proust. Observes that because Richardson never dramatizes incidents, creates tension, or strays outside the mind of Miriam Henderson, the world outside the heroine, which "stands clear and objective" and "never becomes the mind of the spectator" in James, Joyce, and Proust, dissolves into the heroine's mind, so that "nothing . . . has life apart from her thinking about it." Describes Richardson's feminism, a "delightful secret weapon" directed toward "*seeing through* men," as promoting an "emotional solipsism" that marks a retreat from "the many contradictions under which women live."

D308. [Review of Isaac Goldberg, *Major Noah: American-Jewish Pioneer* (Philadelphia: Jewish Publication Society of

America, 1936).] *Jewish Social Studies* 1 (July 1939): 386-87.

Charges Goldberg with a "reverse Stracheyism" which mitigates the flaws and ambiguities of playwright and aspiring Jewish colonist Noah by "slyly imputing better motives than the facts warrant." Calls Noah "a supreme opportunist" saved from serious opprobrium only by "his flamboyant and childlike romanticism."

D309. "Victorian Critics." [Review of John Dover Wilson, *Leslie Stephen and Matthew Arnold as Critics of Wordsworth* (Cambridge: Cambridge University Press, 1939).] *Saturday Review of Literature* 20 (26 August 1939): 16.

Doubts that Arnold's revaluation of Wordsworth, which argued against Stephen in favor of ignoring the poems "most ambitious" in setting forth "a coherent system of thought," has become the "definitive estimate" of Arnold, since it "sacrifices far too much of the poet"; but commends Wilson for taking Stephen's side.

D310. "Determinist and Mystic." [Review of John Dos Passos, *Adventures of a Young Man* (New York: Harcourt, Brace, 1939), and Waldo Frank, *The Bridegroom Cometh* (New York: Doubleday, Doran, 1939).] *Kenyon Review* 2 (Winter 1940): 94-97.

Distinguishes the "therapeutic" despair of *U.S.A.* from the greater, yet inadequately motivated despair of *Adventures of a Young Man*, which "dismisses its very cause and denies importance to the situation from which it arises" by presenting Glenn Spotswood's battle with the American Communist Party without reference to the impulses which first led members to the Party or the tragedy of their political and moral accommodations. Prefer's Dos Passos's determinism, however, to Frank's "Marxian Rosicrucianism," whose "mystic authoritarianism" plays "with radical politics . . . until it ceases to be politics and becomes a kind of activistic Nirvana in which all spiritual burdens are laid down."

D311. "Mr. Lewis Goes Soft." [Review of Sinclair Lewis, *Bethel Merriday* (New York: Doubleday, Doran, 1940).] *Kenyon Review* 2 (Summer 1940): 364-67.

Contrasts the realism of Lewis's fiction from *Main Street* through *Dodsworth* with the "indulgence of Mr. Lewis's dream life" in his more recent work. Remarks that although Lewis, like Henry James, continues to be "curious about the moral life," he displays "little love and no respect for his own art." Defends the expansive looseness of Lewis's "improvisatorial" style as a salutary corrective to the "elegance, allusiveness and complication of form" characteristic of recent serious fiction and attributes his decline in part to the inability of American culture to conceive a novelist's career in terms of development, turning a writer like Lewis into an "event," leading him to mistake "the sense of power . . . for the creative effort which won his success."

Reprinted as "The Unhappy Story of Sinclair Lewis" in A15.

**** "'Elements That Are Wanted.'" [Review of T. S. Eliot, *The Idea of a Christian Society* (New York: Harcourt, Brace, 1939).] *Partisan Review* 7 (September-October 1940): 367-79. See C71.

D312. "The Victorians and Democracy." [Review of Richmond Croom Beatty, *Lord Macaulay, Victorian Rebel* (Norman: University of Oklahoma Press, 1938); E. L. Woodward, *The Age of Reform, 1815-1870* (Oxford: Oxford University Press, 1938); and Benjamin E. Lippincott, *Victorian Critics of Democracy* (Minneapolis: University of Minnesota Press, 1938).] *Southern Review* 5 (1940): 642-47.

Focuses on two opposed figures: Lord Macaulay, "Whiggery's pampered darling," who despite the philistinism of his political beliefs and the limitations of his analytical ability enjoyed notable success, according to Arnold, as "a great *civilizer*" because of his administrative gifts and "the gusto with which [he] lived the life of the intellect" and could communicate the pleasures of literature to an audience like himself; and Fitzjames Stephens, "one of the great pessimistic political teachers from whom liberals hate to learn," who recognized, as liberals still do not, "that the State is always force, however disguised, that government is always coercion, however gentle, and that both are necessary," and whose power of poetic insight equipped him as a liberal "to show the limitations of the liberal assumptions."

D313. "An American in Spain." [Review of Ernest Hemingway, *For Whom the Bell Tolls* (New York: Scribner's, 1940).] *Partisan Review* 8 (January-February 1941): 63-67.

Praises the novel as a recovery from the failure of Hemingway's recent work and a retreat from the belief that "art is to be used like the automatic rifle," but sets its stylistic power against its structural failure--its failure to present the story of Robert Jordan as tragedy rather than "astonishing melodrama." Finds Jordan dull because he "does not reproduce in himself the moral and political tensions which existed in the historical situation." Agrees with Philip Rahv that Jordan falls victim to "the cult of experience": he can . . . 'experience' all the badness, but he cannot deal with it, dare not judge it." Defends Hemingway's preoccupation with death, but notes that, "for Donne, death is the appalling negation and therefore the teacher of the ego, whereas for Hemingway it is the ego's final expression and the perfect protector of the personality," and concludes that despite Hemingway's wish to "celebrate the community of men," his infatuation with individual experience leads him to "glorify the isolation of the individual ego."

Revised and reprinted in B18; in *Ernest Hemingway: Critiques of Four Major Novels*, edited by Carlos Baker (New York: Scribner's, 1962), pp. 78-86; and in A15.

D314. "The Thibaults Were Dull in the Summer of 1914." [Review of Roger Martin du Gard, *The World of the Thibaults: Volume 1, The Thibaults; Volume 2, Summer 1914*, translated by Stuart Gilbert (New York: Viking, 1939).] *PM's Weekly*, 2 March 1941, p. 43.

Finds the second volume of Martin du Gard's social novel less successful than the first because "the drama of the book does not match the actual events it encompasses": when Martin du Gard presents fateful historical events leading to the war, "all that moves us is our own knowledge of the intrinsic importance of these events, not the author's treatment of them."

D315. "Mann's New Work Is a Comedy Ending with a Funeral." [Review of Thomas Mann, *The Transposed Heads*, translated by H. T. Lowe-Porter (New York: Knopf, 1941).] *PM's Weekly*, 8 June 1941, p. 46.

Notes that the philosophical focus of Mann's comic parable--"Where lies the personal identity, in the head or in the body?"--does not keep him from "archness" or "too facile a juggling with large contradictions," and deplores "the notion that Woman is a simple and unmodified Principle."

D316. "Shelley Plain." [Review of Newman Ivey White, *Shelley*, two volumes (New York: Knopf, 1940).] *New Republic* 104 (5 May 1941): 637-38.

Observes that although White does not present "a new Shelley," he presents "a Shelley who can be neither so vulgarly despised nor so vulgarly adored" as he has largely been. Agreeing with Arnold's description of Shelley as an ineffectual angel, traces Shelley's repeated attempts to enact his "perception of the moral good" directly in his life, rejecting first orthodox religion, then orthodox materialism, as inimical to individual freedom. Commends Shelley's reverence for physical and mental facts, suggesting that some of his insights foreshadow Freud and that, although he is "no savior" for contemporary culture, he points to its future.

D317. "The Empire of Angria." [Review of Fannie Elizabeth Ratchford, *The Brontës' Web of Childhood* (New York: Columbia University Press, 1941).] *Nation* 153 (5 July 1941): 16.

Notes earlier biographers' neglect of the Brontës' juvenilia and commends Ratchford's study of the family's fascination with the mythical kingdom of Angria as "one of the few books that may legitimately be used in the psychological study of literary genius." Argues that the difference between Emily and Charlotte Brontë was not, as Ratchford claims, that "Emily's one point of superiority was her full surrender to the creative spirit which Charlotte fought with all the strength of her tyrannical conscience," but concerns the surrender to emotion rather than creativity: "Emily 'surrenders' to the masculinity of her men and the femininity of her women and keeps them distinct," whereas Charlotte "is ambivalent; she does not 'surrender,' she compromises--and continues to struggle."

D318. "The Poet at Bay." [Review of Malcolm Elwin, *Savage Landor* (New York: Macmillan, 1941).] *New Republic* 105 (27 October 1941): 562-63.

Describes Landor as both tragic and boyishly gay, "capable of great perfection and many failures," and urges that his mastery of a formal rhetoric sparing in its use of metaphor "might convince us that we have estimated the value of metaphor too high and the value of poetic sentence too low." Finds Elwin's biography disappointingly unselective, demotic, and thus trivializing.

D319. "The Indispensable Century." [Review of Basil Willey, *The Eighteenth Century Background* (New York: Columbia University Press, 1940).] *Nation* 153 (1 November 1941): 431-32.

Concurs in Willey's estimate of the glaring limitation of eighteenth-century thought as its declining grasp of the tragic. Observes that "amid all this depressing cheerfulness a few figures stand in relieving darkness," and argues that these figures--Swift, Johnson, Butler, and Burke--are most likely to appeal to modern readers. Concludes by agreeing that the eighteenth century is indispensable in the sense that "the philosophical assumptions of no other time are so much taken for granted. . . . The great work of succeeding times has been the correction and augmentation of its ideas."

D320. "Survey of English Literature." [Review of George Sampson, *The Concise Cambridge History of English Literature* (New York: Macmillan, 1941).] *Nation* 153 (29 November 1941): 546.

Praises Sampson's volume as "no mere redaction" of the fourteen-volume Cambridge history despite its lack of any "shaping critical idea." Criticizes Sampson's insensitivity to several important modern writers--James, Forster, Eliot, Joyce, Lawrence--but notes with pleasure Sampson's "slightly bitter sense of modern culture as a whole . . . of book clubs and journalistic criticism and radio and cinema and of how they express and influence modern taste and intellect."

D321. "Greatness with One Fault in It." [Review of James Agee and Walker Evans, *Let Us Now Praise Famous Men*

(Boston: Houghton Mifflin, 1941).] *Kenyon Review* 4 (Winter 1942): 99-102.

Defines a central subject of Agee and Walker's book as the question of how "we [Agee and his middle-class audience] feel about the . . . underprivileged." Notes that Evans answers this question by refusing to make his camera subjects into objects, Agee by conceiving his narrative "as a series of false starts and inadequate attempts--as an inevitable failure, for failure alone can express the inexpressibleness of his matter." Finds Agee's only "failure of moral realism" in his "inability to see these people as anything but good" because of his own "guilt at his own relative freedom," which he records and analyzes but cannot control.

Reprinted with a new headnote as C154, and in that form in A15.

D322. "Mexican Classic." [Review of Jose Joaquin Fernandez de Lizardi (The Mexican Thinker), *The Itching Parrot* (*El Periquillo sarniento*), translated and with an Introduction by Katherine Anne Porter (New York: Doubleday, Doran, 1942).] *Nation* 154 (28 March 1942): 373-74.

Notes the enduring appeal of Lizardi's picaresque novel in Spanish-speaking countries since its first publication in 1830, predicts that readers of Porter's translation will find it "an extraordinarily dull book," and speculates on the reasons for Lizardi's failure to appeal to non-Hispanic readers: though Lizardi himself is "Don Quixote and Sancho Panza all in one," his hero, the Parrot, is "all Panza"; his picaro never fosters the lively ambivalence--the simultaneous impulses to condemn and identify with the hero--represented by other avatars of "the degeneration of the aristocratic ideal" like Lazarillo of Tormes; and the translation omits the wordplay, obscenity, and "moral and political tracts" whose mixture of tones may have provided much of its charm.

D323. "'New Yorker' Fiction." [Review of *Short Stories from the* New Yorker (New York: Simon and Schuster, 1940); Arthur Kober, *My Dear Bella* (New York: Random House, 1941); Benedict Thielen, *Stevie* (New York: Dial, 1941); John Collier, *Presenting Moonshine* (New York: Viking, 1941); Sally Benson, *Junior Miss* (New York: Random House, 1941); James Reid Parker, *Attorneys at Law* (New York: Doubleday, Doran, 1941); and Ludwig Bemelmans, *Hotel Splendide* (New York: Viking, 1941).] *Nation* 154 (11 April 1942): 425-26.

Deplores the transformation of modern literature from a social relation between authors and readers to a "scientific or religious activity" which takes no overt account of its audience, and praises the *New Yorker* as "continuing the old polite tradition of literature," whose intimacy between writers and readers permits a Dickensian, "grimly moral" critique of society. Argues that this intimacy recedes when the stories are presented out of the magazine's context, giving them "a mortuary quality," and turning their moral intensity into a gratuitous and self-serving cruelty absent only from the three collections by Collier, Benson, and Parker. Characterizes Bemelmans, a surviving representative of the polite tradition, as "the most gifted and morally the soundest" of the *New Yorker* writers because his frank acknowledgment of the personal voice with which "he courts the reader" makes his moral judgments "far less intense than his colleagues' but far more just."

D324. "Quennell's Byron." [Review of Peter Quennell, *Byron in Italy* (New York: Viking, 1941).] *Nation* 154 (2 May 1942): 520-21.

Commends Quennell's "quiet worldliness" in assessing Byron's sexual adventures but criticizes his inadequate emphasis on the poet's historical and ideological contexts, and takes particular exception to his assessment of the romantic poets as anarchic, irrational, and ultra-nationalistic.

D325. "The Use of Ideals." [Review of Gladys Schmitt, *The Gates of Aulis* (New York: Dial, 1942).] *Nation* 154 (9 May 1942): 547.

Notes with approval the unusual courage of Schmitt's first novel in criticizing the generally praised "'selflessness' and self-sacrifice" of modern intellectuals--a theme traced back to Hawthorne, Ibsen, and Nietzsche--but finds Schmitt's diffuse and encyclopedic prose as condescending as that of Dorothy Richardson, Waldo Frank, or Thomas Wolfe: "In their insistence on overwhelming us with complete information they are trying in a very aggressive way to substitute their sensibility for the world."

D326. "The McCaslins of Mississippi." [Review of William Faulkner, *Go Down, Moses, and Other Stories* (New York: Random House, 1942).] *Nation* 154 (30 May 1942): 632-33.

Chafes under the demands of Faulkner's manner but applauds the "complicated insights" of the McCaslin stories (excepting only "Pantaloon in Black," which is "merely formal, almost insincere"). Defines the unity and force of Faulkner's analysis of race symbolic rather than literally descriptive or directly prescriptive, and praises "the experience by which [Ike McCaslin's] moral sensibility is developed" as "a kind of compendium of the best American romantic and transcendental feeling."

**** "Tacitus Now." [Review of *The Complete Works of Tacitus*, translated by Alfred John Church and William Jackson Broadribb; edited and with an Introduction by Moses Hadas (New York: Modern Library, 1942).] *Nation* 155 (22 August 1942): 153-54. See C76.

D327. "The Wordsworths." [Review of *The Journals of Dorothy Wordsworth*, edited by Ernest de Selincourt (New York:

Macmillan, 1942.] *New Republic* 107 (24 August 1942): 235-36.

Notes the disservice done to Dorothy Wordsworth's journals by printing her prose as verse, complaining that the word "poetic," unlike "prosaic," is honorific and suggesting that "we have grown callous to the possible virtues of prose and to its claims in its own right." Calls the Grasmere journal fascinating but painful in its "record of a woman terribly betrayed by Nature": the illnesses of Dorothy, William, and Coleridge; William's marriage to Mary Hutchinson; and Dorothy's final madness.

Reprinted in A15.

D328. "The Progressive Psyche." [Review of Karen Horney, *Self-Analysis* (New York: Norton, 1942).] *Nation* 155 (12 September 1942): 215-17.

Sharply criticizes Horney's argument that subjects can therapeutically analyze their own neuroses by attacking Horney's rejection of Freud's theory of unconscious "resistance" to therapy as facile and her contrasting "faith in man" as shallow. Concludes that Horney is "one of the symptomatic minds of our time" in inadvertently revealing "one of the great inadequacies of liberal thought, the need for optimism" and substituting for Freud's biological determinism of self a cultural determinism. Acknowledges that Freud's account of culture is inadequate, but argues that "Freud saw a complex and passionate interplay between biology and culture, whereas Dr. Horney sees the individual infant as a kind of box into which culture drops this or that."

Reprinted in A15.

D329. "Four Decades of American Prose." [Review of Alfred Kazin, *On Native Grounds* (New York: Reynal and Hitchcock, 1942).] *Nation* 155 (7 November 1942): 483-84.

Concurs in Kazin's often low estimate of recent American prose measured against the standards of the nineteenth-century classics, observing that "the pressure of rapid change" in America often encourages a provincial obsession with the present, as in Anderson and Dreiser, and that the insistence that each book "be an event" can inhibit writers like Sinclair Lewis from developing. Continues, however, by demurring from Kazin's habit of defining writers like Dewey and Edmund Wilson by their limitations, and disagrees with his placement of the New Critics "at the opposite pole of critical extravagance from the Marxists," for, despite the inadequacies of their politics, these critics "have helped remind us what poetry is."

D330. "Artists and the 'Societal' Function." [Review of Maxwell Geismar, *Writers in Crisis* (Boston: Houghton Mifflin, 1942); Philo Buck, Jr., *Directions in Contemporary Literature* (New York: Oxford University Press, 1942); and N. Elizabeth Monroe, *The Novel and Society* (Chapel Hill: University of North Carolina Press, 1942).] *Kenyon Review* 4 (Autumn 1942): 425-30.

Characterizes all three books as assigning imaginative writers the role of social physicians, therapists, or messiahs whose function is "to provide the stipulated salvation of the moment." Takes exception to Geismar's criticism of Ring Lardner as "not Freud, Goethe, Marx, Jesus," noting that the weakness of Hemingway and Steinbeck stems precisely from their need for what Geismar calls a "spiritual positive." Ridicules Buck's disappointment that "Proust, Gide, Huxley, Eliot and Mann do not bring specifics for our world-pains but only emotions and ideas" and Monroe's "smug . . . neo-Thomism," which, grading novelists up or down in their approach to orthodox Catholicism, makes her "a kind of Prioresse of criticism," who "will have no farthing of grease on her cup of life, so clean does she wipe her lip."

Reprinted in A15.

D331. "M., W., F., at 10." [Review of William Bradley Otis and Morriss H. Needleman, *A Survey-History of English Literature* (New York: Barnes and Noble, 1937).] *Nation* 155 (21 November 1942): 546-47.

Humorously but trenchantly attacks the *Survey-History* as an indiscrimate farrago of fact, opinion, expressions of taste, and self-canceling judgments about merits and defects, and condemns the academic literary institutions whose cynicism--"the study of literature is the jolliest of the disciplines because in literature anything goes"--encourages the production and use of such books, in which "the written word is being treated without seriousness and respect by the very people who are supposed to be its guardians."

For discussion, see E383.

Reprinted in *One Hundred Years of the Nation*, edited by Henry M. Christman (New York: Macmillan, 1965), pp. 230-33, and in A15.

D332. "Suffer All These Children." [Review of *O. Henry Memorial Award Prize Stories of 1942*, edited by Herschel Brickell (New York: Doubleday, Doran, 1942).] *New Republic* 107 (7 December 1942): 749-50, 752.

Notes the "facility" and "technical competence" of the stories but expresses concern for their emphasis on children and their treatment of adults as children, "without responsibility for their fates and wholly innocent," lacking both "guilt and knowledge." Contrasts the apparent stasis of Chekhov's stories, in which the play of the author's intelligence has the force of action, to the stasis of these stories, whose "first effort is not to disturb . . . but to enshrine" a vision of the world in which "events ha[ve] become too big, or society too big, for any human being to be big himself."

D333. "American Fairy Tale." [Review of Eudora Welty, *The Robber Bridegroom* (New York: Doubleday, Doran, 1942).] *Nation* 155 (19 December 1942): 686-87.

Criticizes the "conscious simplicity" of Welty's manner in transposing a European fairy tale to an American setting and its "facetious air of having a profound meaning for herself"--a feature it shares with Eleanor Wylie's *Venetian Glass Nephew* and Woolf's *Orlando*.

D334. "Last Testament." [Review of Stefan Zweig, *The World of Yesterday: An Autobiography* (New York: Viking, 1943).] *Contemporary Jewish Record* 6 (August 1943): 426-28.

Describes Zweig, though "not a great writer," as a gifted and self-confident citizen of the world, "uniquely supranational," wholly defined by his passion for "the liberal humanistic tradition." Regrets that Zweig did not keep "a little personal wilfulness," reserve, or irony, which might have made him a more discriminating judge, and so a "better humanist," and concludes that for all his courage and good will, "Zweig's temperament . . . responded too easily to something in his tradition which at worst was mortuary and pious and at best academic."

D335. [Unsigned review of Basil Willey, *The Seventeenth-Century Background* (New York: Columbia University Press, 1942).] *Nation* 156 (9 January 1943): 67.

Describes Willey's revealing theme as "the search for the truth of things as they 'really are' and the effect which this dominant concern of science and philosophy had upon religion and poetry."

D336. [Unsigned review of William Gaunt, *The Pre-Raphaelite Tragedy* (New York: Harcourt, Brace, 1942).] *Nation* 156 (9 January 1943): 67.

Points out that although "no one admires Pre-Raphaelite art any more," Gaunt makes its leading figures, especially William Morris, seem admirable and even heroic in their pursuit of the social implications of their aesthetics and in their worldly success "in a post-Raphaelite world."

D337. "The Lower Depths." [Review of Jean Malaquais, *Men from Nowhere* (New York: L. B. Fischer, 1943), and Ramon Sender, *Dark Wedding*, translated by Eleanor Clark (New York: Doubleday, Doran, 1943).] *Nation* 156 (24 April 1943): 602-4.

Charges that few novels about poverty and degradation can reconcile the pathos they evoke with literature's need to give pleasure without sentimentalizing their subject. Notes that Sender's awareness of the "terrible, fantastic pressure" of human misery, as in *Lear*, prevents him from condescending to his characters, but criticizes his climactic descent to "facile optimism."

D338. "The Newest Humanism." [Review of Herbert J. Muller, *Science and Criticism: The Humanistic Tradition in Contemporary Thought* (New Haven: Yale University Press, 1943).] *New Republic* 109 (30 August 1943): 292.

Commends Muller's refutation of the humanistic attack on the straw-man of mechanistic 19th-century scientism, emphasizing Muller's argument that for modern science, "mind is no longer the passive receiver of ideas but their creator." Expresses reservations about Muller's facile acceptance of later revisions of Freud and his enshrinement of Thomas Mann as "the chief of the humanistic pantheon."

**** "Mr. Eliot's Kipling." [Review of *A Choice of Kipling's Verse*, made and with an introduction by T. S. Eliot (New York: Scribner's, 1943).] *Nation* 157 (16 October 1943): 436-42. See C78.

D339. "The Film as Literature." [Review of *Twenty Best Film Plays*, edited by John Gassner and Dudley Nichols (New York: Crown, 1943).] *Film News* 5 (March 1944): 2-3.

Dismisses Gassner's claim that screenplays can be "judged by the standards of the best traditional literature," agreeing with Nichols that the medium is "laconic" and emphasizes reaction rather than action. Concludes that screenplays, despite their value for what they reveal about filmmaking, cannot stand comparison with such novels as *Wuthering Heights*.

D340. "A Seventeenth-Century Psychiatrist." [Review of Bergen Evans, *The Psychiatry of Robert Burton* (New York: Columbia University Press, 1944).] *Nation* 159 (28 October 1944): 532.

Notes several points on which Burton's *Anatomy of Melancholy* advances a psychological theory that anticipates Freud: its detailed symptomatology, its emphasis on the psychogenesis of mental and often physical states, its etiology based on the deprivation of love during childhood and social nurturing later, and its therapy based less on medicine than on "a carefully defined relation between physician and patient."

D341. "Head and Heart of Henry James." [Review of F. O. Matthiessen, *Henry James: The Major Phase* (New York: Oxford University Press, 1944).] *New York Times Book Review*, 26 November 1944, p. 3.

Approves the recent reversal of strictures against James by earlier readers who "resent[ed] being told that the moral life is at least as complex as, say, the New York telephone system." Noting the wide discrepancy between different critics' estimates of James's late novels, observes that Matthiessen's familiarity with James's notebooks gives this dispute "new dramatic interest," but regrets that he did not express more fully "the quality of the pleasure" the late novels offer. Demurs from Matthiessen's distinction between James's analysis of "consciousness" and the "social consciousness" into which it may be "validly translated," and from his ascription of a "coherent dogma" to James's spirituality.

Reprinted as "The Head and Heart of Henry James" in A15.

D342. "The Best of Tennyson." [Review of *A Selection from the Poems of Alfred, Lord Tennyson*, selected and with an introduction by W. H. Auden (Garden City: Doubleday, Doran, 1944).] *Nation* 159 (23 December 1944): 776.

Applauds Auden's emphasis on Tennyson's shorter lyrics and his exclusion of longer poems whose appeal depends on their ideas: "What makes 'In Memoriam' a great poem is not, as the Victorians said, its mastery of large ideas but rather its involvement of large ideas with the bitter, childlike loneliness" characteristic of the poet.

D343. "An International Episode." [Review of *Letters of Thomas J. Wise to John Henry Wrenn: A Further Inquiry into the Guilt of Certain Nineteenth-Century Forgers*, edited by Fannie E. Ratchford (New York: Knopf, 1944).] *Nation* 160 (13 January 1945): 47-48.

Calls the story of Wise's forgeries and his success in selling them to the American financier Wrenn "a Henry James novel in the raw," comparing Wise's personal immunity to the taste he fostered in his patrons to James's treatment of taste as the marketing and acquisition of spiritual values in *The Spoils of Poynton* and casting Ratchford, who indicts Edmund Gosse, Librarian of the House of Lords, and "a conspiracy of guilty Englishmen," as Henrietta Stackpole for her "shrill moral vehemence."

D344. "Are You Sure You're So Clever?" [Review of Carlton Brown, *Brainstorm* (New York: Farrar and Rinehart, 1944).] *Nation* 160 (27 January 1945): 106-7.

Deplores the way Brown's publishers have promoted his "serious and perhaps useful" book about a man who was briefly institutionalized for insanity by playing on the fears of its potential audience in advertisements that ask, "Did you really sleep well last night?" in order to market the "sensational" and "intimate story of a man gone mad."

**** "Sermon on a Text from Whitman." [Review of Samuel Sillen, *Walt Whitman, Poet of American Democracy* (New York: International Publishers, 1944).] *Nation* 160 (24 February 1945): 215-16, 218, 220. See C81.

D345. "John O'Hara Observes Our Mores." [Review of John O'Hara, *Pipe Night* (New York: Duell, Sloan & Pierce, 1945).] *New York Times Book Review*, 18 March 1945, pp. 1, 29.

Describes O'Hara as the sole contemporary heir of Howells and Wharton in his perception of America as "a social scene" and his ability to render typical and individual distinctions at every social level through his selection of sharply observed details. Concedes that O'Hara's work is uneven, but praises him for having restored the Chekhovian impulse to the contemporary short story. Suggests that since "the novel was invented . . . to deal with just the matter that O'Hara loves," O'Hara's greatest talent may be as a novelist rather than an author of increasingly brief short stories.

D346. "A Tragic Situation." [Review of Richard Wright, *Black Boy* (New York: Harper, 1945).] *Nation* 160 (7 April 1945): 390, 392.

Praises Wright's ability to recount the details of an early life oppressed by discrimination without flattering his readers into escape or facile moral indignation, ascribing this integrity to Wright's refusal to become a mere object by masking his anger as passive suffering. Ascribes Wright's resistance to passive suffering to his early inability to understand the difference between black people and white--an inability which prevented him from accepting deliberate oppression as natural and inevitable. Expresses disappointment that Wright does not continue his story past his departure from the South, noting that "the entrance of an aspiring and relatively ignorant young man into the full stream of national life," always a promising theme, would be enriched by Wright's racial problems and his objectivity--an objectivity best illustrated by his pitiless observation of the "flaws of feeling and action" engendered in the victims of oppression.

D347. "A Derivative Devil." [Review of Denis de Rougement, *The Devil's Share* (New York: Pantheon, 1945).] *Kenyon Review* 7 (Summer 1945): 497-502.

Notes the attractions of Rougement's anthropomorphic diabolism (represented in *The Brothers Karamazov* and *Man and Superman*) and its disabling contradiction: having defined the devil in terms of modern secular myth, he uses this myth to support a plea for religious belief. Contrasts Rougement's factitious belief in the devil with Newman's more consistent analysis, and dismisses his attack on psychoanalysis ("an attempt to reduce sin and Evil to subjective meachanisms") as "a failure of moral imagination," an inability to come to terms with Freud's sense of tragedy and pain.

D348. "The Problem of Influence." [Review of Frederick J. Hoffman, *Freudianism and the Literary Mind* (Baton Rouge: Louisiana State University Press, 1945).] *Nation* 161 (8 September 1945): 234.

Praises Hoffman's attack on the assumption that "the creative writer *uses* in his work *the idea* which the systematic thinker *thinks up*, quite as if an idea were a baton that is passed from hand to hand in a relay race," and his perception that ideas change in response to the social circumstances of their transmission, the language in which they are expressed, and the inclination of their audience. Notes the ignorance of Freud's ideas among modern novelists and the resistance to Freud by literary critics.

Reprinted in A15.

D349. "Making Men More Human." [Review of *The Humanities at Work*, Regional Conference on the Humanities, Social Science Foundation, University of Denver (n.p.: University of New Mexico Press, 1945).] *Saturday Review of Literature* 28 (15 September 1945), p. 36.

Ridicules speakers at the Second Regional Conference on the Humanities for "assign[ing] to a high-school course in chemistry all the functions of a whole ideal culture" and "decid[ing] that the universities are to provide permanent peace," charging that academics and politicians alike inflate the social role of education as a "scapegoat for the rest of democractic society" and concluding that educators searching in vain for the social function of the humanities fail to identify "their only effect": "They give a kind of pleasure which, as their name implies, makes men more human."

Reprinted in A15.

D350. [Review of *The Psychology of Sex Relations*, by Theodore Reik (New York: Farrar and Rinehart, 1945).] *Kenyon Review* 8 (Winter 1946): 177-78.

Speaks contemptuously of Reik's "high disdain for biology" in formulating his psychology of love: "It is obvious that Dr. Reik feels that by this formulation he has made a great moral advance over Freud, that he has established love on a much higher plane," overlooking the biological basis of reproduction in his attempt to ground love in an asexual attempt to "escape from the feelings of . . . inadequacy."

D351. "John Henry Newman." [Review of John Moody, *John Henry Newman* (New York: Sheed and Ward, 1945; and Charles Frederick Harrold, *John Henry Newman* (New York: Longmans, Green, 1945).] *Nation* 162 (2 February 1946): 132.

Briefly deplores the fact that although no Victorian "stands the years so well as Newman," neither of these books does him justice, for Moody's is inadequate in its scholarship and intellectual power, and Harrold's so dry that it leaves Newman's ideas "inorganic and remote."

D352. "Mark Twain--A Dominant Genius." [Review of Samuel Charles Webster, *Mark Twain--Business Man* (Boston: Little, Brown, 1946).] *New York Times Book Review*, 3 February 1946, pp. 1, 14.

Reviews Twain's accusations that his nephew and publisher Charles Webster had ruined him and the convincing refutation of this charge by Webster's son, who presents his father as "not so much a business man as the factotum of a grandee." Argues against Van Wyck Brooks that Twain's persistent interest in business schemes was not "a betrayal of his genius at the behest of American philistine ideals," but an expression of "the Faustian will" he shared with Dickens and Balzac.

D353. "The Irrepressible Myth." [Review of Robert Metcalf Smith, in collaboration with Martha Mary Schlegel, Theodore George Ehrsam, and Louise Addison Waters, *The Shelley Legend* (New York: Scribner's, 1945).] *Nation* 162 (23 February 1946): 236-37.

Notes that the posthumous construction, by Mary Shelley and others, of Shelley as "a figure acceptable to Victorian society" depends on Shelley's construction of himself as "a mythopoeic man" and "a culture hero" who created his own mythic self based on "the paradox of strength in weakness, of duty in pleasure, of chastity in passion"--a paradox whose fundamental terms remained unchanged in later versions of the Shelley myth.

**** "Dreiser and the Liberal Mind." [Review of Theodore Dreiser, *The Bulwark* (Garden City: Doubleday, 1946).] *Nation* 162 (20 April 1946): 466, 469-70, 472. See C86.

D354. "Pocket-Size Twain." [Review of *The Portable Mark Twain*, edited by Bernard De Voto (New York: Viking, 1946).] *New York Times Book Review*, 28 July 1946, p. 4.

Notes that Twain is "democratic" in his "assumption that his readers were his equals in all things of the mind" and in his readiness to castigate not merely American institutions but the American people and their country without the anodyne of pious "affirmations": "Twain thought well enough of democracy to suppose that it did not want cheering up and that it gave him full liberty to be gloomy."

**** "The Life of the Novel." [Review of Eleanor Clark, *The Bitter Box* (Garden City: Doubleday, 1946).] *Kenyon Review* 8 (Autumn 1946): 658-67. See C87.

**** "The World of Sherwood Anderson." [Review of *The Sherwood Anderson Reader*, edited by Paul Rosenfeld (Boston: Houghton Mifflin, 1947).] *New York Times Book Review*, 9 November 1947, pp. 1, 67-69. See C88.

D355. "Neurosis and the Health of the Artist." [Review of Sigmund Freud, *Leonardo da Vinci: A Study in Psychosexuality*, translated by A. A. Brill (New York: Random House, 1947); and F. M. Dostoevsky, *Stavrogin's*

Confession, translated by Virginia Woolf and S. S. Koteliansky, with a psychoanalytical study of the author by Sigmund Freud (New York: Lear, 1947).] *New Leader* 30 (13 December 1947): 12.

Announces Trilling's dissatisfaction with C80, and considers questions about the differences between the artist and other neurotics (raised by William Barrett in M990), between the static psychic wound Edmund Wilson associates with artistic creation and the dynamic process of clinical neurosis, and between neurosis and other less benign mental ills. Emphasizes "the complacency with which the literary theorists [unlike neurotics and therapists] regard mental disease," speculating that "those writers who cherish madness and the wounded personality" depend on a narrow, eighteenth-century conception of normality.

Parts incorporated into "Art and Neurosis" in A4, and reprinted in that form in *American Literary Criticism, 1900-1950*, edited by Charles I. Glicksberg (New York: Hendricks House, 1952), pp. 550-66; in *The Study of Literature: A Handbook of Critical Essays and Terms*, edited by Sylvan Barnet, Morton Berman, and William Burto (Boston: Little, Brown, 1960), pp. 214-33; and in *Critical Theory Since Plato*, edited by Hazard Adams (New York: Harcourt Brace Jovanovich, 1971), pp. 959-67; reprinted in its original form in A15.

D356. "Two Analyses of Sigmund Freud." [Review of Helen Puner, *Freud: His Life and Mind* (New York: Howell, 1947), and Emil Ludwig, *Dr. Freud* (New York: Hollman, Wilhelms, 1947).] *New York Times Book Review*, 14 December 1947, p. 4.

Criticizes Puner's "psychograph" as marred by her hostility toward Freud's "masculine and heroic character" and her determination to convict him of some "great crime against himself." Dismisses Ludwig's "crusade against psychoanalysis" as "intellectually discreditable, as disingenuous and as vulgar."

D357. "Family Album." [Review of Van Wyck Brooks, *The Times of Melville and Whitman* (New York: Dutton, 1947).] *Partisan Review* 15 (January 1948): 105-8.

Contends that Brooks, instead of writing literary criticism or literary history, is commemorating "the compost-democracy of the great American family." Notes that despite his book's failure, Brooks is responding to a genuine need: the lack of intimacy the contemporary American audience feels with "a living sense of its past."

Reprinted in A15.

**** "Treason in the Modern World." [Review of Rebecca West, *The Meaning of Treason* (New York: Viking, 1947).] *Nation* 166 (10 January 1948): 46-48. See C89.

**** "Sex and Science: The Kinsey Report." [Review of Alfred C. Kinsey, Wardell B. Pomeroy, and Clyde E. Martin, *Sexual Behavior in the Human Male* (Philadelphia: Saunders, 1948).] *Partisan Review* 15 (April 1948): 460-76. See C91.

D358. "The Legend of the Lion." [Review of *The Legend of the Master: Henry James*, compiled by Simon Nowell-Smith (New York: Scribner's, 1948).] *Kenyon Review* 10 (Summer 1948): 507-10.

Argues that the anecdotes about James collected by Nowell-Smith show the novelist, like his artist-hero Neil Paraday, as a victim of his own public persona, constantly lionized by followers attentive to every nuance of his behavior except for "the nature of James's work, which is, one feels, the one element of James's personality that the memoirists wanted desperately not to observe."

**** "Sigmund Freud: His Final Credo." [Review of Sigmund Freud, *An Outline of Psychoanalysis*, translated by James Strachey (New York: Norton, 1949).] *New York Times Book Review*, 27 February 1949, pp. 1, 17. See C93.

D359. "Orwell on the Future." [Review of George Orwell, *Nineteen Eighty-four* (New York: Harcourt, Brace, 1949).] *New Yorker* 25 (18 June 1949): 78, 81-83.

Attributes Orwell's refreshing "faith in the power of mind" in part to his "connection with his own cultural past," which fostered his "criticism of liberal and radical thought wherever it deteriorated to shibboleth and dogma." Observes that Orwell's "profound, terrifying, and wholly fascinating book" treats utopianism as a dead issue, destroyed by "an image of the impending future" representing not only Soviet Communism but also the potential excesses of "the social idealism of our democratic culture." Praises Orwell's "exposition of the *mystique* of power" and his critique and reversal of the century-long tendency toward salvation through rationalism.

Revised and translated into German in *Der Monat* 2 (April 1950), 84-88, among four contributions "on George Orwell's death"; reprinted in *Twentieth-Century Interpretations of 1984*, edited by Samuel Hynes (Englewood Cliffs, NJ: Prentice-Hall, 1972), pp. 24-28, and in A13.

D360. "Romanticism and Religion." [Review of Hoxie Neale Fairchild, *Religious Trends in English Poetry, Volume III, 1780-1830* (New York: Columbia University Press, 1949).] *New York Times Book Review*, 4 September 1949, pp. 5, 13.

Defends the romantic poets' "report on actuality"--"for some decades . . . the chief expression of spirit of the Western world"--against Fairchild's argument that romanticism poses as a heretical counter-religion, noting "the integral and even symbiotic relationship" between romanticism and orthodox Christianity.

D361. "The Moral Tradition." [Review of F. R. Leavis, *The Great Tradition* (New York: George W. Stewart, 1948).] *New Yorker* 25 (24 September 1949): 98-102.

Praises "forthrightness and downrightness--and rightness" of Leavis's moral criticism, observing that he substitutes "the whole response of his whole being" for any "elaborated theory." Notes in Leavis's strictures against Dickens "a basic error about the nature of art--and of life": his refusal to acknowledge that the deliberate relaxing of moral awareness and the exuberance of virtuoso performance both have "great moral relevance." Defining culture as "the locus of the meeting of literature with social actions and attitudes and manners," contends that Leavis, in continuing "the Cromwellian revolution," sometimes allows his literary judgments to be distorted by "assimilating a social antagonism into his general critical sensibility," but concludes that "it is possible to disagree with half the critical statements Mr. Leavis may make and yet know him to be a critic of the first importance."

Revised and reprinted as "Dr. Leavis and the Moral Tradition" in A7.

D362. "Death of the Spirit." [Review of C. Virgil Gheorghiu, *The Twenty-Fifth Hour*, translated by Rita Eldon (New York: Knopf, 1950).] *New Yorker* 26 (11 November 1950): 157-62.

Examines the success of Gheorghiu's novel of wartime and postwar European disintegration, a success it has enjoyed despite its literary mediocrity and moral inadequacy. Notes that the novel's stale political wisdom--its hatred of technology and its glorification of "the individual life of the spirit" over political life--joins with its identification of the Americans and their military government as the real villains of the war to make it especially attractive to French intellectuals eager to equate American material culture and Russian imperialism as all-encompassing political options equally inimical to individuality.

Revised and reprinted as "A Novel in Passing" in A7.

D363. "Fitzgerald Plain." [Review of Arthur Mizener, *The Far Side of Paradise* (Boston: Houghton Mifflin, 1951).] *New Yorker* 26 (3 February 1951): 90-92.

Compares Mizener's biography favorably to Budd Schulberg's current novel *The Disenchanted*, which gives its author-hero a facile prose style and the gift of observation without showing the true bases of Fitzgerald's legendary status: his moral energy and his "fatal submission to the sanction of social prestige." Links Fitzgerald not only with modern writers like James and Proust but with the romantic poets, especially Wordsworth and Keats, through his nostalgia for youth, his greed for ecstatic happiness, and ultimately his capacity for wonder, which makes him an anachronistic figure, the last of the romantics to take the self as a legitimate object of wonder.

Reprinted in A15.

D364. "Some Are Gentle, Some Are Not." [Review of Irwin Shaw, *The Troubled Air* (New York: Random House, 1951).] *Saturday Review* 34 (9 June 1951): 8-9.

Commends Shaw's belated dramatization of ambivalent liberalism as distinct from "anti-anti-communism," but concludes that his novel about a radio director caught in the crossfire of the Red Scare is too didactic, facile, and factitious to be a successful novel.

D365. "A Man of Heroic Mold." [Review of Gregory Zilboorg, *Sigmund Freud: His Exploration of the Mind of Man* (New York: Scribner's, 1951).] *New York Times Book Review*, 14 October 1951, p. 10.

Criticizes Zilboorg's monograph as dull, "insufficiently informative" about Freud's life and ideas, and too intent on tendentious arguments about Freud's inadequate concepts of art and religion.

D366. "Man of Good Will." [Review of Lewis Mumford, *The Conduct of Life* (New York: Harcourt, Brace, 1951).] *New Yorker* 27 (24 November 1951): 141-46.

After praising Mumford as "something of the prophet" rather than "the public-relations man for high ideals" in his social criticism, linking him to Carlyle, Arnold, Morris, and especially Ruskin, argues against Mumford's injunction to save society by assuming "a sort of provisional perfection" that "we need civilized society just because we are not perfect men," and criticizes the "impulse to synthetic perfection"--for example, the desire to combine the benefits of existing religions without accepting their limitations--as rendering Mumford's conceptions of civilization and politics too idealistic for his pragmatic counsels.

**** "A Change of Direction." [Review of David Riesman, *The Lonely Crowd* (New Haven: Yale University Press, 1950).] *Griffin* 1 (March 1952): 1-5. See C101.

**** "Fiction and History." [Review of Geoffrey Blunden, *The Time of the Assassins* (Philadelphia: Lippincott, 1952).] *Griffin* 1 (June 1952): 1-4. See C102.

**** "Adams at Ease." [Review of *The Selected Letters of Henry Adams*, edited by Newton Arvin (New York: Farrar, Straus and Young, 1951; and Henry Adams, *Democracy* (rpt. New York: Farrar, Straus and Young, 1952).] *Griffin* 1 (August 1952): 1-6. See C103.

**** "The Early Edmund Wilson." [Review of Edmund Wilson, *The Shores of Light: A Literary Chronicle of the Twenties* *and Thirties* (New York: Farrar, Straus and Young, 1952).] *Griffin* 1 (September 1952): 1-5. See C104.

D367. "A Great Man's Instrument of Devotion." [Review of *The Note-Books of Matthew Arnold*, edited by Howard Foster Lowry, Karl Young, and Waldo Hilary Dunn (London: Geoffrey Cumberlege, Oxford University Press, 1952).] *American Scholar* 21 (Autumn 1952): 496-501.

Notes the pathos of Arnold's piety, which conceives personal morality in such simple terms--"the suppression of carnality, of venality, or personality, of inclination"--and imagines it so difficult to maintain.

**** "The Measure of Dickens." [Review of Edgar Johnson, *Charles Dickens: His Tragedy and Triumph*, two volumes (New York: Simon and Schuster, 1952).] *Griffin* 2 (January 1953): 1-7. See C105.

**** "The Personal Figure of Henry James." [Review of Leon Edel: *Henry James: The Untried Years* (Philadelphia: Lippincott, 1953] *Griffin* 2 (April 1953): 1-4. See C108.

**** "Zola's Quality." [Review of Angus Wilson, *Emile Zola: An Introductory Study of His Novels* (New York: Morrow, 1952); and Emile Zola, *Restless House*, translated by Percy Pinkerton and introduced by Angus Wilson (New York: Farrar, Straus & Young, 1953).] *Griffin* 2 (August 1953): 4-11. See C109.

**** "A Triumph of the Comic View." [Review of Saul Bellow, *The Adventures of Augie March* (New York: Viking, 1953).] *Griffin* 2 (September 1953): 4-10. See C110.

D368. "The Adventurous Mind of Dr. Freud." [Review of Ernest Jones, *The Life and Work of Sigmund Freud, Volume I: The Formative Years, 1856-1901* (New York: Basic, 1953).] *New York Times Book Review*, 11 October 1953, pp. 1, 27.

Contrasts Freud's prodigious influence on modern thought with his nineteenth-century, "inner-directed" personality, austere, intransigent, and heroic, citing as an example of Freud's boldness the moment when he "realized that every one of the stories of rape and seduction that his patients were agreed in telling him was untrue." Notes the humanity of Freud's fantasies, superstitions, and petty frustrations, concluding that Jones does justice to both the man and his thought as "a developing idea."

Reprinted as "The Formative Years" in A15.

D369. "A Young Critic in a Younger America." [Review of Van Wyck Brooks, *Scenes and Portraits* (New York: Dutton, 1954).] *New York Times Book Review*, 7 March 1954, pp. 1, 28.

Sets Brooks's early "European orientation"--an inadvertent "tribute to the much-abused genteel tradition"--against the love of America fostered in him by John Butler Yeats, who implanted the idea of "the nation as a means of establishing the claims of the spirit." Notes the waning of Brooks's influence and the irony of his suspicion of current literary and political ideas, and the "tension and conflict" they inevitably generated, "at the very moment when ideas seemed likely to have something of the effect upon the national life that Mr. Brooks had hoped for them."

**** "American Portrait." [Review of David Riesman, *Individualism Reconsidered, and Other Essays* (Glencoe, IL: Free Press, 1954).] *Griffin* 3 (May 1954): 4-12. See C114.

D370. "A Victorian Woman's World and Way." [Review of *The George Eliot Letters, Volumes I-III*, edited by Gordon S. Haight (New Haven: Yale University Press, 1954).] *New York Times Book Review*, 22 August 1954, pp. 1, 16.

Suggests that although Eliot is not a great letter writer, her correspondence shows "a great spirit" capable of "putting us in touch with the solid unbeglamored actuality of her age." Emphasizes the importance of Eliot's early religious commitment, the conflict between her religious faith and her independence and ambition, and her modernist "sense of the extreme danger in which the finely-tempered soul necessarily exists."

**** "Measuring Mill." [Review of Michael St. John Packe, *The Life of John Stuart Mill* (New York: Macmillan, 1954).] *Griffin* 3 (December 1954): 4-11. See C117.

**** "The Novel Alive or Dead." [Review of C. P. Snow, *The New Men* (New York: Scribner's, 1955).] *Griffin* 4 (February 1955): 4-13. See C119.

**** "A Ramble on Graves." [Review of Robert Graves, *Collected Poems* (Garden City: Doubleday, 1955).] *Griffin* 4 (June 1955): 4-12. See C120.

**** "Profession: Man of the Wor[l]d." [Review of James Pope-Hennessy, *Monckton Milnes: Volume I: The Years of Promise, 1809-1851* (New York: Farrar, Straus & Cudahy, 1955).] *Griffin* 4 (September 1955): 4-11. See C121.

D371. "A Victory Built of Faith, Pertinacity and Judgment." [Review of Ernest Jones, *The Life and Work of Sigmund Freud, Volume II: The Years of Maturity, 1901-1919* (New York: Basic, 1955).] *New York Times Book Review*, 18 September 1955, p. 5.

Observes that Freud's later years are "as charged with heroic energy" as his youth, emphasizing his "creative pleasure in himself," which makes him "one of the few great Plutarchan characters of our time,"and his determination to keep "at the center of the intellectual storm he had loosed." Ascribes the "scandal" of psychoanalysis less to its sexual content than to its status as "a new mode of thought." Cites Jones in dispute of the widely-held belief that Freud insisted on orthodoxy among his followers, and mentions the "failings and tragedies" of several of Freud's early followers.

Reprinted as "The Years of Maturity" in A15.

D372. "Her Love of Life Was Very Strong." [Review of *The George Eliot Letters, Volumes IV-VII*, edited by Gordon S. Haight (New Haven: Yale University Press, 1955).] *New York Times Book Review*, 18 December 1955, pp. 1, 11.

Observes that Eliot's later letters, despite her happiness and success, "are not those of a mind and will in embattled progress but rather those of a soul at bay." Cites "the preoccupation with illness and age and death" and the exigencies of "claustal love and duty" as reasons why "so many choice spirits turn against the conditions of life in the Victorian Age in wrath and mockery," and admires the conscious perfection of Eliot's kindness and charity, whose "intention needed to be explicitly expressed."

**** "Mr. Forster's Aunt Marianne." [Review of E. M. Forster, *Marianne Thornton: A Domestic Biography, 1797-1887* (New York: Harcourt, Brace, 1956).] *Griffin* 5 (Summer 1956): 4-12. See C124.

**** "The Farmer and the Cowboy Make Friends." [Review of Douglas Bush, *English Literature in the Earlier Seventeenth Century* (Cambridge: Cambridge University Press, 1952).] *Griffin* 5 (Fall 1956): 4-12. See C126.

**** "'That Smile of Parmenides Made Me Think.'" [Review of George Santayana, *Letters*, edited with an Introduction and commentary by Daniel Cory (New York: Scribner's, 1955).] *Griffin* 5 (February 1956): 4-16. See C127.

**** "Old Calabria." [Review of Norman Douglas, *A Selection from His Works* (London: Chatto & Windus/Secker & Warburg, 1955), and *Old Calabria*, 4th edition, edited by

John Davenport (London: Secker & Warburg, 1957).] *Griffin* 6 (February 1957): 4-10. See C130.

**** "Impersonal/Personal." [Review of *Letters of James Joyce*, edited by Stuart Gilbert (New York: Viking, 1957).] *Griffin* 6 (June 1957): 4-13. See C132.

**** "The Nude Renewed." [Review of Kenneth Clark, *The Nude: A Study in Ideal Form* (New York: Pantheon, 1956.] *Griffin* 6 (July 1957): 4-12. See C133.

D373. "Suffering and Darkness Marked the Years of Triumph." [Review of Ernest Jones, *The Life and Work of Sigmund Freud: Volume III: The Last Phase, 1919-1939* (New York: Basic, 1957).] *New York Times Book Review*, 18 October 1957, pp. 7, 36.

Contrasts the public triumphs of Freud's final years with his personal suffering because of the defection of followers like Rank and Ferenczi, the deaths of his daughter and grandson--which "he experienced . . . as the loss of part of himself"--and the painful cancer in his jaw. Remarks that although indifferent to his life or death, Freud "was never indifferent to himself. . . . His very love seems to spring from pride," a pride closely allied to his conscientiousness, his growing bitterness, and his moral principles.

Revised and reprinted as "Last Years of a Titan" in *Griffin* 6 (December 1957): 4-11, and in A15.

**** "The Story and the Novel." [Review of Isak Dinesen, *Last Tales* (New York: Random House, 1957), and James Agee, *A Death in the Family* (New York: McDowell, Obolensky, 1957).] *Griffin* 7 (January 1958): 4-12. See C134.

**** "Proust as Critic and the Critic as Novelist." [Review of *Contre Sainte-Beuve* in *Proust on Art and Literature*, translated by Sylvia Townsend Warner (New York:

Meridian/World, 1958).] *Griffin* 7 (July 1958), 4-13. See C137.

**** "The Last Lover: Vladimir Nabokov's *Lolita*." [Review of Vladimir Nabokov, *Lolita* (New York: Putnam, 1955).] *Griffin* 7 (August 1958): 4-21. See C138.

**** "Mind and Market in Academic Life, Parts 1 and 2." [Review of Paul Lazarsfeld and Wagner Thielens, Jr., *The Academic Mind* (Glencoe, IL: Free Press, 1958), and Theodore Caplow and Reece McGee, *The Academic Marketplace* (New York: Basic, 1958).] *Griffin* 7 (December 1958): 4-17. See C139.

**** "The Lost Glory." [Review of John Osborne, *Three Plays* (New York: Mid-Century Book Society, 1959).] *Mid-Century*, no. 1 (July 1959), pp. 3-7. See C141.

**** "The Rational Enchantress." [Review of Geoffrey Scott, *The Portrait of Zélide*, new edition (New York: Scribner's, 1959).] *Mid-Century*, no. 1 (July 1959), pp. 21-23. See C142.

**** "'An Investigation of Modern Love.'" [Review of Lawrence Durrell, *Justine* (New York: Dutton, 1957), and *Balthazar* (New York: Dutton, 1958).] *Mid-Century*, no. 2 (August 1959), pp. 4-10. See C143.

**** "All Aboard the Seesaw." [Review of William Gibson, *The Seesaw Log*)New York: Knopf, 1959).] *Mid-Century*, no. 3 (September 1959), pp. 3-12. See C144.

**** "Paradise Reached For." [Review of Norman O. Brown, *Life Against Death: The Psychoanalytical Meaning of History* (Middletown, CT: Wesleyan University Press, 1959).] *Mid-Century*, no. 5 (Fall 1959), pp. 16-21. See C145.

**** "Practical Cats More Practical Than Ever Before." [Review of T. S. Eliot's recorded reading of *Old Possum's Book of Practical Cats* (New York: Spoken Arts, 1959).] *Mid-Century*, no. 6 (November 1959), pp. 11-13. See C146.

**** "Angels and Ministers of Grace." [Review of *The Henry Miller Reader*, edited by Lawrence Durrell (New York: New Directions, 1959).] *Mid-Century*, no. 7 (December 1959), pp. 3-9. See C147.

**** "The Mind of an Assassin." [Review of Isaac Don Levine, *The Mind of an Assassin* (New York: Farrar, Straus & Cudahy, 1959).] *Mid-Century*, no. 8 (January 1960), pp. 11-17. See C148.

**** "Love and Death in the American Novel." [Review of Leslie A. Fiedler, *Love and Death in the American Novel* (New York: Criterion, 1960).] *Mid-Century*, no. 10 (March 1960), pp. 4-14. See C149.

**** "Lawrence Durrell's *Alexandria Quartet*." [Review of Lawrence Durrell, *Mountolive* (New York: Dutton: 1959), and *Clea* (New York: Dutton, 1960).] *Mid-Century*, no. 11 (April 1960), pp. 4-12. See C150.

D374. [Remarks on Philip Rieff, *Freud: The Mind of the Moralist* (New York: Viking, 1959).] *Mid-Century*, no. 12 (May 1960), p. 25.

Calls Rieff's study "one of the the very few . . . books to respond to the intellectual impications of psychoanalysis, especially the moral implications."

Reprinted in several subsequent issues of *Mid-Century*.

**** "Fifty Years of *The Wind in the Willows*." [Review of Kenneth Grahame, *The Wind in the Willows* (New York: Scribner's, 1960).] *Mid-Century*, no. 13 (June 1960), pp. 19-22. See C151.

**** "The Inimitable as an Immortal." [Review of *The Selected Letters of Charles Dickens*, edited by F. W. Dupee (New York: Farrar, Straus & Cudahy, 1960).] *Mid-Century*, no. 14 (July 1960), pp. 9-14. See C152.

**** "The Poem Itself." [Review of *The Poem Itself: 45 Modern Poets in a New Presentation*, edited by Stanley Burnshaw (New York: Holt, Rinehart & Winston, 1960).] *Mid-Century*, no. 15 (August 1960), pp. 10-14. See C153.

**** "An American Classic." [Review of James Agee and Walker Evans, *Let Us Now Praise Famous Men*, revised edition (Boston: Houghton Mifflin, 1960).] *Mid-Century*, no. 16 (September 1960), pp. 3-10. See C154.

**** "The Word as Heard." [Review of T. S. Eliot, *Four Quartets*, sound recording read by Robert Speaight (New York: Spoken Arts, 1960).] *Mid-Century*, no. 17 (Fall 1960), pp. 17-22. See C155.

**** "Masterpieces of Greek Art." [Review of Raymond V. Schoder, *Masterpieces of Greek Art* (Greenwich, CT: New York Graphic Society, 1960).] *Mid-Century*, no. 18 (October 1960), pp. 4-10. See C156.

**** "Bergman Unseen." [Review of Ingmar Bergman, *Four Screenplays*, translated by Lars Malmstrom and David Kushner (New York: Simon and Schuster, 1960).] *Mid-Century*, no. 20 (December 1960), pp. 2-10. See C157.

**** "Three Memoranda on the New Arden Shakespeare." *Mid-Century*, no. 21 (January 1961), pp. 3-11. See C158.

**** "Looking at Pictures." [Review of Sir Kenneth Clark, *Looking at Pictures* (New York: Holt, Rinehart & Winston, 1960).] *Mid-Century*, no. 23 (March 1961), pp. 2-7. See C160.

**** "Curtains." [Review of Kenneth Tynan, *Curtains: Selections from the Drama Criticism and Related Writings* (New York: Atheneum, 1961).] *Mid-Century*, no. 24 (April 1961), pp. 2-9. See C161.

**** "A Poet Newly Given." [Review of *The Complete Poems of Cavafy*, translated by Rae Dalven (New York: Harcourt, Brace & World, 1961).] *Mid-Century*, no. 25 (May 1961), pp. 3-12. See C162.

**** "Yeats as Critic." [Review of William Butler Yeats, *Essays and Introductions* (New York: Macmillan, 1961).] *Mid-Century*, no. 28 (Summer 1961), pp. 3-8. See C163.

**** "Beautiful and Blest." [Review of *Great English Short Novels*, edited by Cyril Connolly (New York: Dial, 1953); *Great French Short Novels*, edited by Frederick W. Dupee (New York: Dial, 1952); and *Great Russian Short Novels*, edited by Philip Rahv (New York: Dial, 1951).] *Mid-Century*, no. 30 (September 1961), pp. 3-9. See C164.

**** "A Comedy of Evil." [Review of *The Short Novels of Dostoevsky*, with an Introduction by Thomas Mann (New York: Dial, 1945).] *Mid-Century*, no. 32 (November 1961), pp. 7-11. See C166.

**** "Rimbaudelaire." [Review of Enid Starkie, *Arthur Rimbaud*, third edition (New York: New Directions, 1961), and *Baudelaire* (Norfolk, CT: New Directions, 1958).] *Mid-Century*, no. 34 (December 1961), pp. 3-10. See C167.

**** "No Mean City." [Review of Jane Jacobs, *The Death and Life of Great American Cities* (New York: Random House, 1961).] *Mid-Century*, no. 37 (March 1962), pp. 14-19. See C168.

**** "'What a Piece of Work Is Man.'" [Review of Claude Lévi-Strauss, *A World on the Wane*, translated by John Russell

(New York: Criterion, 1961).] *Mid-Century*, no. 38 (April 1962), pp. 5-12. See C169.

**** "The Wheel." [Review of Christopher Isherwood, *Down There on a Visit* (New York: Simon & Schuster, 1962); and Iris Murdoch, *An Unofficial Rose* (New York: Viking, 1962).] *Mid-Century*, no. 41 (July 1962), pp. 5-10. See C172.

**** "James Baldwin." [Review of James Baldwin, *Another Country* (New York: Dial, 1962).] *Mid-Century*, no. 44 (September 1962), pp. 5-11. See C173.

**** "Lord of the Flies." [Review of William Golding, *Lord of the Flies*, new edition (New York: Coward-McCann, 1962).] *Mid-Century*, no. 45 (October 1962), pp. 10-12. See C174.

D375. "Out of Darkness." [Review of *Columbia Review*, Spring 1964.] *Columbia Spectator*, 8 January 1964, pp. 2, 3.

Welcomes the *Columbia Review* back to "a new and remarkably bright life" from "its troubled and darkened existence of last year." Commends the length of the issue, the number of writers included, and the "respect that they owe to language," though cordially demurring from assent to the "illogical or non-rational" mode of much of the poetry.

**** "James Joyce in His Letters." *Commentary* 45 (February 1968): 53-64. See C181.

**** "The Freud/Jung Letters." [Review of *The Freud/Jung Letters: The Correspondence Between Sigmund Freud and C. G. Jung*, edited by William McGuire, translated by Ralph Manheim and R. F. C. Hull (Princeton: Princeton University Press, 1974).] *New York Times Book Review*, 21 April 1974, pp. 1, 32-35. See C188.

Section E

Symposia, Interviews, and Miscellaneous

E376. Morand, Paul. "Another Jew Dies." Translated from the French by Lionel Trilling. *Menorah Journal* 14 (April 1928): 369.

A poem ascribing the death of an unnamed German Jew to the totalitarian fears of the state before such a pariah.

E377. Bloch, Jean-Richard. "Napoleon, the Jews, and Modern Man." Translated from the French by Lionel Trilling. *Menorah Journal* 18 (March 1930): 211-19.

Describes Napoleon as "the first modern man" in his pragmatic, impious ability to conquer an entire society, contrasting his ruthless ambition with the millenial promises of Christianity and Islam and arguing that since his triumph, rendering "all mankind . . . elect," has annulled the special status of Jewish social morality and destroyed the balance between this morality and "the frenzy of individualism," it is now "necessary . . . to go beyond individualism."

E378. "Critical Irresponsibility." [Correspondence.] *Nation* 136 (22 March 1933): 319-20.

Condemns Edward Dahlberg's "summary execution of most of his fellow-writers of proletarian fiction" [M1001], pointing out that Dahlberg has deliberately misconstrued an ironic description by John Dos Passos of "the discreditable artistic philosophy of thoughtless and second-rate novelists" as a statement of Dos Passos's own beliefs.

E379. [Letter to the Editor, signed by Trilling, Diana Rubin, and twenty-four other writers, scholars, and intellectuals.] *New Masses* 10 (6 March 1934): 8-9.

Protests the disruption on 16 February 1934 of a Socialist Party rally at Madison Square Garden by members of the Communist Party, criticizing the disruptive tactics of the Communists, reaffirming the signers' partisanship for the working class against imperialism and fascism, and rejecting the compromisingly reformist tendencies of social democracy.

E380. "The Situation in American Writing: A Symposium." *Partisan Review* 6 (Fall 1939): 103-22. [Trilling's contribution, pp. 108-12. Other contributors, responding to seven questions set by the editors, include, in the present issue, Sherwood Anderson, Louise Bogan, Robert Penn Warren, Robert Fitzgerald, R. P. Blackmur, and Horace Gregory; and, in *Partisan Review* 6 (Summer 1939): 25-51, John Dos Passos, Allen Tate, James T. Farrell, Kenneth Fearing, Katherine Anne Porter, Wallace Stevens, Gertrude Stein, William Carlos Williams, John Peale Bishop, Harold Rosenberg, and Henry Miller.]

Identifies the prevailing political tendency in American literature as "a furious romantic revolutionism . . . continuing as an angry self-righteous reformism." Criticizes the resulting "literature of social protest," however sincere in its desire to stimulate moral sensitivity and emotion, as constituting, "because of its artistic failures . . . a form of 'escapism,'" suggesting that the audience "lives in a world of perfect certainties of which critical thought or self-critical feeling are the only dangers." Acknowledges that the American classics "have been far less important to me than the traditional body of European writers." Declines to say whether his own writing expresses his own individuality or his allegiance to a larger group, class, or system, contending that every writer's work necessarily expresses both: "*In a certain limited sense*, there is no such thing as an individual . . . a mind or talent, almost by definition, is a social thing. But once we illegitimately extend that certain limited sense we run into confusion in morality, in politics, in literature." Proclaims his own primary interest "in the tradition of humanistic thought and in the intellectual middle class which believes it continues this tradition" rather than in Marxism or the working class, defining that interest in terms of the contradictions between the intellectual middle class's high inherited ideals and "the badness and stupidity of its action."

E381. "Appreciation of the *Kenyon Review*." *The Kenyon Review: A Statement and Appreciations* [pamphlet], 25 June 1941, pp. 7-16. [Trilling's contribution, p. 10. Other contributors, quoted from published statements or letters in support of a fund drive for the journal, include Clifton Fadiman, George Dillon, Christopher Morley, Charles W. Morris, Justin O'Brien, Philip Wheelwright, Frederick Prokosch, Marianne Moore, R. M. Weaver, Charles Riker, Edouard Roditi, Theodore M. Greene, H. G. Owen, Wen Yuan-ning, and the editors of *Etudes anglaises*.]

Calls the *Kenyon Review* "the only journal which devotes itself single-mindedly to literary and philosophical criticism," noting that the other "two excellent [unnamed] magazines that publish much fine and serious criticism . . . have commitments to other things as well as to literature."

E382. "On the Brooks-MacLeish Thesis: A Symposium." *Partisan Review* 9 (January 1942): 38-47. [Trilling's contribution, pp. 46-47. Other contributors, responding to M994 and M1031, include Allen Tate, William Carlos Williams, John Crowe Ransom, Henry Miller, Louise Bogan, and James T. Farrell.]

Remarks that in marginalizing modern writers like Joyce, Proust, and Eliot as coterie writers in contrast to such affirmative primary writers as Tolstoi, Whitman, and Whittier, Brooks had "made up his mind that literature was divided between Iago and Othello, the base Iago representing negative intellect, the noble Othello representing the Affirmation of Values," and concludes that if Brooks wishes to see literature as a substitute for religion, he "ought to name it properly. He ought not to make Primary Writers into Church Fathers carrying the Torch of Life in a Pageant of Progress." Dissents from Macdonald's "assumption that socialism promises a moral and literary regeneration."

E383. "'Suggested Merits . . . and Defects." [Response to a letter from William Bradley Otis protesting the harsh tone of D331.] *Nation* 156 (6 February 1943): 214.

Replies to the claim that the *Survey-History* serves a valuable function by collecting many contradictory judgments and opinions without assessing their relative merits that unless critics and teachers make such discriminations, all opinions will be equally plausible. Argues that "implying that one opinion about literature is as good as another" effectively "diminishes respect for the written word."

E384. "Under Forty: A Symposium on American Literature and the Younger Generation of American Jews." *Contemporary Jewish Record* 6 (February 1944): 3-36. [Trilling's contribution, pp. 15-17. Other contributors include Muriel Rukeyser, Alfred Kazin, Delmore Schwartz, Ben Field, Louis Kronenberger, Albert Halper, Howard Fast, David Daiches, Clement Greenberg, and Isaac Rosenfeld.]

Describes Trilling's family and upbringing as orthodox, but declines to identify "anything in my professional intellectual life" dependent specifically on his Jewish background. Defines his status as a Jewish writer as the "minimal" position that "I would not, even if I could, deny or escape being Jewish," comparing this "negative" self-definition both to the position of most Jewish American writers and to the position of the contemporary American Jewish community, whose religion serves mainly "to provide, chiefly for people of no strong religious impulse, a social and rational defense against the world's hostility," and whose social institutions (such as the *Menorah Journal*) have "fostered a willingness to accept exclusion and even to intensify it" and withheld any support from "the American artist or intellectual who is born a Jew."

Reprinted in Theodore L. Gross, *The Literature of American Jews* (New York: Free Press, 1973), pp. 358-60.

E385. "On cummings." *Harvard Wake*, no. 5 (1946), pp. 3-77. [Trilling's contribution, p. 57. Other contributors to the magazine's special number on cummings include e. e. cummings, William Carlos Williams, Marianne Moore, Theodore Spencer, Allen Tate, Paul Rosenfeld, Karl Shapiro, Lloyd Frankenberg, Jacques Barzun, Alfred Kreymborg, Harry Levin, John Dos Passos, Horace Gregory and Marya Zaturenska, and Fairfield Porter.]

Protests the dismissal of cummings as "sentimental" by linking his "belief in biology--in, as it were, living"--to "a belief in the life of words." Praises not only cummings's development in *50 Poems* and *1 x 1* away from the "pedantry of metaphor and even of emotion" that weakened his earlier work but also, more generally, "his great act of sticking by himself" for so long.

E386. "An Integral Part of Our Culture." [The Reader's Forum.] *American Scholar* 16 (Winter 1947): 107.

Argues against three brief notes by John Crowe Ransom, Paul Bixler, and Delmore Schwartz in *American Scholar* 15 (Autumn 1946) that little magazines are not "a mere cultural 'symptom,' or . . . a makeshift therapy, but . . . an integral part of our culture," exercising, like individual artists, an influence on the dominant culture disproportionate to their apparent "secession" from that culture.

E387. "The Repressive Impulse." [Trilling's contribution to a discussion on the subject, "The Soviet Attack on Culture--What Happened and What Does It Mean?" in the form of a response to a speech by Nicolas Nabokov.] *Partisan Review* 15 (June 1948): 717-21.

Contends that official Soviet constraints on the freedom of thought and expression are so foreign to the experience of American intellectuals that the situation of Soviet intellectuals is difficult to grasp. Confesses the limitations of the overly rationalistic view--that repression is always exercised deliberately for particular tactical ends--and proposes two analogies to help in understanding the nature of Soviet repression: with "the whole tendency of modern Western culture" toward domination by ideological systems--Marxism, Nazism, radical Zionism--incompletely grasped and increasingly capable of commanding uncritical partisanship (so that "we live in a cultural situation in which it is the mark of intellectual power to deal with everything . . . in terms of polemic"); and with "our private selves," which may well react, as Trilling acknowledges he often does, with loathing and bitterness against "works of art and thought I don't approve of." Concludes that "to understand the situation in Russia we need only conceive the institutionalization of the endemic impulse of our time to overvalue ideology and to associate it with bitterness and violence," noting the roots of institutional repression in "the exclusive and repressive impulse in our own culture and our own hearts."

E388. "The State of American Writing, 1948: A Symposium." *Partisan Review* 15 (August 1948): 855-94. [Trilling's contribution, pp. 886-93. Other contributors, responding to seven questions set by the editors, include John Berryman, R. P. Blackmur, Robert Gorham Davis, Leslie Fiedler,

Clement Greenberg, John Crowe Ransom, Wallace Stevens, and H. L. Mencken.]

Expresses discomfort with the idea of literature as an institution implied by the questions and prefers to speak of it as a trade, a necessity, or an instrument for social change, noting that each of these ideas posits the writer's overt demand for money, attention, or change rather than establishing the writer as a "highly privileged priest who is subsidized by a corrupt society to do it some good." Rejects the "detestable" terms "highbrow" and "middlebrow" as cultural descriptors, arguing that the conception of "highbrow" as "an absolute, high-priced cultural best" is itself a commercialized middlebrow notion and suggesting instead that the middle class, though "paying less lip-service to contemporary highbrow culture" and suspicious of any earlier culture, is developing an impoverished but genuine culture likely to render high culture even more marginal. Characterizes recent experiments in literary form as more superficial than the "permanent experiment" in English "to get the language of poetry back to a certain hard, immediate actuality, what we are likely to think of as the tone of good common speech." Links the new criticism of poetry to other elements of resistance to the "malign materialism pervasive throughout the world and established in Soviet Russia," but concludes that, like other cultural initiatives, this criticism shows, by denying its ideological agenda, that "it doesn't properly estimate the seriousness of the situation."

Reprinted with a brief headnote as "The State of Our Culture: Expostulation and Reply" in A15.

E389. "The State of American Art: A Symposium." *Magazine of Art* 42 (March 1949): 83-102. [Trilling's contribution, p. 100. Other contributors, responding to three questions set by the editors, include Walter Abell, Alfred H. Barr, Jr., Jacques Barzun, John I. H. Baur, Alfred Frankenstein, Lloyd Goodrich, Clement Greenberg, George Heard

Hamilton, Daniel Catton Rich, James Thrall Soby, and John Devoluy.]

Remarks that theories of indigenous, strictly American art, though "certain of their virtuousness" because they proclaim American independence from foreign influence, resemble all nationalistic theories of art in this respect, and rejects all nationalistic theories of art on the grounds that national cultures, like individual artists, borrow freely "both from their neighbors and the past." Ascribes the intimacy among the arts in nineteenth-century Paris to a "greater community of education and tradition" among diverse artists, to their common participation "in the moving spirit of romanticism," and in the more central position of literature among the arts and sciences.

E390. "The Liberal Mind: Two Communications and A Reply [by Richard Chase, Lionel Trilling, and William Barrett]." *Partisan Review* 16 (June 1949): 649-65. [Trilling's contribution, "A Rejoinder to Mr. Barrett," pp. 653-58. Trilling and Chase (M997) are responding to Barrett's comments (G439) on M996 and M998.]

Rejects the false dichotomy of liberalism and religion, describing the Enlightenment as dialectically opposed to Romanticism and citing Freud's work as one possible synthesis of the two tendencies. Limits his earlier criticism of liberalism to the charge that "contemporary liberalism seems incapable of responding to the realistic values of Romanticism which, equally with the idealistic values of the Enlightenment, are properly part of its heritage." Observes that "it is precisely because I am myself a liberal . . . that I am depressed" by liberalism's failure to produce an engaging literature or an authoritative line of philosophical thought. Defines literature's relation to life as "polemical" in the sense that "it is arguing or urging or bullying or tempting or seducing me into certain ways of being which have inevitable reference to ways of acting" and therefore "has ultimately a moral and even a political relevance." Explains the phrase "the moral imagination" as opposed to the assumption common to liberal culture that "the life of man can be nicely settled by a correct social organization, or short of that, by the election of high moral attitudes," arguing instead that "the very election of morality constitutes a kind of moral danger." Indicts "the ideas of our powerful teachers' colleges, the assumptions of our social scientists, the theories of education that are now animating our colleges and universities, the notions of the new schools of psychoanalysis, the formulations of the professors of literature, particularly of American literature" as "the residuary legatees of the Enlightenment" against whom "my own criticism has . . . been directed."

E391. "The Jewish Writer and the English Literary Tradition: A Symposium, Part II." *Commentary* 8 (October 1949): 361-70. [Trilling's contribution, 368-69. Other contributors, responding to four questions set by the editors, include, in this issue, Philip Rahv, James Grossman, Martin Greenberg, Harry Levin, Irving Howe, William Poster, Saul Bellow, Alfred Kazin, and Karl Shapiro, and, in *Commentary* 8 (September 1949) 209-19, William Phillips, Paul Goodman, Louis Kronenberger, David Daiches, Isaac Rosenfeld, Stanley Edgar Hyman, Diana Trilling, Howard Nemerov, Stephen Spender, and Harold Rosenberg.]

Declines to comment on anti-Semitism as "an *essential* characteristic" of English and American literature, observing that since it is only an accidental characteristic, he has never defined his relation to that tradition. Remarks that although he dislikes anti-Semitism in individual writers, he can remain engaged with writers like Lawrence and Eliot despite their anti-Semitism: "I even get a kind of intellectual pleasure from maintaining an attitude of ambivalence toward writers who interest me." Notes his dislike of all ethnic generalizations, flattering as well as unflattering, observing that "the intense Jewish preoccupation with the refinements of cultural difference" tends to legitimize generalizations of both kinds.

E392. "The Teaching and Study of Writing: A Symposium." *Western Review* 14 (Spring 1950): 165-79. [Trilling's contribution, pp. 168-69. Other contributors, responding to eight questions set by the editors, include Allen Tate, Eudora Welty, Walter Van Tilburg Clark, Malcolm Cowley, and Wallace Stegner.]

Asserts that although "the ordinary prose virtues" can be taught by methods now largely dismissed as old-fashioned, more advanced instruction in writing is generally frustrated by the conditions of educational institutions. Remarks that young writers of prose fiction read too little. Expresses impatience with writers' conferences and college courses for aspiring professional writers.

E393. "Seven Professors Look at the Jewish Student: A Symposium." *Commentary* 12 (December 1951): 521-32. [Trilling's contribution, 526-29. Other contributors, responding to three questions set by the editors, include Samuel Middlebrook, Everett C. Hughes, David Riesman, Arnold W. Green, Ludwig Lewisohn, and Oscar Handlin.]

Suggests that the "largely competitive intellectual drive" formerly associated with Jewish students is common to many students whose background is European. Agrees with Morris Freedman that acculturation has made Jewish students accord less with this image, but points out against Freedman's elegiac tone that academic study is not a distinterested activity but "a recognized means of social advancement" subject to "the same moral judgment we direct upon other ways of acquiring prestige." Observes that given the movement of higher education away from mechanical techniques and quantitative goals toward a more "humanistic emphasis," Jewish seriousness and respect for learning no longer seem such exceptional traits. Noting the lack of correlation between academic promise and mature achievement, asks what part "the old 'classical' Jewish student . . . emerged to play in the general intellectual life."

E394. "Our Country and Our Culture: A Symposium." *Partisan Review* 19 (May-June 1952): 282-326. [Trilling's contribution, 318-26. Other contributors, responding to four questions set by the editors, include Newton Arvin, James Burnham, Allan Dowling, Leslie A. Fiedler, Norman Mailer, Reinhold Niebuhr, Philip Rahv, David Riesman, and Mark Schorer. The symposium continues in *Partisan Review* 19 (July-August 1952): 420-50, with contributions by William Barrett, Jacques Barzun, Joseph Frank, Horace Gregory, Louis Kronenberger, and C. Wright Mills, and concludes in *Partisan Review* 19 (September-October 1952): 562-97, with contributions by Louise Bogan, Richard Chase, Sidney Hook, Irving Howe, Max Lerner, William Phillips, Arthur Schlesinger, Jr., and Delmore Schwartz.]

Agrees that in the past ten years American intellectuals have been less aloof from national feeling than ever before, and attributes this change to the unique opportunities America has come to offer, its growing isolation in the face of other nations' hostility, and the bankruptcy of any competing cultural ideals abroad. Notes with approval the closer intimacy of wealth and intellect, allowing the social ascent of "a large class of people whose minds are their only property" and fostering the hope of a more influential intellectual elite. Recommends that "the historical-literary mind," which is "the best kind of critical and constructive mind that we have," consider more critically American culture in all its pluralism and diversity, returning to "the great American tradition of critical non-conformism" instead of taking their inspiration from European culture.

Excerpted in Spanish translation as "El Valor de las Ideas Aumentas en Norteamericana," *Cuadernos* 1 (May-June 1953): 68-69, and published in expanded form as C107.

E395. "Was Orwell Shrewd. . . ." [Letter to the Editor.] *Nation* 176 (24 Jan 1953): 88.

Argues against M1032 that Orwell was correct in seeing the Spanish Loyalist government as fatally compromised by its Stalinist policies and that there is no evidence that he later changed this diagnosis after advancing it in *Homage to Catalonia*.

A rebuttal by Matthews (". . . Or Ill-Informed?") maintains that "Orwell's judgment was based on inadequate knowledge."

E396. "Editor's Commentary." *Perspectives USA* 2 (Winter 1953): 5-10. See B27.

Defends Trilling's "parochial" selection of writers and periodical sources ("American intellectuals" who "are especially aware of the social and political context in which the intellectual and creative life is lived," including many personal friends or colleagues) as proper to his status as "writer" rather than "Cultural Ambassador." Explains that although the Cultural Ambassador sees his culture as monolithic and simply characterized, the writer necessarily sees division and confusion. Hopes that as editor he has "sowed a little confusion" in the reader's mind and "fostered the idea that American culture is no single simple thing."

E397. "Art and Morals: A Symposium." [Excerpts from presentations by Trilling and George Boas at a symposium on Art and Morals held at Smith College, 23-24 April 1953. Other participants, whose contributions are not excerpted, include W. H. Auden, Jacques Barzun, W. G. Constable, Philip Johnson, Archibald MacLeish, Ben Shahn, Allen Tate, and Edgar Wind.] *Art Digest* 27 (15 May 1953): 19-20.

Approaches "the possible deleterious effects of art" as a danger to the will by way of three paradoxes: the effort of artistic will to appear effortless, the effort of moral choice to transcend its defining difficulties and appear as grace, and the wish of grace "to transcend itself and to appear as good works, as the moral law in all its attendant sweat and conditionedness." Emphasizes the dependence of art on "will and desire" but defends the aesthetic elements of art against its concomitant moral elements as necessary to insure the effect of its freedom from the conditions of circumstance and will.

E398. "Decisions on Testifying." [Letter to the Editor.] *New York Times*, 26 November 1953, p. 30.

Corrects the emphasis of M987 by adding that "a refusal to testify [before the House Un-American Affairs Committee] must not be automatically condoned" as well as automatically condemned. Stresses that Trilling's Columbia College committee was not concerned to affirm the right of all Communists to teach--"membership in Communist organizations almost certainly implies a submission to an intellectual control which is entirely at variance with the principles of academic competence as we understand them"--and would certainly not affirm the right of all Fascists to teach.

E399. "The Faust Story." [Program notes.] Charles Gounod, *Faust*. With Victoria de los Angeles, Nicolai Gedda, and Boris Christoff. Chorus and Orchestra of the Théâtre National de L'Opéra, conducted by André Cluytens. RCA Records, no. LM6400, 1953. Libretto, pp. 6-13.

Traces the development of the Faust legend--especially engaging to modern audiences because of "its boundless aspiration and its haunting doubt"--from its first surviving written version in 1587 through Marlowe, the farcical puppet-theater, and Goethe to Gounod, whose opera is notable for "its lyrical sensuousness and its sentimental but perfectly sincere religiosity," which both appealed to Shaw.

E400. Kalb, Bernard. "The Author." *Saturday Review* 38 (12 February 1955): 11.

An interview published as a sidebar to H699 in which Trilling expresses the wish to be identified as a novelist rather than a critic and announces that "from now on I plan to give a good deal of time to [writing fiction]. I'm writing a second novel at the moment."

E401. Nichols, Lewis. "Talk with Lionel Trilling." *New York Times Book Review*, 13 February 1955, p. 21.

An interview in which Trilling, who "could be taken readily for a graduate student," regrets the current absence of literary patriarchs like Twain and Howells, contrasts the rebelliousness of students in the twenties with the social acceptance of contemporary students, and indicates that he is working on three pieces of fiction, "two short, one long."

E402. "Twenty Years of *Western Review*: A Series of Recollections." *Western Review* 20 (Winter 1956): 87-99. [Trilling's contribution, p. 99. Other contributors include Wallace Stegner, Grant H. Redford, George Snell, Brewster Ghiselin, M. L. Nielsen, Alan Swallow, R. W. Stallman, R. V. Cassill, and Allen Tate.]

Applauds the *Western Review* for offsetting "the centralization of our literary culture in the East and the metropolis," fostering the goal of "many centers" for American culture.

E403. "A Conversation with Ernest Jones." [Television interview in the "Conversations with Elder Wise Men" series, National Broadcasting Company. Broadcast 23 September 1956.]

A half-hour television program in which Trilling interviews Freud's biographer Ernest Jones on the occasion of the centenary of Freud's birth; the edited record of conversations filmed in the library of the Psychoanalytic Institute in New York City between 18 and 20 April 1956. Trilling discusses the circumstances of the filming briefly in B35.

E404. Wain, John. "Lionel Trilling: 'The Artist Needs to Take Sides.'" [Literature and Life, #4: An interview.] *Observer*, 29 September 1957, p. 7.

Remarks that the artist not only tends to take strong positions on "the major battles of his time," but needs to do so. The withering of opposition to the "progressive and idealistic views" of Trilling's circle has left him feeling "rather let down. . . . When I settle down to think over possible plots for an interesting novel, I feel the need to choose one that has a direct bearing on public events." Refuses, however, to prescribe meliorative ideas or attitudes for authors. Challenges the organicism of the New Critics: "Obviously literature, and especially fiction, contains a certain discursive or expository element which can be isolated and discussed without any damage." Contrasts British culture, which "produces a *milieu* in which basic questions are never discussed, simply because it's assumed that everyone is too advanced to need to go back over them," with the less sophisticated and continuous American culture, in which, "as a teacher, I find that every job has to be done again from scratch. . . . You're compelled, all the time, to state the rationale of whatever it is you're doing"--a process he finds both "stimulating" and "fatiguing."

E405. "Trilling Addendum." [Letter to the Editor.] *New Leader* 41 (18-25 August 1958): 29-31.

Explains that C137, expressing the hope that the Communist Party of Poland would maintain its independence from the Soviet party, was written and its galleys edited in January 1958, before the capitulation of the Polish party to Russia in July.

E406. "T. S. Eliot Talks About His Poetry." *Columbia University Forum* 2 (Fall 1958): 11-14.

Introduces a reading by Eliot at Columbia University (28 April 1958) by emphasizing the ways in which, despite its allusiveness and frequent obscurity, Eliot's poetry is best "understood as music is understood" by being read aloud, for "sound plays as great a part in it as ideas and images."

E407. "Text." [Letter to the Editor.] *New York Times Book Review*, 20 September 1959, p. 32.

Announces the publication of the complete text of Trilling's speech on Robert Frost [C140], recently attacked in G431.

E408. "On the Death of a Friend." *Commentary* 29 (February 1960): 93-94.

Memorializes Elliot Cohen, founding editor of *Commentary* and managing editor of the *Menorah Journal* who accepted Trilling's first work for publication, as "the *only* great teacher I have ever had," despite his never having taught in a classroom--a man who believed "in the communicabilty of virtually all ideas" and enjoyed, despite the pain of his own life, an unusual openness to "the human wish for the free, the gratuitous" that led him to celebrate and share "his sense of the subtle interrelations that exist between seemingly disparate parts of a culture," from baseball to college traditions.

E409. "The Pleasure Principle in Literature." [A sound recording on audiotape and tape cassette.] New York: McGraw-Hill, 1963.

A recording of a talk Trilling gave at the 92nd Street YM-YWHA Poetry Center in 1963, tracing the pleasure principle in literature from the eighteenth century to the present.

Re-released, New York: J. Norton, 1974.

E410. "Liberal Anti-Communism Revisited: A Symposium." *Commentary* 44 (September 1967): 31-79. [Trilling's contribution, 76-77. Other contributors, responding to three questions set by the editor, Norman Podhoretz, include Lionel Abel, David T. Bazelon, Daniel Bell, Lewis A. Coser, Paul Goodman, Michael Harrington, Sidney Hook, Irving Howe, Murray Kempton, Robert Lowell, Dwight Macdonald, William Phillips, Robert Pickus, Philip Rahv, Harold Rosenberg, Richard H. Rovere, Arthur Schlesinger, Jr., Stephen Spender, Diana Trilling, and Dennis H. Wrong.]

Accepts responsibility as a citizen for the war in Vietnam but denies that "my views as a liberal anti-Communist helped bring about the war," since "the position of liberal anti-Communism . . . has never been influential." Points out the tendency of "clever, thinking people" to find scapegoats like "witches and Jews" for moral corruption, and recalls the charge that "the poets and philosophers of the Romantic movement were responsible for Nazism." Maintains an opposition to Communism based increasingly on political rather than moral grounds, on a growing agreement with Mill's dictum that "the assumptions and habits that make democratic government possible are not present in the tradition of every people." Rejects the charge that the revelation of CIA backing of many cultural projects makes participants in those projects "slaves" or "dupes" of "the darker impulses of American foreign policy," observing that the "good faith" of participants cannot be restored or assessed by such appeals to "bad faith" as these judgments.

E411. "An Open Letter." [A letter signed by Trilling and twenty-six other writers and educators.] *Partisan Review* 35 (Spring 1968): 233.

Protests an early-morning narcotics raid at the State University of New York at Stony Brook and the subpoena of eleven members of the Stony Brook faculty by the Joint Legislative Committee on Crime, claiming that requiring their testimony about students' "confidences" will undermine "the inviolability of trust between teachers and students."

E412. Donadio, Stephen. "Columbia: Seven Interviews." *Partisan Review* 35 (Summer 1968): 354-92. [Interview with Trilling, 386-92. Others interviewed include Immanuel Wallerstein, Peter Gay, Eric Bentley, Mark Rudd and Lewis Cole, Ray Brown and Bill Sales, and Charles Parsons.]

Dismissing the explicit issues provoking the Columbia strike as "largely factitious," identifies the more important issues as symbolic: the more radical students' "alienation from and disgust with the whole of American culture" and a more general attempt by students to win "recognition of their maturity" and assert their involvement in the political process. Suggests that protesting students have challenged the university's concern with its own personnel's rising social status and its position as a repository of cultural values. Notes that political conflicts become more threatening to universities to the extent that they have entered into the mainstream of American life. Predicts the need for greater student and faculty involvement in "the practical life of the University." Acknowledges bewilderment at the motives and desires of protestors--"not the hard-core radical students, the SDS--I think I quite understand them"--but more moderate students whose intense "interest in the university as an institution" has no parallel in Trilling's own undergraduate memories, and contends that "they are wrong in dealing with the university as if it were perfectly continuous with the society, or as if it were the microcosm of the society."

E413. "Jewish Hostages." [Letter to the Editor, signed by Irving Howe, Norman Podhoretz, and Trilling.] *New York Times*, 13 September 1970, Section 4, p. 15.

Deplores the sympathy shown by American leftists and intellectuals to such Arab groups as the self-styled "revolutionaries" in Jordan who kept the Jewish victims of a hijacking as hostages while allowing non-Jewish women and children to leave the airplane and go to a hotel in Amman.

E414. "Jason Epstein et al. Speak." [Letters to the Editor.] *New York Times Magazine*, 16 April 1972, p. 45.

Protests the description of Elliot Cohen in M1036 as "a strange and difficult man who toward the end of his life felt that he was in danger of a physical attack from unnamed Communists," observing that "what actually tormented him was an irrational remorse over the antagonism he had in the past directed to Communists and to sympathizers with Communism."

E415. "The Jameses." [Letter to the Editor.] *TLS*, 20 October 1972), p. 1257.

Disagrees with Leon Edel's contention in his biography of Henry James (recently attacked by Jacques Barzun and defended in Edel's Letter to the Editor of 13 October, which claimed B19 as an ally) that William James declined election to the American Academy of Arts and Letters out of jealousy for his already-elected brother, claiming instead that William's slighting reference to his brother is "a cosy, Brahmin-Boston kind of joke."

E416. "Culture and the Present Moment: A Round-Table Discussion." [The edited transcript of a one-day symposium on the status of American high culture. Participants include Trilling, Edward Grossman, Hilton Kramer, Michael Novak,

Cynthia Ozick, Norman Podhoretz, and Jack Richardson.] *Commentary* 58 (December 1974): 31-50.

Agrees with Kramer that American culture is no longer the property of a single class and that mass culture is falsely opposed to high culture, and suggests that the contemporary avant-garde, unlike the avant-garde of the thirties, has rejected "the vestigial religious intention of art" through its parodistic or ironic stance toward cultural traditions. Deplores the loss of academic standards marked by the inclusion of non-classic writers like Virginia Woolf and Doris Lessing in the college curriculum and more generally by the uncritical acceptance of new artworks. Questions the assumption that art is socially good and important, suggesting that it may blind audiences to the reality it professes to reveal--a proposition debated at length by other participants. Describes the attempt to define criticism as oppositional as "self-defeating," but wonders if modern artistic culture's break with its past is so complete that it cannot be grasped in terms of the past. Notes that the counterculture rejects both "the bourgeois life" and "the high cultural life." Explains Trilling's "despairing shrug" in response to the promise of the counterculture as the product of fatigue rather than cowardice. Ascribes the universal "disaffection from the nature of modern life" in part to the intense cultural self-consciousness generated by art, in part to the influence of mass media like television, which reduce laudatory ideals to bromides undermined by their easy accessibility.

E417. [Walker Evans Tribute (National Institute of Arts and Letters, 22 May 1974).] *Proceedings of the National Institute of Arts and Letters*, Second Series, no. 25 (1975), pp. 22-23.

Commends Evans both for producing "the most perfect, the most profoundly significant and moving achievements of visual art in our time" and for resisting the modern tendency toward "bold and brilliant subjectivity" in the visual arts to affirm "the aesthetic validity of our objective world."

Reprinted as the Foreword to a separate pamphlet, Double Elephant Press, 1975.

E418. "Sincerity and Authenticity: A Symposium." [Panelists at the two-day symposium conducted at Skidmore College in March 1974 included Trilling, Irving Howe, Leslie H. Farber, William Hamilton, Robert Orrill, and Robert Boyers.] *Salmagundi* no. 41 (Spring 1978), pp. 87-110.

Contends in response to Orrill's question that categorical and dialectical modes of thinking do not necessarily contradict each other in A9 or generally, adding that categorical judgments, which are especially appropriate about oneself, offer the modest comfort of "accept[ing] ourselves as we are" without "think[ing] of future developments." Notes that sincerity "relates to one's public image," whereas authenticity is a question of private judgment: "There is . . . a defiant self-assertion in the notion of authenticity so far as it may be said to exist in relation to society at all." Agrees with Boyers that authenticity involves a baneful kind of self-examination, warning that a conscious "concern with sincerity is equally inauthentic and insincere." Acknowledges the value of authenticity in the context of its historical origins as a reaction against philistinism while deploring its degradation as a series of meaningless gestures. Remarks that "I find it difficult to talk about authentic people" because "all people are authentic." Agrees with Howe's connection between the decline of Christianity as the revelation of objective truth and the rise of the concern with sincerity and authenticity, adding that this concern implies that society is fraudulent. Names Ralph Nader as a type of contemporary sincerity, and defends Norman Mailer as a transcendent clown. Asserts with Howe that teaching is "full of subterfuges" and "the opposite of sincere." Stresses the difficulty of defining "an actuality of self" in "a culture permeated by art," given the ambiguous moral power of art, and deplores the growing lack of seriousness and intellectual responsibility among academics and intellectuals, contending that the modern intellectual "never tests his ideas by what it would mean to him if he were to undergo the experience that he is recommending."

E419. "Literary Pathology." [Response to M1035, read at the annual meeting of the American Psychoanalytical Association, 7 December 1962. First published in A15.]

Suggests that Meyer's exploration of Joseph Conrad's "fetishism and sado-masochism" be enlarged to consider the "*mystique* of female power" as a cultural phenomenon, not a pathology specific to the individual, and wonders why such psychoanalytic investigations are usually offered as explanations of artistic failure rather than artistic success, given, for example, the high valuation western culture has placed on "that sado-masochistic genre called tragedy" and the world's "insatiable appetite for the products of neurosis."

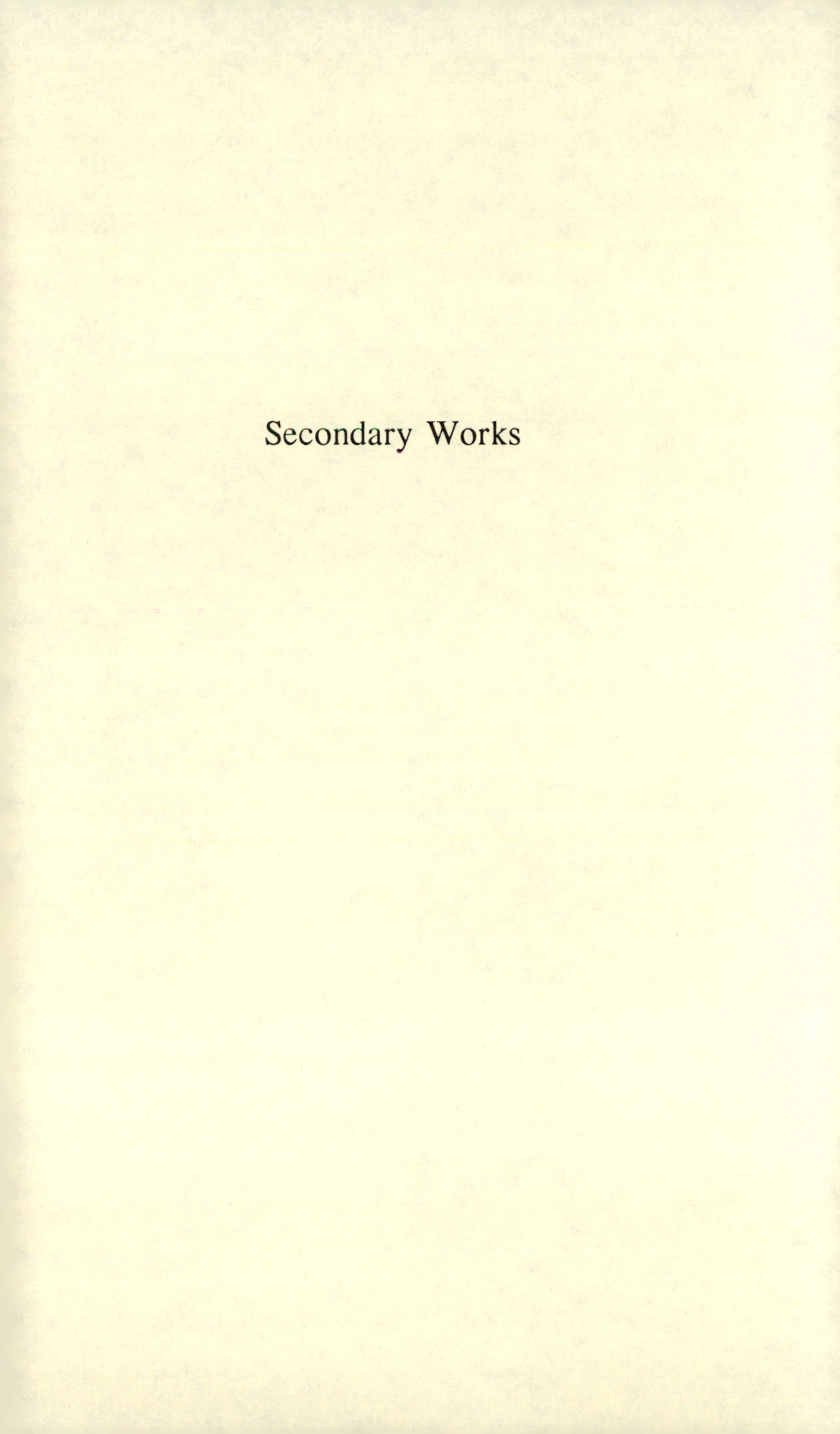

Secondary Works

Section F

Books, Collections of Essays, Special Issues of Journals

F420. Anderson, Quentin, Donadio, Stephen, and Marcus, Steven, editors. *Art, Politics, and Will: Essays in Honor of Lionel Trilling*. New York: Basic, 1977.

Originally planned as a *Festschrift* in honor of Trilling but changed to a memorial volume on his death in 1975. Most of the essays included refer to Trilling only briefly or indirectly or not at all. Includes the following material:

Jacques Barzun, "The Imagination of the Real, or Ideas and Their Environment" (M991)
Gertrude Himmelfarb, "Social History and the Moral Imagination"
Edward W. Said, "Renan's Philological Laboratory"
Stephen Donadio, "Emerson, Christian Identity, and the Dissolution of the Social Order"
Fritz Stern, "The Burden of Success: Reflections on German Jewry"
Irving Howe, "The Pleasures of *Kim*"
Frank Kermode, "Can We Say Absolutely Anything We Like?"
Robert M. Adams, "Religion of Man, Religion of Woman"
Richard Hoggart, "Culture and Its Ministers"
Daniel Bell, "Beyond Modernism, Beyond Self"
Quentin Anderson, "On *The Middle of the Journey*" (G434)

F421. Boyers, Robert. *Lionel Trilling: Negative Capability and the Wisdom of Avoidance.* Columbia: University of Missouri Press, 1977. 74 pages.

Considers the aptness of T. S. Eliot's remark that Henry James "had a mind so fine that no idea could violate it"--a remark noted approvingly by Trilling--to Trilling himself. Focusing on a close reading of B19 and framing its analysis by shorter sections on C77 and C84, argues that in reading Trilling, "what we credit is the cogency and subtlety of the mind working through particular ideas without yielding entirely to them" rather than the premise that these ideas are "practically applicable to our own lives in any perfect way." Commends Trilling's reading of James's novel as a fable of the problems of political action as penetrating and persuasive because of its critique of characters like the Princess who mistake reality for "a thing" instead of recognizing its irreducibly dialectical nature. Criticizes Trilling, however, for calling Hyacinth Robinson's dilemma tragic rather than pathetic or symbolic. Argues that "as something of a symbolic presence himself . . . Trilling [is] unable to think past the function of the symbol to its underlying sources and potential consequences," and mistakes Hyacinth's suicidal "transcendence" of his divided political loyalties (contrasted here with Hamlet's heroically active attempt to avenge his father) for tragedy. Suggests that Hyacinth, and by implication Trilling, makes the opposite mistake from the Princess, conflating "human reality" with the Jamesian sensibility which is a more effective register than agent of political reality. More generally, calls Trilling's use of tragedy as a critical touchstone too indiscrimate, for "it [is] not 'tragic power' Trilling [is] avid to exalt [in his own fiction and the fiction he most admires], but a certain kind of wisdom" leading most often to the resignation or renunciation characteristic of Trilling's own stance.

F422. Chace, William M. *Lionel Trilling: Criticism and Politics.* Stanford: Stanford University Press, 1980. xiv, 207 pages.

Characterizes Trilling as a "sensibility" rather than "historian, philosopher, or theorist," and approaches each of his major works, which are treated in separate, roughly chronological chapters, not through his disciples or his system but through "the representative mind he sought to possess." This mind is quintessentially critical, anatomizing liberalism from within the assumptions of liberalism, and resisting the moral and doctrinal certitudes it seeks in politics, social philosophy, and literature. From politics Trilling derives the "story" most central to his work, the story of "the radical thirties," to which he constantly adverts as indispensable yet repugnant. But his analysis of history substitutes symbolism and "Moral Lesson" for close attention to specific events or figures, and his interest in social behavior subordinates society and history to literary analysis, even though that analysis is typically formulated in moral and social, rather than aesthetic, terms.

Argues that the leading concerns of Trilling's fiction--"the self, death, involvement with others and its costs, and the bitter pleasures of estrangement"--also form the core of his literary concerns. Subordinates Arnold's influence on Trilling to that of that of Hegel, Marx, and especially the later Freud, whose habit of abstracting general, and generally tragic, theories about human behavior from specific evidence is a hallmark of Trilling's work. Acknowledges, however, the importance of Arnold's example of locating himself within the middle-class intellectual audience he addressed. Like Arnold, Trilling constantly criticizes his chosen audience; though he finds in liberalism the only living American intellectual tradition, his own instincts are deeply conservative; and after his critique of liberalism in A4 shows him determined to insure that life and art are kept too complicated to be assimilated to any political program, he adopts a "supervisory" attitude toward culture in the 1950s and finally assumes a frankly adversarial role toward the institutionalized alienation he finds characteristic of modern culture in A8. Describes Trilling's development as marked by an increasing quietism, from the pietistic liberalism of A3 and the call in A4 to a will that can make the imagination politically active to the growing fascination with death as a Freudian absolute and the passivity of A8 and A9.

Sharply criticizes Trilling's choice of European affinities (Arnold, Forster, Wordsworth, Freud) as a means by which "Trilling removes himself from the American intellectual landscape" by apparently rising above its concerns as parochial--a strategy especially important in his treatment of American fiction in "Manners, Morals, and the Novel." Contends, in setting Trilling and Edward Shils against Daniel Bell and Irving Howe, that Trilling is not "satisfied . . . in describing the exhaustions and contradictions" inherent in contemporary culture, but seeks "a resolution of the problem" of an adversarial dominant culture; but concludes that his attempt to move "beyond culture" is defeated by his inconsistent ideas about what it would mean to go "beyond." Criticizes, more generally, Trilling's "enlightened modern liberalism" as "no more than wonderful wordplay" depending on the pretense that its leading abstractions (*moral realism*, *complexity*, *the opposing self*, *authenticity*) are universally accessible even though their meanings are controlled and often shifted by Trilling. This weakness makes A9 an inconclusive "rumination" on its hazily defined central terms and reduces "the kind of history Trilling writes" to a blurred, abstract account whose persuasive power is a function of its rhetorical brilliance rather than "the precise logic of historical argument." Ultimately defines Trilling's sensibility as willfully privatized, gradually retreating from political and circumstantial reality in favor of a controlled universe of moral dialectic.

F423. *Explorations: The Twentieth Century.* Special Series 3 (1989).

The third volume of this annual series, which "attempts to continue the critical tradition of the late Lionel Trilling," includes the following material (pp. 1-100):

Marianne Gilbert Finnegan, "Lionel Trilling: Humanist in the Modern World" (G465)
Bruno Bettelheim, "Notes on Lionel Trilling: Literature and Psychoanalysis" (G445)
J. A. Ward, "Lionel Trilling and Henry James" (G543)
Thomas S. Kane, "The Encompassing Mind: A Note on the Style of Lionel Trilling" (G488)
James Edward Hardy, "Of Tales Untold: Lionel Trilling's Fiction" (G479)

F424. Krupnick, Mark. *Lionel Trilling and the Fate of Cultural Criticism.* Evanston: Northwestern University Press, 1986. x, 207 pages.

Defines Trilling as a cultural critic who invented not only his own persona but his own genre of criticism by displacing the Marxist materialism that dominated his thought during the thirties by an emphasis on ideas, chief among them the idea of the self. Because Trilling's mind is essentially "reactive," it operates most fruitfully within a dogmatic context, defining itself by analyzing and dissenting from its prevailing assumptions. Treats this process in terms of a chronological development from the 1920's, when the context is provided by the "positive Jewishness" associated with the *Menorah Journal*, through the early 1930's, when Trilling becomes a fellow-traveler influenced by the kind of Marxism represented by Sidney Hook, before focusing on Trilling's tenure at Columbia University (which "effectively replaced Marxism as Trilling's cultural context"), where Trilling first planned his dissertation on Arnold as a specifically Marxist critique before turning to a more generally cultural analysis. Trilling's relation to the ideas that enrich his criticism is dialectical, but not in pragmatically Marxist terms; instead, he tends to balance irreconcilable terms (e.g. the "uptown" academic gentleman and the "downtown" engaged Jew, capitalism and socialism, art and politics, self and culture, Schopenhauer's will and idea) by defining an increasingly complex relation between them which resists any synthesis or resolution. Hence his dialectics, intended not "to bring about historical change--but to keep the culture on a steady course and maintain an always threatened equilibrium," are ultimately, like the tension and irony of New Critical theory, static, untranscendent, and unredemptive, for "Trilling decided that he preferred the continued existence of oppositions to any program for resolving them."

By turns praises and criticizes Trilling's static dialectics. The essentially "reactive" nature of Trilling's intelligence makes his critical persona dependent on political institutions and movements to which he no longer feels loyal. Although his apolitical dialectics separate him from the left wing of the New York intellectuals, he continues to define himself with respect to Marxism. Compares Trilling's reaction against the excesses of Communism to Wordsworth's reaction against the excesses of the 1789 revolution, arguing that after positioning himself successfully as a critic of "the liberal imagination," Trilling loses direction because of his loss of Stalinism not as a "god that failed" but as "a steady, dependable object of his polemic"--a loss that leaves his postwar writing "vague and rudderless" until his discovery of a new theme, "the adversary culture," which occupies the same position in his later work. Driven in the 1950's by the increasing poverty of the dominant culture, the threat of totalitarianism, and the discrediting of oppositional politics, Trilling seeks a positive touchstone for his work and finds it in the self which responds to the Nietzschean "weightlessness" of modern society by a humanistic/ biological "shaping" conceived largely in Freudian terms. This "shaped" self represents Trilling's most fundamental belief--the ability of people to create selves in the image of their ideal conceptions--but its invocation by Trilling also represents a retreat from political engagement (a "displacement of politics by [the] ontology" of a "self defining itself not by its choice of actions but by its choice of styles of selfhood") and an entrapment in the terms of political culture. Since "the only way he was able to sustain his totalization was, paradoxically, by raising his own contradictions to the level of an explanatory principle" such as the dialectic between culture and the biological self, "Trilling could only reproduce, not explain, the contradictions of the larger culture."

Maintains however that Trilling's positive, totalizing aims make him "our last Victorian sage." If, like Arnold, he is typically "cogent without being precise," his inveterately dialectical habit of mind, taking him from political activism to the analysis of cultural ideas, leads to the invention of the project of cultural criticism--a project which, for all its limitations, constitutes "his most original act of criticism." Trilling's greatest strengths stem from his own contradictory drives toward political idealism and cultural assimilation. Although his later work eventually, and disappointingly, resolves this conflict in favor of assimilation, the tension between personal and social ideals, perilously maintained throughout the 1940's, is the source of Trilling's best work. His failure to maintain this tension in his later work is traceable to the decline of cultural criticism as a possible response to an increasingly fragmentary and irrational social context. Concludes by lamenting the failure of any more recent critic of Trilling's authority to rise in defense of the shaped self as a critique of recent deconstructions of the self by Derrida and Lacan.

F425. O'Hara, Daniel T. *Lionel Trilling: The Work of Liberation.* Madison and London: University of Wisconsin Press, 1988. xiv, 318 pages.

Proposes that the keynote of Trilling's criticism is its ability, "when confronted by the great achievement of another mind," to generate "imaginative sympathy" rather than "resentful critique." This "magnanimous" critical temper is predicated on a psychoanalytic, largely Oedipal model in which Trilling's father, and his Jewish origins generally, represent a promise or commission given to the second-generation son to fulfill. Analyzing C58 suggests that, "rather than hysterically revise the father, [Trilling] *functions as the father*," considering "the reader-self as one's student-offspring." In Trilling's criticism, the father is displaced successively by several avatars of the "opposing culture" which claim the critic's allegiance and provide him with a framework for debate: "America itself" in the 1930's, "the liberal or Stalinist imagination" in the 40's, "the cold-war polar world" in the 50's, "the academic modernism of the adversarial culture" in the 60's, and increasingly toward the close of his life, "the great dead" whose example and fellowship forms the most "sublimely repressive horizon of opposition." These avatars are used not to break Trilling's career into periods--O'Hara criticizes the neat chronological distinctions in Krupnick, though his own discussion is largely chronological--but to give different forms to the distinctive rhythm of Trilling's critical appreciations.

Traces the origin of this rhythm to the sense of loss, indeed of self-hatred, characteristic of American Jews and Americans generally, and moves through stages of "ambivalence, regression, renewed capacity for love" released by the experience of sympathetic reading and magnanimous criticism--magnanimous in its ability "to imagine . . . as noble a motive for the Other as one can imagine for itself." By reading into Tacitus' *Annals* (for example) "an allegory of the reader's own mental and historical conditions," Trilling develops a "sense of the past," an imaginative response to its gaps and indeterminacies which proposes the work's therapeutic value for modern audiences. Such a response, sufficiently rare even before Trilling, is further endangered in his time by "the paralyzing modern impasse between the revolutionary principle and the conservative instinct" familiar from earlier commentators and became a casualty, with Trilling's death, of the rampant careerism and professionalism which lead critics, instead of honoring classic texts and their authors, to expropriate them to a particular selfish use or political ideology.

Declines to identify Trilling as "the deconstructive bogeyman of phallologocentrism" because the "relentlessly sacrificial cast" of his humanism works against the aggrandizement of its own power; the self Trilling discovers through criticism is inescapably an opposing self which must constantly redefine its identity as its minority challenges become dogmas. (Hence Trilling's discomfort with the liberalism which nurtured him, and later with the official minority culture of postmodernism which he thought too pure and facile in its opposition to high modernism.) Neither, however, does his pietistic reverence toward the past make him a conservative rejoicing in complete submission to the models and precepts of the past, for "the power of repression . . . can become the work of liberation when dramatized, played out in the creation of a self-critical text." Since Trilling conceives "culture (repression's other name)" as "an intermediate realm between (yet still informed) by the anarchic desires of the self and the political struggles endemic to the social world," his brand of critical humanism "arranges the associative dimension of words to produce culture as an earthly paradise where power temporarily overcomes itself in reflexive play and yet retains its very real potential for violent transgression or equally violent repression." The purgatorial rhythm of Trilling's criticism produces, for the critic and his audience, a pleasure necessarily against the grain of the unconscious pleasures naturalized within the dominant culture.

In his later work, Trilling, dismayed at the ascendancy of "the established liberal pieties that would reform all aspects of human life by bringing them progressively under the enlightened rule of law," maintains his distance from liberalism by posing as its demonically benign parody, "a subversive image of the patriarchal tradition of romantic individualists in modern literature" which projects "a canon of subversive patriarchy to mirror ironically the absurd orthodoxy of the dominant culture of enlightened permissiveness." As postmodernism defines itself as modernism's Other, Trilling thus becomes liberalism's Other, differing however in his refusal to accede to the "weightlessness" of postmodernism, the superficial radicalism he deplores. But this pose, competing with the earnest pleasures of liberal culture and the weightless pleasures of postmodernism, is not as obviously pleasurable, and Trilling often yields to temptation when he "subverts the most forbidding implications of his own insights by succumbing to the spectacle he creates from his essays," eventually misreading Rousseau and Hegel in an "opportunistic and distorted formulation" in A9 and, in several late essays, "withdrawing his credence from the humanistic ideology that animated his career," refusing to accept the illusion of a usefully oppositional culture his students now eagerly adopt and proposing instead "an ideal of selfhood wholly textual in nature."

F426. *Salmagundi*, no. 41 (Spring 1978). Special issue in honor of Lionel Trilling.

Comprises pp. 3-110 of the Spring 1978 issue, including the surprisingly critical G535, G467, G466, and G542 among the following contributions:

Mark Shechner, "Lionel Trilling: Psychoanalysis and Liberalism" (G535)
Joseph Frank, "Lionel Trilling and the Conservative Imagination" (G467) and "Appendix (January 1978)" (G466)
Robert Langbaum, "The Importance of *The Liberal Imagination*" [misidentified in the Table of Contents as "Lionel Trilling and his Time"] (G500)
Helen Vendler, "Lionel Trilling and the *Immortality Ode*" (G542)
Lionel Trilling, Irving Howe, Leslie H. Farber, William

Hamilton, Robert Orrill, and Robert Boyers, "Sincerity and Authenticity: A Symposium" (E418)

F427. Shoben, Edward Joseph, Jr. *Lionel Trilling: Mind and Character*. New York: Ungar, 1981. x, 278 pages.

Describes Trilling in sympathetically psychoanalytic terms--the author is a clinical psychologist and former Columbia colleague of Trilling's--as an "opposing self" whose dialectical stance toward all ideology is essential to his own conception of himself as teacher and writer and to his conception of selfhood as such. Reviews the events of Trilling's career at Columbia, contending that Trilling "left nothing behind" but insisted on maintaining a critical distance from even his most sustaining social and institutional affiliations and emphasizing the importance of Trilling's profession as a teacher and aspirations as a novelist. Sees the leading motif of Trilling's temperament as an ambivalence which serves similar functions in his fiction and criticism, discusses the aptness of this ambivalence for a novelist, and speculates at length on Trilling's possible motives for abandoning fiction after A3 and on the likelihood that Trilling worked extensively on a second novel between 1955 and 1965.

Identifies four interlinked themes in Trilling's work to be treated in successive chapters: the dialectical relation between the individual and the culture that both confers and constrains identity (Trilling's clearest legacy from Freud), the conflict between personal freedom and social necessity, the perils of utopian fanaticism, and the uses of imagination in dealing with social reality. Names Arnold and Freud as Trilling's primary models, focusing on the tragic matrix of Trilling's thought but discussing in detail its indebtedness to Arnold's emphasis on feeling, especially the joy that confirms the individual's sense of selfhood. Argues that Trilling's faith in the success of liberal democracy is based on three tenets never articulated explicitly in his writings but underlying them all: the need to maintain a distinction between the realm of ideas or ideals and the realm of practical politics, the need to retard the application of ideals in the political realm through the legislative and executive processes, and the need to cultivate "the sentiment of being," the sense of oneself as "distinctive, existent, *real*," and ultimately irreducible to any social or ideological norms.

Defends Trilling against several earlier critics, citing especially their "distortions" of his refusal to commit himself categorically to any political ideology. Describes Trilling's "virtually deliberate development of anomie" as a Keatsian negative capability dramatizing his concept of selfhood as alienation, allowing him to entertain incompatible ideas about politics, morality, and the good life without necessarily taking sides or demanding resolutions, and argues against F421 and G467 that Trilling's suspicion of ideology represents a mode of engagement and continual openness rather than a retreat to neutrality or olympian detachment. Asserts that given doubts about the consequences of one's behavior and the efficacy of accepted moral standards, "the issue is less one of what he should *do* than one of what he will *become* as a result of his choosing." Largely accepts Chace's analysis in F422 of the primacy of death and the corruption of doctrinaire politics in Trilling's thought but contends that Trilling subordinates the fact of death to a more general concern for human mortality and institutional politics to a more generally moral view of culture, so that Trilling sees literary works as cultural situations, which are in turn "fights about moral issues," and adds a third primary area of concern: "issues of individual identity and integrity." Defends Trilling's hostility toward student radicals at Columbia on the grounds that "for Trilling, ideology was perhaps the prototypical form of an irritable grasping for fact or reason as a way of escaping from serious and complicated questions," concluding that his resistance to New Left fanaticism is consistent with the earlier resistance to socialist or religious fanaticism portrayed in A3, dismissing the charge of G525 that Trilling was unable to adapt to the sixties by replying that "Trilling had no wish to 'adapt' to the spirit of that time. He deplored it, opposed it, and suffered real anxieties about its probable consequences." Concludes with a brief bibliographic essay.

F428. Tanner, Stephen L. *Lionel Trilling*. Boston: Twayne, 1988. xiv, 150 pages.

Defines Trilling as "essentially a conservative--a conserving mind--nurtured in a liberal-radical environment," arguing that "despite his emphasis on politics, he was, in terms of partisan or ideological or practical politics, distinctly apolitical. His concern was literature and culture, and in his literary and cultural views he was singularly conservative." Reviewing Trilling's early association with the left, concludes that "his political 'activities' in the thirties consisted mainly in writing letters to the editor and signing petitions," adding that "it was Marx's method more than his conclusions that interested him." Contends that "the elusiveness [of such central terms as *liberal*, *moral*, *culture*, and *will*] combined with his courteous dialectical temperament enabled him to win a liberal audience for what, from a cultural standpoint, are really very conservative views." Sees the burden of Trilling's career as his attempt to reconcile the liberal and conservative habits of his mind.

After a general introductory chapter, proceeds to close readings of the major texts of the Uniform Edition, grouped chronologically. Traces Trilling's leading themes to his engagement with Arnold, probably encouraged by the recent prominence of the New Humanists, in A1: the social import of literature, the value of critical distinterestedness, the notion of culture as combining reason and faith, and the uses of historical dialectic. Defends the consistency of Trilling's work against critics' charges of non-development, emphasizing especially the third of these themes in Trilling's subsequent writing. In A4, which "propelled Trilling beyond criticism that merely explains the work of others to criticism that is literature in its own right, manifesting original and weighty ideas of its own," the central terms *moral*, *liberal*, and *culture* carry both rational and transcendental connotations. Notes that Trilling's intellectual quarrel with liberalism makes several of his titles ambiguous. The title of A4 "can be construed as positive only in the sense of constituting an ideal by which the actual imagination of liberalism is measured and found wanting." Despite its title, A5 does not simply invest the opposing self as Trilling's hero; instead, Trilling "admires Keats because of his firm grip on the essential fact that the destiny of the self is always to confront the difficult and limiting actualities of circumstances." More generally, since "a firm and vibrant sense of self . . . is achieved only within the social context, it must not be allowed to triumph over the sentiment of society." Discusses the ways A8 and A9, even from their titles, explore the threat of a self conceived as liberated from or operating in absolute oppposition to social constraints--a threat which engenders the leading ideas of Trilling's later work: the premise that modern literature is animated by aggression directed against society as such, the diagnosis of "the mystique of unpleasure" as a distinctive type of modern spirituality, and the conclusion that will has lost its value, and mind is under attack, in modern high culture. The essays of A5 mark a conservative retreat from modernism to the social values of the nineteenth-century novel; in A9, which is "a synthesizing rather than an original effort," Trilling achieves "a level of seriousness and breadth . . . [at which] terms like *liberal* and *conservative* cease to have much relevance."

Defends Trilling against many of his hostile critics, noting that his imputed defects of conceptual imprecision, evasiveness, secularism, anti-aestheticism, and lack of practical political commitment are necessary to enable his critique of ideological absolutism, his focus on the relations between literature and culture, and his insights into the complex legacy of such secular thinkers as Rousseau, Marx, and Freud. Points out that cultural critics, unlike literary critics, "put at risk the credibility of their shaping cultural vision each time they approach an individual subject as a cultural manifestation." Defends the ambivalence of C77 against reductionist commentators and of C84 against G463, which "simply confirms the existence of the tendencies Trilling was attacking." Argues that critics who consider A3 abstract and undramatic place undue restrictions on the form of the novel, and concludes more generally that Trilling's propensity for rhetorical qualification does not preclude moral and political purpose. Observes that although Trilling has been rejected by the current critical avant-garde, his reputation continues secure among readers and teachers "uninitiated into the mysteries of recent critical theory or repelled by them."

Section G

Essays and Review Articles

G429. Abel, Lionel. "Lionel Trilling and His Critics." *Commentary* 82 (November 1986): 56-63.

Notes recent retractions of critical attacks on Trilling by Mark Krupnick (F424) and Irving Howe (G485 and G486) and defends Trilling against attacks by Howe (M1017), Joseph Frank (G466 and G467), Delmore Schwartz (G531), and Robert Boyers (F421), rejecting Frank's opposition of Trilling's political quietism to Camus's political commitment and his contention that Trilling glorifies "the actualities of ordinary life." Argues that Trilling's work is organized around "a *critique of hubris* in modernist literature, in left-wing politics, and more generally in the moral life," agreeing with Trilling that "liberals [like Frank] will do almost anything in preference to taking a clear stand . . . against political radicalism."

Revised and reprinted in *Important Nonsense* (Buffalo: Prometheus, 1987), pp. 3-15.

G430. Adamowski, T. H. "Lionel Trilling: Modern Literature and Its Discontents." *Dalhousie Review* 55 (Spring 1975): 83-92.

Dissents from Trilling's arguments in C159 against teaching modern literature, arguing that apart from its new emphasis on sexual experience, modern literature is no more "personal" or "shocking" than *King Lear* or *Great*

Expectations and that writers like Lawrence are attacking particular cultures, not the idea of culture itself. Contends that Trilling's assumption of the "truth" of modernism's fascination with "the irrational, the demonic, and the barbaric" would render any rational discourse about modern literature contradictory. Suggests that the lack of "historical specificity" in Trilling's abstract conception of modernism causes him to overlook modernists like Williams, Stevens, Faulkner, and Sartre, who are marking "the loss of confidence in the standards and norms held up to us for twenty-five centuries by Western Civilization" rather than celebrating the triumph of the irrational over civilization.

G431. Adams, J. Donald. "Speaking of Books." *New York Times Book Review*, 12 April 1959, p. 2.

Attacks Trilling's speech at Robert Frost's 85th birthday party [C141] as an example of "literary snobbery," speculating that "Frost had difficulty in recognizing himself" as the "terrifying" poet Trilling described. Charges that Trilling, as "a native New Yorker . . . showed little understanding of the United States," a failure "widely shared by other American intellectuals" and by D. H. Lawrence, who, like Trilling, was "too lost in the Freudian wood." Concluding that "all this country needs is to recapture its earlier vision," claims that Frost, like Emerson, "simply sees the universe as it is and accepts it. He isn't terrified by what he sees, and neither should we be." Asks Trilling to surrender the confusion he shares with Lawrence--"Don't take Lawrence so seriously"--and "face the facts of life."

G432. Akmakjian, Hiag. "Psychoanalysis and the Future of Literary Criticism." *Psychoanalysis and the Psychoanalytic Review* 49 (Spring 1962): 3-28.

Examines the fallacies of Trilling's remarks on psychoanalysis as exemplary of the limitations of current literary criticism in its most sustained and thoughtful engagements with psychoanalysis. Charges that Trilling often misreads Freud and his disciples, especially Ernest Jones, because of a professional jealousy that expects psychoanalysts to respect the expertise of literary critics but does not reciprocate, arguing that Trilling's attack on Jones's Freudian reading of *Hamlet* confuses Jones's "psychoanalytic (or metapsychological) esthetic theory" with "literary criticism." Concludes that because Freud's scientific study of the importance of emotions in so many cultural fields has revolutionized the study of language and thought, future literary critics who wish to avoid Trilling's errors will need to supplement their humanistic education by undergoing a successful psychoanalysis.

G433. Alexander, Edward. "Lionel Trilling." *Midstream* 29 (March 1983): 48-57.

Examines the extent to which Trilling's writing and thinking was shaped by his Jewish identity: "Not enough to serve as a key to the complex unity of his mind but more than has usually been supposed." Emphasizes the decisive impact of the Holocaust on Trilling's later work, linking Trilling's surprising but characteristic pose in C96 of being "as Jewish among the goyim as he had formerly been goyish among the Jews" not only to Trilling's generally dialectical temperament but to his determination to "respond, in the only way he saw open to him, to the Jewish calamity." Considering C122 a paradigmatic attempt to find an adequate way to respond to the Holocaust as a shattering actuality before which "the mind stops," ascribes the failure of this attempt to Trilling's refusal either to become "a Holocaust Jew, one for whom the event was the existential reference point," or "to admit that his two chief values, mind and liberal culture," were not merely compromised but revealed as bankrupt by the Holocaust and its intimations of European cultural suicide. Concludes that in neglecting the postwar image of Jewish resurgence, particularly through the state of Israel, Trilling "showed no signs of attraction to a form of

Jewish existence committed to life rather than redolent of death" but that his work displays and fosters an unappeased yearning for faith, transcendence, and peace.

G434. Anderson, Quentin. "On *The Middle of the Journey*." *Art, Politics, and Will* (F420), pp. 254-64.

Describes A3's attack on "the pieties of middle-class radicalism" as so "grave and inclusive" that it had to be ignored rather than directly confronted. Traces the "confusion of the aims of the American Communist Party with the belief that the world could be remade in accord with our personal demands" to the "persisting American habit of appropriating political ideals as narcissistic supplies for a self which demanded nothing less than imaginative possession of its world" in Emerson, Thoreau, and Whitman, who differ in precisely this regard from the more dialectical British Romantics with whom they are often misleadingly classed. Ascribes "American individualism" ("the denial of conditioned human reality") to "the impoverished imagination of the human subject" linked to the exclusive concern of contemporary criticism with formal patterns rather than human subjects and their relations, and charges Trilling's increasingly apocalyptic leftist critics with a "refusal of the human condition" through a "love affair with an authoritarian politics which served their personal needs rather than those of the community"--leading them rather than Trilling to abandon "the politics of liberal democracy."

G435. Anon. "How Terrifying a Poet?" *Newsweek* 54 (27 July 1959): 89.

Briefly reviews the controversy between "eminent high-brow critic" Trilling and "eminent middle-brow critic" J. Donald Adams (G431) over Trilling's speech at Robert Frost's 85th birthday party (C140). Quotes Adams as saying that he had attacked Trilling on Frost's behalf because "he felt he had been maligned"; Trilling as having received a letter from Frost saying that "he was a little taken aback, but that he had enjoyed it," and acknowledging that he had had Adams in mind as one of the "admirers" who had not "understood clearly what [Frost has] been doing in [his] life in poetry; and Frost as not "upset. . . . His was serious criticism, and I couldn't be anything but pleased with serious criticism."

G436. Anon. "A Sad, Solemn Sweetness." *Time* 106 (17 November 1975): 74, 76.

An obituary notice recalling Trilling's tenure at Columbia, his refusal to testify against Whittaker Chambers at the Hiss perjury trial, and his arguments in A10 against affirmative action. Calls Trilling a critic "with neither an ideology nor an all-encompassing aesthetic theory" who relied on his "historical sense" in criticism.

G437. Anon. "Trilling Says 'Race' Doesn't Have Meaning." *Columbia Spectator*, 15 December 1939, p. 1.

Reports an address to the Jewish Students Society in which Trilling contends that race is "a modern superstition" with "no meaning at all," argues that Jews are a religious rather than a racial group, and concludes that "the meaning of Jewishness lies largely with the action of non-Jews. It is not a racial fact; it is not a religious fact to any great extent; it is not a positive cultural fact. It is wholly a social fact."

G438. Barrett, William. "The Authentic Lionel Trilling." *Commentary* 73 (February 1982): 36-47.

Describes Trilling as "a virtuous man without any touch of the prig" and "the most intelligent man of his generation--or at least the most intelligent I knew." Traces the animosity between Trilling and Delmore Schwartz to Schwartz's belief that Trilling had blocked his academic appointment at Columbia and Philip Rahv's willingness to allow his attack (G531) because of his suspicions that Trilling had become too "bourgeois" for *Partisan Review*. Sides with Trilling's reading of Proust in C90 against Schwartz's, and acknowledges that the "Classless Society" Schwartz felt Trilling to be opposing has come to seem frankly utopian, but agrees with Schwartz that Dostoevsky's characters tend to be motivated by "an *idea*"--by reason cut off from "the deepest instincts of life"--rather than by questions of class or money. Calls Trilling's adherence to Freud a substitute for religious faith, noting that his "'successful' psychoanalysis" led him to a transference directed not toward his analyst but toward Freud himself, and suggests that Trilling retained a nineteenth-century sensibility that made it, as Schwartz charged, difficult for him to appreciate modern literature. Sees C159 and the course it describes as Trilling's belated reply to Schwartz, praising the essay as "stimulating and fertile" but supplementing its analysis of modernism by emphasizing the "*detachment from feeling*" characteristic of modern literature and "the continuing secularization of our culture." Ascribes Trilling's resolute secularism to his revulsion from ghetto culture, wonders if his own funeral (which is briefly described) was secular or religious, and asks how religious forms, once emptied of meaning, can be renewed.

Revised and reprinted in L896.

G439. Barrett, William. "What Is the 'Liberal' Mind?" *Partisan Review* 16 (March 1949): 331-36.

Responds to Richard Chase's broad attack on progressive liberalism [M996 and M998] by indicating the roots of liberalism in the rationalism of the Enlightenment and inviting Chase to demonstrate his commitment by attacking the Enlightenment directly in the name of the religious convictions he admires in Father Zossima. Worries about the limits of Trilling's use of "liberal" to describe the targets of his attacks: does it include only avowed Stalinists like Max Lerner and Harold Laski, or leftists like Sidney Hook and Bertrand Russell as well? Suggests that critics of liberalism consider more directly the legacy of the Enlightenment instead of wasting their energy attacking "the degradation of a doctrine" in "minor targets."

For Trilling's rejoinder, see E390.

G440. Barzun, Jacques. "The Critic, the Public, and the Sense of the Past." *Salmagundi*, nos. 68-69 (Fall 1985-Winter 1986), pp. 206-25.

Deplores the decline of historical criticism in the face of the New Critics' misconception of formal analysis as "scientific," observing that the triviality of earlier historical and biographical criticism at least "left the work of art untouched," capable of engaging new readers, whereas contemporary criticism, which leaves the work "methodically, surgically invaded," threatens to cure students of the love of art. Commends instead the "cultural criticism" adopted in A4, explaining how it arose in a graduate seminar first taught by Barzun and Trilling in the mid 1940's, informed by principles of non-exclusion and non-coerciveness: "no method, no terminology, no system-based exclusions," and "no holds barred" in proposing evidence and background knowledge for the reading of each text, so that "the clarity and openness of the historical outlook gave individual judgment free play." Argues that modern political history and literary biography too often express the impulse toward "collecting" sociological data in the absence of an informing narrative sense, so that "the cultural scene resembles that of the seventeenth and early eighteenth centuries, when contemporary art alone was intelligible and history had not yet come to sophisticate the critical mind." Describes cultural criticism, directed by a "sixth sense" born of experience rather than theory, as a necessary corrective to the contemporary "drive to reduce the many and various to oneness."

G441. Barzun, Jacques. "Memoir: Remembering Lionel Trilling." *Encounter* 47 (September 1976): 82-88.

Traces Barzun's long friendship with Trilling from their years together as college students--when Trilling "affected a languid, sauntering elegance" despite his "invincible ignorance in maths"--to their Columbia colloquium on great books to their coeditorship with W. H. Auden of the Reader's Subscription. Distinguishes Trilling from Arnold, a moralist fearful of "massed philistines and democrats" who seeks refuge in a poetry unsullied by political forces, ascribing the more "political and intellectual" focus of Trilling's work to the political matrix of his upbringing and coming-of-age. Describes Trilling's "possibilist mind" as deeply suspicious of the coerciveness of ideology and endlessly open to new complexities, citing as advantages in his critical project his continual rereading for his classes and his relative insulation from the French humanists who influenced Babbitt and Eliot, though blaming his immersion in teaching, along with lack of encouragement by publishers and editors, for his failure to publish any novels following A3. Ascribes Trilling's "unwarrantably subdued reputation" during his lifetime to his shyness and the academic appointment that was inimical to the image of a "thinker-pathfinder."

G442. Bender, Thomas. "Lionel Trilling and American Culture." *American Quarterly* 42 (June 1990): 324-47.

Charts Trilling's development as a spokesperson for the American middle class, from his earliest influences in the 1920's--not Marx, but John Dewey, the Greenwich Village writers (Randolph Bourne, Van Wyck Brooks, and Edmund Wilson), Columbia College, and the *Menorah Journal*--that "prefigured the complex pattern of exploration and evasion" of the ideological constraints Trilling preferred "to work *within*, not *against*." Links Trilling's growing success to the rise of the educated middle class he took as his audience and the later decline of his influence to the fragmentation of the middle class into "the diverse public he confronted in the 1960s." Contends that Trilling's synthetic, consensual criticism "no longer provides a model" for a contemporary culture whose territory is so closely contested.

G443. Beresnack, Lillian. "The Journey of Lionel Trilling." *Perspective* 1 (Spring 1948): 177-83.

Praises A3 for its "sensitive blending of realism with something higher than realism," its ironic humor, and the "relevance" and "modernity" of its style, regretting only "the exclusiveness of its appeal," since it is unlikely to appeal to "those who are concerned more with social action than with the ideas behind social action." Describes two dangers implicit in choosing a political attitude--abandoning political activity to professional politicians, and adopting "a political ideology as a religious faith"--and stresses the importance of avoiding both dangers by "remaining ambivalent today," as John Laskell does. Notes Trilling's emphasis on death as "almost a kinetic symbol" connected to both "the guilt of modern liberals" and "the relaxation of the will" in love, tolerance, or the distrust of abstract ideals, and compares Laskell's ambivalence to that of Billy Budd (against Gifford Maxim's religious reading of Melville).

G444. Berger, Peter L. "'Sincerity' and 'Authenticity' in Modern Society." *Public Interest*, no. 31 (Spring 1973), pp. 81-90.

Attempts to place the "intellectual drama" of *Sincerity and Authenticity* in a sociopolitical context by arguing that "ideas do not triumph in history because of their intrinsic truth, but because of their affinity to pragmatic concerns and interests," and tracing the connections between the growing asymmetry between self and society Trilling studies and the growing "weightlessness" of social institutions originally effective in anchoring the individual's sense of self. Discusses the rise of the private social sphere, exemplified by the family and the novel, in fostering "the production and maintenance of identity," its pluralization and consequent decline as a stable guarantor of identity since the industrial revolution, and the dangerously nostalgic appeal of totalitarianism as a replacement for the private sphere. Suggests that the results of the 1972 Presidential election indicate that "American society is still much more a world of bourgeois sincerities than of the desperate drama of authenticity-versus-alienation," but predicts that the modern crisis in identity Trilling describes will make "more drastic political remedies" seem more attractive.

G445. Bettelheim, Bruno. "Notes on Lionel Trilling: Literature and Psychoanalysis." *Explorations: The Twentieth Century* (Special Series) 3 (1989): 29-44.

Hails Trilling as Freud's principal explicator to the literary community and his defender against revisionary theorists and a reductively optimistic American public who denied the importance of the death drive. Suggests that the internal conflicts F424 ascribes to Trilling attracted Trilling to Freud's conflictual view of human nature and his conviction that "the best we can gain out of life is to be able to love well and to work well, despite our inner conflicts and the knowledge that death is life's inescapable end." Contrasts Trilling's dialectical view of psychological conflict with the "fascination with disintegration" he finds characteristic of postwar modernism, identifying Trilling's central theme as "the affirmation of the self."

G446. Blackmur, R. P. "The Politics of Human Power." [Review of A4.] *Kenyon Review* 12 (Autumn 1950): 663-73.

Notes that Trilling "cultivates a mind never entirely his own," a mind he identifies variously with that of contemporary society and a prophetic and corrective old European society, in dealing with the problems of the "mass urban society" and its distrust of the intellect despite its commitment to universal education. Defends Trilling against R. W. B. Lewis's charge in G502 of stoicism, calling him "an administrator of the affairs of the mind" who "is everywhere against the passive as he is against escape into the long view or aggression into the moral view," and citing "the difference between saying that the job [of mediating between the contradictory powers of mind, emotion, and will] cannot be done and saying that the job must be done over again at the cost of any insurrection and any initiative." Calls Trilling "primarily a literary critic" who "teeters into the social or the historical" only in his excesses or errors. Identifying Trilling's masters as Arnold and Freud, discusses the ways their emphasis on "incentive and dread" and "the intellectuality and sanity of art" collide in Trilling, who defines ideas not in terms of "'thought,' which is a subject for history, but . . . thinking, which is a matter of experience." Observes that the failure of liberal democracy to support a distinguished literature should be ascribed not to the particular shortcomings of liberalism but to the necessary hostility of literature to all institutionalized power, and suggests that when Arnold and Freud overpower Trilling and "make him think too much," he forgets that the true business of literature and intellect is "to remind the powers that be . . . of the turbulence they have to control."

Revised and reprinted in *The Lion and the Honeycomb: Essays in Solicitude and Critique* (New York: Harcourt, Brace & World, 1955), pp. 32-42.

G447. Borklund, Elmer. "Lionel Trilling." *Contemporary Literary Critics*. Edited by Elmer Borklund. New York: St. Martin's, 1977. Pp. 485-90.

Defines Trilling's leading subject as "the conflict between the self and culture" and the power of art to liberate the self from the tyranny of culture. Bases Trilling's concept of the free and unconditioned self in his self-critical liberalism, noting his growing pessimism about contemporary attempts to define a self apart from cultural norms. Concludes that the appearance of A8 and A9 refutes "the established view of Trilling as a genteel moralist" by developing the implications of the dialectic between self and culture.

G448. Boyers, Robert. "*The Middle of the Journey* and Beyond: Observations on Modernity and Commitment." *Salmagundi* 1, 4 (1966-67): 8-18.

Describes John Laskell's development as "the liberal intellectual's journey from detachment to alienation" because his "destructive, analytical cast of mind" not only "calls all commitments, all sympathies, into question" but "eats the heart out of its own pleasures by perpetually judging them by standards which it knows to be arbitrary or facile." Noting the bad faith of Arthur Croom and Laskell's "disgust" at "the inauthenticity of his [own] response" to Duck Caldwell, argues that "the horror of the modern world, its rampant criminality, is largely attributable to the unwillingness of all men . . . to implicate themselves in actions in which they ostensibly believe," and recommends that artists and intellectuals reject moderation in their views and expressions and commit themselves to "embarrass[ing] those in positions of power and influence," concluding that "the emergent culture to which artists and intellectuals must contribute is a culture of anarchic, but not random, dissent, in which the powerful and influential feel forever threatened, challenged."

G449. Bradbury, Malcolm. "Lionel Trilling: End of the Journey." *New Statesman* 90 (19 November 1975): 619.

A memorial notice describing Trilling's movement into literature "not as an escape from politics, but in pursuit of a deeper politics," distinguishing his liberalism from British liberalism, and emphasizing the centrality of A3's argument that "a good politics is a politics of whole persons."

G450. Brustein, Robert. "Lionel Trilling, Memories of a Mentor." *Yale Review* 76 (March 1987): 162-68.

Recalls Brustein's days as a student under Trilling and Trilling's paternal encouragement of him as a critic by help and example despite his prejudice against theater as "a poor stepsister of the arts." Notes that in the late 1960's, Trilling came under attack by radicals like his former student Norman Podhoretz for his conservatism, just as he would later be attacked by Podhoretz, "now turned rabidly neoconservative," for his liberalism. Recounts how an attempt by Brustein and his wife to repair the friendship between the Trillings and Lillian Hellman was ruined by Hellman's "incensed" response ("'the most conservative thing I ever heard'--a phrase she often used") to "something that Lionel or Diana said." Asserts that Trilling, to whom Brustein dedicated *The Culture Watch* shortly before Trilling's death, "penetrated deeper into life and literature than any American critic before or since," and predicts "a less ideological day" when readers will rediscover him.

G451. Casalandra, Sister Estelle. "The Three Margarets." *Sewanee Review* 81 (Spring 1973): 225-36.

Suggests that the Margaret of Hopkins's "Spring and Fall" and the two Margarets of C84 "dramatize . . . three modes of realizing or confronting the human condition" of mortality and susceptibility to sin: through inarticulate intuition, through "a developing rational process" of self-consciousness which is equally intimidating, and through an angry refusal of one's flawed humanity. Quotes two letters in which Trilling acknowledges that he had Hopkins's poem in mind when he wrote the story, but not in its first conception.

G452. Chace, William. "Lionel Trilling: The Contrariness of Culture." [Review of the first four volumes of A11.] *American Scholar* 48 (Winter 1978-79): 49-59.

Contrasts the "adulation" accorded Trilling by many of his contemporaries with the "condescension or disregard" of younger critics, noting that in its constant critique of "intellectual life," Trilling's work "provided the kind of sustenance needed by those who would, in later times, find him wanting." Emphasizes the necessarily adversary role Trilling conceived for critics of culture and for culture itself. Identifies art as a mediating or transcendent force in the struggle Trilling perceives between self and "the erosiveness of culture," but concludes that for Trilling art, though it may relieve the contradictions between self and culture, cannot resolve them. Calls Trilling a "sensibility" rather than a historian, philosopher, theorist, or critic, noting that his work is a praxis rather than a systematic exposition of thought.

G453. Chace, William M. "*The Middle of the Journey*: Death and Politics." *Novel* 10 (Winter 1977): 137-44.

Disagrees with Trilling's recollection that the figure of Maxim in its political associations displaced death as the primary subject first planned for A3, observing that the novel reveals little new "about politics, about communism, or even about anti-communism," and that Laskell's attempt to transcend the political will is based on his "love affair" with death. Argues that Maxim's more active awareness of death gives his opposition to Laskell's merely pious humanism, which "exists only to be threatened," a decisive force: "Laskell we might sympathize with, but it is Maxim who imposes himself on us."

G454. Conant, Oliver. "The Hunger and the Journey: Communism in the Thirties." *Book Forum* 6 (Winter 1982): 248-56.

Discusses A3 in conjunction with Richard Wright's *American Hunger* as seminal studies of "the Communist mentality" in the thirties. Describes Trilling as briefly a fellow-traveler whose opposition to the Party "found an important outlet" in 1937 with the transformation of *Partisan Review* from an organ of the John Reed clubs to an independent review. Argues that both Wright's and Trilling's novels prescribe "the attainment of maturity," the acceptance of identity and the possibility of action apart from a single absolute political imperative, as a means to facing "the disenchanted life." Concludes that Wright and Trilling show the hunger that led American intellectuals to Communism also leading them beyond it by virtue of their "capacity to act, feel, and think in [a] human way."

G455. Cowan, S. A. "Parrington, Woolley, and Reality: A Note on Trilling's 'Of This Time, of That Place.'" *English Language Notes* 26 (December 1988): 56-59.

Following Trilling's autobiographical commentary on the story in B40, identifies V. L. Parrington as a prototype for the figure of the disapproving older critic Frederic Woolley. Notes the similarity between Woolley's and Parrington's programmatic theories of literature and their language in having "hymned . . . the struggle for wheat in the Iowa fields," and suggests that Trilling would have expected readers of the story to notice the resemblances.

G456. Curley, Dorothy Nyren. "Lionel Trilling." *A Library of Literary Criticism: Modern American Literature*. Fourth enlarged edition. 4 volumes. Edited by Dorothy Nyren Curley, Maurice Kramer, and Elaine Fialka Kramer. New York: Ungar, 1969. 3: 273-78.

Excerpts brief passages from G469, H555, H595, H602, H610, H626, H641, H647, H693, H695, H696, H700, H728, H760, H777, L959, and M1027.

G457. Daiches, David. "Keats or the Upanishads?: Reflections on Lionel Trilling's 'Lost Cause.'" *Encounter* 11 (December 1958): 3-12.

Takes issue with Trilling's contention in C135 that the decline of the study of English literature is linked to the decline of England as a world power, ascribing the attack on British literature survey courses in the 1930's to the rise of New Criticism and other critical and pedagogical debates. Notes the different kinds of importance literary works can have (as historical background, as influences on history, as texts significant to a large fraction of the world's population) and argues against pursuing "the will-of-the-wisp of world knowledge" apparently threatened by the decline of British literary study and for a closer appreciation of "the nature and formal qualities" of individual works of art as each a microcosm of the creative transformation of knowledge and ideas.

G458. Dickstein, Morris. "The Critics Who Made Us: Lionel Trilling and *The Liberal Imagination*." *Sewanee Review* 94 (Spring 1986): 323-34.

Recalls Trilling as "more playful than genteel" in his inveterate habit of self-criticism and his preference for "art and imagination" to politics: "He would puckishly refuse to say whatever was most expected of him, to the consternation of his neoconservative admirers." Criticizes Trilling's strictures against the American "social fiction" of Dreiser and Richard Wright, remarking that Trilling's fictional desiderata of "variousness and possibility" are better fulfilled by the "loose baggy monsters" of Tolstoy and Dostoevsky than by James's novels. Notes that Trilling's divided sensibility, adopting "a lacerating gesture of introspection," refuses to turn literature into an object of knowledge or a repository of fixed ideas, but prefers "to amplify the cultural contradictions of the moment" through its own dialogue with itself, and suggests that Trilling's later work suffered from "the complete rout of his radical adversaries."

G459. Donoghue, Denis. "The Critic in Reaction." [Review of A5.] *Twentieth Century* 158 (October 1955): 376-83.

Acknowledges Trilling's achievement but denies A4 the importance of Ransom's *The World's Body*, Winters's *Maule's Curse*, or Leavis's *The Great Tradition* because its focus is ideological rather than literary. Observes that Trilling has little interest in the particular language of lyric poems or passages from longer works, and suggests that he "is drawn to the novel rather than to the poem because in dealing with the novel he can more plausibly move out along his pet sociological tangents." Describes the power of A5 as closely akin to that of "sociological studies such as David Riesman's *The Lonely Crowd*." Contends that Trilling has been erroneously acclaimed "the Whole Critic" because he writes without jargon, his writing conveys a sense of abundance and range, and he represents a survival of a comfortably belletristic tradition. Suggests that Trilling will ultimately be remembered as a novelist rather than a critic.

G460. Donoghue, Denis. "Trilling, Mind, and Society." *Sewanee Review* 86 (Spring 1978): 161-86.

Traces Trilling's preoccupation with "the mutual bearing of mind and society," which nurtures or blights it and in which its actions have consequences. Agreeing with R. P. Blackmur [G446] that Trilling cultivated a mind "never entirely his own," notes that this mind combined Trilling's own purposes with "the purposes he ascribed to the best intentions of a possible society rather than of the particular society in question and in force." Compares Trilling to structuralists who emphasize cultural conditioning, but distinguishes "Trilling's sense of the cost of a human act" from the fatalistically self-chosen "slavery" of structuralist theories of mind. Emphasizes Trilling's distrust of absolute freedom or consciousness as a self-gratifying activity: "The end is given as social consequence. . . . He is interested not in the possibilities of mind but only in its consequences" and "judged mind upon its results." Suggesting that "mind" is a more hierarchical, "practical," and unifying term than "imagination," argues that Trilling's confidence in the social and moral efficacy diminished dramatically in his later work, leading him to propose "culture" as a redemptive intermediary between an unfashionably active mind and a hypostasized, inhumane society, and finally to express outrage in A8 over the degradation of oppositional cultural attitudes through mass-production and vulgarization. Criticizes Trilling's mournful emphasis in C159 on the idea of social alienation from society promoted by the teaching of modern literature, noting that institutions assimilate such disruptive ideas to ultimate ideas of order, and that even such a powerful idea always competes for allegiance with many other ideas. Disputes Trilling's readings of Hawthorne, James, and Kafka in C177, concluding that Trilling's dialectics are sustained by abstract ideas of society and language ("*eloquentia*") providing "reasonable energies at work, fair purposes and consequences, more nonchalance than self-consciousness, and just enough tension to foster and maintain validity."

G461. Eisinger, Chester E. "Trilling and the Crisis in Our Culture." *University of Kansas City Review* 25 (Autumn 1958): 27-35.

Defends A3 against the charge that its characters are "intellectuals enacting a bit of highbrow history" by setting it within a context of Trilling's essays, especially his two essays on Freud (A6 and C69). Argues that Laskell's incorporation of both a death instinct and a reality principle, allow his movement "from an uncritical liberalism to a new, humanistic liberalism," making it possible for him to avoid both "the simplistic optimism about man" of liberals like the Crooms and "the God-dependence and guilt-obsession" of fervent neo-conservatives like Maxim. Concludes that the temptations offered by Maxim and the Crooms are designed "to make Laskell's position desperate, because Laskell must test whether the self alone can survive in modern society," and that Laskell succeeds by rejecting both absolute individual freedom and absolute responsibility.

Revised and reprinted in *Fiction of the Forties* (Chicago: University of Chicago Press, 1963), pp. 135-44.

G462. Elledge, W. Paul. "The Profaning of Romanticism in Trilling's 'Of This Time, of That Place.'" *Modern Fiction Studies* 29 (Summer 1983): 213-26.

Describes the pivot of the story as "the clash of romantic with classical values" within both Joseph Howe and Ferdinand Tertan. Notes that although "Howe no less than Tertan begins as *potentially* a full-fledged, full-throated romantic," he gravitates increasingly toward such classical values as "traditionalism, practicality, decorum, political conservatism, reasonableness"--values represented in purer form by the Dean and in a debased version by Theodore Blackburn--while Tertan, who "has in his own view transcended time and place and even parentage" from the moment Howe first sees him, "does not himself appear the paradigm of romanticism--is not, in fact, without alloy--until after his official disposition by the College--a disposition which "has neither deprived him of power nor sheltered the namers."

G463. Farrell, James T. "A Comment on Literature and Morality: A Crucial Question of Our Times." *New International* 12 (May 1946): 141-45.

Defines two approaches to moral problems, based on social morality, which seeks to understand and change the social conditions that produce moral inequities, and personal morality, which emphasizes "the regeneration of the individual." Argues that Henry James is "not a moralist in the sense that Tolstoy was," since he merely reflects moral conflicts, transforming them into individual conflicts, rather than urging change. Puts forth Doestoevsky and Ibsen as exemplary modern moralists, contrasting them to Trilling, whose dramatization of a moral problem in C84 is trivialized by its omissions (no sympathetic lower-class characters, no responsibility for the protagonist to act on his principles) and rendered unfair by the spokespersons for each position (Mark Jennings [sic], reserving moral responsibility to each individual, is opposed by his daughter Lucy [sic], "an inexperienced thirteen-year-old girl who is still too young to appreciate the painting by Rouault," parroting her unseen teacher's belief that society is responsible). A characteristic riposte to C86, as its footnotes make clear.

Revised and reprinted as "The Other Margaret" in *Literature and Morality* (New York: Vanguard, 1947), pp. 3-14.

G464. Fergusson, Francis. "Three Novels." [Review of A3; Robert Penn Warren, *All the King's Men* (New York: Harcourt, Brace, 1946); and James Gould Cozzens, *Guard of Honor* (New York: Harcourt Brace, 1948).] *Perspectives USA* 6 (Winter 1954): 30-44.

Compares A3 to Robert Penn Warren's *All the King's Men* and James Gould Cozzens's *Guard of Honor*, suggesting that all three authors, seeing "their characters in relation to social forces which dwarf them," seem "not sure of the meaning of their narratives." Notes that Trilling's attempt "to write the spiritual epic of our time" has opened a promising new line in contemporary fiction, but finds John Laskell's conflicts with the Crooms and Gifford Maxim "hardly enough to substantiate either Laskell or the philosophies at issue," since unlike Cozzens's hero, who remains despite his imaginative thinness convincingly "responsible for immediate practical decisions" which establish his "moral being," Laskell, whose "diet of thinking" diminishes the power established by his earlier illness and convalescence to give him "some of the ghostliness of the concepts themselves," is finally "responsible only for rejecting Maxim and the Crooms."

G465. Finnegan, Marianne Gilbert. "Lionel Trilling: Humanist in the Modern World." *Explorations: The Twentieth Century* (Special Series) 3 (1989): 1-28.

Reviews Trilling's affinities with Arnold, emphasizing his defense of literature as a rational, civilizing moral force. Discusses Trilling's early modification of Arnold's classical literary humanism in favor of a romantic aesthetic championing "a strong individual self" as an antidote to "a world of titanic upheavals," and traces his later critique of this aesthetic in response to the modernist cult of unpleasure, the narcissistic hedonism of the youth movement, and the cultural determinism of Marxism early and late. Notes that in A9, Trilling, indisposed to prescribe "wisdom" as an essential concomitant of great literature and unable to follow Arnold in allying literature to such other dependably civilizing forces as "the State and the Christian religion," fails to work out a reasoned defense of literature as a cultural force. Concludes that despite Trilling's small direct influence on American culture, his search for a dialectical awareness of complexity remains "*the* moral necessity for the multiple and intersecting cultures of the contemporary world."

G466. Frank, Joseph. "Appendix (January 1978)." *Salmagundi*, no. 41 (Spring 1978), pp. 46-54. See G467.

Discusses his turn against A5 in terms of his earlier enthusiasm for A4 as the exemplary American attempt to fuse political radicalism with "an openness to the cultural *avant-garde*." Reiterates his critique of Trilling's development, citing the shift from defining "the given" in A4 as "the metaphysical limits of life itself, to all those human appetites and desires that have always proven refractory to the demands of the social-political will," to defining it in A5 as "an acceptance of circumstances whatever they might be." Traces this shift to the influence of the later Freud, noting the discrepancies between the penetration of Trilling's particular cultural analyses--though he underrates the ways in which modernist works "reveal their own destructiveness as a problem and a dilemma"--and the misleadingly Freudian terms in which he generalized those analyses. Stresses Trilling's achievement as a literary critic, and discerns in his emphasis on "mind" in C185 a useful alternative to "biology."

G467. Frank, Joseph. "Lionel Trilling and the Conservative Imagination." [Review of A5.] *Sewanee Review* 64 (Spring 1956): 296-309.

Contends that Trilling rose to prominence at the same time as the New Critics because he expressed their "disillusionment with politics" as an explicitly political critique of liberalism from an aesthetic viewpoint not constrained by political limitations, implying an "immediate practical and political revelance" for his retreat from political actuality. Argues that the tension between art and politics animating A4 is resolved in A5 by wholesale "rejection of the political imagination" through the exaltation of the "abnegation of the will," which tends to "endow social passivity and quietism *as such* with the halo of aesthetic transcendence" by conflating "the tragic sense of the conditioned in Donne, Pascal, and Tolstoy" with the "social trivia" celebrated by Howells, making no distinction between Keats's heroically aestheticized "self-realization and a blind and dumb submission to destiny," a condition which shares with Keats "only an absence of will." Describes the movement from A4 to A5 as a shift from a liberal attack on "the tyranny of the will in wishing to impose its aims on other modes of apprehending reality" to a conservative defense of "the virtues of acknowledging necessity," claiming that "in adopting the positive standpoint of the conservative imagination, Mr. Trilling has taken over its weakness": its readiness to abandon the active intervention of will even "in areas where the will may fruitfully intervene." Notes regretfully that whereas Trilling's "defense of art and the tragic" in A4 marked a useful corrective to the "shortsighted [American] optimism and utilitarianism," his defense of the conditioned in A5 merely encourages the prevailing tendency toward conformism.

Revised and reprinted in *The Widening Gyre: Crisis and Mastery in Modern Literature* (New Brunswick: Rutgers University Press, 1963), pp. 253-74, and in F426.

G468. Freedman, William. "*The Middle of the Journey*: Lionel Trilling and the Novel of Ideas." *The Forties: Fiction, Poetry, Drama*. Edited by Warren French. Deland, FL: Everett/Edwards, 1969. Pp. 239-48.

Observing that A3 "reads at times as though it were first serialized in *PMLA*," acknowledges that its ideological discussions, "usually almost guaranteed to be boring, are often dramatic and rarely tire or bore us," adding that the rest of the novel is far less dramatic. Aligns the novel ideologically with such "anti-revolutionary or anti-reformist novels" as *The Possessed* and *Darkness at Noon* as expressing greater skepticism about "the possibilities of the human will and its capacity to resist corruption" than novels like *Man's Fate*, *The Grapes of Wrath*, or *The Fixer*. Traces the novel's weakness to the limited nature of Laskell's acceptance of conditioned responsibility, a political awakening which has no impact on either others or himself. Remarks that although it is Trilling's intention to dramatize "the void left by [the failure of] the Party," still "one never feels that it matters much, that the void is filled even partially by the pain of loss or a subsequent commitment," and that Laskell's insight "is by definition untranslatable into signficant action." Concludes that the lack of "distance between author and protagonist" prevents Trilling from indicating "just how pathetic the John Laskells truly are."

G469. Frohock, W. M. "Lionel Trilling and the American Reality." *Southwest Review* 45 (Summer 1960): 224-32.

Notes that Trilling's style implies a close correspondence between his ideas and those of his readers; characterizes Trilling as a cultural critic rather than a literary analyst whose perspective is bounded by New York; and criticizes his understanding of American culture as parochial. Defines the characteristic experience of American fiction as confrontation with "an unfamiliarity with life in America itself" which leads to conflicts between different subcultures and their values, and cites Dickinson and Millay as illustrating "the experience of such variation" as Trilling typically overlooks.

Revised and reprinted in *Strangers to This Ground: Cultural Diversity in Contemporary American Writing* (Dallas: Southern Methodist University Press, 1961), pp. 19-35.

G470. Galliano, Luciano. "Lionel Trilling: Critica et Narrativa." *Studi Americani* 2 (1956): 243-59.

Distinguishes Trilling from other American writer-critics like Eliot and Kenneth Burke by virtue of his intellectualism, stemming from Arnold, which imparts a European cast to both his criticism and his fiction through his Arnoldian challenge to the liberal mind to return to the ideals of complexity, difficulty, and variety.

G471. George, Diana L. "Thematic Structure in Lionel Trilling's "'Of This Time, of That Place.'" *Studies in Short Fiction* 13 (Winter 1976): 1-8.

Discusses the irreconcilable conflict between science and morality represented by the image of Hilda Aiken's deceptively imprecise camera and the relationship between art and life dramatized by an exploration of the poet's social role that emphasizes the similarities between the dangerous "madness" of Howe's "personal" poetry and Tertan's insanity.

G472. Goodheart, Eugene. "Lionel Trilling, 1905-1975: A fusion of baroque, often witty elegance and classic lucidity." *Chronicle of Higher Education* 11 (17 November 1975): 15.

Observes that Trilling's teaching and writing were both marked by a concern to link politics and literature--one of A3's "deep attractions" for the young Goodheart was that "it did not foreclose the possibility of a radical position"--and by an unequalled historical sense, and describes his "essential theme" as "the historical life of the modern self," a "shaped self" he took as his "doctrine" even when it came most sharply under attack.

G473. Green, Martin. "Lionel Trilling and the Two Cultures." *Essays in Criticism* 13 (October 1963): 375-85.

Defends C. P. Snow against Trilling's attack on him in C170 by disputing Trilling's reading of *The Two Cultures*: Snow is recommending that the traditonal pattern of British education, not traditional culture, be broken; he does not use "literary" and "traditional" interchangeably; he does not imply that whatever the future scientists "have in their bones" is necessarily good. Deplores Trilling's insistence on analyzing Snow's motives for his argument about the dangers of literary culture instead of responding directly to that argument, as he does in C159, which Green quotes at length against Trilling, concluding that "Trilling himself has shown us that contemporary literature is the most *dis*loyal opposition imaginable, disloyal not just to science and the future, but to every stable and organized undertaking, to society itself." Recommends that instead of attempting to impeach science as "a non-humane intellectual discipline," literary figures join scientists in moving "toward a middle mode [of education], a more genuinely intellectual mode."

Revised and reprinted as Part II of "Two defences of 'The Two Cultures,'" in *Science and the Shabby Curate of Poetry* (New York: Norton, 1965), pp. 1-30.

G474. Greenfield, Robert M. "The Politics of the Liberal Imagination." *Perspectives on Contemporary Literature* 11 (1985): 1-9.

Contends that Trilling's achievement depends on his having juxtaposed "divergent conceptions of liberalism"--as attenuated radicalism, as the dominant American intellectual tradition, and as a receptiveness to variousness and possibility--"in vital opposition with one another." Maintains that A4 attacks American Stalinists' neglect of ideas, the institutional tendency to separate ideas from their contingent circumstances, and Parrington's description of American culture in terms of a single predominant "current," commending instead the power of "the decentralized local intelligence in its efforts to confront contemporary reality." Describes the liberal imagination as "both literal and intransigent in character" in Trilling's critique, calling Trilling by contrast "a moralist with no simple moralism to recommend."

G475. Greenwood, E. B. "The Literary Criticism of Lionel Trilling." *Twentieth Century* 163 (January 1958): 44-48.

Describes A4 and A5 as both more centrally concerned with "the drama of dialectic" which gave them focus and force than with the specific quality of the authors and works they considered--A4, for example, dealt largely "with a single main theme, the ambiguities latent in the word 'real,'" and the dialectic of A5 "stemmed less from the process of criticizing the inadequate views of others than from an attempt to establish certain views of his own about the self and its relation to society and culture"--whereas A7, marking a lapse from Trilling's earlier commitment, is "the least unified and most mellow of the three"; to borrow Trilling's own distinction between Eliot and Forster as essayists, it relaxes readers rather than stimulating them.

G476. Grumet, Elinor. "The Apprenticeship of Lionel Trilling." *Prooftexts* 4 (May 1984): 153-73.

Traces the course of Trilling's affiliation with the *Menorah Journal* from his early friendship with Henry Rosenthal and Elliot Cohen to his refusal to serve on the editorial board of Cohen's new journal *Commentary* in 1945. Uses Trilling's unpublished 1929 letter of endorsement of the *Menorah Journal* to define his commitment to the journal as social and cultural rather than religious or political (it "did not include longings for Zion," nor did it express "a longing for Jewish study in its own terms"). Observes that Trilling found contemporary Judaism "contentless because the classics of the tradition were inaccessible to him," and that he therefore took his guiding principles for reviewing and judging Jewish writing from the European literary tradition. Describes Trilling's widely-criticized use of "we" as part of an attempt to create "a community-by-incantation which shares and validates the culture as he perceives it." Concludes that "Trilling used the composition and criticism of 'Jewish fiction' to exorcise his ethnic habits of mind," refusing to let the minimal, passive identification with Judaism he describes in E384 "legislate his emotional or intellectual life."

G477. Hagopian, John V. "A Reader's Moral Dissent from Lionel Trilling's 'Of This Time, of That Place.'" *American Literature in Belgium*. Edited by Gilbert Debusscher. Amsterdam: Rodopi, 1988. Pp. 227-38.

Ascribes his resistance to the story to his inability to identify with Joseph Howe, whose acquiescence on Theodore Blackburn's success--he gives Blackburn a passing grade without reading his paper--is "reprehensible and professionally immoral." Calls Howe "a moral opportunist . . . who fails Trilling's own test of moral realism," and identifies him with "the author himself," who does not establish an ironic distance from Howe because he is himself an "opportunistic, self-serving, status-driven academic entrepeneur," as "the candid memoirs of those who knew the real Lionel Trilling" [L944, L964, and M1026] attest.

G478. Hagopian, John V. "The Technique and Meaning of Lionel Trilling's 'The Other Margaret.'" *Etudes anglaises* 16 (July-September 1963): 225-29.

Summarizes the progress of Stephen Elwin's moral revelations in C84, contrasting the story's adult point of view with the adolescent point of view common to such stories of moral awakening as "My Kinsman, Major Molineux," "The Egg," "The Killers," and "That Evening Sun," and concluding that Trilling's presentation of an ongoing conflict between the perspectives of youth and age makes his story meditative rather than dramatic and ironic, and "makes it possible for him to comment explicitly on the moral issue in the story" rather than "putting the burden of meaning completely on the reader."

G479. Hardy, James Edward. "Of Tales Untold: Lionel Trilling's Fiction." *Explorations: The Twentieth Century* (Special Series) 3 (1989): 81-100.

Analyzes the theme of the untold story in the stories collected in A12. Notes the narrator's attempts in C53 to avoid Hettner's story altogether; Elwin's reluctance in C84 to recount his experience on the bus because of the ways it implicates him in "the 'insupportable fact' of *death*"; the status of C58 as "not a story told, but only a story, or stories, that could be told"; the withheld revelation in C85 of Garda Thorne's story and the unwritten stories of Hammill's students; and the omission in C77 of any sample or authorial account of Howe's poetry or any suggestion of a significant future for him: although it is difficult to predict what will become of Tertan, it is clear that "not much" will happen to Howe.

G480. Hartman, Geoffrey H. "Between the Claims of Self and Culture." [Review of A9 and A10.] *New York Times Book Review*, 4 February 1973, pp. 1, 28-31.

Observes that despite long attention to the counterclaims of self and culture, Trilling "has no grand philosophy or overview of the conflict"; instead of attempting to resolve the debate between morality and art, he has preferred to remain in the middle, analyzing the ways his contemporaries strenuously resist conditions they have not chosen while allowing themselves to be seduced by conditions--ideologies and their terms--they have. Traces Trilling's critique of ideology to Arnold's distrust of Hebraism in favor of the "'disinterested' play and circulation" of the ideas given political currency by the French Revolution, regretting the absence, as in Arnold, of "that more forceful and trenchant kind of comment" typical of Philip Rahv and Irving Howe. Explains the absence of Kierkegaard from Trilling's analysis of the ways sincerity and authenticity displace good as a moral criterion by Trilling's refusal "to define authentic moral experience in terms of a transcendent religious perspective. . . . He acknowledges but does not explore deeply the demonic side of the psyche." Notes that moments like Trilling's attack on R. D. Laing's "upward psychopathic mobility" make him "another last Puritan, or displaced Hebraic consciousness, roused from his Arnoldian flirtation with modern Hellenism." Pronounces A10, like most "lay sermons," a failure because of its oversimplifications, its "unremitting solemnity," and its overidealization of the historical sense, pointing out that "Trilling's achievement elsewhere is precisely that he exemplifies rather than prescribes a 'sense of the past' which intervenes between us and the easy solution."

Revised and reprinted as "Lionel Trilling as Man in the Middle" in *The Fate of Reading and Other Essays* (Chicago: University of Chicago Press, 1975), pp. 294-302.

G481. Harvey, W. J. "Editorial Notes: *Kulchur* and Culture in America." *Essays in Criticism* 10 (October 1960): 441-50.

Suggests that Trilling's laudable attempt to mediate, as "critical entrepeneur," between high culture ("*Kulchur*") and mass culture is often undercut by his reliance on a "bland, pontifical, soporific" rhetoric designed to reassure his readers that they "are now in touch with *Kulchur.*" Charges that the "hypnotic charm" of Trilling's prose often masks weaknesses in argument, indiscriminate cultural references, and evasions in judgment.

G482. Hirsch, David H. "Reality, Manners, and Mr. Trilling." *Sewanee Review* 72 (Summer 1964): 420-32.

Attacks Trilling's failure in C90 to "recognize the 'problem of reality,'" arguing that he is uncertain "whether to locate reality in the subject or in the object" and accusing him of falling into the same errors he had uncovered in V. L. Parrington in C68 by using "'manners' conceived from the vantage point of *haute culture*" as the defining feature of reality in the novel. Ascribes Trilling's strictures against the novel in America to the fact that American novelists have rarely been interested in "the serious portrayal of a traditional aristocracy," but instead have sought, as in *Moby Dick*, to "explore the ultimate problems of all men," and contends that even in those European works Trilling values most highly, he defines "the 'problem of reality' as merely a question of social hypocrisy."

Abridged and incorporated into *Reality and Idea in the Early American Novel* (The Hague: Mouton, 1971), pp. 32-36.

G483. Holloway, John. "Varieties of Dialogue." [Review of A11; L920; William Walsh, *F. R. Leavis* (London: Chatto & Windus, 1980); and F. R. Leavis, *Education and the University* (1943; rpt. Cambridge: Cambridge University Press, 1980).] *Encounter* 56 (February-March 1981): 67-77.

Describes Trilling's work as essentially political in its focus on "the whole social and public life of man," motivating his interest in literature as "important" rather than "interesting." Analyzes the ways Trilling's faith in his dialectical analysis of self and society was shaken by two crises dramatized in A8: his sense of despair over the power of modern literature to shape intellectual and political life, and his discovery of a radical counterculture as stultifying in its institutionalization as the culture it condemns. Although "Trilling can a little overdo it," the power of his prose is "an index of great gifts, of largeness and nobility as well as disciplined, dedicated intellect."

G484. Howe, Irving. "Lionel Trilling: A World of Remembrance." *Salmagundi*, no. 35 (Fall 1976), pp. 3-5.

Notes Trilling's growing interest in the play and pleasures of literature, his enduring fondness for *Kim*, and his wish to write a book on Wordsworth. Recounts a conversation in which Trilling, asked if new developments in critical theory made him anxious, replied, "I always feel anxious," adding, "I don't even know whether I have a critical method."

G485. Howe, Irving. "On Lionel Trilling: 'Continuous Magical Confrontation.'" *New Republic* 174 (13 March 1976): 29-31.

Describes Trilling as a critic who seeks "to melt ideological posture into personal sensibility" rather than offering "primarily . . . literary guidance." Disputes Trilling's premises that "liberalism as a politics cannot avoid a reductionist and smug militancy" and that liberals believe "'all' human problems can be solved merely through social action," encouraging a combination of Trilling's sensitivity with a will to active political action. Emphasizes Trilling's "radical" faith in literature, even the modernist literature against whose power he warned, concluding that "Trilling spoke for the imperilled autonomy of our life."

G486. Howe, Irving. "Reading Lionel Trilling." [Review of A9.] *Commentary* 56 (August 1973): 68-71.

Identifies Trilling's growing ambivalence toward modernism as the leading theme of his work, which presents "a drama of self-recognition." Despite reservations about the discontinuity and obliqueness of A9, praises its "tentativeness" in dramatizing "a deep, abiding theme." Notes that sincerity, standing for "a conduct of *should*," is "an attribute of Romanticism," and authenticity, standing for "a potential of *is*," is "a straining of modernism," whose triumph "is signalled by a shift from impersonal truth to personal sincerity." Suggests that Trilling's "deepest interest" is not in literary criticism but in "searching for the animating biases" that shape cultural history through thematic and stylistic conventions, and that his "guiding norm" is the operation of a "will" that might warrant "his own sense of authenticity."

Reprinted as "Lionel Trilling: Sincerity and Authenticity" in *Celebrations and Attacks: Thirty Years of Literary and Cultural Commentary* (New York: Horizon, 1979), pp. 213-20.

G487. Jay, Gregory S. "Hegel and Trilling in America." *American Literary History* 1 (Fall 1989): 565-92.

Differentiates "Hegelian dialectics" as "a method for undoing reified cultural categories" from the "American oppositional thought" represented by Trilling's motivic "lapses into static contradictions" between the coercive apparatus of culture and the individual who "transcends the contradictions of the national experience." Traces in detail Trilling's influential "psychological" appropriation of Hegel, which "locates the struggle for unity in the individual self," from his attack on Parrington in C68, which "erases writing by making the mind of the artist (rather than language itself) the agency of negation and mediation," through the Preface to A5, which attempts "to use writing as a technique for overcoming determination" despite its recognition that writing is coercively implicated in cultural history, to the argument of A9, which attempts "to universalize the American quest for freedom and selfhood" by adapting it to the terms of Hegelian dialectic, which becomes "specific to the destiny of the nation." Suggests that "Hegel and American literary history bequeathed to Trilling the search for an authenticity that would not be conditioned by the social"--an authenticity he eventually discovers in Freud's "mythic and universal" theory of an "irreconcilable dialectic of will and negation, something that goes on within the self and within society, not simply in the adversarial relation between them." Concludes that "Trilling's agon with Hegel should mark the death of the subject of literary history" because it demonstrates the impossibility of using writing to transcend and so analyze the dialectic of history.

G488. Kane, Thomas S. "The Encompassing Mind: A Note on the Style of Lionel Trilling." *Explorations: The Twentieth Century* (Special Series) 3 (1989): 69-79.

Analyzes Trilling's diction as distinguished by a rhetorical economy and a careful use of figurative language producing flashes of "revealing brilliance"; the organization of his encompassing, allusive prose as urging an experience of specific literary events "within the wholeness of western culture"; and his rhythmic sentence structure as creating "an audibility of mind" and "a reticulation of [literary] experience, ever expanding, ever vibrant."

G489. Keech, James M. "Trilling's 'Of This Time, of That Place.'" *Explicator* 23 (April 1965), Item 66.

Suggests that the title of Trilling's story comes from *The Prelude*, III, 77-82, in which Wordsworth recalls his disturbing alienation and his fellow students' suspicions of his madness during his residence at Cambridge. Contends that Tertan is a misunderstood figure of distinctive promise like Wordsworth, not "a pathetic grotesque."

G490. Kendle, Burton S. "Trilling's 'Of This Time, of That Place.'" *Explicator* 22 (April 1964), Item 61.

Identifies several references to "The Rime of the Ancient Mariner" and "Kubla Khan" in Trilling's story, noting the kinship between Tertan and Coleridge's poet and seer and between Howe and the Mariner, another figure consumed with guilt for his "apparently motiveless" destruction of an innocent.

G491. Kermode, Frank. "Lionel Trilling, New York's secular rabbi." *Observer*, 9 November 1975, p. 10.

A memorial notice emphasizing Trilling's indebtedness to Freud as intellectual hero and guarantor of the mind's "tragic dignity," a notion under assault by revisionary psychoanalysts and the adversary culture, whether institutionalized in the classroom or laying siege to the campus.

G492. Kim, Chrysostom. "Lionel Trilling on 'The Self in Its Standing Quarrel with Culture.'" *American Benedictine Review* 27 (September 1976): 332-56.

Links Trilling's "double-mindedness" toward modern literature to Freud's ambivalence toward the coercive power of civilization and to Trilling's habit, described in G446, of "cultivat[ing] a mind never entirely his own," a mind rooted in "what he understands to be the mind of society." Argues that since this understanding is based on the conditioned elements of everyday life, neglecting these elements leads both to social alienation and "losing one term of life's dialectic" between spirit and circumstance.

G493. Krupnick, Mark. "Lionel Trilling: Criticism and Illusion." [Review of B41.] *Modern Occasions* 1 (Winter 1971): 282-87.

Criticizes Trilling's turn in the fifties to "premature resignation, social passivity, and relentless privatism," marked for example by his "insistence on tragedy," which "anaesthetizes our moral feelings," becoming "a rationalization for giving in too soon, too easily." Argues that Trilling is unable "to respond fully to any subject but that of loss and defeat, which he proceeds to dignify in the rhetoric of tragic grandeur," and that his mandarin distaste for the radicalism of modern literature leaves him "straining after the quotidian" in C98 and C177. Characterizes the ideology of B41 ("How I Learned to Hate the Revolution") as narrow, antipolitical, and nondialectical in its avoidance of alternative viewpoints, and concludes that Trilling's present revulsion is neither conservative nor liberal.

G494. Krupnick, Mark. "Lionel Trilling and the Politics of Style." *American Literary Landscapes: The Fiction and the Fact.* Edited by Ian F. A. Bell and D. K. Adams. New York: St. Martin's, 1989. Pp. 152-70.

Observes that in his early essays, "Trilling used literature as the standard by which to correct the errors and refine the dullness of [the] liberal-progressive mind," and traces the widening gap in his later writings between his ideal of selfhood and his distrust of modernist literature. Notes that C66 praises an ideal of authenticity established through "style and tone" that Trilling would later criticize in A9, arguing that although Trilling appeals to Dewey's *Ethics* for a rationale for this commendation, it is actually based on "the work of art as model" for the self--a model Trilling does not set against politics because he defines "political choice" in terms of "personal quality." Contends that "Trilling presents contradictory notions of the relation of self to style": the self is fashioned from the choices of personal style, but it is the uncontrollable "external manifestation of a spiritual condition" reserved for "the authentic few." Calls into question on the basis of this ambiguity the oppositions Trilling establishes "between a morality of action and a morality of being, between the social world and the individual, between politics and literature." Suggests that although Trilling attempts in A5 to define society as well as the self in terms drawn from modernist art rather than mass culture, his awareness that mass culture had endowed him with his own power and prestige led him to suspect the modern reliance on self-invention through style and to commend in C116 and A9 an "archaic" categorical morality based on a "unified" and "self-identical" notion of self apparently outside culture and history, but actually valorized by the historical concept of "middle-class individuality." Hence Trilling, in seeking "to oppose the modernist morality by which we intimate superiority by style," simply ended by "urging one style at the expense of another," urging qualities of "hardness, density, and weight in the self he admired" without realizing that these qualities were as deliberately chosen, as much a question of style, as those he distrusted.

G495. Krupnick, Mark. "Lionel Trilling, 'Culture,' and Jewishness." *Denver Quarterly* 18 (Autumn 1983): 106-22.

Reviews the details of Trilling's first years, proposing that his awareness of "Anglo-Saxon culture," figured in Arnold's ideal of Hellenism, gained ascendancy over the conflicting "parochialism" of Arnoldian Hebraism. Suggests that Trilling associated himself after his graduation from Columbia with the *Menorah Journal* because "he was a social man who needed institutions to be part of and cultural situations to which he could respond," and that his early short stories, dramatizing his ambivalence toward a "dream of freedom and sometimes even of wildness," unite modernist motifs with a Jewish "tradition of rebellion." Notes the discrepancies between G540 and M1013, and concludes by tracing the "new firmness and authority of

Trilling's writing" beginning with A1 to his identification with the "liberal-humanist culture" from which he had earlier been deflected, "first by 'positive Jewishness,' later by Marxism," noting that Trilling attempts years later in C96 to "make peace" with the Jewish identity he had suppressed in the thirties.

Revised and reprinted as Chapter 2 of F424.

G496. Krupnick, Mark. "Lionel Trilling, Freud, and the Fifties." *Humanities in Society* 3 (Summer 1980): 265-81.

Contends that Trilling's turn to Freud in his later work marks a change from his defense of mind in A4 to an affirmation of "the mindless life of the instincts as a necessary corrective to culture." Freud's view of the human subject as both within and beyond culture becomes a corrective to revisionary psychiatrists like Horney and Fromm who define the self "*exclusively* in terms of culture." But Trilling's "saving biologism sounds a good deal like culture, its supposed opposite," because Trilling, in contrast to a radical Freudian like Norman O. Brown, "remained preeminently a defender of culture who could only praise biology after first humanizing and defusing it." Concludes that the biologism implied by the catchphrase "sentiment of being" allowed Trilling to appeal to political conservatism by providing a tragic dimension to his quietism and supplied "the ideal of rest as the positive goal of human striving."

Revised and reprinted as Chapter 7 of F424.

G497. Kubal, David L. "Lionel Trilling: The Mind and Its Discontents." *Hudson Review* 31 (Summer 1978): 279-95.

Searches Trilling's earlier work for harbingers of the double-edged critique of aesthetic modernism in A8 and A9: "It had lost . . . the tension between the concept of individual will as opposed to that of necessary limit," and "its complex truths were domesticated and reduced to cant as part of a general diatribe against the possibilities of ordinary existence." Discovers the roots of this disaffection in the portrayal of Maxim's "radical denial of life" in A3, in Trilling's perception of "a nascent counter-culture" in C101, in his shifting emphasis from "the intractable nature of existence" in A4 to "the self's possibilities in culture" in A5 and A7, and in his search in A5 for "an imagination of health . . . independent of any ideology"--an imagination he often discovered in such non-literary authors as David Riesman and Kenneth Clark. Concludes that although "during the Fifties it seemed to him that the literary mind might recover from its acculturation," he acknowledged in A8 the bankruptcy of literary modernism and in A9 the success of the widespread attack on rationality as a possible corrective, even though his final view, emphasizing the mind's ability "to imagine us *becoming* other than we are," never permits "the comfort of pessimism, that perverse relief from the necessity of thought."

Revised and reprinted in L947.

G498. Kubal, David L. "Trilling's *Middle of the Journey*: An American Dialectic." *Bucknell Review* 14 (March 1966): 60-73.

Notes the formal affinities of A3 with "epic structure" (division into twelve parts, title taken from the *Inferno*, opening *in medias res*) and argues that these affinities support Trilling's critique of the liberal imagination by posing a mental and moral discipline the author and his surrogate hero establish their humanity by mastering, "working *within the range of possibility* to re-create and improve the existing social forms" rather than succumbing to the conservative compromises described in G467. Describes Emily Caldwell as "a catalyst for [John Laskell's] union of the *me* and the *not-me*," validating through her physical love Laskell's abstract ideas of wholeness and selfhood. Concludes that the novel is central to Trilling's achievement since it exemplifies "his major political ideas and validates . . . his critical theory."

Revised and reprinted in L947.

G499. Lang, Hans-Joachim. "Lionel Trilling: Ein Nachfolger Matthew Arnolds in Amerika." *Die neuren Sprachen*, Neue Folge 6 (August 1957): 374-81.

Remarks that Trilling is aptly described by his own characterization of Eliot's criticism--"The form of the dialectic gives us pleasure; we are connected with large issues"--although his articulation of those issues changes after the Moscow Trials and the Nonaggression Pact, when his criticism of liberalism comes from the right rather than the left. Citing the misgivings in G439 and G531 about Trilling's lack of conceptual clarity, and noting the contradictions between Trilling's dim view of modern culture in A6 and his more sanguine view in C101, suggests that he is most consistent in his status as a strict Arnoldian who criticizes the class with which he aligns himself and adopts the shifting concepts cherished by that class as his points of attack instead of defining terms like "liberal" and "culture" more clearly himself.

G500. Langbaum, Robert. "The Importance of *The Liberal Imagination*." *Salmagundi*, no. 41 (Spring 1978), pp. 55-65.

Emphasizes the complementarity between Trilling and the New Critics, whose criticism showed a similarly "conservative drift." Identifies the target of A4 as "the unreconstructed liberalism that got reflected as Stalinism," judged against the standards of "social context and the tragic sense," without which liberals seduced by "self-aggrandizing abstractions" can become Stalinists. Describes "the typical plot" of Trilling's essays in dialectical terms: "Trilling sets forth a positive position and then says all that can be said against it before returning to the advancement of his original position." Notes Trilling's late opposition to structualism as still "another system antithetical to will and individual freedom," and contends that critics like Trilling will always be valued for the defense they provide against such deterministic systems.

G501. Leary, Lewis. "Lionel Trilling 1905-1975." *Sewanee Review* 84 (Spring 1976): 302-4.

A memorial notice stressing Trilling's "beguiling seriousness," which subordinated "the aesthetics of literature" to its social and culture import and gave him a "messianic commitment to the inevitability of man's tragic recompense." Describes as "the mind's final and fatal presumption" Trilling's "insistence that art must submit to intellect."

G502. Lewis, R. W. B. "Lionel Trilling and the New Stoicism." [Review of A4.] *Hudson Review* 3 (Summer 1950): 313-17.

Calls Trilling "capable at once of more range and more exactness than almost any other critic in America today," praising his criticism of unduly narrow versions of reality in C68, C69, and C72, but intimating that his "own idea of reality," though "it evidently touches mind as well as matter," still "resists formulation." Notes the high value Trilling ascribes to literature as a social force and his distrust of "absolute values," and proposes the term "new Stoicism" for his "centrist position," which offers, "not a program for creative action, but a device for shoring up defenses." Compares Trilling's "doctrine of sustained tensions" to the "comic vocabulary" Kenneth Burke develops in *Attitudes Toward History* that "transcends acceptance or rejection" without achieving true transcendence.

G503. Lopate, Phillip. "Remembering Lionel Trilling." *American Review*, no. 25 (October 1976), pp. 148-78.

Recalls Lopate's experiences of Trilling as cultural icon, teacher, advisor, and friend. Describes Trilling as "a rather impressionistic lecturer" who "had very little faith in the value of democratic opinion" but whose classes were characterized by an "honesty and modesty" which gave his students "a glimpse of an older way of being": "He taught himself better than he taught any of the books." Recounts Lopate's unsuccessful attempt to enlist Trilling's support for his protest against Columbia's withdrawal of funding from the 1963 *Columbia Review*, and quotes the opening paragraphs of Trilling's warmly responsive review [D375] of the Fall 1963 issue, under Lopate's editorship, and three letters Trilling wrote to Lopate about his former student's writing.

G504. McAfee, Tom. "A Note on 'The Other Margaret.'" *Western Review* 14 (Winter 1950): 143-44.

Dismisses Farrell's political critique of C84 in G463, which looks for "propaganda" in a story showing "the universal man in a universal situation--that of growing older and realizing he must work it out or assume some moral code."

G505. McCarthy, P. J. "Lionel Trilling's Matthew Arnold." *Arnoldian* 15 (Winter 1987-88): 81-86.

Noting the similarities between Trilling and Arnold and their situations and programs (especially in A4, which submits liberalism to an Arnoldian critique), emphasizes one difference between the two: Trilling's lack of transcendent religious beliefs, a lack he attributes to Arnold as well. Reviewing the widely-held view that Trilling undervalues the playful aspect of literature, "language as self-delighting or heuristic," argues that Trilling does not politicize literature and culture but observes its inescapably political cast, especially striking in a period beset by the absolutist demands of Communism, philistinism, and later the uncompromising hostility to the idea of society. Asserts the continuing relevance of Arnold's and Trilling's attempt to find a middle ground between individual will and the constraints of culture.

G506. MacRae, Donald. "Mr. Trilling Sees It Through (Almost)." [Review of A4.] *Interim* 4 (1954): 67-73.

Describes Trilling's analysis of culture as imaginative or literary rather than historical, set forth in terms of a tragedy whose ideal liberalism is "subverted by liberalism as fact"--by "the good but superficial man" like Emerson or Parrington who tries to ignore or domesticate "the 'demons' that everywhere conspire against his goodness." Agrees with Trilling's analysis but sees it as limited by his "indifference to the complex drama of historical liberalism," which may mark modern liberalism as a contradictory expression of "political disorganization as an ideal." Contrasts Trilling's trenchant reading of James in B19 with the blindness of Osborn Andreas to James's "electric qualities of mind."

G507. McSweeney, Kerry. "Lionel Trilling as a Literary Critic." [Review of A11.] *Canadian Review of American Studies* 14 (1983): 195-206.

Reviews the range and incisiveness of Trilling's specifically literary criticism from his early reviews, commending especially B22, C73, C83, C116, C159, C181, and D313, and criticizing B20, B23, C96, C177, and C192. Contends that A9, which deals "principally if not exclusively with ideas" rather than literary works, is open to the same charges of oversimplification Trilling levels at the "history-of-ideas approach to literature" in C75. Compares Trilling to Edmund Wilson as a general critic, observing that "Wilson's cultural base and social context is much wider than Trilling's and the 'we' for whom he writes correspondingly larger and more catholic."

G508. Marcus, Steven. "Lionel Trilling, 1905-1975." *New York Times Book Review*, 8 February 1976, pp. 1-2, 30, 32-34.

Defining the "agenda" of A4 as "a running argument with Stalinism in both its political and cultural forms," contends that, having placed Stalinism "within the historical tradition of Western enlightenment and rationality" in order to deal with it "from the perspective of the very tradition of which it is an aberration," Trilling departed from that agenda in his later work: as the adversary current of modernism became institutionalized in "a factitious or pseudo-autonomy," his defense of the self as against ideological imperatives developed into a critique of the "irrationalism and self-abandonment that the 'success' of the adversary culture had made popular and even *chic*." Praises Trilling for "his exigency and his minimalism," his ability to affirm, however cautiously, values of mind and culture rejected by his contemporaries, and his uncompromising insistence on the historical and cultural significance of literature, its effect on "the world 'out there.'" Calls Trilling "our historian of the moral life of modernity, our philosopher of culture," who "came to conceive of the modern self as an endangered species" that "was certainly worth conserving."

Reprinted in F420.

G509. Marx, Leo. "Mr. Eliot, Mr. Trilling, and Huckleberry Finn." *American Scholar* 22 (Autumn 1953): 423-40.

Rejects Trilling's and Eliot's defenses of the novel's ending as formally apt (see B20), arguing that its farcical tone and ascription of Jim's freedom to Miss Watson's unmotivated act seriously undermine Huck's heroic and "unpremeditated identification with Jim's flight from slavery." Argues that in the ending, Twain, "having revealed the tawdry nature of the culture of the great valley, yielded to its essential complacency" by showing "a failure of nerve" in declining to provide a conclusion acknowledging that "a partial defeat [of Jim's quest for freedom] was inevitable." Attributes Trilling's and Eliot's uncritical praise of the ending to their preoccupation, in "reaction against the mechanical sociological criticism of the thirties," with questions of individual morality at the expense of "social or political morality."

Reprinted in *Interpretations of American Literature*, edited by Charles Feidelson, Jr. and Paul Brodtkorb, Jr. (New York: Oxford University Press, 1959), pp. 212-28.

G510. Monteiro, George. "The Doubloon: Trilling's Melville Problem." *Canadian Review of American Studies* 17 (Spring 1986): 27-34.

Sets Trilling's comments on "Bartleby the Scrivener" and *Billy Budd* in A4, A9, and B40 against Gifford Maxim's religious analysis of *Billy Budd* in A3, noting that in his discussion of "Bartleby" in A9, "Trilling teeters . . . on the verge of defining the social world as totally inauthentic" despite his own enduring faith in society, whereas Maxim reads the tale as showing, in his words, "the tragedy of Law [and "its child, Spirit"] in a world of Necessity." Concludes that although John Laskell apparently rejects Maxim's reading of Melville as "an impassioned plea . . . for the *status quo*," Trilling in A9 seems more inclined to take Maxim's view seriously himself.

G511. Montgomery, Marion. "Lionel Trilling's *The Middle of the Journey*: A Good Book Gone Wrong." *Discourse* 4 (Autumn 1961): 263-72.

Argues that despite a few successful scenes, the ambitious theme of A3--"to what extent . . . is a man to commit himself, body and soul, to mankind?"--is vitiated by Trilling's lack of appreciation of the comic nature of his story, his failure to surround Laskell with convincing antagonists, the undue prominence he gives to Laskell's consciousness, his repeated slackening of tension by presenting events out of chronological sequence or interrupting them with Laskell's ruminations, and his generally "trite and lifeless" descriptions and dialogue.

G512. Moore, Susan. "Lionel and Diana Trilling of New York." *Quadrant* 27 (August 1983): 29-34.

Compares the Trillings to F. R. and Q. D. Leavis as uniquely distinguished literary couples, observing that both Trilling and F. R. Leavis have been widely attacked and neglected, attacks on Trilling, unlike those on Leavis, date mainly since his death. Defends Trilling against "false analyses . . . sometimes malicious, sometimes simply obtuse" by Robert Boyers and others. Argues that the Trillings together depended on an unusual intimacy with their audience, including the anonymous audience they never met, and that their "intellectual base" has now disappeared, discredited by suspicion of the anti-communist Left, of the belief in social class as an established fact, and of ethical criticism generally. Predicts that the eclipse of the Trillings will end with "the recent wave of intellectual madness."

G513. O'Connor, William Van. "Lionel Trilling's Critical Realism." [Review of A4.] *Sewanee Review* 58 (July-September 1950): 482-94.

Describes A4, like A3, as encouraging a greater awareness of the pitfalls of liberal assumptions by using Romanticism to interrogate Enlightenment dogmas of reality and the prestige of scientific knowledge. Commends Trilling's resistance to the "magnificent strategies" of systematic thought and political commitment (except perhaps in the case of Lawrence), noting that he "shows with great acuteness and insight what literature *does*," rather than emphasizing "what it *is*," and that his particular readings are always placed at the service of a functional analysis of literature. Proposes "the search for myth" as a complement to Trilling's suggestion that novels in the future will anatomize the ideological bases of social manners in an attempt to "see reality in its multiple characteristics."

G514. O'Hara, Daniel. "The Resistance of Style: Response to Bloom." *American Literary History* 2 (Winter 1990): 781-83.

Protests I866's reductive discussion of the "academic politics" of Trilling and O'Hara, deploring the "fashionable and 'throwaway' radicalism" originally intended to resist the "commodification of all things in our postmodern culture" and contending that Trilling's persona and style are designed to "resist easy assimilation and so are not 'easily consumable.'"

G515. Pickrel, Paul. "Lionel Trilling and *Emma*: A Reconsideration." *Nineteenth-Century Fiction* 40 (December 1985): 297-311.

Calling Trilling's observations in C131 "inexact, willful, even naive," contends that Emma's alleged snobbery is only a cover for her other motives, unacknowledged or disguised; that the "national spirit" of the novel "has little to do with the yeomanry"; and that the novel's "bad actions," all "informed by economic considerations," make it impossible to consider it, in Trilling's terms, "a pastoral idyll." Suggests that Trilling's fondness for "bringing to bear on [*Emma*] an immense range of reading" blunts his insights and misrepresents the heroine as another Don Quixote or Emma Bovary.

G516. Pickrel, Paul. "Lionel Trilling and *Mansfield Park*." *Studies in English Literature 1500-1900* 27 (Autumn 1987): 609-21.

Disputes Trilling's "indictment" of the novel in C116 as "all for fixity and stasis and enclosure against freedom and openness," rejecting his descriptions of Lady Bertram as maternal and Sir Thomas Bertram as unintelligent and opposed to the theatricals in his house. Ascribes Trilling's contradictory assessments of the Crawfords to their change under the influence of Mansfield and London. Argues that Fanny Price, though placed in a position of enforced passivity--"the big discovery must be made by others about her"--is not temperamentally passive, and concludes that her relationship toward Mansfield Park gives the novel the dialectical quality Trilling denies it in A9, though his reading, despite its inaccuracies, "has some kind of psychological truth" in its correspondence to the experience of the novel's readers.

G517. Podhoretz, Norman. "The Arnoldian Function in American Criticism." [Review of A4.] *Scrutiny* 18 (June 1951): 59-65.

Sees Trilling as Arnold's successor in expressing "a committed responsiveness to the problems of his age." Notes that Trilling's critique of liberalism is less systematic than Eliot's in *The Idea of a Christian Society* because, unlike Eliot, he believes that liberalism itself "has a native 'primal' strength to maintain it" and so attacks the attitudes of liberals rather than the doctrines of liberalism. Emphasizes Trilling's belief that "the future of our world depends upon the infusion of something European into the American pattern"--specifically, a greater awareness of "class-thinking" and of "the presence of ideas" in works of art.

G518. Raleigh, John Henry. "Editor's Page: Matthew Arnold and Lionel Trilling." *Arnoldian* 3 (Winter 1976): 1-4.

Compares Trilling to Arnold on the basis of their focus on past European thinkers rather than contemporaries, their focus on the tragic tension between the ideology of the French revolution and the individuality of the Romantic self, and their view of their own vocation as a friendly but disinterested critique of liberalism that would help their readers "to find their true selves within themselves." Describes Trilling as "the director of a resident stock company" whose members--Freud, Hegel, Rameau's nephew, Werther, Austen, Wordsworth, Conrad, Rousseau, Arnold--appear in surprising new roles in A9.

G519. Ricks, Christopher. "Lionel Trilling and Death." *Listener* 94 (27 November 1975): 727-28.

A memorial notice emphasizing the importance of death in Trilling's thought as a seductively charismatic preoccupation of contemporary culture, a scandal to the unimaginative liberal imagination, and a test for ideologies of the self.

G520. Robinson, Jeffrey. "Lionel Trilling: A Bibliographic Essay." *Resources for American Literary Study* 8 (Autumn 1978): 131-56.

Lists Trilling's most important publications, correcting two errors in Barnaby's bibliography (see J874) and describing C57 as a fictional story; briefly indicates the location of principal collections of manuscripts and letters; reviews the autobiographical portrait that emerges from excurses in several essays; and devotes most of its length to an extended analysis of the development of Trilling's criticism. Finds in the early reviews for *Menorah Journal* the seeds of Trilling's charge that liberalism "inadequately represented the American experience critically" and his prescriptive exhortation: "the full treatment of the individual" without reduction to ideological abstraction. Contends that this emphasis develops during the 1940's into a concern for "the place of emotion and instinct in social life" and "the 'saintliness' that stands in the objects of the Western tradition--embodiments of the Holy Spirit of creative energy," which perceives that "divinity is in things when they aggravate the mind in a free opposition to them," so that "things for Trilling become a kind of modern sublime." Describes Trilling's later career as focused on the attempt to "mak[e] pleasure play a significant role in our experience of modern life" by attacking the modern cult of unpleasure, celebrating figures like Keats capable of "restoring the pleasure principle to the reality principle," and to urge on his audience the subversive pleasures of criticism and mind.

G521. Robinson, Jeffrey Cane. "The Immortality Ode: Lionel Trilling and Helen Vendler." *Wordsworth Circle* 12 (Winter 1981): 64-70.

Defends Trilling's reading of the Ode against Vendler's attack in G542. Argues that Wordsworth's passion arises from two sources--sexual jealousy and political frustration--which "disrupt his whole-hearted entry into the elegiac convention," concluding that the poem dramatizes the necessary failure of the attempt "to dissolve the threats of passion into the classic proportions of elegy." Agrees with Trilling in describing the poem as analytical rather than therapeutic, suggesting that it "points toward the Romantic goal of the integrated personality while it defends against it," attempting to transcend personal loss and its attendant passions through the consolations of elegy while warning that such attempts at transcendence fail to face them completely.

G522. Robinson, Jeffrey Cane. "Lionel Trilling and the Romantic Tradition." *Massachusetts Review* 20 (Summer 1979): 211-36.

Links the technique of Trilling's occasional essays--the process by which they reveal the truth about their subject at the same time they advance Trilling's larger argument--to his reading of the English Romantics by noting the link in both Trilling and the Romantics between "felicity and manly energy" and by treating Trilling's essays as "idylls" which "represent mind becoming a second nature." Traces

Trilling's dialectic between pleasure and reality in B22 and C175 and his presentation of Tertan's "archaic" power over Howe's humanistic perspective in C77 to Arnold's reading of the Romantics. Sees Trilling's view of the Romantics as offering a kind of "comfort . . . related to our need for community" as a corrective to Blake's "reactionary acceptance of alienation as though it were a permanent truth of human life"--a corrective which underlies his preference for the occasional essay as a form prophesying a systematic account of a subject it does not pretend to treat systematically.

G523. Robson, W. W. "Professor Trilling and the 'New Critics.'" *Dublin Review* 454 (Fourth Quarter 1952): 54-62.

Takes Trilling's strictures against the New Critics in C75 and C95 as the impetus for an examination of whether "historicity," "intellectual cogency," and "relevance" are "to be 'regarded' or 'disregarded' in good literary criticism." Grants that literature and purely literary readings exist, but argues that these assumptions do not help the critic "decide what his job is or how to do it," since all interpretation entails contextualizing lines like "Beauty is truth, truth beauty" or "Ripeness is all"--either within the works in which they appear or within biographical, historical, or ideological situations that can give them currency for readers. Agrees with Trilling that New Criticism does not convincingly establish "what factors *should* govern the operation of this mode of attention."

G524. Rosenthal, M. L. "The Robert Frost Controversy." *Nation* 188 (20 June 1959): 559-61.

Agrees with Trilling's description of Frost in C140 as having "dark depths which make him something more than a rural Longfellow." Ridicules J. Donald Adams's estimate in G431 of Frost's sensibility as "simply" indigenous, recalling that Frost first developed as a poet and was first published in England. Notes the "panicky edge" that underlies many of Frost's "exotic" descriptions of natural scenes-- "Something there is in him that does not love a pure, simple, extroverted affirmation"--and identifies Frost's ambivalence as "very American--also very European, human, Emersonian, Freudian, or what have you."

G525. Sale, Roger. "Lionel Trilling." [Review of A9.] *Hudson Review* 26 (Spring 1973): 241-47.

Attacks Trilling as oppressively self-serious, dated in his concerns and his assumption of centrality ("Trilling treats himself as an institution, and so he can never speak with anything less than full assurance. . . . He never gives the impression of having read anything for the first time"), unable to "let his subject live separately from him," and monotonic in his prose ("reading Trilling in bulk" is like "eating a meal consisting entirely of Thousand Island dressing"). Calls the lecture Trilling's "most congenial form," and treats A9 as a series of lectures whose initial promise is dissipated by Trilling's shift from the "interesting and difficult" analysis of sincerity to the more facile and familiar analysis of authenticity: "We have all been here before, and a good deal of the time Trilling himself has been our guide." Concludes that because he is unresponsive to "quirkiness and eccentricity," Trilling "needs centrality of concern [in his subjects] to be himself central," and wonders why he has not written on the late eighteenth-century writers who would most likely evoke this centrality.

Revised and reprinted in *On Not Being Good Enough: Writings of a Working Critic* (New York: Oxford University Press, 1979), pp. 148-57.

G526. Samet, Tom. "Lionel Trilling and the Social Imagination." *Centennial Review* 23 (Spring 1979): 159-84.

Emphasizes the dialectical tension constant throughout Trilling's work, acknowledging his ambivalence, given his continuing attraction to society, toward the "moral aggression" of an "actively radical" modern literature, but noting that Trilling, like Lawrence, values society "precisely . . . as a field for the achievement and fulfillment of selfhood," to which he grants "primacy and . . . privilege." Contrasts Trilling's dialectic with those of Leftist thinkers "whose notion of a struggle was keyed to an anticipation of the end of all struggle." Traces the earliest version of Trilling's ambivalence toward the claims of a dominant culture through his early fiction, which poses the motivic question, "What does it mean to be a Jew here and now, at this time, in this place?" and answers by developing a paradoxical conception of the "a self conceived within culture and beyond it."

Incorporated into J878 as Chapter 1.

G527. Samet, Tom. "The Modulated Vision: Lionel Trilling's 'Larger Naturalism.'" *Critical Inquiry* 4 (Spring 1978): 539-57.

Sets Trilling's critique of modernism's "fierce impatience with the conditioned nature of human experience and its attendant devaluation of man's life in society" against Virginia Woolf's argument in "Mr. Bennett and Mrs. Brown" that people have become radically disconnected from the social and material contexts which were once assumed to define them. Argues against G482 and G531 that Trilling conceives character and consciousness as operating both within and beyond culture, defined by a dialectical relation to social reality, contending that Trilling's emphasis on social manners as the nexus between self and society, far from narrowing the focus of the novel, attempt to "restor[e] the genre to what he regards as its appropriate fullness and complexity," and citing John Laskell's determination to maintain a belief in human beings as "both responsible and conditioned" and Raymond Williams's observation that modern fiction has suffered an impoverishing split into "the 'social' novel and the 'personal' novel." Criticizes the "reflexiveness and insularity" of John Barth and other contemporary novelists as rooted in "a characteristically modern impulse to deny the reality of social and material conditions," urging instead a return to Trilling's "'double truth' of liberty and limitation."

Incorporated into J878 as Chapter 3.

G528. Samet, Tom. "Trilling, Arnold and the Anxieties of the Modern." *Southern Quarterly* 16 (April 1978): 191-208.

Discusses the relation between self and society in Trilling in terms of the "organic conception of society" Trilling ascribes to Arnold, which offers a way of conceiving social relationships set against the anti-social imperatives of the authentic unconscious. Contends that "the organic assumption lodges the constraints of history and of circumstance against the dream of perfection," acting as a check on both the untrammeled self and "the eschatological politics" of modern totalitarianism. Contrasts Arnold's faith in the cultural organism with Trilling's skepticism about "the omnipotence of culture," which leads him to Freud as an exemplary theorist of the individual's alienation from a culture in which everyone is necessarily implicated: "Incapable of Arnold's harmonious synthesis, Trilling can offer only proximate adjustments and permanent strain--the endlessly conflicting claims of self and culture."

Incorporated into J878 as Chapter 2.

G529. Sarchett, Barry W. "From Arnold to Plato: Lionel Trilling's *Beyond Culture* and the End of Modernist Criticism." *Western Humanities Review* 42 (Summer 1988): 93-111.

Argues that Trilling's highly critical analysis of the adversary culture in A8--a culture "guided by the very ideal of personal autonomy he seeks also to validate"--is undermined by his need "to suppress the connections between the adversary culture and modes of production and consumption under capitalism." Notes that Trilling sees adversary culture as an attack on the middle class which "has all the look of a class itself," which "protects and sanctions [the social and political orthodoxy] . . . it was created to oppose," leaving "the self to rely on its own rational intellect in a desperate isolation." Contends that the dominant and adversary cultures are more than structurally similar, since the adversary culture is "largely a sham" which, in its substitution of aesthetic spirituality for materialistic analysis and political action, "stands squarely in the middle of the liberal bourgeois tradition." Concludes that Trilling fails to resolve his contradictory attitude toward adversary culture "because he refuses to analyze cultural phenomena otherwise than through broad moral and psychological categories," thus overlooking the ways that "the self has become the ultimate commodity in consumerist culture," as "the consumer becomes the consumer rather than the producer of its self."

G530. Scholes, Robert. "The Illiberal Imagination." *New Literary History* 4 (Spring 1973): 521-40.

Urges structuralism as the logical "illiberal" successor to liberalism, noting that although Trilling's use of a liberal ideal to criticize liberal ideology left the ideal itself "virtually inscrutable," its notion of liberty is based on a view of the universe as chaotic or itself inscrutable--a view that valorizes "variousness" and individuality as desiderata. Counters W. J. Harvey's argument in *Character and the Novel* that great novels must necessarily be independent of Christian or Marxist ideology by proposing the synoptic gospels, the *Commedia*, and *Pilgrim's Progress* as great Christian novels and arguing that even the most closely rendered characters in nineteenth-century fiction were typical as well as individual because of novelists' faith that "the nature of reality is determinate and discoverable but has not yet been discovered--until now." Defines the movement of twentieth-century fiction as a movement "from naturalism to archetypal vision," commending the fiction of Robert Coover, John Barth, Iris Murdoch, and John Fowles as displaying the power of structuralism as against existentialism ("the last and finest flower of liberal thought") to "envision a new world," and inviting "a politics of structure (and a politics of love)" based on the duality of "sexual differentiation" to follow by envisioning "illiberal political forms of government" beyond communism and fascism.

G531. Schwartz, Delmore. "The Duchess' Red Shoes." *Partisan Review* 20 (January 1953): 55-73.

Attacks Trilling's emphasis on observed manners as the basis of the novel arguing that throughout C90 he oscillates between a broad definition of manners as "a culture's hum and buzz of implication" and a more narrow definition of "the manners of particular social classes and groups in a given social hierarchy." Maintains that *The Brothers Karamazov* "is not . . . in any literal sense about manners, society, and the social world" and that Trilling denigrates American fiction by applying a narrow definition of manners which applies equally well to the novels he values most highly. Charges that Trilling's use of "literary standards and values" to criticize modernist writers as hostile to liberalism would be "intolerable" if it were not excused by his concern for "the welfare of the educated class." Dismisses John Aldridge's argument in M984 that recent American fiction has failed because of the virtual absence of manners from American society as simply deploring the passing of the kind of "good manners" prescribed by Amy Vanderbilt, accusing Aldridge of wanting a corrupt Proustian social milieu for the sake of its literary opportunities, whereas "part of what Mr. Trilling is trying to do as a critic of literature and society is to salvage some of the lost or hurt pride of the middle class in its human inheritance."

Reprinted in *Selected Essays of Delmore Schwartz*, edited by Donald A. Dike and David H. Zucker (Chicago: University of Chicago Press, 1970), pp. 203-22.

For discussion, see K888.

G532. Sennett, Richard. "On Lionel Trilling." [Review of A11.] *New Yorker* 55 (5 November 1979): 204, 207-10, 215-17.

Identifies Trilling with the generation of Americans first forced to recognize in the failure of Russian Socialism "the limits that history put on one's faith" in individual opportunity, noting that he responded by attempting to discover--using as a foundation his Jewishness, his belief in psychoanalysis, and his fascination with the coherence of literary works--how modern culture had been "victimized" by credulity and despair because of its lack of will. Calls Trilling's remark, "Between is the only honest place to be," evidence of an "anti-liberal" reluctance to surrender completely to aesthetic fervor as well as ideological positions--a dilemma culminating in A9, "his greatest, and least appreciated, book," which traces the growing inability to know the self to the modern feeling "that the modern self is somewhere else" which condemns each quest for authenticity to alienation and despair.

G533. Sharma, D. R. "Cultural Criticism: A Critique of Trilling's Position." *Indian Journal of American Studies* 4 (June and December 1974): 53-65.

In defending Trilling's cultural criticism as pluralistic and inclusive, distinguishes F. R. Leavis's "moral emphasis," a stern and explicit commitment which "makes him virtually a latter-day Cromwellian saint," from Trilling's "moral realism," a sharply self-critical awareness of the problems and contradictions involved in living the moral life. Compares Trilling's dialectical, comprehensive conception of culture to William James's image of experience as "a huge spider-web suspended in the chamber of consciousness." Defends Trilling against Joseph Frank's indictment of his "conservative imagination" in G467 by arguing that Trilling allies imagination to will instead of opposing them, as Frank claims. Raises several questions about Trilling's conception of culture--"Isn't [it] class-oriented? If culture is a debate with life, then is counter-culture really a part of culture? If everything that happens in life goes to make culture, then can there be anarchy?"--but praises its strength and utility.

G534. Shechner, Mark. "The Elusive Lionel Trilling, Parts I and II." *Nation* 225 (17 and 22 September 1977): 247-50, 278-80.

Describes Trilling as ethnically "cosmopolitan" in his "Jewish internationalism," his "easy familiarity with European ideas," and his "special proclivity" for Victorian literature and social thought: as opposed to more "pugnacious" New York intellectuals like Irving Howe, Trilling "was going Protestant America one better by becoming a thoroughly accomplished British man of letters." Traces Trilling's cosmopolitan "preference for defining himself by negatives" to his own "interior quarrels," a "devil's advocacy" which offered no positions to replace the ones it criticized and therefore risked nothing. Notes Trilling's "strange fondness for the conditioned and the circumstantial as it was wedded to a thoroughgoing idealism," and deplores "how easily his efforts at transcending vulgarity have lent themselves to a *haute vulgarisation* of their own" in recent issues of *Commentary*.

G535. Shechner, Mark. "Lionel Trilling: Psychoanalysis and Liberalism." *Salmagundi*, no. 41 (Spring 1978), pp. 3-32.

Discusses the "climate of aggressive malaise" in which "psychoanalysis moved into the conceptual vacuum left by the retreat of socialism" in the 1940's, noting that Freudian concepts were congenial to the libertarian socialism, compounded by "rage and guilt," of the American left, to whom psychoanalysis promised both "ideology and cure." Compares Trilling's interest in psychoanalysis as "a codification of the great urge of self-discovery and self-healing" to Tennyson's faith and Wordsworth's sentiment. Defines "Freudian man" as "a step upwards from liberal man in his complication and mysteriousness," a figure whose "fondness for self-defeat . . . made his failures seem more like genuine expressions of will than his successes." Describes the characters of A3 as "literally sick with modern thought," and Laskell in particular as an example of the "'disintegrated consciousness' that Trilling would later attribute to the modern character," and the essays in A4 "both as chapters in a moral autobiography and showcases for the acculturated ego in the process of its self-reconstruction." Argues that psychoanalysis becomes for Trilling "a principle of approbation rather than a tool of radical analysis," citing his inclination toward "applied *Civilization and Its Discontents*" rather than rigorously psychoanalytic readings (except in B22), and his appropriation of Freud's ego psychology and cultural dialectic rather than his emphasis on guilt, dreams, infantile sexuality, and "the dynamic unconscious." Concludes that although "Trilling was captivated by the *idea* of the inner life," his high-minded radicalism was compromised by a fastidiousness that made his "dialectics [sound] like mere habits of fussiness," suggesting that Trilling's essays are most illuminatingly seen as chapters in his own self-psychoanalysis.

G536. Simpson, Lewis P. "Lionel Trilling and the Agency of Terror." *Partisan Review* 54, 1 (1987): 18-35.

Links Trilling to his contemporary Allen Tate by positing, largely on the basis of C195, two warring aspects of Trilling--an aspiring novelist who admired Hemingway's indifference toward society and a dominant man of letters and critic of society--illuminated by Tate's argument that

Emily Dickinson and the Elizabethan poets dramatized "the modern self's emergence as a historical entity and its struggle to define its existence" by its continued fascination with the images of moral systems that no longer compelled belief. Sees Trilling's rejection of graduate teaching in American literature in favor of a return to undergraduate teaching in 1951 as "a last-ditch effort to separate the self of the critic from that of the imaginative writer" by refusing to remain a part of American literature. Calling A5 Trilling's crucial work for its "compelling meditations on the idea of the modern self," finds "the climactic moment . . . in Trilling's search for vocational identity" in his identification in C116 of Austen as "the agent of the Terror of the secular spirituality" that is the modern self's "only moral resource," aligning Trilling himself with Austen as an agent of the modern "terror he beheld in our self-conscious existence in history."

G537. Sriraman, T. "E. M. Forster, Lionel Trilling and the Liberal Imagination." *Indian Journal of American Studies* 10 (July 1980): 67-73.

Finds Trilling and Forster similar in several paradoxical ways: both are spokesmen of metropolitan culture whose views are anti-metropolitan, both sought ways of connecting "the life of the intellect and the life of the instinct," both were capable of entertaining remarkably contradictory ideas. Notes Trilling's appreciation of Forster's forthright treatment of social class, the importance he attaches to tradition, and his ironic comedy. Concludes that both Trilling and Forster share a paradoxical attitude toward will: "Even as Trilling is fascinated by a cessation of the will's function, he speaks of the task of the Liberal as the renovation of the will."

G538. Stanford, Derek. "A Note on Literary Liberalism." *Contemporary Review* 205 (August 1964): 401-5.

Analyzes Trilling as a representative of contemporary liberal humanism (here equated with rationalism). Summarizes Trilling's critique of liberalism's inability to come to terms with evil, death, and tragedy, noting his fascination in A3 with death and his later "correcting reflection on the despairing precipice-leap into total religious pessimism." Contends that Trilling's work focuses on the "collision" between two attitudes toward death--millenial hope and dread, and stoic *apatheia*--which perhaps can never be resolved.

G539. Tanner, Stephen L. "Lionel Trilling and the Challenge of Modernism." *Literature and Belief* 5 (1985): 67-78.

Examines Trilling's value for Christian readers, admiring his defense of the tradition of Arnoldian humanism in a hostile environment and his determination to come to terms with modern writers to whom he was often unsympathetic--two interests together inspiring his "distinguished pioneer work in delineating the main issues in the conflict between traditional edification conceptions of literature and modernist theory and practice"--but criticizing his habitual ambivalence, which "prevented him from taking a firm position when he probably should have," and the secular perspective that found in "the social relationship . . . the only source of obligation and authority."

G540. Trilling, Diana. "Lionel Trilling: A Jew at Columbia." *Commentary* 67 (March 1979): 40-46.

Recounts the years before Trilling's appointment by Nicholas Murray Butler, president of Columbia, to an assistant professorship in 1939. Describes Trilling's middle-class parents--his indigent, ineffectual father David, shipped to America after breaking down during his Bar Mitzvah service in Bialystok, and his strong-willed, British-educated mother Fanny, who wanted her son to have an Oxford Ph.D.--and Trilling's financial support of them after his father lost his fur business in the Depression. Recalls that Trilling taught at the University of Wisconsin and Hunter College between 1926 and 1929 and that upon his marriage in 1929 he took on additional jobs--an assistant editorship at the *Menorah Journal*, part-time teaching, book reviewing, tutoring, addressing women's clubs--to the detriment of his dissertation on Matthew Arnold. Describes Trilling's decision to appeal his termination in 1936--a dismissal motivated not so much by anti-Semitism or anti-Marxism as by his unsatisfactory progress on the dissertation--as "the single most decisive move of his life," the basis for his completion of the book, his sending a copy on the advice of Irwin Edman to Butler, and Butler's decision, provoked in part by the University of Berlin's refusal to accept Felix Adler in an exchange of philosophy professors, to make the point that "at Columbia . . . we recognize merit, not race" by appointing Trilling as an assistant professor. Notes that shortly after Trilling's promotion, his dissertation director Emery Neff called at the Trillings' home to express the hope that Trilling would not use his position "as a wedge to open the English department to more Jews."

Revised and reprinted in A15.

G541. Vallette, Jacques. "Lionel Trilling, Critique et Createur." [Review of A3 and A4.] *Mercure France* 312 (August 1951): 720-22.

Identifies the leading similarities--penetration, lucidity, freedom from dogmatism, a taste for general ideas--between Trilling's essays and recent European criticism. Calls Trilling an example of the liberal imagination he celebrates in Hemingway and Faulkner, suggesting that reading A4 is a necessary preliminary to appreciating A3. Concludes that earlier objections to novels of ideas as unduly narrow do not apply to A3 because, as A4 demonstrates, the boundaries of both literature and ideas have been so enlarged that Trilling properly refuses to treat them as separable.

Reprinted in a one-paragraph abridgment in *Etudes anglaises* 5 (February 1952): 82-83.

G542. Vendler, Helen. "Lionel Trilling and the *Immortality Ode.*" *Salmagundi*, no. 41 (1978), pp. 66-85.

Disputes Trilling's reading of Wordsworth's poem in C73, rejecting both its conclusions about the structure of Wordsworth's argument and its assumptions about the "discursive" nature of poetry, and asserting against Trilling that the poem is essentially elegiac in character. Observes that Trilling "feels no impulse to delight in Wordsworth's invention or his manner" but is interested solely in his paraphrasable assertions. Argues that because Trilling overlooks the satiric and "naturalistic" tone of stanza 7's portrait of socialization and the "supernatural" images in stanzas 9-11, he too readily sees the poem as offering dynamically opposed theories of maturity, instead of a single "self-therapeutic" conclusion--"that the [poet's] feelings of despair are a waystation on the path to his ultimate powers of adulthood"--set forth most abstractly in stanza 9, which affirms the value of "thought arising from feeling," associating it with "the realm of questioning and misgiving" rather than "the splendor of transfigured sense."

G543. Ward, J. A. "Lionel Trilling and Henry James." *Explorations: The Twentieth Century* (Special Series) 3 (1989): 45-68.

Explores a wide range of affinities between Trilling and James, for Trilling the exemplary novelist of social realism. Compares Trilling's reading of "The Pupil" in B40 to his handling of a similar relationship between teacher and student in C77; notes the Jamesian character of "the moral obligation to be intelligent"; describes James as creating "a nearly perfect" version of Trilling's dialectic between self and society. Notes Trilling's impatience, however, with novelistic form as "an annoying irrelevance." Noting

Trilling's unqualified praise of *The Princess Casamassima* in B19 as a prophecy of modernism, argues that Trilling's covert discomfort here with the hard details of social and political circumstance, which recasts the novel's conflicts in mythic, autobiographical, and psychoanalytic terms, becomes explicit in C159, whose voice is akin to those of James's characters most fearful of experience, and in Trilling's critique of James's Hawthorne in C177, which aligns Hawthorne with Kafka, dismisses James's reading of Hawthorne as denying his dark power, and identifies James, despite a disavowing footnote, as a Philistine because of his worldly sensibility. Concludes that despite a reassertion of conservatism in A9, Trilling in most of his later work sees "moral realism" as "a failure of nerve."

G544. Warshow, Robert. "The Legacy of the Thirties." [Review of A3.] *Commentary* 4 (December 1947): 538-45.

Identifies the legacy of the thirties as a preoccupation with Stalinism that left Americans too disillusioned and corrupted by political ideologies to establish any fuller relation to their own past experiences than intellectual analysis. Takes Trilling as an example of the novelist who "finds at every turn that he is unable to realize and respond to his experience in any way that seems valid and fruitful to him." Compares A3 unfavorably to Wilson's *Memoirs of Hecate County* and, at great length, to Forster's novels, contending that Trilling does not face "the problem of feeling--and thus the problem of art"--because "he is removed from experience *as* experience." Criticizes Trilling's assumption that Maxim's motivations and the primary appeal of Stalinism to the Jewish middle class do not "count." Contends that Trilling, unlike Forster, is often "taken in" by his characters and so is reduced through his hero to rebuking them for their political views, suggesting instead that "the novelist's function is not to argue with his characters--or at least not to try too hard to win the argument." Concludes that in his failure to imagine his fictional experience more fully and specifically by establishing an imaginative relation to his own past, Trilling, as a representative of his generation, "has not yet solved the problem of being a novelist at all."

Reprinted in B36.

G545. Wellek, René. "The Literary Criticism of Lionel Trilling." *New England Review* 2 (March 1979): 26-49.

Groups Trilling with Edmund Wilson as "critics of culture, in particular American culture," reviews his political development, and notes Trilling's dismay, as he analyzes the political concomitants of literature, that the "adversary relation of the artist (of which he obviously approves) has been most successfully stated by writers who . . . often hold illiberal and reactionary opinions." Cites Trilling's indebtedness to Marx and Freud, calling Freud "the key figure in Trilling's thinking," and adding that "Freud as a person is Trilling's hero," but concludes that "Trilling cannot be called either a Marxist or a Freudian critic." Reviews Trilling's disagreements with New Criticism, focusing especially on C75 and noting that his emphasis on the rhetorical dimension of literature sets Trilling against the idea that "literature is primarily an art analogous to painting or music." Attempts to refute Trilling's rejection of Wellek's position, set forth in *Theory of Literature*, that ideas operate in literature only to the extent that they become symbols or myths. Noting Trilling's emphasis on the novel as the literary mode best suited to examine the conditioned will and his preference for European over American novelists, concludes that "the sharp contrast between the English and the American novel seems overdrawn." Asserts that "Trilling does not think much about form," arguing that he borrows in his close analyses the organicist terms and methods of the New Critics. Concludes that Trilling's place in American criticism is "extremely complex," emphasizes his "strong yearning for absolutes" despite his "historicism and relativism," and observes that "he seems to have been very certain of . . . [his possession of a] 'shaped self' he misses in his contemporaries, an impression that established and enhanced his authority as wise man."

Revised and reprinted in *A History of Modern Criticism, 1750-1950* (New Haven: Yale University Press, 1955-92), 6: 123-43.

G546. West, Cornel. "Lionel Trilling: Godfather of Neo-Conservatism." *New Politics*, new series 1 (Summer 1986): 233-42.

Argues that the rediscovery of the New York intellectuals, provoked by a "nostalgia for a time when ideas really mattered," overlooks the relatively minor nature of their contributions to American thought. Focuses on Trilling's development from prescient absorption in the debate over cultural hegemony in A1 to his use of the occasional essay to create a rhetorical "illusion of superiority" to his adversaries and substantive issues and his refusal throughout the 1950's to follow Keats in linking "tragic vision to redemptive political struggle" until the militancy of the New Left drove him to an apocalyptic Manicheism. Commends Trilling, despite the "dead-end" to which his increasingly conservative critique led, as "an effective critical organic catalyst" who can serve as a useful model for such "oppositional communities" as women, workers, ecologists, and minorities too ready to see themselves as "perennial pariahs."

G547. West, Paul. "Romantic Identity in the Open Society: Anguished Self-Scrutiny Among the Writers." *Queens Quarterly* 65 (Winter 1959): 578-85.

Identifies the dilemma of American intellectuals like Trilling as the need "to reconcile his greater awareness with his correspondingly greater craving for identification." Warns of the dangers of cultivating intellectual snobbery as a defense against "a society which fosters snobberies very different from theirs." Observes that Trilling, a "self-obsessed" romantic like Santayana and Malraux, seeks in agnostic spirituality "a coherence both cosmic and personal." Wonders whether freedom of opportunity in a democracy places too great a value on personal identity and personal commitment; whether personal contentment must lie in "a devised coherence rather than in an attentive resignation"; and whether the American intellectuals' anxiety about their alienation is likely to devalue that status of intellectuals or lead to a return to the novel of manners.

Section H

Reviews of Books by Trilling

Matthew Arnold [A1]

**** Chace, William. "Lionel Trilling: The Contrariness of Culture." [Review of the first four volumes of A11.] *American Scholar* 48 (Winter 1978-79): 59-59. See G542.

H548. "J. B." [Jacques Barzun.] "Trilling's Matthew Arnold." *Columbia University Quarterly* 31 (March 1939): 69-71.

Praises A1 as scholarly without being either dry or "superficially faultfinding": It "has the order and fidelity we expect from a report and the accent we expect from a living man." Applauds Trilling's success in translating Arnold's language into the deceptively similar language of his audience, emphasizing his renewal of Arnold's claims to relevance as poet and social philosopher.

H549. Moore, T. Sturge. *English* 2 (Autumn 1939): 386-87.

Despite Trilling's "prolixity," his insensitivity to Arnold's poetry, and his blindness to "the fact that Arnold made a point of not addressing everybody in general nor yet himself alone," concedes that his discussion of Arnold as "politician and theologian" is useful, and that A1 as a whole is "interesting, sometimes almost fascinating."

H550. Colum, Mary M. "Matthew Arnold's Times." *Forum and Century* 101 (March 1939): 141-42.

Acknowledges that Trilling has "attempted to write a biography on new lines" by relating Arnold's life and work so closely to the events of his time, when "literature . . . affected people with an impact that only political ideologies have now"; but criticizes Trilling's emphasis of social and political events over psychological insight, adding that "he often forgets that he is discussing Arnold's ideas and puts forward too many of his own."

H551. Warren, Robert Penn. "Arnold vs. the 19th Century." *Kenyon Review* 1 (Spring 1939): 217-21.

Commends Trilling's "therapeutic" progress toward a history of the nineteenth-century conflict between "the scientific attitude and the poetic sensibility," which underlies Arnold's career and his period but continues unresolved to the present. Notes that Trilling generally avoids close analysis of Arnold's poems, even in relation to their ideas, and undertakes a brief analysis, concluding that the effort to synthesize the traditions of romanticism and rationalism that Trilling ascribes to Arnold is fully "dramatized only in his life," for "he could not assimilate a fluctuating and various world of actualities to his obsessive theme."

H552. Allott, Kenneth. [Review of A1d.] *Modern Language Review* 59 (July 1964): 468-69.

Calls A1 still "the best introduction we have to Arnold's ideas and the best-proportioned treatment of his literary achievement as a whole" but finds it distinctly less successful in discussing Arnold's poetry.

H553. Harrold, Charles Frederick. [Review of A1 and Carleton Stanley, *Matthew Arnold* (Toronto: University of Toronto

Press, 1938).] *Modern Philology* 37 (November 1939): 220-22.

Regrets A1's inability to take advantage of forthcoming scholarly editions of Arnold's poems and notebooks and its "lack of sharp contour, of integrating conclusions," but finds it "the most thoroughgoing and the most penetrating" book on Arnold, especially welcome in its attempt to show Arnold's legacy from his father, its sensitive criticism of his literary theory, and his relevance to contemporary thought.

H554. Lovett, Robert Morss. "The Mind of Matthew Arnold." *Nation* 148 (11 March 1939): 297-98.

Notes Trilling's success in writing a biography of Arnold's mind despite his lack of access to unpublished sources, and approves his critique of Arnold's apology for the status quo and his definition of religion. Concludes that although Trilling "does not attempt to work Arnold's ideas into Marxist formulas," he establishes Arnold as a forerunner of twentieth-century socialism.

H555. Wilson, Edmund. "Uncle Matthew." *New Republic* 98 (22 March 1939): 199-200.

Expresses reservations about the lack of biographical detail concerning Clough and Mrs. Arnold, but emphasizes Trilling's success in presenting Arnold as the most modern of the Victorians, the one who "saw the realities of his time, stated sharply the problems they presented, and would not desist from worrying about them even though he was never able to produce any solution of which the inadequacy was not absurd and patent." Commends Trilling's presentation of Thomas Arnold as a corrective to Strachey's satiric portrait, the connections he draws between Arnold's politics and religion, and his emphasis on Arnold's dialectical habits of thought, and calls A1 "one of the first critical studies of any solidity and scope by an American of [Trilling's] generation," and "a credit both to his generation and to criticism in general."

H556. Whicher, George F. "Seeing Matthew Arnold Whole." *New York Herald-Tribune Books*, 5 February 1939, p. 2.

Identifies A1's greatest stength as its demonstration of unity throughout Arnold's work and between his ideas and those of his father. Observes that despite avoiding new biographical material, Trilling shows "convincingly in how many ways Arnold was connected with his age by underground roots."

**** Broyard, Anatole. "Four by Lionel Trilling." [Review of the first four volumes of A11.] *New York Times*, 10 June 1978, p. 17. See H823.

H557. Lowry, Howard F. "The Mind of Matthew Arnold." *New York Times Book Review*, 29 January 1939, p. 2.

Finds A1, despite its neglect of ongoing biographical research and its plethora of "diverting" comparisons, useful for "its psychological criticism," which corrects the pervasive fragmentation of Arnold's coherent thought into a "catalogue of his manoeuvres."

H558. Hansen, Harry. "Lionel Trilling's 'Matthew Arnold' a Scholarly Discussion of the Man, His Ideal of Order, Peace, Unity." *New York World-Telegram*, 28 January 1939, p. 23.

Notes that "to America, Arnold was the personification of culture, and the Americans of 1883 took it out on him." Commends Trilling for treating Arnold not as "a reactionary philosopher" but as "a great individual who was vitally affected by the social philsophies of his day" and whose work provides "a key to the mental confusion of the mid-Victorian period."

H559. Phillips, William. "Whitman and Arnold." [Review of A1 and Newton Arvin, *Whitman* (New York: Macmillan, 1938).] *Partisan Review* 6 (Spring 1939): 114-17.

Argues that although A1 is "somewhat diffuse and overburdened with details and quotations," it resists Arvin's tendency to bring its subject up to date by "find[ing] in our consciousness the necessary detachment for a more objective view of the past than it was able to have of itself" and so takes its place as "one of the best works of historical criticism produced in this country."

H560. Orrick, James. "Arnold's Influence." *Saturday Review of Literature* 19 (28 January 1939): 5-6.

Praises Trilling's ability to take "Arnold seriously without being pious about him" by presenting "a comprehensive study of the whole man" based on the insight that Arnold "was really a social critic." Though Trilling neglects "the poetry for his own sake," he succeeds in showing Arnold's striking similarities to his father "as a social reformer" and urging his enduring significance.

H561. Knickerbocker, William S. "Thunder in the Index." [Review of A1 and Carleton Stanley, *Matthew Arnold* (Toronto: University of Toronto Press, 1938).] *Sewanee Review* 47 (July-September 1939): 441-45.

Dissents from the eulogistic tone of H556 and H565, citing H557 in support of the view that "a *total* Arnold" cannot yet be reconstructed. Calls A1 a combination of three books: a biography of Arnold's mind, a digressive parade of "great thinkers supposed to have influenced Arnold," and "an instructive, edifying, and occasionally stodgy, revelation of Mr. Lionel Trilling's own solutions of our present difficulties and his corrections of Matthew Arnold's deficiencies." Suspects that Trilling, who offers no clear explanation of Arnold's method, "has not the slightest inkling of the meaning of 'oscillatory' or 'dialectical action' in criticism."

H562. Blackburn, William. "Arnold's Mind." *South Atlantic Quarterly* 38 (October 1939): 462-64.

Commends Trilling's emphasis on the unity of Arnold's poetry and criticism, which accounts for "the transformation of a shy, melancholy poet . . . into the robust critic of society and sanguine prophet of Culture" by placing the State, as the salvation of a modern society reduced to chaos following the French Revolution, at the center of Arnold's thought.

H563. Blackburn, William. [Review of A1a.] *South Atlantic Quarterly* 49 (January 1950): 106.

Describes A1 as "an exploration not only of Arnold's mind but also of those problems which stirred his age and continue to harass our own."

H564. Jones, W. Melville. *Southern Literary Messenger* [new series] 1 (September 1939): 635-36.

Calls A1 "in no sense a biography of Matthew Arnold" but rather "a biography of Arnold's mind and thought," emphasizing Trilling's success in presenting Arnold as a controversialist whose most characteristic and influential essays arose from his engagement with Carlyle, Newman, Mill, Gladstone, and Huxley.

H565. Sackville-West, Edward. "The Modern Dilemma." *Spectator*, 28 April 1939, p. 716.

Commends Trilling's "thrillingly interesting" book, "the most brilliant piece of biographical criticism issued in English during the past ten years," as especially timely in marking and continuing Arnold's attempt to integrate "Action and Contemplation."

H566. Anon. [John Middleton Murry.] "Matthew Arnold To-day." *TLS*, 11 March 1939, pp. 148, 150.

Indicates that the current crucial American debate about the positive values of the State explains why the best book about Arnold, for whom this problem is central, should be written by an American. Concurs with Trilling's insistence that style and society are closely linked in Arnold. Notes Arnold's "emphasis on the necessity of continuity" in moral, social, and religious thought, criticizing Trilling's dismissal of Arnold's "counsel of perfection" in the evangelization of Christian society as unsympathetic and impatient.

Reprinted in *Poets, Critics, Mystics: A Selection of Criticisms Written Between 1919 and 1955 by John Middleton Murry*, edited by Richard Rees (Carbondale: Southern Illinois University Press, 1970), pp. 69-77.

H567. Bald, R. C. "Lives of the Poets." [Review of A1; DeLancey Ferguson, *Pride and Passion: Robert Burns, 1759-1796* (New York: Oxford University Press, 1939); and E. K. Chambers, *Samuel Taylor Coleridge: A Biographical Study* (Oxford: Clarendon, 1938).] *Yale Review* 28 (June 1939): 855-59.

Begins by describing A1 as confined to its subject's work (as opposed to his life or personality) but judges it virtually "a study of the nineteenth century, with Arnold as its focal point." Notes Trilling's originality in emphasizing Arnold's legacy from his father and Arnold's continued critical powers despite his decline as a poet, concluding that "the struggle to be whole may only produce premature exhaustion."

H568. Bishop, John Peale. "Matthew Arnold Again." In *Collected Essays of John Peale Bishop*. New York: Scribner's, 1948. Pp. 353-56.

Asserts that A1 "might be taken as an example of contemporary scholastic criticism in America" because of its copious quotations (Trilling "writes a book the way Tom Sawyer white-washed the fence") and its diffidence toward Arnold's poetry except insofar as its ideas can be abstracted. Contends that "Arnold was a poet and at his best can only be read as a poet."

Explains in a headnote that "this review was written for *Partisan Review*, but the editors declined to print it."

E. M. Forster [A2]

H569. Daiches, David. *Accent* 4 (Autumn 1943): 61-62.

Praises Trilling's self-effacing skill in introducing salient comparisons that elucidate Forster's distinctive achievement, but notes that "he is too often content with extracting, explaining and criticizing the 'message' of the novels, and letting the result stand as a literary judgment," unhelpfully merging description and evaluation by conflating "defects in your author's imagination and defects in your author's works."

H570. Anon. *Booklist* 40 (15 October 1943): 56.

A brief notice describing Forster as "an English writer whose intellectual books have an enduring but limited appeal."

H571. Anon. "Re-Discovering E. M. Forster." [Review of A2, and E. M. Forster, *A Room with a View*, *The Longest Journey* (Norfolk, CT: New Directions, 1943), *Howards*

End, and *Where Angels Fear to Tread* (New York: Knopf, 1943).] *Christian Science Monitor*, 25 September 1943, p. 13.

Briefly reviews Forster's reputation, noting in passing that A2 "voices appreciation in critical terms."

H572. Hicks, Granville. *Common Sense* 12 (October 1943): 380.

Finds A2 "always stimulating and almost always right in its comments on particular books," though less satisfactory in the opening chapter's generalizations, in which "Trilling ties himself in knots with a private definition of liberalism."

H573. Wright, Cuthbert. "The Damned and the Saved." [Review of A2, and E. M. Forster, *A Room with a View*, *The Longest Journey* (Norfolk, CT: New Directions, 1943), *Howards End*, and *Where Angels Fear to Tread* (New York: Knopf, 1943).] *Commonweal* 38 (24 September 1943): 557-61.

Praises the "guiding radiance" of "Mr. Trilling's packed, penetrating little book," though dissenting from its assessment of James and Meredith as Forster's masters, citing instead the "vernacular" tradition of Austen and Butler.

H574. Kristol, Irving. "The Moral Critic." *Enquiry* 2 (April 1944): 20-23.

Focuses on the incongruities between Trilling's two criticisms of leftist thought--its surrender of its "traditional moral vision," and its blinding by that same vision to "the true principles of humanism"--and suggests that the second critical strain has dominated Trilling's recent work, especially A2.

An addendum signed "H." (pp. 23-24) warns of the "special brand of smugness" of "the Trilling-Forster emphasis" on the "negative guideposts" of moral realism over ethical idealism.

H575. Willis, Katherine Tappert. *Library Journal* 68 (15 April 1943): 327.

Calls A2 more "scholarly" than Rose Macaulay's 1938 volume on Forster, describing both as "valuable to any library that makes a point of literary criticism."

H576. Zabel, Morton Dauwen. "A Forster Revival." [Review of A2, and E. M. Forster, *A Room with a View*, *The Longest Journey* (Norfolk, CT: New Directions, 1943), *Howards End*, and *Where Angels Fear to Tread* (New York: Knopf, 1943).] *Nation* 157 (7 August 1943): 158-59.

Hails recent reprints of Forster's novels as relieving both "the doldrums of fiction" and "the greater atrophy or abdication of human and moral values--or the simplifying rigor of militant action on their behalf." Praises A2 as "an examination of the conscience of contemporary literature and thinking," agreeing with Trilling that "a consideration of Forster's work is useful . . . in time of war."

H577. Mayberry, George. "The Forster Revival." [Review of A2, and E. M. Forster, *A Room with a View*, *The Longest Journey* (Norfolk, CT: New Directions, 1943), *Howards End*, and *Where Angels Fear to Tread* (New York: Knopf, 1943).] *New Republic* 109 (6 September 1943): 341.

Compares A2 favorably to Rose Macaulay's "rambling appreciation" of 1938, agreeing that Forster is "preëminent among the survivors" of the native tradition of English fiction, though wondering if Trilling and his reviewers have "taken Forster too seriously" in comparing him to the non-English Conrad, James, and Joyce.

H578. Pryce-Jones, Alan. *New Statesman and Nation* 26 (6 November 1943): 303.

Notes that "the apparently narrow margin by which [Forster] avoids the commonplace" allows him a tone which has been infectiously well-received since *Howards End*, and commends the skill of Trilling's "concise critical guide-book" in catching that tone despite its lack of familiarity with Cambridge, which sometimes leads him to overlook Forster's "subtleties of nerve and complexion and bearing."

H579. Whicher, George F. "A Modern Rational Mind." *New York Herald-Tribune Weekly Book Review*, 5 September 1943, p. 7.

Describes A2 as a "manifesto" for the "renascent spirit of free intelligence" which the critic has rescued from the novelist's self-doubt, providing "a notable study of a culture in disintegration, along with exciting premonitions of a new faith about to rise from the ashes of the old."

H580. Broyard, Anatole. [Review of the Uniform Edition reprint.] *New York Times*, 2 April 1980, p. C26.

Calls Forster "a congenial subject" for Trilling, who "would have liked to write a novel of 'infinite modulation'" like Forster's, and who was perhaps "the only man who could have refined on Forster" in discussing his work.

H581. Baker, Carlos. "New Biography of E. M. Forster." [Review of A2, and E. M. Forster, *A Room with a View*, *The Longest Journey* (Norfolk, CT: New Directions, 1943), *Howards End*, and *Where Angels Fear to Tread* (New York: Knopf, 1943).] *New York Times Book Review*, 15 August 1943, p. 4.

Calls Forster's novels "a continual delight" and A2 "only less so because it is a critique rather than a novel." Urges further scrutiny of the "line of descent from Hawthorne through James to Forster" Trilling indicates. Disagrees with Trilling's contention that "Forster's comic manner prevents a greater response to his work," but agrees that Forster is capable of "serious moral intention" through comedy.

H582. Fadiman, Clifton. "E. M. Forster." [Review of A2, and E. M. Forster, *A Room with a View*, *The Longest Journey* (Norfolk, CT: New Directions, 1943), *Howards End*, and *Where Angels Fear to Tread* (New York: Knopf, 1943).] *New Yorker* 19 (14 August 1943): 60, 62.

Calls A2 "unsettling" in its demonstration that other contemporary novelists are "bright, earnest, passionate children," less serious than Forster "though incomparably more solemn." Praises both Trilling's analysis of Forster and his penetrating remarks "about literature in general, about the novel, and about England."

H583. Arvin, Newton. "Two Cheers for Forster." [Review of A2, and E. M. Forster, *A Room with a View*, *The Longest Journey* (Norfolk, CT: New Directions, 1943), *Howards End*, and *Where Angels Fear to Tread* (New York: Knopf, 1943).] *Partisan Review* 10 (September-October 1943): 450-52.

Commends Trilling for avoiding the sharp distinction between seeing "poetry as knowledge" or "poetry as action": he "has a suppleness denied to the men in both camps." Notes Trilling's affinity to Forster's protest against "pedantry and priggishness," criticizing only his inconclusiveness about "Forster's rather subtle . . . 'refusal to be great.'"

H584. Jones, Howard Mumford. "E. M. Forster and the Liberal Imagination." [Review of A2, and E. M. Forster, *A Room with a View*, *The Longest Journey* (Norfolk, CT: New Directions, 1943), *Howards End*, and *Where Angels Fear to

Tread (New York: Knopf, 1943).] *Saturday Review of Literature* 26 (28 August 1943): 6-7.

Suggests that Trilling is moved to reread Forster mainly because of the precipitous decline of contemporary fiction, "killed by the publicity men." Recommends celebrating "the glories of the liberal imagination in literature" rather than joining Trilling in criticizing that imagination's deficiencies.

H585. Hardy, Barbara. "The Personality of Criticism." [Review of A2b; David Shusterman, *The Quest for Certitude in E. M. Forster's Fiction* (Bloomington: Indiana University Press, 1965); Alan Wilde, *Art and Order: A Study of E. M. Forster* (New York: New York University Press, 1964); John A. Clair, *The Ironic Dimension in the Fiction of Henry James* (Pittsburgh: Duquesne University Press, 1965); Naomi Lebowitz, *The Imagination of Loving: Henry James's Legacy to the Novel* (Detroit: Wayne State University Press, 1965); Jean Frantz Blackall, *Jamesian Ambiguity and "The Sacred Fount"* (Ithaca: Cornell University Press, 1965); George H. Ford, *Double Measure: A Study of the Novels and Stories of D. H. Lawrence* (New York: Holt, Rinehart and Winston, 1965); L. D. Clark, *Dark Night of the Body: D. H. Lawrence's "The Plumed Serpent"* (Austin: University of Texas Press, 1964); and Helen Corke, *D. H. Lawrence: The Croyden Years* (Austin: University of Texas Pres,, 1965).] *Southern Review*, new series 3 (Autumn 1967): 1001-9.

Uses A2 as a standard of "personal presence" against which to measure, mostly unsatisfactorily, a range of "impersonal-sounding" recent critics. Finds Trilling's "I" "more appealing than his more notorious 'We'"--"natural, relaxed, never awkward, affected, cold, or deceptive"--the sign of "a man speaking to men about a man," intent on "justifying and expressing the individual encounter with the work of art." Concludes that the current "cult of impersonality . . . springs from a dissociation of the critic's sensibility, from an inhibition encouraged and perpetuated by our academic establishments."

H586. Anon. "'Undeveloped Hearts': Mr. E. M. Forster and the Modern World." *TLS*, 7 October 1944, p. 481.

Endorses Trilling's view of Forster's work as "gestures of scorn at the ossified or the undeveloped heart," though finding him vague in his analyses of Forster's use of nationalistic judgments and sudden death as "deeply related to Mr. Forster's view of life." Notes that Trilling, like Forster and Chekhov, thinks artists should raise social questions rather than answer them.

H587. Anon. "Forster and the Human Fact." *Time* 42 (9 August 1943): 98, 100, 102, 104.

Calling A2 "the first important Forster study in English," ascribes the Forster revival to "the recent renewal of interest in India" as well as the revaluation of Forster as "the most distinguished living English novelist." Quotes extensively from Trilling's "successful attempt to set Forster in the context of his time."

The Partisan Reader [B18]

H588. "D.S." "The Decline of Culture." *Christian Science Monitor Magazine*, 21 September 1946, p. 12.

Identifies a leading theme of the anthology, which is surprisingly free from stridency and factitious erudition, as "the growing separation between intellectuals and the nation, or the disappearance of that shared cultural tradition in which the past found its canons of criticism and value."

H589. Davis, Robert Gorham. "Politics and Imagination." *Nation* 163 (12 October 1946): 411-12.

Notes the variety of angles from which *Partisan Review* has attacked the liberal imagination, observing that its resulting alienation has left it "little positive ground . . . to stand on." Recommends that the "highly discriminatory intelligence" of the journal be supplemented by "techniques of actualizing fraternity" in order to fulfill the promise of its "humane Marxism."

H590. Schorer, Mark. "Art and Dogma." *New Republic* 115 (11 November 1946): 634, 636.

Criticizes the *Review*'s anti-Stalinism as "exactly as rigid as the Stalinism it attacks," adding that the journal's best work, including the "beautiful" C74, "has been apolitical, even asocial." Argues that the rift Trilling diagnoses between imagination and politics continues even "between the writers the editors seek out and the ideas the editors themselves espouse."

H591. Stauffer, Donald A. "Partisan Anthology." *New York Times Book Review*, 8 September 1946, pp. 3, 28.

Wonders whether the deepest loyalty of the *Review* is to politics or art. Suggests that despite his attack on the "neo-Americanism" of Van Wyck Brooks, Trilling is similarly impelled to regard "art as a means toward politics as an end." Criticizes the intellectual modishness of many of the essays included, but concludes with relief that "the editors' literary tact keeps destroying the political pattern" of their thought.

H592. Anon. *New Yorker* 22 (14 September 1946): 103.

Applauds the editors' resolve "to print only superior writing which treats of ideas and cultural questions without bothering about their current popularity."

H593. Foff, Arthur. *San Francisco Chronicle*, 4 December 1946, p. 14.

Commends B2 as a uniquely valuable anthology, and suggests the compilation of a supplement reprinting essays omitted from this collection.

H594. Redman, Ben Ray. "Magazine of Ideas." *Saturday Review of Literature* 29 (28 December 1946): 18-19.

Finds stories like C77 refreshingly free of formulas, and concludes that the *Review* is an avant-garde magazine whose "steady and profitable contact with the main body of culture" has kept it free of obscurantism and experimentation for its own sake.

The Middle of the Journey [A3]

**** Warshow, Robert. *Commentary* 4 December 1947): 538-45. See G544.

H595. Rago, Henry. *Commonweal* 47 (14 November 1947): 121-22.

Notes with pleasure the developing tragicomic discrepancy between Laskell's perceptions of his friends and their ideas and "what they tell him about them." Hopes the novel will achieve widespread success, not because the public "ought" to read it, but "because this is what it really wants to read . . . and what it is really seeking in those books in which zombies speak advertising-copy to each other and life has the depth and reality of an illuminated jukebox."

H596. "R." [Review of A3i.] *Encounter* 44 (June 1975): 35-36.

Emphasizes the historical value of the novel indicated by its preface identifying Maxim as Whittaker Chambers, which adds to its literary merits its importance as "a kind of artist's note in the margin of history."

H597. Nye, Robert. "A bit of a drag." [Review of A3i; Gore Vidal, *Myron* (London: Heinemann, 1975); Cormac McCarthy, *Child of God* (London: Chatto and Windus, 1975); Elaine Feinstein, *Children of the Rose* (London: Hutchinson, 1975); Anna Kavan, *My Soul in China* (London: Peter Owen, 1975); Anna Kavan, *Who Are You?* (London: Peter Owen, 1975); and Sally Rena, *The Sea Road West* (London: Weidenfeld and Nicolson, 1975).] *Guardian*, 10 April 1975, p. 12.

Offers A3, "a fruit of what is finest in the American imagination," as an antidote to the travesties of Vidal and McCarthy: "The book has more than historical or biographical fascination. Anyone who has been caught up at all in the intellectual currents of the twentieth century will find here a lucid dream-picture of political dilemmas."

H598. Wall, Melvyn. "Quite Trilling." [Review of A3i; Edward G. Hannon, *Man Alive--Man Dead* (London: Mitre Press, 1975); Sally Rena, *The Sea Road West* (London: Weidenfeld and Nicolson, 1975); and Charles McCarry, *The Tears of Autumn* (London: Hutchinson, 1975).] *Hibernia* 39 (11 July 1975): 25.

Places A3i "on a far higher level than the other three" under review because of its "delicate and subtle probing of the mind" haunted by politics and death and its awareness of "the strangeness of human relationships."

H599. Brittain, Victoria. "Recent fiction." [Review of A3i; Iris Murdoch, *A Word Child* (London: Chatto and Windus,

1975); Len Deighton, *Yesterday's Spy* (London: Cape, 1975); and P. D. James, *The Black Tower* (London: Faber, 1975).] *Illustrated London News* 263 (June 1975): 63.

Commends Trilling's exclusion of "any spurious excitement or glamour [from] the novel's characters, events or locations," and calls A3 "a more ambitious, thoughtful and satisfying work than the best of the generation of novels which succeeded it."

H600. Anon. *Kirkus Reviews* 15 (1 August 1947): 407.

Describes A3 as "a first novel of some acumen and almost no physical motion, of considerable conscious intellectualization but an equal emotional sterility," and observes that "the ideological confusion [and] emotional instability of the literati [are] reproduced with fidelity (and probably from experience) but providing little sympathy, often very little interest."

H601. Barrett, Mary L. *Library Journal* 72 (15 September 1947): 1271.

A brief notice calling A3 "exceptional in offering a solution to, as well as analysis of, modern man's problem."

**** Vallette, Jacques. "Lionel Trilling, Critique et Createur." [Review of A3 and A4.] *Mercure France* 312 (August 1951): 720-22. See G541.

H602. Zabel, Morton Dauwen. "The Straight Way Lost." *Nation* 165 (18 October 1947): 413-16.

Calls A3 "a novel of remarkable . . . austerity" which concedes "little or nothing . . . to the conventional inducements of current fiction"--its characters "are suspended in a kind of social and moral void," and "their talk is strung to a painful pitch of personal abstraction"--and describes it as helping define a new novelistic genre: the "dialectic novel," which "succeeds not only as a brilliantly sustained argument but as the record of an essential experience and milieu of our age, one fully equal in validity to the actualities of proletarian fiction." Concludes that A3 "brings the best critical intelligence now discernible in America into play with an absolutely honest creative talent."

Revised and reprinted in *Craft and Character in Modern Fiction: Texts, Method, and Vocation* (New York: Viking, 1957), pp. 312-17.

H603. Flint, R. W. "From Vertigo to Tears." *New Leader* 30 (October 1947): 10.

Compares A3 favorably to such recent failed novels of ideas as *The Death of Vergil* and *Under the Volcano*, labeling it "didactic" fiction in the tradition of Plato's dialogues, *Don Quixote*, *Wilhelm Meister*, and *The Brothers Karamazov*, and describing Trilling's "field of intellectual action," despite its unnecesaary opposition of religion to sensibility, as the largest and most "serious" in American fiction since James.

H604. Mayberry, George. *New Republic* 117 (13 October 1947): 29.

Finds A3, compared to Trilling's short stories, anemic in its story and unoriginal in its characters, though "all done with an intelligence and a Forsterian feel for that strange mixture which is the tragi-comedy of our times" that lift it "far above the general level of recent fiction."

H605. Samet, Tom. "Reconsideration: Lionel Trilling." [Review of A3j.] *New Republic* 176 (23 April 1977): 29-30.

Defends Trilling against the charge of quietism by arguing that A3, which is ultimately "a story of recovery and renewal, resolution and independence," confronts "the temptations of acquiescence" but denies them "full or final authority," affirming instead "the specifically *social* virtues . . . of reason and decorum and restraint."

H606. Fuller, Roy. "Trilling at 70." [Review of A3i.] *New Review* 2 (April 1975): 57-59.

Denies that Trilling is "a born novelist" but finds A3 "deeply intelligent" and surprisingly successful in its rendering of the distinctions of social class despite its insulation of its principals from such political problems as unemployment, agitation, and "the social stigma of evil mild left-wing activity," and its "deficient" irony in presenting Maxim and Nancy Croom.

H607. Ricks, Christopher. "Tennysonian." [Review of A3f; John Updike, *Pigeon Feathers* (London: Deutsch, 1962); Brian Glanville, *The Director's Wife* (London: Secker & Warburg, 1963); Rex Warner, *Pericles the Athenian* (London: Collins, 1963); and Edmund Wilson, *I Thought of Daisy* (Harmondsworth: Penguin, 1963).] *New Statesman* 65 (8 February 1963): 208.

Calls A3 "humorless and nagging" despite its status as a "distinguished . . . document," comparing it unfavorably to Mary McCarthy's "My Confession," and warning that it may be misunderstood in England, "mainly because we didn't have exactly this crisis of liberalism."

H608. Caute, David. "Summer people." [Review of A3i.] *New Statesman* 89 (11 April 1975): 486.

Though finding Trilling "too direct a writer" in his exposition of thoughts and motives and uneven in his success in creating the "thick social texture" he admires in C90, commends the novel's "quiet, mature style, its sudden flashes of feeling, its professional capacity in stimulating interest while not pretending that anything more dramatic than dawning awareness is likely to happen."

H609. Morris, Lloyd. "Ideas and Intellectuals in Close Conflict." *New York Herald-Tribune Weekly Book Review*, 12 October 1947, p. 4.

Describes A3 as a successful novel of ideas, praising its analysis of liberalism as "not a particular program, but an attitude of mind" whose "only absolute doctrine is to hold no doctrine absolutely." Notes that Trilling's "strongest effects lie in what is implied and suggested rather than in what is directly represented."

H610. Schorer, Mark. "The Vexing Problem of Orientation." *New York Times Book Review*, 12 October 1947, pp. 4, 40.

Contends that although A3 lends itself to discussion in moral rather than dramatic terms, "the dramatic terms are always in the fore, and sometimes almost as brightly as in a comedy of manners" whose wit is paramount. Notes that the novel's high lucidity is disturbed only by Trilling's obvious revulsion from the Crooms, which is not reflected by Laskell's weariness toward them.

H611. Howe, Irving. "On *The Middle of the Journey*." [Review of A3j.] *New York Times Book Review*, 22 August 1976, p. 31.

Salutes the republication of A3, which "still seems feverishly topical" in exploring "the moral consequences of being caught up with ideologies." Criticizes Trilling's neglect of "concrete particulars," which often makes A3 "closer to a highly intelligent rumination about a fiction than a fiction itself," but praises Maxim as a "major triumph" compared to the tepidly admirable Laskell, and describes A3 as a novel that "need not always act upon us through concrete incident" because it lives "in the reflecting intelligence of its narrator."

H612. Lalley, J. M. "Two Journeys and a Pastoral." [Review of A3; C.-F. Ramuz, *When the Mountain Fell*, translated by Sarah Fisher Scott (New York: Pantheon, 1947); and Mollie Painter-Downes, *One Fine Day* (London: Hamish, 1948).] *New Yorker* 23 (25 October 1947): 126, 129, 130, 132.

Identifies the interest of A3 as "topical rather than aesthetic," emphasizing the "remarkably oblique" style of its dialogue, which resembles the "elegant journalism" of *New Masses* and *Partisan Review*, and its shadowy, allegorical characters and enervated tone.

H613. Toynbee, Philip. "Confrontations." [Review of A3i.] *Observer Review*, 4 May 1975, p. 27.

Notes that with the passing of its political topicality; A3 emerges as a "fine novel . . . judged by any standard--literary, political, moral or psychological." Observes that "nearly all [of Trilling's characters] are given enough reality to save the novel from the very real danger of turning into an allegory." Commends Trilling's "prophetic insight" into modern-day Hisses and Chamberses even for readers who know nothing of their originals.

H614. Sypher, Wylie. "The Political Imagination." *Partisan Review* 15 (January 1948): 123-27.

Describes A3 as an "intellectual history of the thirties interpreted through Laskell's sensibility of skepticism." Remarks that although the texture of the novel is generally psychological, its "most daring feats"--Susan's death, the confrontation between Maxim and mild Reverend Gurney--break through its psychological plane, establishing its continuity with "Victorian narrative." Compares Trilling to Arnold as "a liberal attempting a moral critique of liberalism" by dramatizing the "strenuousness of choice from moment to moment that removes apocalyptic visions and programs into the distance of irrelevancy."

**** Beresnack, Lillian. "The Journey of Lionel Trilling." *Perspective* 1 (Spring 1948): 177-83. See G443.

**** Fergusson, Francis. "Three Novels." [Review of A3; Robert Penn Warren, *All the King's Men* (New York: Harcourt Brace, 1946); and James Gould Cozzens, *Guard of Honor* (New York: Harcourt Brace, 1948).] *Perspectives USA* 6 (Winter 1954): 30-44. See G464.

H615. White, Warren Ragan. "Emily and Her Friends." *San Francisco Chronicle*, 1 December 1947, p. 12.

Suggests that Trilling's position that "the middle should be defended as stanchly and tenaciously as the extremes" sometimes requires "supersubtle" behavior of both his characters and himself, and expresses relief, considering the heavy quality of Trilling's jocularity, that "his characters don't get gay very often."

H616. Cordell, Richard. "Clash of Ideas." *Saturday Review of Literature* 30 (11 October 1947): 25.

Calls Trilling's characters "more interesting than credible," observing that they "speak elegantly, like characters in a play by Behrman," but concluding that despite the novel's potentially chilly intellectual cast, Trilling writes of intellectual problems "with acumen and compassionate understanding."

H617. Hazard, Eloise Perry. "First Novelists of 1947." [Brief profiles of twelve first novelists, including Trilling, Lionel Shapiro, Willard Motley, Percy Winner, Oswald Wynd, Robert McLaughlin, A. B. Guthrie, Jr., Robert Lewis Taylor, Gabrielle Roy, David Davidson, Esther Carlson, and

Herman Wouk.] *Saturday Review of Literature* 31 (14 February 1948): 8-12.

Describes Trilling as "one of the most important literary figures among America's left-of-center intellectuals," noting the range that allows him to respond to both James and Baudelaire and serve on the editorial board of "both the explosively political, avantgardiste, Marxist, anti-Soviet *Partisan Review* and the more restrained, non-political, gracefully academic, and mildly experimental *Kenyon Review*." Reports that Trilling is at work on a second novel.

H618. Anon. "Disunited States." *TLS*, 16 October 1948, p. 581.

Calls A3 "the best book to come out of America for some little time," commending not only Trilling's mastery of his subject--"the peculiar combination of arrogance and imbecility found at certain levels of intellectual life"--but also his "grasp of character and capacity for handling suspense."

H619. Bayley, John. "Middle-Class Futures." [Review of A3i.] *TLS*, 11 April 1975, p. 399.

Calls the novel "a masterpiece" whose status as "one of the most original humanist novels of its generation" has been "confirmed--even emphasized"--by the passage of thirty years. Emphasizes the contrast between the novel's unoriginal, "Anglican" manner and the "turmoil of ideas, guilts, intellectual anxieties and vulnerabilities" it presents, echoed by a contrast between the characters' middle-class preoccupation with the future and the novel's absorption with death and the past. Compares Trilling to Lawrence and Tolstoy in his presentation of Duck, and notes that "the sad, clownish, but somehow not degraded" portrait of Whittaker Chambers as Maxim confirms the suspicion that "the nicer and better people had none the less somehow got it wrong."

H620. Anon. "Soul Searcher." *Time* 50 (20 October 1947): 106, 109.

Describes A3 as "a good and honest novel about the modern inability to accept such a hell and heaven as Dante imagined," but calls "critic Trilling, author of neat books about Forster and Matthew Arnold . . . not yet a finished novelist": despite his sensitivity in writing of children and their elders and his Forsterian mastery of "surprise and anticlimax," he "mishandles the Dostoevskian character of Maxim" and devotes too much time to "earnest psychologizing."

James, *The Princess Casamassima* [B19]

H621. Flint, R. W. "The Politics of Exclusion." *Hudson Review* 1 (Autumn 1948): 418-20.

Calling Trilling's introduction "highly suggestive," suggests that its focus on the novel's "political superstructure" be supplemented by a consideration of Hyacinth Robinson's peculiarly sexual anguish: "James deprives him of love *by the mere accident of size*," which makes it impossible to earn the love of the people he loves. Agrees with Trilling's suggestion that James cared little for culture or social justice "in the knowing, systematic and fanatical way they are often cared for today."

H622. Chase, Richard. "Folk Hero." *Nation* 166 (19 June 1948): 695-96.

Emphasizes Hyacinth Robinson's affinity with the heroes of folklore and "the Ishmael figures" in Melville and Hawthorne as well as the Young Man from the Provinces in Stendhal, Dickens, and Flaubert, and compares the novel's "moral-political consciousness"--atypical of American fiction--to that of *The Blithedale Romance*, *The Confidence Man*, and A3.

The Portable Matthew Arnold [B21]

H623. Johnson, W. Stacy. [Review of B5a.] *College English* 19 (February 1958): 277.

Commends Trilling's representation of the range of Arnold's interests, and his omission of "the rather fuzzy writings on religion," and the coherence his introduction establishes for Arnold's thought.

H624. Anon. *New Yorker* 25 (17 September 1949): 115.

Notes that Trilling's "long and interesting introduction" correctly ascribes the oft-damned phrase "sweetness and light" to Swift.

H625. Redman, Ben Ray. *Saturday Review of Literature* 32 (27 August 1949): 38.

Agrees with Trilling's "capital introduction" that Arnold's "predicament is ours--he just knew it a little earlier"--and that "he is also founder of the faith--which claims eminent adherents--that modern poetry should be 'a complete magister vitae.'"

The Liberal Imagination [A4]

H626. Rolo, Charles J. *Atlantic* 85 (June 1950): 82, 84.

Admires Trilling's "flexible, undoctrinaire modernism," which "asks of liberalism that it pay its neglected dues to the irrational," though citing the disconcerting "group-centeredness" of some of his observations as still another example of "liberalism's narrowness of outlook."

H627. Anon. *Booklist* 46 (1 March 1950): 209-10.

A short notice calling Trilling's approach "intellectual" and "some of his points debatable," but describing A4 as "readable and thought-provoking."

H628. Wilson, Milton. "Turning New Leaves." *Canadian Forum* 30 (October 1950): 160-61.

Reviews the arguments of C68, C80, C86, and C90, emphasizing Trilling's "willingness to accept the writer on his own terms," a function of his exemplary "humility" before works of art, artists, and other human beings.

H629. Dinkins, Paul. "Four Critics of the Writing Craft." [Review of A4; Bernard De Voto, *The World of Fiction* (Boston: Houghton Mifflin, 1950; Maxwell Perkins, *Editor to Author*, edited by John Hall Wheelock (New York: Scribner's, 1950); and Robert Gathorne-Hardy, *Recollections of Logan Pearsall Smith* (New York: Macmillan, 1950).] *Catholic World* 172 (November 1950): 104-10.

Asks, "What is the business of the novel?" and contrasts De Voto's answer ("It is blasphemy to ask of art what art cannot do," i.e. "to change the world") to Trilling's faith, despite his running critique of liberalism, in the humanist proposition that "the cure [to the "universal accident" of neurosis] lies in the realm of culture." Contends that Trilling's humanism collapses into De Voto's in the absence of "any absolute beyond man," though it is too early to tell whether Trilling's quarrel with humanism will lead to "nihilism" or "something else."

H630. Engle, Paul. "A Perceptive Analysis of Our Culture." *Chicago Sunday Tribune Magazine of Books*, 16 April 1950, p. 16.

Notes that Trilling's "maturity of perception and control and information" offer some hope for an end to the cultural immaturity he finds in America, singling out C68 and C86 as especially penetrating. Regrets that Trilling's emphasis on "the social factor" sometimes makes him slight "the power of literary form as itself an order of verbal society with its own impact on any writer."

H631. Spender, Stephen. "Beyond Liberalism." *Commentary* 10 (August 1950): 188-92.

Finds Trilling's critique of liberalism only intermittently at the center of his essays. Charges that although this critique is often apt, Trilling does not take "the conservatism of W. H. Auden, Ezra Pound, T. S. Eliot, Allen Tate, Robert Lowell, Peter Viereck, and others" seriously as an ideology and so overlooks a more fundamental challenge to liberalism than his own.

H632. Hay, John. *Commonweal* 52 (5 May 1950): 105-6.

Calls A4 "remarkable" in its "readiness not to take refuge" in pursuing its ambitious attempt "to reestablish criticism in a living context" by "restor[ing] and reconstitut[ing] the will." Demurs from Trilling's call for a theory of criticism "in terms of manners, or social class, or politics," arguing more generally for an appreciation of the "unpredictable, implausible, and even dissociated" aspects of literature.

H633. Rovere, Richard H. "Fever Chart for Novelists." [Review of A4; Alex Comfort, *The Novel and Our Time* (Denver: Swallow, 1948); Bernard De Voto, *The World of Fiction* (Boston: Houghton Mifflin, 1950); Calder Willingham,

Geraldine Bradshaw (New York: Vanguard, 1950); John Kerouac, *The Town and the City* (New York: Harcourt, Brace, 1950); Maxwell E. Perkins, *Editor to Author*, edited by John Hall Wheelock (New York: Scribner, 1950); William Saroyan, *The Twin Adventures* (New York: Harcourt, Brace, 1950); Kathleen Winsor, *Star Money* (New York: Appleton Century-Crofts, 1950); and Charles Jackson, *The Sunnier Side* (New York: Farrar, Straus, 1950).] *Harper's* 200 (May 1950): 114-23.

Defends Trilling against De Voto's charge that he is "a schematizer," asserting that "Trilling's view of the novel, 'a summary and paradigm of our cultural life,' comes closer to accounting for all its triumphs than De Voto's prescription that the novel "tell the reader what is happening inside him," and agreeing with Trilling that "experience is always in some sense social."

**** Lewis, R. W. B. "Lionel Trilling and the New Stoicism." *Hudson Review* 3 (1950): 313-17. See G502.

**** MacRae, Donald. "Mr. Trilling Sees It Through (Almost)." *Interim* 4 (1954): 67-73. See G506.

**** Blackmur, R. P. "The Politics of Human Power." *Kenyon Review* 12 (Autumn 1950): 663-73. See G446.

H634. Anon. *Kirkus Reviews* 18 (15 February 1950): 123.

Describes A4 as "a highly intellectualized, precious collection . . . united by an underlying concern for liberalism as an intellectual tradition," and constituting "first ranking literary criticism" despite its "limited market."

H635. Roth, Claire W. *Library Journal* 75 (15 March 1950): 492.

A brief notice identifying Trilling's "core of unity" as "the relationship of ideas to literature."

H636. Read, Herbert. "The Paradox of Liberalism." *Listener* 45 (26 April 1951): 671.

Notes the differences between British and American definitions of liberalism, demurring from Trilling's association of liberalism with "the organizational impulse." Contends that in the American opposition between reality and mind, "Mr. Trilling is always on the side of mind." Suggests that Trilling has moved over the past ten years from "an American conception of liberty" to a more agile, critical, "European conception."

**** Vallette, Jacques. "Lionel Trilling, Critique et Createur." [Review of A3 and A4.] *Mercure France* 312 (August 1951): 720-22. See G541.

H637. Howe, Irving. "Liberalism, History, and Mr. Trilling." *Nation* 170 (27 May 1950): 529-30.

Stresses Trilling's ideological critique of literature, arguing that a concern with moral problems "is no adequate substitute for an *active* moral passion against social injustice" and that "much of the imaginative barrenness Mr. Trilling rightly finds in liberalism has been due less to intransigent commitment than to the shabbiness of what that commitment has become." Suggests that the failure of liberal ideals to inspire writers as distinguished as Stendhal, Dickens, Turgenev, Byron, and Wordsworth indicates their lack of political success, citing especially the bankruptcy of modern capitalism, and argues that "Trilling's attempt to invigorate the liberal imagination from within the liberal orbit" is "without historical basis or urgency and excessively dependent on that mere will whose dangers he has so often observed." Praises Trilling's literary essays, though noting that C80 fails "to acknowledge the role of social 'alienation' in shaping the artist's psychic condition."

H638. Hicks, Granville. "The Shortcomings of Liberalism." *New Leader* 33 (19 August 1950): 22-24.

Notes that Trilling's interest in the relation between literature and society has set him against both the New Critics and the sociological critics, and identifies his own bias "in favor of sound ideas" in such moral realists as James and Forster. Argues that just as "it is foolish to condemn James for not doing what Dreiser did, it is not exactly wise to dismiss Dreiser and Anderson because they didn't write like James." Wonders whether liberalism can survive in a world marked by "the development of a mass society, potentially world-wide in its scope," and recommends that Trilling's analysis of liberalism's shortcomings be supplemented with "a bold, positive, imaginative setting forth of liberalism's potentialities."

H639. Lind, Sidney E. "The Use of Liberalism." *New Republic* 123 (3 July 1950): 18.

Praises Trilling for avoiding the pendantry of "mechanical scholarship and the arrogance of much of modern criticism," adding that he most values the humanistic virtues: "compassion, breadth of understanding, depth of vision and genius for expression." Wonders why Trilling persistently arrives at such "negative conclusions" about liberalism in the face of liberalism's "inextinguishable optimism."

H640. Anderson, Quentin. "Reconsideration: Lionel Trilling." *New Republic* 176 (23 April 1977): 30-32.

Argues that Trilling's faith in "inward variousness" and "recognition of the full existence of others" freed him to discuss class and society as conditioning, but not determining, individual identity. Cites Trilling's favorite authors as having "shouldered the burden of being a self" in a world whose loss of faith in the self had created the idea of society, and suggests that contemporary literary theory extends the resulting tendency toward "depersonalization" despite Trilling's "stubborn biological faith in human possibility," which gave "dignity, force and clarity to our own attempt to marry individual perception to individual act."

H641. Whicher, George. "A Liberal Critic's Far-Ranging Essays." *New York Herald-Tribune Book Review*, 9 April 1950, p. 5.

Agrees with Trilling in deploring the failure of contemporary liberals to question their own dogmas, which are "in danger of perishing from inanition," and praises him for exposing the "complacent paralysis" of "Parrington, the most liberal of our prophets." Finds A4 less important in the cogency of its individual essays than in raising "a banner round which the badly dispersed forces of liberalism may rally."

H642. Toynbee, Philip. "An Attack on Our Cultural Idols." *New York Times Book Review*, 9 April 1950, pp. 5, 13.

Stresses Trilling's distinctiveness in attacking liberalism "from inside that political citadel," noting that he remains stubbornly liberal in his insistence that "the modern novel must be political." Argues that social class is not at the heart of novels like *Moby-Dick*, *The Brothers Karamazov*, or even *The Charterhouse of Parma*. Warns that Trilling's "extreme persuasiveness" should not too easily vanquish alternative viewpoints.

H643. Fadiman, Clifton. "Lionel Trilling and the Party of the Imagination." *New Yorker* 26 (22 April 1950): 115-18.

Hails Trilling as a possible successor to H. L. Mencken in his ability to address a general educated audience. Suggests that Trilling, like James and Fitzgerald, can hold in fruitful suspension two opposed commitments: to political liberalism, and to an aristocratic tradition of tragic irony. Remarking that Trilling "presses liberalism where it is weakest--on its philosophical and emotional front"--concludes that Trilling's criticism is "constructive" in attempting to win adherents from "the party of the Party, whatever its political orientation," to "the party of the Imagination."

H644. Anon. "Baffled Trilling." *Newsweek* 35 (10 April 1950): 85-86.

Calls A4 "old-fashioned" in its "effort to add balance and perspective to the country's intellectual life," suggesting that "Trilling seems constantly baffled by a lack of material to work on, like a surgeon performing an elaborate operation without realizing that the patient is made of straw."

H645. Nicolson, Harold. "The Free Mind." *Observer*, 25 March 1951, p. 7.

Suggests that Trilling, perceiving the "sad uniformity" and "mechanical literacy" of American culture, attempts more successfully than Edmund Wilson "to induce the youths and maidens of the United States to think and feel more variously" in order to prevent their ideas from deteriorating into ideology.

H646. Snell, George. "The Critic and the American Writer." *San Francisco Chronicle/This World Magazine*, 16 April 1950, p. 23.

Distinguishes the "historico-radical" group of critics with which Trilling is aligned from the less political liberal New Critics, though noting that Trilling's group "has become less and less political in its appraisals of literature." Calls A3 evidence that Trilling is "among the half-dozen most gifted creative writers in America," and applauds this new reminder that "an eminent novelist can also be a distinguished critic."

H647. Redman, Ben Ray. "Reality in Life and Literature." *Saturday Review of Literature* 33 (15 April 1950): 44-45.

Notes approvingly the formidable range of Trilling's interests, but wonders, in considering the essays' principle of unity, what Trilling means by "the liberal imagination" or "liberal" generally. Criticizes the "parochialism" of Trilling's dismissal of conservatism as an intellectual tradition and his assumption that "our educated class" once looked to the Communist Party for cultural leadership: at such times "Mr. Trilling speaks not for a class but for a small group within a class."

**** Podhoretz, Norman. "The Arnoldian Function in American Criticism." *Scrutiny* 18 (June 1951): 59-65. See G517.

**** O'Connor, William Van. "Lionel Trilling's Critical Realism." *Sewanee Review* 58 (July-September 1950): 482-94. See G513.

H648. Anon. "A Creative Critic." *TLS*, 20 April 1951, p. 24.

Groups Trilling with Forster, Huxley, and Edmund Wilson, agreeing that "liberal humanism is no longer enough," and emphasizing his "passion for literature and moral virtue." Notes that although Trilling may sometimes become duller than Wilson, his judgments are never as perverse as Wilson's can be. Joins Trilling's call for the rebirth of social democracy "as a faith likely to inspire poets and novelists."

H649. Bush, Douglas. "The Critical Spectrum." [Review of A4; W. H. Auden, *The Enchafèd Flood* (New York: Random House, 1950); and *Perspectives of Criticism*, edited by Harry Levin (Cambridge: Harvard University Press, 1950).] *Virginia Quarterly Review* 26 (Summer 1950): 472-76.

Calls Trilling "a temperate, civilized liberal" with "an appropriately Arnoldian platform," identifying him with the New Critics in "his recognition of literary form and style" but noting his contrary insistence on "the pastness of the past."

H650. Clark, W. P. *Western Humanities Review* 4 (Autumn 1950): 353-54.

Praises Trilling's resistance to the recent "insurgence against reason" in criticism, his "sense of the essential importance of ideas," and his rejection of the tendency to blame artists and writers for current social problems.

H651. Copeland, Thomas W. "Critics at Work." [Review of A4; Kenneth Burke, *A Rhetoric of Motives* (Englewood Cliffs: Prentice-Hall, 1950); and Harry Levin, editor, *Perspectives of Criticism* (Cambridge: Harvard University Press, 1950).] *Yale Review* 40 (September 1950): 167-69.

Praises Trilling's "universal alertness, which makes it possible for him to watch what is going on in a dozen arenas at the same time," and his freedom from jargon, his own or others'.

The Selected Letters of John Keats [B22]

H652. Anon. *Booklist* 47 (1 June 1951): 344.

Observes that Trilling's introduction describes Keats's "geniality as his most outstanding characteristic."

H653. Engle, Paul. "Sharp, Witty Letters from Poet Keats." *Chicago Sunday Tribune Magazine of Books*, 17 June 1951, p. 4.

Maintains that Keats's letters prove that only a "noble and intense" person can write noble and intense poetry. Commends Trilling's introduction as "perhaps the best brief account of the man and poet I have seen."

H654. Chapin, Ruth. "'Vale of Soul-Making.'" *Christian Science Monitor*, 27 September 1951, p. 13.

Commends Trilling's "stimulating and provocative" introduction and his selection of letters, though regretting the absence of letters which would have revealed "the brave front Keats showed the world" apart from Fanny Brawne.

H655. Rugoff, Milton. "The Letters of Keats and Byron." [Review of B6 and *The Selected Letters of Byron*, edited by Jacques Barzun (New York: Farrar, Straus & Young, 1953).] *Griffin* 2 (August 1953): 20-23.

Remarks that Trilling's attempt (which "digs . . . deeper indeed than we have reason to expect an introductory essay to go") to reconcile Keats's sensuous appetites with his Platonic morality "does not quite take into account the fact that much of Keats's 'sensuality' was plainly wishful."

H656. Barker, Shirley. *Library Journal* 76 (1 April 1951): 596.

Observes readers equipped with Trilling's selection of the letters, together with his introduction and an edition of the poems, "could come to know the poet as well as most of us are likely to."

H657. Howe, Irving. "The Honey Gorged." *Nation* 172 (9 June 1951): 543-44.

Admires Keats's "manliness," as opposed to "the false American strut," and deplores, on the evidence of his letters, the modern decline in prose: "His style can be related, as the good styles of our day cannot be, to a general level of literary cultivation." Finds Trilling's introduction, though overlong, "an act of genuine criticism" mercifully free from "mimicry of the subject."

H658. Stauffer, Donald. "Cowper and Keats." [Review of B6 and *The Selected Letters of William Cowper*, edited by Mark Van Doren (New York: Farrar, Straus and Young, 1951).] *New Republic* 125 (22 October 1951): 20.

Contrasts Cowper's "closed world" with Keats's attraction to "a romantic expanding universe." Calls Trilling's introduction "one of his profoundest and most shapely pieces of criticism," concluding that despite Keats's youth, his letters "live up to Trilling's heroic portrait."

H659. Whicher, George. "The High Heroism of Keats' Letters." *New York Herald-Tribune Book Review*, 3 June 1951, p. 3.

Observes that as a compelling model of spiritual and moral health, "Keats's letters are [even] more serviceable than his poems." Agrees with Trilling's brisk dismissal of the myth of Keats as an "indolent hedonist," calling him instead "one of the best-balanced poets this side of Shakespeare, and until tuberculosis overtook him, one of the most healthy minded," as against Edmund Wilson's paradigm of the neurotic artist in L981.

H660. Quennell, Peter. "'Your Ever Affectionate John Keats.'" *New York Times Book Review*, 27 May 1951, pp. 4, 24.

Sets Keats's "marvelous maturity" against his superficial marks of "immaturity, even crudity," his limited knowledge of the world, his "schoolboyish greed," and his "coloring of the poetaster," remarking that Keats was able to transform "the symbols of voluptuous childhood" into "the poetic imagery of the adult life-worshipper." Notes that in Trilling's selection of the letters--though not, by implication, in his introduction--"the impassioned adolescent and the adult artist appear with equal clarity."

H661. Anon. *New Yorker* 27 (15 December 1951): 159.

Notes Trilling's correction of earlier writers' neglect of Keats's supposedly "rather coarse" buoyancy, "which was as much Regency as it was Romantic."

H662. Auden, W. H. "Keats in His Letters." *Partisan Review* 18 (November-December 1951): 701-6.

After briefly commending Trilling's introduction, goes on to distinguish between letters "in which the poet is in control of his situation--what he writes about it is what he chooses to write--and those in which the situation dictates what he writes," calling the second kind mere "'human documents'" in which Keats has "ceased to be a poet and become a poetic subject." Praises Keats's "maturity of outlook" and his freedom from "hushed reverence before the artistic mystery" and financial irresponsibility. Notes the striking contrast between the "calm and majestic" style of the Odes and the protean "helter-skelter rush" of the letters, and concludes that Keats's letters suggest that he "died before he found a style and form in which he could incarnate all sides of his sensibility"--a narrative form that "would have made him the equal of and only successor to Chaucer."

H663. Anon. *Saturday Review of Literature* 34 (14 July 1951): 47.

Calls Trilling's "admirable" introduction, which calls attention to the "startling intimacy" with which Keats displays his "naked mind and sensibility," "one of the main treats of the volume."

H664. Anon. "In the Mouth of Fame." *Time* 58 (16 July 1951): 94.

Emphasizes the extent to which the letters, and Trilling's "sparkling" introduction, destroy the "romantic legends that have grown up around Keats."

Orwell, *Homage to Catalonia* [B24]

H665. Parry, Hugh J. *Annals of the American Academy of Political and Social Science* 284 (November 1952): 219-20.

Ascribes the neglect of B24, which traces Orwell's disillusionment with "the techniques of Ends-before-Means," to Orwell's "swimming against the vulgarly obvious current of history."

H666. Rolo, Charles J. *Atlantic* 190 (July 1952): 85.

Agrees with Trilling that Orwell, "a man willing to die for a cause and unwilling to lie for it," was "a virtuous man."

H667. Anon. *Booklist* 48 (1 June 1952): 318-19.

Describes B24 as a modern Iliad introducing "chapters of political orientation" with "chapters of straight narrative."

H668. Ames, Ruth C. *Catholic World* 175 (July 1952): 318.

Notes that Orwell's "transparently honest" account may well furnish ammunition to readers who disagree with his politics.

H669. Ames, Alfred C. "Orwell's Delayed Story of a Communist Betrayal." *Chicago Sunday Tribune Magazine of Books*, 18 May 1952, p. 3.

Regrets that the first American publication of B24 was delayed "until anti-Communism had become fashionable," but judges its frontline reportage and its critique of the Spanish Communists as still timely.

H670. Garrison, W. E. *Christian Century* 69 (30 July 1952): 878.

Though resisting the suggestion that all Spanish loyalists were Communists, commends Orwell's portrait of the Communists' "betrayal of the republican cause for the promotion of their own."

H671. Harrison, Joseph G. "Communist Betrayal in Spain." *Christian Science Monitor*, 21 May 1952, p. 13.

Notes the helpfulness of Orwell's analysis of "the mistakes which democracy must avoid if it is to compete successfully with totalitarianism of both the Right and the Left."

H672. Ashe, Geoffrey. "The Bell Tolled." *Commonweal* 56 (20 June 1952): 277-78.

Suggests that readers familiar with Orwell will be prepared alike for his courage and honesty and his "recurring confusion and bewilderment."

H673. Anon. *Kirkus Reviews* 20 (1 May 1952): 293.

Calls B24, though "not a book to create sensation in a day when much of what was happening at Barcelona has been realized," still "as exciting as it is meditative."

H674. Willis, Katherine Tappert. *Library Journal* 77 (15 May 1952): 891.

Agrees with Trilling that B24, "a classic in its interpretation of totalitarianism--left or right"--is "one of the important documents of our time."

H675. Mayberry, George. "Orwell in Spain." *New Republic* 126 (23 June 1952): 21-22.

Criticizes Orwell's utopian socialism as naive, pointing toward "the sloughs of despond of his last books," which suffer from "abstractness" and "spleen."

H676. Wolfe, Bertram D. "What Orwell Saw in Spain Before He Wrote '1984.'" *New York Herald-Tribune Book Review*, 18 May 1952, p. 7.

Calls B24 "no less a work of art" than *1984* and more direct in "its moral impact," agreeing with Trilling that Orwell "is one of those rare figures who live their visions as well as write them."

H677. Hicks, Granville. "George Orwell's Prelude in Spain." *New York Times Book Review*, 18 May 1952, pp. 1, 30.

Emphasizes Orwell's revulsion from the Spanish Party's lies about the P.O.U.M. rather than their brutal suppression of the group. Concludes that all Orwell's work is "a call to action, not a cry of despair."

H678. Anon. *New Yorker* 28 (17 May 1952): 142-43.

Calls B24 "one of Orwell's very best books and perhaps the best book that exists on the Spanish Civil War."

H679. Fuller, Edmund. "No Middle Stool!" *Saturday Review* 35 (12 July 1952): 17, 35.

Suggests that without Trilling's introduction, which relates B24 "to the whole of Orwell's life and work," the book, "a minor document" that overestimates the political responsibility of the Spanish anarchists and other opponents of Franco, would probably "not carry its proper weight today." Wonders if Orwell would have reassessed the Spanish Civil War if he had lived to prepare a revised edition of B24.

H680. Vogler, Lewis. "George Orwell's Vivid Report Of the Civil War in Spain." *San Francisco Chronicle/This World Magazine*, 8 June 1952, pp. 19, 22.

Remarks that despite Orwell's warnings "against his own bias and possible errors," his dispassionate exposition of political issues "compels belief." Agrees with Trilling that B24 is "a testimony to the nature of modern political life."

H681. Anon. *Time* 59 (19 May 1952): 112.

Regrets that the American publication of B24, "still the best book on the Spanish civil war," was delayed by its unfashionable anti-Communism until Orwell had achieved fame for *Animal Farm* and *1984*.

The Opposing Self [A5]

H682. Linscott, Robert. *American Scholar* 24 (Summer 1955): 360-66.

Calls the essays in A5 less unified and striking than those in A4 but asserts that it confirms Trilling's shared position with Edmund Wilson as one of the two pre-eminent American critics. Suggests against B23 that contemporary fiction reveals emptiness rather than a preoccupation with evil.

**** Chace, William. "Lionel Trilling: The Contrariness of Culture." [Review of the first four volumes of A11.] *American Scholar* 48 (Winter 1978-79): 49-59. See G452.

H683. Anon. *Booklist* 51 (1 March 1955): 280.

A brief notice citing "the affirmation of the self against the imprisonment imposed upon it by nature and society" as Trilling's "keynote."

H684. Faverty, Frederic E. "Lionel Trilling: Our Present Day Matthew Arnold." *Chicago Sunday Tribune Magazine of Books*, 6 March 1955, p. 12.

Notes the difficulty of saying something new about "19th century immortals," and maintains that although Trilling always manages to say something new, it is not always something significant. Concludes that even when Trilling presses the idea of the opposing self too far, his incidental observations and his "delightful" style provide compensating pleasures.

H685. Pickrel, Paul. "The Voice Beyond Ideology." *Commentary* 19 (April 1955): 398-400.

Remarks that Trilling, "a true son of the age of ideology," argues that "the universe speaks in a voice beyond ideology," and that writers like Keats achieve heroic stature by attending to that voice, which takes the form of conditions and circumstances in modern fiction. Identifies the novelty of A5 as the insight that "the iron law" of social conditions is "a source of joy and pleasure," indeed "a religious priniciple." Argues that the "self" Trilling opposes to culture ought more properly to be called "being," which differs from self "as a blueprint differs from a building": "a building is conditioned and a blueprint is not."

H686. Mercier, Vivian. "The Modern Writer's Quarrel with His Culture." *Commonweal* 61 (4 March 1955): 587-88.

Noting Trilling's estrangement from both Judaism and Christianity, argues that "Trilling's quarrel with culture began before he had ever really possessed a culture": though essays like C116 can be brilliant performances, Trilling, like other writers for *Partisan Review*, harps too much on "our" alienation, overlooking the dangers of his own "secular self-righteousness."

H687. Arrowsmith, William. "All About Ripeness." [Review of A5; Marianne Moore, *Predilections* (New York: Viking, 1955); and Leslie Fiedler, *An End to Innocence* (Boston: Beacon, 1955).] *Hudson Review* 8 (Autumn 1955): 443-49.

Defines Trilling's position as honoring the "tension between the best of Arnold and the best of Freud," and notes his recent tendency to favor "Arnold the poet" over Freud. Notes that Trilling's "villain" is the modern appetite for pure evil and unconditioned spirit, but contends that the values he commends have been threatened less by social circumstance than by "the bad habits of innocence."

H688. Anon. *Kirkus Reviews* 23 (1 January 1955): 25.

Pronounces A5 "as distinguished and richly rewarding a book of criticism as has appeared in America in many years," one which confirms Trilling's "place among all the all too few critics who have anything real to say." Describes the way Keats's letters set the program for the volume's emphasis on "the development of the self."

H689. Libaire, Beatrice B. *Library Journal* 80 (1 February 1955): 368-69.

Remarks that Trilling's analysis, "though often eloquent and delightfully thought-provoking, is not for the rapid reader."

H690. Anon. *Listener* 54 (18 August 1955): 265.

Calls A5 "shorter and perhaps slighter" than A4 but equally wide-ranging and intelligent. Notes the "philosophical unity" implied by Trilling's ability to illuminate the conflict between self and culture in such unlikely texts as *Bouvard and Pécuchet*.

H691. Fuller, Roy. [Review of A5a and Stephen Spender, *The Making of a Poem* (London: Hamish Hamilton, 1955).] *London Magazine* 2 (November 1955): 87-90.

Observes that Trilling's assessment of the most oppositional writers depends on "what, and what amount, they are able to accept of life." Defends his essays as justified in their apparent digressiveness and "daring comparison" by their illuminating central premise, but expresses disappointment that neither Trilling nor Spender, "having abandoned any clear conception of the structure and movement of society," offers any specific idea of how writers are to overcome their social alienation.

H692. Daiches, David. "The Broad View." *Manchester Guardian*, 23 August 1955, p. 4.

Criticizes Trilling's habit of using literary subjects as pretexts to indulge in "baffling generalisation" about "life in general."

H693. Miller, Perry. "'Romantic' Image of the Self." *Nation* 180 (5 March 1955): 203-4.

Observes that Trilling discovers a "romantic" image of the self in "certain figures [Austen, Howells, James] resolutely prized in these days by the anti-romantics." Since Trilling seeks "an element of redemption" in literature, unwary readers "may find him insidiously leading them back to didacticism" in his use of literature to attack "the dominant anti-intellectualism of this age." Admires Trilling's "advocacy of literary underdogs," though expressing occasional discomfort "at being so cavalierly included in Mr. Trilling's 'we.'"

H694. Alvarez, A. "Problem Critic." *New Statesman and Nation* 50 (13 August 1955): 193-94.

Contends that Trilling's insistent emphasis on "twentieth-century values" rather than literature "elevate[s] the prejudices of his earlier book into a critical method" which allows "the particularity of the works of art . . . to elude him."

H695. Daiches, David. "Essays by Lionel Trilling." *New York Herald-Tribune Book Review*, 3 April 1955, p. 4.

Cites several dangers in Trilling's critical method: his conversational lack of rigor in developing cultural generalizations familiar to him, his "habit of bringing in as analogies whatever he has been reading or thinking about recently"; his frequent rush from evaluative criticism to genetic explanation. Concludes that because "it is civilization, we feel, that he really wants to talk about," he sometimes forces his literary observations to fit broader cultural arguments.

H696. Levin, Harry. "An Urgent Awareness." *New York Times Book Review*, 13 February 1955, pp. 3, 30.

Describes Trilling's mood as "a pathos of the present" rather than "nostalgia for the past" in which writers defined themselves in opposition to their culture. Notes that Trilling has become "more concerned with values than motives," but concludes that he is "only rarely . . . swept away with the largeness of his generalizations" in B23 and B25.

***** Broyard, Anatole. "Four by Lionel Trilling." [Review of the first four volumes of A11.] *New York Times*, 10 June 1978, p. 17. See H826.

H697. Anon. *New Yorker* 31 (19 February 1955): 132.

A brief notice listing the subjects of individual essays, which "are linked . . . by grace, by clarity, and by Mr. Trilling's own and admirable perception."

H698. Magid, Nora. "The Creative Criticism of Lionel Trilling." *Reporter* 12 (7 April 1955): 44-45.

Observes that Trilling "writes very little, really, but what he does write is uniformly excellent" and eagerly received in several essays' reappearances "as lecture, article, introduction, and book chapter." Remarks that the "loosely linked" essays collected in A5 are distinguished by Trilling's sensitivity to "much that we may well have missed in our own reading."

H699. Jones, Howard Mumford. "Nine Glimpses of Our Selves." *Saturday Review* 38 (12 February 1955): 11-12.

Aligns A5 with the European traditon of *feuilletons* and "the love of books . . . not synonymous with bookishness," suggesting that Trilling's essays have more vitality than the ephemeral work of popular reivewers concerned only with new work. Suggests that in Trilling's reading, "the modern self" has "mistaken the limitations of society for the limitations of life." Quarrels with Trilling's occasional verbosity and lack of a center and his misidentification of Little Dorrit with Beatrice but finds his importance in his "dar[ing] to utter unfashionable terms like duty, joy, . . . and culture."

**** Frank, Joseph. "Lionel Trilling and the Conservative Imagination." *Sewanee Review* 64 (Spring 1956): 296-309. See G467.

H700. Wain, John. "A Daniel come to judgement." *Spectator* 195 (29 July 1955): 171-72.

Praises Trilling's Arnoldian success in addressing "those who are directly on a level with the critic himself" and his gift of "describing *exactly* the thing he is talking about." Criticizes C111 as responsive to Dickens without identifying the specific causes of that response, and concludes that Trilling excels in "*moral* definition" rather than structural analysis.

H701. Anon. "Preoccupations of a Critic." *TLS*, 26 August 1955, p. 492.

Notes that Trilling has ruled his own project--"a critique of the moral imagination"--impossible. Expresses disappointment at the "quietism" of Trilling's moral concerns following the social and political emphasis of A4, and suggests that Trilling "has failed to match the growing intensity of his moral preoccupations" with a corresponding selectivity concerning subjects. Remarks that Trilling's "greatest gift is for admiration," a kind of "wary generosity," but complains, in a passage quoted in the Preface to A8, of the slipperiness of Trilling's "we," charging that the ambiguity of the pronoun frequently makes it unclear whether Trilling is discussing alienation as a condition of the modern self or of a particular social group like the New York intellectuals.

H702. Francis, Sister Mary. "Literature and Art." *Thought* 30 (Winter 1955-56): 611-13.

Describes Trilling's subjects as "nine 'selves' that win the quarrel against culture, and are not destroyed by it."

Notes that despite Trilling's hesitations and qualifications, his conclusions are typically conservative, though he is often undecided about whether the principle or the quality of an action can best serve as the basis for the opposing self. Criticizes Trilling's moral conflation of literature and life.

**** Donoghue, Denis. "The Critic in Reaction." *Twentieth Century* 158 (October 1955): 376-83. See G459.

H703. Martz, Louis L. "The Energy of Mind." [Review of A5; R. P. Blackmur, *The Lion and the Honeycomb: Essays in Solicitude and Critique* (New York: Harcourt, Brace, 1955); and Eliseo Vivas, *Creation and Discovery: Essays in Criticism and Aesthetics* (New York: Noonday Press, 1955).] *Yale Review* 45 (September 1955): 142-46.

Compares A5 unfavorably to both A4 and Blackmur's collection; except for B22, the essays are "pale and limited."

The Collected Stories of Isaac Babel [B29]

H704. Rolo, Charles J. *Atlantic* 196 (August 1955): 85-86.

Notes that Trilling's Introduction "does much to sharpen the reader's appreciation of this remarkable writer," and adopts Trilling's dialectic of violence and sensitivity as the basis for a discussion of Babel's work.

H705. Anon. *Booklist* 52 (15 September 1955): 33.

Praises Babel's "semiautobiographical sketches" and "vignettes of Jewish life," as well as Trilling's "illuminating introduction."

H706. Engle, Paul. "Where Is the Joy-Giving Revolution? No Answer." *Chicago Sunday Tribune Magazine of Books*, 3 July 1955, p. 5.

Regrets that "a personality independent enough, and undeceived enough, to portray his people as they really were could not possibly have fitted into the rigid Soviet conception of a writer."

H707. Popkin, Henry. "Stories from the Spirit of This Age." *Commonweal* 62 (26 August 1955): 523-24.

Remarks that Babel, "a better artist than a politician," "prefers showing events to drawing conclusions." Suggests that he is most interested in "human qualities that are most like pictorial qualities--skill, grace, ease, power, confidence, authority."

H708. Anon. *Kirkus Reviews* 23 (1 May 1955): 308.

Emphasizes the "contradictions and anomalies" of Babel's preoccupation with both violence and "spiritual values," which makes B29 "an important contribution to modern literature." Commends Trilling's "masterly introduction."

H709. Oboler, Eli M. *Library Journal* 80 (1 June 1955): 1381.

Observes that the "universal appeal" of Babel's "deep insight into human morals and values" transcends his stories' "autobiographical . . . content."

H710. Howe, Irving. "The Right to Write Badly." *New Republic* 133 (4 July 1955): 16-18.

Calls Babel "one of the literary masters of our century." Criticizes Trilling's neglect of Babel's Yiddish affinities and his transformation of Babel's treatment of "the problem of historical action" into "a kind of timeless moral dialectic," which overlooks his specific commitment "to the fate of a desperate revolution" and the unique historical importance of his "straining toward a union of passion and tenderness."

H711. Deutsch, Babette. "Whiffs of New-Mown Hay, Gunpowder and Garlic." *New York Herald-Tribune Book Review*, 10 July 1955, p. 3.

Emphasizes the contrast between Babel's aesthetic craftsmanship and the extreme experiences of his stories and his own life.

H712. Slonim, Marc. "A Storyteller, Ironic and Lyrical." *New York Times Book Review*, 26 June 1955, p. 4.

Compares Babel's "terse manner" to "physiological naturalism," but observes that the "romantic . . . tension and melancholy" of his world are "perfectly controlled." Commends Trilling's analysis of "Babel's literary genius and his peculiar racial and psychological characteristics."

H713. Marcus, Steven. "The Stories of Isaac Babel." *Partisan Review* 22 (Summer 1955): 400-11.

Argues against Trilling that Babel's stories are marred by his inveterate irony, which often undercuts the premises of his stories, his hatred of Polish Jews, and his "overinvestment in violence." Suggests that the dialectic Trilling finds between Babel's attractions to violence and spirituality is "more accurately a duality," a strategic and inconclusive search for a force moderating his infatuation with violence, and concludes that "Babel's ironies and contradictions often tend to destroy, rather than create, each other."

H714. Lewisohn, Ludwig. "Russian Grotesques." *Saturday Review* 38 (9 July 1955): 11.

Attacks Babel's writing as "hasty, jumbled," and "spasmodic," lacking any "shred of creative tranquility," and pronounces his current reputation inflated by partisan political sympathies and a perverse delight "in nothing but the vulgar and sordid."

H715. Anon. *Time* 65 (27 June 1955): 94, 96, 98.

Emphasizes the unsparing cruelty Babel observes in his world and shows toward himself, as his narrator wonders, "not, 'Can I take it?' but 'Can I dish it out?'" Praises Trilling's "perceptive introduction."

Freud and the Crisis of Our Culture [A6]

H716. Daly, John K. "Freud, Catholics and Culture." *Commonweal* 63 (9 March 1956): 596-98. Discussion, *Commonweal* 64 (13 April 1956): 49-50.

Argues that Trilling's biological emphasis is complemented by his concern "with the need of re-establishing communication between persons." Draws a parallel between the Freudian self beyond culture and the Catholic soul and conscience. Contrasts the conceptual sophistication allowed by Trilling's critical terms with the conceptual bluntness and poverty fostered by "scholastic training and terminology."

Three letters in the later issue defend scholastic thinking against Daly's charges; none mentions Trilling more than briefly.

H717. Sacksteder, William. *Ethics* 66 (July 1956): 306.

Calls A6 "a tossed salad made up variously of remarks on the views of Freud, generalizations concerning literature, popular philosophy, and random social comment."

H718. Sandrow, Edward T. *Jewish Social Studies* 19 (January-April 1957): 87-88.

Links Freud's Jewish resistance to cultural hegemony to his biological account of selfhood, the liberating "central idea that has prevented playwrights and philosophers from making peace with our culture as it is" and provided "a dynamic force against all forms of totalitarianism."

H719. Barron, Louis. *Library Journal* 81 (15 January 1956): 196.

Briefly summarizes the argument of A6, recommending it "for all libraries."

H720. Hicks, Granville. "The Grounds for Dissent." *New York Times Book Review*, 8 January 1956, p. 7.

Commends Trilling for "trying to find the right grounds on which to quarrel with contemporary society," though wondering if "he might have built a firmer foundation" by relying on a more "pragmatic" base than Freud's thought.

H721. Anon. *New Yorker* 31 (21 January 1956): 122.

Notes that Trilling's style in this "important statement" "increasingly resembles T. S. Eliot's."

H722. Anon. "For 'Sloppy Thinkers'?" *Newsweek* 47 (30 January 1956): 100.

Finds Trilling's strength in his loyalty to "well-worn truths about society and literature" temporarily obscured by changing fashions. Notes that his "pithy, if polysyllabic," lecture opposes self and culture in Freud's thought and urges that this opposition "can clear up some of our own sloppy thinking" about the two.

H723. Brien, Ivor. "Vestigial Organ." [Review of A6 and H. L. Philp, *Freud and Religious Belief* (New York: Rockliff, 1956).] *Spectator* 197 (21 September 1956): 394.

Briskly dismisses Freud's claims as a religious thinker, arguing that his mistakes about literature are consistently more useful than his mistakes about religion, a subject he never took seriously. Praises both "authors' ability to cut away some of the undergrowth that has grown up around Freud, concealing his real importance."

H724. Anon. "Freud and the Arts." [Review of A6 and Herbert Marcuse, *Eros and Civilization* (London: Routledge and Kegan Paul, 1956).] *TLS*, 4 May 1956, pp. 261-62.

Analyzes at length the disrepute into which Freud's theories of artistic expression, as opposed to the applications of his work to the psychology of artists, have fallen. Observes that both Trilling and Marcuse try to rescue Freud from the "lively New World optimism" of recent sociological revisionists by emphasizing the biological basis for his discussion of human identity.

H725. Bremner, Marjorie. *Twentieth Century* 159 (May 1956): 516, 518, 520.

Notes that Trilling's defense of Freud's apparently "reactionary" resistance to cultural conditioning has been supported by Anna Freud's later work showing that "even a highly desirable environment cannot always prevent neuroses in children." Suggests that the fear of cultural conditioning is more pervasive in America than in Britain or France.

A Gathering of Fugitives [A7]

H726. Linton, Calvin D. *American Scholar* 26 (Spring 1957): 251, 258.

Notes that the "relaxed atmosphere" of A7 proves that "a good critic . . . mellows as he matures."

**** Chace, William. "Lionel Trilling: The Contrariness of Culture." [Review of the first four volumes of A11.] *American Scholar* 48 (Winter 1978-79): 49-59. See G452.

H727. Frenz, Horst. *Books Abroad* 21 (Summer 1957): 315.

Observes that the essays collected in A7 "go far beyond ordinary book reviews," giving "background, amplification, and original thought to the particular subject under discussion," as in C101, which ascribes the changing attitude of American intellectuals toward their country to the waning influence of Europe and the "considerable improvement in the cultural situation in this country" over the past thirty years.

H728. Daiches, David. "The Mind of Lionel Trilling: An Appraisal." *Commentary* 24 (July 1957): 66-69.

Calls Trilling "the perfect New York intellectual" but argues that his metropolitanism is in many ways provincial, isolating him from large areas of the American scene and leading him to generalize too easily about his own isolation. Concludes that Trilling's "well-stocked mind" can observe and analyze data only if they have been written about; hence his growing interest in "American society as a *subject*" stems from David Riesman's writing.

H729. Anon. *Listener* 58 (7 November 1957): 751.

Pronounces Trilling, together with Edmund Wilson and F. R. Leavis, one of three masters of criticism in English; his reading is not as broad or his work so wide-ranging or frequently ephemeral as Wilson's, nor is he as preoccupied as Leavis with "permanent judgments." Instead an essay like C101, which shows how the American intellectual class "has lost touch with the major forces--the revolutions in technology, economics, administration, journalism--which are transforming the Western culture it is their business to comprehend," shows him "poised . . . between involvement and dedication."

H730. Stewart, J. I. M. "Academic Persons." [Review of A7; David Cecil, *The Fine Art of Reading* (London: Constable, 1957); and John Wain, *Preliminary Essays* (London: Macmillan, 1957).] *London Magazine* 4 (November 1957): 69-72.

Praises the lightness and firmness of Trilling's essays, concluding that it is "wonderful that Mr. Trilling should be able to emerge from all those lectures and seminars, all those freshmen and sophomores, and address--so zestfully, so wittily, and presumably so much to his reasonable economic advantage--a general and adult American reading public."

H731. Balakian, Nona. "Reviews by Trilling." *New Leader* 40 (25 February 1957): 24-25.

Admires Trilling's care in checking "traditional values and stock responses against his own experience of reality" and "sense of fact"--a habit which produces "often delightfully unexpected" results, especially when Trilling persuades his audience to join him in scrutinizing unsympathetic or equivocal figures like Henry Adams or Ethan Frome.

Reprinted in *Critical Encounters: Literary Views and Reviews, 1953-1977* (Indianapolis: Bobbs-Merrill, 1978), pp. 132-35.

H732. Edel, Leon. "The Critic en Pantouffles." *New Republic* 135 (19 November 1956): 25-26.

Traces Trilling's preoccupation with defining culture both to Arnold and to a long-standing American uneasiness about culture. Contends that because America is too large and various to have a single cultural capital, American culture can be conceived only in regional terms. Approves the sensitivity of Trilling's literary essays but disputes his argument that American intellectuals are enjoying a period of ascendancy, claiming that corporations prize cleverness rather than intellectualism and that the country, for all its wealth and power, is becoming less literate.

H733. Davis, Robert Gorham. "Personal Reader." *New York Times Book Review*, 4 November 1956, pp. 5, 28.

Applauds Trilling's escape from "chatty impressionism" and from the "transvaluative prestidigitation" of Marxists and Freudians, noting approvingly the controversy C101 has aroused in questioning "the stock responses of his own intellectual and academic kind."

**** Galliano, Luciano. "Lionel Trilling: Critica et Narrativa." *Studi Americani* 2 (1956): 243-60. See G470.

H734. Anon. "A Critic Speaks." *TLS*, 23 August 1957, p. 509.

Stresses Trilling's relaxation into an "almost distressingly colloquial" style, observing that the "modest and reasonable" tone with which he occupies "the middle ground between textual and interpretive criticism" often hides such unorthodox opinions as his sympathy for British writers like Graves and Snow.

**** Greenwood, E. B. "The Literary Criticism of Lionel Trilling." *Twentieth Century* 163 (January 1958): 44-48. See G475.

The Life and Work of Sigmund Freud [B35]

H735. Slavens, Thomas P. *Christian Century* 79 (11 July 1962): 865-66.

Strongly criticizes the abridgment's omissions as rendering the edition "of little interest to the scholar" or even the general reader.

H736. Braceland, Francis J. *International Journal of Social Psychiatry* 8 (Summer 1962): 232.

Observes that Freud's "biographers," who have preserved the essence of Jones's work and sacrificed little of value, "make no effort to defend or to explain him." Emphasizes Freud's unfortunate lack of "spiritual leanings" and religious faith.

H737. Barron, Louis. *Library Journal* 86 (1 November 1961): 3784.

Recommends the "well-proportioned" abridgment "even for public libraries that already have the original edition."

H738. Hyman, Stanley Edgar. "Images of Sigmund Freud." [Review of B35; C. G. Jung, *Freud and Psychoanalysis*, translated by R. F. C. Hull (New York: Pantheon, 1961); Peter Madison, *Freud's Concept of Repression and Defense: Its Theoretical and Observational Languages* (Minneapolis: University of Minnesota Press, 1961); J. A. C. Brown, *Freud and the Post-Freudians* (Baltimore: Penguin, 1961);

and Henry Denker, *A Far Country* (New York: Random House, 1961).] *New Leader* 45 (5 February 1962): 26, 27.

Contends that the editors' excisions of "technical discussions and scholarly documentation . . . along with digressions, trivia and some of Jones' whimsies" have improved the book for the non-specialist audience, and that Trilling's introduction focuses the story "more sharply . . . as heroic."

H739. Mairet, Philip. "Beyond analysis." *New Statesman* 63 (22 June 1962): 908-9.

Commends the editors for having produced a book "still quite bulky enough to read with comfort." Points out in response to Trilling's introduction that the inseparability of psychoanalytic theory from "the individual subjectivity of Freud the seer" is "in the nature of the case."

H740. Anon. *New York Herald-Tribune Books*, 12 November 1961, p. 14.

A brief notice observing the deletion of material dealing with "technical aspects of Freud's work."

H741. Steiner, George. "Titan Abridged." *Reporter* 25 (7 December 1961): 68-70.

Praises the "great skill and tact" of the abridgment, "a trim, authoritative piece of work," but emphasizes the inevitable losses "even when one fully supports the grounds for abridgment"--for example, the "deceptive impression of ease" conveyed by omitting false steps in the development of Freud's theories and the de-emphasizing of Freud's courage in confronting his final illness documented so exhaustively in Jones's original biography.

H742. Brown, Ralph and Marian. *Social Education* 26 (May 1962): 275-76.

Notes that the abridgment emphasizes Freud's "life and development" rather than his work.

Warshow, *The Immediate Experience* [B36]

H743. Anon. *Booklist* 58 (15 March 1962): 471.

Describes Warshow's "philosophic rather than sociologic" approach to his material as "incisive" and "biting" in its revelation of writers' and the public's "self-delusion."

H744. Griffin, Hilary. *Catholic World* 195 (July 1962): 253.

Regrets the absence of "enough essays here to delineate the author's predominant themes and critical points of view," which would investigate the relation between the "pervasive and disturbing power" of popular culture and "the superior claims of the higher arts."

H745. Weisberger, Bernard A. "Krazy Kat and Others." *Chicago Sunday Tribune Magazine of Books*, 21 January 1962, p. 4.

Finds Warshow's essays more impressive individually than as a humorless book which does "not quite jell."

H746. Anon. *Christian Century* 79 (16 May 1962): 631.

Finds many of the essays "dated," but praises those on gangster films, *Monsieur Verdoux*, and *Day of Wrath*.

H747. Croce, Arlene. "Conscience of His Generation." *Commonweal* 76 (16 April 1962): 42-43.

Commends Warshow's unique ability "to relate the ephemera of taste to a historic totality," and ascribes this ability to his legacy as a "dispossessed leftist intellectual." Concludes that Warshow "obviously was not a movie critic"; instead, "his subject was politics; he was a critic of culture" whose greatest weakness is his political condescension to the products of popular culture as completely determined by their economic means of production.

H748. Anon. *Kirkus Reviews* 29 (1 November 1961): 994.

Calls B36 "the finest collection of essays on popular culture since Mary McCarthy's . . . *Sights and Spectacles*," noting that Warshow, though he lacks McCarthy's stinging contempt, is "more civilized, cultivated and committed."

H749. Adelman, George. *Library Journal* 87 (1 February 1962): 560-61.

Describes Warshow's essays as "criticism of the highest order."

H750. Kauffmann, Stanley. "An Intellectual and the Movies." *New Republic* 146 (22 January 1962): 16-17.

Finds Warshow's essays on specific plays and films far inferior to his social and political essays, and criticizes his ponderous approach to A3, leading to the obvious conclusion that "Forster is a novelistic genius, Trilling is not." Attacks Trilling's introduction as "windy" and "puffed with pomposities."

H751. Fiedler, Leslie. "His World Was New York." *New York Times Book Review*, 4 February 1962, p. 12.

Attributes Warshow's political outlook on popular culture to his close association, both "catholic" and "provincial," with New York and *Commentary*, and his belief that "the key experience of our time" was "the drift toward communism in the Thirties and the revulsion from it thereafter."

H752. Alpert, Hollis. "The Images Behind the Screen." *Saturday Review* 45 (20 January 1962): 23.

Describes Warshow's point of view as "entirely intellectual," despite its freedom from jargon and snobbery, and suggests that his theory of film tended toward "the espousal of documentary realism."

H753. Lynn, Kenneth S. "On American Society." [Review of B36; Daniel J. Boorstin, *The Image: Or What Happened to the American Dream* (New York: Atheneum, 1962); Paul Goodman, *Utopian Essays and Practical Proposals* (New York: Random House, 1962); and Harvey Swados, *A Radical's America* (Boston: Atlantic-Little, Brown, 1962).] *Yale Review* 51 (June 1962): 649.

Excepts B36 from the long list of books (including all three of the others under review) that "simply create new illusions by the very act of 'exposing' the illusion-makers." Praises Warshow's tonic "awareness that the radical intellectuals of a generation ago who placed a premium on conventionalized intellectual 'responses' have left an enduring mark on our emotional and moral capacity."

Beyond Culture [A8]

H754. McGovern, Hugh. [Review of A8 and Carl Bode, *The Half-World of American Culture* (Carbondale: Southern Illinois University Press, 1965).] *America* 114 (15 January 1966): 90-91.

Ridicules the Freudian preoccupations of both Trilling and Bode, which make American culture seem "dark and grim indeed." Concludes that the "pedantic pussyfooting" implicit in Trilling's refusal to define leading concepts like "life" and "culture" vitiates his argument and invalidates his title.

**** Chace, William. "Lionel Trilling: The Contrariness of Culture." [Review of the first four volumes of A11.] *American Scholar* 48 (Winter 1978-79): 49-59. See G452.

H755. Duffy, Dennis. "The Middle of the Journey." *Canadian Forum* 45 (March 1966): 284-85.

Praises Trilling's "ability to write a number of essays around a topic without riding a hobby-horse" but criticizes his insularity in coming so recently to the widespread recognition that "style rather than substance" is at the center of modern intellectual and aesthetic culture. Concludes that "whether or not the teller realizes it, *Beyond Culture* points to a course beyond liberal humanism."

H756. Dowell, Peter W. *College English* 28 (November 1966): 183.

Contrasts Trilling's "cool urbanity" to his "strong sense of mission" in opposing "the hegemony of the adversary culture," especially in C159 and C179.

H757. Jacobsen, Dan. "Beyond Whose Culture?" *Commentary* 41 (March 1966): 87-93.

Contrasts Trilling's pose as spokesman for genteel bookmanship in A7 with his role as spokesman for "a self-consciously tense, exhausting" modernism. Notes the "frustrated courage and despair" behind Trilling's continued attempt to be "seditious and upsetting" about the cultural establishment, but finds the attempt undermined by his increasingly fussy style and his complicity with the "second environment" he deplores. Excoriates the apologetic tone in which Trilling notes his disenchantment with the institutionalizing of modernism. Ascribes the success of A4 to its political importance, arguing that "the fate of the progressive political impulse" was a more resonant subject than the second environment, whose proponents Trilling too easily assumes "have pre-empted all the available literary and intellectual space."

H758. Kostelanitz, Richard. "Men of the '30s: A Contemporary Look at Five Literary Figures." [Review of A8; Alfred Kazin, *Starting Out in the Thirties* (Boston: Little, Brown, 1965); Philip Rahv, *The Myth and the Powerhouse: Essays on Literature and Ideas* (New York: Farrar, Straus and Giroux, 1965); F. W. Dupee, *The King of the Cats* (Farrar, Straus and Giroux, 1965); and Granville Hicks, *Part of the Truth* (New York: Harcourt, Brace & World, 1965).] *Commonweal* 83 (3 December 1965): 266-69.

Compares writers and critics who came of age during the 1930's, including all five of those under review, unfavorably to earlier and later generations. Claims that the importance of A4 is based more on "its influence upon the fashionable thought of the time than any lasting ideas or judgments." Takes Trilling's disapproval of modernist writing as evidence that he thinks critics more rational, socially aware, and important to society than artists. Contrasts his rhetorical complexity with "the simplicity of his ideas," and calls the essays in A8 "wandering and diffuse commentaries." Concludes that "the thirties must be rejected as completely as possible."

H759. Anon. *Economist* 219 (28 May 1966): 970.

Notes that "the ambiguity of [Trilling's] title is deliberate," and sets Trilling's "serious doubts about the power of literary studies" against the tonic effect of C131, which makes criticism appear as "truly a civilised and civilising enterprise."

H760. Tanner, Tony. "Lionel Trilling's Uncertainties." *Encounter* 27 (August 1966): 72-77.

Identifies the conflict between self and world as underlying all Trilling's criticism, and remarks that "his ambivalent attitude to the problematical reationship between self and society . . . is tending [in A8] towards direct contradiction." Finds this contradiction clearest in C177, which commends Hawthorne for maintaining rather than resolving "the dialectic between human imagination and material circumstances which Trilling finds most rewarding." Disputes Trilling's argument that "poetry is necessarily antipathetic to, and lower than, philosophy," expressing regret that Trilling's conclusions to his leading questions--"what is happening to the self in our culture? what can we learn from modern literature? what are we doing when we set out to 'teach' literature? what are the possibly undesirable effects of the power of modern criticism?"--are so tentative and incomplete.

H761. Pickrel, Paul. "Edmund Wilson, Lionel Trilling, Philip Rahv." [Review of A8; Edmund Wilson, *The Bit Between My Teeth: A Literary Chronicle of 1950-1965* (New York: Farrar, Straus and Giroux: 1965); and Philip Rahv, *The Myth and the Powerhouse: Essays on Literature and Ideas* (New York: Farrar, Straus, and Giroux, 1965).] *Harper's* 232 (January 1966): 95-96.

Notes that Trilling and Rahv draw more direct connections than Wilson between reading and other moral behavior. Contends that Trilling's achievement is to place the opposition between individuals and society in a cultural context that shows the institutionalizing of opposition, and suggests that Trilling's hostility toward modernist oppositional culture, which he "takes . . . too seriously," is stronger than he usually acknowledges.

H762. Cevasco, George. *Library Journal* 90 (15 November 1965): 4982.

Observes that Trilling "gives the impression that he views himself as another Arnold." Praises the essays in A8 but declines to subscribe to all their conclusions.

H763. Hough, Graham. "'We' and Lionel Trilling." *Listener* 75 (26 May 1966): 760-61.

Excuses himself from membership in Trilling's "we" on the grounds that the unhealthy intimacy Trilling sees between the university and modern culture is an American, not a European, phenomenon and that he cannot share Trilling's "monotonously apocalyptic" view of the adversary culture. Charges that Trilling's ambivalence as a teacher of modern literature does not place him outside culture but rather situates him precisely within it, concluding that Trilling's place as an East Coast American academic intellectual commands respect and close study but not the universal authority Trilling's rhetoric seems to invite.

H764. Lerner, Laurence. *London Magazine* 6 (July 1966): 108-12.

Calls Trilling "probably the finest critic we have today" on the basis of his "response to literature," his "interest in ideas," and his "sensitivity to the spiritual needs of contemporary society." Poses "the basic question" of A8--"Can the central place of literature in our education be justified from the nature of modern literature?"--and contrasts "the greatness of the modern movement," which "came from having to fight for its despair," with its facile acceptance by the academic establishment. Contends that Trilling escapes this subversion of the formally subversive modernist impulse because "he believes in politics" as a means to achieving the social ideals modernist writers wish to attack or transcend.

H765. Williams, Raymond. "Beyond Liberalism." *Manchester Guardian*, 15 April 1966, p. 8.

Concurs in Trilling's revulsion from conformist modernism, but argues that his critique is not radical enough. Contends that Trilling's adversary culture is actually a "post-liberalism" that clings desperately "to a liberal idea of the self at a point where the liberal idea of civil society had broken down"--a variation rather than an adversary of liberalism, whose illusions can only be prolonged by such attempts to rationalize them from within.

H766. Alter, Robert. "A Necessary Uncertainty." *Midstream* 12 (March 1966): 77-80.

Deplores the critical reception of A8, singling out H771 as especially "obtuse" in its demand for unearned "dramatic finalities." Observes that Trilling has once again declined to produce the "Big Book" favored by both "position-takers" and "system-builders" because his criticism, "the history of a mind's self-questioning as it feels the pressures of changing cultural forces," is necessarily "occasional" and "provisional."

H767. Hoffmann, Frederick J. "The New Gentility." [Review of A8 and Philip Rahv, *The Myth and the Powerhouse* (New York: Farrar, Straus and Giroux, 1965).] *Nation* 201 (8 November 1965): 334-36.

Criticizes collections of occasional pieces as less continuous and intense than a sustained work, and finds both collections disappointing because of "what they settled for *not* doing." Distinguishes aesthetic culture from "*total* culture--to which manners and technology and beliefs integrally belong"--identifying Trilling's adversary culture with this "noble or unwashed marginal culture . . . which strikes at the conservative heart of social life." Criticizes Trilling's conclusion in C175 that "if you are both interested in pleasure and doubtful of its ultimate value you have reached some point of intellectual balance," and concludes that "Trilling too often appears to want to save himself . . . from the ultimate commitment which the humanistic engagement involves."

H768. Rosenthal, Raymond. "Wrestling with the Angel." *New Leader* 49 (17 January 1966): 24-26.

Describes A8 as "a polemical book in an unpolemical manner" and "an interim, agonizingly uncertain book" written "with the unreasonable hope that its readers will take it for a peremptory cultural pronouncement." Contends that Trilling's analysis of adversary culture is weakened by his failure to notice the "severe break and discontinuity" between high modernists like Joyce, Yeats, and Eliot, and "third-rate heirs" like William Burroughs, Norman Mailer, and Allen Ginsberg, who espouse "a debased and uncritical romanticism." Regrets the fact that in attacking the conformism of modern aesthetic culture, Trilling has been backed "into the ranks of those who submit to an even greater coercion . . . to conform to the reigning norms and standards of existing industrial society." Although he deplores the failure of criticism to wrestle with the angelic powers it ascribes to literature, maintains that "the means for wrestling with that angel that Trilling provides his critics are startlingly meager."

H769. Enright, D. J. "Literature as suicide." *New Statesman* 71 (15 April 1966): 539-40.

Observes that although Trilling clearly "enjoys ideas," the "undertaker's chill" of these "egregiously sensible" essays and their "strikingly tidy" passions suggest that he may not enjoy literature. Contends that "the idea-men, the intellectuals, the professors" are more directly responsible than Tolstoi or Dostoevsky for the establishment of modern anti-establishment culture. Suggests that Trilling, confronted with unpleasant choices (should modern literature be dropped or kept as a subject of instruction?), "seems to prefer neither."

H770. Steiner, George. "An Overture to Silence." *New York Herald-Tribune Book World*, 31 October 1965, pp. 4, 39.

Expresses disappointment that since 1955 Trilling has published only "a handful of essays and lectures" instead of "a major statement" and that he adopts a "sybilline" tone instead of forthrightly defending his provocative premise that "art does not always tell the truth" and "can even generate falsehood and habituate us to it." Argues that "an education founded decisively on the *written word* . . . may gradually enfeeble our awareness of the real."

H771. Mazzocco, Robert. "Beyond Criticism." *New York Review of Books* 5 (9 December 1965): 20-23.

Criticizes Trilling's "wearily genteel" later style, which is like "trudging uphill," obscuring potentially illuminating insights with abstractions and qualifications. Dissents from Trilling's assumption that the unconscious is beyond cultural manipulation, describing phrases like "biological reason" (in A6) and "intelligent love" (in B16) as "evasive effusions" about the relation between individuals and their culture, and expressing impatience with the satisfaction he takes in Hawthorne's ambivalence in C177, and concludes that "if one wishes to strike through the mask, one should not be masked oneself."

**** Broyard, Anatole. "Four by Lionel Trilling." [Review of the first four volumes of A11.] *New York Times*, 10 June 1978, p. 17. See H826.

H772. Macauley, Robie. "From the Particular to the Universal." *New York Times Book Review*, 14 November 1965), pp. 5, 38.

Marks Trilling's focus on the adversary culture as overriding "all that is idiosyncratic and excursional" even in his occasional essays.

H773. Lehan, Richard. [Review of A8; John Henry Raleigh, *Time, Place, and Idea* (Carbondale: Southern Illinois University Press, 1968); Louis D. Rubin, Jr., *The Curious Death of the Novel* (Baton Rouge: Louisiana State University Press, 1967); Howard Mumford Jones, *Belief and Disbelief in American Literature* (Chicago: University of Chicago Press, 1967); Vernon W. Grant, *Great Abnormals* (New York: Hawthorn, 1968); John Walsh, *Poe the Detective: The Curious Circumstances Behind "The Mystery of Marie Roget"* (New Brunswick: Rutgers University Press, 1968); *Regionalism and Beyond, Essays of Randall Stewart*, edited by George Core (Nashville: Vanderbilt University Press, 1968); and *Six American Novelists of the Nineteenth Century*, edited by Richard Foster (Minneapolis: University of Minnesota Press, 1968).] *Nineteenth-Century Fiction* 23 (December 1968): 368-75.

Attacks Trilling's critique of Hawthorne as proto-modernist in C177 on the grounds that his values are "inclusively . . . twentieth-century," his definition of "modernity" too narrow, and his defense of the heroic individual against the encroachments of culture debatable, since it would endorse the behavior of Rappaccini, Chillingworth, and Aylmer. Observes that Hawthorne's vision of "the individual fulfilled . . . within society . . . keeps him this side of cultural anarchy."

H774. Gross, John. *Observer Weekend Review*, 10 April 1966, p. 20.

Agrees with Trilling that the adversary culture has been uniquely successful in the mass media and on college campuses. Praises the penetration and ironic wit of Trilling's critique of the institutions of modernism, though criticizing his refusal to distinguish sharply Arnold's call for a rationally better-educated society and Dickens's rebellion "against the necessary limitations of any society whatsoever."

H775. Raleigh, John Henry. "Culture and Beyond." *Partisan Review* 33 (Summer 1966): 429-35.

Identifies Trilling as Arnold's successor in the double role of conservator of the past and "proponent of the free play of the critical intelligence on the present." Analyzes the ways Trilling sets the self as "an almost irresistible force" against culture as "an almost immovable object," remarking that "whichever proves the more potent Mr. Trilling sees . . . a failure of the critical intelligence." Argues that the modern mind is less fatigued than contemporary literary criticism, and indicates some ways its contradictions are expressed by the paradoxically aggressive yet passive behavior of college students.

H776. Sklar, Robert. "Culture and Cant." [Review of A8 and Susan Sontag, *Against Interpretation and Other Essays* (New York: Farrar, Straus and Giroux, 1966).] *Progressive* 45 (April 1966): 45-46.

Observes that Trilling opposes "the faculty of reason" to the adversary culture, seen as "a party of art," but wishes for "a more direct confrontation of the rational intellect with the power and ideology of contemporary art."

H777. Edel, Leon. "Literature and Life Style." *Saturday Review* 48 (6 November 1965): 37-38.

Attributes Trilling's authority to his critical stance--"half aggressive, half cautious"--praising his continuing attempt to define culture but criticizing his "needlessly subjective" generalizations and his apparent embrace of advertising as a "cultural ally." Suggests that his blindness to the "power hunger" of Leavis and Snow and his "uneasiness before the politics of the artist" stem from his own unexamined assumptions about "egalitarianism."

H778. Stafford, John. "Scholars and Gentlemen in American Literature." [Review of A8; Jay B. Hubbell, *South and Southwest: Literary Essays and Reminiscences* (Durham: Duke University Press, 1965); Robert E. Spiller, *The Third Dimension: Studies in Literary History* (New York: Macmillan, 1965); Carl Bode, *The Half-World of American Culture: A Miscellany* (Carbondale: Southern Illinois University Press, 1965); Albert F. McLean, Jr., *American Vaudeville as Ritual* (Lexington: University of Kentucky Press, 1965); and R. W. B. Lewis, *Trials of the Word: Essays in American Literature and the Humanistic Tradition* (New Haven: Yale University Press, 1965).] *Southern Review*, new series 3 (Autumn 1967): 1062-76.

Contrasts Trilling's wish "to circle and circle the fact" of each cultural event, drawing out its possible social significance, with Lewis's directness in confronting adversary reactions. Suggests that although Trilling is capable of "confrontation" in C170, he usually prefers to "sidle off after having demonstrated fully the complexity of the fact," as in C131.

H779. Cox, C. B. "Trilling's journey." *Spectator* 216 (15 April 1966): 470-71.

Notes that Trilling, like Babel and Forster, distrusts aggression but feels that intellectuals need it to withstand corruption by his society; hence he admires Austen because she appreciates "self-preservation." Finds his customary dialectic more fretful and incomplete in A8 than usual, as "he asserts the values of reason and will, but lacks the aggressive self-confidence needed to create large structures of thought," but concludes that he retains the strength of his own self-awareness, so that "his struggles, even his indecisions, have helped his readers as they follow the same quest" toward self-knowledge.

H780. Anon. "The Middle Way." [Review of A8 and R. W. B. Lewis, *Trials of the Word: Essays in American Literature and the Humanistic Tradition* (New Haven: Yale University Press, 1965).] *TLS*, 28 April 1966, p. 368.

Observes that Trilling has "a liberal imagination" in the sense of seeing every side of an argument, so that although he is concerned with the growth of power in the modern university and the ideological effects of teaching modern literature, he does not take sides in either case.

H781. Newman, Charles. "On American Culture." [Review of A8 and R. W. B. Lewis, *Trials of the Word: Essays in American Literature and the Humanistic Tradition* (New Haven: Yale University Press, 1965).] *Yale Review* 55 (Spring 66): 450-55.

Compares the reception of A8 to the disappointing response to Arthur Miller's *After the Fall*, describing Trilling's perspective as increasingly "cranky and diffuse" despite his sensitivity to individual authors. Notes that "while Trilling may be beyond the adversary culture, he may well be behind the bourgeois," who have simply absorbed the disenchantment of modernism in the course of a typical generation and who take it as their starting hypothesis. Suggests that "the adversary culture may have in fact been unionized, but it is not yet a closed shop."

The Experience of Literature [B40]

H782. Richardson, Jack. "What Every Freshman Should Know." *Chicago Tribune Book World*, 24 September 1967, pp. 18, 21.

Gently criticizes the cumbersome size and relatively narrow scope of B40, which is largely an anthology of British and American literature, but commends Trilling's warmly intelligent commentaries, which express "an easy, very human friendship with literature."

H783. Stock, Irvin. *College English* 29 (November 1967): 160-68.

Places the "startling radicalism" of the anthology in the context of Trilling's career, a developing attempt "to awaken us to the discrepancy between our habitual ideas and the experience they pretend to describe." Argues that although A4's "critique of simplemindedness" was well-received as hallowed by "the lessons of modern literature," A5 and A8, which showed "the literary community itself as given to simplification" of "the complex actuality of experience," were attacked as vague and inconclusive. Contrasts Trilling's emphasis on "the *experience* of literature" with Brooks, Purser, and Warren's formal orientation, which implies that "the act of reading itself is the property of specialists," and suggests that many college teachers will be "shocked" at the "unaccustomed *nudity*" of his selections, unarmored by any systematic critical apparatus.

H784. Donoghue, Denis. "A Literary Gathering." *Commentary* 45 (April 1968): 92-96.

Describes B40--"no ordinary anthology," but ambitious and important, "a significant document in contemporary American culture"--as "a Sacred Book of the Arts" intended for the fictional class Trilling dramatizes in C77.

Commends Trilling's sensitivity to "the order of the book"--the network of relations within each work, between different works, and between a work and the society which produces and receives it--and his complementary awareness of the "peremptory" energies of chaos, as in his sympathetic portrayal of Tertan: "One of the most compelling visions in modern criticism is the sight of Mr. Trilling falling over backwards to be fair to intransigence. . . . The sight of Tertan has made Mr. Trilling so guilty that he is prepared to make the world all over again in his favor." Complains about the textual accuracy of a dozen poems reprinted here.

H785. Macauley, Robie. "Unrequired but Unavoidable." *New York Times Book Review*, 31 December 1967, p. 3.

Compares B40 to Brooks and Warren's *Understanding Poetry* as having "surmounted pedagogy in order to teach," distinguished from competing anthologies because it "is after the Quick" rather than "the Dead." Identifies the "life-force" Trilling seeks at the heart of each selection as an "idea-theme" the commentaries attempt to isolate. Criticizes Trilling's inclusion of Brecht's "very bad and very deceitful play" *Galileo*, and wonders whether his modernist omission of "all the great and noble bores of literature" will "inspire certain subversive students into a clandestine reading of Spenser, Chaucer, Turgenev, Schiller, and Zola."

Literary Criticism: An Introductory Reader [B41]

**** Krupnick, Mark. "Lionel Trilling: Criticism and Illusion." *Modern Occasions* 1 (Winter 1971): 282-87. See G493.

H786. Rosenthal, M. L. "Criticism: What Do We Want?" *Nation* 211 (19 October 1970): 375-76.

Uses the equivocal tone of B41's preliminary disclaimer, which explains that the book was not originally intended for a general audience, to explore the ambiguity in contemporary criticism and education about anthologists' (and teachers') relation to their audiences. Concludes that Trilling's selection and introduction will appeal mainly to an audience whose commitment to criticism is already firm--but neither a general audience nor an audience of contemporary students increasingly likely "to have acquired more set attitudes toward art" that need to be stripped away by more pointed and immediately engaging selections.

H787. Lehmann-Haupt, Christopher. "Must Reading, But Will They?" *New York Times*, 27 August 1970, p. 33.

Expresses gratitude that such a "lucid and unpedantic" college textbook should be made available to a wider audience. Though acknowledging that "the case for the ultimate autonomy of art stands up pretty well" in Trilling's selections, wonders whether they ought to take closer account of the current political ferment on campuses and within academic disciplines.

H788. Benedikt, Michael. *Poetry* 113 (December 1968): 214-15.

Calls Trilling's selection of poems "excellent" and his introductions "remarkable," but disputes his judgment in restricting the selection to poems in English, especially considering the vitality and influence of modern European poetry.

Sincerity and Authenticity [A9]

H789. Spiller, Robert E. *American Literature* 45 (November 1973): 482-83.

Finds in Trilling's discussion "chronological progress rather than historical evolution." Suggests that another book could be written on the proposition, noted briefly by Trilling, that the ideal of authenticity could illuminate "the American 'self'" and American literature.

H790. Vernon, John. "On Lionel Trilling." [Review of A9 and A10.] *Boundary* 2 2 (Spring 1974): 625-32.

Criticizes Trilling's refusal to acknowledge that "society today as it exists is insane"; he "talks about society in the abstract, but he doesn't really talk about this society," and so focuses, in his critique of authenticity, on the symptoms of cultural malaise rather than the disease itself. Concludes that although "the book is certainly the most intelligent and complex one that Trilling has written," it is too abstracted from the actualities of modern culture, and calls for a history based on "the body and its gestures" rather than a cultural critique that diminishes the power of mind, as A10 does, by insisting on its autonomy.

H791. Anon. *Choice* 10 (May 1973): 441.

Remarks the novelty of Trilling's addressing a subject of "almost impossible largeness" in "an intriguing and stimulating volume" which, though "not systematic," reveals "lightning-flashes of insight."

**** Howe, Irving. "Reading Lionel Trilling." *Commentary* 56 (August 1973): 68-71. See G486.

H792. Erdoss, Trisha. [Review of A9 and George Steiner, *After Babel* (New York: Oxford University Press, 1975).] *Cresset* 39 (January 1976): 23-25.

Notes that both Trilling and Steiner call for a balance between a "totally translatable" sincerity and a solipsistically "incomprehensible" authenticity, concluding that both critics condemn the loss of either ideal as "a denial . . . of humanity, of divinity, of the possibilities of life."

H793. Wain, John. "The single mind." *Critical Quarterly* 15 (Summer 1973): 173-79.

Calls A9 "an amplified discussion of the problems raised" in W. W. Robson's essay "Purely Literary Values." Summarizing in detail a passage from Chapter 5, notes the uncommon denseness and "exhilarating rough ride" produced by Trilling's "double focus" on sincerity and authenticity as abstract ideals and historical values and his habit of arguing not with stationary opponents but with himself in a discussion whose flow often seems to reverse direction. Concludes that although Trilling has "firm convictions," A9 "offers a series of illuminations" on a "crucially important set of ideas" rather than "a central thesis."

H794. Graff, Gerald. "On Culture and Society." *Dissent* 20 (Spring 1973): 230-34.

Links Trilling, despite his insistence that his views are "archaic" or "anachronistic," to a line of American critics including the early Van Wyck Brooks, Richard Chase, John W. Aldridge, and Alfred Kazin, prescribing the self-alienating dialectic fostered by a resistant, oppositional social culture as the basis for the "sharply individuated character type." Regrets Trilling's failure to explain the reasons the contemporary avant-garde has lost its truly oppositional character, and suggests that the adversary culture's "resistance to co-optation" has been lowered by its susceptibility to an increasingly superficial mass society cut off from its formative "religious, moral, and intellectual convictions."

H795. Holloway, John. "'Sincerely, Lionel Trilling.'" *Encounter* 41 (September 1973): 64-68.

Links Hegel and Gerard Manley Hopkins to suggest the importance of "selving" both in A9, which charts the way the self "comes to be a self as it departs from [the] primal simplicity" underlying the unity of thought and action and "comes to have reservations about what [it] is doing," and in Trilling's own career, marked by an exemplary ambivalence toward the claims of self and civilization. Quarrels with Trilling's definitions of "sincerity" and "authenticity" but acknowledges that these disagreements are minor given his emphasis on the question of "how and where literature bears on the tension between society and the individual." Notes that Trilling's attempt "to enter into everything but never lose his balance one iota" projects the "hundred modes of authenticity" through which Trilling "selves" as a sympathetic, responsible complement to Rameau's Nephew.

H796. Rogers, Timothy. [Review of A9; Bernard Bergonzi, *The Turn of a Century: Essays on Victorian and Modern English Literature* (London: Macmillan, 1973); Malcolm Bradbury, *Possibilities: Essays on the State of the Novel* (London: Oxford University Press, 1973); Roger Sale, *Modern Heroism: Essays on D. H. Lawrence, William Empson, and J. R. R. Tolkien* (Berkeley: University of California Press, 1973); and David L. Kubal, *Outside the Whale: George Orwell's Art and Politics* (South Bend: Indiana University Press, 1972).] *English* 23 (Spring 1974): 39-40.

Praises Trilling as less abstract than Bradbury and more gratifyingly reflective than younger critics like Kubal.

H797. Raleigh, John Henry. *English Language Notes* 11 (June 1974): 320-25.

Suggests that Trilling's "sinuous and elegant" discussion overemphasizes the temporary outbreak of American irrationalism and anti-intellectualism during the 1960's and defines *authenticity* in four different ways: as a historically evolving concept, as the "false or bogus" concept of R. D. Laing, as the call of high literature to "fullness and strength of being," and the secular, though religiously-rooted, Freudian injunction that "guilt is not mocked."

H798. Tomlinson, Peter. "Sincerity." *Essays in Criticism* 24 (October 1974): 417-22.

Argues that sincerity, "the less pretentious . . . [but] the more valuable" of Trilling's leading terms, equivocally mixes "truth and pretence" even in Shakespeare and Sidney. Denying that "the mind can and should be self-subsistent," dissents from Trilling's uncritical acceptance of "the notion of spiritual autonomy," claiming that it makes his account of authenticity diffuse and leads to "a tacit self-commitment which one is invited to endorse."

**** Sale, Roger. "Lionel Trilling." *Hudson Review* 26 (Spring 1973): 241-47. See G525.

H799. Bond, E. J. *Humanities Association Review* 25 (Spring 1974): 146-48.

Agrees that the search for authenticity through "the assertion of the dark, passional side" of experience has led to a self-alienating rejection of social imperatives rather than a reformation of individuated selves, but argues that since "the morality which provides the foundation for a decent and civilized society can be shown to grounded in reason," it requires none of the "metaphysical underpinning" whose loss has been proclaimed by Nietzsche, Sartre, and now Trilling.

H800. Flower, J. E. *Journal of European Studies* 3 (March 1973): 70.

Regrets the absence of further historical cross-references linking figures as remote in time as Rousseau and Marcuse, and of any discussion of the plastic arts. Observes that in his final chapter Trilling's measured tone "betray[s] an anguish and concern that recent developments need to be checked--and quickly."

H801. Chisholm, A. R. *Journal of the Australasian Universities Language and Literature Association*, no. 41 (May 1974), pp. 104-5.

Compares Trilling to Spengler in the depth and scope of his analysis. Wonders at the omission of Rimbaud, Valéry, and Rilke. Notes that when the quest for authenticity "pushes self-revelation to the point of exhibitionism," the act of revelation is neither sincere nor authentic.

H802. Hogan, Patricia M. [Review of A9 and A10] *Library Journal* 98 (1 January 1973): 72.

After dismissing the argument of A10 as "not particularly inspired," describes A9 as expanding the theme of "the diminished status of rationality" through an analysis of "the triumphant rise of authenticity as an ideal and as a power."

H803. Lomas, Herbert. "The Critic as Bourgeois." *London Magazine*, new series 12 (February-March 1973): 140-44.

Criticizes Trilling's historical account of individuality as arising during the seventeenth century and Trilling's defense of Freud against Sartre's critique: "Biological determinism or an immutable unconscious superego" are "reassuringly conservative: they put guilt out of the area of human responsibility and turn it into an irrational nonsense--a 'tragic' affliction." Concludes that A9 "fails in daring," preferring "the old stable ego" to "the revolutionary flux" of R. D. Laing; but acknowledges that Lomas's own critique is "one-sided," and that "this is . . . an enjoyable book with which to exercise oneself, and see where we've come from."

H804. Davie, Donald. "Mind at the end of its tether?" *Manchester Guardian*, 19 October 1972, p. 10.

Contends that Trilling's assumption that sincerity has been superseded by the "unnecessary frenchified refinement" of authenticity is parochial (sincerity enduring as an admired virtue in England) and self-alienating, leading to a "panicky and painful" critique of "the assumptions on which [he] has proceeded through an admirably responsible lifetime." Suggests that human progress in controlling and directing histrionics or "play-acting" may offer Trilling a "glimmer of consolation" in the impasse produced by revisionary critiques of Freud's ennobling account of selfhood.

H805. Webb, W. L. "Literature and the arts." *Manchester Guardian Weekly*, 30 December 1972, p. 22.

Citing H804, names A9, "an unavoidable book by a 'touchstone' critic of the liberal enlightenment," among "the most memorable [publishing] events of the year."

H806. Hoagwood, Terence. *Masterplots 1973 Annual: Magill's Literary Annual*, edited by Frank N. Magill (Englewood Cliffs: Salem Press, 1974), pp. 325-28.

Calls A9 "a study of morality rather than literary criticism" before proceeding to a detailed, noncommittal summary. Praises Trilling's success in "bringing unheard-of relations [e.g., among Rousseau, Wordsworth, and Joyce] to lucid understanding."

H807. Gindin, James. "The Syncretic Self." [Review of A9; David Goldknopf, *The Life of the Novel* (Chicago: University of Chicago Press, 1972); and Edward Engelberg, *The Unknown Distance: From Consciousness to Conscience, Goethe to Camus* (Cambridge: Harvard University Press, 1972).] *Michigan Quarterly Review* 13 (Summer 1974): 302-6.

Welcomes the return of generalizing or syncretic criticism in all three books, observing that "very few contemporary critics can stand any evaluative comparison with Trilling," whose "Coleridgean" imagination "glides from idea to idea so easily that one frequently needs to stop to let his thoughts catch up."

H808. Peacock, R. *Modern Language Review* 70 (January 1975): 131-34.

Notes that Trilling's "breadth of explicit and implicit reference to social culture and civilization," which asserts a not always convincing "relation between aesthetic and culture-policy areas," increases the richness of his analysis but also "intensifies [his] socio-literary thesis and the simplified interpretation it produces," so that the resulting argument is provocative but oversimplified by the kind of imprecision produced by inveterate "summaries of theory and counter-theory."

H809. Molesworth, Charles. "The Problem of Conscious Virtue." *Nation* 216 (29 January 1973): 153, 155-56.

Describes A9, a "small but magnificent book," as an attempt to understand the terms of contemporary ignorance about "who we are" and "what we might be" by asking, "how have we come to be so confused?" and invoking in response a distinction between "assent" and "credence" as "our chief malady." Criticizes Trilling's ambivalence toward the "heroically radical honesty" of modern culture, noting the "hint of sadness, something like defeat," pervading the analysis.

H810. Mano, D. K. *National Review* 24 (22 December 1972): 1417.

Praises the "wisdom" of "Trilling, a traditional and now superannuated liberal," in his defiance of the New Left's narcissism.

H811. Lerner, Laurence. "Past & present." *New Statesman* 84 (20 October 1972): 558-60.

Commends the breadth and freshness of Trilling's analysis but sharply criticizes his reading of Rousseau's "sentiment of being" as referring to the self rather than existence as such. Suggests that Trilling, having "the academic virtues," is less convinced, hence less convincing, by his attempts "to go beyond them to the deeper virtues of paradox."

H812. Foot, Philippa. "Sincerely Yours." *New York Review of Books* 20 (8 March 1973): 23-24.

Reviews the importance of Rousseau, Diderot, and Nietzsche in the transformation of the self, charging that Trilling "fails to confront the modern apostles of authenticity" by refusing to render judgments on Sartre and Nathalie Sarraute, who see "the reflexes of shame and disgust as so closely connected with a truthful attitude to life," and neglecting Nietzsche's more radical critique of a selfhood based on moral judgment.

H813. Broyard, Anatole. "'Each One of Us a Christ.'" *New York Times*, 25 October 1972, p. 45.

Groups Trilling with pathologists of society whose grandeur gains from the sorry state of the culture they describe. Describes sincerity and authenticity as increasingly vain and masochistic attempts to define and authorize a self, leading finally to the assertion: "I'm authentic: therefore I am." Welcomes Trilling's attempts to rescue his audience from "the hydra-headed distortions of the idea of authenticity."

**** Hartman, Geoffrey H. "Between the Claims of Self and Culture." *New York Times Book Review*, 4 February 1973, pp. 1, 28-31. See G480.

H814. Britton, Karl. *Notes and Queries* 220 (May 1975): 211-13.

Suggests that Trilling, like Hegel (whose transitions also "spring from contradictions"), focuses on "the Varieties of Reflective Consciousness." Notes without surprise Trilling's lack of interest, despite his range of reference, in "philosophy as professed by English and American university departments."

H815. Kermode, Frank. "True voice of feeling." *Observer Review*, 22 October 1972, pp. 55-60.

Reviews in approving detail Trilling's historical argument, noting that "his deeply considered modernism belongs to a period he admits to be dead," but asserting that in its analysis of "autonomy of judgment" as "a superannuated ideal," A9 "has *weight*" in the sense of trying with Freud "to remedy the weightlessness brought to the world by the death of God."

H816. Letwin, Shirley Robin. "The birth and death of the individual." *Spectator* 229 (21 October 1972): 624-26.

Disputes Trilling's historical analysis of sincerity as a Renaissance phenomenon, indicating Plato, Cicero, and Augustine as earlier examples. Criticizes more generally Trilling's insistence on opposing the genuinely authentic individual, determined by a Freudian biological necessity, to society, urging instead an understanding of people as "shaping their lives out of wants that they could neither have conceived of nor satisfied apart from social life," and human life as "an activity of composing a harmonious arrangement out of disparate materials" rather than "a process of repression or a struggle for authenticity."

H817. Anon. "Real selves and social selves." *TLS*, 27 October 1972, pp. 1269-70.

Calls Trilling's "delicately scrupulous" prose "a tribute . . . to the 'honest' consciousness" while observing that his qualities of mind "exist in a state of acute tension because they can find no anchorage in the present cultural scene." Suggests on the other hand, however, that A9 escapes from the "oversensitivity" of some of Trilling's earlier work through "a manner of presentation that quite transcends local deformations." In repudiating his earlier reliance on the university as a shelter for intellectual ideals, Trilling "has become a lonelier writer and a stronger one."

H818. Anon. *Virginia Quarterly Review* 49 (Spring 1973): pp. xc-xci.

Calls the perspective of Trilling's "sketch" "interesting and revealing."

**** Eckhardt, Caroline D. "Collected Works." [Review of A9 and A15.] *World Literature Today* 44 (Summer 1981): 477-78. See H841.

H819. Wimsatt, W. K. "We, Teiresias." *Yale Review* 62 (Spring 1973): 431-38.

Describes A9 as presenting "a cultural landscape of 400 years, lavishly populated with speaking figures": Rousseau, whose status as a devotée of both sincerity and authenticity makes his place in the argument problematic; Nietzsche, whose "centrality" here is "out of proportion to the fact that he is never dramatically developed"; Freud, whose insistence that the superego's demands will never be satisfied makes him "a 'lion' standing against the hopes of the liberal social imagination" urged by A10; and "We," Trilling's own "strenuously developed . . . subtle, pervasive, ingratiating, and coercive" speaking persona, "a menacing superego of our twilight society."

Mind in the Modern World [A10]

**** Vernon, John. "On Lionel Trilling." [Review of A9 and A10.] *Boundary 2* 2 (Spring 1974): 625-32. See H790.

**** Hogan, Patricia M. [Review of A9 and A10.] *Library Journal* 98 (1 January 1973): 72. See H802.

H820. Cameron, J. M. "Trilling, Roszak, & Goodman." [Review of A10; Theodore Roszak, *Where the Wasteland Ends: Politics and Transcendence in Postindustrial Society* (Garden City: Doubleday, 1972); and Paul Goodman, *Little Prayers and Finite Experience* (New York: Harper & Row, 1972).] *New York Review of Books* 19 (30 November 1972): 18-21.

Agrees with Trilling that "the intense energy with which the processes of mind themselves are now examined both exhibits the power of mind and makes plain its impotence," and concludes that "nothing quite like this has ever been known in the world before."

**** Hartman, Geoffrey H. "Between the Claims of Self and Culture." [Review of A9 and A10.] *New York Times Book Review*, 4 February 1973, pp. 1, 28-31. See G480.

H821. Anon. *Virginia Quarterly Review* 49 (Autumn 1973): clxx.

Notes that Trilling "is less harsh on his contemporaries" than Arnold was "because he shares many of their doubts and fears" despite his defense of intellect and objective understanding against political attacks.

The Oxford Anthology of English Literature: Romantic Poetry and Prose [B42] and *Victorian Prose and Poetry* [B43]

H822. Low, D. A. *Journal of European Studies* 4 (September 1974): 300.

Commends especially Trilling's selection and introduction of non-fictional prose, but regrets the exclusion of prose fiction, considering the Victorian period's achievement in the short story and the novel.

The Works of Lionel Trilling [A11]

**** Chace, William. "Lionel Trilling: The Contrariness of Culture." [Review of the first four volumes of A11.] *American Scholar* 48 (Winter 1978-79): 49-59. See G452.

H823. Langbaum, Robert. "Lionel Trilling in Retrospect." [Review of A11 and F427.] *American Scholar* 52 (Winter 1982-83): 132-38.

Contends that in following Arnold's critique of liberalism, "Trilling was helping prepare the twentieth-century mind that would accept the welfare state rather than communism as the alternative to untrammeled capitalism." Sees Trilling's defense of the novel of manners as based on his opposition to communism and other deterministic forms of totalitarianism, reports that Trilling had announced shortly before his death his opposition to structuralism "as another system antithetical to will and individual freedom," and suggests that in watching the growing influence of anti-social ideals of personal freedom, "Trilling must have felt that his work of criticizing self-destructive liberal idealism had to be done all over again." Notes that Trilling has little interest in literary "form, imagery, or texture"--for him, "literature differs from other modes of discourse only in the superior complexity of its ideas"--and calls him a man of letters rather than a literary critic.

Praises F427's "clear account of Trilling's thought," though noting its failure to assess Trilling's stylistic authority or his status among other critics. Answers charges of Trilling's later conservatism by emphasizing Shoben's recollection that Trilling refused in 1948 to testify against Whittaker Chambers before the HUAC and supported "the ultraliberal Stevenson against Eisenhower" in 1952.

**** McSweeney, Kerry. "Lionel Trilling as a Literary Critic." *Canadian Review of American Studies* 14 (1983): 195-206. See G507.

H824. Cain, William E. "Making Judgments: Criticism Past, Present, and Future." [Review of A13; A14; Richard Ohmann, *English in America: A Radical View of the Profession* (New York: Oxford University Press, 1976); Frank Kermode, *The Genesis of Secrecy: On the Interpretation of Narrative* (Cambridge: Harvard University Press, 1979); Harold Bloom et al., *Deconstruction and Criticism* (New York: Seabury Press, 1979); Eugene Goodheart, *The Failure of Criticism* (Cambridge: Harvard University Press, 1978); and F. R. Leavis, *The Living Principle: 'English' as a Discipline of Thought* (New York: Oxford University Press, 1975).] *College English* 42 (September 1980): 25-34.

Calls A13 and A14 "uneven and disappointing" and questions Trilling's aptness as the representative humanist critic despite "his well-lubricated prose" because "he responds poorly to the language of texts" and inveterately "exploits the texts he uses as examples, misreading and under-reading them in order to fit them into [his] grand scheme." Suggests that Leavis is "the superior critic" and avatar of the humanist sensibility.

H825. Shrimpton, Nicholas. "The end of the journey." *New Statesman* 103 (11 June 1982): 19-20.

Contrasts Diana Trilling's account of her husband's early years in G540 with his own account in C194, which notes as formative "his ambition to write novels" and "Columbia in the 1920s" as a spiritual home for Trilling despite its racial and ethnic prejudices. Emphasizes the interplay of Marx and Freud throughout Trilling's critique of liberalism, praising C84 and A3 as dramatizing ambivalence more memorably than any of his essays, and singling out C116 as "one of the finest acts of criticism ever performed in our language" because of its profound grasp of the nature of moral discrimination. Pronounces Trilling's work "an *oeuvre* which merits, as few critical gatherings do, reading as an entity."

**** Atlas, James. *New York Times*, 9 July 1979, p. C15. [Review of A12.] See H830.

H826. Broyard, Anatole. "Four by Lionel Trilling." [Review of the first four volumes of A11.] *New York Times*, 10 June 1978, p. 17.

Praises Trilling as "a remarkable phenomenon" whose insights make American culture seem "infinitely more dimensional than I had supposed," so that even his frequent "disapproval bathes us in reflected glory."

H827. Broyard, Anatole. "Lionel Trilling Encores." [Review of A13 and A14.] *New York Times*, 26 October 1979, p. C28.

Calls Trilling, like Arnold, "a labor mediator of the imagination, which in our time is given to walkouts and wildcat strikes." Praises both the broad scope of the essays in A14 and the relaxed intimacy of the commentaries in A13.

**** Broyard, Anatole. [Review of the Uniform Edition of A2.] *New York Times*, 2 April 1980, p. C26. See H580.

**** Sennett, Richard. "On Lionel Trilling." *New Yorker* 55 (5 November 1979): 204, 207-10, 215-17. See G532.

Of This Time, of That Place, and Other Stories [A12]

H828. Anon. *Antioch Review* 37 (Fall 1979): 506.

Asserts that "some authors can't manage to say eight dollars worth in a hundred pages. Trilling can." Wonders "what the publishers mean by calling this a uniform edition of Trilling's works."

H829. Lainoff, Seymour. "Trilling's Jewish Persona." *Midstream* 27 (December 1981): 54-56.

Emphasizes the importance of C53 and C58 in dramatizing the question, "What is the Jew's relation to the outside world?" Notes Tertan's Jewish-influenced traits in C77 and C84's close thematic relation to A3.

H830. Atlas, James. *New York Times*, 9 July 1979, p. C15.

Emphasizes the autobiographical value of the stories, despite their "didactic" and "pedagogical" weaknesses, as dramatizing "conflicts that manifested themselves only subliminally in [Trilling's] criticism"--for example, the question posed in C58 "whether a Jew could lay claim to the wider realm of Western literature and culture."

H831. Garrett, George. "Technics and Pyrotechnics." [Review of A12 and seventeen other volumes of short fiction.] *Sewanee Review* 88 (Summer 1980): 412-23.

Calls Trilling "a good and thoughtful critic and a custodian of ideas" who "had the courage to produce creative work" and who "told his stories very well for a critic."

H832. Halio, Jay L. *Studies in Short Fiction* 17 (Summer 1980): 354-55.

Aligns Trilling's fiction with that of Austen and James rather than the Jewish milieu of Alfred Kazin, and regrets Trilling's decision to publish no more fiction after A3.

H833. Furbank, P. N. "The Gravities of Grown-Upness." *TLS*, 21 August 1981, p. 951.

Describes "criticism as the whole theme of [Trilling's] stories," and "growing up" as the leading concern of all his fiction and indeed "Trilling's central preoccupation" in his critical essays, which are typically moved by the consideration of apparently conflicting facts "dialectically toward some new vantage-point." Finds C77 and C84 "remarkably fine and likely to live," but criticizes the climactic debates of A3 as "self-indulgent and not really worthy of Trilling," overblown for their place in a realistic novel.

H834. Belkind, Allen. *World Literature Today* 55 (Winter 1981): 103-4.

Notes Trilling's criticism of insensitivity toward "the mentally ill and toward racial, religious and economic minorities"--attitudes which have now partly changed. Describes the other Margaret (in C84) as "gradually breaking all the family's china."

Prefaces to The Experience of Literature [A13]

**** Cain, William E. "Making Judgments: Criticism Past, Present, and Future." [Review of A13; A14; Richard Ohmann, *English in America: A Radical View of the Profession* (New York: Oxford University Press, 1976); Frank Kermode, *The Genesis of Secrecy: On the Interpretation of Narrative* (Cambridge: Harvard University Press, 1979); Harold Bloom et al., *Deconstruction and Criticism* (New York: Seabury Press, 1979); Eugene Goodheart, *The Failure of Criticism* (Cambridge: Harvard University Press, 1978); and F. R. Leavis, *The Living Principle: 'English' as a Discipline of Thought* (New York: Oxford University Press, 1975).] *College English* 42 (September 1980): 25-34. See H824.

**** Broyard, Anatole. "Lionel Trilling Encores." [Review of A13 and A14.] *New York Times*, 26 October 1979, p. C28. See H827.

**** Donoghue, Denis. "Of Self and Society." [Review of A13 and A14.] *New York Times Book Review*, 20 January 1980, pp. 9, 26-27. See H837.

The Last Decade [A14]

**** Cain, William E. "Making Judgments: Criticism Past, Present, and Future." [Review of A13; A14; Richard Ohmann, *English in America: A Radical View of the Profession* (New York: Oxford University Press, 1976); Frank Kermode, *The Genesis of Secrecy: On the Interpretation of Narrative* (Cambridge: Harvard University Press, 1979); Harold Bloom et al., *Deconstruction and Criticism* (New York: Seabury Press, 1979); Eugene

Goodheart, *The Failure of Criticism* (Cambridge: Harvard University Press, 1978); and F. R. Leavis, *The Living Principle: 'English' as a Discipline of Thought* (New York: Oxford University Press, 1975).] *College English* 42 (September 1980): 25-34. See H824.

H835. Hovey, Richard B. "The Humanist as Ghost?" *Modern Age* 25 (Summer 1981): 318-21.

Finds "no falling-off" in Trilling's late essays, which are centrally concerned with "the fatty degeneration of the intellect" in the latter-day anti-intellectual heirs of William Morris. Agrees that the structuralist dream of "bringing order into human affairs by ending the conflict of wills would foster not liberalism, but totalitarianism."

**** Broyard, Anatole. "Lionel Trilling Encores." [Review of A13 and A14.] *New York Times*, 26 October 1979, p. C28. See H827.

H836. Anon. *New York Times Book Review*, 10 January 1982, p. 35.

Briefly describes the contents of A14 on the occasion of its publication in paperback.

H837. Donoghue, Denis. "Of Self and Society." [Review of A13 and A14.] *New York Times Book Review*, 20 January 1980, pp. 9, 26-27.

Describes Trilling's criticism as "meditative rather than analytic, a pondering of themes" indicated by the relations among the terms "society," "self" ("sometimes elucidated in terms of will," sometimes, more honorifically, in terms of "mind" or imagination), and "culture" (which refers to "the work that a serious mind does to persuade society to act on its promises and live up to its principles." Notes the "rueful and occasionally dispirited" detachment of Trilling's later work and the relative buoyancy of C191. Concurs in Trilling's therapeutic "care for the nature and quality of society," but calls his work most exhilarating when it challenges his social principles in response to a particular writer's gifts, as in C122 or C181.

H838. Hauptman, Robert. *World Literature Today* 54 (Summer 1980): 436-37.

Criticizes Trilling's obliqueness as leading to rambling and "sophomoric" summary and making A14 "generally disappointing." Makes exceptions for C188, C190, and especially C185, which shows "the life of the mind . . . in trouble," but "*not* at the end of its tether."

Speaking of Literature and Society [A15]

H839. Pritchard, William H. "Criticism as Literature." [Review of A15; Clive James, *First Reactions: Critical Essays, 1968-1979* (New York: Knopf, 1980); Edmund Wilson, *The Thirties*, edited by Leon Edel (Farrar, Straus & Giroux, 1980); and Mary McCarthy, *Ideas and the Novel* (New York: Harcourt Brace Jovanovich, 1980).] *Hudson Review* 34 (Spring 1981): 117-24.

Calls the Uniform Edition "wholly benign" despite its air of "canonization" and the unevenness of the posthumous volumes A14 and A15, and identifies A4, A5, and A8--"the collections of essays on speculative topics and particular writers"--as Trilling's "great contributions as a writer." Commends Trilling's early sympathy to Cather, Lewis, Dos Passos, and O'Hara; his sane determination to consider literature a trade rather than an institution; and his surprising sensitivity to aesthetic form.

H840. Alter, Robert. "From Books to Cultural Questions." *New York Times Book Review*, 12 October 1980, pp. 3, 38.

Dissents from the prevailing view of Trilling's decline in A8, criticizing instead A9 because its speculative, discontinuous generalizations are better suited to individual essays than extended argument. Describing the reviews collected in A15 as "discriminating, judicious, never mean-spirited or carping but always demanding," contrasts Trilling's centrifugal response to the centripetal methods of the New Critics. Notes Trilling's unresponsiveness in C138, despite his insight into *Lolita*, to Nabokov's sense of play, and concludes that Trilling's emphasis on literary connections and contexts made him withdraw from "the absolute individuality of the original work."

H841. Eckhardt, Caroline D. "Collected Works." [Review of A9 and A15.] *World Literature Today* 55 (Summer 1981): 477-78.

Suggests that A15 reveals "the essential Trilling": his emphasis on literature's moral importance despite his lack of allegiance to any simple morality; his "tendency to read literature at once personally and socially"; and his lucid, often aphoristic style. Describes Trilling's mind as balanced, though not neutral, and "mature" in its insistence on complexity despite the currently fashionable "attack upon all meaning" foreshadowed by the closing pages of A9.

Section I

Reviews of Books About Trilling

Quentin Anderson et al., eds., *Art, Politics, and Will* [F420]

**** Samet, Tom H. "Trilling and Cultural Criticism." [Review of F420 and F421.] *Sewanee Review* 86 (Spring 1978): 306-9. See I842.

Robert Boyers, *Lionel Trilling: Negative Capability and the Wisdom of Avoidance* [F421]

I842. Samet, Tom H. "Trilling and Cultural Criticism." [Review of F420 and F421.] *Sewanee Review* 86 (Spring 1978): 306-9.

Argues against Boyers that Trilling does not celebrate the "conditioned" nature of life as such but rather the "dialectic of spirit and matter, self and culture, freedom and necessity," as in A6, C68, and C86. Observes that the reconsideration of this dialectic in a large number of essays in F420 gives it an unusual degree of unity.

Incorporated into J878 as Appendix II.

I843. Bayley, John. "The way towards sanity." *TLS*, 30 December 1977, p. 1518.

Agrees with Boyers that Trilling's "critical temper was less drawn to genius--Dostoevsky, Dickens, Lawrence, Kafka--than to writers [like Howells and Orwell] in whom the force of moral realism is more cogent than creative power," and that his own fiction reflects this disposition as well. Observes that Trilling "was sure of himself, however tentative he may seem. . . . The mode of diffidence was for him a necessary aspect of the civilization he sought to defend."

I844. Cain, William E. "Trilling in Our Time." *Virginia Quarterly Review* 54 (Summer 1978): 565-70.

Criticizes Boyers's emulation of Trilling's style and tone, arguing that he restricts his discussion to too narrow a range of texts and too seldom pursues insights into Trilling or the criticisms of him he registers incidentally. Contends that "Trilling's themes are few and remain constant" throughout his work, with "minimal advance in sophistication and insight," and that a serious defense of his relevance for contemporary criticism would have to engage more closely the post-structualist concept of a decentered self, as against Trilling's assumption of a centered self, and consider more critically the political stances of both Trilling, whose "worried withdrawal from the world" too often becomes "mere distance and disengagement," and contemporary theorists, whose politics are "intense but unserious and self-promoting."

Revised and reprinted in *The Crisis in Criticism: Theory, Literature, and Reform in English Studies* (Baltimore: Johns Hopkins University Press, 1984), pp. 125-29.

William M. Chace, *Lionel Trilling: Criticism and Politics* [F422]

1845. Sutton, Walter. *American Literature* 53 (March 1981): 156-59.

Calling Chace "skillful in analysis but perhaps too generous in judgment," presents Trilling as "primarily a psychologically rather than socially oriented critic" whose political ideal is "cultivated apathy." Describes A9's history as based on a simple New Critical conceptual dualism comparable to that of T. S. Eliot's positing of a "dissociation of sensibility."

1846. Schwartz, Sanford. *Ethics* 93 (October 1982): 189-90.

Noting that "the days when one could conceive of a solidly progressive if excessively rationalistic educated class, or an inordinantly large adversary culture threatening the stability of bourgeois democracy, have long passed," commends Trilling's cultural criticism as a corrective to intrinsic analysis, especially for a contemporary audience which "suffers less from the defects of its commitments than from the want of any definable commitments at all."

1847. Homberger, Eric. *Journal of American Studies* 15 (December 1981): 438-39.

Criticizes Chace's detachment of Trilling's work from its Jewish and radical backgrounds, which "obscures the extent to which Trilling was always more polemical and partisan, even in the cause of a lofty and disengaged intellectuality." Contends that in "disentangling" Trilling from his milieu, Chace presents a figures whose "youthful indiscretions and unfortunate bits of background" are "neatly swept under the carpet."

I848. Ashton, Jean. *Markham Review* 9 (Summer 1980): 79-80.

Agrees with Chace in identifying the accord Trilling achieved between "the deepest concerns of art and history," assimilated as dogma by many college students of the fifties seeking an "alternative to the stringent methods of the New Criticism," as "merely a passing stage" in the evolution of Trilling's dialectic between public consciousness and private unconsciousness. Criticizes Chace's failure, encouraged by Trilling's generous use of large ideas, to answer more precisely the questions, "What did Trilling write *about* and what was he?"

I849. Goodheart, Eugene. "Lionel Trilling." *Partisan Review* 48, 3 (1981): 469-78.

Defining "all of the changes in Trilling's intellectual career" as "the tracings of 'an idea in modulation,'" takes John Laskell's liberalism in A3--"not a piety, but an anxiety"--as exemplifying "a necessarily inadequate response to the twin temptations of Stalinism and ideological anticommunism" further complicated by "the spectre of Nazism." Notes that Trilling's presentation of "the view of man as conditioned" as "noble" is threatened "when the polarities exclude alternatives" because "the test of heroism, of courage is in the capacity one has to persist against those conditions and the grace which one finally submits to them." Though asserting that "Trilling never conflated Stalinism with radicalism," misses in his work "a sharper discrimination between a possible radicalism and an absolute radicalism" which tends to blunt Trilling's later hostility to modern culture as "an expression of the aggressive will." Observes however that even A9, allowing "the adversarial view its full claim upon us," shows that, "unlike Stalinism, modernism remained an object of deep ambivalence for Trilling."

Revised and reprinted in *Pieces of Resistance* (Cambridge: Cambridge University Press, 1987), pp. 9-18.

1850. Cox, R. G. "Criticizing the Critics: Leavis and Trilling." [Review of F422; L921; and R. P. Bilan, *The Literary Criticism of F. R. Leavis* (Cambridge: Cambridge University Press, 1979).] *Sewanee Review* 89 (Winter 1981): 118-25.

Notes Chace's emphasis on Trilling's refusal to choose sides in cultural debates, observing that Trilling fought both Stalinism in the forties and "bourgeois optimism and conformism . . . and the simpler conservative reactions" in the fifties: "Trilling characteristically wrestled with the contradictions in the hope of arriving at a new synthesis." Remarks that Trilling's "rejection of all doctrinaire formulas and all systematizing," which made him suspicious of New Criticism, made him overlook "the possibilities of a criticism starting from the New Critical disciplined attention to the words on the page but leading outward to larger issues--the sort of thing that Leavis advocated and practised."

1851. McWilliams, John P., Jr. *Studies in American Fiction* 9 (Autumn 1981): 282-84.

Remarks the contradiction implicit in Chace's isolation of Trilling's work from its social context, which produces "a New Critical reading of the political and literary thought of a cultural humanist who intensely disliked the New Criticism." Commends Chace's analysis, but hopes for further work considering Trilling's involvement in New York intellectual circles, contemporary politics, and the Columbia faculty.

1852. Delany, Paul. "Varieties of Liberal Experience." [Review of F422 and Louis Hyde, *Rat and the Devil: Journal Letters of F. O. Matthiessen and Russell Cheney* (Hamden, CT: Archon, 1978).] *TLS*, 5 December 1980, p. 1391.

Argues that Trilling's suspicion of left-wing politics as dehumanizing its adherents by promoting totalitarianism and coarsening social relations made him "set politics in opposition to society or, at least, to the social." Notes that Trilling's oscillation between considering Stalinism as inhumanly dogmatic and as narcissistic led him to propose different remedies for it and to consider conflicts between impulse and obligation not as operating between self and world but rather within "the very structure of consciousness" as "problems to be lived with rather than solved"--as Trilling, unlike Matthiessen, succeeded in carrying on "a continuous, civil and productive dialogue with himself." Suggests that the Columbia humanities program, which Chace does not discuss, "explains much about Trilling's concept of culture."

Mark Krupnick, *Lionel Trilling and the Fate of Cultural Criticism* [F424]

I853. Tuttleton, James W. *American Literature* 58 (December 1986): 669-70.

Agreeing with Krupnick that "Trilling shaped his cultural opinions to fit the moment, to serve as a corrective to what he perceived as the prevailing view," concludes that "his positions over time became manifestly self-contradictory" and that this "chronic indecision about ultimate values" led to the decline in his reputation.

I854. Murphy, Geraldine. "Back to Basics." *Boundary 2* 15, 1-2 (1987): 381-94.

Commends Krupnick as a close reader but argues that his attempt to recuperate Trilling as an exemplary cultural critic contextualizes Trilling too easily on Trilling's own terms, glossing over his aversion to political action and accepting uncritically his dialectic of self and culture, overlooking the poststructuralist insight that "'self' is a construction to be investigated." Suggests that Krupnick's turn from

Displacement, his earlier "collection of essays on Derridean topics," to a sympathetic account of Trilling's varied appeals to centrism indicates "a shift in loyalties . . . from oppressed and invisible minorities . . . back to what Trilling referred to as 'our educated classes.'"

I855. O'Hara, Daniel T. "Between Marx and Freud: The Authority of the Commonplace in Cultural Criticism Today." [Review of F424 and Bruce Robbins, *The Servant's Hand: English Fiction from Below* (New York: Columbia University Press, 1986).] *Contemporary Literature* 28 (Fall 1987): 409-15.

Suggests that Trilling's later work reflects the search for a standard of critical judgment that would allow him to continue to practice "oppositional criticism magnanimously" and the use of "the commonplace" as "a sensible brake upon the always accelerating apocalyptic or utopian hopes of modern American society." Places Freud, "the psychoanalytic 'servant' of an ennobled reason to come," at the center of the "counter-historical ideal community" Krupnick discovers as the positive principle underlying Trilling's continuing cultural critique, and concludes that any new cultural criticism will depend on having "worked through" the "critical tradition of infectious apocalypse" Trilling scrutinized.

I856. Claridge, Henry. [Review of F424 and Terry Comito, *In Defense of Winters: The Poetry and Prose of Yvor Winters* (Madison: University of Wisconsin Press, 1986).] *Journal of American Studies* 22 (August 1988): 300-302.

Links Trilling, Winters, and Edmund Wilson as moral polemicists for the imagination whose methods are empirical rather than theoretical. Criticizes Krupnick's emphasis on figures and schools who influenced Trilling, contending that such an analysis does nothing to support Krupnick's claims for Trilling's importance. Concludes that "Winters is the greater critic . . . because he proceeded with far less ambition" and "knew the proper limits of critical inquiry."

1857. Baym, Nina. [Review of F424 and Daniel R. Schwarz, *The Humanistic Heritage: Critical Theories of the English Novel from James to Hillis Miller* (Philadelphia: University of Pennsylvania Press, 1986).] *Journal of English and Germanic Philology* 86 (April 1987): 277-81.

Distinguishes between the contemporary notion of cultural studies, which "posits individual works of art as instances of cultural production which do not transcend their context and which may fruitfully be described in terms of the complicated network of overlapping cultural forces that they disclose," and Trilling's brand of cultural criticism, which "looked in each work for some supposedly supracultural element that might serve as a platform from which one could view life steadily and whole." Finds "little to admire" in Trilling, who, like Leavis, "used novel criticism to scold his readers" from an unusually parochial perspective uninformed by deep knowledge of philosophy, poetry, drama, or the nonliterary arts, and inaccurate in its analyses of the texts it used as examples, concluding that Krupnick's book is "peculiarly important because of the way in which it undermines its own case" for a return to cultural criticism.

1858. Birnbaum, Milton. "The Ambivalences and Ambiguities of Lionel Trilling." *Modern Age* 30 (Summer-Fall 1986): 289-92.

Agreeing with Krupnick that Freud was "the only 'god' that Trilling clung to for most of his life," contends that Trilling's temperamental ambivalence is heightened by "a longing to be freed from the stresses of living an involved life," which makes art a means of "anaesthetizing" life's pressures. Concludes that his late work makes it apparent that "Trilling's quest for self and certitude was never completed."

1859. Steeves, Edna L. "A University Set on a Hill." [Review of F424; *The Selected Letters of Mark Van Doren*, edited by George Hendrick (Baton Rouge: Louisiana State University Press, 1987); and Jacques Barzun, *A Word or Two Before You Go . . .* (Middletown: Wesleyan University Press, 1986).] *Modern Language Studies* 18 (Fall 1988): 91-94.

Agrees with Krupnick that "Trilling is best judged in the context of the New York intellectual group to which he belonged." Noting that "Trilling's experiences at Columbia in the early thirties may not have been altogether happy," asks, "Whoever imagined the academy to be an ivory tower?" Approvingly cites Krupnick's comment that Trilling's continued ambivalence is a sign of the uncertain fate of cultural criticism in America.

1860. Shechner, Mark. "Trilling Man." *Nation* 242 (31 May 1986): 767-69.

Distinguishes Trilling from the other New York intellectuals as the most productive, scholarly, and challenging, the only teacher by vocation rather than expediency, and a public figure entirely self-created: "Long before deconstruction became a fashion in the academy, Trilling was practicing it on himself." Explains Trilling's present eclipse by describing his mind as "cautiously incandescent and stealthily adventurous" rather than fashionably "ferocious and polemical" or "arcane and theoretical."

1861. Boyers, Robert. "Too Smart to Be Correct." *New York Times Book Review*, 13 April 1986, p. 19.

Suggests that Trilling is a more radical thinker than Krupnick's "strikingly unified" portrait shows because Krupnick accepts the "popular view of politics as telling us more about reality than anything else can," whereas Trilling "knew that there were aspects of experience utterly beyond the reach of a narrowly pragmatic political discourse" espoused by the Princess Casamassima and other naively political activists, from Stalinism to the 60's, heedless of the consequences of their beliefs; for him "the sustaining dialectic was not a doctrine of inevitable progress but a means of nurturing a rich ambivalence."

1862. Rischin, Moses. "When the New York Savants go Marching In." [Review of F424, L906, L911, and L978.] *Reviews in American History* 17 (June 1989): 289-300.

Suggests that "a more penetrating grasp of the 'family'" of New York intellectuals "must be grounded in big biography" rather than the group biographies of Bloom or Wald, and praises Krupnick's focus on Trilling as exemplary, especially in its revelation of "the high price that acculturation ultimately exacted" on this group of "non-Jewish Jews," heirs both to "a mythic nineteenth-century new Russsia" that brought writers and critics to new prominence and to such "turn-of-the-century ghetto and Park Row forerunners" as Hutchins Hapgood and his circle of journalists at the *New York Commercial Advertiser*. Urges an attempt to place the New York intellectuals in the larger context of American cultural history.

1863. Edmundson, Mark. "On Lionel Trilling." *Salmagundi*, nos. 74-75 (Spring-Summer 1987), pp. 161-68.

Commends the "endless work of critical self-invention" Krupnick finds in Trilling, noting that "the victory of one's own principles is, to the dialectitian, simply a motive for assaulting them from a new perspective." (Hence Trilling "could be polemical without being doctrinally committed to any one position.") Distinguishes between deconstructionists like Derrida and Foucault, who advocate open revolt against "the reigning forms of authority" and who find Trilling's dialectical stance toward culture too timid and compromised by its own participation in that culture's language, and the traditionally American Emersonian strand of cultural critique, which seeks neither to refurbish or dissolve cultural vocabularies but to "mint new tropes, arrive at fresh ways of seeing and saying those that have failed to work," concluding that present-day Emersonians could learn much from Trilling despite their justified suspicion of his complicity with the style and categories of the dominant culture.

1864. Jay, Gregory S. *South Atlantic Review* 52 (January 1987): 103-7.

Contends that Krupnick's implicit leading question--why has Trilling, once so influential, become so completely forgotten?--is best answered by considering the indifference of Trilling as "representative man of American literary humanism" to questions of language: "Trilling has a theory of the self (as tragic moralist), a theory of modernity (culture's self-ambivalence), but no theory of literature or language, or of how the structures of language inform the shape of culture." Infers that, although Trilling never confronted the work of post-structuralists like Derrida or Lacan, his reaction to them would be to reject "the structuralist argument that language is the model for deciphering the subject's conditioning by history," and concludes that "it is only because Trilling never entertained the question of language that he was able for so long to defend the myth of the self."

1865. Symons, Julian. "Opposites Unresolved." *TLS*, 5 September 1986, pp. 959-60.

Compares Trilling's continuing attachment to the political and intellectual movements he criticized to Orwell's, but notes that whereas Orwell took pains to "spell out his differences from socialist orthodoxy," Trilling "did his best simultaneously to assert and conceal his differences from what he was attacking." Judges Trilling's ambivalence as "damaging to Trilling as a critic" despite the subtlety it allows him, concluding that "Polonius would have approved" the strategic omissions and qualifications in B18. Sees Trilling's emphasis on the shaped self as against an instrumental society in A6 and later as a maneuver against the Marxist theorists who emphasized society over the individual, but observes that Trilling's use of Freud led him to a new dialectic between the pleasure principle and the reality principle rather than to a resolution. Finds Trilling more "assured, humorous, and tolerant" in B23, B40, and his fiction than in his his formal essays, and judges C77, C84, and A3 Trilling's finest achievements, for "only when wearing the mask of the fiction writer was he able freely and confidently to approach the contradictions inherent in his own personality."

Daniel T. O'Hara, *Lionel Trilling: The Work of Liberation* [F425]

I866. Bloom, James D. "Fellow Travelers: A Canon for Critics." [Review of F425; Greig E. Henderson, *Kenneth Burke: Literature and Language as Symbolic Action* (Athens: University of Georgia Press, 1988); *The Legacy of Kenneth Burke*, edited by Herbert W. Simons and Trevor Melia (Madison: University of Wisconsin Press, 1989); and Samuel Southwell, *Kenneth Burke and Martin Heidegger: With a Note Against Deconstruction* (Gainesville: University of Florida Press, 1987).] *American Literary History* 2 (Winter 1990): 772-80.

Groups Trilling and Burke as older critics whose "commitment to historically and politically minded antiformalism" appeals to "the desire to preempt, to assimilate, and, at the same time, to subvert deconstructionism" by correcting its revisionary radicalism and careerism. Distinguishes both Trilling and Burke from "militant demystifiers" who deny the existence of "*God* or *nature* or *class* or *gender* or *history*" except as terms of discourse, concluding that their work thus mixes "agnosticism toward both insurgent and establishment absolutisms and a humble regard for conceivable absolutes."

For a response by O'Hara, see G514.

I867. Bové, Paul A. "The Love of Reading/The Work of Criticism: F. O. Matthiessen and Lionel Trilling." [Review of F425 and William E. Cain, *F. O. Matthiessen and the Politics of Criticism* (Madison: University of Wisconsin Press, 1988).] *Contemporary Literature* 31 (Fall 1990): 373-82.

Observes that O'Hara "uses Trilling against the current state of critical affairs" in two ways: he "ventriloquizes through Trilling" about postmodern critical studies, and he reenacts Trilling's stance by offering an "ethics of critical magnanimity" toward his academic opponents despite his own critique of their "postliberal, oppositional rhetoric, values, and performances," and so showing "narcissistic postmodernism" struggling "to renew the dread capacity of love."

I868. Armstrong, P. B. *Journal of Aesthetics and Art Criticism* 48 (Winter 1990): 103.

Criticizes O'Hara for undermining his tribute to Trilling's "magnanimity" through a reductionistic and dismissive account of his cultural criticism and an undue emphasis on Trilling's own subversive potential.

I869. Simpson, Lewis P. "Trilling in the Tradition." [Review of F425 and F428.] *Partisan Review* 57 (Summer 1990): 474-82.

Regrets that F428 follows Trilling's "own debatable principle of literary inquiry" in presenting Trilling's critical assumptions as sympathetically as possible, describing the resulting portrait as "a nostalgic survivor of a [humanistic] lost cause" who may "engage our sympathies but cannot truly engage our minds." Remarks the "ironic pathos" of O'Hara's "magnanimity in having chosen not to pillory Trilling as a psychopath" in his misreading of Freud as replacing his failed father as the figure validating his diagnosis of culture, concluding that O'Hara misreads Trilling, who "never appeared to his audience save as a mediated self," in the same deliberate, self-empowering way he claims Trilling misreads Freud.

Edward J. Shoben, Jr., *Lionel Trilling: Mind and Character* [F427]

**** Langbaum, Robert. "Lionel Trilling in Retrospect." [Review of A11 and F427.] *American Scholar* 52 (Winter 1982-83): 132-38. See H823.

I870. Martin, Jay. *South Atlantic Quarterly* 82 (Spring 1983): 216-18.

Finds "Trilling's reputation . . . immensely greater than his achievement," an attempt to fulfill promises of success given to his mother and his older colleagues at Columbia and avoid the kind of personal failure that had driven his father from Lithuania. Although his positions were "personally derived," Trilling succeeded "in transforming his anxieties into a series of literary examinations which have proved to be useful to others."

Stephen L. Tanner, *Lionel Trilling* [F428]

**** Simpson, Lewis P. "Trilling in the Tradition." [Review of F425 and F428.] *Partisan Review* 57 (Summer 1990): 474-82. See I869.

Philip French, ed., *Three Honest Men: A Critical Mosaic: Edmund Wilson, F. R. Leavis, Lionel Trilling* [L921]

**** Holloway, John. "Varieties of Dialogue." [Review of A11; L921; William Walsh, *F. R. Leavis* (London: Chatto & Windus, 1980); and F. R. Leavis, *Education and the University* (1943; rpt. Cambridge: Cambridge University Press, 1980).] *Encounter* 56 (February-March 1981): 67-77. See G483.

I871. Shechner, Mark. *New Republic* 186 (17 February 1982): 32.

Calls L921 "a compendium of commonplaces" distinguished by the juxtapostions that foster insights, for example, into the shared cultural and intellectual "Protestantism" of its three subjects, all "ministers without a church" who "admitted no distinction between literary values and social or spiritual ones."

**** Cox, R. G. "Criticizing the Critics: Leavis and Trilling." [Review of F422; L921; R. P. Bilan, *The Literary Criticism of F. R. Leavis* (Cambridge: Cambridge University Press, 1979); and William Walsh, *F. R. Leavis* (Bloomington: Indiana University Press, 1980). *Sewanee Review* 89 (Winter 1981): 118-25. See I850.

Nathan A. Scott, *Three American Moralists: Mailer, Bellow, Trilling* [L972]

1872. May, John R., S. J. "Faith, History and the Ironic Imagination." [Review of L972; William F. Lynch, S. J., *Images of Faith: An Exploration of the Ironic Imagination* (South Bend: University of Notre Dame Press, 1973); and Charles Moeller, *Man and Salvation in Literature*, translated by Charles Underhill Quinn (South Bend: University of Notre Dame Press, 1970).] *New Orleans Review* 4 (9 June-3 July 1974): 370-73.

Links Scott to Lynch in his faith in irony as the capacity "for holding together contraries," a capacity "singularly uncharacteristic of American literature," which is riven by unresolved opposites, except in such writers as Mailer, Bellow, and Trilling who persist in "grappling with the finitude of human existence" in its implication in "the duties and contingencies of our life in history."

Section J

Dissertations

J873. Alspaugh, Elizabeth Norton. "The Formation of Lionel Trilling's Moral Dialectic: A Study of His Fiction and Criticism, 1939-1955." University of Maryland, 1979. 367 pages.

Proposes an autobiographical matrix for Trilling's major criticism and fiction of the 1940's. Establishes as a basis for his dialectical mode of thinking a thesis--"joy," discovered in the ideal of "pure perception" that drew Trilling to Arnold and brought him into close sympathy with Arnold's renunciation of poetry (a renunciation foreshadowing Trilling's own retreat from fiction)--an antithesis--"responsibility," dramatized in Forster's critical quarrel with liberalism, which Trilling pursues throughout the forties--and a synthesis--"conditioned responsibility," urged by the essays collected in A4. Analyzes in detail the autobiographical incarnations of each of these terms in Trilling's contemporaneous works of fiction: joy in the untrammeled appetite for life Tertan defends in Captain Alving in C77, responsibility in the moral maturation of Stephen and Margaret Elwin in C84, and conditioned responsibility in John Laskell's response to the thesis of the Crooms' childlike Stalinism and the antithesis of Maxim's authoritarian sense of individual responsibility. Argues that both Howe's betrayal of Tertan and Trilling's insistence in B40 that Tertan is insane, based on fear of his power, lead to a sense of guilt (Howe's concerning Tertan, Trilling's concerning his model Allen Ginsberg) that Trilling attempts to resolve by emphasizing the need in his writing for resistance to passive ideology as a form of social action, and finally for a conditioned sense of responsibility that balances a self-gratifying sentiment of being against the pressures of social implication. Suggests that this attempt fails to sustain Trilling's fiction because although he can renounce the solitary pleasures of pure perception, he maintains an ambivalent attitude toward social imperatives, making the proposed hero of his synthesis, Laskell, less clear and engaging than his principal tempter Maxim. Ascribes Trilling's decision to write no more fiction after 1949 to his fear of the imaginative regression that would enable him to confront and master his fears directly, observing that he prefers to come to an accommodation with those fears by identifying with a series of other writers--Forster, James, Keats, and Freud--who have achieved "autonomous selfhood" through dialectic.

J874. Barnaby, Marianne Gilbert. "Lionel Trilling: Modulations of Arnoldian Criticism at the Present Time." University of Connecticut, 1975. 226 pages.

Presents Trilling as an inheritor of Arnold's dialectical temper of thought who in his most influential period (1946-55) used a dialectic of self and world to mediate between the commitment of Marxist ideologues and the New Critics' claims of textual autonomy. Remarks the irony of Trilling's valorizing of the literature of the sixty years following the French Revolution--a period whose literature Arnold had dismissed as inadequate to its ideas--suggesting that Trilling, like Arnold, may have placed an "ultimate messianic burden" on literature because of the failure of so many political, social, and religious systems to provide a "repository for value." Contends that Trilling follows his dialectical defense/critique of liberalism by diagnosing in A6 a cultural crisis stemming from a misunderstanding of the true nature of the self and recommending Freud's model of a "strong sense of individual resilient identity within the framework of civilization" rather than the "fierce strain of asserting the ego apart from all conditions of surrounding reality" prescribed by modern literature. Argues that since Trilling's analysis of the leading modernist writers--Proust, Joyce, Yeats, Kafka, Gide--is rarely supplemented by close analysis of any individual works, his attitude toward them becomes more deeply ambivalent when he teaches their work, generating fundamental reservations about his own Arnoldian humanism--reservations he explores in A8--questioning his former assumption of the moral adequacy of literature and literary study and his preference for the literary dramatization of ideas over their exposition in philosophical works, and charging that modern literature, for all its power and grandeur, "has created a split between morality and imagination"--and attempts to rebut in A9 by positing literature as a means for developing the Hegelian Spirit "from the external tangible condition toward the realm of pure Being" and for releasing readers from their dependence on possessions to focus with Marx on "true value in terms of natural existence." Notes that despite the value Trilling continues to attach to literature, he finds that the uncritical, quasi-religious investiture of literature as a source of wisdom exacerbates the split Freud diagnoses between the desires of the self and the values of the external world; hence to the implicit questions which shape A9--Is literature "a force for *good*"? Is Arnold's faith in its moral force is still justified?--Trilling can give no conclusive answers; and in C185, "since he uses literature to give evidence of all positions and all opinions, it does not serve him as the committed champion of the mental life."

The appended bibliography was originally published in *Bulletin on Bibliography* 31 (January-March 1974): 37-44.

J875. Bucho, Louella Mae. "The Literary Criticism of Lionel Trilling: Trilling and the Novel." Indiana University of Pennsylvania, 1990. viii, 273 pages.

Distinguishes Trilling's cultural criticism from his theoretical and applied literary criticism, surveying the field of Trilling studies to demonstrate that the literary criticism, theoretical and applied, has been relatively neglected. Contends that Trilling's theory of the novel, though nowhere explicitly set forth, can be reconstructed from his literary essays, especially B41. Identifies four principal influences on this theory: John Erskine's idea of intelligence, which prescribes moral realism and an explicit treatment of ideas as the ideal basis for the novel; Trilling's belief in the value of literature as "an ethical agent" for moral education; Freudian psychology; and political liberalism. Traces Trilling's early advocacy of the proposition that novels ought to "rescue the will and society" by reconstituting or renovating the will and his later movement away from this meliorist position to a more general prescription: the novel should present ideas in a dialectical mode, combining "ideas and life." Adds a single stylistic prescription: the novel should be, in contrast to Sartre's ideal of an authorless, impersonal fiction, "an authored story written in a natural prose," explicitly concerned with ideas rather than form. Notes that Trilling's applied criticism of fiction is difficult to pigeonhole--his orientation has been variously described as social, psychological, cultural, historical, and biographical--because of his enduringly interdisciplinary interests, but emphasizes the lasting influence of Arnold's conception of literature as a support and critique of social and political culture. On the basis of B41, argues that Trilling conceives criticism's primary tasks as interpretation and judgment. Describes four steps in the process of interpretation: description of the literary work in terms of its genre and structure, in accordance with New Critical practice; consideration of the work's historical and "cultural causation"; consideration of the author's biography; and psychoanalytic investigation. Similarly differentiates three modes of judgment: assessment of the work's technical accomplishment, of its "right to power" in light of the sources of its authority, and of its cultural significance. Adds that all Trilling's criticism of the novel, theoretical and applied, is directed to an audience including professional and non-professional readers. Reviews Trilling's applied criticism of the novel--with special attention to A2, B19, B20, B23, B25, C98, C111, C116, C131, and C180, and briefer analysis of a group of reviews including C66, C102, C147, and C173--in the light of three general propositions: the essays focus on ideas central to Trilling's theory of the novel; they employ historical, sociocultural, and psychological perspectives; they are artfully composed. Concludes by identifying "the idea and ideal of a *social novel*" as Trilling's most significant legacy to the study of the modern novel.

J876. Du Quesnay, William. "The Sense of the Dialectical in Lionel Trilling's Criticism." Louisiana State University, 1977. 151 pages.

Seeks to "establish the critical method" of Trilling by a close examination of the Prefaces to A4, A5, and A8, and an extended analysis of C185. Defining Trilling as a dialectician of self and world, argues that his dialectic is available only through the imagination, the "chief dialectical faculty of the human mind," and that Trilling's principal legacy from the nineteenth century is his sense of culture as dialectical (as opposed to earlier conceptions of culture as an inherited tradition received by the self). Notes that despite Trilling's allegiance to this romantic conception of culture, he criticizes romanticism whenever it moves away from dialecticism, since he regards the consequent ideological certitude as "the greatest perversion of human knowledge," adding that although he follows Emerson in distinguishing an unconditioned self from the conditioned world, he rejects Emerson's unitarian vision of self and world for Freud's starker model of an embattled self ultimately resistant to assimilation by the world. Finds "the center, the stance of Trilling's criticism" in the concluding passage from the Preface to A5, positing "the modern imagination of autonomy and delight" as making "a new idea in the world" whose shifting forms and fortunes Trilling traces. Suggests that once the adversive imagination of the romantics is tenured in as the adversary culture, Trilling comes to admire his nineteenth-century heroes--Wordsworth, Keats, Flaubert, Hegel, Arnold, Mill, Freud--less for their radicalism than for their anti-ideological conservatism. Compares C185--in which the term "dialectic" never appears, its place having been taken by the phrase "Jeffersonian ideal"--to a Ciceronian oration, noting the correspondence of its four parts to the *exordium*, *narratio*, *confirmatio*, and *peroratio* prescribed by classical rhetoric. Agrees with Trilling's attack on affirmative action directives, which threaten the "aggression and authority of mind," on behalf of "a democracy whose citizens are no longer made anxious by the sacrifice and discipline required by the life of mind."

J877. Grumet, Elinor Joan. "The Menorah Idea and the Apprenticeship of Lionel Trilling." University of Iowa, 1979. 315 pages.

Traces the development of Trilling's work for the *Menorah Journal* as the "most honest and fullest record of a struggle with Jewish identity in secular terms." Discusses at length the rise of Menorah Societies, whose founder Henry Hurwitz defined negatively as umbrella groups to bring together the greatest number of Jewish college students without offending or alienating any potential members by insisting on religious affiliations, as organizations which paradoxically sought to promote "pure Jewish spirit" by means of assimilation to secular university culture. Examines Trilling's close affiliation with Hurwitz's *Menorah Journal* from 1925 to 1931, when Hurwitz laid off Elliot Cohen as editor, contending that Trilling, ultimately finding "Jewish cultural nationalism an intellectual dead-end," and refusing implication in "Jewish cultural agony," turned from the Menorah Idea of self-realization through a separatist attack on literary anti-Semitism--a negative ideal he excoriates in C53 and inadvertently displays in C55--to an alignment with literary modernism and the English literary canon. Focusing on C192 and Trilling's reviews of contemporary Jewish fiction, argues that Trilling's movement from culturally Jewish social and aesthetic ideals to "a purer, more idealist form of modernism" is indicated by his Kantian realization that reality exists only as it is apprehended through the perceiving mind, weakened by Trilling's tendency, inherited from Symbolist aesthetics, to identify reality with the perceiving mind (as in C68). Concludes that although Trilling's "attempt to reconcile the claims upon secular allegiance of an individualst, elitist modernism, and the people's tradition of realism," fails in its heroic quest to identify the conservative moral authority of Western culture with the culturally pluralistic moral authority of the liberal, often radical, strain of rebellion against that tradition, "Trilling matured when he came to understand maturity as the individual's constant bargaining with society, and not as a separation from it."

Much of the dissertation, especially Chapters 3 and 4, giving historical information about Trilling's affiliation with the *Menorah Journal*, is based on original research, and the dissertation contains a great deal of information about Trilling's earliest publications not available elsewhere.

J878. Samet, Thomas Harold. "The Problematic Self: Lionel Trilling and the Anxieties of the Modern." Brown University, 1980. 228 pages.

Traces Trilling's dialectical presentation of "the complexities and vicissitudes of the life of the self under the circumstances created by culture and history" from his earliest stories to A9, which Samet calls his greatest book. Examines Trilling's attempt to dramatize and maintain a tension between self and society in his stories about the problems of Jewish identity, his inheritance from Arnold of an "organic" conception of society capable of mediating between the anti-social claims of the self and the compromising demands of the culture--a conception Trilling regards more warily than Arnold because of the strains placed on an organic society by the brutality of modern ideologies and the intransigence of the individual--his turn toward Freud as theorizing the tragic necessities of social implication and social alienation, and his insistence, against modernists like Woolf, on the social matrix of personal identity and, against post-modernists like Alain Robbe-Grillet and Leo Bersani, on the continued integrity of character. Finds in C191's dialectic of life and art a dialectic of ways of being foreshadowed by Trilling's studies of Babel's fascination with violence and peace (C122) and David Riesman's distinctions between inner- and other-directed personalities (C102). Argues that critics of A9 have commonly misread it as an attack on authenticity, urging instead that Trilling endorses the values of both sincerity and authenticity, despite their frequent opposition, even though he deplores such extreme or oversimplified celebrations of authenticity as R. D. Laing's. Criticizes Trilling for overlooking the other-directed, chameleon-like aspect of Keats's negative capability, and notes that his defense of the shaped self may constitute a rearguard action against the deconstructed self proposed by Bersani and others; but contends that this deconstructed self, far from marking a liberation from social ideology and its repressions, may mark a collaboration with a social actuality that has itself been decentered or deconstructed, and concludes that recent attacks on the self have given Trilling's dialectics a new urgency.

Includes two appendices reviewing the 1975 reissue of A3 and the publication of F420 and F421.

J879. Sarchett, Barry Wayne. "Lionel Trilling in Historical and Critical Context: A Critique." University of Utah, 1988. x, 318 pages.

Premising that Trilling too often ignores the material circumstances and effects of his own discourse, examines the ideological structures and implications of his work--especially the essays collected in A4, A5, and A8--from an avowedly radical perspective. Stresses the importance of Heisenbergian uncertainty ("to perceive is to transform") in Trilling's emphasis on "the intentionality of knowledge" as early as A1, which follows Arnold in defining knowledge as a series of "provisional attempts at truth" eschewing certitude, but sees the liberal legacy Trilling inherits from Arnold's humanism as riven by contradictions. Argues that Trilling's distinction in A4 between ideas and ideology, "a methodological mistake" comprising "the foremost intellectual sin of his age," though couched in terms of manner--ideology is an unconscious habit of mind substituting for a more active apprehension and criticism of ideas--is actually reducible to a distinction involving the content of ideas: ideology, involving a hidden agenda of the will triumphing over the advance of rationality, is by definition anti-Enlightenment, anti-humanist, anti-liberal. Compares Trilling to Wayne Booth as another liberal primarily interested in opposing radical thought by attenuating social conflict, and follows G467 and F421 in describing "the real quarrel" of A4 as not between constricted and open political visions but between the literary imagination and the exigencies of any political action whatever. Finds Trilling's attempts "to pursue the health of the self apart from the health of society" persistently undermined by his repression of the economic determinants of society in favor of a purely moral and psychological critique of the dominant liberal culture and, later, the adversary culture, and his consequent determination to "portray present reality as absolute reality" by magnifying the Stalinist betrayal into "a cosmological defeat, a stoic metaphysics of accommodation." Charges that Trilling, despite his criticism of modernist writers' political millenialism, shares their disgust with politics and their utopianism (rooted in his case in a nostalgia for a nineteenth-century balance between culture and individual will), and expresses this disgust and utopianism in A5, his "most claustrophobic book," by forsaking dialectic for a protective identification of quotidian reality with "middle-class existence" which attempts to "find essential reality in literal reality" while overlooking the way bourgeois values are part of the weightlessness from which he wants them to rescue the modern self. Contends that although all his later work is an extended gloss on A5, Trilling renews his faith in dialectic in A8, whose argument is rendered "confused and confusing" by his yearning for the autonomy fostered by the indignant perception of the modern self and his contradictory loyalty to "the ideology of classical liberalism," which he wishes to protect from hostile criticism. Concludes that Trilling's resolutely moral and psychological analysis of the adversary culture's attack on the shaped self is compromised by his unawareness of the extent to which "the self has become the ultimate commodity in consumerist culture."

Chapter 6 is revised and reprinted as G529.

Section K

Miscellaneous

K880. Anon. "Lionel M. Trilling." *Columbian*, 1925, p. 168.

Trilling's college yearbook identifies him with "the Hartley Corporation" who "tried to monopolize 'Sweetness and Light' a few years ago," notes that "Li hid his genius under a bushel-basket . . . for two years" before beginning to write for the *Morningside*, and reveals that "this master mind used to play marbles--in the dirt!"

K881. Anon. "Key Novel." *Observer*, 25 March 1951, p. 5.

A sidebar to H645 that calls A3 Trilling's "most profoundly thoughtful book," identifies its principals with Whittaker Chambers and Alger Hiss, Trilling's "fellow students at Columbia," and suggests that it "probably provides the correct psychological background" to the Hiss case.

K882. Anon. "Personal Expression." *TLS*, 7 October 1944, p. 487.

An addendum to H586 that takes up Trilling's question of the relative values of impressionistic and systematic criticism, observing that Trilling attempts to strike a balance between the two, and agreeing with Forster that criticism is at heart subjective.

K883. Anon. "Trilling reveals all." *Observer Review*, 6 April 1975, p. 34.

Reports London publisher Tom Rosenthal's "coup" in persuading Trilling to reissue A3 with a new introduction. Notes that "even if novelists do use real people they rarely admit it," contrasting Trilling's straightforward identification of Maxim with Whittaker Chambers.

K884. Bentley, Eric. "Fun with Art." [Letter to the Editor.] *New York Times Book Review*, 23 November 1980, p. 46.

Dismisses as "bunkum" Robert Alter's contention in H840 that "Trilling didn't have fun with art," arguing that Trilling, unlike Nabokov, took both aesthetic play and its real-world consequences for granted, "and *went on* to explain in what context he, as historian and humanist, could see any phenomenon."

K885. Bradbrook, Frank W. "Emma." [Letter to the Editor.] *Encounter* 9 (October 1957): 70.

Agrees with K889 that *Emma*, like Austen's other novels, is "quite clearly written to show the inadequacy of the social virtues alone," opposing Chestertonian ideals of social behavior to "the Johnsonian virtues of endurance and stoicism" incarnated in her heroes.

K886. French, Philip, moderator. "Lionel Trilling, New York and the American Imagination." [An abridgment of a radio discussion with Daniel Aaron, Quentin Anderson, Jacques Barzun, Morris Dickstein, Stephen Donadio, John Hollander, Irving Howe, Alfred Kazin, Steven Marcus, and Norman Podhoretz.] *Listener* 98 (15 December 1977): 783-84, 786.

A roughly chronological discussion in which Anderson distinguishes Trilling from Philip Roth as one of "those who would take Jewishness . . . for granted"; Barzun identifies his early Marxism as cultural, focusing on "Marx's revelations" rather than "the machinery" of the Communist Party; Hollander emphasizes Trilling's effort in A3 in resisting the turn of the American novel toward romance; French and Barzun agree that after A3, Trilling's writing becomes less explicitly political; Howe distinguishes Trilling's "conservative" liberalism as a "moral, imaginative stance" from his own "concrete politics" of socialism; Kazin suggests that Trilling's audience, though determined to repudiate its Marxist leanings, "did not want to resolve its contradictions" concerning liberalism; and Donadio, disagreeing with Dickstein's observation that Trilling's last work marked a retreat into "19th-century realism" from the "modernism in the streets" of the counterculture, contends that Trilling "resisted . . . the facile acceptance of apocalyptic notions . . . as if they had no social consequences."

For a more comprehensive transcript, see L921.

K887. Herman, William. "A Letter to Mr. Trilling." *Mid-Century*, no. 5 (Fall 1959), p. 22.

Rejects Trilling's comparison in C141 of Osborne with Chekhov, arguing that although they both deal with defeated characters, "Osborne is a petulant child and Chekhov was a man of compassion." Suggests that Osborne's popularity is due to the novelty of seeing "a play about the English middle class," whose effect is like that of "the vicar losing his pants."

K888. Ramsey, Paul, Jr. "Manners and Values." [Letter to the Editor.] *Partisan Review* 20 (May-June 1953): 362-68.

Complains that Delmore Schwartz in G531 is guilty of bad manners in unfairly identifying Trilling's and John W.

Aldridge's concern with manners (see C90 and M984) as snobbery. Suggests that Schwartz's indifference to literary and social ideas that "lack political utility against, say, [Senator Joseph] McCarthy" shows his "lack of faith in his own vocation."

Schwartz replies that "manners stand to values as religious ceremonials [not, as Aldridge claims, religion itself] stand to religious belief," charging that "values are prior to manners and that unless our values have a direct and sincere relation to our manners, we are abysmal hypocrites."

K889. Statham, M. H. "Emma." [Letter to the Editor.] *Encounter* 9 (September 1957): 69-70.

Questions Trilling's neglect in C131 of the "central theme" of *Emma*: the relationship between Emma and Knightley, which ends in betrothal when Emma, who "has adhered to . . . 'social' values," accepts the supremacy of Knightley's "modern individual consciousness." Suggests that tracing the development of this conflict to its resolution would dispel the "difficulties" Trilling finds in the novel.

K890. Tate, Allen. "On *The Fathers*." [Letter to the Editor.] *Partisan Review* 6 (February 1939): 125-26.

Praises the sensitivity and disinterestedness of D306 but disputes Trilling's conclusion that *The Fathers* is "an indictment of the Old South," ascribing the social problems it represents to "human nature" and suggesting that they could as easily have arisen in a Marxist society. Emphasizes his admiration for "the ante-bellum values" of the South, despite their limitations, compared to "what we are likely to get in fact" rather than any such "political absolute" Trilling seeks in Tate.

The editors respond briefly by describing Tate's conception of human nature as embodying "an absolute of *limitation*," set against a historicized Marxist analysis.

**** Trilling, Lionel; Howe, Irving; Farber, Leslie H.; Hamilton, William; Orrill, Robert; Boyers, Robert. "*Sincerity and Authenticity*: A Symposium." *Salmagundi*, no. 41 (Spring 1978), pp. 87-110. See E418.

In a discussion of problems raised by A9, Howe argues that Trilling's ambivalence toward categorical and dialectical modes of thinking is not problematic because "every serious person" nostalgically yearns for moral absolutes while still keeping that yearning in check, goes on to identify sincerity with romanticism and authenticity with modernism, and worries that the proliferation of paperback books may represent "a debasement of precious commodities." Farber suggests that memory and imagination allow individuals to identify the self that exists beneath its various roles and proposes "serious" as a common synonym for "sincere"--to which Howe adds "genuine" as a synonym for "authentic."

K891. Weeks, Edward, et al. "Letters to the Editor." *New York Times Book Review*, 3 May 1959, p. 24.

Includes eleven letters on the Trilling-Adams-Frost controversy (see C140 and G431). Joseph Gold and Morton D. Paley defend Trilling against Adams's attack; the other writers--who include *Atlantic* editor Weeks, Freudian analyst Anne Steinmann, novelist August Derleth, poet Norman Rosten, and Trilling's dissertation director Emery Neff--take Adams's side. Neff's letter is typical: "Mr. Trilling had that rebuke coming to him. For years he has disregarded similar warnings of his ignorance given privately by old acquaintances. . . . Frost might have had a Nobel Prize if so many New York critics hadn't gone whoring after European gods."

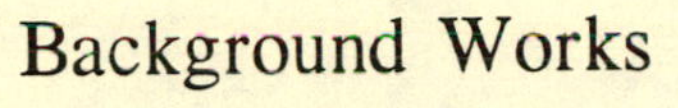
Background Works

Section L

Books

L892. Aaron, Daniel. *Writers on the Left*. New York: Harcourt, Brace and World, 1961.

Disputes the assumption that only neurotic, unworldly misfits were drawn to American Communism by defining the matrix of American literature as an ongoing battle between writers and their society and analyzing the drift, between 1912 and 1940, of artists and intellectuals toward Communism--a party few of them joined, and most broke away from after a short time--as one more instance of a normal historical cycle beginning with the optimistic "pursuit and discovery of a philosophical system," proceeding to a manifesto turning philosophical to social criticism--offering, in this case, an alternative to widespread disillusionment with capitalism and a means of challenging fascism--and finally ending to a decline of literary radicalism and a reabsorption of all but a few intellectuals into the American mainstream following the traumas of the Moscow trials, the Spanish Civil War, and the Non-Aggression Pact between Germany and the Soviet Union.

L893. Anderson, Quentin. *The Imperial Self: An Essay in American Literary and Cultural History*. New York: Knopf, 1971.

Extends Trilling's assertion in C90 that the best American writers have turned away from society by theorizing American individualism as a flight from culture and community most fully figured in Emerson's discovery of the divine within the "secular incarnation" of the individual, Whitman's "assimilationist" consciousness whose goal is "the unliving of our bodily and cultural set," and the conquest of "the great world of European culture and art" by the imperial self which "carries it home in triumph" in *The Golden Bowl*. Argues that the sense of the self as imperially expansive entails "a sharp diminution in our sense of ourselves as as agents whose lives are known through what we do to and with others," until the active self of the classical imagination is displaced by "the hypertrophied self," prepotent yet utterly disengaged, of modern consciousness.

L894. Arac, Jonathan. *Critical Genealogies: Historical Situations for Postmodern Literary Studies*. New York: Columbia University Press, 1987. See pp. 166-67, 310-12.

Argues that Trilling's "independence from Stalinism" came only at the price of a monistic, ahistorical view of Stalinism, that forced him to ignore the work of F. O. Matthiessen, which belied his claim that contemporary liberals could take no interest in literary modernism, and which led to his "integration into the cold war" as an "independent" authority on the newly institutionalized modernists.

L895. Avorn, Jerry L. et al. *Up Against the Ivy Wall: A History of the Columbia Crisis*, edited with an Introduction by Robert Friedman. New York: Atheneum, 1969. See pp. 69-70, 88-89, 132, 179, 231.

Describes Trilling's unsuccessful attempts, as one of the three members of the faculty group charged with establishing a tripartite commission of students, faculty, and administrators to resolve the issues raised by the student strike at Columbia in 1968, to mediate between the demands of students insisting on amnesty and administrators reserving the right to bring disciplinary charges against them, and details the violent confrontations between demonstrators and the police after negotiations broke down.

L896. Barrett, William. *The Truants: Adventures Among the Intellectuals*. Garden City: Doubleday Anchor, 1982. See especially pp. 161-86.

A memoir of the New York intellectuals by the longtime editor of *Partisan Review*, framed by elegiac portraits of Philip Rahv and Delmore Schwartz, and including a detailed, warmly sympathetic, but not uncritical portrait of Trilling as "the most intelligent [man] . . . I knew" (see G438).

L897. Barzun, Jacques. *Romanticism and the Modern Ego*. Boston: Atlantic Monthly/Little, Brown, 1944. Reprinted as *Classic, Romantic, and Modern* (New York: Doubleday, 1961). See pp. 87, 119, 275, 290, 319.

After a dedication "to Lionel Trilling with gratitude and admiration," repeatedly cites D316's argument that Shelley's romantic tradition is coeval with modernism, anticipating even Freud.

L898. Bayley, John. *The Uses of Division: Unity and Disharmony in Literature*. New York: Viking, 1976. See Chapter 1.2, "Sincerity and Authenticity," pp. 17-25.

Suggests that the authenticity Trilling describes in A9 "could consist in one assertion: 'I am the hero of a novel and therefore authentic.'" Notes that although "the modern reflective consciousness cannot in some sense but see itself as taking part in a novel," novelists from Austen to Proust typically dramatize dialectical confrontations between sincerity and authenticity, embodied in different characters, as in Austen, or within the shaping consciousness of the author, as in Balzac.

L899. Bazelon, David T. *Nothing but a Fine Tooth Comb: Essays in Social Criticism, 1944-1969.* New York: Simon and Schuster, 1969. See pp. 260, 266.

Recalls a "frightening" meeting in which Trilling "told me how much trouble he had caused himself in trying to undercut literary snobbishness in [John] O'Hara's favor." Notes that by 1960 Trilling "appears to have been wearied by his thankless, uphill effort."

L900. Bell, Daniel. *The Cultural Contradictions of Capitalism.* New York: Basic, 1976. See pp. 40-41, 143.

Contends that what Trilling calls "adversary culture" has now "triumphed over . . . society" and "come to dominate the cultural order" because its members form a group of signficant size and cohesiveness, this group influences or dominates even mass "cultural establishments," and bourgeois society has "no intellectually respectable culture of its own." Identifies the ideology of this "counter-culture" as "an attack on reason itself."

L901. Bell, Daniel. *The End of Ideology: On the Exhaustion of Political Ideas in the Fifties.* Second edition. Cambridge: Harvard University Press, 1988. See "The End of Ideology in the West: An Epilogue," pp. 393-407.

Finds by the end of the 1950's "a disconcerting caesura" among American intellectuals unable to believe in "the old politico-economic radicalism" and unable to redress "the stultifying aspects of contemporary culture" in political terms.

L902. Bell, Daniel. *The Reforming of General Education: The Columbia College Experience in Its National Setting.* New York: Columbia University Press, 1966.

A report, dedicated to Trilling, to the faculty of Columbia College on the fate of its fifty-year-old mission of general education, proposing to substitute for "a single [cultural] tradition and a single past" reducible to a parochial list of great books of the Western tradition "the *idea* of tradition . . . and the *idea* of the past," and making specific recommendations for strengthening the core curriculum of general education courses and the position of the College in a university increasingly dominated by powerful graduate and professional schools. Endorses Trilling's ambivalence to modern culture, rather than Norman O. Brown's narcissistic nihilism, as a model for a university committed to mediating between "the technocratic and apocalyptic modes" of institutional culture.

L903. Bell, Daniel. *The Winding Passage: Essays and Sociological Journeys 1960-1980.* Cambridge: ABT Books, 1980. See "The 'Intelligentsia' in American Society," pp. 119-37.

Distinguishes three senses in which classes of intellectuals have been defined--as clerical guardians of learning, as ideologues, and as advisors on social policy--focusing on the second, especially on "the New York Jewish intelligentsia, 1935-65," whose union of "political radicalism and cultural modernism" and whose accession to institutional power after the war were rooted in their "desire to find a *home*," since "the ideological impulse in this country . . . has paradoxically been a hunger for inclusion." Contends that Trilling wrote best on British subjects--Arnold, Forster, Austen--which "gave a great sense of coherent social structure or of nuanced relationships" impossible in America, where "we are a *nation*, but not a *community*."

L904. Bender, Thomas. *New York Intellect: A History of Intellectual Life in New York City, from 1750 to the Beginnings of Our Own Time.* New York: Knopf, 1987. See especially pp. 316-17.

Emphasizes Trilling's ambivalence toward John Dewey, Charles Beard, and the liberalism they represented in politics, history, and pedagogy, noting that Trilling, together with Richard Hofstadter and C. Wright Mills, formed "an intellectual generation" which resisted "the temptation of expertise" in the name of "the public significance of the academic mind."

L905. Bewley, Marius. *The Eccentric Design: Form in the Classic American Novel.* New York: Columbia University Press, 1959. See especially pp. 13-24.

Perhaps the most influential extension and codification of Trilling's argument, in C90 and C92, that "the novel in America diverges from its classic intention." Contends that the thinness of American society has forced American novelists into symbolism, abstraction, and radical subjectivity: "There was really only one subject available to the nineteenth-centry American novelist: his own unhappy plight." Contrasts the normative English novel to the resulting American romance, which was shaped by a "tension between the democratic and the aristocratic attitudes" peculiar to America.

L906. Bloom, Alexander. *Prodigal Sons: The New York Intellectuals and Their World.* New York: Oxford University Press, 1986. See especially pp. 190-98, 248-50, 382-85.

Suggests that the principal value of A4, whose essays were "more speculative than comprehensive," was to reclaim for American intellectuals an active role at a crucial historical moment ten years after their marginalizing by Stalinist politics. Reviews the actions of Trilling's 1953 Columbia committee on political freedom within the university, noting Trilling's emphasis in E398 on the issue of anti-communism rather than that of academic freedom. Concludes that Trilling's rise to "supreme intellectual eminence" is confirmed not by his legacy of a "unified intellectual or cultural conception" but his continuing influence on a large and uniquely diverse group of students.

L907. Blotner, Joseph. *The Modern American Political Novel.* Austin: University of Texas Press, 1966. See pp. 315-20.

Contrasts A3 with *Barbary Shore*, Mailer's equally ambitious but less successful novel of political disillusionment, focusing on the range of political beliefs dramatized by the novel and praising "its richness in statement and symbol" and suggesting that its "static quality is probably inevitable in all but the greatest" novels of ideas. Compares Laskell's "limited central intelligence" formally to Strether's in *The Ambassadors*, "though Laskell is no Strether," and the novel in its seriousness and skill to Warren's *All the King's Men.*

L908. Caute, David. *The Fellow-Travellers: A Postscript to the Enlightenment.* New York: Macmillan, 1972. See especially pp. 250-66.

Traces the development of Communist sympathies in America, Britain, France, and Germany from 1928, when the first Soviet Five-Year Plan released a store of pent-up optimism and good will, to 1956, when the suppression of the Hungarian revolution made fellow-travelling virtually impossible. Sees fellow-travelling--"commitment *at a distance*" both geographical and intellectual to the goals and programs of the Soviet Union--as marking a resurgence in the Enlightenment belief in progress and rationality against the irrationalistic nineteenth-century challenges from the Romantics to Freud. Distinguishes Marx's conviction that the triumph of reason demanded a classless society to fellow-travellers' belief in the rational perfectibility of all classes and their frequent revulsion from the proletariat, and roots the fellow-travellers' rationalistic ideology of "left-wing technocratic totalitarianism," as against Marxist socialism, in both Communist theory and the practice of Soviet planning.

L909. Chase, Richard. *The American Novel and Its Tradition*. Garden City: Doubleday Anchor, 1957.

Pursuing Trilling's suggestion in C90 that American novels deviate from the social realism of their European counterparts, argues that the American literary imagination is typically riven by irresolvable contradictions which take the form of a "broken circuit" best represented by the romances and non-realistic novels of Brockden Brown, Hawthorne, Melville, Twain, and Faulkner, and the displaced psychological romances at the heart of James's realistic novels and such novels of manners as *The Great Gatsby*. Probably the most sustained and influential attempt to construct a canon of American fiction based on Trilling's theory of the novel.

L910. Chase, Richard. *The Democratic Vista: A Dialogue on Life and Letters in Contemporary America*. Garden City: Doubleday Anchor, 1958. See especially pp. 27, 125, 159-62.

Approvingly cites Trilling's account of culture as a dialectic rather than a stream or confluence in the course of a dialogue prescribing a new orientation for American culture based on a dialectic between the liberal-radical views of Chase's spokesman and the conservative, middlebrow views of his principal interlocutor, who agrees with him that "the real danger is not in a dialectical view but in a view that is not dialectical enough" because it may seem to erase or resolve contradictions by recasting them from debates between different thinkers to conflicts within the minds of divided thinkers.

L911. Cooney, Terry. *The Rise of the New York Intellectuals: Partisan Review and Its Circle.* Madison: University of Wisconsin Press, 1986. See especially pp. 217-22.

Focusing on the formative period from 1937 to 1945, emphasizes the cosmopolitanism the New York intellectuals sought, their search for "a rich and inclusive American culture--and especially an American literature--that could measure up to the traditions of Europe," their attempt to root a cosmopolitan outlook in their predominantly Jewish heritage, and their gradual turn away from Stalinism, first "in the name of a more genuine radicalism," then away from the left entirely. Stresses Trilling's continuities with the *Partisan Review* circle in these regards, noting that his skepticism about scientific and political progress was at odds with the tenor of the review but was largely subsumed by his desire for intellectual balance.

L912. De Voto, Bernard. *The World of Fiction.* Boston: Houghton Mifflin, 1950. See pp. 267-68, 294-99.

After praising A3 as "a brilliant and moving novel" which solves the diffcult problem of making ideas fictionally salient, takes sharp exception in its closing pages to Trilling's assertion in C92 that the novel should "change the world," arguing that all but the greatest novels undertake simply to entertain, enlighten, and reassure their readers in their loneliness by presenting "the truth about experience or, failing that, something that will seem true," and warning that "it is blasphemous to ask of art what art cannot do."

L913. Dickstein, Morris. *Gates of Eden: American Culture in the Sixties*. New York: Basic, 1977. See especially pp. 253-54, 262-66.

Describes Trilling's critique of liberalism as occupying an "ambiguous ground, neither left nor right--though in some ways to the left of left"--by simultaneously aerating the ideological mind and restoring the social and historical imagination to the literary mind. Recalls Trilling's frustration with the New Left, whose rebellion against the adversary culture left him feeling "that a spiritual abyss had opened up at [his] feet," and argues that although Trilling never "joined the ranks of backlash intellectuals," his admiration of bourgeois values is to be distinguished from Marcuse's belief that "the paternalistic structure of bourgeois society gives the young person something firm to rebel against."

L914. Draper, Theodore. *American Communism and Soviet Russia: The Formative Period.* New York: Macmillan, 1960.

Continues the analysis of L915, focusing on the period from 1923 to 1929. Contends that all the important decisions within the American Communist Party have been made by surviving members of the first generation of its members, who came to the Party from diverse native radical movements before it was fully formed or established, and argues that as American Communism has shifted from another expression of an American radical impulse to a function of the Soviet party, it has been unable either to develop a consistent central ideology or to command the following Marx predicted for it.

L915. Draper, Theodore. *The Roots of American Communism.* New York: Viking, 1957.

Charts the transformation between 1919 and 1923 of the American Communist movement "from a new expression of American radicalism to the American appendage of a Russian revolutionary power," emphasizing its tendency throughout this period to split into warring factions and concluding that the dualities in terms of which the movement became defined--doctrine and reality, political orthodoxy and mass influence, inner development and outer control--insured its early decline from revolutionary doctrine to ideological dogma.

L916. Ellis, William. *The Theory of the American Romance: An Ideology in American Intellectual History*. Ann Arbor: UMI Research Press, 1989.

Attacks Trilling's theory of American "exceptionalism" on the grounds that it exaggerates the consensus of nineteenth-century American culture and its differences from a European culture far from homogeneous itself, assumes too simple a correlation between class struggle and literary form, and contradicts his own belief in a pluralistic American culture in order to assert that American novels differ in their formal and thematic concerns from European novels. Ascribes the influence of this theory, despite its inconsistencies, to the postwar quest for a distinctively American national identity expressed most directly by consensus historians like Daniel Boorstin and Robert Dahl. Argues that critics of Trilling have typically accepted this consensual view of American culture despite their exceptions to his theory of American romance. Observes that just as the consensual view came under serious attack in the 1970's, it "dropped out of sight--taking with it the challenges themselves"--and proposes Trilling's "old criticism"--his Arnoldian account of literature as a criticism of life--as a promising alternative not only to the new criticism and the politically progressive criticism of the 1940's, but to the deconstructive critique that has largely displaced it.

L917. Erskine, John. *My Life as a Teacher*. Philadelphia: Lippincott, 1948. See "Great Books," pp. 165-75.

Describes Erskine's rationale for introducing a program at Columbia College devoted to reading literary classics in translation without the aid of scholarly resources or any pretense to covering the works exhaustively--a program that Trilling often described as central to his experience of university teaching--recalls the opposition which greeted his proposal, and briefly outlines the history, and some of the problems, of the program at Columbia, St. John's College, and the University of Chicago.

L918. Erskine, John. *The Moral Obligation to Be Intelligent*. New and enlarged edition. New York: Bobbs-Merrill, 1921.

The title essay, best remembered as supplying the unofficial rallying cry for the General Education program, reviews the well-established opposition in British literature between virtue and wisdom and urges consideration of intelligence as "the infinite order, wherein man, when he enters it, shall find himself."

L919. Fiedler, Leslie A. *Waiting for the End*. New York: Stein and Day, 1964. See pp. 148-54, 165-66.

Cites as evidence of the drama of contemporary academic life the "extraordinary kind of fame" of C77, calling it Trilling's most successful work of fiction, noting its affinities with J. D. Salinger's *Franny and Zooey*, and crediting it with the "invention" of Allen Ginsberg's "mythic life" as a public figure.

L920. Fraiberg, L. B. *Psychoanalysis and American Literary Criticism*. Detroit: Wayne State University Press, 1960. See "Lionel Trilling's Creative Extension of Freudian Concepts," pp. 202-24.

Describes Trilling as perhaps the best-informed about Freud of any contemporary critic while emphasizing his ambivalence toward Freudian concepts and characterizing this ambivalence as based on compromise, inconsistency, or incomplete understanding. Notes that the critique of Freud's theory of art in C69 is based on Freud's early work, though Trilling acknowledges his position is different in his later work. Argues that Freud considers art an evasion of reality only within a therapeutic context, when it may substitute for other kinds of adaptation to reality. Defends Ernest Jones's Oedipal reading of *Hamlet* as not seeking to displace other readings. Against these reservations, approves Trilling's critique of Freud's positivism, his recognition that Freud sees normal mental processes as poetic, and his emphasis on the death instinct as a uniquely valuable contribution to the understanding of human nature. Commends Trilling's later work, especially C80 and D355, as less critical of Freud.

L921. French, Philip. *Three Honest Men: A Critical Mosaic: Edmund Wilson, F. R. Leavis, Lionel Trilling.* [Participants include Daniel Aaron, Quentin Anderson, Jacques Barzun, Morris Dickstein, Stephen Donadio, John Hollander, Irving Howe, Alfred Kazin, Steven Marcus, and Norman Podhoretz.] Manchester: Carcanet New Press, 1980.

Transcripts of three BBC programs assembled from radio interviews conducted by French. Interviewed about Wilson, Trilling emphasizes his early shyness, compares him to Sainte-Beuve "as a disinterested, detached commentator on literature in all its aspects," calls *To the Finland Station* his most important book, and suggests that he has been more widely admired than imitated.

In speaking of Trilling, Kazin emphasizes his Americanness--obscured by his fondness for Britain and British writers--Anderson notes the importance of "will" in Trilling's later writings as indicating a political involvement that is not simply a search for "proper fullness of being"; French recalls that Trilling testified for the defense at the obscenity trial of Wilson's *Memoirs of Hecate County*; Aaron notes the ways Trilling's commitment to teaching made him less "free-wheeling" than Wilson; Marcus traces Trilling's fascination with the "enigmatic" nature of his mind and considers the vexed political dimension of his criticism; and Anderson, asked what future critics will take from Trilling, notes Trilling's distrust of methods and systems, leading to his adjuration that "we must bear full responsibility for our lives, whether we talk about art, about politics or about morality. . . . One should make one's judgments fully personal."

The transcript of the Trilling interviews was originally published in *PN Review*, no. 10 (August 1979), pp. 48-55, and reprinted in abridgment in K886.

L922. Gilbert, James Burkhart. *Writers and Partisans: A History of Literary Radicalism in America.* New York: John Wiley & Sons, 1968. See especially pp. 274-75n.

Interrupts his history, focusing largely on *Partisan Review* and its predecessor and successor journals, to decline speculation on the possible degree of CIA influence on the editorial policies of *Partisan Review*, concluding only that "a good many intellectuals and America's leading spy agency came to the same conclusions at much the same time about America's role in world society."

L923. Goldstein, Philip. *The Politics of Literary Theory: An Introduction to Marxist Criticism.* Tallahassee: Florida State University Press, 1990. See pp. 15-17.

Describes Trilling as an anticommunist critic who shares Georg Lukács's belief that although "literary ideas grasp sociohistorical reality accurately," great artists, specifically modernist artists who adopt an oppositional stance toward the prevailing ideology, can escape ideological determination. Criticizes Trilling's attempt to blame Stalinism alone rather than "racial prejudice, social injustice, and class conflict" for preventing the complete, ahistorical unification of "the Western subject."

L924. Goodheart, Eugene. *The Failure of Criticism.* Cambridge: Harvard University Press, 1978. See especially pp. 8, 21-22, 28.

Links the ideal of the "shaped self" animating Trilling's humanist criticism, like that of Edmund Wilson, Raymond Williams, and Ortega y Gasset, to nineteenth-century religious ideas and the English Protestant tradition. Commends Trilling's resistance in C159 to "the destructive element" of the scientistic pretensions of structuralism, but suggests that modern humanist critics' intimidation by a history that valorizes modernism prevents Trilling and other critics from developing this resistance beyond a cultured ambivalence.

L925. Goodman, Walter. *The Committee: The Extraordinary Career of the House Committee on Un-American Activities.* Foreword by Richard H. Rovere. New York: Farrar, Straus and Giroux, 1968. See pp. 328-29.

Recalls Trilling's leading role at Columbia in protesting the 1953 dismissal of two Rutgers instructors for membership in the Communist Party--a position vindicated by the Supreme Court's 1967 decision annulling New York State's loyalty laws for teachers.

L926. Gorak, Jan. *The Making of the Modern Canon: Genesis and Crisis of a Literary Idea.* London: Athlone, 1991. See pp. 76, 227.

Briefly enlists Trilling in the ranks of American "anti-canonism" that created a "radical counter-canon" based on "conformity to established patterns of nonconformity." Cites B41 as having "imprinted the new scepticism on college curricula" by questioning the validity of normative canons.

L927. Graff, Gerald. *Professing Literature: An Institutional History.* Chicago: University of Chicago Press, 1987. See pp. 136, 172-73.

Suggests that Trilling's critique of the liberal imagination valorized the perspective of Columbia's General Honors course against the historicism of its Contemporary Civilization sequence. Agrees with Trilling's pessimistic diagnosis in C189 that the theory of general education has tended toward platitude, but argues that in the absence of a consensual culture which shares pedagogical principles, the only way to formulate goals without lapsing into platitude is for "the old universals" to be "thoroughly historicized."

L928. Green, Martin. *Transatlantic Patterns: Cultural Comparisons of England with America*. New York: Basic Books, 1970. See Chapter 15, "America After 1945 III: Criticism and the Social Contract Now," pp. 215-34.

Speculates on the autobiographical motives behind A9, comparing Trilling to Isaac Babel in his divided loyalties to sincere piety and authentic heroism, and contrasting Trilling's choice--an ironic version, after Arnold and Forster, of sincerity--with Norman Mailer's choice of authenticity, as against Robert Lowell's sincerity. Suggests that Trilling, more than any other critic, has "defined the situations and set up the terms for his younger contemporaries," even those like Mailer who reject him by way of rejecting all criticism, since his patient attempts to understand them have "re-established criticism's reign over them." Compares Trilling to Northrop Frye and Green himself as demonstrating the affinity between criticism and liberalism, since liberals are both the defenders and the critics of high culture.

L929. Gunn, Giles. *The Culture of Criticism and the Criticism of Culture*. New York: Oxford University Press, 1987. See especially pp. 19-40, 93-115.

Defends the relevance of evaluative questions to critical discourse by examining the institutional assumptions and conventions of "the genre of cultural criticism"--taking Trilling as exemplary--which has most insistently pressed these questions.

L930. Habegger, Alfred. *Gender, Fantasy, and Realism in American Literature.* New York: Columbia University Press, 1982. See Chapter 25, "Who Made James the Modern American Master, and Why?," pp. 289-302.

Sees Trilling's and Philip Rahv's rediscovery of James as illustrating the continuity between the genteel tradition and modernism--both defining themselves against a coarse, dominant American cultural tradition. Argues that James's "highbrow fantasy masquerading as realism" in *The Bostonians*, accepted uncritically as an attack on the "radical social reform" threatened by contemporary feminists, "supplied the ideal material prop . . . for mandarins of the margin of American political life." Reads Laskell's withdrawal from politics in A3, which too easily conflates "denounc[ing] radical politics" with "abandon[ing] political reform," as Trilling's own version of *The Bostonians*, his "denunciation of progressive reform" in the name of "the private life."

L931. Hart, Jeffrey P. *Acts of Recovery: Essays on Culture and Politics.* Hanover, NH: University Press of New England, 1989. See pp. vii-xiv.

In a Preface "in honor of Lionel Trilling," cites Trilling's assertion in the Preface to A4 that liberalism is "the sole intellectual tradition" in American culture. Proposes a broader alternative tradition, descending from Johnson to Hazlitt, Arnold, G. K. Chesterton, Eliot, Edmund Wilson, and Trilling, based on "conversation about literature" as "a vital human activity, central to civilization as we know it."

L932. Hellman, Lillian. *Scoundrel Time.* Boston: Little, Brown, 1976. See pp. 83-84.

Hellman's memoir of her 1952 appearance before the House Un-American Affairs Committee sharply disputes Trilling's description of Whittaker Chambers in C190 as "a man of honor" and wonders "how Diana and Lionel Trilling, old, respected friends, could have come out of the same age and time with such different political and social views from my own."

L933. Hoffman, Frederick J. *The Modern Novel in America, 1900-1950.* Chicago: Regnery, 1951. See especially pp. 195-97.

Identifies "the burden inherited by the sensitive liberal who has outlived the pertinence of his naïvely held principles . . . a remarkably rewarding subject for a novelist," and calls A3 the most successful fictional treatment of this subject to date.

L934. Hofstadter, Richard. *Anti-Intellectualism in American Life.* New York: Knopf, 1963. See pp. 393-432.

Uses Howe's quarrel with Trilling over whether intellectuals should accommodate themselves to the social mainstream (see E394 and M1017) as the basis for an analysis of American intellectuals as a social class willfully alienated from a larger society they regard as inimical to their interests.

L935. Hollinger, David A. *In the American Province: Studies in the History and Historiography of Ideas.* Bloomington: Indiana University Press, 1985. See especially pp. 56-91.

Analyzes the implications of conceiving America as "a province of a civilization that also embraces the national cultures of Europe," emphasizing the distinctness of American intellectual history and the attitudes of recently assimilated cosmopolitan American intellectuals toward contemporaries they often considered more provincial than themselves.

L936. Honan, Park. *Matthew Arnold: A Life.* London: Weidenfeld and Nicolson, 1981. See pp. 322, 454.

Though conceding that A1 is "often brilliant" in its assessment of Arnold's humanism, attacks Trilling's ignorance of much of Arnold's reading, unpublished correspondence, and manuscript notes--which leads him to discover "unintended contradictions" in Arnold--and his "remorseless politicizing of Arnold's thought."

L937. Horowitz, Irving Louis. *C. Wright Mills: An American Utopian.* New York: Free Press, 1983. See pp. 84-87, 252-53, 284-85.

Quotes Mills's paraphrase of Trilling's criticism of *White Collar*--"Too absolute a doctrine. . . . You must acquire a more chaste style. . . . Destroy your illusion of creative literature and put in its place standards of exposition"--after a meeting in 1952, and an exchange of letters in November 1955 following Mills's attack on C107 in L957--in which Mills accuses Trilling of overlooking the Luce publications' misuse of the talented minds they seek, and Trilling in turn accuses Mills of anti-ideological elitism for dismissing the value of "technician[s]"--as revealing "a debate . . . between a celebration and a critique of American scholarship."

L938. Hough, Graham. *The Dream and the Task: Literature and Morals in the Culture of Today.* London: Duckworth, 1963. See p. 55.

Compares Trilling, "the finest untechnical critic of our own day," to Arnold in his habit of turning from literary to moral and social criticism, a habit which has made him "less a literary critic than a general cultural mentor to modern America."

L939. Howe, Irving. *A Margin of Hope: An Intellectual Autobiography.* New York: Harcourt Brace Jovanovich, 1982. See especially pp. 128-61, 229-32, 323-25.

A memoir shaped by Howe's conviction that "the years of my life coincided with the years of socialist defeat" in America. Chapter 6 ("Literary Life: New York"), recording Howe's years at *Partisan Review*, presents the controversy over Ezra Pound's 1948 Bollingen Prize as presaging Trilling's later revulsion from literary modernism. Later episodes recall Howe's 1954 attack (in M1017) on Trilling's approval of the growing accord between "wealth and intellect" in America (in C107). Suggests that Trilling did not grasp the quietistic implications of his ambivalence toward liberalism, despite attacks by Howe and others throughout the 1950's, until much later. Admires the "liberalism of spirit" with which Trilling sought "imaginatively to encompass extreme states of being that in his own moderate life he might never encounter directly," thus preventing his liberalism from lapsing into mediocrity, and wonders if it would be possible to combine Trilling's subtle dialectical reflectiveness with Howe's penchant for political activism.

L940. Jacoby, Russell. *The Last Intellectuals: American Culture in the Age of Academe.* New York: Basic, 1987. See pp. 25, 78-85, 102.

Criticizes Trilling as sharply limited in "the brilliance, originality, or force of his thought" whose social theory was "thin" and grasp of philosophy "weak." Reviews Trilling's disagreements with C. Wright Mills during the the 1950's, and argues that Trilling's occasional writings on Freud have overshadowed Norman O. Brown's *Life Against Death* only because of his membership in the influential New York intellectual circles that have marginalized Brown.

L941. Kadushin, Charles. *The American Intellectual Elite*. Boston: Little, Brown, 1974. See pp. 30, 105, 370, 376.

Names Trilling as one of the ten "most prestigious American intellectuals" in a poll taken in 1970, describing his position as a "reasserted liberalism" as against neoconservatism. A chapter by Thomas J. Conway places Trilling's 1950's work among that of "liberal-leftist Stalwarts" who, opposing "critical supporters" and "recalcitrants" during the cold war decade, generally supported American attacks on Communism.

L942. Kahn, Roger. *The Battle for Morningside Heights: Why Students Rebel*. New York: Morrow, 1970. See p. 193.

Briefly reviews Trilling's role in the Joint Committe on Disciplinary Affairs, concluding with a cameo of him "standing on the steps, looking at all the wreckage. A wonderful critic, a person like that. He seemed in shock. He was stooped and gray and crushed, as though *he* had been beaten."

L943. Kaul, A. N. *The American Vision: Ideal and Actual Society in Nineteenth-Century Fiction*. New Haven: Yale University Press, 1964.

Revises Trilling's premise of C90 that "American writers of genius have not turned their minds to society" by arguing that the uniqueness of the American novel is rooted "not in the [impoverished] social reality of America but rather in the novelists' conception of it," defined in terms of a vision of a closed, ideal community in its relation to the existing social order rather than of the manners appropriate to that existing order. Contrasts the institutional preoccupations of European novelists with the more general, idealized social critique of American novelists.

L944. Kazin, Alfred. *New York Jew*. New York: Knopf, 1978.

Kazin's third volume of autobiographical memoirs, despite describing Trilling as "an intense intellectual admiration of mine," paints an unusually ungenerous portrait of him as assuming the "conscious air" of the "voice of tradition" who would "meet the world only halfway" and who told Kazin that "he would not write anything that did not 'promote my reputation.'" Contrasts Trilling's affected cosmopolitanism, his determined defense of himself "from the many things he had left behind," with the ethnic forthrightness of Saul Bellow and Kazin himself, whom Trilling "would always [find] 'too Jewish,' too full of my lower-class experience." A propos of recalling meeting Trilling for coffee during the early 1950's, Kazin describes him as the propototype of "the ex-radical intellectuals [who] were . . . total *arrivistes* and accommodating in their thinking," an "expressive Hamlet of the intellect" distinguished by his capacity for "dramatizing his mind on paper."

For responses to Kazin's portrait of Trilling, see O1079.

L945. Kempton, Murray. *Part of Our Time: Some Ruins and Monuments of the 30's.* New York: Simon & Schuster, 1955. See pp. 121-23.

Describes Slesinger's novel *The Unpossessed* as a *roman a clef* documenting the political "hysteria" of a group of New York intellectuals whose revolutionary fervor represents "an aesthetic rather than a social tendency" and whose originals include "a critic of notable powers"--a reference to himself Trilling disputes in C180.

L946. Kostelanitz, Richard. *The End of Intelligent Writing: Literary Politics in America.* New York: Sheed and Ward, 1973. See especially pp. 50-53.

Identifies Trilling as "chief" of "the New York literary mob," and deplores his "over-inflated" reputation as "an elder statesman before his years."

L947. Kubal, David. *The Consoling Intelligence: Responses to Literary Modernism.* Baton Rouge: Louisiana State University Press, 1982. See especially pp. 27-32, 124-57.

Calls Trilling's attacks on the counterculture in A8 "the most cogently expressed criticism of modernism and of the truths that it holds sacred and self-evident," but argues that his critique of "the efficacy of the aesthetic mode" overlooks or marginalizes the attempt of many writers, from Bellow, Cheever, and Angus Wilson to Trilling himself and his surrogate John Laskell, to create "humane centers" whose function is "to affirm and to console while taking into account the worst that man has endured."

L948. Laing, R. D. *The Divided Self: An Existential Study in Sanity and Madness.* Second edition. Harmondsworth: Penguin, 1961. See pp. 39-40, 70.

Quotes B22 at length as a useful illustration of the difference between "*primary ontological security*" (here, in Keats and Shakespeare) and "*primary ontological insecurity*" (here, in Kafka and Beckett). Compares one of his case-studies to the situation of Tertan in C77.

For Trilling's reaction to the book, see A9.

L949. Lasch, Christopher. *The Minimal Self: Psychic Survival in Troubled Times.* New York: Norton, 1984. See pp. 200-201.

Aligns Trilling with Philip Rieff and Daniel Bell as "neoconservatives" who "see a strong social superego as the only reliable defense against moral anarchy," setting them against advocates of enforced social conformity, "liberal humanists" who adopt a laissez-faire attitude toward social behavior, and the revolutionary critique of the New Left.

L950. Lasch, Christopher. *The New Radicalism in America (1889-1963): The Intellectual as a Social Type.* New York: Knopf, 1965. See especially pp. ix-xviii, 286-349.

Examines the "new radicalism" of the American twentieth century--as distinct from progressivism, populism, and earlier left-wing movements--as resulting from the rise of intellectuals as a social class whose "fantasies of omnipotence" and "concomitant fears of hostility and persecution" made them see themselves as an embattled minority allied with other disempowered social classes and movements. Using Reinhold Niebuhr, Sidney Hook, Arthur Schlesinger, Dwight Macdonald, and Norman Mailer as examples, argues that postwar intellectuals' "confusion of politics and culture" focused their debates on the abstract confrontation between liberalism and radicalism as "rival myths of history" rather than on "the relation of cultural values to political action."

L951. Leavis, F. R. *Nor Shall My Sword: Discourses on Pluralism, Compassion and Social Hope.* London: Chatto & Windus, 1972. See pp. 39-74.

Reprints "Two Cultures? The Signficance of Lord Snow," the acrimonious response to Snow's Rede Lecture that provoked Trilling's assessment of the conflict in C170, with an additional note accusing Trilling of "*la trahison des clercs*" for questioning the relevance of Leavis's attack on Snow's novels. Includes Trilling in the group of commentators who have recoiled from Leavis's attack on Snow's credentials as a spokesperson for science while making no attempt to deal with the substance of Leavis's arguments in favor of the central position of literary culture.

L952. Leitch, Vincent B. *American Literary Criticism from the Thirties to the Eighties.* New York: Columbia University Press, 1988. See "The New York Intellectuals," pages 81-114.

Finds Trilling representative of the second (post-1940) phase of the circle of New York intellectuals whose earlier exemplar, in his socialist commitment, is Philip Rahv. Recognizing the frequently unconscious and antagonistic ways cultural conventions and beliefs operate, Trilling's criticism moves outside a narrowly sociological framework to psychoanalytic and dialectical perspectives. Describes Trilling as "the most committed to *Freudian* psychoanalysis" of the New York writers, but emphasizes his arguments in C80 against Freud's conception of the artist as neurotic and concludes that "Trilling 'saved' art from the charge of illness by bringing in not only sociology but aesthetics." Trilling's insistence on defining realism in terms that combined objective and subjective aspects leads him to urge as a critical method a dialectical "moral realism"--"a Jamesian theory of literature that never really caught on."

L953. Lewis, R. W. B. *The American Adam: Innocence, Tragedy, and Tradition in the Nineteenth Century.* Chicago: University of Chicago Press, 1955.

Recasts nineteenth-century American literature as a dialogue between the party of Hope, which saw the young republic as a new Adam unsullied by the European past, and the party of Memory, which deplored the emergence of the American Adam as dehumanized by severing its ties with the past. Identifies the central American literary tradition with a party of Irony--including Hawthorne, Melville, the theologian Theodore Parker, and the historian Orestes Brownson--which, following Trilling's dialectical conception of literature, aimed "both to undermine and to bolster the image of the American as a new Adam" by exploring the tragic implications of the Adamic figure in historical time.

L954. McCormick, John. *Catastrophe and Imagination.* London: Longmans, Green, 1957. See pp. 67-83.

Considers the evolution of the novel from social comedy celebrating the integration of individuals and society to social tragedy marking their dissolution and finally the novel of ideas. Argues that Trilling's pathology of the novel, based on an "Edwardian" sensibility, narrows the definition of social comedies to novels of manners and ignores the emergence, especially in America, of novels of ideas analyzing society in terms of the conflicts it poses between appearance and reality, despite the contrary evidence of Fitzgerald, Dos Passos, Bellow, and A3 itself.

L955. Marx, Leo. *The Machine in the Garden: Technology and the Pastoral Ideal in America.* New York: Oxford University Press, 1964. See especially pp. 341-45.

Notes the decisive influence of Trilling's "dialectical theory of culture" in C68 and Chase's dialectical reading of American fiction in L909, and proposes the rapid industrialization of America--"within the lifetime of a single generation, a rustic and in large part wild landscape was transformed into the site of the world's most productive industrial machine"--as the historical basis of the "profound contradictions of value" typical of American literature.

L956. Millgate, Michael. *American Social Fiction: James to Cozzens.* New York: Barnes and Nobel, 1964. See especially pp. 199-201.

Calling Trilling "the author of an impressive socio-economic novel," quotes his observation of the inferiority of recent American fiction to sociology in its sense of actuality, adding that the novelist cannot hope to compete successfully with "the sociologist proper" in this area. Concludes that despite Americans' lack of interest in writing novels of manners or picaresques, "the social novel may be more common in America, and commonly more distinguished, than Trilling allows."

L957. Mills, C. Wright. *Power, Politics and People: The Collected Essays of C. Wright Mills.* Edited with an introduction by Irving Louis Horowitz. New York: Oxford University Press, 1963. See "On Knowledge and Power," pp. 599-613.

Deplores the decline in the growing estrangement of power from learning, noting the small number of people who are both powerful and knowledgeable. Dismisses Trilling's view in C107 that a new intellectual class is rising to power as based on his observation that old intellectual groups have achieved limited measures of power and prosperity, and his "confusion of knowledge as a goal with knowledge as a mere technique and instrument."

For discussion, see L937.

L958. Mills, Nicolaus. *American and English Fiction in the Nineteenth Century: An Antigenre Comparison and Critique.* Bloomington: Indiana University Press, 1973.

Attacks Trilling's distinction in C90 between the American romance and the English novel of manners, deploring Trilling's influence in "initiating a series of critical misreadings of American fiction," and arguing, by means of comparisons of four pairs of American and English novels, that "American fiction gives an ultimate importance . . . to certain ideational or visionary concerns . . . transcendent of the social context" to which English fiction makes these concerns subordinate or coextensive. An appendix reviews A. N. Kaul's revision of Trilling's argument in L943, praising its important "corrections" but criticizing its oversimplified contrast between the institutional focus of European fiction and the idealized social concerns of American fiction.

L959. Milne, Gordon. *The American Political Novel.* Norman: University of Oklahoma Press, 1966. See pp. 139-49.

Concentrates on Trilling's use of major characters to express different political views, noting also his skill in observing the quirks that make both these characters and minor figures like Miss Paine and Mr. Gurney lively and individual, and his "clever and sophisticated style," which maintains "a coolness of tone . . rather unusual for a political novelist." Identifies "the need for human beings to adopt a responsible attitude" as the focus of Trilling's ideological critique and his "speculations about the large subjects of death and love."

L960. Minogue, Kenneth. *The Liberal Mind.* London: Methuen, 1963.

Defines liberalism as "goodwill turned doctrinaire," relying on peaceful persuasion and a secular world-view, whose ideological unity arises from its ambivalent impulse toward social reform.

L961. Pells, Richard H. *The Liberal Mind in a Conservative Age: American Intellectuals in the 1940s and 1950s.* New York: Harper and Row, 1985. See especially pp. 135-38.

Continues the historical exploration of L962 by examining the ambivalence of American intellectuals during the 1940's and 1950's to an increasingly conservative American culture. Identifies Trilling as one of a group of liberal intellectuals (Reinhold Niebuhr, Sidney Hook, Arthur Schlesinger, Daniel Boorstin, Seymour Lipset, Daniel Bell, Richard Hofstadter, Louis Hartz, John Kenneth Galbraith, Dwight Macdonald) who regarded the postwar drift toward prosperity and social conformism with "a mixture of contentment and uneasiness." Emphasizes the continuities between the "conservative" 1950's and the "radical" 1960's by noting the conservative values often preached by the New Left, stressing the "cultural rather than political or economic" nature of sixties radicalism, and establishing the roots of this radicalism in liberal intellectuals' critique of American culture in the 1950's.

L962. Pells, Richard H. *Radical Visions and American Dreams: Cultural and Social Thought in the Depression Years*. New York: Harper and Row, 1973.

Taking the Depression as a matrix of long-standing American social problems and the ideological debates surrounding them, characterizes American intellectuals of the 1930's as "both radical and conservative" in their attraction to collectivist ideals, their distaste for capitalism, and their admiration of Trotsky as an exemplary "cosmopolitan Jew" rendered more attractive by his political failures. Observes that because writers of the period wanted "not only a new party but also a new relationship between the intellectual and society" revealed in philosophy and art as well as political action, their social criticism was "as much cultural as political or economic." Along these lines, emphasizes Trilling's Freudian critique of capitalism as dehumanizing rather than economically exploitive and the "aesthetic" attack of *Partisan Review* on Stalinism as hostile to modernist art and literature rather than politically oppressive. Traces the deradicalizing after 1935 of ideals of community and central planning into calls for conformity and social control as "the demand for a conflict of classes became an appeal for national unity," calls for dissent were subsumed by calls for national unity, and philosophies of collectivism were superseded by the quest for personal survival in an absurd and tragic world.

L963. Phillips, William. *A Partisan View: Five Decades of the Literary Life*. New York: Stein and Day, 1983. See especially pp. 70-75.

Responds to the neoconservative bias of L896 and L965 by presenting an avowedly more liberal-minded memoir of the *Partisan Review* circle. Identifies Trilling as a "marginal" member of this circle, emphasizing his reserve, his habitual sense of complexity and ambiguity, and his aloofness from controversy (though mentioning arguments Trilling had with Norman Podhoretz over politics and with Donald Barthelme over the value of A3). Defends Trilling against Barrett's description of him in L896 as a forerunner of neoconservatism and against Kazin's charge in L944 that he "played down his Jewishness," citing his "strong support of Israel" and his temperamental reluctance to "wear one's star on one's sleeve."

L964. Phillips, William. *A Sense of the Present: Essays, Stories, and Reviews* (New York: Chilmark, 1967). See "What Happened in the 30's," pp. 12-29.

An important general analysis of radical politics and literature which notes the renewed interest in the 1930's with the turn toward radical politics, "temperate solutions having failed." Ascribes the contradictions between the universality of the Left's programs and "the sectarian crudity" of its activities to "the needs of the Communist party," which entangled American radicalism, naturally an "urban, intellectual, and critical" movement, with "the freewheeling, grass-roots tradition" at the same time disillusionment with Soviet Communism made "concern with socialism . . . wither away" rather than addressing its specific political problems. Describes the position of Phillips and other *Partisan Review* contributors as "for purity in politics and impurity in literature," an awareness of the dangers for literature of ideological orthodoxy. Distinguishes the New Left as concerned with humanity rather than politics, as "the avant-garde questions of the 30's have become the mass questions of today," finding the milder opposition of contemporary writers like Nabokov as operating "within the accepted world," and concluding that "the radical movement of the 30's broke the radical spirit of literature by lowering its sights and making it more palatable for popular consumption" and recommending that radical literature and radical politics be kept separate.

L965. Podhoretz, Norman. *Breaking Ranks: A Political Memoir*. New York: Harper & Row, 1979. See especially pp. 276-82, 295-304.

Sets Podhoretz's conversion from fifties radicalism to sixties neoconservatism against the cautionary figure of Trilling, who is repeatedly accused of a "failure of nerve" for declining, despite his revulsion from the New Left, to enlist in *Commentary*'s "no-holds-barred campaign . . . against the Movement." Agrees with Trilling's attacks on the valorization of insanity in C184 and on affirmative action in C185 but finds both essays intolerably freighted with "academic baggage" that muffles their point.

L966. Podhoretz, Norman. *Making It*. New York: Random House, 1967.

This notoriously self-promoting account of the success of the self-described "first son born to the family [of New York intellectuals] in the third generation" cites Trilling in its Acknowledgments as having "taught me more than he or I ever realized--though not, I fear, precisely what he would have wanted me to learn." Trilling appears briefly and sporadically throughout Podhoretz's memoir as his mentor at Columbia and later as the surprisingly resourceful, candid, and politically astute advisor who shocks him by asking what kind of power he wants and who, alone of all his Columbia friends, expresses pleasure when Podhoretz is invited to write for the *New Yorker*.

L967. Poirier, Richard. *The Renewal of Literature: Emersonian Reflections*. New York: Random House, 1987. See p. 192.

Suggests that Trilling's response to "what seemed to him the authentic historical pressures within a New York intellectual coterie that flourished in the 1940's and 1950's" marks a temporary detour from the the American tradition of thought that descends from Emerson to more recent American literary theorists.

L968. Raleigh, John Henry. *Matthew Arnold and American Culture*. Berkeley: University of California Press, 1957. See pp. 220-45.

Sets Trilling's "socioliberal" Arnold against the "poetic-religious" figure who influenced T. S. Eliot, noting that Trilling, seeing Eliot as "the proper Coleridge of his time" whose positions must be addressed however antipathetic they may be, often responds to Eliot's quarrels with Arnold's secular humanism in Arnold's name. Identifies the French Revolution and the ensuing romantic movement as Trilling's intellectual heritage, observing that he inherits from Arnold a tendency to continue the work of the Revolution through a friendly but often astringent criticism of liberalism in the manner of Forster. Like Arnold, who anoints poetry as the successor to religion, Trilling considers literature a criticism of life whose meliorative social function is too often overvalued by liberal critics who distrust any literature that does not simply reflect their own views. Notes Trilling's affinities with Freud as a descendant of romanticism, and describes A3 as a scaled-down version of *The Possessed*. Concludes that despite his frequent criticisms of Arnold, Trilling reaffirms his centrist literary judgments, opposing the excessive specialization and narrow technical focus of much academic criticism by emphasizing "the civilizing function of the novel."

L969. Reising, Russell. *The Unusable Past: Theory and the Study of American Literature*. New York: Methuen, 1986. See especially pp. 93-107.

Attacks Trilling's "notion of reality and his strategies for discussing it" as having exercised a prodigious but baneful influence on "both American historiography and literary criticism," contending that Trilling displaces the Progressive emphasis on "what, *in fact*, was the reality of history" with a counter-emphasis on "how people *felt* about reality and how their myths, images, and symbols dramatized these feelings." Argues that although Trilling's insistence on "the integrity of individual consciousness and the complexity of social reality" verges on "a critique of ideology far ahead of its time," this critique is compromised in Trilling (unlike Adorno and Marcuse) by his conception of the "literary idea" as insulated by formal ambiguity and balance from any ideological commitment, so that his dialectic ends by "functioning almost counter-dialectically as a tool for a kind of stasis" by abstracting ideas from the social contexts that would give them more than aesthetic potency.

L970. Riesman, David. *The Lonely Crowd: A Study of the Changing American Character*. New Haven: Yale University Press, 1950.

Distinguishes three personality types--the tradition-directed, formed by a society whose rituals control its behavior closely in order to encourage its survival and success; the inner-directed, accustomed to coping with a changing society by maintaining a balance between goals implanted early in life and the demands of the immediate surroundings; and the other-directed, whose main goal is approval by peers and authority figures and internalization of the changing goals urged upon it--and analyzes the rise of the other-directed personality in contemporary America. Exerts perhaps the greatest influence of any single book on Trilling's work of the 1950's (beginning with C101, his first essay for the *Griffin*) and after.

L971. Said, Edward W. *The World, the Text, and the Critic*. Cambridge: Harvard University Press, 1983. See pp. 142, 164-65.

Identifies Trilling as "the critic whose work in the United States had most assuredly placed English studies centrally on the literary agenda," excepting his work from the "endemic flaccidity" of English studies by noting his receptiveness in C159 and elsewhere to modernist writers from outside England and America.

L972. Scott, Nathan A., Jr. *Three American Moralists: Mailer, Bellow, Trilling*. Notre Dame: University of Notre Dame Press, 1973. See pp. 151-216.

Characterizes Trilling's position as a secular, centrist humanism attempting to mediate between the positivistic rationalism of the Enlightenment and the subversive powers of Romanticism--a position weakened in A3 and elsewhere by Trilling's unwillingness "to brook any theological possibility," which leads him to undermine Maxim's religious conversion by unsubstantiated hints of his continued opportunism. Notes that in the absence of religious belief, Trilling "appropriate[s] the testimony of the literary imagination as the material for a phenomenology of selfhood," but charges that the irreducible fact of self Trilling wants to maintain "beyond culture" is not biological but spiritual. Observing that A5 follows Jacques Maritain's critique of "angelism"--the pursuit of a life of unconditioned spirit rather than of particular manifestations of that spirit, argues that Trilling's "deepest misgiving" about modern adversary culture in A8 concerns its perversely unpleasurable angelism. Calls Trilling's humanism "anxious" not because it lacks self-confidence but because its allies, constantly failing to keep a distance from Romanticism or rationalism, dilute their commitment to a dialectical humanism. Criticizes Trilling for skirting the "large and genuinely philosophical effort" his criticism seems, like Coleridge's, to demand as its complement, but hopes that his tendency in A8 and A9 "to set aside his earlier Arnoldian faith in the redemptive power of art" is a sign of his readiness to engage in this further inquiry.

L973. Shechner, Mark. *After the Revolution: Studies in the Contemporary Jewish American Imagination*. Bloomington: Indiana University Press, 1987.

Defines the enabling condition of modern Jewish American writers as "the emergence of a demanding and intricate *self*," a self arising from the collapse of the social ideologies of the 1930's and crystallizing in the minds of such "non-Jewish Jews" as Trilling, Reich, Rosenfeld, Bellow, Mailer, Ginsberg, and Roth in the form of "psychoanalysis as a social idea" rather than "an evolving theory of mind" or "a therapeutic practice." Contends that espousing the "ideology" of psychoanalysis transformed Jewish-American writers "from revolutionists to convalescents." Describes Trilling, in contrast to his contemporary Jewish-American Adams, as "the Sartor Resartus of his generation," and compares his darkly Freudian politics of the 1940's to those of Arthur Schlesinger's Americans for Democratic Action as set forth in his anti-progressive *The Vital Center*.

L974. Slesinger, Tess. *The Unpossessed*. New York: Simon and Schuster, 1934.

A novel satirizing the social and political commitments of a group of thirties leftists whose private lives are variously devoted to aimless sexual relationships and the founding of a new little magazine. After sketching the relations among three central couples--Margaret Banner and Miles Flinders, Bruno Leonard and his cousin Elizabeth, and Jeffrey and Norah Blake--climaxes with a long chapter, "The Party," whose title and setting (a party to celebrate the launching of the new magazine) pun on the heroes' rootless commitment to American communism, and with Margaret's return home after aborting the child whose birth Miles has persuaded her would be a betryal of their leftist vocation. Widely received as a *roman a clef* about the Menorah circle whose leading figures included Slesinger herself (Margaret, or "Missis Flinders"), her husband Herbert Solow (Miles), Elliot Cohen (Bruno), and perhaps Trilling himself (though Trilling denies this in C180).

For discussion of the novel's historical and biographical import, see C180, L945, and M992. For a new edition with an afterword by Trilling, see B38.

L975. Snow, C. P. *The Two Cultures: And a Second Look: An Expanded Version of The Two Cultures and the Scientific Revolution*. Cambridge: Cambridge University Press, 1964. See pp. 94-97, 106-7.

Reprints Snow's 1959 Rede lecture, which had urged humanists to overcome their hostility to scientific education, with a long epilogue that cites C159 as posing, through its static, romantic conception of the artist's hostility to society, an unhealthy temptation to dismiss the claims of social justice in the name of a modernist aesthetic, and a footnote that complains that Trilling's attack on Snow in C170 misconstrues Snow's views and misrepresents Trilling's own.

The essay and its epilogue are reprinted in *Public Affairs* (New York: Scribner's, 1971), pp. 13-79.

L976. Tuttleton, James W. *The Novel of Manners in America*. Chapel Hill: University of North Carolina Press, 1972. See pp. 7-27.

Accepts Trilling's definition of manners in C90 but not the concomitant argument that the novel, or indeed the novel of manners, has not flourished in America. Argues that the novel of manners, occupying a midpoint between the two poles--the individual and society--between which all novelists mediate, is central to the tradition of the novel. Sets the unfortunate nineteenth-century prestige of the "romance as epic" reflected in Hawthorne against "the fundamental impulse of American fiction--a realistic impulse grounded in the commonplace actualities of our everyday experience"--

and notes that although Cooper, James, and Wharton all disparaged the thinness of social manners in America, their own novels "surprisingly transcend conditions that seem to them insurmountable."

L977. Tynan, Kenneth. *Curtains: Selections from the Drama Criticism and Related Writings* (New York: Atheneum, 1961). See "Culture in Trouble," pp. 375-79.

Briefly describes a television program in which Trilling, Jacques Barzun, and W. H. Auden "discussed 'The Crisis in Our Culture' with such fussy incoherence that they seemed to be not so much debating the crisis as embodying it." Observes that Trilling, who "leaned so far forward in cerebration that he appeared, in close shots, about to butt the camera," "had plenty to say, but seemed devoid of individuality" or appeal to a television audience.

L978. Wald, Alan M. *The New York Intellectuals: The Rise and Decline of the Anti-Stalinist Left from the 1930s to the 1980s*. Chapel Hill: University of North Carolina Press, 1987. See especially pp. 33-37, 46-75, 226-49.

Surveys the history of the New York intellectuals from an avowedly Trotskyite perspective, deploring their "deradicalization," a process in which Trilling was a leading figure, during and after the war. Accordingly finds Trilling's early work, including his stories and reviews for the *Menorah Journal*, more congenial than C84 and A3.

L979. Wallerstein, Immanuel. *University in Turmoil: The Politics of Change*. New York: Atheneum, 1969.

Analyzes in general terms the issues--the relation between universities and the government, the governance of universities, the ideals and tactics of social change--underlying the unrest at Columbia and other colleges during the 1960's. Dedicated to Trilling and Alexander Erlich.

L980. Webster, Grant. *The Republic of Letters: A History of Postwar American Literary Opinion.* Baltimore: Johns Hopkins University Press, 1979. See pp. 252-60.

Denies Trilling, the leading figure among the "Intellectual Men of Letters . . . a permanent place in critical history," since despite his important role as "the Intellectuals' consciousness," he "does not show us a new way to read and respond to literature." Observes that Trilling is the first of the Intellectuals to transcend Jewish provincialism and the first to "make the move from the avant-garde to the intelligentsia" by choosing an academic career. Calls "Trilling's application of literary standards of complexity to the politics of 1940 . . . his most important act as a critic" for its influence in critical politics, finding thereafter in Trilling's stubbornness in remaining within the humanistic tradition and his "compulsive attachment to dualistic forms of thought" the seeds of his growing irrelevance during the fifties. Ruling that "by reality . . . Trilling means that part of the world which is bourgeois, liberal, physical, scientific, positivistic, Philistine, and evil," suggests that Trilling at his best is able to maintain a fruitful tension between "bourgeois reality and avant-garde imagination," but that his failure to adapt to changing times destroyed this dualism, so that by the time of A8 "he has given up the struggle to comprehend contemporary life altogether" and can produce only the "threnody" of A10 and the "pointless" meditations of A9.

L981. Wilson, Edmund. *The Wound and the Bow: Seven Studies in Literature.* Boston: Houghton Mifflin, 1941.

Theorizes in seven essays a link, made most explicit in the concluding essay on *Philoctetes*, between artistic power and psychological disability as its enabling precondition.

For Trilling's reaction, see C80 and D355.

L982. Wise, Gene. *American Historical Explanations*, second edition, revised. Minneapolis: University of Minnesota Press, 1980. See Chapter 8, pp. 223-295.

Uses Trilling and Reinhold Niebuhr to illustrate the creation of a new "explanation-form" or paradigm shift in American studies from activist Progressive social and political optimism to a counter-Progressive perspective normalizing irony and ambiguity, rejecting "the Progressive-liberal belief in straight lines of experience" formed by liberalism and conservatism as tenable alternatives. Suggests that counter-Progressives like Trilling and Niebuhr "were once nourished on Progressive assumptions, but have come to sense life is more complicated than that, and have gone on to use this 'moment of truth' as the base point in their thinking." Argues that Trilling, who overlooks the "variously conservative, pessimistic, skeptical, ironical," counter-Progressive strain in Parrington, makes this strain central to his own thinking, which promotes sustained debate within liberalism rather than victory over conservatism. Contends that since Trilling defines experience as "basically paradox" and culture in terms of "what it *talks about*" rather than "what it *is*," his analysis is "*spectatorial*" rather than taking an active "*participant's*" role, but that he and Niebuhr nonetheless foster a crucial tendency among American historians like Arthur Schlesinger, Jr., and Henry Nash Smith to take "their basic categories from outside politics."

Section M

Essays

M983. Aaron, Daniel. "The Occasional Novel: American Fiction and the Man of Letters." *Studies in American Fiction* 5 (Spring 1977): 127-41.

Describes the occasional novel--the novel written by a critic, poet, or philosopher not by profession a novelist--as "schematic, unspontaneous, programmatic, self-conscious," subordinating character and situation to a moralistic or didactic purpose often articulated by a hero who stands for the author. Considers in detail four such novels--Edmund Wilson's *I Thought of Daisy*, Kenneth Burke's *Towards a Better Life*, George Santayana's *The Last Puritan*, and A3--concluding that they are limited not by their commitment to topical or didactic ideas, but because "they are too contrived or too theoretical or too constricted by the force of inner needs." Finds A3 in particular to offer "a dim sense of the events that, given the involvements of [its] main characters, might have been expected to press upon their lives," though acknowledging the pleasures offered by its style and penetration and agreeing with Trilling that "intellectual content can add an aesthetic dimension to the novel."

M984. Aldridge, John W. "Manners and Values." *Partisan Review* 19 (May-June 1952): 347-48, 350.

Following C90, maintains that "manners are the organized public manifestations of those dogmas, codes, myths, and moral ideosyncrasies which comprise the value system of a culture," and ascribes the passing of the novel of manners in America to a universal cultural homogenization from which only Boston and the Deep South have been exempt, since "without dogma . . . there can be no personality."

Enlarged and reprinted as Chapter 3 of *In Search of Heresy: American Literature in an Age of Conformity* (New York: McGraw-Hill, 1956), pp. 70-109.

M985. Alter, Robert. "Epitaph for a Jewish Magazine: Notes on the 'Menorah Journal.'" *Commentary* 39 (May 1965): 51-55.

Deplores the "self-consciously British and literary" tone of C55, remarking that "it is almost as if Trilling, himself the son of an immigrant, had invented a persona through which to speak" in distancing himself from "the alien Jew of mediocre talents." Takes C96 as evidence of "how much more securely placed the Jewish writer had become in the Anglo-American intellectual world by the 1950's."

M986. Alter, Robert. "On Walter Benjamin." *Commentary* 48 (September 1969): 86-93.

Reviewing Hannah Arendt's new selection of Benjamin's work, praises Benjamin by comparing him to Trilling as a Jewish-American critic of comparable scope, learning, and subtlety whose career, unlike Benjamin's, is "an achieved process of hyper-acculturation." Cites passages by Trilling and Benjamin on snobbery, on the novel, and on Kafka, observing that Trilling writes from a "psychologically protected" vantage, Benjamin as a socially implicated outsider; that Trilling regards the novel as "an extraordinary instrument of self-knowledge," Benjamin as a means of exposing a culture's insoluble problems; and that Trilling considers Kafka's parabolic fiction in the imprecise terms of dream and nightmare, Benjamin more profoundly as "lore in quest of Law."

Revised and reprinted as "Walter Benjamin: The Aura of the Past" in *Defenses of the Imagination: Jewish Writers and Modern Historical Crisis* (Philadelphia: Jewish Publication Society of America, 1977), pp. 47-66.

M987. Anon. "Educators Attack Congress Inquiries." *New York Times*, 18 November 1953, p. 28.

Reports the adoption by the faculty of Columbia College of a statement calling congressional investigations of the political backgrounds and sympathies of college teachers "unnecessary and harmful." Quotes the statement, drafted by a committee chaired by Trilling, as defending the right of teachers to invoke the Fifth Amendment without automatically furnishing sufficient grounds for their dismissal.

For Trilling's response, see E398.

M988. Anon. "Parnassus, Coast to Coast." *Time* 67 (11 June 1956): 65-70.

A cover story (Jacques Barzun is pictured on the cover) asking: "What does it mean to be an intellectual in the U.S.?" Contends that the opposing accusations of anti-intellectualism and anti-Americanism are becoming muted as "the Man of Protest" gives way to "the Man of Affirmation" as intellectuals have realized in the wake of the debunking of practical knowledge by the Depression that "they are true and proud participants in the American Dream." Cites C86 in support of the observation that "the easy liberalism of the past . . . has proved completely inadequate" as an article of intellectual faith," and C107 as evidence that "the alienation of intellectuals [from national life] may be a thing of the past."

M989. Barrett, William. "Art, Aristocracy, and Reason." *Partisan Review* 16 (June 1949): 658-65.

Reviews the debate initiated by Richard Chase in M996 and M998 and continued by various correspondents in G439, M997, and E390. Welcomes Trilling's remarks in E390 clarifying the focus and scope of his critique of liberalism, but contends that "the evil that corrupts liberal minds has its root, not in liberalism itself, but in some deeper condition of our culture." Criticizes Chase for having "tried to make of Mr. Trilling's critique what it cannot be: a *Weltanschauung*, a complete philosophy, a total view of life."

M990. Barrett, William. "Writers and Madness." *Partisan Review* 14 (January-February 1947): 5-22.

Dissents from Trilling's dismissal in C80 of the connection between neurosis and artistic talent, arguing in a note that the literary "process does . . . imitate the neurotic process and does exploit neurotic material"; that writers and other artists are "compelled by an excessive need for the winning of love"; and that "the writer's neurosis . . . attempts to square itself with reality--but only in the work," not, as Trilling suggests, in the writer's life as well. Contends that authors' tendency toward insanity through "identification with the objects of fantasy," as in Swift, has been greatly magnified by the distortions of modern society, which provide both authors' material and the frustration of their desires and forces them into an ever more "absorbing and terrifying" quest for personal authenticity.

For Trilling's rejoinder, see D355.

M991. Barzun, Jacques. "The Imagination of the Real, or Ideas and Their Environment." *Art, Politics, and Will* (F420), pp. 3-27.

Cites, in a "Prologue on Origins" to Barzun's discussion of the advent of the railroad, Trilling's and Barzun's

Colloquia on Modern Books at Columbia as representing "an original way of understanding both literature and history" in the face of the orthodoxies of Marxism and New Criticism, focusing on the study of ideas in the context of their historical "antecedents and concomitants *of whatever kind*" and their consequences, without reducing them to either "resultants" of their circumstances or hypostasized essences. Defines the leading difficulty of this "methodless method" as choosing the most illuminating historical conditions and avoiding "the fatal error of slipping into a new determinism" concerning these conditions.

M992. Biaggi, Shirley. "Forgive Me for Dying." *Antioch Review* 35 (Spring-Summer 1977): 224-36.

Briefly recounts the life of Tess Slesinger, identifying the originals of the principals of L974 as Elliot Cohen (Bruno Leonard), Max Eastman (Jeffrey Blake), Herbert Solow (Miles Flinders), and Slesinger herself (Margaret Flinders).

M993. Brooks, Van Wyck. "What Is Primary Literature?" *Yale Review* 31 (September 1941): 25-37.

Excoriates the neglect of universal primary literature, which "favors the life-drive" and "expresses the states of mind by which the race has risen," for the "coterie" and "sectarian" enthusiasms of Eliot, Pound, and Yvor Winters, who, elevating literary above "human values," judge poetry entirely on the basis of its language and form. Aligns Eliot's recasting of literary history with James's dismissal of Tolstoy and Joyce's impudent experimentalism, and suggests a return to such American writers as Whittier, who is "important for us" because of "his passion for freedom" and his ability to convey "a sense of one's group history."

For discussion, see M1030 and E382.

M994. Calinescu, Matei. "Modernity and Popular Culture: Kitsch as Aesthetic Deception." *Sensus Communis: Contemporary*

Trends in Comparative Literature/Panorama de la situation actuelle in Littérature Comparée. Edited by Jano Reisz et al. Tübingen: Gunter Narr, 1986. Pp. 221-26.

Follows the premise in C175 that modern high art dissociates itself from pleasure to pursue three theories of the deceptive nature of pleasure in popular art or kitsch: Adorno's "demonic" theory of popular art as an ideological ploy to control the masses, Abraham Moles's more ambivalent theory of kitsch as an aesthetic system of mass communication parasitic on the high art it emulates, and Umberto Eco's contrastingly "serene" theory of kitsch as "structural lying" by means of citing "a culturally 'prestigious' message in a context . . . whose general structure does not have the same characteristics of homogeneity, complexity, and necessity of the original context"--a theory which avoids both Adorno's diabolism and the cultural pessimism of conservative theorists like Trilling.

M995. Chanda, A. K. "The Young Man from the Provinces." *Comparative Literature* 33 (Fall 1981): 321-41.

Refines the paradigmatic nineteenth-century hero described in B19 by distinguishing the Young Man from the Provinces more sharply from the Sensitive Young Man (Pierre Bezukhov and Prince Myshkin), the self-made man (the heroes of Samuel Smiles and Horatio Alger), the parvenu (Bounderby and Silas Lapham), and the hero of the *Bildungsroman* (Wilhelm Meister and Ernest Pontifex). Examines the Young Man's descent from the picaro and the figures of Rousseau, Napoleon, and Benjamin Franklin, emphasizing his attempt to synthesize "romance and realism, the aristocratic and the bourgeois, the civilized and the pastoral, ambition and happiness, poetry and prose," defining himself through a romantic, compromised career of social climbing and an ensuing fall. Notes the Young Man's survival in "the modern existential hero" first personified by Raskolnikov.

M996. Chase, Richard. "Dissent on Billy Budd." *Partisan Review* 15 (November 1948): pp. 1212-18.

Argues that *Billy Budd* has been misread as a tragedy, since the social forces represented by the paternalistic Captain Vere and Claggart, a "self-righteous Liberal" like the Confidence Man, are opposed not by "Isaac or the fallen Adam or Oedipus," but by "the beatified boy of the liberal-progressive myth, the figure who gets 'pushed around.'" Concludes that Billy's "suffering and death are without moral content."

For discussion, see E390.

M997. Chase, Richard. "Liberalism and Literature." *Partisan Review* 16 (June 1949): 649-53. See E390.

Defines liberalism as "a belief in freedom and a copiousness and openness of mind and sentiment" whose modern instruments are "democratic, libertarian politics and the doctrine that the human reason, in its secular function, is capable of establishing the social conditions of freedom," and adding that unlike other disputants, he wishes "to make of liberalism a somewhat broader and more octopus-like ideal." Presses his attack on liberals like William Barrett who deny the power or political relevance of religion and literature, defends his description of Iago's behavior as a challenge liberalism has been unwilling to face and Claggart as "a fake liberal," and concludes that modern liberalism's commitment to Enlightenment ideals must be tempered by a critical attitude.

M998. Chase, Richard. "The Progressive Hawthorne." [Review of *The Portable Hawthorne*, edited by Malcolm Cowley (New York: Viking, 1948); Robert Cantwell, *Nathaniel Hawthorne: The American Years* (New York: Rinehart,

1948); and Randall Stewart, *Nathaniel Hawthorne* (New Haven: Yale University Press, 1948).] *Partisan Review* 16 (January 1949): pp. 96-100.

Dismisses Cowley's assessment of Hawthorne as necessarily either a progressive social liberal or a sacramental religious writer and ridicules Cantwell's reading of "My Kinsman, Major Molineux" as "rollicking" and his indictment of Aylmer in "The Birthmark" as "undemocratic."

For discussion, see E390.

M999. Connolly, Cyril. "E. M. Forster." *Britain To-day*, no. 104 (December 1944), pp. 20-24.

Uses Trilling's description of Forster's leading theme as "the undeveloped heart" as the basis for an examination of Forster's religion--"a primitive pantheistic paganism to which has been afterwards added an oriental preoccupation with non-attachment and abnegation, all worked upon by his inherited moral temperament"--and concludes that Forster sees virtue as having to be "punctiliously enforced, like vaccination."

Revised and reprinted as "The Art of Being Good: II. The Undeveloped Heart" in *The Condemned Playground: Essays 1927-1944* (London: Routledge, 1945), pp. 254-59.

M1000. Cook, Richard M. "The Public Critic and Poetry: A Case of Avoidance." *Modern American Cultural Criticism: Proceedings of the Conference, 17-18 March 1983*. Edited by Mark Johnson. Warrensburg: Central Missouri State University, 1983. Pp. 46-57.

Contends that the reason "public critics" like Trilling, Edmund Wilson, and Alfred Kazin neglect poetry in their work is because they oppose the generally technical and hermetic bias of contemporary criticism of poetry by emphasizing the ability of literature to provoke speculation on questions outside particular literary works, revealing their uneasiness not only with poetry but "literature in general." Observes that Trilling uses Keats's letters in B22 to encourage a reconsideration both of Keats and of the modern assumption that poetry is to be valued as autonomous and unconditioned, since he believes that "in demanding everything from poetry we have settled for too little," insuring the "approaching irrelevance" of poetry by blindness to its heroic sense of its own limits. Concludes that public critics, like Plato, refuse the suspension of their rational and moral engagement with historical reality which poetry seems to invite; Trilling in particular considers literature a function of human beings, not the reverse, and regards literature as proclaiming both the historical and ideological contingency of the human subjects and their ultimate and irreducible freedom.

M1001. Dahlberg, Edward. "Erskine Caldwell, and Other Proletarian Novelists." [Review of Erskine Caldwell, *God's Little Acre* (New York: Viking, 1933).] *Nation* 136 (8 March 1933): 265-66.

Links the inarticulate and derivative sterility of Caldwell to the "rattling puerilities and gawkish perambulations" of Dos Passos's recent introduction to *Three Soldiers*, which plays to "the left band-wagonists" by treating novels as commodities like ice cream.

For Trilling's response, see E378.

M1002. Dembo, L. S. "Dissent and Dissent: A Look at Fiedler and Trilling." *Contemporary American Jewish Literature: Critical Essays*. Edited by Irving Malin. Bloomington: Indiana University Press, 1973. Pp. 134-54.

Analyzes the connections between Fiedler's thunderous dissent from American cultural orthodoxies and Trilling's urbane critique of modern liberal culture. Traces Trilling's advocacy of the self in its quarrel with culture from A6 and

C159 back to C77, which shows Joseph Howe, despite his sympathy for Tertan, is "guilty of the same pigeonholing and categorization that marks the classroom domestication of modern literature." Concludes that both Fiedler and Trilling are in their antiformalism "victims of . . . methodologies and a priori conceptions" that make them, like all exclusively social critics, "prone to hyperopia."

M1003. Ellison, Ralph. "Society, Morality, and the Novel." *The Living Novel: A Symposium.* Edited by Granville Hicks. New York: Macmillan, 1957. Pp. 58-91.

Quotes at length a passage from C90 which has made "a single statement of Henry James more prominent in our thinking than all the complex aesthetic ideas spelled out in the Prefaces and the essays," arguing that Trilling has "missed the point" that the thinness James ascribes to American culture is "appalling [only] for the French and English imagination." Wonders what Trilling means by the "joke" that remains to Americans shorn of social rituals and "what the state of novel criticism would be today if Mr. Trilling had turned his critical talent to an examination of the American joke."

M1004. Epstein, Joseph. "One Cheer for E. M. Forster." *Quadrant* 29 (December 1985): 8-18.

Argues for the centrality of Forster's homosexuality to his work, suggesting that if Trilling had known about it when he wrote A2, he would have seen Forster's "emancipatory liberalism" as hiding a "homosexual utopian." Concludes that Forster's "polemical and didactic" novels have now been rendered obsolete by the widespread realization that the emancipation Forster so desired, like the liberal British culture he criticized, is "itself thin, hollow, and finally empty."

M1005. Fiedler, Leslie A. "*Partisan Review*: Phoenix or Dodo?" *Perspectives USA*, no. 15 (Spring 1956), pp. 82-97.

Notes that the "two-fold avant garde, political and artistic," championed by *Partisan Review* marks both a rift between its political progressivism and its nostalgia for the high modernism of the 1920's and a reason for its surprising influence. Traces the survival of the magazine's "old political passion" in the secular, sociological literary analysis of Trilling and Edmund Wilson. Observes that despite being a New York Jewish "exploiter of . . . anguish and alienation," Trilling "manages to preserve a remarkable aura of respectability not granted any of his colleagues" because of his "soft-spoken style."

M1006. Geertz, Clifford. "Found in Translation: On the Social History of the Moral Imagination." *Georgia Review* 31 (Winter 1977): 788-810.

Follows C191 in asking why "significant works of the human imagination . . . speak with equal power to the consoling piety that we are all like to one another and to the worrying suspicion that we are not." Contending that observers can apprehend a foreign culture "not by looking *behind* the interfering glosses which connect us to it but *through* them," indicates the influences of contrary ideals of Balinese culture as both "Shangri-La and Pandaemonium" on European observers' beliefs about their own culture, concluding that "other people's creations can be . . . utterly their own and . . . deeply part of us."

Revised and reprinted in *Local Knowledge: Further Essays in Interpretive Anthropology* (New York: Basic, 1983), 36-54.

M1007. Geertz, Clifford. "'From the Native's Point of View': On the Nature of Anthropological Understanding." *Bulletin of the American Academy of Arts and Sciences* 28 (January 1975): 26-45.

Uses the publication of Bronislaw Malinowski's *A Diary in the Strict Sense of the Term* to raise questions about how ethnographers, unless they are gifted with an unusual degree of sensitivity and empathy, can understand the foreign cultures they study. Contends that the ethnographer, proceeding not by intuitive empathy but by a study of the symbolic forms people use to project ideas of themselves, does not . . . perceive what his informants perceive," but rather "what they perceive 'with.'" Concludes that ethnographic understanding, which requires "a continuous dialectical tacking between the most local of local detail and the most global of global structure," is more like getting a joke or reading a poem than like achieving communion.

Revised and reprinted in *Local Knowledge: Further Essays in Interpretive Anthropology* (New York: Basic, 1983), pp. 55-70.

For Trilling's response, see C191.

M1008. Gunn, Giles. "The Moral Imagination." *Modern American Cultural Criticism: Proceedings of the Conference, 17-18 March 1983*. Edited by Mark Johnson. Warrensburg: Central Missouri State University, 1983. Pp. 26-38.

Urges against "the progressive discrediting and displacement of . . . traditional norms of evaluation" the examples of Edmund Wilson and Trilling as developing the position that literature has the moral function of challenging the official sanctions of received tradition and showing how they might be revised in the name of "some irreducible element within the self . . . beyond the reach of cultural control." Notes that Wilson located the obstacles to the intellect and imagination in the deficiencies of the environment and pursued them in biographical speculations, whereas Trilling rooted them within the individual and conceived them in more overtly political terms. Points out that Arnold, not Freud, provides Trilling's model for how culture transcends its limitations through the critical function of art, which renders potential modes of experience as actual. Criticizes Trilling's subordination of imagination to will, suggesting that "the moral function of the imagination might consist precisely in its ability to transcend the will and its own dream of virtue," as indicated by James and Nietzsche.

Revised and reprinted as "The Moral Imagination in Modern American Criticism" in L929.

M1009. Gunn, Giles. "The Semiotics of Culture and the Interpretation of Literature: Clifford Geertz and the Moral Imagination." *American Critics at Work: Examinations of Contemporary Literary Theory*. Edited by Victor A. Kramer. Troy, NY: Whitston, 1984. Pp. 396-420.

Reviews the discussion between Geertz (M1006 and M1007) and Trilling (C191) in order to indicate the relations between Geertz's cultural semoitics and Trilling's moral criticism based on "literary hermeneutics." Emphasizes Trilling's argument that self-critical thinking reveals the ability of the imagination to "obtain a knowledge of what we are not--namely, of other minds, even of alien cultures." Finds this dialectical nature of the imagination potentially fruitful to Geertz's conception culture as "an interwoven system of functional . . . symbolic forms." Agrees with Geertz that "art forms are generative as well as refractory" of experience, but raises with Trilling the question of what kinds of pragmatic changes cultural knowledge does and does not effect, suggesting that the relations between artists and their audiences "need to be reconceived as reciprocal rather than merely representational," enabling not "a reunification of humankind in allegiance to a wider humanism" but a dialogue of writers and readers "even across the divide of historical time and cultural space."

Revised and reprinted as "The Semiotics of Culture and the Diagnostics of Criticism: Clifford Geertz and the Moral Imagination" in L929.

M1010. Harder, Kelsie B. "Inside-Dopestered Critics: The Invasion of Literary Criticism by Sociologists." *Modern Age* 3 (Spring 1959): 143-47.

Warns of the ascendancy of a new generation of critics who either "eschew detailed analysis" (Leslie Fiedler and John W. Aldridge) or insist on reading "for a purpose" informed by psychology, sociology, history, economics, anthropology, or theology (Kenneth Burke, David Riesman, Alfred Kazin, Frederick J. Hoffman, Susanne Langer, and Trilling) rather than "for aesthetic appreciation." Praises Trilling as a "sane and clear" close reader of Wordsworth, but argues that when his individual essays are collected in A4 his ideological agenda displaces his literary interests.

M1011. Hollinger, David A. "Ethnic Diversity, Cosmopolitanism, and the Emergence of the American Liberal Intelligentsia." *American Quarterly* 27 (May 1975): 133-51.

Traces the rise during the 1930's of the intellectual ideal of cosmopolitanism--defined, as opposed to cultural pluralism, as the belief that ethnic and cultural differences within an assimilating culture are neither to be eradicated nor parochially preserved, but "viewed as repositories for insights and experiences that can be drawn upon in the interests of a more comprehensive outlook on the world." Notes Trilling's attraction to Edmund Wilson's broad learning and his personal "incarnation of the great tradition of Greenwich Village." Ascribes the assimilation of Jewish intellectuals to American literary culture largely to the anti-Stalinism and anti-Fascism that fostered cosmopolitan ideals and allowed the new cosmopolitans to show "selective appreciation for American provincialism" in books like *Let Us Now Praise Famous Men*. Observes the rift between cosmopolitan and parochialism debated in (and between) the *New York Review of Books* and *Commentary*, and suggests that cosmopolitans ideals have flourished most vigorously in connection with intellectuals' conceptions of themselves as separate and comfortably elite rather than obliged to justify their intellectual beliefs and styles to a non-intellectual audience.

Revised and reprinted, with a headnote, in L935.

M1012. Honan, Park. "Arnold, Eliot, and Trilling." *Matthew Arnold in His Time and Ours: Centenary Essays*. Edited by Clinton Machann and Forrest D. Burt. Charlottesville: University Press of Virginia, 1988. Pp. 171-82.

Contends that grappling with Arnold's conception of culture helped both Eliot and Trilling to become important critics. Identifies A1, despite its limitations and inaccuracies, as valuable for having helped Trilling to purge "his debilitating emotions about Arnold." Suggests that culture, a notion that emphasizes the relation between art and society, provides a corrective in Eliot's writing to his early aestheticism and a continuing basis for Trilling's dialectics, even when it is own "faith in Arnoldian humanism" that comes under attack in his later work, by focusing his awareness of both the release and the dangers of irrational atavism on "the emotional basis" of gestures in support of or attack on culture.

M1013. Hook, Sidney. "Anti-Semitism in the Academy: Some Pages of the Past." *Midstream* 25 (January 1979): 49-54.

Recalls Trilling's threatened termination as an instructor at Columbia in 1936, despite his love of teaching and his "satisfactory progress" on the dissertation that became A1, as motivated by anti-Semitism. Reports that Trilling asked Hook for advice and Hook suggested that Trilling confront his chair with an accusation of anti-Semitism, a strategy that proved successful when Trilling was appointed the first Assistant Professor of English at Columbia.

For a sharply contradictory account of this episode that calls Hook's story "a bargain-basement version of the actual scenario," see G540.

M1014. Hook, Sidney. "The Strange Case of Whittaker Chambers." *Encounter* 46 (January 1976): 78-89.

Identifies Trilling as having arranged Hook's first meeting with Chambers in spring 1934 in order to have Hook explain his theory of "social-fascism" to Chambers, and recounts Chambers' determined attempts, like Maxim in A3, to give himself a public identity after his defection from the Communist Party in 1938.

For discussion, see O1079.

M1015. Howe, Irving. "James T. Farrell--The Critic Calcified." *Partisan Review* 14 (September-October 1947): 545-52.

Defends C84 against Farrell's attack in G463 as "not a thesis or an argument" but "a work of art" whose purpose is "to dramatize a situation" in all its "*emotional ambiguity.*" Observes that Farrell's position as "the Yvor Winters of the left," which makes his criticism unremittingly reductive, would render him unworthy of attention if he did not raise exemplary questions, as a figure who is "becoming the center of a myth," about why so few contemporary novelists write criticism and whether concurring in his political values necessarily entails agreeing with his kind of criticism.

M1016. Howe, Irving. "The New York Intellectuals: A Chronicle and a Critique." *Commentary* 46 (October 1968): 29-51.

This seminal discussion of its subject describes the New York intellectuals as the only true intelligentsia in American history, an exception to the native tradition of isolated individuality. Traces their roots to "the world of the immigrant Jews" they struggled to leave behind by espousing the political Left, the literary avant-garde, and more briefly and fitfully, the sociology of mass culture. Observes that the intellectuals were never "at the center of cultural life in the 30's," since "their best hours were always spent on the margin, in opposition." Acknowledges that as the leading figures of the circle--Rahv, Phillips, Trilling, Rosenberg, Abel, Kazin, Hook, Schwartz, Bellow, Goodman, Rosenfeld, and Schapiro--emerged clearly after the war, "their internal distintegration" had already begun to take them "racing or stumbling from idea to idea," but vigorously defends their anti-Communism throughout the fifties, and identifies this period as the richest for critics like Trilling, Rahv, Chase, and Dupee. Suggests that "the remarkable absorptiveness of modern society" could accommodate the intellectuals' challenging critical essays for the sake of their excitement as performance. Ascribes the group's survival to the appeal of their complex, ironic style; their identification with a pre-eminent American city, and their continuing institutional force, if only as an influence to be shaken off. Contrasts the intellectuals with their generational challengers, loosely identified with Norman Mailer, Norman O. Brown, Herbert Marcuse, Marshall McLuhan, and the New Left, whose "*psychology of unobstructed need*" assumes that "everything touched by older men reeks of betrayal." Condemns the guaranteed success of this "new sensibility," its trivializing of cultural problems like alienation, and its abdication of judgment, but expresses pessimism that the New York intellectuals will be able to mount a serious challenge to its avatars.

M1017. Howe, Irving. "This Age of Conformity." *Partisan Review* 21 (January-February 1954): 7-33.

Deplores Trilling's satisfaction in C107 with the current accord between "wealth" and "intellect," arguing that "culture has acquired a more honorific status" because "'intellect' no longer pretends to challenge 'wealth'"; instead, tamed intellectuals have been largely absorbed into government bureaucracies and "the constantly growing industries of pseudo-culture" as "the ideology of American capitalism" has come to dominate all modes of cultural expression.

M1018. Jumonville, Neil. "The New York Intellectuals' Defense of the Intellect." *Queen's Quarterly* 97 (Summer 1990): 290-304.

Dissents from recent political explanations (in L906, L911, and L978) of the New York intellectuals' "apparent journey from the political left to the centre," arguing that their gradually changing political orientation, "prompted by their need to define the proper function of the intellectual" after the war, was predicated on their identity as intellectuals rather than the other way around. Describes the postwar intellectuals' hostility to the New Left and counterculture movements as based on an anti-absolutism--a fear of romantic irrationality threatening to their "vision of what it meant to be free, independent, unbeholden intellectuals" and their "right to continue questioning"--consistent with their earlier anti-totalitarianism. Notes that Trilling's fear that his students would be "fatally undermined" by the very modernism that had nurtured him is developed by Daniel Bell into a distinction between a high adversary culture and a mass counterculture.

M1019. Kramer, Hilton. "Unreal Radicalism." [Review of John W. Aldridge, *In Search of Heresy: American Literature in an Age of Conformity* (New York: McGraw-Hill, 1956).] *Partisan Review* 23 (Fall 1956): 553-56.

Ridicules the attempt by Aldridge, who "would like to be radical without being political," at a social analysis of contemporary fiction that relies on Trilling and David Riesman for its analysis of the Age of Conformity, emphasizing the decline of the novel of manners and never mentioning the Cold War or the political tensions that continue to animate American fiction.

M1020. Krupnick, Mark. "An American Life." [Review of L944.] *Salmagundi*, nos. 44-45 (Spring-Summer 1979): 197-204.

Attacks L944 as trading too facilely on Kazin's Jewishness, using the Holocaust to counterpoint his own personal success, and settling scores with "'refined' Jews" like Trilling by dismissing them as more interested in "manners" than politics, even though Kazin himself is equally interested in manners and equally uncommitted politically. Suggests that Kazin's awareness of the American tendency toward endless self-creation, rather than the Holocaust, gives meaning and form to his own life and work.

M1021. Krupnick, Mark. "Fathers, Sons, and New York Intellectuals." [Review of L903.] *Salmagundi*, no. 54 (Fall 1981): 106-20.

Noting that the New York intellectuals produced "little in the way of abstract thought" or "original art," defines their "project" not in terms of their relation to Marxism but in "their self-conscious relation to their origins," especially their ambivalence about their immigration, alienation, and acculturation as Jews to a Gentile world. Calls Bell's cultural "antimodernism" a generational development of Trilling's "conservatively toned liberalism" that omits Trilling's "liberal-humanist emphasis on individual autonomy and self-realization" in its "rediscovery of religion" and renewed "fidelity to 'the old system,' which is more fundamental than ideology."

M1022. Krupnick, Mark. "The Menorah Group and the Origins of Modern Jewish-American Radicalism." *Modern Jewish Studies Annual* 3 (1979): 56-67.

Examines the initial attraction of Jewish-American intellectuals to thirties radicalism by linking it to the cultural Jewish radicalism of the *Menorah Journal* under Elliot Cohen. Notes that the writers Cohen recruited for the *Journal*--Clifton Fadiman, Herbert Solow, Anita Prenner, Tess Slesinger, Albert Halper, Felix Morrow, Henry

Rosenthal, and Trilling--were joined by their hostility toward "the institutions and ideology of the organized Jewish community" that expressed itself initially, as in C56, in cultural criticism, but later, after the 1929 stock market crash, broadened to a more general political critique of the American Jewish Committee and the capitalistic politics of Zionism which led to Cohen's resignation, at editor Henry Hurwitz's request, and the departure of Trilling and the other writers.

M1023. Krupnick, Mark. "The Neoconservative Imagination." [Review of L965.] *Salmagundi*, nos. 47-48 (Winter-Spring 1980): 202-8.

Notes the tendency of "New York literary intellectuals of his time [to] measure themselves against Trilling," observing that Podhoretz attacks Trilling for "his lack of wholeheartedness in repudiating the Left" in A8 and A9. Remarking Podhoretz's tendency to borrow more from Trilling's uncharacteristic political polemics than from his carefully ambivalent analyses of culture, identifies Podhoretz as "the true heir not of Trilling but of Trilling's enemies, the would-be American Lenins Podhoretz professes to despise."

M1024. Krupnick, Mark. "The Two Worlds of Cultural Criticism." *Criticism in the University*. Edited by Gerald Graff and Reginald Gibbons. Evanston: Northwestern University Press, 1985. Pp. 159-69.

Offers several explanations for contemporary leftist critics' neglect of such American precursors as Trilling, Philip Rahv, and Harold Rosenberg: the impatience of the New York critics with close analysis and even sustained argument, their indifference to technical philosophy and their consequent lack of an assimilable critical method, and their affinities with popular journalism. Argues nonetheless that "the central tradition in American criticism" is "culturally oriented and journalistic." Explores the drift from this tradition and its potential recovery by contrasting the careers of Trilling, who gradually retreats from politics into the university, and Edward Said, whose growing eclecticism in "bring[ing] his philosophical interests to bear on immediate cultural issues is bringing him ever closer in method and tone to New York-style cultural criticism."

M1025. Lehan, Richard. "Dreiser and the Hostile Critics." *Old Northwest* 10 (Fall 1984): 307-17.

Defends Dreiser against Trilling's attack in C86 by arguing that critics can appreciate both James and Dreiser without choosing between them; that Dreiser's inchoate philosophy does not muddle his fiction because he is attempting to dramatize conflict rather than embody a system; that Dreiser is more fairly compared to Howells and Richard Wright than to James, who drew on very different social material; and that Dreiser is much less inclined toward didacticism or moral suasion than Howells and Wright, and so "is able to say more about the [social] machine than a Howells, and willing to say less than a Wright." Concludes by criticizing Trilling's unawareness of the "dualism [that] was the source of Dreiser's vision and his salvation as a novelist."

M1026. Lelchuk, Alan. "The Death of the Jewish Novel." *New York Times Book Review*, 25 November 1984), pp. 1, 38-39.

Illustrates the declining prestige of Jewish-American ethnic fiction by telling how "inappropriate" Trilling pronounced Saul Bellow's informal autobiographical remarks about "Jewish ghetto life" at a Brandeis commencement.

For a reply by Diana Trilling, see O1078.

M1027. Levine, Paul. "American Bards and Liberal Reviewers." *Hudson Review* 15 (Spring 1962): 91-109.

Reviews the weaknesses in the "liberal" critics responsible for "virtually all the signficant attempts to define American culture for our times." Notes the shifts in the meaning of "liberal" between V. L. Parrington and Van Wyck Brooks and a later generation that includes Trilling, Alfred Kazin, Leslie Fiedler, Richard Chase, and Norman Podhoretz. Calls Trilling the most influential and interesting of liberal critics, arguing that the "intellectual elitism" common to liberal critics, which motivates his attempt to "separate liberalism form political reality" by conflating intellectualism with liberalism and linking the imagination insistently with politics, leaves him with "a chronic inability to accept the totality of American society as it actually exists."

M1028. Longstaff, S. A. "The New York Family." *Queens Quarterly* 83 (Winter 1976): 556-73.

Outlines several transformations of the New York intellectuals between 1936 and 1966, focusing on their shift from left-wing politics to avant-garde cultural issues with the coming of war, their unexpected assumption of "a leading part in the cultural Cold War," their division by their different stands on the American Committee for Cultural Freedom in the 1950's, their renascence with "the ascendancy of 'Jewishness' in American letters," and the final rupture of the group over American involvement in Vietnam.

Revised and incorporated into N1070 as Chapter 1.

M1029. Longstaff, S. A. "*Partisan Review* and the Second World War." *Salmagundi*, no. 43 (Winter 1979), pp. 108-29.

Argues that "the very Marxist beliefs and habits of mind that . . . fortified the [*Partisan Review*] editors and their collaborators in their early opposition to the party and its Popular Front allies also led to their disablement a few years later as they tried to come to grips with World War II."

Uses the lukewarm (and aesthetic rather than political) response of Trilling and others to Dwight Macdonald's call for repudiation of the Brooks-MacLeish thesis (see E382, M993, M1030, and M1031) to contrast their "narrow, evasive, and ultimately debilitating" recasting of radicalism in literary terms with Macdonald's more forthright and consistent political commitment.

M1030. Macdonald, Dwight. "Kuturbolschewismus Is Here." *Partisan Review* 8 (November-December 1941): 442-51.

Characterizes M993 (and inferentially M1031) as "a Dadaist gesture in reverse," evidence of a "swing back to bourgeois values" so hysterical in its rejection of "the living tradition of our age" that it makes Brooks, once the leading progressive critic in America, "our leading mouthpiece for totalitarian cultural values." Links Brooks's dismissal of modernist writers as coterie writers in the name of his devotion to "a sapless respectability" to the Moscow Trials' indictment of the political heterodoxy of Soviet writers. Asserts that "in an age of social decay, it is only by rejecting the *specific* and *immediate* values of society that the writer can preserve those *general* and *eternal* human values with which Brooks is concerned."

For discussion, see E382.

M1031. MacLeish, Archibald. "The Irresponsibles." *Nation* 150 (18 May 1940): 618-23.

Deplores the split of the man of letters into the modern scholar and writer. Charges that the factitious professionalism of literary scholars, coupled with contemporary scholars' and writers' indifference to moral values in the name of "objectivity," has allowed the rise of fascism by declining to oppose it.

For discussion, see M1030 and E382.

M1032. Matthews, Herbert L. "Homage to Orwell." *Nation* 175 (27 December 1952): 597-99.

Disputes Orwell's analysis of the Spanish Civil War as a "betrayal of the social revolution by the communists" as undermined by Orwell's local partisanship and political naivete, which prevented him from realizing until after writing *Homage to Catalonia* that "the government was not run or controlled by Communists." Criticizes C100 for "tak[ing] Orwell literally and uncritically."

For Trilling's response, see E395.

M1033. Mazzeo, Joseph. "Comments on Trilling Talk of October 25, 1973." *[Columbia University] Seminar Reports* 1 (7 December 1973): 4.

Traces the conflict between liberal and general education back to Athens and the Renaissance, but contends that the problem Trilling discusses in C187 has become far more serious in the U.S. because America's "commitment to universal education, technology, and longevity" have created "the most heterogeneous and variegated system of education in the world"--a problem likely to be further exacerbated by the current movement toward greater professional specialization.

M1034. Merrill, Robert. "Another Look at the American Romance." *Modern Philology* 78 (May 1981): 379-92.

Argues that the novel, not the romance, is the central mode of American fiction, and that *The Scarlet Letter* has repeatedly been misread as a romance by critics who, following the "hints" of C90 and C92, overlook the "identification and empathy" with the principals which gives readers the experience of tragedy rather than the more disengaged, analytical experience of romance.

M1035. Meyer, Bernard. "Psychoanalytic Studies on Joseph Conrad: II. Fetishism." *Journal of the American Psychoanalytic Association* 22 (April 1964): 357-91.

Uses Conrad's fascination with hair and his ambivalent portraits of idealistic heroes slavishly devoted to demanding women as evidence of a castration anxiety which links his fiction, especially such "poorer works" as "The Return," "The Planter of Malata," and *The Arrow of Gold*, to Sacher-Masoch's *Venus in Furs* as a revealingly autobiographical account of masochistic fetishism.

For Trilling's response, see E419.

M1036. Miller, Merle. "Why Norman and Jason Aren't Talking." *New York Times Magazine*, 26 March 1972, pp. 34-35, 111-18.

Describes at length the "feud" between Norman Podhoretz, editor of *Commentary*, and Jason Epstein, a founder of the *New York Review of Books*, tracing their relationship from their years together at Columbia to their current mutual disenchantment.

For Trilling's response, see E414.

M1037. Mizener, Arthur. "The Novel of Manners in America." *Kenyon Review* 12 (Winter 1950): 1-19.

Observes that the leading problem for contemporary novelists is to absorb their discriminating personal awareness into an awareness of the larger social scene, adding that most recent American novelists choose one kind of awareness over the other instead of attempting to incorporate both, as in the novel of manners described in C90. Predicts that the novel of manners is more likely to grow out of Fitzgerald's concern with individual moral problems than the more abstractly conceived social pageantry of Dos Passos, which "hardly ever gets around to manners at all."

M1038. Moynihan, Daniel P. "An Address to the Entering Class at Harvard College, 1972." *Commentary* 54 (December 1972): 55-60.

Commends A3, along with Joseph A. Schumpeter's *Capitalism, Socialism, and Democracy*, to a freshman class that is "living in the future about which they wrote." Discusses the relation between Schumpeter's prediction that capitalism would be destroyed by an anti-capitalist intellectual class it had fostered itself and Trilling's observation that intellectuals entering into politics would become hypocritical and corrupt, leading to a decline in both "the language of politics" and "confidence in politics." Notes that although Laskell's *via media* has not yet been discredited in the academy, it is no longer confidently espoused, and enjoins his audience to resist the attack on the academy by ideological extremists from either left or right.

Revised and reprinted in *Coping: Essays on the Practice of Government* (New York: Random House, 1973), pp. 405-19.

M1039. Murphy, Geraldine. "Romancing the Center: Cold War Politics and Classic American Literature." *Poetics Today* 9, 4 (1988): 737-47.

Analyzes the tendency of Trilling, Richard Chase, and others to read American novels as romances as "a way to square American literature with the aesthetics of high modernism and thereby wrest it from the cultural sphere of the left." Contends that the modernist ideology of American romance, which "staked out the cultural center between realism and nativism on the left and elitist, New Critical modernism on the right," is parallel to "the struggle for control of the political center" as the New York intellectuals "withdr[ew] from the left under the colors of the left" by endorsing a narrative form which "promoted freedom," as against the novel's "coercive" insistence on verisimilitude and social integration.

M1040. Nichols, Lewis. "In and Out of Books." *New York Times Book Review*, 12 April 1959, p. 8.

Noting J. Donald Adams's attack (G431) on Trilling's birthday speech on Robert Frost (C140), quotes Frost in response: "I don't mind being brought out this way. . . . I avoid so much writing about me that it's good to hear some of it." Notes Frost's nervousness during the reading that followed Trilling's remarks: "I'm still investigating myself. I'll be investigating myself for a week. . . . Oh, dear, I haven't been given to think about myself so much in my whole life."

M1041. Niebuhr, Reinhold. "Ten Years That Shook My World." *Christian Century* 56 (26 April 1939): 542-44.

Anticipates the preface to A4 in its charge that as bourgeois culture has appropriated the achievements and insights of liberal Christianity (chiefly a "faith in man" and human history) to the requirements of a rootless contemporary skepticism or a facile optimism, "liberal culture has not seen the problem of mankind in sufficient depth to understand its own history."

Reprinted as "The Liberal Illusion" in *The Strenuous Decade: A Social and Intellectual Record of the 1930s*, edited by Daniel Aaron and Robert Bendiner (Garden City: Doubleday Anchor, 1970), pp. 493-98.

M1042. Ohmann, Richard. "Teaching and Studying Literature at the End of Ideology." *The Politics of Literature: Dissenting Essays on the Teaching of English*. Edited by Louis Kampf and Paul Lauter. New York: Pantheon, 1972. Pp. 160-89.

Attributes the "second environment" described in C179 to the New Critics' revival of literary studies by withdrawing from politics--though actually embodying a profoundly bourgeois ideology "identified with a pluralism that would help preserve individual freedom," and so masking its ideological program--elevating both the literary imagination and critical discourse above social engagement or effects. Calls for humanists to examine more critically the political implications of contemporary literary studies, in which humanism itself has played such an oppressive role.

Revised and reprinted as Chapter 4 of *English in America: A Radical View of the Profession* (New York: Oxford University Press, 1976), pp. 66-91.

M1043. Pearce, Roy Harvey. "Historicism Once More." *Kenyon Review* 20 (Autumn 1958): 554-91.

Cites C75 in support of the conception of criticism, against the New Critics, as a form of historical understanding, and A6 as providing an account of the "absolute *humanitas* which sets the creative writer's intention to create an ideally possible whole out of historically conditioned cultural data."

Revised and reprinted in *Historicism Once More: Problems & Occasions for the American Scholar* (Princeton: Princeton University Press, 1969), pp. 3-45.

M1044. Pease, Donald E. "The Cultural Office of Quentin Anderson." *South Atlantic Quarterly* 89 (Summer 1990): 583-622.

Analyzes Anderson's shifting use of A4 between 1957 and 1983, first to establish the terms validating the triumph of the receptively liberal imagination in fitting the demands of the self to the requirements of the social scenes, then later to recovering such political threats as Stalinism and the counterculture as "vulgarizations of internal attitudes," or heresies of the imperial self. Argues that after Trilling's own liberal imagination became "a political issue dividing his generation from his students" in the 60's, effectively removing him from the political scene rather than empowering him in or over it, Anderson, driven by the continuing "compulsion" to re-enact his mediatory position between Trilling and the political Philistines and blind to the specific political circumstances that conditioned the dialectic between self and society, invoked Trilling through "a powerful negation," defining the imperial self as the absence of the liberal imagination in order to claim the "utopian energies" released by the counterculture for "the dominant cultural realm that Trilling and [Richard] Chase had previously cordoned off from politics."

M1045. Pecora, Vincent P. "Adversarial Culture and the Fate of Dialectics." *Cultural Critique*, no. 8 (Winter 1987-88), pp. 197-216.

Cites the Preface to A5 in an attempt to ascertain whether there are ruling ideas. Argues that Trilling's image of an internal prison to describe the adversarial culture "both reveals and obscures the sense of anything called a ruling idea," since it exemplifies Marx's belief that "a general suspicion toward one's ruling ideas may after all be the bourgeois mode of thought par excellence" by ascribing to the revolution a dialectical suspicion actually rooted in the "market economy that promotes . . . suspicion of everything beyond what can be blindly appropriated." Discusses the difficulty of mounting a cultural critique outside the terms of a dialectic that can be appropriated by the market economy and its discourses.

M1046. Philipson, Morris H. "Some Reflections on Tragedy." *Journal of Philosophy* 55 (27 February 1958): 197-203.

Cites C95 at the climax of a discussion of the mimetic aspect of Aristotle's definition of tragedy ("What is life *like*?") as indicating that "it is possible to apply a pragmatic test to the form of a literary work" which can "tell, by the satisfaction one takes in the experience of a literary work, what kind of life one would actively lead." Suggests that future criticism is likely to develop in the direction marked out by Trilling and Kenneth Burke, "where the psychological and ethical questions are brought into conjunction, in the special light of the 'philosophy of literary form.'"

M1047. Poirier, Richard. "The Art of Poetry II: Robert Frost." *Paris Review*, no. 24 (Summer-Fall 1960): 88-120.

An interview in which Frost points out that Trilling's birthday speech was not "correcting some sort of public ignorance" about Frost's work but a mistake Trilling had made himself, and recalls that Frost "thought at first he was attacking me" and was still puzzled "when he began comparing me to Sophocles and D. H. Lawrence," but found "his defense of it" (in C140) "very clever . . . very interesting."

M1048. Rahv, Philip. "Proletarian Literature: A Political Autopsy." *Southern Review* 4 ([Winter] 1939): 616-28.

Argues that the revolutionary program calling for writers to "*ally [themselves] with the working class and recognize the class struggle as the central fact of modern life*" doomed writers to an alliance with the Communist Party, which, by focusing on the private lives and political beliefs of individual authors rather than on the literature they produced and by proscribing the empirical analysis of ideas characteristic of the novel, killed the attempt it sought to foster toward a serious proletarian literature. An important anticipation of much of Trilling's writing on literature and ideology.

Revised and reprinted in *Literature and the Sixth Sense* (Boston: Houghton Mifflin, 1969), pp. 7-20.

M1049. Renfrow, Jack N. "Hamlet and the Psychologists." *Shakespeare Newsletter* 13 (April 1963): 20.

Concluding a review of Freudian readings of *Hamlet* by Ernest Jones, Theodore Reik, Norman Symons, Frederic Wertham, and James C. Maloney and Lawrence Rockelein, agrees with C69 that Oedipal readings, despite their occasional excesses, have uncovered "a new point of interest" in the play.

M1050. Richler, Mordecai. "Literary Ids and Egos." [Review of L944.] *New York Times Book Review*, 7 May 1978, pp. 1, 38-39.

Expressing wonder at "what self-serving rascals most of our literary heroes are," approvingly cites several anecdotes Kazin tells about Trilling's determination to avoid appearing "too Jewish" or publishing anything that did not help his reputation.

For discussion, see O1079.

M1051. Rosenberg, Bernard. "Mr. Trilling, Theodore Dreiser (and Life in the U. S.)." *Dissent* 2 (Spring 1955): 171-78.

Argues that Dreiser, despite Trilling's charges to the contrary, excels in reporting "the social fact," and that Trilling's "incapacity to see the strength and the truth in Dreiser's novels," which tell "what it means to live in the country of the dollar," is "deeply related" to his recreation of *Bouvard and Pécuchet* in C112 as a novel about "life" rather than the bourgeoisie, removing "the sting and the pain" from Flaubert's social analysis.

M1052. Rosenberg, Harold. "Twilight of the Intellectuals." *Dissent* 5 (Summer 1958): 221-28.

Agrees with Raymond Aron's distrust of intellectuals in *The Opium of the Intellectuals*, but argues that American attempts to vanquish or supplant the intellectual class have led to the rise of a group of "intellectual[s] without ideas" whose function, "to stand guard against ideas as a disintegrating force," has led to a viewpoint as doctrinaire as the ideological viewpoints they oppose. Warns that intellectuals and ideologues are still necessary because "the absence of ideologies will not save the world for the skeptic and the pragmatist. Rather will a dream of unreason supply what the dream of reason could not."

M1053. Rosenthal, Henry. "Inventions." *Menorah Journal* 14 (January 1928): 49-61.

A short story echoing C53 in the conflict it develops between Starobin, a "Zionist" based on Rosenthal himself, and the assimilated Dolman, a "blithe and literate" figure based on Trilling. Describes Starobin's attempts to persuade Dolman that he is "ashamed of being a Jew" and Dolman's measured and unashamed response to Starobin's efforts to "convert" him: "*Find* your God before you try to sell Him to me." As in C53, the authorial surrogate comes off less well than his opponent.

M1054. Rosenzweig, Saul. "The Ghost of Henry James." *Partisan Review* 11 (Autumn 1944): 436-55.

Reads James's career in the psychoanalytic terms made popular by L981, emphasizing the importance of James's "obscure hurt" in crystallizing his perceived inferiority to his dominating father and brother into "a passional death" repeatedly re-enacted in stories from "The Story of a Year" (1865) to "The Jolly Corner" (1908) and motivating not only the ghosts representing the unlived life who appear throughout his work but his own energetic relief work in World War I as an expiation for his non-participation in the Civil War. Agrees with Wilson's analysis of "the sacrificial roots of [artistic] power."

For Trilling's response, see C80.

M1055. Said, Edward W. "Comments on Trilling Talk of October 25, 1973." *[Columbia University] Seminar Reports* 1 (7 December 1973): 3-4.

Disagrees with Trilling's implication in C187 that "secondary education is the A from which B, or university education, follows," arguing that secondary schools take their cue from liberal arts programs in exposing their students to wide reading in translation, turning the study of literature from a progressive, philologically-based discipline to a "monochromatic" activity without any "rhetorical center."

M1056. Santirocco, Matthew. "Comments on Trilling Talk of October 25, 1973." *[Columbia University] Seminar Reports* 1 (7 December 1973): 3.

Urges, in conjunction with C187, that Greek and Latin be "more widely and imaginatively taught as electives in secondary schools." Suggests that the continuity between European secondary and higher education is purchased at the price of earlier specialization and weaker general education.

M1057. Shapiro, Charles. "On Our Own: Trilling vs. Dreiser." *Seasoned Authors for a New Season: The Search for Standards in Popular Writing*. Edited by Louis Filler. Bowling Green: Bowling Green University Popular Press, 1980. Pp. 152-56.

Offers the difficulty in evaluating Dreiser's novels as a test of the general problem of literary evaluation. Defends Dreiser against Trilling's attack in C86, arguing that Trilling overlooks Dreiser's philosophical evolution and his success at "incorporat[ing] his ideals into his realistic architectonics" and making audiences care about his characters.

M1058. Showalter, Elaine. "R. D. Laing and the Sixties." *Raritan* 1 (Fall 1980): 107-27.

Contrasts Laing's "tribute" to Trilling in *The Divided Self*, which "shares with Trilling a sense of the modern self asserting its integrity in opposition to an imprisoning and increasingly internalized social reality," with Trilling's passionate denunciation of Laing in the concluding paragraph of A9, though acknowledging that "even in his hostility Trilling took Laing seriously," unlike most commentators on Laing's work since.

M1059. Staats, Armin. "'Genteel Tradition' und 'Liberal Imagination.'" *Mythos und Aufklärung in der amerikanische Literatur/Myth and Enlightenment in American Literature.* Edited by Dieter Meindl. Erlangen: Universitätsbund Erlangen-Nürnberg, 1985. Pp. 353-73.

Compares the liberal imagination, as a dialectical stance opposed to the utopian quest for power and individual selfhood, to the genteel tradition Santayana set against Americans' consuming personal ambition. Contrasts the unresolved conflict in Howells's *A Modern Instance* between a genteel tradition allied with the negative dialectic of Calvinist morality (and more recently incarnated in the Frankfurt School's denigration of the individual) and moral progressivism with the more openly ambivalent dialectic Fitzgerald establishes in *The Great Gatsby* between Nick Carraway's pluralistic liberal imagination and Gatsby's symbolic imagination and romance of self-definition, which Nick admires despite himself.

M1060. Torgovnick, Marianna. "The Politics of the 'We.'" *South Atlantic Quarterly* 91 (Winter 1992): 43-63.

Analyzes the ways the use of "we" in critical discourse creates a homogeneous inner circle into which readers are invited or bullied even as it erases the writer's historical specificity. Objects to "the easy slide from 'I' to 'we'" that "is often the essence of cultural criticism"--for example, in Trilling's use of "we," democratically emphasizing the acculturative power of the university and the canon, but often "chillingly coercive" in effect. Recalls the way Trilling's classroom performance often transformed himself rather than his students into "the anonymous third-person that his 'we' always resembled." Sees in Dinesh D'Souza's demonizing of leftist intellectuals as outsiders a newer version of this process of coercive acculturation, and calls for "a more open and personal, more fluid and tentative" use of "we."

M1061. Trilling, Diana. "The Other Night at Columbia: A Report from the Academy." *Partisan Review* 26 (Spring 1959): 214-30.

Intercuts an account of a reading by three Beat poets--Allen Ginsberg, Gregory Corso, and Peter Orlovsky--at Columbia with reminiscences of Ginsberg's flamboyant, troubled years as a student of Trilling's, climaxing in Ginsberg's reading of "Lion in the Room," dedicated to the absent Trilling.

Revised and reprinted in *Claremont Essays* (New York: Harcourt, Brace & World, 1964), pp. 153-73.

M1062. Van Doren, Mark. "Jewish Students I Have Known." *Menorah Journal* 13 (June 1927): 264-68.

Describes Trilling, sixth among seven unnamed students Van Doren describes, as a "fastidious" and increasingly melancholy man who "spoke diffidently, with a hushed and harmless voice," and who "found it hard to decide what to write about," carefully maintaining an "amateur standing" as a storyteller and poet. Predicts that "what he will eventually do, if he does it at all, will be . . . the fruit of a pure intelligence slowly ripened in not too fierce a sun."

M1063. Walcutt, Charles Child. "*Sister Carrie*: Naturalism or Novel of Manners?" *Genre* 1 (January 1968): 76-85.

Argues against Trilling that *Sister Carrie* is not a naturalistic novel marked by "materialistic determinism," but a novel of manners which "does not reject the values of its society," and whose principals, "impelled *not* by values conceived and held in the intellect but by animal impulses of desire and self-preservation," do not revolt against social norms but attempt to master them.

M1064. Wald, Alan. "The Menorah Group Moves Left." *Jewish Social Studies* 38 (Summer-Fall 1976): 289-320.

Charts the increasing intimacy between writers for the *Menorah Journal*, maintaining that Herbert Solow, despite his protests to the contrary, "was consciously trying to move his circle toward Communism." Describes how the 1934 Communist Party disruption of a Socialist Party rally at Madison Square Garden led to the drafting of E379, indicating Trilling's movement away from Communism, and reviews attempts made in L945 and M992 to identify characters in L974 with Trilling and other members of the *Menorah Journal* group.

Revised and reprinted as Chapter 2 of L978.

M1065. Wald, Alan. "The Politics of Culture: The New York Intellectuals in Fiction." *Centennial Review* 29 (Summer 1985): 353-69.

Using a distinction between Philip Rahv's pragmatic radicalism, which sees art as capturing and preserving non-ideological experience, and Terry Eagleton's Marxist epistemology, which defines experience as necessarily ideological, contends that Trilling's fiction shows "the enfeeblement of American Marxism at the hands of pragmatism" in its regression from Howe's ambivalent "acquiescence" in a corrupt social order in C77, whose outcome Trilling regards "in a half-bemused, half-tragic manner," to Stephen Elwin's self-justifying "antiradicalism" in C84, "the first anti-affirmative action short story," conceived perhaps in response to Richard Wright's *Native Son*. Groups A3 with Edmund Wilson's *Memoirs of Hecate County* and Mary McCarthy's *The Oasis* as political novels that prophetically advocate the "end of ideology" described ten years later by Daniel Bell and Seymour Martin Lipset.

Revised and reprinted as Chapter 8 of L978.

M1066. Weiland, Steven. "Teachers, Truants, and the Humanities." *Georgia Review* 37 (Fall 1983): 481-99.

Notes the sharp disagreement within the academy about the ideological implications of teaching, and criticizes William Barrett's assumption in L896 that "the right ideas about communism and capitalism are at least as important" to teachers in the humanities "as good taste in the arts and a sophisticated historical sensibility." Deplores Barrett's use of Trilling as both a neo-conservative "master" who avoided the truants' mistake of "cultivat[ing] politics as if it were a purely aesthetic discipline" and a target of his critique of reactionary tastes and modern secularism, concluding that "Trilling is an exemplary humanist not because he avoided intellectual truancy nor because he anticipated currently fashionable ideas," but because of "his good taste and generosity . . . his synthesis of literary and social ideas and ideals, and his consistently liberal if not intensely ideological views."

M1067. Wisse, Ruth R. "The New York (Jewish) Intellectuals." [Review of L904, L906, L940, L973, and L978.] *Commentary* 84 (November 1984): 28-38.

Deplores the tendency of recent studies of the New York intellectuals to discredit or ignore their ideas in favor of sociological analysis. Argues that the continuing attraction of these figures is rooted in their attempt to maintain "unequivocal independence"--not from Stalinism, "a system to which they were not subject," but from Zionism and the defense of Jews and the "Jewish polity" incarnated in Israel. Discusses E384 as an example of the intellectuals' view that "an 'adjustment' to Judaism may have seemed more neurotic than separation from it," noting its timidity in expressing only "sorrow at the massacre then going on," and suggesting that A3 misses greatness because Trilling declines to give Laskell a Jewish past and a Jewish consciousness. Remarks that since independence is "an ideal of unencumbered boyhood," most of the group were more comfortable as alienated sons than as father-figures, citing as successful exceptions such neoconservatives as Irving Kristol, Norman Podhoretz, and Saul Bellow.

Section N

Dissertations

N1068. Barry, Michael Gordon. "Recovering Meaning from the Irony of History: American Political Fiction in Transition." State University of New York at Buffalo, 1989. 190 pages.

Discusses four political novels of the 1940's--*The Grapes of Wrath*, *Native Son*, A3, and *All the King's Men*--arguing that in each case, a suspicion of totalitarian politics redirects the search for political solutions to injustice (especially in Steinbeck and Wright, whose sharp sense of social injustice leads to a surprisingly ambivalent attitude toward political meliorism) to "a search for personal meaning." Contends that this search leads Warren and Trilling to a rediscovery of tragedy, as they realize that political inaction is no more efficacious or authentic, and much less meaningful, than political action, however flawed, observing that Trilling, having argued through Maxim humankind's universal responsibility for evil, goes on to prescribe "a limited activism."

N1069. Longstaff, Stephen A. "The New York Intellectuals: A Study of Particularism and Universalism in American High Culture." University of California, Berkeley, 1978. xiii, 473 pages.

Disputing the "intellectual subsociety hypothesis" that American intellectuals are typically cosmopolitan, broadly assimilative and only marginally ethnic, argues that a postwar return to Jewishness is a primary thrust of the New York intellectuals, providing an agenda to replace their earlier attack on cultural anti-Stalinism and defense of modernist literature. Considers the ways in which the predominantly Jewish figures in this circle, most of whom had earlier neglected their own cultural heritage in favor of "Enlightenment creeds that dominate Western intellectual discourse," were moved to a return by buried loyalties to Judaism, by a renewed recognition of the power of the sacred, or by a view of Judaism as a locus of morality. Cites the American opposition to Nazism, and later the realities of the Holocaust, as specific catalysts for the large number of intellectuals' public acknowledgments of their Jewish roots in the early 1950's, as "Jewishness" became a replacement theme for the cold war. Emphasizes the importance of Trilling's own such acknowledgment in C95, which "seemed to many to signal an important change in the intellectual atmosphere" because of his earlier non-Jewish gentility. Suggests that Trilling's and Saul Bellow's close identification with literary modernism gave their critique of the avant-garde during the 1960's a power surpassing its originality. Concludes, largely on the basis of 84 anonymous interviews with 76 figures associated with the New York intellectuals, that the circle was defined by a continuing tension between its members' culturally ethnic heritage, by turns repressed and celebrated, and their drive toward assimilation as Americans and accredited Western thinkers.

Chapter 1 appeared in an earlier version as M1028; parts of Chapters 5 and 6 are revised and reprinted as M1029.

N1070. Moore, David Walter. "Liberalism and Liberal Education at Columbia University: The Columbia Careers of Jacques Barzun, Lionel Trilling, Richard Hofstadter, Daniel Bell, and C. Wright Mills." University of Maryland, 1978. x, 440 pages.

Explores Trilling's role in defining and developing Columbia University's commitment to a program of liberal education between 1915 and 1968 and maintaining its mission in the face of New Left challenges (represented here by Mills) and the new ideal of the "technocratic university." Follows C113 in describing the ideal of a liberal education as a reaction against the vocationalism and individualism of an elective system of college courses and its preference for the Oxford model to the scientific and professional models offered by German universities and Johns Hopkins. Noting that Trilling's attack on Parrington is not a retreat from a material reality but an insistence on its incompleteness, argues that Columbia's commitment to the new program of General Education was intended in part "to restore a proper sense of reality and possibility to the intellectual community, making for a better political climate." Notes the ways in which Trilling is left behind as "the liberal impulse becomes increasingly politicized [in the 1950's and 1960's], moving beyond liberalism" as supporters of liberal education no longer subscribe to a liberal ideology, until Trilling's attempts to mediate between students and the administration in the 1968 strike end in failure.

N1071. Murphy, Geraldine Anne. "The Ideology of American Romance Theory." Columbia University, 1985. 251 pages.

Roots the development of American romance theory--the distinction of the romance from the novel on the basis of its freedom from social norms and resolutions--in the postwar "new liberalism" marked by left-wing writers retreat from the Marxism and Stalinism of the 1930's to the anti-Communist liberalism described and fostered by Arthur Schlesinger's *The Vital Center*. Argues that Trilling's rejection of ideological commitment in favor of conceiving himself as a "battleground" for conflicting cultural imperatives prepares for Richard Chase's projection of this personal longing for ideological freedom onto the form of the American romance as codified by Trilling, Chase, and Marius Bewley.

N1072. Platzker, Doris A. "Public Vistas, Private Visions: Aspects of the Modern American Political Imagination." Yale University, 1966. 230 pages.

Uses *Man's Fate*, *Democracy*, and *The Princess Casamassima* to lay the groundwork for a detailed discussion of three recent political novels: Warren's *All the King's Men*, A3, and Cozzens's *Guard of Honor*. Contends that Trilling's novel, which is concerned with "*ideas about political power* rather than power itself," is flawed, like Cozzens's, "because the public experience portrayed overwhelms the novelistic imagination." The "*dubito ergo sum*" represented by Laskell's rejection of absolutist ideology marks a failure of Trilling's imagination, a withdrawal into "oppressive cerebralness," but indicates as well "its strength as moral history": its "extraordinary compression of values," and the clarity and urgency with which it represents "the reality of both freedom and necessity."

N1073. Shapiro, Herbert Eugene. "*Partisan Review*: The Forging of a Jewish-American Literary Aesthetic." University of Rochester, 1980. 209 pages.

Argues that *Partisan Review*, though beginning as a political journal, became defined by an aesthetic of alienation specific to the New York Jewish intellectuals, an aesthetic which allowed the journal to anticipate *Commentary* in "liberat[ing] Jewish intellectual magazines from their traditional parochialism." Noting that *alienation* has been correlated with such diverse concepts as powerlessness, meaninglessnesss, normlessness, cultural estrangement, social isolation, and self-estrangement, suggests that the fiction and essays in *Partisan Review* achieved a new level of general appeal by declining to choose among these concepts, shifting from an apolitical "'cult' of alienation" characteristic of aesthetes in the 1920's to "a [political] 'school' of alienation" by means of radical politics, then withdrawing from Communist sponsorship to a more generalized notion of alienation. Analyzes C77 and C84 as exemplary transformations of autobiographical or sociological motifs of specifically Jewish alienation, observing that C84 originally encourages its audience to side with Margaret against her mother's dislike of their maid before educating them in moral realism through a critique of Margaret's "'masscult' version of liberalism." Connects the dissolution of a cohesive New York Jewish intelligensia to the founding in 1962 of the non-alienated *New York Review of Books*. Proposes Isaac Rosenfeld as "the 'perfect' *Partisan Review* radical," Delmore Schwartz as "the quintessential *Partisan Review* type," and Trilling as the "most eloquent spokesman" for the aesthetic of alienation.

N1074. Tsai, Yuan-Huang. "Men of Words and Ideas: Intellectuals in the Post-World War II American Novel." State University of New York at Binghamton, 1981. 285 pages.

Links A3 to *All the King's Men*, *Pale Fire*, and *Herzog* as studies of a fictional writer/intellectual's struggle to "balance an inner life with an increasing commitment to the outer world" by means of a new ideological perspective "concerning the proper use of words." Uses Nabokov's John Shade, "a paragon of the healthy encounter with reality," as a measure of each of the other heroes' alienation, attributing John Laskell's "dissociation and depersonalization" to a "lack of conviction of reality" which leads him initially to an attempt to escape from the present into the past instead of using the past to achieve a sense of "connectedness." Maintains that Laskell's rejection of the Crooms' rootless Stalinism and Maxim's religious millenialism shows him increasingly "grasping the present as the basis of the future" without "abstracting himself from his community and the community of intellectuals" by realizing that "he and the Crooms are 'parts of history, elements in the dialectic' of the situation." Calls Laskell's "present-oriented illumination . . . a middle way" that is "not a plea for expediency or compromise," and A3 "a novel of tension without resolution."

N1075. Wright, Palmer. "The New Liberalism of the Fifties: Reinhold Niebuhr, Lionel Trilling, David Riesman, and the American Intellectual." University of Michigan, 1966. vii, 268 pages.

Defines New Liberalism, which flourished between 1948 and 1957, as "a dialectical view of mind inherited from depth psychology" rather than "a consistent political ideology." Situates New Liberalism at "a convergence of three traditions: pragmatic empiricism, romantic modernism, and institutional practicalism"--that is, a recognition of the necessities of social conformity--generalizing all three as "traditions of 'realism'" which seek to chasten "the liberal spirit . . . by the 'pragmatic' disciplines of inquiry, by the psychoanalytic and religious disciplines of self-awareness, and by the 'stoic' disciplines of provisional and critical accommodation to 'lesser-evil' institutional and political roles." Aligns Trilling's "man of 'negative capability' with Niebuhr's "Christian realist" and Riesman's "autonomous man" as exemplary figures of this dialectic, each "the product of 'autonomous' decision arising from a sense of personal identity, rarely achieved in full." Cites as a basis of the similarities among these three figures the liberal view of Freudian ideology presented by Philip Rieff in *Freud: The Mind of the Moralist*. Traces the increasing disinclination of "progressive liberals" like F. O. Matthiessen and Henry Steele Commager to call themselves "liberals," especially after the split between progressives and such "pragmatic liberals" as Trilling opened or revealed by Henry Wallace in 1947. Emphasizes Trilling's anti-progressive polemic against culture, noting that "culture" in A4 stands for "both the mindless culture of [the] educated liberal American middle class, and the potentialities of an essential imagination of mind of the opposing self as developed in literature," and that in A5 "culture is the opponent."

Section O

Miscellaneous

O1076. Stern, Daniel. "The Liberal Imagination of Lionel Trilling." *New Letters* 52 (Winter-Spring 1986): 5-32.

Not an essay on Trilling, despite its misleading title, but a short story whose anonymous narrator recounts, in the course of an elegy on Katherine Eudemie, his meeting with her years earlier at a party at Trilling's home, his seduction of her immediately after, and his determined and successful attempt to prevent any further development of their affair by blindfolding himself upon leaving to avoid observing the location of her house. Trilling and Steven Marcus are briefly glimpsed at the party "talking about fishing," and the gulf Trilling identifies in A3 between modernist writers and liberal ideology is invoked to help explain the narrator's willed isolation from the doomed heroine.

O1077. Trilling, Diana, and Anderson, Quentin. [Letters to the Editor.] *New York Times Book Review*, 23 December 1984, pp. 21, 23.

Both letters protest Alan Lelchuk's recollection in M1026 that Trilling had objected to the autobiographical informality of Saul Bellow's remarks about his Jewish background at the 1978 Brandeis commencement as "not credible to those who knew Trilling." Diana Trilling additionally corrects the date of the incident to 1974: "In 1978 my husband had been dead for three years."

Lelchuk replies that Trilling "made his considerable mark on the literary world precisely by *making* judgments, not by avoiding them," and adds that his original talk had referred to Trilling and Bellow as "two princes of Jewish sensibility."

O1078. Trilling, Diana, and Hook, Sidney. "Remembering Whittaker Chambers: An Exchange." *Encounter* 46 (June 1976): 94-96.

In a letter to Hook, Diana Trilling disputes his recollection in M1013 that Lionel Trilling arranged a meeting between Hook and Whittaker Chambers on the grounds that the Trillings saw little of Chambers after Diana Trilling refused to receive the mail that Chambers had asked her, like Nancy Croom in A3, to accept for him. Hook in his reply defends his memory, insisting that Trilling would likely have had a lively interest in "socio-fascism," since this theory led to the Communist disruption of a Socialist Party rally that led to Trilling's public criticism of the Communists the following year.

O1079. Warren, Robert Penn, and others. [Letters to the Editor.] *New York Times Book Review*, 25 June 1978, p. 56.

Warren objects to the portrait of Trilling's social and professional vanity advanced in L944 and M1050. A second letter, labeling this portrait "a grotesque misrepresentation," is signed by M. H. Abrams, Quentin Anderson, Eric Bentley, Morton Bloomfield, Frank Kermode, Leslie Fiedler, Charles Frankel, Richard Howard, Howard Mumford Jones, Stanley Kauffmann, Steven Marcus, Robert K. Merton, Edward Said, Arthur Schlesinger Jr., Fritz Stern, Barbara Probst Solomon, Aileen Ward, Michael Wood, and Paul Zweig.

O1080. Warshow, Robert. "'This Age of Conformity': Protest and Rejoinder." [Correspondence.] *Partisan Review* 21 (March-April 1954): 235-38.

Defends Trilling against Irving Howe's attack on him in M1017 by ridiculing Howe's demand that in order to qualify as a non-conformist, "you must not be pleased at anything in the present cultural situation. (That's where Lionel Trilling made his mistake.)"

In a rejoinder, Howe contends that "to debate with Lionel Trilling about the present state of American culture is in no way to impugn his 'chastity.'"

Index of Authors

Italicized listings refer to entries written (or edited, translated, or introduced) by the author; subsequent listings refer to discussions or reprintings of entries by the authors (but not the editors, translators, or introducers) of italicized entries.

Index of Titles

Citations in italics refer to primary listings; citations following italicized listings refer to reprintings of or references to the primary listing. Each reprinting under a new title is listed separately. References to a given essay are listed under the essay's most widely known title--generally the title of its first book publication. All foreign-language titles are listed in the language in which they were originally cited.